Turning to Political Violence

Turning to Political Violence

The Emergence of Terrorism

Marc Sageman

PENN

UNIVERSITY OF PENNSYLVANIA PRESS

PHILADELPHIA

Published by
University of Pennsylvania Press
Philadelphia, Pennsylvania 19104-4112
www.upenn.edu/pennpress

Printed in the United States of America on acid-free paper
10   9   8   7   6   5   4   3   2   1

Library of Congress Cataloging-in-Publication Data
Names: Sageman, Marc, author.
Title: Turning to political violence : the emergence of terrorism / Marc Sageman.
Description: 1st edition. | Philadelphia : University of Pennsylvania Press, [2017] | Includes bibliographical references and index.
Identifiers: LCCN 2017010333 | ISBN 978-0-8122-4877-7 (hardcover)
Subjects: LCSH: Political violence—History. | Radicalization—History. | Terrorism—History. | Terrorists—Psychology—History.
Classification: LCC JC328.6 .S24 2017 | DDC 363.32509—dc23
LC record available at https://lccn.loc.gov/2017010333

For Jody and Joseph

Contents

Preface

On April 15, 2013, at the end of the Boston Marathon, two bombs exploded in the crowd of spectators, killing 3 people and injuring more than 250 others. Within a few days, the perpetrators were identified as two brothers, Tamerlan and Dzhokhar Tsarnaev, who were Chechen refugees. Tamerlan, the older one, was killed in the ensuing police dragnet, but Dzhokhar survived despite being wounded multiple times. By all accounts, he seemed to be a well-assimilated and sociable young man, attending college and smoking marijuana with his friends.

Shortly after the bombing, my usually silent phone started ringing off the hook. Journalists called to ask the same question: how could an apparently normal young man like Dzhokhar do this, seemingly out of the blue? I was just emerging from a long involvement with the U.S. intelligence community, during which I was banned from speaking with journalists. Although now free to talk to them, I was still at a loss to provide a short and pithy answer. Despite spending over a decade straddling government and academia working on terrorism issues, I still did not entirely understand what leads a person to turn to political violence. How does one start to make sense of this senseless violence? Do these individuals have something psychologically wrong with them, as many people believe? Are they victims of a mysterious process of brainwashing or indoctrination, as many others believe? More fundamentally, how does one conceptualize terrorism, terrorists, and the process by which a very few people become terrorists? I concluded that only with a radical change of perspective could scholars hope to answer these questions.

What leads people to turn to political violence? This haunting question has obsessed me ever since the tragedy of 9/11. This book originated as a short historical introduction to a book on the current wave of global neojihadi[1] attacks against the West. However, this attempt to contextualize this current wave of terrorism proved far more complicated as I dug deeper into each historical case. Parallel to this revelation were developments in various academic disciplines, changes in the political climate, and not least, insights gained through actual encounters with politically violent people.

The political climate since 11 September 2001 has changed. In the decade following 9/11, the anticipated onslaught of terroristic violence in the United States did not materialize. This allowed some scholars to step back and take some distance from the devastation of that day. Alarmist voices among self-promoting experts no longer rang true when faced with the paucity of actual global neojihadi attacks in this country. I was privileged to examine the evidence for many of the government claims from the inside and was struck by the lack of substance behind many of them. I also investigated many alleged instances of political violence, including interviews with alleged perpetrators, and realized that many of the claims were somewhat overblown. This does not mean that there is no threat, but overall the risk is quite small, especially when compared with fatalities from accidents and other forms of human violence in this country.

At the same time, there were many developments in academic fields that have always been a source of inspiration for my work. New scholarship on the perpetrators of the Holocaust and violence during the French Revolution challenged many of my fundamental assumptions about political violence. These studies focused on how political actors conceived of and understood themselves and their actions at the time they committed their acts. New developments in cognitive and social psychology, especially in the social identity perspective, have reinterpreted classical experimental evidence that had defied interpretation. These research findings have direct relevance on political violence, and I have incorporated them into this work.

My interviews with perpetrators of political violence and review of transcripts of interviews of others made me aware of the importance they attributed to government action against them in their explanations of their actions. Political violence necessarily involves contested narratives, and perpetrators defined themselves in contrast to governmental agents and their actions, which gave meaning to their violence in the context of a conflict between them and the state. They viewed their actions as response to state aggression. In their minds, their violence could not be understood outside this escalating conflict. Indeed, as some scholars have previously pointed out, much political violence involves competition with the state, in a cycle of escalation culminating in ever-increasing violence. Like a boxing match, it is impossible to understand a fight without looking at both combatants: the actions of each are the context to which the other reacts. To understand the violent effects of any conflict requires an examination of both belligerent parties.

This raises the sensitive issue of the state's potential contribution to non-state political violence. Because funding for terrorism research comes exclusively from the state, the subtle temptation is simply to overlook the role of the state so as not to jeopardize one's funding. I was fortunate to be in position to do this project on my own, without any government support, and was therefore free to explore this important topic. This book brings the state back into the investigation of non-state political violence by analyzing violence as emerging out of a conflict between the perpetrators and the state.

Prolonged immersion in the archival material and very detailed legal evidence to which I had access, extensive interviews with actual perpetrators, and time to think without any imposed deadlines, interruptions from work, or other demands on my time allowed me to explore the subject of political violence more deeply by comparing this current wave with previous campaigns of political violence. As a result, this is not another quickly written book exploiting great tragedies, like the vast majority of popular books on terrorism. It is the result of my own gradual intellectual journey to try to consolidate disparate insights originating in very different disciplines—historical, psychological, political, sociological, and cultural.

Time and further study eroded my original conceptual and methodological foundations and reshaped the emotional commitment that drove me on. I became more skeptical of the conventional perspective on my original subjects—terrorism and radicalization—to the point that I have avoided use of these concepts. This study is a first, tentative, and imperfect step to understand what leads people to become politically violent. My goal is to inform the debate on this issue and draw attention to relevant questions. I hope to raise the level of this debate, unmask our preconceived and often mistaken notions imbedded in it, and subject all arguments to empirical and critical examination. One of my goals is to provide the missing facts that may transform future debate from stale polemical repetition of the same worn-out and simplistic arguments to consideration of more fruitful ones. I tried to collect as complete and reliable a set of historical details as possible to give readers an opportunity to study them within their own perspective and challenge some of my conclusions. This explains the length of this study, which I hope will become a source book for future work and lead to future debates based on evidence rather than speculations about the worst possible scenario. Such speculations on terrorists' possible use of nuclear or biological weapons have unfortunately largely shaped the debate about political violence in the West. Of course, one must protect oneself against these catastrophic scenarios, but one should not allow them to completely transform one's everyday life. Instead, I suggest getting into the minds of violent political actors in order to understand them and to avoid preventable future instances of political violence. All of these insights allowed me to go beyond the tyranny of labels and question some of the conventional wisdom based on prejudice, polemics, and a paucity of data to understand politically violent actors. The result is a paradigm shift in how to look at political violence.

This book is not a sweeping narrative of Western non-state political violence—often referred to as terrorism. It is a theoretical examination of a process, the turn to political violence, with historical illustrations of it whenever there were adequate primary sources that I could understand. It is not a comprehensive historical survey of political violence, as it obviously skips over three of its most prominent instances, namely Irish, Balkan, and colonial violence.

To understand this violent turn, one must understand the perpetrators from the inside, an enterprise fraught with danger. The murder of innocent victims inherent in political violence is an appalling act that rightly deserves condemnation. However, an outside perspective on such crimes obscures an internal one that is more fruitful in understanding and preventing them. The perspective of the scholar must be detached and dispassionate and assume that political violence is ultimately explicable. Like a surgeon needing to cut a person, a temporary harm, in order to cure or alleviate that person's suffering— a greater good—the scholar must therefore put aside the victims' cries that the perpetrator is pure evil, craving and enjoying the suffering of the victims. A scholar must assume that these crimes have a meaning for the perpetrators and try to capture their subjectivity to understand this meaning. In suspending his moral judgment for the sake of long-term prevention, he or she must adopt the perpetrator's point of view. It is natural for the public to identify with victims of political violence especially when they are members of the same group. The perpetrators are naturally categorized into stereotypes that distinguish them from the general public. To even try to look at them as normal human beings, similar to the public at large, may seem like an act of betrayal of the victims' group norms and values, especially in time of real danger to one's group, when the emotional need is for support and sympathy.

An illustration of the public's rejection of the normality of terrorists was the mass protest against a *Rolling Stone* cover picture and (accurate and detailed) story of Dzhokhar Tsarnaev, the surviving Boston bomber, resulting in a boycott of that issue of the magazine because he looked like the typical teenager that he was.[2] The press is complicit in presenting distorted portraits of terrorists with active editorial suppression of any facts that might reflect positively on a suspected perpetrator. Dedicated journalists have complained to me that their stories were edited to provide a negative picture of the suspects to conform to the conventional stereotype. Such distortions challenge the reliability of flawed newspaper accounts as sources for terrorism research.[3] Terrorism arouses strong emotion that obstructs scientific dispassionate investigation; anything seen as slightly sympathetic to them is viewed as a betrayal of the community. So, to the public, a detached and dispassionate scrutiny of a perpetrator might seem to "make excuses" for him, "justify" the violence, or worse, "blame the victim."

This book's approach may be initially hard for people to share because terrorists are heroes in their own minds and taking their perspective may seem like glorifying them. To lessen this concern, I stayed away from recent atrocities still fresh in people's minds and analyzed historical examples of political violence, hoping that time has granted us some distance from the victims' suffering and the panic these attacks generated. Nevertheless, my enterprise may still seem like an insult to the memory of the victims or a betrayal of one's natural sympathy for them. I understand and respect this view. The aim of this study is to understand political violence in order to minimize it and save lives in the future. Meaningful understanding of perpetrators requires transcending one's natural and rightful inclination to identify with victims. Even those interested in understanding the causes of this type of violence may reject this necessary detached perspective as simple forgiveness. I am not an apologist for terrorists and agree that we ultimately need to come back to the perspective of innocent victims and make individuals responsible for their actions. In carrying out their crimes, each perpetrator believed that he or she acted out a virtuous sacrifice. To them, the innocents killed were unfortunate collateral damage, the cost of doing business.[4] This is no excuse for the victims and justice demands taking their perspective. However, this study is not an attempt to bring justice to the victims but to understand how the crime emerged in order to prevent future ones. Taking the perpetrator's perspective is just a means to an end. Eventually, perpetrators must be held accountable for what they did—as must governments[5]—and punished appropriately.

In a sense, this book reverses the chronology of my evolving understanding of political violence. I first traced the process of turning to violence in the present wave of global neojihadi terrorism and compared it to detailed historical accounts of campaigns of violence. I then searched for cognitive and social psychological theories that provided a foundation for this process. In this book, I first present a model of this process by distilling it from relevant cognitive and social psychological perspectives that frame the later empirical chapters. Those interested in the theoretical model should focus on Chapters 1 and 8, while those more interested in the history of political violence might first read the empirical chapters, 2 through 7, before returning to the theoretical chapters explaining these events. The cumulative narrative in the empirical chapters traces the emergence of modern terrorism from mob violence in the eighteenth century during the French Revolution to a wave of regicides and finally indiscriminate mass murder in the early twentieth century. Chapters 2 and 3 describe the emergence of all the elements of modern political violence that occurred in France from the French Revolution to the Paris Commune. Chapter 4 portrays the transformation of peaceful activists into full-time terrorists in nineteenth-century Russia, which is often taken as the starting point of terrorist historiography. Chapter 5 shows how targeted political violence expanded into more indiscriminate killing through the evolution of anarchist violence in France and the United States in the late nineteenth century. Chapter 6 returns to Russia to describe the specialization of political violence with the creation of the Combat Unit of the Russian Socialist Revolutionary Party. Chapter 7 shows the further degeneration of political violence into the banditry of the Bonnot Gang in France and the indiscriminate bombings of the Galleani group in the United States. Between these two campaigns of violence came the assassination of Archduke Franz Ferdinand of Austria in Sarajevo, which inadvertently ushered decades of carnage bracketed by the two world wars and destroyed the old regime in Europe.

Chapter 8 returns to the theoretical model to discuss the dynamics of continuous campaigns of political violence and draw the policy implications of the model for both the prevention of political violence or, failing that, the termination of campaigns of political violence in liberal democracies. In the appendix, I present evidence that the model is generalizable to even the recent global neojihadi campaigns of violence by testing it in an expanded sample of campaigns of political violence. I also compare it against two alternative explanations for the turn to political violence, namely the ideological thesis and rational choice theory, the reigning paradigm in political science.

Methodology

It is unfortunately quite common for studies on political violence to dive into the subject without providing an outline of methodology, resulting in a series of narratives, often based on secondary sources and told in an authoritative voice, to illustrate the author's claims.[6] There is no acknowledgment that many facts in such tales are deeply contested, undermining their validity. Here I outline my methodology and discuss the scope and limitations of this study.

This book combines three strategies to understand the process of turning to political violence. First, Chapter 1 outlines this process by deductively deriving it from cognitive and social psychological theories. Second, the major part of the book presents detailed descriptions of campaigns of political violence, which illustrate the model I present and sometimes compare it to popular alternative explanations. These descriptions generate inductive generalizations about this process that, in turn, guided me to the relevant theories that framed the deductions of the first chapter. Third, the appendix tests this model empirically by adding other campaigns of political violence to the ones already discussed.

This book is an exploration trying to identify variables and processes relevant to the turn to political violence. As in all science, its findings are at best temporary, tentative, and incomplete. Nevertheless, I hope that the reader will realize that they are based on much more extensive historical and comparative data than previous works, covering two centuries, two continents, multiple goals, ideologies, and social settings. The theoretical framework presented in the next chapter also provides a deep understanding of the underlying mechanisms in turning to political violence. Previous discussions of terrorism have too often been based on few facts and many prejudices, and lacked any systematic methodology. I hope that this book will contribute to raising the quality of discourse on non-state political violence.

In the second part of this study, I analyze a series of incidents of political violence, defined broadly, and lump them into campaigns of violence. The aim is to elaborate causal mechanisms and conditions for this complex process of turning to violence. Within each instance, I trace this process, moving from original conditions to the outcome, political violence. For each case, I use a within-case analysis, comparing people before and after their turn to violence, using them as their own control group, in an attempt to understand their journey. I also compare them to their peers who did not turn to political violence in a loose approximation of a control group, to identify the specific factors distinguishing them from their controls. I also compare cases to each other to understand their commonalities and differences. This approach therefore combines qualitative within-case and cross-case analysis. Incidents of political violence often come in larger campaigns, which give meaning to each of their incidents. Therefore, on this collective level of analysis, I conduct a within-campaign analysis comparing politically violent clusters before and after their turn to violence as well as cross-group analysis comparing them with their larger nonviolent political protest communities to understand their violent emergence from their original communities.[7]

Process tracing requires detailed and reliable data on the turn to political violence. The lack of comprehensive open source data on recent political violence[8] required to test the model led me to turn to historical cases, where the evidence is available to scholars. Before speculating about the process of turning to political violence, we need to know the facts. Much of the historiography of terrorism relies on superficial interpretations of deeply contested facts. I have reconstructed the relevant events mostly from primary sources into detailed narratives and hope that this may serve as a source book for future research.

There are two major perspectives on violent actors: the usual outsider stance from out-group observers and an insider one from in-group members.[9] All too often, terrorism scholars take the outside perspective of the state, reducing terrorists into stereotypes. This adversarial strategy impedes insightful understanding of perpetrators and results in a re-hashing of counter-terrorists' prejudices, full of unexamined assumptions, which masquerades as social science. It comforts the readers by stressing their essential differences from terrorists.

To study what leads people to turn to political violence requires at least some understanding of what is going on in their minds, a peek into their subjectivity. The investigation needs to proceed from an insider's point of view. This study does not assume that people are completely self-aware, as social science has documented for at least half a century the wide gap between what people believe or say and what they do.[10] However, we should at least consider their own insights, without necessarily taking their words at face value, as they may very well try to deceive us. Their words are only a starting point for this inquiry, for we cannot conduct participant observation, which is illegal or inadvisable even if possible. Participation in political violence is against the law in most countries and severely punished. From a scientific perspective, it is inadvisable, as shown by Bill Buford's cautionary tale of his attempt to understand soccer hooligans in England, which resulted in him becoming one of them.[11] Participation involves the danger of identifying with one's subjects and, in this case, actually becoming a terrorist and losing one's ability to observe in an unbiased way. Surreptitious observation is now possible with various types of recording devices, but they did not exist at the time of most the cases in this study.

Political violence in this study is deliberate: it is meaningful and intentional for the perpetrators. The turn to political violence is embedded with meaning for them. To capture this meaning and more generally the actors' subjectivity requires a detailed description of the incident,[12] in contrast with the superficial coding of large databases available for terrorism research.[13] Such databases do not capture the significance of the act for the perpetrators. In contrast, this inquiry aims to go beyond the bare facts and provide details, context, emotions, meanings, and significance of the act for the actor as well as the web of interactions among actors. Through this meaning, the analysis brings the context and relevant social structural features into the process under study. The empirical chapters attempt to accurately describe and interpret social actions within the context in which they happen.

The strategy is to analyze perpetrators' actions from an insider perspective, the opposite strategy of the vast majority of terrorist studies. This puts the reader within the context of meanings of the act in order to understand it. There is an understandable reluctance for readers to adopt this perspective, for they might feel that they are indifferent to the suffering of the victims. Nevertheless, an insider understanding of perpetrators is necessary and the first step for prevention of violence. Without perpetrators, there is no political violence. It is therefore crucial to develop an adequate understanding of the actor, from his or her perspective, to understand political violence and select appropriate interventions to prevent it.

To capture the subjectivity of political actors, one must rely on their words and actions rather than just their ideology.[14] Their relevant words and actions are the accounts generated by the actors themselves about their paths to violence. It is important to focus on the violent actors themselves and not just the ideologues of their communities. The two are often confused, and many scholars substitute the ideologues' rationales for the motivations of the actual perpetrators. The perpetrators' accounts are found in primary sources, and one of the major tasks in this study was to collect them to generate the detailed descriptions in the following chapters.

I searched for archival material where perpetrators' voices were documented, either in trial transcripts where their testimony was recorded, articles they authored, diaries they recorded, interviews they gave, or letters or memoirs they wrote. For each case, I attempted to reconstruct the meaning imbedded in the context of the violence. I tried to capture the thoughts, feelings, and behaviors of the conspirators when they became politically active, when they turned to political violence, and sometimes when they disengaged from it. In short, I tried to understand terrorism from the ground up. I assume that violence is an extension of how they made sense of their social world and thought about themselves in it, especially with respect to members of their group and enemies. I focused on the emergence and evolution of these groups within their respective social movements. How did they conceptualize what they were doing within their ideological context, structure of opportunities, and constraints they were facing to accomplish their goal? What was the emerging sense of shared social identity within their respective groups and in comparison to their enemies, especially when this identity was threatened? What was their relationship with allies and people on behalf of whom they were acting? Again, it is crucial to understand their view of salient out-groups that helped define them. For many, these out-group members were the agents of the state, such as high government officials or the police threatening them. For anarchists and workers, these out-groups also included the bourgeoisie—factory owners and financiers. These out-groups became the targets of their violence.[15]

However, with the possible exception of diaries and contemporaneous letters, where the actor records all his or her passing thoughts, these accounts are problematic, for they had a specific purpose and were not always accurate records of events for posterity. They were intentionally composed to address an audience with a specific agenda: a prosecutor, a judge, an imagined future public, relatives at home—the author wanted to influence these specific audiences in a certain way. The surviving archival traces often focus on theoretical or ideological justification for violence. Indeed, much research on political violence concentrates on how these justifications evolved over time according to experience and context. This is because such documents are what is left from history, and they privilege ideology as a motivation for political violence. This methodological artifact gave rise to the assumption that, by looking at the justifications, one can understand violence. I believe that this is not enough to recreate the relevant subjectivity of the actors. In a sense, our job starts where the documents end. The key is to transcend the biased accounts left by the actors trying to justify what they did or by their enemies trying to discredit and condemn these same acts. By the nineteenth century, most Western systems of jurisprudence gave voice to both sides of a trial and allowed actors to explain themselves within that context. The researcher sifting through these legal documents, must understand their origin and intent, and try to reconstruct how the actors felt, thought, and behaved leading up to and at the time of the violence.

Many historical accounts left behind are self-serving. Even in the few instances when the writer tried to be as honest as possible, his or her memories were full of unconscious or sometimes deliberate distortions. These sources must be handled with caution, but this is not an impossible task, thanks to the emerging understanding of some of the normal cognitive distortions of memory and thinking.[16] These biases can also be dealt with through corroboration in the analysis of the data. Nevertheless, retrospective memory must be viewed with at least some skepticism, as people reinterpret their past actions in light of their present beliefs. For instance, people often retrospectively explain their decision to join an ideological or religious group in terms of its ideas and neglect the importance of social bonding, which field studies have demonstrated to be one of the most important factors in that process.[17]

Even under the best circumstances, people view the same events differently, generating conflicting evidence. I let actors speak for themselves by trying to find contemporaneous quotes indicating their state of mind at the time. Getting a real flavor of their thoughts through quotes helps in understanding how they viewed themselves in their particular context. Sometimes, actors lived long enough to write memoirs, which gave a hint of their motivations at the time. However, memoirs and memory as a whole may be deceiving, as they often reconstruct personal history in as favorable light as possible for the writer. This must be taken into account as well. Most often, narrators skip over events that might not fit into the image they want to project at the time of writing. Nevertheless, these recollections are our only window into their minds and cannot be completely discounted, and so I have treated them as simple data points for the narrative.

Relatively few subjects of this study left autobiographical accounts behind. People who survived their acts of political violence were often captured and tried, and judges and juries were always interested in what motivated the defendants to commit such horrible acts. Trial testimonies and pre-trial interrogations, which allowed the defendants to explain their actions and the meaning these actions had for them, probably constitute the largest source of information for this study. The recent posting of such material online, especially for the French cases, courtesy of the Bibliothèque Nationale de France, greatly facilitated the collection of relevant trial transcripts. Testimonies in Russian were also widely reported and translated into English or French. Of course, such material must be viewed with caution, as defendants tried to diminish their culpability in court or simply use the courtroom for propaganda purposes.[18] Therefore, each piece of archival material was evaluated in terms of who was speaking to whom, for what purpose, and under what circumstances. After this assessment, I analyzed each piece in terms of what it indicated about that person's turn to political violence. In many cases, the defendants who had been caught in *flagrant délit* knew that they faced the most severe penalties, no matter what, and decided to provide a fairly plausible and comprehensive account of their trajectory to political violence. These accounts are instructive because they dispel many of the common beliefs about people committing such acts.

Despite my attempts to collect as much data as possible for each incident, only fragments of evidence survived. I do not know whether these fragments were representative of what these actors thought and felt or if I missed some significant pieces of information. Nevertheless, this book covers the subjectivity of the subject actors in these campaigns of violence in greater detail than others have attempted before. Although no new ground is broken here and no new source of evidence discovered, I brought together in one volume material that was scattered in many different places. While scientific research is never perfect or complete, it does try to further one's understanding of a given subject. The hope is that this deeper scrutiny might uncover some patterns that have been overlooked as well as test competing explanations of the process of turning to political violence.

The uneven documentation imposes its own rhythm on the construction of the narrative of past events. Sometimes, there is a lot of information, lots of testimony and documents, and here the description is rich and thick. These dense periods are interspersed with much longer intervals when there is very little left, leaving large gaps in our understanding. This emphasizes short bursts of dramatic events over longer, mundane periods in the lives of militants, when, overshadowed by competing social identities such as being a loving spouse, parent, or trusted friend, political identity and activities waned. I left these gaps alone and resisted the temptation to fill them with unwarranted speculations. The result is a narrative that collapses these long periods and strings together significant events in the actor's retrospective self-understanding. Although these uneventful periods did not play a significant role in the actor's understanding of him- or herself and the outside world around him, they probably contributed to the turn to violence. For instance, happily married and working people without grievances usually do not get involved in violent protest politics. These two mundane conditions may be the most significant factors in keeping people from traveling down the path to political violence, but scholars often neglect to mention their absence in favor of dramatic events that provide a more sensational and superficial explanation of their turn to violence. Therefore, it is important to collect as much information in as much detail as possible to reconstruct a narrative of events that will help us trace the process of turning to political violence. The many gaps in the historical evidence interfering with our understanding of this process impose a substantial limitation of this study.

People also react more to recent events than to long-past events.[19] Too many studies of terrorists collapse time, leading to erroneous causal attribution of behavior to long-forgotten events, like childhood "traumas" and slights to family honor evolving into indelible obsessions that the child avenges in adulthood. Such pathological long-term childhood obsessions are rare and seldom the cause of political violence. The very few cases of murderous obsessions described in the present study were generated in adulthood.

When I started this historical exploration into what led people to turn to political violence, it was clear that most of them acted as part of a conspiracy or were inspired by a political community that gave meaning to their action. It makes more sense to treat the conspiracy or incident itself as the unit of analysis rather than the individual narratives of each of the conspirators. Even loners, except for those suffering from mental disorders, were connected to a political community; their individual actions can be understood only within the web of meanings of this subculture and their relationships to in-group and out-group members. The aim, then, is to create a nuanced account of the evolution of each plot, a collective story rather than a collection of individual tales. The collective stories take place within a specific subculture of common history, tradition, norms, and values, creating shared social identities defined in comparison to relevant out-groups and existing within specific social, political, and economic conditions. These stories are also accounts of cooperation, mutual influence, and other emergent factors of group life, which must be included in the narrative. Overall, the cases come in clusters within a given historical community, a campaign of political violence, so to speak. I describe each of these campaigns of political violence in a narrative structure, paying close attention to chronology. I believe that only a narrative approach can hope to capture the drama and meanings of the various plots constituting a campaign of political violence. The stories of these campaigns form the six empirical chapters of this book.

The requirement for adequate and reliable data necessary to support a detailed description needed for process-tracing forced me to focus primarily on countries that held legal proceedings that allowed defendants to speak for themselves and recorded their words. This limits the scope of inquiry to Western countries, creating narrow geographical and historical boundaries for this study and precluding the selection of cases that may constitute a different type of political violence, such as the campaigns in colonies struggling for independence during the nineteenth and twentieth centuries. Colonial powers rarely bothered to leave behind extensive records of these campaigns from the challengers' perspective; they simply tried to eliminate them without much concern about their civil rights. The neglect of anti-colonial campaigns of violence is another serious limitation in this study, because they represent the type of cases that achieved the greatest percentage of political success, namely independence from foreign rulers.[20] However, this political outcome has not been necessarily due to the violence, as demonstrated by the successful, generally nonviolent campaign for independence in the Indian sub-continent. People there were not especially peaceful, as shown by the massive bloodbaths from Hindu-Muslim communal riots during the partition of the sub-continent. Independence was granted for complex political reasons in the metropolitan capitals, and violence did not seem to have been the determining factor in this decision. I invite other scholars to fill this gap of campaigns of political violence for independence with solid evidence.

The history of political violence in this study shows that violent political actors in the West generally modeled themselves on predecessors, establishing some continuity from the French Revolution, the regicides of the nineteenth century, People's Will, anarchists in Europe and America, Russian socialist revolutionaries, and Young Bosnia. They rarely referred to the long struggle of the Irish to gain independence from Britain, and therefore I did not include this otherwise extremely important instance of political violence in this book. Let me repeat, I have not attempted to write a comprehensive survey of political violence in the past two centuries. Instead, I have accumulated historical illustrations for the model described in the next chapter, which amount to a history of the turn to indiscriminate political violence. Fortunately, my linguistic limitations—English and French—did not force me to narrow the scope of this book since there is abundant documentation of Russian populists and socialist revolutionaries in both languages enabling me to incorporate them into this study. I ended this study when political violence, which over the nineteenth century had been careful to avoid unnecessary deaths, became indiscriminate with the targeting of civilians around World War I.

Although the inspiration for the study was the current global neojihadi campaign of violence in the West, I wanted to temporarily stay away from violence carried out in the name of Islam because of the present contentious debate on the importance of Islamist ideology in contributing to violence. Instead of contributing to this polemical mudslinging, I decided to look at history to assess the importance of ideology and more generally the model presented of the turn to political violence in different contexts and on a very different set of data before returning to more recent campaigns of violence in the appendix. I hope the reader will gain some insights from these historical campaigns that may facilitate a fresh look at the present violence.

Chapter 1

A Model of the Turn to Political Violence

Making Sense of Terrorism

What leads people to turn to political violence? A good starting point is to analyze how President George W. Bush mobilized Americans to fight against al Qaeda in the aftermath of the 11 September 2001 attacks on the United States. On 20 September, he addressed a joint session of Congress. His eloquent and moving speech framed the American understanding and response to this form of political violence against the West for the next decade and a half.

> Americans have many questions tonight. Americans are asking: Who attacked our country? The evidence . . . points to a collection of loosely affiliated terrorist organizations known as al Qaeda . . . Its goal is remaking the world—and imposing its radical beliefs on people everywhere . . . The terrorists' directive commands them . . . to kill all Americans, and make no distinction among military and civilians, including women and children . . . They are recruited . . . and brought to camps in places like Afghanistan, where they are trained in the tactics of terror. They are sent back to their homes or sent to hide in countries around the world to plot evil . . . Our enemy is a radical network of terrorists, and every government that supports them. Our war on terror begins with al Qaeda, but it does not end there. It will not end until every terrorist group of global reach has been found, stopped and defeated.
>
> Americans are asking, why do they hate us? . . . They hate our freedoms—our freedom of religion, our freedom of speech, our freedom to vote and assemble and disagree with each other . . .
>
> Americans are asking: How will we fight and win this war? We will direct every resource at our command . . . to the disruption and the defeat of the global terror network . . . We will pursue nations that provide aid to or safe haven to terrorism. Every nation, in every region,

now has a decision to make. Either you are with us, or you are with the terrorists. From this day forward, any nation that continues to harbor or support terrorism will be regarded by the United States as a hostile regime . . . This is not, however, just America's fight. And what is at stake is not just America's freedom. This is the world's fight. This is civilization's fight. This is the fight of all who believe in progress and pluralism, tolerance and freedom. We ask every nation to join us . . .

Americans are asking: What is expected of us? . . . I ask you to uphold the values of America, and remember why so many have come here. We are in a fight for our principles, and our first responsibility is to live by them . . .

Great harm has been done to us. We have suffered great loss. And in our grief and anger we have found our mission and our moment . . . The advance of human freedom—the great achievement of our time and the great hope of every time—now depends on us. Our nation . . . will lift a dark threat of violence from our people and our future. We will rally the world to this cause by our efforts, by our courage. We will not tire, we will not falter, and we will not fail.[1]

Let us analyze how President Bush's speech mobilized the nation to use violence against al Qaeda. He addressed the nation, and the world, as an American—"our country"—and not as an individual. As the nation came under attack, he reminded us of our common bond—our social identity as Americans—and asserted that any attack on one American, or three thousand, was an attack on all Americans. This threat to "us" made our self-conception as Americans far more relevant than our individual identities. This view of Americans-in-danger stressed our shared identity, dwarfed our individual differences, and focused us on the threat, the people who attacked us. He eloquently compared and contrasted us, freedom-loving people, from "them," freedom-hating people. This maximized our differences from the evil-doers and stressed our commonalities as Americans. He simplified the terrorists' essence to that of indiscriminate murderers whose intolerance betrayed their religion. He then went on to draw sharp boundaries between us and our allies, and them and their allies: "Either you are with us, or you are with the terrorists." Given the proximity of the 9/11 tragedy, this definition of the situation resonated with most Americans.

Indeed, as the leader of the country, President Bush had to help the nation make sense of these extraordinary, puzzling, and threatening events and provide guidance for the rest of us about how to think, feel, and act in this situation. His repeated phrase "Americans are asking" was followed by explanations and guidance. This set up expectations for thoughts, feelings, and behavior as

Americans especially with respect to these terrorist outsiders. Through a shared social identity as Americans or Westerners, he set the tone for mobilization of Americans to fight the threat. This sense of shared social identity as non-terrorists included our allies in this fight[2] and formed the basis of collective action against terrorists. By this stress on the virtuous "us," "who believe in progress and pluralism, tolerance and freedom," President Bush reached out and extended his in-group to include the rest of the world that he hoped to mobilize in a "global" war against terrorism. Getting people to feel engaged in the post-9/11 events, to feel outrage at the perpetrators as if they had been attacked themselves, was the necessary condition for counterterrorism, or the fight against "them."

With his speech, President Bush became the prototypical in-group member, providing guidance to the appropriate feelings, thoughts, values, and behaviors we should adopt as Americans vis-à-vis terrorists. His fondness for Texan boots, jeans, and leather jackets and his malapropisms only enhanced his image as the prototypical American. The day after the speech, the vast majority of Americans (78 percent) felt that the president did a good job explaining the goals of any military action that might result as a part of the war of terror.[3] By crafting this sense of shared social identity in a project to fight terrorists, he mobilized the country for war. President Bush's approval rating soared to a record 90 percent the day after the speech, according to a poll conducted by CNN/USA Today/Gallup.[4] His high approval rating was partly due to the fact that he had captured the mood of the country and moved to where it wanted to go. Fully 75 percent approved of his proposed military response, and an additional 19 percent complained that it was not enough. A week before the speech, 88 percent of Americans already thought that the country should take military action in retaliation for the 9/11 attacks. With this speech, Bush jumped into the locomotive of a moving train. The nation looked to him for leadership and internalized his sense of shared social identity and norms. He did not have to order Americans to join the national security apparatus; there was no need for coercion or material incentives. Tens of thousands volunteered and became soldiers in the fight against al Qaeda.

This process of mobilizing Americans to fight al Qaeda is similar to that of turning to political violence for those who are now called terrorists. A political community, in an escalating conflict with an outside group, disillusioned with peaceful means of solving the conflict and outraged by this group's unwarranted aggression, will generate volunteers, who view themselves as soldiers, to defend it against this outside group. Although this book deals with what is usually called "radicalization," or the process of becoming a "terrorist," both terms are so full of embedded assumptions that it is necessary to first deconstruct them by laying a foundation of a perspective or paradigm[5] of political behavior before defining them. Likewise, the turn to political violence can only be understood within this paradigm, which frames the model presented in this book. This paradigm implies some counterintuitive findings that otherwise defy explanation.

A Social Identity Perspective of Political Violence

According to this paradigm, all attempts to understand the social world start with an automatic and natural cognitive process of self-categorization. My analysis of President Bush's mobilization of Americans to fight al Qaeda shows that self-categorization was the basis of Americans' understanding of themselves and their enemies. Self-categorization is the core concept of a social science project analyzing the behavior of groups, known as the social identity perspective (SIP).[6] This perspective allows us to transcend the intuitive but unexamined and erroneous assumptions guiding our understanding of how people become terrorists, which have resulted in stagnation in terrorism research.[7]

The most popular explanation for "radicalization into terrorism"[8] is that future terrorists are predisposed to carry out terrorist operations because of some personal characteristics.[9] While a few people still believe that terrorists are insane,[10] most laypersons believe that they are "true believers"[11] guided by wrong ideas. This view that they are fanatics driven by ideology is the ideological perspective. As the president's speech suggested, they are seen as naïve, vulnerable, or "at-risk" young people spotted at home and developed by recruiters, who indoctrinate them and send them to terrorist camps abroad. Once their brainwashing and tactical instruction are completed, they are ordered back home to carry out mayhem. This view implies a theory of social influence to explain the acquisition of novel ideas so strong that one is willing to sacrifice oneself and kill others for them. One of the most common of such theories postulates that people are rational actors whose behavior is the observable result of cost/benefit calculations according to a predetermined set of preferences.[12] This is the rational choice theory (RCT), whose simple assumptions allow scientists to precisely calculate probabilities of choices and predict behavior. This perspective, which has been one of the most fruitful paradigms in the social sciences,[13] provides a simple explanation for the adoption of a new ideology as the result of indoctrination that selectively rewards its acceptance (through the provision of love and inclusion in a desirable group) and punishes its rejection (through ostracism or retribution). This study will frequently compare the social identity perspective, ideological, and rational choice theory paradigms as suitable explanations at key milestones in the turn to political violence in the empirical chapters that follow.

In contrast, when perpetrators of political violence are asked to explain their use of violence, they blame it on grievances. However, this answer quickly fails to satisfy because the same grievances are shared by a huge number of people, yet only a few turn to violence. When probed deeper, they blame circumstances.[14] These explanations stress the doubt and uncertainty they felt when they had to choose among several alternatives in a complex and confusing situation. Their explanations clash with the linear and simplistic determinism of analysts who never participated in these events.[15] The certainty and linearity of pundits come only retrospectively, when the complexity of circumstances can be reduced to an abstraction of what we know post hoc to be the significant factors. This ignores the considerable trouble actors have at the time detecting true signals from noise. This popular analysis focuses on a person's decision making to explain behavior. In fact, modern Western culture favors this lay explanation of behavior with its elaborate causal vocabulary of how mental states, especially emotions, lead to certain actions. In contrast, there is an absence of an equivalent lexicon of situations leading to specific behavior, with the exception of threats, experienced as fears.

Before dismissing perpetrators' explanations of their behavior as merely exculpatory justification for their crimes, let the reader consider the robust evidence that circumstances exert strong pressure, or force, on people to behave in a certain way. The French capture this sense of being compelled by circumstances by calling it *la force des choses*, literally the force of things, which is an ambiguous expression lumping together grievances, static circumstances, and the dynamics of events. The static dimension captures the structural context of events and includes the opportunity structure to use violence.[16] As events unfold in a certain way, the dynamic dimension suggests that the evolution of circumstances favors some actions over others at a given time.

When experts are asked about reasons for the turn to political violence, some continue to use pathological psychological explanations[17] or cite frustration from relative deprivation.[18] Most, however, point to classical social psychological experiments dealing with conformity,[19] obedience to authority,[20] and the power of assigned roles.[21] These experiments reveal the power of situations—*la force des choses*—to dramatically affect behavior without the actor even being aware of subtle experimental manipulations of the environment,[22] which show that randomly chosen experimental subjects are willing to kill others in the name of science or to sadistically torture prisoners. A few scholars have used these insights as building blocks for an explanation of radicalization.[23] However, these experiments, whose findings are robust and have been duplicated, have long lacked an adequate theoretical explanation. Recently, the SIP has provided this explanation.[24] In the rest of this chapter, I describe this perspective and its relevance to understanding the turn to political violence. I do not suggest that the SIP is the only explanation for this process, but it is probably its most significant one.

Like many other developments in social psychology, the social identity perspective began as an attempt to understand catastrophic events like the Holocaust.[25] The SIP comes from the work of Henri Tajfel, a Polish Jew who had immigrated to France and joined the French army to fight the Nazis. He was captured and survived a series of prisoner of war camps in Germany. After his liberation, he dedicated his life to studying what had made the Holocaust possible.

In order to find out the minimal elements that led to prejudice and intergroup conflict, Tajfel randomly assigned subjects to arbitrary groups (of which in fact they were the only member) and found that this assignment was enough to generate in-group favoritism and out-group discrimination. This group bias involved identification with one's group or, as his student John Turner would later argue, self-categorization. These minimal group conditions showed that loners spontaneously acted out on behalf of a group with which they had no contact.[26] Political examples of such loners acting out on behalf of a group because they imagine themselves to be one of its members are lone terrorists committing acts of violence on behalf of a larger social category: "jihadis," "anarchists," "liberators," "defenders of the constitution," "defenders of unborn babies," or any member of a vanguard striking out against the public in the name of some virtue. These loners do not require a special explanation for their violence and do not warrant a special label, like lone wolf. In fact, the empirical chapters show that a large number of politically violent people in history were loners.

Tajfel's minimal group experiments imply that people categorize themselves into different groups and this simple process of categorization leads to prejudice, group bias,[27] and is the key to understanding collective behavior, including social movements,[28] terrorism, and counterterrorism. Self-categorization, or the acquisition of a shared social identity, is what makes collective behavior possible. Categorization is a quick, natural, associative, emotional, effortless, and automatic process of simplifying our environment in order to make sense of it by creating categories of objects sorted out on the basis of apparently common attributes.[29] In terrorism research, this process centers on the categorization of terrorists in contrast to ourselves, as Bush did in his speech.

Bush mobilized the country by crafting a common sense of identity for his audience: American. This category made them all the same when compared with the salient out-group, the terrorists, and by portraying the war on terrorism as a defense of American virtues, values, and priorities threatened by this out-group. With his rhetorical skills, Bush answered key questions on Americans' minds: "Who attacked our country?" "Why do they hate us?" "How will we fight and win this war?" "What is expected of us?" Through his guidance, he generated the appropriate norms for Americans, our common in-group, and positioned himself as its prototype for others to follow or emulate. His arguments resonated strongly with Americans, and through them he became the true leader of the nation, as illustrated by his dramatic approval rating.

Through his address, Bush became the uncontested leader of the fight against terrorism. First, he consistently used language that showed that he was not only one of us, but indeed the prototype representing us. Second, he laid out a vision and project that clarified and promoted our group interests. Third, he crafted a sense of what it meant to be us, creating a compelling vision of our identity and our norms, with its implications for action. He told us how to act by telling us who we were. He mobilized us to fight against those that threatened who we were. Instead of asking, why did they attack us, Bush asked, "Why do they hate us?" He assumed that they attacked us because they hated us; and his simple answer was because of our norms, which we had to defend. Unfortunately, this answer was misinterpreted by some who took his argument to a more extreme position and argued that the values and norms of Islam were inimical to our "American values" and the guiding force of the terrorists.[30] Fourth, he used this identity to make us feel that we mattered: we were engaged in a global fight against terrorism for the future of the world. These four dimensions of leadership—being one of us, doing it for us, crafting a sense of us, and making us matter—define the dynamics of real leadership, people who use a sense of shared social identity to generate influence and power.[31] Followers often endow their in-group prototypes with a special quality—"charisma."[32]

The SIP implies that the way we think about ourselves varies according to the context. We think of ourselves at different levels of abstraction, ranging from a human being (humans versus animals) to a member of a group (us versus them) to an individual (me versus you), according to what is significant to us in a particular context. For example, we may see ourselves as part of the human race in the context of a natural catastrophe like an earthquake; as part of a nation in the context of international competition like sport, war, or trade; as part of a group defined by race, religion, gender, or citizenship status in the context of national comparison; or simply as an individual in the context of comparison with other individuals. In other words, our concept of self is fluid, varying according to the relevant contextual comparison. We have multiple significant identities that compete with one another according to the relevant context. There is nothing like an existential threat against one of them to bring its salience to the fore. An outsider attack on Americans, because we are Americans, makes our identity as Americans extremely relevant. Likewise, an attack on Muslims by Western nativists makes a Muslim identity especially salient.

A social identity means that one views oneself as an interchangeable member of a social group. This is a very important insight: one's own personal and individual identity does not come to mind since it is not relevant in that situation. Much like athletes during a game, members think of themselves not as individuals, but as teammates. In this context, individual perception becomes depersonalized: people think of themselves as team members and not as individuals—it is more important for the team to win than to pad one's personal statistics. Indeed, it is this process of depersonalization—being a team member rather than an individual player—that makes group phenomena possible.[33] This relative neglect of the individual self in favor of group identity is a natural process that all of us experience when immersed in events as sports fans or patriots.[34] In-group members are teammates and no longer different individuals.

Likewise, opponents or out-group members are viewed not as individual players but as members of the opposite team. Self-categorization glosses over intragroup differences and sharpens intergroup differences. This accentuation of in-group similarity and out-group differences simplifies social reality into clear, concise, and manageable categories.[35] It also erases out-group members' individual differences and reduces them to one-dimensional stereotypes. This depersonalization of out-group members combined with reduction to a stereotype may lead to their dehumanization. Some have argued that such a process is necessary as a mechanism of moral disengagement to carry out political violence.[36] What the SIP implies is that this dehumanization of out-group members may be natural and automatic, part of self-categorization. There is no need for any additional process of desensitization, indoctrination, or brainwashing for this to occur.

Most people engage in political violence not for personal motives, but for group motives. As the president argued, any threat or injury to another group member is viewed and felt as a threat or injury to oneself, just as any negative turn of events for a sports team is experienced as negative by each team member. This is not a pathological process of losing one's own identity and mysteriously merging with that of the group. It is not indicative of a "true believer"[37] or "weak personality"[38] or some sort of brainwashing. It is not conformity, compliance, or obedience. It is simply part of categorizing oneself as a member of a group. It is a natural and direct consequence of self-categorization: in that context, one's identity is the group identity.

The shift from individual to social levels of identification underlies the social identity perspective, which investigates group processes, intergroup relations, and the self-concept. This shared social identity both creates and is created by the group. With a sense of shared social identity, we tend to see events in the world in terms of their significance to ourselves as group members rather than their implications for ourselves as individuals. A shared social identity transforms the relationship among members of an in-group to enable coordinated and effective collective action. When people view others as belonging to the same group as they do, they are more likely to trust, respect, and cooperate with them; seek out agreement and coordinate with them; give them help and develop a feeling of group belonging. In other words, shared social identity makes collective behavior possible.[39]

People have multiple social identities. Which one is activated in a given situation? People self-categorize within a particular social identity when, in a given situation, they have more in common with one another than with the rest of the population. This is the meta-contrast principle, which predicts that we lump people into a single group when their in-group differences are less significant than their differences with out-group members within a comparative context.[40] The perception of these two sets of differences activates the salient social identity that contrasts best to this out-group. By accentuating in-group similarities and out-group differences, we simplify our social world in order to navigate it more easily. Danger, like perceived out-group aggression against members of one of our potential in-groups, immediately increases its salience to us. Self-categorization is always in contrast to an out-group.

Self-categorization is facilitated by quick accessibility of the activated social category to one's mind—that is, it is commonly available from one's repertoire of categories.[41] This carving of the social world into given categories must also fit the categorizer's understanding of the world. Thus, activation of a given category among a multitude of potential ones is contextual, reflects a person's relevant concern at the time of the self-categorization, and conforms to the meta-contrast principle, its accessibility in his or her mind, and fitness to this context.[42] Social categories are therefore not fixed, absolute properties of the observer but are relative, fluid, and context dependent.[43]

The Terms *Radicalization, Terrorism,* and *Terrorist*

The process of turning to political violence is commonly called *radicalization*. However, this term has a double meaning: it refers both to the acquisition of extreme or radical ideas and to the readiness to use violence. The two are not the same. Many people share radical ideas, but the vast majority do not go on to use violence in their pursuit. The literature unfortunately confuses these two very separate processes and assumes that belief in radical ideas inevitably leads to violence. I focus on the process of turning to political violence and use this more precise expression rather than the word *radicalization* to avoid confusion. Turning to political violence is what is commonly thought of as becoming a terrorist.

Alex Schmid opened his classical survey of more than one hundred definitions of the term *terrorism* with the conclusion, "There is no clear and generally accepted definition of what constitutes terrorism."[44] This remains true today. As the quip goes, one man's terrorist is another's freedom fighter. The social identity perspective helps us understand this conundrum of terrorist/ freedom fighter and the difficulties of generating objective definitions of terrorism and terrorists. These terms simply refer to the categorization of out-group members (the terrorists) by members of an in-group (state agents, society) in conflict with this out-group. In-group members accentuate their differences with out-group members and reduce them to their essential characteristic distinguishing them from the in-group, namely to the fact that they commit illegal acts of political violence. This categorization lumps all terrorists together and endows them with a uniformity that erases their differences. In other words, to a particular in-group, all terrorists as members of the out-group are essentially the same. To King George, American patriots in the 1770s were terrorists. Communists and Nazis in the Weimar Republic were terrorists to each other, but not to their comrades. So were Afghan rebels to Soviet forces in the Soviet-Afghan War of the 1980s.

The meanings of the terms *terrorism* and *terrorist* change according to the constructed stereotype of this out-group and the context in which this categorization takes place. What the words mean depends on where the observer stands at the time.[45] "The question of definition of a term like terrorism cannot be detached from the question of who is the defining agency."[46] If members of a politically violent group are on our side, we often imbue them with a virtue common to our in-group: they are freedom fighters. If they are on the opposite side, we see only their tendency to violence, which we assume constitutes their essence: they are terrorists. Therefore, the meaning of the terms changes over time and context. For example, we called an Afghan *mujahed* like Jalaluddin Haqqani a freedom fighter in the 1980s when he was on our side but denounced him as a terrorist 20 years later for doing exactly the same thing: defending his country against foreign invaders. He did not change; the invaders of Afghanistan did, from the Soviets in the 1980s to the U.S.-led coalition forces 20 years later. His categorization into a freedom fighter or a terrorist depends on who is doing the labeling, not any internal characteristic of the man.[47]

Violent political actors define themselves according to the nature of their beliefs (royalists, republicans, anarchists, socialists, communists, religious believers) or their membership in societies (Freemasons, Carbonaris, revolutionary societies, or even religious sects). They usually do not define themselves according to their use of a tactic (terrorism).[48] Very few terrorism scholars have been terrorists themselves, and terrorism research is an activity of outsiders. Indeed, most researchers approach this subject from a national security or counterterrorism perspective, adopting the state categorization of terrorists as hostile out-group members. In doing so, they define these outsiders according to some essence that identifies them as terrorists. The scientific requirement of an unbiased definition of the subject of research has led to countless attempts to generate an objective definition of a term defined by subjective categorization. To my knowledge, no one has provided a self-reflexive definition of terrorism that included the defining agent. Of course, there is no consensus definition because different definers have different groups and different research questions in mind. They focus on different aspects of this issue and different context. They cannot agree on a common definition of terrorism because they were looking at different things.

Scholars of terrorism often define their subjects by a single act, albeit a very significant one. They decontextualize their subjects' actions, disconnect them from their intended meaning, and ignore the complexity of their subjects' lives and contexts. Instead, a small majority (51 percent) focuses on the effect of terrorist actions on the public, namely fear and terror.[49] However, there is a huge gap between terrorists' intent and the results of their actions. Whether acts of political violence are intended to terrorize an audience is an empirical question that can be answered only after careful study and should not be included in the definition of the act or the perpetrator. For instance, biological and chemical attacks by some groups were carried out clandestinely without the population being aware of them at the time and were only detected much later, when the perpetrators themselves revealed what they had done in the past.[50] These acts are labeled as terrorism despite the fact that the targeted population was not aware of them as the time and therefore not terrorized by them. The empirical chapters show that politically violent actors were seldom motivated by the *psychological* consequences of their actions. Basing a definition on these effects is anachronistic and limits the scope of any study of terrorism.

When terrorists talk about their violent act, they refer to its *political* purpose, which changes according to the context. This purpose gives meaning to their deed. For example, some may say they acted in order to bring certain political grievances to the attention of an audience and raise its political consciousness. However, after the violence, this audience rarely pays attention to these grievances but instead focuses on its moral outrage at the violence and its effect on them, namely the fear and terror they feel. This may well be the fundamental paradox of domestic political violence as a strategy: it seldom has its intended effect—bringing attention to a set of grievances—but focuses attention, including that of scholars, on the violence and its perpetrators and on how they differ from the rest of society. In carrying out acts of political violence, perpetrators see themselves as acting out the norms, values, and meanings of their group, while out-group members focus on their acts and construct a stereotypical profile of people who can carry out such acts.

The context and meaning of violent political acts generally fade away after their commission. Language reflects this cognitive focus on the actor rather than the situation leading to the action. It is easy to create a name for a person taking an action: committing a criminal act makes one a criminal; carrying out an act of terrorism makes one a terrorist. However, the circumstances that generate a criminal or terrorist act elude labeling and usually do not become a focus of study. Once a word is created, it defines a category and acquires a life of its own. It includes many associated thoughts, emotions, and memories that are immediately activated along with the category. A word like *terrorist* comes fully loaded with emotional associations and preconceived notions of the types of people who commit such acts of political violence. These categories are very difficult to change and require a strong cognitive effort to do so.[51] By default, the now decontextualized concept of *terrorist* is explained by some stable characteristic or essence of the person that allegedly drives him or her to commit political violence. This has led to the search for some predisposition to carry out such acts and a set of personal indicators or profile that might help us detect a terrorist before he or she carries out his or her act. So far, scholars have failed to uncover a terrorist personality, but since there is no other explanation for the decontextualized violent act, laypeople and security officials persevere in this search.

This muddy conceptualization of terrorists, embedded in the use of the word *terrorist,* generates a strong bias against them that is universally shared by the public, and has real-life consequences for both their victims and arrested suspects. Indeed, in the West this form of violence is all the more mysterious because it is so rare. I try to unpack this complex set of prejudices and biases that prevent us from understanding the turn to political violence. I am not trying to defend murderers. Terrorism is not excusable or justifiable,[52] but my task is to make it understandable.

I define terrorism as a categorization of out-group political violence during domestic peacetime. Terrorists are simply people who carry out acts of terrorism, as viewed from an outside and therefore critical perspective. The word refers to the disapproving categorization of individuals who commit acts of political violence. The actual content of this category varies according to the definer and the context of the act. One public's freedom fighter is another's terrorist, depending on whether the defining public categorizes the actor as an in-group or out-group member, respectively. In the classic example, Palestinian bombers are viewed as terrorists by an Israeli public but freedom fighters by an Arab one. As seen in the example of Jalaluddin Haqqani, the same person can be categorized as either one or the other by the same public along the same in-group/out-group axis. The word *terrorists* refers only to our enemies, not our friends. The usage of the term has degenerated to the point that authoritarian governments label as terrorists any political dissenters in their country. Liberal democracies should not adopt the terminology of these ruthless and brutal tyrants.

The self-reflexive definition of terrorism does not mean that the notions of political violence and its perpetrators are arbitrary and relative, or that the study of terrorism is just a semantic game. However, we need to use an expression that allows us to transcend the prejudices built into this terminology to uncover the process of turning to violence. Therefore, I shall use the terms *terrorist* and *terrorism* only in those instances when the actors themselves used them and will not project them back anachronistically onto these historical actors. Instead of terrorism, I use the more neutral expression *political violence* throughout this book.

The term *terrorism* is commonly used by a public that identifies with the state and its agents. In this instance, the out-group is a non-state actor. This usage was not always so. Political violence clearly can be carried out by either state or non-state actors. A state may be in the hands of a minority ruling over a generally hostile majority and use its monopoly of "legitimate" violence to intimidate this majority. After the widespread adoption of the term *terrorism* in the 1930s, it mostly referred to state violence—Nazism and Communism—or vigilante violence—like the Ku Klux Klan—that terrorized a population.[53] In fact, state violence has been far more devastating by several orders of magnitude than non-state political violence, with a ratio of perhaps a thousand to one. Today, global neojihadis deny that they are terrorists and instead accuse the United States of being the real terrorist because of the great destruction it caused in Muslim countries and its use of drone strikes that terrorize Muslim populations. State violence is much simpler to explain than non-state violence. Police, soldiers, and other state agents carry out violence as part of their roles and their identification with the state. Although it is usually explained with the concept of obedience to authority, the notion of carrying out orders does not completely explain state-sanctioned political violence. Some state agents sometimes refuse to carry out legitimate orders, and more do so with orders that they consider illegitimate.[54]

Only after the 1950s did states, their constituencies, and scholars limit their investigation of terrorism to non-state political actors. The above definition can be used by both those who identify with the state and state challengers. In this study, I focus on non-state actors, not because I identify with the state but because non-state political violence is more challenging to understand. The following chapters show that many violent political actors paradoxically start out as explicitly rejecting violence. Their transformation and use of violence require explanation.

In the above definition of terrorism, political violence is the deliberate collective attempt to use force against people or objects for political reasons. The word *political* refers to a community affected by a set of grievances, often a threat of violence or aggression by a contrasting out-group. This community can be members of an occupation, a family, tribe, town, society, nation, or any group defined by self-categorization. Politics in this sense harks back to its original Greek meaning relating to affairs of the community of people living in a city (*polis*) rather than the more modern focus on power. In Roman law, aggressions against the Roman community were *crimen majestatis populi romani imminutae*, "crimes diminishing the dignity of the Roman people." *Majestatis* refers to the grandeur of this community. When rulers captured power within a community and became identified with it, such crimes became *crimen laesae majestatis*—crimes harming the grandeur of the king—or crimes of *lèse-majesté* in French. In the course of time, these political crimes evolved into high treason, sedition, subversion, sabotage, mutiny, and, I would now add, terrorism. Their history had a different trajectory than that of ordinary crimes.

In modern times, a threat or aggression against one's group is political if this group is a large community, like a city or country. This use of the word *political* with respect to crimes follows a tradition in political science and jurisprudence.[55] "Violence or even, discrimination against an ethnic group, as well as a proscribed labor strike or picketing against a private employer, can be perceived as a political crime when those in power [and often the rest of society] see such conduct as undermining the political stability of the state"[56] or society—the perceived in-group. The meaning of the word *political* evolves according to how groups self-categorize or are categorized by out-groups. For instance, the violence of the Molly Maguires in Pennsylvania in the second half of the nineteenth century was considered criminal, not political, because it was both meant and viewed as revenge on cruel industrial supervisors. However, a few years later, the same violence committed by anarchists was viewed as political by both its perpetrators and the rest of society because both sides saw the violence as "propaganda by the deed," intended to spark a revolution. The violence was the same, but its meaning had changed.[57] Therefore, violence or threats are political when those who feel targeted view the acts of aggression as attempts to undermine them as a community.

I use the word *deliberate* to eliminate the cases of accidental use of violence. The term *collective* implies that the act has to be seen in the context of a political community. This eliminates people with serious and persistent mental disorders, whose ideas are only in their heads and not shared with others. They are self-motivated and not sensitive to their social context. Lack of responsiveness to social cues is part of the definition of mental illness. In other words, they are not part of a political protest community. Such lone political assassins, whose mental disorder is the major contributing factor to their political violence, have existed throughout history. Although the consequence of their action was political, they did not belong to a political community that gave meaning to their act. As such, their act was not political within the above meaning of political violence. Likewise, lone mass murderers often suffer from such mental disorders and have a political ideology on behalf of which they strike out. They should not be considered political actors; they are simply violent people with mental disorders, which were the major contributing factor of their act. Their delusional ideas of persecution do not reflect participation in a political mass movement. I have excluded them from this study when they did not belong to a politically active community trying to change society. Such people are still dangerous, especially when they are still able to function socially and therefore not institutionalized. However, their violence is not political in the sense of being carried out in the name of any group and has no group meaning.

I use the word *attempt* to include only serious threats or use of violence. For a threat to become serious, there must be clear acts in furtherance of violence, and not merely talk about violence. In present times, as communication is increasingly mediated through electronic media, states can easily capture words of political malcontents. States can now prosecute them for conspiracy to commit terrorism for just using violent words despite the fact that there was no act in furtherance. Violent complaints against one's government are universal and often lead to agreements between friends to do something about grievances, but such resolutions quickly fade away and seldom result in actual violence. Their prosecution undermines the meaning of liberal democracy.

I further limit this study to political violence in peacetime or acts not carried out at times of ubiquitous violence. Acts of political violence during foreign and civil wars, insurgency, or general breakdown of law and order can usually be considered part of the general violence, from which they derive their meaning. In wars and insurgency, the belligerents are soldiers fighting for their respective sides. In a general breakdown of law and order, such as in ungoverned areas or during times of revolution, many acts of violence are tit-for-tat revenge or carried out in the perpetrators' self-interest, but thinly disguised as political. In such a state of lawlessness, these violent acts acquire different meaning, and people react to them differently. They seem analytically distinct to me. Many large databases kept on terrorist incidents include insurgent attacks against foreign troops or government facilities.[58] To me, these attacks are part of the insurgency or war and should not be included in the same database as peacetime political violence. Local populations often see the presence of foreign troops as illegitimate, regardless of claims by their own often unrepresentative government, and fight the occupiers just as they would a foreign enemy. It is simply war, and such attacks are not included in this study. However, political violence carried out for domestic political reasons in a peaceful area even during wartime with a foreign enemy, fought in a distant place, and not attributed to the foreign enemy is part of this study.[59] I recognize that this may generate some confusion, but political violence by its nature is very messy, and it is not possible to avoid all ambiguity.

In the following empirical chapters, I do not include an analysis of violence during such important events as the Revolution of 1848 in France, the Paris Commune, or the Russian Revolution of 1905 because of the above considerations. The exception is an analysis of the violence of the *journées révolutionnaires* during the French Revolution. The reason is that, at the time of these *journées* before the Terror, the Revolution was generally peaceful and many instances of modern political violence evolved from these *journées* as an attempt to trigger a mass uprising and control the masses to overthrow a government and bring about political change. This transition came during Babeuf's conspiracy, which became the prototype of later revolutionary violence.[60] Without an understanding of this transition, later instances of non-state political violence become difficult to comprehend.

Many scholars include the targeting of innocent civilians in their definition of terrorism. The following chapters show that it is not until the early 1890s that civilians were deliberately targeted. Such a definition would eliminate the first hundred years of the history of modern non-state political violence. The use of indiscriminate violence against civilians came after a long evolution in the use of political violence. Starting at this point would be like studying only the tip of the iceberg, neglecting the rich history that led to this degeneration. Because early perpetrators of indiscriminate violence were inspired by earlier violence, starting with them, at almost midpoint in this history, would prevent a full understanding of them and the evolution of modern political violence.

This definition of terrorism does not negate the responsibility of politically violent people. Political violence results in deaths, injuries, and suffering, and on rare occasions in an outrageous number of deaths. These deaths, injuries, and sufferings are real, as the victims' grieving families can attest. This is even more reason to achieve a realistic understanding of this phenomenon, peeled off from unnecessary prejudices, in order to prevent such future atrocities. This desire to prevent violence does not mean that this book automatically assumes the stance of the government. Although governments traditionally cloak their interest in self-preservation behind the veil of national security, they are not neutral observers in the perpetration of this type of political violence. The role of governments in the causation of non-state terrorism is an empirical issue that must be addressed. My stance in this study is akin to that of a physician, trying to understand illness and suffering with equanimity. To describe political violence and try to understand it from the insider's point of view does not mean that I accept, agree with, or glorify this perspective. Nor does it mean that I forgive such heinous acts of violence. On the contrary, my sympathies, like those of the public, are firmly with the innocent victims and, as a physician, I try to understand the process leading to this suffering in order to alleviate it.

Activation of a Politicized Social Identity

Let us return to the process of turning to political violence. The first step in this process consists of the activation of a politicized social identity, which forms an imagined political protest community. In the presence of an escalating conflict with a contrasting out-group (often the state), disillusionment with peaceful protest, and moral outrage at out-group aggression, some militants start thinking of themselves as soldiers protecting their political community. This second self-categorization into a martial social identity leads a few to turn to violence in defense of their imagined community. In the following sections, I describe the activation of a politicized social identity that creates an imagined discursive political protest community and show how the social identity perspective implies a counterintuitive theory of social influence and group dynamics, which frames our model of the turn to political violence.

A politicized social identity is activated when people with a serious grievance realize that they have more in common with one another in terms of the grievance than they do with the rest of the population. The collection of people with a politicized social identity creates a vague and diffuse political community. One of the findings of the empirical chapters is that politically violent actors often did not originally view themselves as political. Many were students, workers, or citizens with some sort of grievance whose peaceful demonstration was violently repressed by the state. This aggression against the group, for instance, using the police or the army to crush a peaceful crowd, shocked its members into experiencing this attack not as neutral observers but as threatened members of a collective. This common fate and state aggression politicized the victims, who self-categorized in contrast to the army and police. All the politically violent groups in this study had self-categorized into a political social identity before they became violent. This self-categorization transforms the personal into the political and activates a politicized social identity.

It does not make sense to study political violence in a vacuum without looking at out-group intervention because political actors define themselves in comparison to this out-group and their actions acquire meaning in the context of out-group behavior. In effect, any analysis of political violence including terrorism must be dialectical in the context of an escalating conflict between two political groups. With the exception of previously mentioned people with mental disorders, it is impossible to understand the turn to political violence without the context of out-group activity. The way political challengers make sense of this *danse macabre* between themselves and out-group members, often agents of the state, contributes to their turn to political violence.

Discursive Political Protest Community

A collection of people united by a common politicized social identity form an active political protest community of meaning, shared through discursive practices. It is an imagined community, in the same sense that a nation is an imagined community, as each member imagines that he or she shares something in common with other members of this community.[61] It is anchored by specific symbols, shared ways of thinking and feeling about the world, and common rituals and behaviors, which may amount to a lifestyle, deepening the commitment of its members. Group members often acquire a specific vocabulary, manner of speaking, preferred references and standards, dress code, diet, types of relationships, and ways of behaving. In short, this discursive political protest community often becomes a counterculture.

Members of such a community become politically active through a repertoire of protest activities, which may include writing, discussions with intimate circles of friends and with strangers in public spaces, formal meetings, proselytizing, demonstrations, civil disobedience, strikes, disruptions, confrontations, and riots. The magic ingredient that makes all these activities possible is the constant discussion that is going on, which is why it is a discursive community. It is through discussion that political activists learn about current events as well as the fate of their friends, encounter new ideas, and develop an understanding of the world around them.

All the cases in this study predate the Internet. To expand from their small face-to-face communities, many of these activists or small groups wrote letters to each other and put out newsletters, telling their followers about relevant and significant events, new ideas, and especially social meetings. These newsletters functioned like information boards, with personal notices, announcement of local meetings, and celebration of marriages, births, and holidays. While one purpose of these publications was propaganda to recruit newcomers to the cause, they were even more important in forging a sense of social identity among the writers, subscribers, and readers. Even during intense repression by the state, many of these groups understood the importance of a printing press and tried to maintain one, no matter what the risk to them personally.

The advertised social meetings often included forums for political discussion along with social enjoyment such as dancing and picnicking. Local meetings about pressing issues solidified their common identity. Regional and national gatherings allowed them to meet other like-minded people or simply catch up with old friends. Members also traveled to meet people they knew through the informal grapevine and newsletters. They provided shelter for each other and hid members on the run. In all these interactions, there was constant discussion, from which emerged a sense of shared social identity. This continued social (and sometimes sexual) intercourse transformed their abstract identity into strong emotional bonds of friendship.

The informal epistolary network of such a community is a good indicator of its size and structure. It is usually centered on multiple informal prominent circles discussing political events. People drift in and out of this nascent community, which is amorphous and fluid, with fuzzy and porous boundaries. This collection of people is not yet a community until its members start thinking of themselves as such members, and this often involves the intense efforts of some individuals who help shape and structure this loose assortment of people.

Often such communities evolve into a rejection of mainstream culture and norms, which members view as being hypocritical and decadent. Such a critique is easy to formulate, since all societies inevitably breed some degree of social injustice, which is either glossed over by elites or justified in self-serving terms. This critique elicits a backlash against the protest community from mainstream society, which often adopts the hegemonic ideology of the elites. The triumph of nationalism in the nineteenth century in the Western world made people in a given country believe that they all belonged to the same in-group, the nation. By challenging the social foundations of this in-group, the social rebels are seen as deviant in their own society. This patriotic hostility toward these deviants is usually greater than that felt toward similarly critical foreigners. Those who loudly reject society are often viewed as traitors by the rest of society. It is easy to believe that their betrayal is due to a secret allegiance to a foreign entity, hence the constant search for a foreign and international hand. Society and its official representatives are typically disproportionally hostile to these internal rebels, and we see that attitude sanctioned in the wide-spread terrorist enhancement provisions of modern jurisprudence. It is a com-mon reaction of group members to subject in-group deviants to greater denigration and rejection than that accorded to comparable out-group mem-bers, and to punish them disproportionately for acts committed against the group. This robust finding in the social identity perspective is called the "black sheep effect,"[62] and this study will show much evidence for this, as political crimes are more severely punished than common crimes.[63]

Members of a protest community come to view political events from the group's point of view. News is rarely perceived objectively, but is interpreted through the prism of one's social identity and acquires different meanings for different groups. Al Qaeda members celebrated 9/11 as a great victory and a source of great pride, while Americans saw it as a great tragedy and a source of moral outrage. In a deeply polarizing subject like terrorism, facts are vigor-ously contested. To understand perpetrators of political violence, we must rely on their interpretation of these facts and not the state's spin on them.

This trendy rejection of the mainstream culture gives rebels panache and makes them attractive to some youths, who find it cool to be part of this group. Not only do the political rebels view themselves as more enlightened or ad-vanced than the rest of society, but many young people in society also regard them as such and join them in order to be fashionable. They all feel part of this flamboyant community that is different and more interesting than the rest of society.

A Theory of Social Influence

People are not born terrorists; they become terrorists. The turn to political vi-olence requires a theory of personal change or a theory of social influence acting on an individual to transform him or her into a politically violent per-son. The social identity perspective provides such a theory.

The social identity perspective suggests that in adopting a particular so-cial identity, people seek to discover the meanings and norms associated with their social category (for example, "warriors don't do this"). They view these norms positively and try to follow them. From this process emerges a certain social cohesion and coordination, making collective action possible. To un-derstand the meaning and norms of their group, people turn to its most repre-sentative members, who serve as models for them to emulate and thereby exert a strong social influence on the rest of the group.[64] They often come to define the group.

People think about categories not in terms of criteria clearly defining their boundaries but in terms of its most representative member.[65] This thinking in terms of representativeness means that the boundaries of categories themselves are not set in stone but change with its most representative element. As self-categorization is always activated in contrast to a salient out-group, a social category varies according to its comparative context: it is a fuzzy set with elastic and permeable boundaries.[66] Its most representative members are its prototypes; that is, its members most similar to other in-group members *and* most different from out-group members. As sources of guidance and emulation, these prototypes exert strong influence on other in-group members.

The social identity perspective sees social influence very differently than rational choice theory, which suggests that social influence is achieved through the manipulation of an individual's incentives, rewarding good behaviors and punishing bad ones. However, this overt manipulation of one's incentive structure often creates resentment and leads to paradoxical resistance to utilitarian leadership. On the contrary, the social identity perspective argues that social influence within a group is effectively exercised through the attraction that members feel for group norms, not the semi-coercive manipulation of people in power. This explains their enthusiasm and initiative in carrying out group goals. In the political arena, state elites control social incentive structures and reward conformity. Here rational choice theory has trouble explaining the very existence of political dissent and non-state violence, which involve tremendous self-sacrifice for the challengers. On the other hand, the social identity perspective argues that such self-sacrifice for the in-group is one of the major characteristics of group behavior, especially among its most prominent members.[67]

One of the findings of the following chapters is that politically violent groups rarely had a formal leader.[68] Instead, members of these informal groups looked up to their prototypical members, who set a model for others to emulate. These prototypes led by example within a given context: by their words and actions, they provided guidance for other members to follow. Members of politically violent groups in general were not forced or ordered to carry out violence: they actually wanted to do it, which explains why so many acted on their own. The views, actions, and feelings of a prototypical member of a group shape group norms. When ordinary members do not clearly grasp the meaning of a situation or know which norms are supposed to guide them, they seek out the prototypes. People viewed as in-group prototypes provide these meanings and guidance either explicitly through their words or implicitly through their actions. Other in-group members adopt these meanings, follow this guidance, and imitate these actions. As members think, feel, and act to conform to their prototype, these thoughts, feelings, and behaviors become the group norms. We all belong to multiple social groups, such as father, husband, worker, voter, or member of a racial or religious category. How we perceive events and behave will vary from context to context, as different social identities and their inherent norms become salient.

Effective leaders turn group members into dedicated actors, who want to do what the group would like them to do because it is who they are. There is no need for extrinsic rewards for doing what members believe and feel should be done in the first place. They adopt these beliefs and feelings from their most prototypical members, whom they emulate. In violent political groups, they carry out acts of political violence because they want to do it. There is no brainwashing or mysterious process of radicalization. These group members just carry out their social identity, like soldiers carrying out violence because that is who they are and what they do, and not because of their need for approval, fear of sanction, or group pressure to conform. The beliefs, desires, and feelings embedded in their social identity vary according to the context, especially the salient out-group. Information not consistent with their self-categorization is usually ignored.[69]

In an informal group where no one can enforce leadership through force, potential leaders need to be viewed as champions for the group, acting on its behalf, which implies trustworthiness and fairness toward in-group members. Indeed, the use of force to try to impose one's leadership shows that one's social influence has failed to elicit members' duty to the group. Too much concern about themselves or blatant self-promotion discredits potential leaders in the eyes of their comrades and undermines their appeal as source of inspiration.

Leadership in this perspective is not a passive reflection of "reality." It is an active attempt to influence the in-group and shape its "reality" though the manipulation of social categories and projects for the future. Let's return to President Bush's speech to illustrate this point. He consolidated his leadership of the Western world by crafting a shared sense of social identity belonging to a common social category (Westerners in contrast to al Qaeda). He established in-group norms, values, and priorities for action. By arguing that such a task mattered for world history, he gave a new sense of self-importance to those willing to carry out this global war on terrorism. He did not order the U.S. population to mobilize for the global war on terrorism, but influenced it to volunteer to carry out such a war and to zealously silence those citizens opposed to his project. Although he was already the formal leader of the nation, his approval rating and his ability to mobilize the nation behind him showed that he was also the prototypical member of the nation. The definition of who is included in the in-group (category boundaries) determines the extent of the mobilization of a wider audience into the group. By including Western nations, Bush hoped to mobilize all of them in the "global war on terror." The definition of what it means to be an in-group member (category content) determines the target of the mobilization. Bush defined Americans as fighting against terrorism in general, including al Qaeda and Iraq together. When France limited the fight against terrorism to al Qaeda and rejected its link to Iraq, refusing to take part in the invasion of Iraq in 2003 despite being an ally of the United States against al Qaeda, it earned disproportionate American anger—an example of the black sheep effect. Finally, the definition of who best exemplifies the in-group (category prototype) determines the leadership of the mobilization. Bush clearly was the prototype of the group defining itself in contrast to al Qaeda. True leadership is the exercise of this social influence as opposed to ordering people around even if allowed by one's legitimate authority. This is especially true in loose informal groups like violent political groups where formal legitimate authority is often lacking.

Discursive political protest communities, based on a sense of shared social identities, do not emerge by themselves. They are created through the intense efforts of political organizers, who craft this new sense of social identity in a potential constituency. Nevertheless, the political context determines the relevance of this identity at any given time. They must not be too far ahead or behind of their constituency. Continuing with the Bush analogy, an example of the power of context was the ability of a clique of neoconservatives to mobilize the nation to start a war against Iraq. At the beginning of Bush's presidency, they were considered far too extreme to be allowed to eliminate Saddam Hussein and drag the United States into a transformation of the Middle East according to their vision. The attacks of 9/11 changed the political landscape, giving their aggressive belligerence against Saddam Hussein new life and precipitating the war with Iraq in 2003. By that time, the nation was solidly behind them to punish those who were not "with us" and therefore "against us." President Bush, who at first believed their theory that al Qaeda was linked to Saddam Hussein, was able to mobilize the nation behind them. As just mentioned, France did not follow as it was too far removed from the neoconservatives' influence and saw no evidence for such a link.

Informal leadership also depends on the goals of the community. Early in its formation, members of a political protest community attempt to distinguish themselves from others in their original group, and intellectuals play a prominent role in this definitional task. When it is time to carry out its mission, organizers come to the fore and leave intellectuals behind. The practical problems of carrying out violent attacks, such as the manufacture of weapons, lead technical experts to displace organizers. Thus, the context and the task of a group elevate different members into positions of prominence.

Finally, besides crafting a sense of social identity and being a champion for the group, an effective leader needs to make members of the group feel important.[70] He needs to convince other members that being part of the group matters and what they do is significant. Political protest may be a high-risk enterprise, especially where states are very hostile to dissidents. To anticipate the argument, all violent political actors studied were willing to sacrifice their lives for comrades and the cause, and many did so without hesitation. Some went proudly to the scaffold or the guillotine, and one or two even volunteered for it to share their comrades' fate. They wanted to do something significant with their lives, and some decided to go down in a blaze of glory.[71] This self-sacrifice for the group reaches its logical conclusion in the current phenomenon of suicide bombers. These militants actually want to sacrifice themselves and are not coerced to do so through cynical manipulation by their leaders.

In taking prototypes as guides and models for thought, feelings, and behavior, the rest of the group respects, trusts, and wants to agree with them. In a sense, their followers endow them with charisma and attraction that is especially evident among group members. Prototypes are especially attractive to members of the opposite sex, who compete for their intimate favors. Given this temptation, leaders of many political groups were quite promiscuous, which was especially remarkable given the sexually repressive atmosphere of their time. This is not gender specific, but the vast majority of prototypes are male, and women throw themselves at them regardless of their objective physical attributes. However, more rarely and recently, women, like Bernardine Dohrn of the Weathermen,[72] can build up a collection of male consorts. This attraction need not be purely sexual—women also admired Dohrn's poise and look and tried to imitate her.[73]

Members of political groups felt part of a vanguard trying to change their societies. Their participation in such a difficult mission gave them a sense of pride. Unanticipated successes, like an effective demonstration, intensified this feeling. When others validated the emotion, it became even more attractive to be part of this community. When this community is viewed as special and prestigious, with delightful members, the quality of the companionship becomes a major attraction to its potential constituency. A pleasant sense of belonging to an attractive group helps maintain a strong sense of social identity and may strengthen faith in its professed ideology. As successful churches have long understood, a very active social community helps maintain faith in the group's beliefs.

This type of community attracts new members, who want to become part of it or be part of the action. They join relatives or friends who are already members of this community. Indeed, coming into such informal groups is mostly organized through preexisting bonds of friendship and kinship.[74] Unlike religious cults, which proselytize with active recruitment campaigns, political groups do not actively try to recruit passive or reluctant strangers. In the following chapters, all the protestors encountered were active, in apparent control of their actions, and guided by their sense of shared social identity. None saw themselves as vulnerable to some ideology, or at risk, or brainwashed into joining or participating. They were attracted by the in-group and volunteered to join it. Out-group members postulate an active recruitment process because they cannot understand how people could willingly join such communities that are hostile to the state and sometimes hold such extreme beliefs. Newcomers join a political protest community because of their identification with in-group victims, and their entry into the community was facilitated by friends or relatives.

The resulting political protest community involves a progression of activities that deepens its members' sense of shared social identities and further commits them to the community. There is a continuum of intensity of activism, ranging from nominal participation to complete and exclusive dedication of one's time and efforts. Such a community, therefore, has poorly demarcated borders with varying degrees of permeability and expands or contracts according to the political context. This amorphous, pulsating, internally fluid community is more akin to a social blob than a stable and formal network of people. Its internal composition is of course a loose network of people, but it is not stable. Its members (nodes in graph theory), are not stable entities, since the activation of shared social identity at a given time depends on salient contextual events, mostly the action of its relevant out-group at that time. Nor are relationships (links in graph theory) stable; friendships of varying intensity are constantly formed and broken according to their internal rhythms. Social identities and networks evolve over time, and a relationship at a given time will not stay the same later on. This lack of stability in nodes and edges greatly limits the usefulness of social network analysis as a tool to understand political protest communities.

A Theory of Group Dynamics

The previous sections argued that the turn to political violence does not require either a specific ideology or style of leadership. It comes from a process of self-categorization, with group prototypes that embody group ideology and norms. However, in addition to these internal group—or pull—factors that influence this process, external—or push—factors arising from the context at the time of categorizing play a critical role.

Just as it required a theory of social influence, the process of turning to political violence requires a theory of group dynamics to explain the transformation of a generally nonviolent political community into smaller violent groups. This theory needs to take into account unexpected developments and be more consistent with the vicissitudes of real life than the usual deterministic and static explanations of this process. The social identity perspective provides such a theory. Crowd phenomena, surprisingly common in historical cases of the turn to political violence, serve as a good frame to develop this theory.

A crowd is usually an unstructured group with no formal lines of command that congregates for a specific goal: celebration, entertainment, or protest. It consists mostly of strangers who had no time to agree on group norms beforehand. They therefore try to make sense of their situation as members of the crowd, activating a member-of-a-crowd social identity and look at the words and behavior of typical members of the crowd for cues on how to think and behave. Individuals in a crowd join it with different agendas. A few may come with the intention of inciting violence, but the vast majority consider themselves good citizens exercising their legitimate right to protest. They see the police as neutral protectors of the social order and therefore reject these advocates of violence as outliers, not representative members of a peaceful crowd, and may even actively discourage those prone to violence. In a situation where the crowd is monitored by the police in a fair and respectful manner, the prototypical member of a crowd is peaceful. Peaceful protest crowds constitute the overwhelming norm, but because "nothing" happens (there are no "historical" events except perhaps for their size), they do not make history books and fade from collective memory.

However, the police monitoring the crowd also self-categorize into police officers in contrast to crowd members, whom they lump together as an outgroup, stereotyping and not distinguishing among its individual members. When provoked by a few violent individuals in the crowd, their tendency is to see all members of the crowd as identical and respond to them accordingly. Sometimes the size of the crowd intimidates and frightens some police officers, who, lacking the discipline to hold their fire, panic and shoot at the crowd. Indiscriminate police brutality shifts the crowd prototype from moderation to radicalism. As members of the crowd feel attacked because they are crowd members, many panic, try to escape, or defend themselves. They now view themselves as victims in contrast to violent police officers. Their understanding of the situation is now consistent with that of the previously rejected advocates of violence against the police and others who are lumped in that out-group category. The extremists' perspective of violent conflict between crowd members and the police becomes more credible, and some members are now willing to defend themselves with violence if necessary and express their outrage through the destruction of property that the police are there to protect. This reconceptualization of their social identity as victims of police brutality, combined with solidarity with other group members and overwhelming advantage in terms of numbers, gives them a sense of empowerment and willingness to challenge the police. This dynamic mutual self-categorization of both crowd members and police officers escalates into a riot or massacre, depending on the number of victims, which is often one-sided since the police are usually well armed while the crowd is not.[75]

Participation in a crowd event may have long-lasting consequences, for it often leads to a long-term change in identity. People who were not politicized and came simply to express nonpolitical grievances (such as campus issues for students, work conditions for workers) are transformed as the event activates a politicized social identity. People who came to the demonstration in solidarity with their more militant friends start to share their friends' social identity after their participation and later adopt their friends' beliefs. Although not politicized before their participation in the event, their experience, especially when faced with police brutality, activates a new self-categorization that leads them to later adopt the beliefs and norms of their new shared social identity.[76] In addition, participants may experience a newfound confidence to resist and make claims against the police and other authorities. They may also experience new feelings, such as pride in themselves and their effectiveness in confronting the police, as well as moral outrage, which not only motivates them to mobilize against police brutality but also makes them more receptive to violent revenge against the state. In effect, indiscriminate police brutality against a peaceful crowd at the very least activates a political social identity and mobilizes victims and those who identify with them to address the perceived aggression. This threat against their social identity contributes to the activism of a political protest community.

This crowd shift to extremism is an illustration of a more general process combining contextual prominence with the meta-contrast principle. As argued earlier, prototypical members of a group are its most representative members, meaning that they are most similar to other in-group members and most different from the out-group (lumped into one stereotype). This sharp contrast between in-group similarity and out-group difference is called the meta-contrast principle. Members best representing this contrast are prototypes for the group. The meta-contrast principle implies that, as perceptions of the out-group change, so do in-group prototypes. In other words, the prototypicality of the same individual within the same in-group varies as a function of the context, namely the in-group relationship with the out-group. With friendly, cooperative out-groups, advocates of collaboration are prototypical, as in peaceful demonstrations. On the other hand, with hostile and violent out-groups such as a brutal police force, belligerent advocates are seen as prototypical of the in-group.[77] This is very important because prototypes are models generating in-groups' norms, and they exert strong social influence on other group members. Hostile police empower extreme crowd members, as the rest of the crowd sees these extremists as prototypical and endows them with great social influence over the crowd, thereby shifting the entire crowd to a more extreme position. The context of a hostile salient out-group is understood by in-group members as forcing them to adopt a more extreme and radical attitude, consistent with their blame of *la force des choses* for their turn to violence.

Returning to our analogy, President Bush would undoubtedly have failed to mobilize the country to fight against al Qaeda without the attacks on 11 September 2001. On 10 September 2001, a plan to mobilize the whole country to fight al Qaeda in Afghanistan and later invade Iraq would have been seen as too extreme. A strong threat to a social identity immediately increases its salience. The president was able to organize his constituency because they felt threatened as Americans, as 9/11 was experienced as a clear attack on America and Americans. Here, the nature of the threat to Americans from the salient out-group, al Qaeda, also drew the boundaries of the threatened in-group: Americans, including civilians, women, and children. After framing 9/11 as an attack on American social identity, President Bush could easily motivate his constituency and organize it in a massive counterterrorism campaign.

The salience of a specific social identity is temporary, depending on the context. Outrage at a perceived moral violation fades with time, and people move on. In a liberal democracy, the boundaries of a political protest community tend to be porous since peaceful political dissent is tolerated. On the other hand, authoritarian states do not tolerate political dissent and punish even temporary protest. In this case, the state determines the boundaries of the protest community by closing off the possibility of the dissenter's return to normal life. By punishing dissidents severely and bestowing on them a permanent outlaw status, authoritarian states endow extremists with more social influence with the dissident community. Some of its members turn to violence for self- and group protection. By treating peaceful protestors as dangerous, authoritarian states force dissidents to either submit to punishment or turn to self-defense and violence, in a self-fulfilling prophecy.

In a liberal democracy, dissent is supposed to be tolerated, but the state can apply pressure on protestors in more subtle ways and close off their opportunity to return to normal life. One method to persecute political protestors is to use rarely enforced laws to punish them harshly for usually trivial violations that would not ordinarily have elicited an arrest. As a result, those at large and now in judicial limbo are forced to go underground and live a clandestine life, preventing them from escaping their political dissident social identity. Another, more informal method is state notification of prospective employers of dissidents' past political activities, resulting in withdrawal of a new job offer or an immediate dismissal from an existing one. As political protestors are denied decent jobs that would allow them to integrate back into society, such measures force them to depend on illegal means to survive. Police harassment can also take the form of stop-and-frisk, constant questioning, informal brutality, and so forth. All of these methods remind dissidents of their outlaw status and social identity, reinforce the image of the hated police officer, and contribute to the escalation of violence between the unfairly treated protestors and their enemies, the police.

To be fair, law enforcement agents undergo the same process of self-categorization as dissidents. The police view dissidents as a very dangerous out-group and themselves as the virtuous protectors of society, prevented from effectively doing their job by the naïve constraints of liberal laws. Police officers believe in a simplistic behavioral rational choice theory:[78] if you punish dissidents enough, they will stop protesting. This works for animals, but not for humans. Instead, the social identity perspective suggests that dissidents self-categorize as victims and may seek revenge, resulting in the opposite of the intended effect. Sophisticated protestors understand the radicalizing effect of police persecution of their group. They try tactics to provoke indiscriminate police repression on their community, hoping to attract newcomers who self-categorize as militants in the context of police brutality against them.[79]

Conditions for the Emergence of Political Violence

With this foundation, we are now ready to discuss the emergence of violence from a peaceful political protest community: it involves a second self-categorization into soldiers defending their community, which completes the turn to violence when these soldiers act out their identity. This second self-categorization into a martial social identity occurs under three conditions: escalation of the conflict between two groups, including a cumulative radicalization of discourse; protestors' disillusionment with nonviolent tactics; and moral outrage at state aggression against the community.

Escalation of Conflict

The turn to political violence often results from an escalation in the conflict between political protesters and their salient out-group, often the state. The relationship between state and protesters is dynamic and leads to unexpected developments. Each party responds to the other in real time. The social identity perspective requires a dialectical analysis of this relationship, as group members define themselves in contrast to a salient out-group, which, for political challengers, is the state. The group dynamics previously outlined show how an escalation by the out-group results in a shift to extremism in an in-group. Any analysis of the emergence of political violence cannot focus on just one of the belligerent parties. Such a one-sided focus on terrorist groups prevents any comprehensive and nuanced understanding of their behavior that responds to its context, namely the behavior of its salient out-group—the state. In an escalation of their conflict, both parties are usually responsible and therefore any scientific analysis of this escalation must address the state's contribution to this outcome.

This state contribution to the emergence of political violence has been neglected in terrorism research.[80] Of course, it is easy to attribute this to the fact that states fund most terrorism research, but this cynical explanation is not the whole story. The social identity perspective provides a more nuanced account. Honest scholars in the field self-categorize on the side of the victims and the state, and, like any other in-group member in a conflict, are blind to their own in-group's contribution to the situation and completely blame the out-group for any violence. In fact, in-group members reject any suggestion that the state might have contributed to the outbreak of violence as subversion or even treason, eliminating this topic from scholarly consideration. The state contribution to the emergence of political violence may be the most important still unexplored topic in the field. Acknowledgment of this contribution will help us understand this process and may even start a counter process that can defuse this type of political violence before it erupts.

Concomitant to the physical escalation of conflict is a rhetorical escalation on both sides. Each group sees its out-group's most extremist voice as most representative of the out-group,[81] ignoring general out-group condemnation of this type of speech and its own in-group's violent words. Fueled by popular media focusing on the most sensational and extreme, out-group extremist speech predominates in in-group perceptions of its rival, gives credibility to in-group extreme positions, and justifies the in-group's hatred of its enemy. This vicious cycle of mutual reinforcement of opposite extremes raises the volume of voices for violence in the cacophony of in-group noise. As long as out-group threat remains clear and present, in-group moderate voices are muted because they lack credibility in defense of their group. Extremist contenders for group leadership (protypicality) exaggerate the threat and danger to rally neutral members around them and discredit internal rivals as being too soft on the out-group and unable or unwilling to adequately protect the in-group against its enemy. By mobilizing their group against its enemy, they hope to increase their social influence, which they can wield for their own purposes.[82] They become intolerant of internal challenges in this alleged emergency and accuse these challengers of betraying the group, triggering the black sheep phenomenon. The suggestion that the in-group might have contributed to this dire state of affairs is simply viewed as a betrayal of the in-group.

The dominance of verbal extremism over concrete and reasonable proposals to deal with the situation is important. Extremist discourse precludes dispassionate discussions in the search for fair and just solutions to a group's grievances. Extremist speakers create a polarized atmosphere, and, as they use extremist concepts to interpret their group's experience of reality, they propose extreme solutions. Such speakers take a few incidents out of context and then blow them out of proportion. Violent discourse helps extremists shape how people feel about or make sense of events, thus influencing how they act. This discourse obscures the mutual dynamics that lead to retaliation and self-defense. War metaphors are especially harmful as they imply violent action, justify physical violence, and decrease the threshold for it. In retrospect, the situation is never as dire as portrayed in the speech of extremists nor is the struggle with the out-group as significant as they claim. But extremists come to believe their rhetoric and delude themselves about the grandeur of their fight.

While this book deals with history, the present situation, especially the Internet, exacerbates this escalation. Without any obligation to check facts, the Internet allows amplification of rumors through constant repetition. It allows each polarized side to harden its positions and prevent any dialogue between opposite parties posting their extremist messages. Some social media further aggravate this situation by reducing complex issues to 140 characters. To top it off, the absence of the physical presence of an adversary allows Internet-mediated communication to shed the last vestige of civility.

While hate speech must not be equated with violence, this cumulative radicalization of discourse rather than ideology per se favors extreme solutions and encourages violence.[83] These very violent words are often mistaken for violence, as reflected in the dual meaning of the word *radicalization*. However, there is a huge gap between words and deeds. This virulence of discourse from political protesters is mirrored in the speech of champions of the state or society. Such extremist speech contributes to the political atmosphere that allows violence to emerge.

Disillusionment with Nonviolent Strategy

In a replication of Philip Zimbardo's famous Stanford Prison Experiment,[84] Alexander Haslam and Stephen Reicher found that their subjects did not behave according to role expectations. Guards were reluctant to impose their authority and agreed with inmates to set up a more egalitarian prison system. When this proved unsustainable, all the subjects became resigned to allow their more authoritarian colleagues to impose a more tyrannical system.[85] The researchers interpreted their puzzling results in terms of social identity. They argued that the original reluctance of their subjects to act out their assigned roles was due to identity failure, an inability to identify with their assigned social role. The failure of the new egalitarian system adopted with great enthusiasm disappointed them and led to a second identity failure, this time with the egalitarian group. Most gave up and allowed more efficient, but authoritarian, colleagues to emerge, take over, and impose a more tyrannical regime.[86]

Disappointment with the efficacy of one's group may lead to acceptance of a more efficient but extremist leadership. This is mediated by the strength of one's identification with the group. This strength may be approximated as weak, moderate, and strong, by the degree of personal sacrifice one is willing to provide for the group. People with a weak sense of social identity with the community are not willing to make any effort for it. They can be viewed as free riders,[87] letting activists take on all the costs of participation and benefiting from these efforts at no or little cost to themselves. When faced with any adversity or with the inefficacy of the community to bring about reforms, they quickly lose interest, leave the community, and fade from history. This scenario is consistent with Albert Hirschman's famous argument that members in a declining group either leave it (exit) or voice their discontent (voice) to redress this decline, and these two options are mediated by group loyalty.[88] If loyalty is viewed as the strength of one's identification with the group, then those with little or no investment in this community are the ones who exit quickly when faced with the first sign of adversity or disappointment with the community. Vindictive states are counterproductive in preventing these weak protestors from giving up their political social identities and melting back into society.

On the other hand, moderate group members are willing to sacrifice some time, effort, and resources for their community. They can be expected to voice their displeasure at the ineffectiveness of the community to redress group grievances. They complain that what their leaders are doing is ineffective: they "just talk, talk, talk—and nothing happens." Over time, feeling disappointment with the group or confronted with punitive measures from the state, they will also leave the community and fade away, but later than the free riders.

Members who have sacrificed too much to give up their political activism can be expected to persist and even redouble their efforts to negate the decline of the group or its ineffectiveness.[89] Within this subset of members willing to sacrifice themselves for the cause, some convince themselves that the rules of the political game are unfair and that extralegal forms of protest are necessary. They escalate their activism to include more extreme and perhaps illegal measures. Other members, disillusioned with the inability of the protest community to achieve significant progress in terms of their grievances, are willing to let more radical members use more extreme tactics on behalf of comrades and cause. Very few are willing to join the extremists in their use of violent tactics, fully aware that their sacrifice means imprisonment or even death.

Disillusionment with the gains of a political protest community may explain the common observation that political violence often erupts at the tail end of a legal political protest campaign. When most members exit, activists disappointed with the results of the campaign may escalate to violence in a last-ditch effort to redress the original grievances. At the same time, the state, which did not dare crack down on a very large social movement, may decide to do so when the community of protestors diminishes to a more manageable size. This leads to a mutual escalation of violence.

Moral Outrage at State Aggression

Disillusionment, by itself, is usually not enough to turn politicized people to violence. Often there is a triggering incident, like a disproportionate outgroup aggression against the in-group. In a group, all members feel an attack on one is an attack on all, eliciting strong feelings of moral outrage against out-group aggressors and calls for punishment.

Moral violations are of course in the eyes of the beholder. In-group aggression against out-group members does not cause outrage in the in-group. In-group favoritism and out-group discrimination are results of the process of self-categorization. In-group members often see the result of their own aggression as "collateral damage," either necessary or accidental in the the struggle against the out-group. In-group members dismiss such collateral damage as unfortunate, because it was not intended in the first place (and thus does not generate any sense of guilt or even responsibility within the in-group). However, out-group members experience the egregious damage and do not dismiss it so casually. Instead, they see it as intentional on the part of the in-group. They believe the damage was indeed the goal or intention of the aggression, not an accident as the in-group claims. Social events are never neutral: people interpret and react to them through the prism of their social identity.

What about third parties, members of neither the in-group nor the out-group? Third parties are not an undifferentiated mass. Many have a latent social identity with one or the other group, and as this social identity is made salient and activated through an aggression against it, they are transformed into either in-group or out-group sympathizers or even members. The aggression politicizes them and makes them imagine that they are part of the active political community. Returning to our 9/11 analogy, Americans in Georgia watching 9/11 immediately felt American (rather than Southerners disliking northern Yankees) and took the attack on the United States very personally as an attack upon themselves. On the other hand, many Muslims who strongly sympathized with Muslim victims of previous Western aggression celebrated the abstract success of the blow against America, symbolizing the West in general. They did not celebrate the loss of life per se but the symbolic victory against an abstract West that had previously persecuted them. This does not mean they delighted in the horrendous loss of life; their feelings were a normal result of self-categorization. However, except for very few extremists, their identification was not strong enough to make them feel that they were part of the militant Islamist social movement.

But what about true third parties, not leaning toward one group or the other? Here, it is easier to identify with concrete victims, whose vividness facilitates imagining oneself as one of them, than with members of a mysterious terrorist group. This explains the widespread sympathy for Americans in the immediate post-9/11 era, including from most Muslims the world over.

People with conflicting latent social identities may experience a dilemma: dual loyalty to various potential groups can be transformed into divided loyalty when these groups are in conflict. For instance, after 9/11, Muslim political activists who self-categorized both in contrast to the West and as potential victims of al Qaeda extremism were divided on how to think about themselves. The resolution of such dilemmas probably depends on the specific context at the time.

Aggression against one of many social identities threatens this specific identity and propels it to the top in terms of salience and importance at the time. This violation and threat become the relevant context, which activates the specific social identity not only for one individual but also for many other people sharing this social identity. The threat activates a sense of shared social identity, which forms a self-categorized community. This is a normal and automatic reaction to perceived moral violations, which create or, through the conversion of latent into active members, expand a politicized imagined community.

A modern state, attempting to keep the peace by monopolizing violence within its territory, must intervene in disputes between competing groups that become violent. If it appears biased in favor of one group and uses violence against the other,[90] victimized group members will blame it for having committed a moral violation. Such a state intervention in a private dispute politicizes the victimized group, which now self-categorizes in contrast to the state as its salient out-group and creates a political protest community. For instance, blatant state intervention on behalf of industrialists transformed bloody labor disputes into political violence.[91]

The most obvious act of aggression against a group is the killing of one of its members, who, in death, becomes a hero or a martyr as he or she is viewed as killed for belonging to the group. Those viewed as dying fairly, in either combat or deserved execution for crimes committed, are viewed as heroes for the in-group. Regardless of their previous background, with their death, they become group prototypes: sources of celebration, inspiration, and imitation for the rest of the group. As models to emulate, they influence others in the group to turn to violence. Group members psychologically experience the death of martyrs differently from that of heroes, for martyrs' fate is seen as very unfair or disproportionate to what they have done.[92] For members, the death of a martyr is the ultimate sacrifice for the group. It instantly endows him or her with virtue and cleanses the person's reputation of any previous flaws. Deaths of martyrs cry out for revenge. They inspire strong motives for action: some members turn to violence, while others harden their resolve and press forward along their violent paths. These actions are not about ideology but about injustice done to the group. While heroes become inspirational models to follow, they do not elicit the same moral outrage as martyrs' deaths, which generally push comrades to action.[93] Martyrs are important in the turn to political violence because their deaths call for vengeance, igniting retaliatory escalation resulting in full-blown violence. An unfair murder of a member that goes unpunished by authorities can be seen as an egregious attack on the group, rousing its surviving members to defend themselves and avenge their martyr. This can quickly degenerate into a cycle of retaliatory violence: revenge for the martyr is met by unfair prosecution fueled by mass hysteria about an exaggerated danger, leading to greater retaliation and so on.

An out-group threat to completely wipe out the in-group also causes in-group moral outrage. A threatened community at the very least tries to arm itself in self-defense, which increases the probability of violence, for, once many people are armed, any incident may trigger large-scale violence. Armed crowds are especially dangerous—even very small events can trigger violence within them. Such crowds may take preemptive revenge against minorities allegedly allied to political challengers to the state and society through large-scale violent actions, riots, or pogroms. These mass explosions of violence are unfortunately still too common.

Another common moral violation is unfair and disproportionate state punishment against in-group members. In these circumstances, when the police try to arrest them, they may as well resist arrest and die in a blaze of glory.

In the process, the dead member is transformed into a hero and a source of emulation for the in-group. What started as an individual act of resistance spreads into more generalized political violence.

Another form of out-group aggression is undermining the sense of social identity through the recruitment of in-group spies or traitors. When group membership entails great personal risks, traitors generate intense anger and desire for punishment of the culprit, for they threaten the group's existence and undermine the meaning of its social identity. An insider betrayal undermines the trust that makes group activities possible and endangers its existential viability, hence the disproportionate anger and venom toward the traitor. An insider attack leads group members to reaffirm the value of their shared social identity far more strongly than a similar outsider attack would. The urge to punish the traitor severely, often with death, is especially strong. The black sheep effect describes this tendency to punish in-group deviant members more severely than out-group counterparts who commit a similar action.[94]

It is important to note that this form of punishment of traitors or cheaters within a community is far more common than expected by rational choice theory. A growing body of experimental evidence shows that total strangers will spontaneously punish cheaters, even at a cost to themselves, hence the name of third-party or altruistic punishment for this research project. This type of punishment, arising from a sense of indignation at the cheater, may promote cooperation in society. Without it, society as we know it might not be possible.[95] The social identity perspective may provide an explanation for this phenomenon. People tend to think of themselves as virtuous and cooperative with friendly others. If they are truly neutral and do not share a latent social identity with either of the parties (cooperator or cheater), they find it easier to identity with the victim when witnessing an instance of cheating. They feel the same moral indignation as victims. Desire for punishment of a cheater occurs naturally, and those who carry it out to restore their sense of a just world may be viewed as third-party or altruistic punishers. On the other hand, for people sharing a latent social identity with the cheater, the violation may not trigger a desire for third-party punishment. A cheating incident against an out-group may well activate a social identity with the cheater and won't trigger a desire to punish the cheater because of in-group favoritism. Cheating out-group members on behalf of the in-group is not only accepted, but on the contrary, celebrated.

If a group prototype is a traitor, this is especially devastating to the group, and even the most severe punishment may not rehabilitate its social identity. Instead, the betrayal may well lead to the disintegration of the group as members come to realize that their group norms and inspiration generated by the deceiving prototype were based on lies. If one's leader turns out to be a traitor, what is then the meaning of all one's efforts and risks on behalf of the group? Are the followers simply dupes? Nothing could be more demoralizing.

This fear of betrayal is not paranoia, but is grounded in reality. Attempts to penetrate a politically violent community and use of agents provocateurs, encouraging members to break the law so as to arrest and eliminate them, rank among the more effective means to end a campaign of political violence. When a traitor is found, not only do group members try to punish him, but so do others who share the general social identity of the targeted group. The elimination of traitors in a political protest community and preservation of its meaning trumps petty internal squabbles.

On a societal level, this black sheep effect may also account for the disproportional severity of punishment for domestic political violence. Mainstream members of society, and especially state agents protecting it, feel angry at the apparent betrayal of their national social identity. Tasked to maintain the social order, these agents often self-categorize in favor of pillars of society, which include prominent industrialists and landowners, and view challengers as members of an out-group rejecting the social order. Indeed, society questions the patriotism of political dissenters, asking them, "Don't you love this country?" while reaffirming its own unwavering support for the government, "My country, right or wrong!" Violent protestors are seen as betraying their own country, hence the desire for "terrorism enhancement" that punishes political crimes far more severely than ordinary crimes.

Aggression against symbols of one's social identity also elicits moral outrage and violence to avenge this insult, as seen in the recent wave of attacks against people drawing cartoons denigrating the Prophet Muhammad. This is especially so in groups for whom honor is important. Violence is more likely to result from a threat to social identity in a culture of honor than it is in a more modern society with less emphasis on honor.[96] Aggression against symbols representing a social identity, such as burning or debasing flags, crosses, or religious books or drawing insulting caricatures of one's emblematic founder, elicits anger and retaliation as a personal insult would. Criticism of group prototypes or praise of enemy prototypes can similarly be interpreted as intentional insults demanding some form of apology or redress.

Out-group aggression can shift in-group understanding of the social world to that of a dangerous one in which it needs to defend itself. In this atmosphere, any self-defensive action that crosses the threshold of violence may prompt a further slide down the slippery slope to full-blown violence. The pressure to support one's comrades in such a belligerent context may transform single acts of violence into a full campaign of political violence. The violent action becomes incorporated into the group repertoire of possible political actions and inspires other members to follow suit or escalate. The freshness of the group's violent retaliation is readily available in the minds of comrades, who may view it as legitimate, especially if the state overreacts to this first act of violence. This cognitive availability of acts of violence may explain the copycat phenomenon in which many violent acts seem to cluster together.

However, isolated out-group aggression is usually not enough, by itself, to lead to political violence. For that to happen, violations triggering moral outrage must find the fertile ground of disillusionment with the political protest community's effectiveness in the context of an escalation of conflict. This combination of escalation, disillusionment, and moral outrage is powerful and leads some of the most dedicated activists to question nonviolent forms of protest, which have resulted only in increased state repression that they cannot prevent through legitimate means. A few exasperated activists, too invested in the community to leave and tired of "just talk, talk, talk," react to the latest outrage with the attitude "enough is enough, and we need to do something about it."

Activation of a Martial Social Identity

A few of these exasperated activists may further self-categorize into soldiers for their victimized comrades and the cause. This martial identity is always activated in contrast to a salient belligerent out-group and then more recently and commonly against all potential enemies. This further self-categorization into a violent group is the second major step of the process of turning to political violence.

In the face of mounting threats and attacks from an out-group, with no legal recourse to prevent or stop them, a few in-group members will step up and volunteer to defend their imagined community. Are these few distinguishable from their comrades? At this point, there is no solid empirical evidence allowing us to make any such distinction. As previously mentioned, a strong sense of honor may play a role.[97] Another possible factor may be sensitivity to disrespect for an inflated sense of social identity.[98] Both factors cannot be simply reduced to just a psychological component as they both have a strong cultural component. In any case, we must leave this issue of personal predisposition unresolved since it completely lacks any reliable database of detailed violent political perpetrators' personality that could be scientifically analyzed. Any comment now would be speculation.

This activation of a martial social identity does not usually come as a conscious epiphany (some sort of "cognitive opening").[99] Neither is it a gradual evolution due to careful reasoning or something derived from a specific ideological interpretation. In the following chapters, no one attributed his or her turn to political violence to a better understanding of an ideology. Self-categorization is an unconscious process,[100] resulting from an understanding of the ever changing in-group/out-group relationship. Most of the time, there is no key event identifying the precise moment of this self-categorization, but at some point, the actor views him- or herself as a soldier, fighting for comrades and cause. The duration of this process may be very short. It is always possible to go back into the background of violent individuals and, with the help of hindsight, pick out episodes from childhood as indicative of a personal predisposition to violence. However, this type of analysis completely ignores the overwhelming amount of evidence that simply does not fit into this preconception and instead points to the collective nature of this new shared social identity.

Trying to draw a strict timeline of this process, commonly known as radicalization, by delineating the boundaries between a normal social identity, politicized social identity, and the narrower martial social identity suggests a degree of self-awareness that simply may not exist. The process of self-categorizing and making sense of the social world is ongoing, as people are always reinterpreting their position and role in their changing environment. Picking out a "stage" of this process is essentially arbitrary. Nevertheless, people who have undergone this process think about it in retrospect as an evolution. There was a period in their lives when they did not think of themselves as soldiers or defenders of their community, and there was a later period when they did. In retrospect, many attribute this change to specific events: police brutality at peaceful demonstrations, unfair prison time, or learning about egregious injustice against comrades.

Emerging violent militants understand and react to key events according to their personal and group conceptual evolution, much of which is gradual, natural, and largely outside of self-awareness at the time. With some rare exceptions, they generally do not set out to become violent political actors. On the contrary, many start out as explicitly rejecting violence, but once they adopt a martial social identity, or the state treats them as violent enemies, they act out their new identities. They start to go on short paramilitary excursions, learn paramilitary skills, practice martial arts, get weapons, take target practice to improve their skills, and so forth. These activities reinforce their social identity as soldiers for comrade and cause.

The use of violence against one's enemies raises the issue of the legitimacy of killing for the cause. Some political activists, endowed with delicate sensibilities, are willing both to use violence and also to sacrifice themselves, rationalizing that they earn the right to kill through their self-sacrifice. Their own death is the price of murder and reestablishes their belief in a just world, balancing their clearly illegal acts with their willingness to kill themselves or receive capital punishment for them.[101] However, most violent political actors do not share these scruples. Activation of a martial social identity legitimizes political violence: the perpetrators are just soldiers fighting for their imagined communities. Soldiers fight; violence is what they do. Self-categorization into a martial social identity in a political community means that violence is imminent because people with this new social identity may act out who they think they are. They want to carry out violence: there is no brainwashing or other mysterious process.

There is some debate as to whether this turn to violence is logical or emotional; rational or expressive; and the result of deliberate long-term strategy or the gut reaction of irrational people. Earlier, I stressed the element of moral outrage, but this does not negate rational thinking. Recent discoveries in the neurocognitive basis of moral thinking suggest a close integration between cognition and emotion, especially when it involves actions. Brain areas of feelings and thought are closely associated and too intertwined in moral reasoning to be neatly separated, as is so often done in abstract analysis.[102] Indeed, in the following chapters, violent militants all expressed deep feelings of indignation, moral outrage, hope, fantasies, and loyalty, but as a group they were surprisingly "intellectual," trying to understand and analyze their situation to find guidance for what they should do in their circumstances. Their evolving self-conception was the result of self-categorization activated in contrast to a belligerent group and extensive collective deliberations.

Some newly self-categorized members of the larger community act on their own as loners or couples. There is nothing about them to warrant a special label, like lone wolf. They simply act out their sense of shared martial social identity. Indeed, the social identity perspective emerged from an explanation of individual behaviors in studies of "minimal groups" consisting of a loner who imagined that he was part of a group. These loners showed the same behavior as regular members of larger groups. Self-categorization into an in-group and out-group in order to make sense of the world was enough to elicit the social dynamics of intergroup behavior.[103] Lone wolves are examples of this self-categorization, like any other real group members.

This new self-categorization indicates a willingness to sacrifice one's life for comrades and the cause. In the chapters that follow, some perpetrators explicitly stated they wanted to do something significant with their lives before they died. Indeed, a few were convinced that they would soon die for medical reasons, were afraid they might die without doing something that might give meaning to their lives, and decided to go down in a blaze of glory. Frantz Fanon argued that fighting back reestablishes pride and self-esteem in a discouraged and disillusioned community.[104] The willingness to sacrifice oneself for a cause means that the cause is worth personal risks and gives meaning to one's life.

Self-glorification can also play a part in the turn to political violence. Most subjects in the following chapters felt important as part of a vanguard and that their lives mattered, but most kept these feelings private and were willing to sacrifice themselves anonymously. They frowned upon comrades suffering too blatantly from the Herostratos syndrome and shied away from these self-promoting braggarts. Those willing to sacrifice themselves humbly for the group were celebrated as heroes: prototypes sacrifice themselves for the group and not for self-promotion.

Very few volunteer to defend their political community, and the vast majority take a free ride and let others bear the burden of protecting it.[105] These self-appointed soldiers for their community become frustrated and even angry with other members of the community who are resigned to their lot and do not join the soldiers in their new violent enterprise. The soldiers' willingness to use violence gradually isolates these self-selected few from their comrades in the larger political protest community, who do not want to get into trouble with the authorities and who avoid the violent militants. Many of their former comrades view them as undermining and discrediting their common cause by using violence and are angry that this violent faction has hijacked their movement. For their part, the soldiers gradually see their former comrades as wimps, lose their trust in them, and stay away from them.

The self-conceived soldiers start feeling and thinking of themselves as special, different from the rest of their community, believing that they are creating history as they go along. They believe they are the vanguard of the revolution and, like soldiers everywhere, develop a strong esprit de corps. The greater the sacrifice, the greater their self-esteem and the closer they feel to each other. Their baptism through risk, hardship, and common experience of violence transforms them. They prefer to hang out together because they feel part of the same group willing to brave extreme dangers and do not have to constantly explain themselves, their views, and actions to former comrades. Just being among like-minded companions who understand them, accept them for who they are, and share their social identity, beliefs, and fate is pleasant, comfortable, and relaxing. As the violence builds up, pressure intensifies for the violent group, and its members end up spending all their time together.

Gradually, the violent militants redraw the fuzzy and porous boundaries of their imagined community, excluding their former comrades from their new in-group. Their concept of the out-group enemy gradually expands from state agents and their allies to former comrades rejecting violence and finally incorporates the population as a whole for its support of the state. For the militants, all members of this expanded out-group become legitimate targets of violence. The history of Western political violence shows this pattern of evolution from narrowly targeted to indiscriminate violence against the population.

To escape arrest, these self-categorized soldiers go underground. Their social isolation narrows their exposure to events, ideas, feelings, perspectives, and interpretations of the world, which they now share only with their clandestine companions. They naturally dismiss any critique of violence from the out-group or the general population because of obvious bias. Likewise, they reject any warning about the misuse of violence from their nonviolent comrades because they feel superior to and believe they know better than their former friends. Their isolation and exclusive intercourse with like-minded extremists lead to mutual approval and reinforcement of their views, feelings, and behavior, validating and hardening their beliefs about the social world and the necessity for violence. Without exposure to a wider gamut of ideas, they experience a narrowing of their cognitive horizon,[106] often centered on an obsession with their enemies. Isolated, they become more self-referential and develop a private language that soon becomes incomprehensible to outsiders, including former comrades. This narrowing of cognitive horizons gives outsiders the impression that the violent militants are irrational because of the opacity of their beliefs, fanatic because of the strength of these beliefs, and rigid because of these beliefs' resistance to outside arguments. These adjectives reduce a complex dynamic group phenomenon to personal attributes, fostering the belief that there is something wrong with the thinking of these militants, like pathological hatred, as President Bush suggested in his speech to Congress.[107]

Violent militants start to convince themselves that violence may bring about reforms or is more widespread than it actually is: they delude themselves that revolution is around the corner in a triumph of wishful thinking over reality. This bizarre groundless optimism probably comes from the availability heuristics (they think about revolution all the time), their gradual isolation from the general population in the absence of convincing opinion polls, and the narrowing of their cognitive horizons, which leads them to overestimate the popularity of their own beliefs. When the public fails to follow their lead, they turn against the society, which they now view as made up of cowards.

More often than not, the result of their violent campaign brings about the opposite of what they intended, not state concession but further polarization and anger from the general public. In the larger society, a mirror self-categorization takes place, and militant violence causes a shift in favor of extremist champions of state repression, who succeed in imposing ever-stronger repressive measures.

A Bunch of Violent Guys

This martial self-categorization produces self-appointed soldiers willing to use violence on behalf of their threatened community, a bunch of violent guys emerging from the political protest social blob. Returning to the 9/11 analogy, after the tragedy and the president's speech, many young people volunteered to join the military, work for national security agencies, or become contractors in this industry. The state has institutions to facilitate their acceptance and transition into their new position to achieve their mission. This is usually not the case for political challengers. With the exception of a combat unit in a formal party representing a larger political community, this is a bottom-up process based on self-categorization, which has specific consequences for the composition, structure, and dynamics of these violent groups.

The formation of such groups is an informal process, not linear, often haphazard and difficult to determine in advance because of the contextual contingencies involved. They usually emerge out of discussions among committed members of the larger community occurring at informal meetings, study circles, prisons, restaurants, public places where protestors hang out, and now more commonly on the Internet. Their social identity is mutually negotiated through discussions within a specific context and converges around the need to use violence. Such discussions are dangerous, for the state is often vigilant, and therefore take place among trusted friends and relatives, who over time become a bunch of violent people—women can be as violent as men. This process results in small clusters, which are much more internally homogeneous than the larger political community because they are self-selected from networks of friends and relatives. These small clusters of self-conceived soldiers are fluid with fuzzy boundaries between them and their original political community. This makes the nascent violent group difficult to detect from the rest of the community and explains the usual difficulty state agents have in identifying all the conspirators in a plot. Group boundaries are porous at first but harden and become less permeable as the newly formed group progresses to violence because violent militants' status as outlaws prevents them from fading back into society.

These informal clusters lack any top-down authority that might appoint a clear legitimate leader to resolve inevitable internal disputes, causing instability in these groups. Personality conflicts frequently erupt among rivals and threaten to undermine their mission. Rivalries often masquerade as ideological disputes or degenerate into accusations of betrayal. I suspect that most accounts of campaigns of political violence greatly underestimate the extent of these disputes. History is written retrospectively, starting at the end—the political violence—and tracing it back to its origin in a linear fashion. Historiography ignores the many splinter groups that faded into oblivion because they failed to cross the threshold of historical attention. This historiographical artifact attributes a sense of determinism to the group whose violence helped it achieve notoriety. Viewed prospectively, these violent groups were plagued by internal rivalries. In reality, much energy is devoted to these disputes among conspirators, sometimes distracting them from the execution of their plans and at other times, on the contrary, facilitating violence in competition with their rivals.[108] This internal strife is hidden from outsiders because of secrecy and the tendency to lump all out-group members into a single stereotype, giving violent clusters a deceptive appearance of cohesion. In reality, many people drop out of the nascent violent group to be replaced by other, more compatible militants still sharing a martial social identity.

Quite often, there is no clear leader, but an active core, engaged in constant discussions, egging each other on. The core usually consists of two to four prominent members of the informal group who initiate and drive the violent conspiracy. It is not fixed, but evolves according to dynamics of internal rivalry and of its salient out-group influencing in-group prototypes. In contrast to the traditional static view of leadership, the emerging picture of this leadership core is a fluid one, waxing and waning according to the dynamics of the context. This explains why it is sometimes difficult to identify the leader of these informal clusters.

The context, especially violent state aggression, gives these emerging clusters greater social influence within their original community. I found no case in the following chapters where these champions of violence gave an ideological reason for their advocacy of violence to former comrades in the larger political community. They already shared the same ideology, but the active core attributed the necessity for violence to the state's escalation of violence against them. This context gave them more credibility in explaining what was happening to their community and justified their violent response to state violence. Ideological justifications were usually directed at outsiders to the larger political protest community.

The willingness of the active core to use violence and sacrifice themselves for the whole political protest community in the context of a belligerent out-group makes them prototypes for some members of this larger community, attracting them, especially younger ones, to the cause of violence. These newcomers, who share the martial social identity, want to join the new violent cluster. The growth of the new bunch of violent guys usually does not involve much effort by the active core to "recruit" like-minded comrades. Newcomers either eagerly volunteer, begging the active core to take them, or simply accept an invitation to join in their violent enterprise. Usually, the active core's views are well known in the larger community, especially to friends and relatives, who often go along out of solidarity. The growth of these violent clusters is often based on preexisting networks of trust, commonly grounded in friendship and kinship. This allows for last-minute "recruitment" based on the demands of the operation. There is no need for a prolonged period of development, indoctrination, or brainwashing, as is usually assumed for recruitment for clandestine activities or religious cults.

This analysis implies a continuum of commitment and activism in the new violent groups, ranging from a dedicated active core, to associate companions who tag along, and finally to peripheral comrades. These marginal friends might know about the conspiracy and help their violent comrades in minor ways, but otherwise do not actively participate in violent operations. What distinguishes the three levels of participation in political violence is that only the active core initiates and drives violent plots; associates are full participants but, on their own, would not have initiated or pushed the plot along; peripheral comrades suspect but do not know the details of the plot. Peripheral comrades still feel loyalty and solidarity for their friends or relatives, which translates into the provision of help in terms of shelter, money, and protection by keeping silent. Indeed, in many political communities persecuted by the state, such help was a sacrosanct duty and could not be refused to a comrade, no questions asked. These peripheral comrades constitute a large, loose network of potential supporters. They may not share a sense of martial social identity and sometimes explicitly reject violence. Nevertheless, they feel they have no choice but to show solidarity with their violent comrades despite strong disagreement with them over their tactics.

The degree of participation in political violence is not static. Indiscriminate punishment of peripheral comrades may prompt them to become more violently active. The disproportionate punishment of low-level support for friends and relatives may drive these peripherals to violence as it may trigger a feeling of moral outrage and activate a new martial social identity. The empirical chapters describe how a significant number of people who, feeling they had been unfairly punished, joined their more violent comrades.

The new bunch of violent guys is not self-selected based on an inherent violent predisposition. In the following chapters, there were a few who were probably already leaning to violence, but the vast majority had no record of criminal violence before participation in political violence, and most were explicitly nonviolent when they first became politically active. However, in the context of the escalating struggle with the salient out-group, they did not hesitate to carry out acts of political violence.

Many political activists come from families sympathetic to social change. They may even have internalized in childhood core family values of generosity, fairness, and justice. Many of the revolutionaries in the following chapters were "red diaper babies."[109] However, I do not wish to draw a straight line between parents' political social identity and that of their children. The children's path to political violence was not linear, and there was plenty of generational rebellion between them and their parents. Even for red diaper babies, the turn to political violence is quite complex, involving personal confrontation with out-group injustice and aggression threatening their social identity. I suspect that their core family values made them especially outraged when personally faced with inequity from the out-group.

Participation in a violent conspiracy becomes gradually more time consuming as it reaches its conclusion. Intense political commitment demands time. This means that deeply committed political activists and violent political conspirators must clear their schedule of other demands on their time. This is easier to do for students, the unemployed, or casually employed. Some students are particularly attracted to political activism. It is a time of transition for them, as they leave their family of origin. In a new environment and surrounded by new friends, they are more open to new possibilities, young enough to have energy to do things, and free of commitment, enabling them to sacrifice themselves for their ideals. When competing social identities, such as those involving new family or job responsibilities become more salient and significant, many drop out of violent political activism. Those who remain seem comfortable with a sense of indeterminacy toward their future. As political activism becomes their major preoccupation and identity, they reject traditional occupations, trades, or professions that cannot accommodate their time-consuming engagements.

The strong bonds forged in adversity and violence consolidate an "all for one, and one for all" attitude and make for a "band of brothers" unlike any other. Companions see themselves as self-sacrificing, fighting heroes battling the out-group, personified as the forces of evil. Increased personal danger and a shared fate cement their common sense of social identity into strong affective bonds, like the esprit de corps of soldiers, sailors, airmen, policemen, and firemen. These bonds create a special trust among them, and give more credibility to other in-group members. This strong fraternity demands that they share equally in the risks, costs, and sacrifices experienced by other companions. They do not want to feel that they are not carrying their load of the burdens and dangers or that they are letting their buddies down. This fraternity and indeed love increase their desire to protect and defend their companions from outside threat. This may make violence more likely when companions are eager to take risks to rescue an endangered brother.

This natural and automatic affection adds a sense of joy when companions meet, interact, and carry out their activities together. Strong emotional relationships reinforce this turn to political violence. When a spouse does not support a militant's new martial identity or discourages involvement in violent activities, the militant must make a choice and give up either the spouse or the violence. Militants feel strong emotional and often sexual bonds among themselves, which encourage, reinforce, and accelerate their paths to violence. Political commitment is not gender specific. The intensity of the sexual relationships formed in these violent groups is hard to match and is just one illustration of the intense affective bonding among the companions. Not infrequently, lovers are willing to gamble everything to save their mates.

In the context of two belligerent groups, even an attempt to understand out-group members and portray them as anything but pure evil may be seen as a betrayal of this strong in-group loyalty. Indeed, any attempt to try to understand out-group members in anything but the most evil light immediately brings accusations of betrayal and sympathy with the out-group: "Whose side are you on?" Although this is true for violent clusters, this is even truer for society, which, in a mirror self-categorization, feels the same way toward the political challengers. Any attempt to understand the challengers' subjectivity is met with shouts of betrayal of society. An attack on society demands repressive measures. Violent clusters retaliate, eliciting greater state repression and persecution, which in turn leads to greater retaliation in an escalating cycle of mutual violence.

As a bunch of violent guys pursues its political path, its activities gradually cross the line into full-fledged illegality. There is a gradual increase in suspicious activities. Conspirators show a keen interest in previous instances of political violence. They read about past attacks or learn chemistry in order to make bombs. They discuss ideas, previous political attacks, and plans for possible attacks of their own. They may practice their skills in laboratories or on camping trips. They show unusual interest in potential targets and start casing them. They need money for their planned operations and raise it through personal income or wealth, solicitation from rich sympathizers, loans, fraud, or robberies. They go about acquiring necessary weapons, ranging from knives and firearms to materials to build bombs. Many realize that their operation may result in their deaths, and make appropriate preparations for it by writing or recording their wills or just saying goodbye, partially explaining their upcoming action. Finally, just before executing the operation, in order to blend into their surroundings as they approach their target, they take steps to change their appearance, such as putting on a uniform, or changing the color, style or size of their hair. At this point, violence is a solid part of their repertoire of political activities, and the turn to political violence has been completed.

The French Revolution and the Emergence of Modern Political Violence

The history of modern political violence should start with the French Revolution. This period has been ignored by historians of terrorism, despite the fact that the word *terrorism* comes from its time of Terror. Instead, they start their history in 1878, with Vera Zasulich's attempt to assassinate St. Petersburg Governor-General Fyodor Trepov. However, as we shall see, the French Revolution inspired these Russian populists. Zasulich was compared to Charlotte Corday, whose assassination of Jean-Paul Marat was one of the triggers of the Terror, and the Russians militants called themselves terrorists in honor of Maximilien Robespierre, the head of the government during the Terror. Indeed, the French Revolution framed political violence in the West and inspired violent militants ever after. In fact, without the French Revolution as a reference, later political violence is difficult to understand. The next two chapters fill this crucial gap of almost a century in our understanding of modern political violence.

Expansion of the Political Arena at the Eve of the French Revolution

The French Revolution forever changed the nature of politics, including political violence. It politicized society and dramatically expanded the political arena. A partial expansion had already occurred during the American War of Independence, as private citizens fought off the British army. This politicization of American patriots generated local mobs that intimidated British sympathizers.[1] However, mobs as a new form of political violence involving all citizens of a nation capable of overthrowing a régime became the outstanding feature of the French Revolution.

Up to the French Revolution, politics was the prerogative of nobles, fighting among themselves to rule society and using violence to extend their authority over a given territory. In the run-up to the Revolution, the French king centralized power in his hands[2] and tried to monopolize the use of violence within his kingdom.[3] Although violence was still omnipresent in daily life, it was rarely political, and the king's progressive monopoly over its use contributed to its dramatic decrease in France.[4] By 1788, the king through his state had managed to pacify the country, and Paris got the reputation of being a relatively safe city, especially at night, thanks to the efficiency of its municipal police.[5] However, noblemen and burghers resented this state expansion of power and viewed it as too absolute, arbitrary, and unfair. They demanded political, economic, and social reforms to roll it back. A fiscal crisis in the late 1780s forced the king to search for new revenues, but these elites refused to consent to new taxes without reforms and urged the king to convene the General Estates. In August 1788, he reluctantly agreed to do so in May 1789. From then on, politics was constantly on the mind of the French. Electoral campaigns among the notables[6] of France immediately sprung up, along with a flood of political pamphlets allowed by the de facto relaxation of press censorship. Local grievances were recorded in notebooks, *cahiers de doléances*, and sent to the court. As the General Estates had not met for a century and a half, disputes about election and voting methods pitted wealthy commoners, making up the Third Estate, against the privileged classes constituted by the clergy (First Estate) and the nobility (Second Estate). This polarization activated a politicized self-categorization dividing common people from the privileged aristocracy (top clergymen were also aristocrats).

On the eve of the Revolution, France had become a nation after a century of active myth-making around the celebration of Great Frenchmen (and a few women) and the attempt to establish French as a common language.[7] From loyal subjects of an absolute divine right king, they had become citizens of a nation, France, with the king as its prototypical member. Unlike the state, which is a large umbrella institution, a nation is more ephemeral and difficult to define. A nation is essentially an imagined community, a community of people sharing a common political and cultural social identity—in this case, the community of French people. It commands profound emotions in its members, who are willing to die and kill for it.[8] This affective fraternity uniting nationals scattered across a vast territory trumped other political relationships linking rulers and ruled. This social identity, activated in a specific context (often vis-à-vis foreigners, usually Englishmen), gave dignity and pride to its members.

A popular pamphlet on the eve of the election, *Qu'est-ce que le tiers état?* (What is the Third Estate?), noted that the Third Estate represented almost the entire French nation, yet had no influence in French politics. It urged that the

Third Estate be given as much influence as the other two estates combined in the upcoming General Estates meeting—that is, its size should be equal to the other two and voting should be carried out by head count and not by estate in order to prevent it from being outvoted two to one on every issue.[9] The pamphlet's author, the abbé Sieyès, clearly identified with commoners, whom he viewed as the only legitimate members of the French nation. He excluded aristocrats from it, for they descended from a German tribe, the Franks, and not the Gauls, like the rest of France. In fact, he seemed to categorize real Frenchmen in contrast to these aristocrats.[10]

On top of this financial and political upheaval came a huge hailstorm that ravaged crops, a terrible harvest, and a very harsh winter, which led to food shortages and inflation. This triple catastrophe shattered the long period of political calm and led to 289 riots from the fall of 1788 to the spring of 1789.[11] The autumn of 1788 saw the first instance of collective blood flowing in the streets of Paris in about 150 years.[12] This storm of violence, blamed on mysterious outsiders and brigands, caused much confusion and fear, and local notables created municipal militias for self-protection.

By early 1789, election fever affected the French for the first time in their history. In this extraordinary atmosphere, people were uncertain about how far to push legal limits that might trigger repression by the Ancien Régime backed up by its efficient police. Common people feared that their "enemies," stereotypical "aristocrats" or their "brigand" agents, would not give up their privileges without a fight and might try to block their hopes for reform. The idea of an aristocratic plot against them quickly became an obsession.[13] There was some justification for this fear, as aristocrats in fact were trying to maintain their privileges. But in this politically charged atmosphere, people exaggerated the power of privileged elites to mythic proportions and attributed to them or their mysterious agents blame for all kinds of natural disasters, like food shortages, inflation, and even accidents. The 27–28 April 1789 Réveillon riot illustrates how this politicized social identity transformed a labor and food riot into a political mob.

At the end of April 1789, Jean-Baptiste Réveillon, a self-made man who had amassed a fortune in the manufacture of wallpaper and liked to flaunt his newly acquired wealth by giving ostentatious parties at this house, ran for election for the Third Estate. He gave a speech complaining about high wages, which increased his manufacturing costs and prevented him from competing with cheap goods imported from England. The news of the speech spread quickly to workers who interpreted it as a threat to cut their wages at a time when they were spending three-fourths of their daily pay on the purchase of bread alone. This triggered two days of rioting when Réveillon's house was stormed as well as several local food stores. Military troops reestablished order by shooting into the crowd, killing hundreds. In the next few days, the police identified some of the prominent rioters and hanged a few of them.[14] The bloody repression showed Parisian commoners that the state would not hesitate to slaughter them in a serious confrontation and reinforced their social identity in contrast to those wanting to maintain their privileges.

Some scholars consider this riot a prelude to the Revolution.[15] What made it different from other food riots? While looting, the rioters screamed, "Long Live the Third Estate!" This slogan is surprising because Réveillon was of course a member of the Third Estate. So, it seems that the riot was not directed at him personally: he was well-liked, paid his employees well, and even financially supported people he had laid off. In fact, none of his employees participated in the riot. The slogan indicates that not only did the political atmosphere contribute to the disturbance but the rioters were striking at rich people in the abstract. They identified with the Third Estate, with whom they also placed their hope for a better future. At this stage, they shared the Third Estate's self-categorization in contrast to the rich and privileged—the aristocracy.

As political rules were being challenged, agents of state authority, the army and police, became confused and paralyzed, searching for guidance. Some sympathized with and even joined the challengers. When confronted with hostile crowds protesting against food shortages or high prices, military leaders did not know how to react for fear that their soldiers might desert them. This indecision, compounded by confusion about the legitimacy of the authority of the General Estates, started the process of internal collapse of the monarchy. The Réveillon riot might have been the last popular unrest when lines of authority were still clearly defined as the police and royal troops did not hesitate to put down the rebellious mob.

Although the French Revolution is famous for its violence, it started out in relative peace. There was no call for violence among the people or recorded in the cahiers de doléances. Third Estate reformers never mentioned violence in their early debates and tried to convince aristocrats to give up their privileges through persuasion.[16] Third Estate deputies were not ideologues, but mostly pragmatic and cautious lawyers who had achieved great success within the system and reflected a wide variety of interests and opinions.[17] When they first met in Versailles a week after the Réveillon riot, their most aggressive demands were for legal and fiscal equality with the nobility and clergy: the end of all tax privileges, a single constitution for all citizens, state job opportunity based on merit, and voting based on a head count. They all self-categorized in contrast to the aristocrats, whose arrogance and intransigence they resented.[18] Within seven weeks of their first meeting, without originally even dreaming of the possibility, the Third Estate transformed itself into a revolutionary National

Assembly, claiming sovereignty over the nation—all accomplished without violence. What happened?

The Birth of the National Assembly

The day after the royal inauguration of the General Estates on 5 May 1789, each of the estates met in separate rooms. At their first gathering, Third Estate deputies discovered that they shared a common desire for all the General Estates deputies to meet in one chamber and vote according to a head count. They refused to start deliberations until this happened. In terms of strategy with respect to the other two estates, none preached violence, but they differed on whether to use conciliation or confrontation. The Dauphiné delegation, which had been elected in harmony with the other two estates, preached conciliation and negotiation. On the other hand, the delegation from Brittany, which had experienced bitter elections plagued by hostility and violence from the other estates, advocated confrontation. In the hopeful and thrilling first days, the Dauphiné's strategy won handily, and the Third Estate sent deputies to negotiate with the other estates.[19]

The clergy was divided on this issue, but its aristocratic leaders won a narrow vote against common deliberation and voting. The nobility, whose aim was to protect itself from commoners' "threats," met in "a mixture of frivolity of manners and pedantry of opinion; and all this combined with an utter disdain for ideas or intelligence."[20] Noblemen declared they would never accept any compromise and overwhelmingly rejected common deliberations. They allied themselves with court conservatives, led by the king's younger brother, the Comte d'Artois, and the Austrian-born queen. Despite mediation efforts by popular royal adviser Jacques Necker,[21] the negotiations went nowhere.

The arrogance and intransigence of the nobility moved the Third Estate to the Bretons' confrontational position. This extremity shift appears puzzling from the ideology and rational choice perspectives. The ideology of the deputies had not changed over three weeks, nor had their incentive structure. Instead, as suggested by the meta-contrast principle discussed in the previous chapter, the intransigence of the nobility empowered hardline deputies, as the prototypical leadership approach in the commoners' in-group shifted from cooperation to confrontation in response to the hardline strategy of the aristocratic out-group. The Third Estate deputies also discovered they shared feelings of intense fraternity for one another, fortifying their common social identity in contrast to the aristocracy and giving them courage to press on. They did not blame the king, whom they believed was misled by his conservative courtiers. Crowds constantly cheered them on from the tribune at their meetings, showered them with adoration on the streets, and bolstered their growing confidence. Such relentless demonstrations of popular enthusiasm convinced the deputies that they embodied public opinion or the people's "general will."[22] After days of frustrating negotiations, they now believed that the nobility's intransigence justified their more radical demands and adopted with near unanimity the Breton abbé Sieyès's resolution to invite all the privileged deputies to join with "all the representatives of the nation" for a joint verification of their respective credentials.[23] Despite the fact that only a few low-ranking priests came to the joint session, the Third Estate deemed the procedure adopted and moved on to declare itself the National Assembly, a sovereign body, on 17 June. Shortly thereafter, these deputies unanimously took a solemn oath to this assembly and passed a motion granting themselves complete control over taxation—threatening that payment of all taxes would cease if the government dissolved the assembly. They congratulated themselves, to the wild cheers of the public in the galleries.[24]

This unprecedented and still peaceful development (the word *revolution* had not yet entered the political vocabulary) was completely unexpected; it had not even crossed anyone's mind only six weeks earlier. The deputies knew that they had committed sedition and were anxious about the king's reaction. Their courageous defiance generated feelings of exhilaration, fear, and fraternity from the knowledge that they would all share the same fate. Two days after their momentous declaration, low-ranking priests and a handful of liberal bishops squeezed out a narrow victory within the First Estate, allowing them to join the Third Estate, but the king sent soldiers to prevent this meeting and closed down their meeting hall. Spurred on by the crowd, the deputies reconvened in an indoor tennis court three blocks away and swore that they would not separate until they had established a constitution for France. In response, the king summoned them to a full session of the General Estates on 23 June. When he addressed them, he adopted a hard line, annulled the deliberations of the past few days, and implied he would dissolve the entire meeting if the deputies rejected his proposal. After he left, the Third Estate deputies remained in the hall in defiance of a direct order to leave. Instead, the Comte de Mirabeau (elected with the Third Estate) captured the mood of his colleagues: "We shall only leave at the point of bayonets."[25] They rejected the king's proposals and declared themselves covered by parliamentary immunity, for they feared that they might be arrested at any moment. The tension was palpable: troops monitored their movements, let them meet in their own chamber but barred other deputies from attending, and closed down the spectators' gallery.[26]

But the crowds kept on cheering them in the street, and the majority of the clergy, true to their vote, breached the king's barriers and joined their

Third Estate colleagues, who welcomed them with tears of joy in this moment of doubt and fear. Finally, on 25 June, 47 liberal noblemen, led by the king's cousin, the liberal Duc d'Orléans, also defied their estate and joined the rest in the common hall. At the same time, law and order seemed to break down as many French soldiers openly comingled with the crowds. Unsure of the loyalty of his troops and fearing for his life, the king capitulated and invited the rest of the General Estates deputies to join the National Assembly. This was the tacit end of the General Estates and approval of the National Assembly—a bloodless revolution so far.

The news prompted widespread celebration and fireworks in Paris. Jubilant crowds breached the courtyard of the royal palace, as soldiers let them in. Rumors spread that whole companies in Paris had deserted and were toasted by crowds at the Palais Royal, the Duc d'Orléans's personal property in the middle of Paris, a large entertainment and commercial mall where he allowed free speech, protected from the king's men. The conservatives felt threatened by the seditious crowds and the shifting loyalty among the troops. Alarmed by the possibility of a general mutiny, the king called to Versailles and Paris 20,000 foreign mercenaries, most of whom spoke no French. This buildup and positioning of cannons targeting Paris alarmed its inhabitants, in whose mind the memory of the bloody repression of the Réveillon riot was still fresh. The introduction of foreign troops raised an identity dilemma for some French soldiers. Most people now understood the situation as a conflict between conservative courtiers supported by foreign troops on one side and patriotic Frenchmen on the other. In early July, there were altercations between French and foreign soldiers in Versailles. Many French troops leaned to the side of patriotism: "We are citizens before soldiers."[27] On 9 July, the assembly declared itself the Constituent National Assembly to emphasize its overall mission. But on 11 July, the king believed he was secure enough with the arrival of his foreign troops to dismiss and send into exile Necker, who had earned the hostility of his conservative advisers.[28] This triggered the first outbreak of political violence of the Revolution.

The Storming of the Bastille

The news of Necker's dismissal arrived in Paris on Sunday, 12 July, when a crowd was enjoying the holiday at the Palais Royal. A few agitators protested the dismissal, which they interpreted as the prelude of a massacre by the foreign troops, and urged the crowd to arm itself. The crowd, already in an angry mood from the severe food shortage, went to search for weapons and broke into gunsmith shops. As the crowd swept through the nearby Place Vendôme, a small company of German troops tried to clear the area. The crowd ran into the adjacent Tuileries gardens, where it saw a protestor dragged behind a German horse. The rumor that Germans and Swiss were "massacring the people" spread rapidly around Paris. Local units of patriotic French troops arrived at the scene in superior numbers, confronted the German company, and forced it to back down. Fearing a mutiny, the commander of the police and all military forces in Paris (he was located in Versailles) withdrew his troops from the city, eliminating the last vestige of royal law and order in Paris, as its police, left without any guidance from above, did not interfere.[29] During the night and the next day, crowds took advantage of this breakdown of law and order to loot food warehouses. They also destroyed most of the hated customs gates, burning their papers and tax records. These gates controlled access to the city and taxed goods entering it, thereby raising prices to the detriment of the poor.

Concerned about the breakdown of law and order, Parisian district assemblies recently created to elect Third Estate deputies formed a committee at the Hôtel de Ville, the city hall, to act as the provisional government of the city and raise a municipal militia for protection against the indiscriminate arming of the whole population. Lacking a distinctive uniform, the new citizen-soldiers were required to wear a red and blue cockade—the colors of Paris—for recognition and distinction from royal troops. They asked the provost of Paris to provide them with weapons, but the provost stalled and sent them on several wild goose chases throughout the city. He finally sent them to the Hôtel des Invalides garrison, where 30,000 muskets and dozens of cannons were stored. Its commandant delayed acting on the demands of the crowd by requesting permission from Versailles. Meanwhile, as crowds continued to search for weapons throughout the city, there were minor instances of looting, but the newly constituted militia restored some semblance of law and order by hanging some of the looters.[30]

On the morning of 14 July, rumors emerged that 30,000 troops were marching on Paris to put down the insurrection. An impatient crowd returned to the Invalides, ignored its commandant, and stormed the garrison. Many soldiers stationed there joined the insurgents and helped them from inside. Several protestors were crushed in the confusion. The crowd grabbed muskets and cannons but found very little gunpowder, which had recently been transferred to the Bastille fortress. It went there to get the powder.

Meanwhile, about 900 local militiamen, composed of craftsmen, shop owners, and defecting soldiers, had already gathered at the Bastille, which was guarded by 82 retired and disabled soldiers, supplemented by 32 Swiss guards. The militia demanded the powder, but the Bastille governor replied he needed instructions from Versailles and raised the drawbridge to the outer gate of the fortress. He invited two delegates from the Hôtel de Ville committee to lunch with him to resolve the situation. The militia grew restless during the delay and became suspicious that the governor had arrested the delegates. Jumping into the fortress from a nearby house, a protestor succeeded in cutting the cables of the outer drawbridge, which came crashing down, killing a demonstrator. The militia rushed into the courtyard of the fortress. Shots were fired, with each side later accusing the other of firing first. The invaders believed that they had been lured into a death trap—the courtyard was a closed space with no place to hide from defenders' fire. Everyone panicked, leading to indiscriminate firing from both sides.

At the same time, reinforcement from the Invalides, now armed with muskets and cannons, joined the attackers and aimed their cannons at the inner gate of the fortress. The disabled defenders were becoming increasingly reluctant to prolong the fighting, as they had no reserve of food or water to sustain a siege. The governor hesitated. Should he blow up the entire storage of 30,000 pounds of powder, destroying the fortress and a large part of the city, or surrender? His troops persuaded him to surrender. The second drawbridge came down, and the crowd rushed in to take control of the rest of the Bastille. The fatalities amounted to about a hundred attackers and only one to seven defenders. The disproportionate numbers of fatalities show that this was not a violent mob lashing out indiscriminately since it spared the defenders. This was not true of the onlookers. The governor was taken to the Hôtel de Ville, but was killed en route by a cook, who had not taken part in the assault on the Bastille. Likewise, when the provost left the Hôtel de Ville that evening, he was shot by someone in the crowd. Universal acclamation proclaimed the head of the National Assembly, Jean-Sylvain Bailly, as the new mayor of Paris and Gilbert du Motier, Marquis de La Fayette as the commander of the new municipal militia, which took the name Parisian National Guard.[31]

This insurrection was a spontaneous event, driven by fear of a possible massacre by foreign troops. The heroes of the day were relatively unknown, like former Swiss Guard sergeant Hulin who defected and was part of the original militia around the Bastille or second lieutenant Elie who came with the reinforcement from the Invalides. The Constituent National Assembly played no role in the uprising. Its deputies had self-categorized in contrast to not only the conservative courtiers (and the fear that they might convince the king to dissolve the assembly) but also the mob (mass military mutiny, unruly crowds, and chaos). The unpunished Bastille insurrection effectively ended exclusive royal sovereignty in France, for the crown could no longer control the crowd. The king recognized the National Assembly the next day and vowed to work with it for the salvation of the nation. The deputies cheered him on, embraced, wept with joy, and some fainted from emotional exhaustion. The leaders of the conservative clique, including the Comte D'Artois, left Versailles and sought refuge abroad. The next day, the remaining deputies from the first two estates, who had boycotted the National Assembly, joined it. On 17 July, the king visited the Hôtel de Ville and implicitly legitimized the uprising by accepting a tricolor cockade from La Fayette uniting the insurgents' blue and red colors of Paris with the royal white, still the color of the French flag today. The crowd cheered, peace was temporarily restored, and Necker was called back.[32]

The violence of these fateful three days is consistent with the social identity model of the turn to political violence. The shifts in the crowd followed the dynamics described in the previous chapter. Ideology had little to do with these events: with the Réveillon massacre still fresh in their mind, Parisians feared for their safety and armed themselves. The shooting and sacking of the Bastille were in response to fire from the defenders. Rational choice theory is also consistent with the rapid shifts in the schedule of utilitarian incentives faced by the crowds, especially when their lives were at stake. However, it does not explain the skirmishes between French and foreign troops in the weeks before the riot, the behavior of French troops confronting the German contingent on 12 July, and the reinforcement of forces coming from the Invalides to invade the Bastille. The social identity perspective suggests that, in all three cases, the helping forces had developed a shared sense of social identity with the crowd and acted on the basis of this self-categorization.

The Great Fear and the Declaration of the Rights of Man and the Citizen

The confusion and uncertainty of the mid-July 1789 crisis ushered in one of the most bizarre episodes in French history, the Great Fear.[33] In this time of confusion, fear was everywhere, and rumors of enemies—their identity was vague and varied according to location, but usually included combinations of aristocrats/foreigners and their paid agents, brigands and beggars—coming to seek revenge on French people filled the air. Towns and cities formed municipal militias for self-protection, and any accident could cause panic and result in violence. One of the most famous incidents was the explosion of Quincey Castle near the Swiss border late in the evening of 19 July. The day before, M. de Mesmay, the local nobleman, had invited citizens to celebrate the reinstatement of Necker at his castle the next day. Given his well-known conservative views, he did not want to spoil his guests' celebration by his presence and excused himself. During his absence, an explosion occurred, killing four celebrants and wounding four others. Influenced by the rumor of an aristocratic plot, local people jumped to the conclusion that Mesmay had lured them into a trap to blow them up.[34] The news of the explosion fueled the Great Fear, which spread throughout France, with peasants ransacking and burning manors and tax archives. It later turned out that the explosion had been an accident caused by three drunken revelers who went looking for more wine and inadvertently set off a powder keg with their torch.[35] This incident shows that the emergence of panic does not require any intentional act. It is a natural consequence of any natural or manmade incident that seems to target a population, especially if its origin is not well understood. In a politicized atmosphere, it is easy to blame alleged political enemies for any negative event.

The social identity perspective sheds some light on this strange panic. Common people had self-categorized in contrast to imagined enemies (aristocrats), and any imputed aggression from these enemies against fellow in-group members was experienced as an attack on all. Panic and revenge against any out-group member, lumped together by the crowds, ensued. This was not due to a sudden change in ideology. Rational choice points to the careful destruction of tax archives as an incentive for this series of castle burnings, but utilitarian calculation fails to explain the intense emotions of the crowds.

The National Assembly deputies were appalled by these reports of widespread violence. This nationwide breakdown of law and order was now foremost on the deputies' mind. They debated how to restore order and created a Committee of Reports to organize information and approve local appointments, as well as a Committee of Investigation, charged with police functions. The 60 electoral districts of Paris sent two members each to the Hôtel de Ville to form a municipal council replacing the previous committee, and each raised a company of National Guards which also collectively came under the overall command of La Fayette. To give the guards a new identity, La Fayette ordered them to wear the tricolor cockade.

While Paris regained a modicum of calm, the Great Fear's uprisings in the countryside continued unabated. The deputies were in a bind. They were aware that they owed their success to crowds intervening on their behalf in Paris and Versailles when it appeared that the Comte d'Artois's partisans were about to defeat them. On the other hand, they simply could not tolerate the spreading lawlessness that was destroying France—and in many cases their own property back home. Almost a full house, about a thousand deputies, was in attendance on the evening of 4 August to discuss this crisis. Since coming together over the past two weeks and facing threats from the right and left, the deputies from all three estates had experienced a sort of honeymoon period, from which was emerging an esprit de corps—in other words, a strong shared social identity, which set up this remarkable night.[36]

The session started routinely enough, with a proposal addressing the need to respect people and property. But then two very rich but liberal aristocrats took the podium. They denounced the unrests, but blamed them on the peasants' servitude and wretched living conditions. They proposed, therefore, to eliminate these conditions by abolishing the privileges of feudalism. Their admission of their own responsibility for the peasant unrests set the tone for the rest of the session and their generosity framed the ensuing debates. They opened a floodgate of denunciations of feudal and clerical privileges, with each speaker outdoing his predecessor in self-sacrificial patriotic fervor. The participants' diaries and letters attest to the feeling of solidarity akin to inebriation and exhilaration that reigned over the debates that night,[37] "a universal madness, a frantic delirium,"[38] which effectively abolished feudalism in France. The deputies spent the next week codifying the main themes of that fateful night, culminating in the Declaration of the Rights of Man and the Citizen, which was enacted three weeks later and eventually became the preamble of the French Constitution.

What happened that night? This apparent collective folly was an enigma to the participants themselves, as attested by their letters home. A historian cited "the inner dynamic of the Assembly and the force of events themselves"[39]—*la force des choses*. According to the social identity perspective, the deputies were vying for leadership of their group by escalating their demonstrations of self-sacrifice for it (and the nation) and by giving their group a sense of maximum significance.[40] Again, ideology played a small role in this remarkable night, which puzzled its participants because they had so obviously acted against their self-interest, a clear violation of rational choice theory.

The Transfer of Power to the National Assembly

This solidarity did not last long. Once the urgency of outside threats from the courtiers and the mob faded, some aristocrats had second thoughts about their prior enthusiasm. Soon, the deputies sorted themselves out into two major factions: conservatives, who called themselves monarchists, sat together at the right of the assembly's president, and demanded absolute royal veto power over legislation; and liberals, who called themselves "patriots," sat on the left, and opposed royal veto power. A compromise was found with the idea of a temporary veto, which could be overridden by three adoptions of a vetoed bill. Since all the deputies were prominent local citizens concerned about protecting some of their privileged position with respect to the vast majority of poor people, power within the Assembly shifted to the right, and the king refused to accept the Declaration of the Rights of Man and the Citizen. Patriot newspapers led by polemicists like Jean-Paul Marat demanded that the king be moved from his insulation in Versailles to Paris, where he would feel the power of the people.

Meanwhile, in Paris, the bread shortage was getting worse, leading to frequent small skirmishes in front of bakeries. Women were demanding bread: rumors of aristocrats hoarding grain to punish people and cause a famine became louder. Meanwhile, the king called his Flanders Regiment to Versailles for better protection, and patriot newspapers reported that at its welcoming banquet its officers had intentionally desecrated the tricolor cockade by stepping on it, with the foreign-born queen's approval. Women in the markets focused their wrath on her for the food shortage and resolved to march on Versailles to demand bread. At the sound of the tocsin at dawn on 5 October, a crowd of 6,000, mostly women, gathered in front of the Hôtel de Ville. They confronted the National Guard battalion protecting the building and ransacked it looking for weapons, leaving money and other valuables untouched. They then started on the road to Versailles in a hard rain, picking up support along the way. When La Fayette later arrived at the Hôtel de Ville, his National Guards were ready to follow the women. They had also taken offense at the alleged insult and wanted to replace the Flanders Regiment as the rightful protectors of the king. La Fayette tried to dissuade them, but, when he realized he had an impending mutiny on his hands, he went along with them to limit the potential damage.

The crowd of women arrived in Versailles in early evening. They were blocked from entering the palace grounds and instead flooded the National Assembly, demanding bread. They seemed fairly well informed about the political leanings of the deputies and threatened the monarchists. Intimidated by the size and proximity of the insurrection, the king notified the assembly that he was now ready to accept the Declaration of the Rights of Man, abolishing feudalism. La Fayette and 15,000 National Guards arrived around midnight. He tried to defuse the standoff by going alone to negotiate with the king. He suggested that the situation would be resolved if the king allowed the National Guards to protect his person, guaranteed adequate food delivery for Paris, and consented to return to his palace in Paris. The king agreed to the first condition, but said he had to consult his family for the third one. La Fayette reported back to his men and the National Assembly, and the rest of the night passed.

At dawn the next day, the crowd found a relatively unprotected palace gate and broke into the queen's wing. Two of her bodyguards fired at the mass of people climbing the stairs, and the crowd killed them both. The noise alerted the queen, who escaped to the king's apartment. A company of National Guards confronted the crowd and succeeded in controlling it, saving the royal family. La Fayette, awakened by the commotion, rushed to the palace and found the royal family badly shaken and huddled in the king's apartment. Under his guidance, the king approached the National Guards, who immediately swore their loyalty to him. Three hours later, the crowd and National Guards escorted the royal family back to Paris. The city again welcomed the king and his family as they settled in the Tuileries Palace.[41]

The National Assembly also followed the king from Versailles to Paris. Shortly after its arrival, a mob lynched a baker. The frightened deputies decreed the right to temporarily impose martial law to restore law and order, and created the crime of *lèse-nation* (the crime of harming the nation—that is, treason) to pursue enemies of France.[42] They also delegated police powers to local authorities, and the municipality of Paris wasted no time in creating investigation committees and rebuilding its police force on the same basis as that of the old regime. A good harvest in 1789 improved the food situation in the city, and the unrest of the spring and summer gradually disappeared from the capital. As many badly shaken monarchists resigned from the National Assembly, its right and left factions became more evenly matched and competed for the allegiance of the much larger nonaligned center. The patriot Bretons found a meeting hall in a monastery near the new assembly site, and people started referring to them by the name of their new location: the Jacobins.[43]

The move to Paris by the king and National Assembly was crucial in the evolution of the French Revolution for it left them vulnerable to the whims of the Parisian crowd, although at this point no one had thought about manipulating it to intimidate enemies. Crowds had saved the revolution when it seemed headed for defeat and their violence was spontaneous, in response to threats. These events show that the consequences of political crowd phenomena are often far more important than the political violence of smaller groups, which is commonly defined as terrorism. These phenomena have been neglected in the literature on terrorism.[44] Political crowd violence or its violent repression is often the prelude to terrorist campaigns, which cannot be understood without reference to their origins. This type of collective violence must be incorporated in terrorism studies on par with the rest of the repertoire of political violence.

The King's Betrayal of the French Nation and the Massacre at the Champ de Mars

In 1790, France had another excellent harvest and its financial situation improved: there was little popular protest. The cooperation of the king and his moderate cabinet helped shift influence to moderate constitutional monarchists within the Constituent National Assembly as implied by the social identity paradigm. These empowered moderate monarchist deputies dominated

their more revolutionary colleagues—hardline aristocratic deputies had emigrated.[45] The two-year calm allowed the Assembly to pass laws, govern France,
and draft a constitution. The deputies kept a constant flow of communication
with their respective constituencies and started to think of themselves as the
expression of the nation's general will.[46] However, they were conscious of the
unprecedented aspect of their task and knew that their revolutionary gains
were still fragile and might be swept away by counterrevolutionary forces—
hence the continued obsession with aristocratic or counterrevolutionary plots.

Within the Assembly, factionalism exacerbated this feeling of precarious-
ness: patriots suspected monarchists of conspiring with counterrevolutionary
forces, while monarchists suspected patriots of manipulating popular discontent into mass political violence. In fact, patriot deputies like their monarchist
colleagues were too frightened of popular uprisings to even think about using
them as a political tool.[47] Although there was still a great deal of popular anxiety and uncertainty, it did not rise to the level of the Great Fear of 1789 or
degenerate into mass unrest even when frightening incidents occurred.

One of them was the first instance of suicide bombing I have found anywhere, but it has been forgotten despite the fact that it was the most devastating indiscriminate bombing for more than a century. In the town of Senlis, a
clockmaker named Rieul-Michel Billon had been thrown out of a newly organized municipal militia for having charged an excessive interest rate in a loan
to an innkeeper. Billon felt humiliated, became depressed, and secretly swore
revenge. He accumulated gunpowder at his house, which also doubled as his
shop. On 13 December 1789, his former unit paraded in front of his house.
From inside, Billon shot at it, and, as he expected, the unit stormed into the
house. Barricaded upstairs in his booby-trapped house, Billion waited for the
militiamen to completely fill up his downstairs before setting fire to the gunpowder. The resulting explosion blew up the house and caused extensive damage in his neighborhood. He killed himself as well as 25 others and wounded a
further 41.

Billon's crime was declared *lèse-nation*: his cadaver was recovered from
the ruins of the house, desecrated, and dumped in the forest to be eaten by
wild predators. However, an extensive investigation found no trace of conspiracy or any link to an enemy. Although it caused great fright and was labeled a
political crime at the time, his suicide bombing of the local militia did not
trigger a new wave of mass unrest, as had the Quincey Castle explosion five
months earlier.[48] Indeed, despite the large number of fatalities and casualties,
unequaled until the twentieth century, Billon's suicide bombing also disappeared from the history books. Had he been active in any political circles or
clubs at the time, he would certainly have been viewed as the first prominent
terrorist in the modern sense of the term. So, despite the fact that the incident

had all the characteristics of what we have come to expect from terrorism in its modern sense—indiscriminate bombing, targeting innocent agents of the state (local militia), causing great fear in the population—his case has been ignored in the historiography of terrorism and even forgotten in that of the French Revolution. This shows that it is not the severity of the damage or ensuing panic or even the use of a particular method of violence that defines an act as political violence in the popular mind. Rather, it is the link to a political community or a politicized social identity that gives specific meaning to such violence.

Far from being the bloodthirsty vandals portrayed by Edmund Burke,[49] the French revolutionary deputies advocated nonviolence. In May 1790, the king requested the assembly to authorize expenditures for 14 warships in order to enter a maritime war on the side of Spain against Britain. This raised the issue of who had the right to declare war, the king or the National Assembly? The deliberations divided monarchists and patriots. Maximilien Robespierre, the future leader of the Terror, argued, "In contrast to principles that make people unhappy, the French nation, happy to be free, does not want to get involved in any war and instead wants to live in fraternity with all the nations as commanded by nature."[50] The assembly decreed that only it could declare war, subject to later royal approval, and that the "French nation renounces any war of conquest and will never use its forces against the freedom of any people."[51]

Over the course of the next year, the assembly took over more of the king's privileges, and the king felt his situation to be increasingly precarious, especially after the April 1791 death of Mirabeau, who had become his greatest ally in the assembly. He felt trapped, a captive in Paris, prevented even from spending Easter at his palace in nearby Saint-Cloud. Encouraged by the queen, he plotted his escape abroad with his family and secretly left in the middle of a June night. The slowness of his enormous carriage allowed a commoner, Jean-Baptiste Drouet, to recognize him and convince the municipal authorities of the village of Varennes to stop him on the evening of 21 June 1791. Emissaries from the Assembly led by revolutionary Jérôme Pétion were already in hot pursuit after discovering the king's absence, caught up with him there, and brought him back to Paris.[52] The king's attempted flight revealed his identification with émigrés rejecting the Revolution, therefore a traitor to the nation, and discredited his allies in the National Assembly. Radical journalists called for the establishment of a republic (in effect abolishing the monarchy) and fueled small popular demonstrations in Paris mostly of "passive citizens," people unable to pay three labor days' worth of taxes, which excluded them from voting, bearing arms and holding public office. The revival of popular unrest upset the "active citizens," who made up the National Guards since they were authorized to bear arms. Social inequalities piled on top of political differences and divided the nation.

On 16 July, radicals drafted a petition to convene a new assembly and establish a new type of government—minus the king. They invited people to come to the Champ de Mars the next day to sign the petition. About 50,000 people, mostly passive citizens, showed up and about 6,000 had already signed the petition when La Fayette showed up with his National Guard. He told the peaceful crowd that the mayor had declared martial law, and ordered it to disperse. When the crowd refused, he ordered his troops to march onto it. Some demonstrators responded by throwing stones at the advancing guards, some of whom panicked and fired back. Between 12 and 50 people were killed and an unknown number wounded. More than 200 people were arrested over the next few days.[53] This Champ de Mars massacre of a peaceful and unarmed demonstration discredited constitutional monarchists, especially La Fayette, in the eyes of the participants. The incident consolidated the passive citizens' social identity as sans-culottes[54] (literally "without breeches," more on them later) in contrast to richer active citizens, who wore them. The severe repression against the organizers of the Champ de Mars meeting hardened their hostility toward notables, including National Assembly deputies allied to the king.

Even the Jacobin Club split between a faction of constitutional monarchists and a republican faction that wanted to abolish the monarchy. Nevertheless, as the monarchists were in the majority at the assembly, the new constitution adopted on 3 September 1791 was a constitutional monarchy as if the king's attempted flight had never taken place. Ten days later, the king came to the assembly to accept it. With its mission accomplished, the Constituent National Assembly dissolved itself, but not before granting a general amnesty to all those arrested for political crimes dating back to May 1788, which released the imprisoned Champ de Mars participants. It also banned its own members from running for reelection to flush out remaining hardline aristocrats from the next assembly. The subject of the king's fate, precipitated by his flight, was shelved for the future. Its successor, the Legislative National Assembly, took office in early October 1791.[55] The apparent calm masked the deep polarization of society.

The social identity perspective clarifies the significance of the king's failed flight for the future of the French Revolution. Until this event, he was still seen as the prototype of the French nation. However, Varennes exposed his rejection of membership in this national group, leading revolutionaries to view him as a traitor to their in-group, an enemy of the nation. Demands for his elimination, and eventually his death (the black sheep effect), were a logical consequence of the new national self-categorization.[56]

The Overthrow of the King and the Bloody Second Revolution

A new set of deputies made up the Legislative National Assembly. They were generally more conservative than the previous assembly and only a very small minority decided to join the Jacobin Club. The former republican deputies did not completely vanish from political life as their participation in Jacobin Clubs that sprang everywhere in France allowed them to continue to hold sway over public opinion. In Paris, they were certainly not forgotten as Pétion, now popular republican, easily defeated La Fayette in an election to replace the retiring Paris mayor.[57]

Popular unrest returned in 1792, as inflation soared and sugar became scarce due to a revolt in Haiti, France's sugar-producing colony. Parisians again blamed the sugar shortage on alleged hoarders trying to undermine the revolution. Mayor Pétion was able to calm them down and defuse more serious unrest. He tried to bolster the dignity of passive citizens by letting them arm with pikes and bridge the gap between them and active citizens.

Meanwhile in the Legislative Assembly, the issue of war returned in a new context. The king and his allies wanted war because they counted on the rapid defeat of the degraded French army as all senior officers were aristocrats and many had emigrated. The king hoped that a foreign army of his royal relatives would help him reestablish his absolute authority over the nation. Surprisingly, an incoming faction of provincial Jacobins led by the eloquent Jacques-Pierre Brissot[58] also championed war, but for the opposite reason. Brissot calculated that war would unite the French nation, force the king to choose between patriots and émigré aristocrats, and mobilize troops from the provinces. He expected that large numbers of volunteers driven by nationalism would lead to a quick victory, strengthen the provinces against Parisian dominance in French politics, and allow him to establish a federal form of government. Within the Jacobin Club, he was opposed by a faction led by Robespierre, who feared that war might lead to the emergence of a military dictator who might usurp power. The disagreement between these two Jacobin factions escalated into strong personal hate.

Brissot prevailed and, on 20 April 1792, the Legislative Assembly, with the king's approval, declared war on the heir to the Austrian throne, who had encouraged émigrés to gather in Coblenz and plot to reconquer France.[59] The result was disastrous, as the poorly disciplined and reluctantly led French army suffered a quick succession of defeats. The enemy was approaching Paris. War began eroding the distinction between active and passive citizens. The previous year, 50,000 people of both categories had volunteered for the army, and in 1792 the number rose to 70,000. Sans-culottes strongly identified with the Revolution, which to them was synonymous with the nation, and petitioned the mayor to parade at the assembly with their weapons in a show of support for the assembly and the war. Pétion granted their request but was careful to surround them with an escort of National Guards to maintain law and order. For the first time, National Guards paraded with sans-culottes, armed with spikes. This demonstration temporarily consolidated their common social identity in contrast to the "Austrian Committee," as the internal enemy was perceived at the time. War was also radicalizing the sans-culottes' attitude against moderates, for in a belligerent context, extremists become the prototype of a nation. In war, neutrality, pacifism, or even moderation is often viewed as treason.[60]

The situation in France continued to deteriorate, with civil unrest in the provincial cities and the war. The king vetoed decrees persecuting refractory priests, who refused to swear allegiance to the constitution, and, under the advice of La Fayette, dismissed the Brissotin ministers of the government. The poor Parisian sections again asked the mayor for permission to parade in arms at the Legislative Assembly in support for the dismissed Brissotins and plant a liberty tree commemorating the anniversary of the tennis court oath, 20 June. Pétion granted it with the same conditions as before. After the ceremony, on its way back home, the crowd found a side entrance of the adjacent Tuileries Palace poorly guarded and stormed into the royal apartment. It forced the king to don a cap of liberty and listen to their grievances; thousands of armed people walked past him for hours. Alerted, Pétion came to the king's rescue and was able to peacefully disperse the crowd.[61]

This humiliation of the king produced a massive backlash of protests from his supporters, both in the wealthier sections of Paris and especially among the outraged émigrés. Pétion was suspended for three weeks before being exonerated by the Legislative Assembly. Meanwhile Prussia had joined Austria in the war and Prussian troops under the Duke of Brunswick were making steady progress toward Paris. On 11 July, the Legislative Assembly declared *la patrie en danger*, a state of national emergency. Federal troops (*fédérés*) from patriotic parts of France were called to Paris and quartered among the population. One detachment from Marseille marched in, singing a new war song that acquired the name of this unit, *La Marseillaise*, the future French national anthem. The newly arrived fédérés intermingled with likeminded Parisians and forged a common social identity of nationalist republicans defending the Revolution against external and internal enemies, including the king.

The successful demonstration of 20 June had empowered the Parisian radical sections, which found themselves in a growing conflict with the Legislative Assembly that was attempting to crack down on people criticizing its new conservative government and on prominent militant activists, whom the sections tried to protect. The sections were losing trust in the ability of the assembly and the Paris municipal council to protect them and address their political grievances.[62] Parisian National Guards' twin chains of command were now in conflict. They were recruited locally under the control of their respective sectional assemblies but were also under an umbrella command of a municipal general staff, discredited by the Champ de Mars massacre the previous year. As their dual loyalty became divided loyalties, the guards, like any part-time reservists, chose their respective sections, friends, and families over the more conservative municipal general staff. The state of emergency allowed the sections to stay in permanent session and they immediately abolished the distinction between passive and active citizens on their own initiative. This allowed the sections to greatly expand their armed forces and mobilize all their men, who self-categorized as soldiers defending Paris and the nation in response to foreign aggression.[63]

Around that time, the Duke of Brunswick threatened Parisians, who might touch the royal family or enter the royal palace, with "an ever memorable vengeance by delivering the city of Paris over to military execution and complete destruction, and the rebels guilty of the said outrages to the punishment that they merit."[64] This threat reached Paris in early August, and, far from scaring republicans away from any action, this clear escalation provoked moral outrage at the king and his allies—now clearly perceived to be on the side of the foreigners. Popular agitators immediately demanded the king's ouster. A secret committee of the leaders of the fédérés and radical Parisian sections was formed to coordinate their action and seize the Tuileries Palace to prevent the king's escape. Despite general agreement on the necessity of this action, its members could not agree on any plan or leadership. They simply assumed that the mass of people would carry the day, as it had before. This discussion was the first deliberate attempt to use a mass uprising in France to overthrow a government.

Pétion knew that the palace was well defended and wanted to avoid unnecessary bloodshed. He asked them to postpone any plan until after the Legislative Assembly had a chance to act on a petition that he had delivered asking the assembly to depose the king. On August 9, the assembly avoided taking any decision on it.[65] That evening, the radical Parisian sections set up a new formal committee, the Insurrectional Commune, with full power over troops and local administration. With its command over the armed forces, this new committee was now the real power in Paris, taking over from either the legitimate Paris commune (and its mayor) or the Legislative Assembly, which lacked any forces of its own. The Insurrectional Commune ordered the tocsin to ring at dawn on 10 August, and two large columns of National Guards and sans-culottes from the poor sections of the city, reinforced by disciplined fédérés, converged on the Tuileries Palace. Early in the morning, the king, who had been forewarned, tried to gauge the loyalty of his troops, consisting of about 1,000 Swiss mercenaries and 2,000 French troops. He saw some of his French soldiers fraternizing with arriving armed patriots, and, alarmed, he and his family took refuge inside the nearby Legislative Assembly building. He abandoned his guards to face on their own the gathering mob, already some 20,000 strong.

So far, the *journées révolutionnaires* (revolutionary days, as these popular uprisings came to be called, sometimes just *journée*) had been relatively peaceful affairs, albeit with the threat of violence.[66] This was about to change in a dramatic way. The Marseille detachment walked into the palace courtyard to fraternize with its defenders, but was greeted with a volley of fire coming from the Swiss guards. As at the Bastille, the attackers thought that they had been lured into a trap, panicked, and started firing in earnest. Adding to the confusion, the king ordered his troops to surrender to prevent further loss of life, but it was too late. Without effective leadership or discipline to prevent a massacre, the assailants slaughtered and mutilated the Swiss guards who tried to surrender, while the king's French troops defected to the mob. The result was an orgy of blood, and the macabre tally at the end of the day was about 600 Swiss troops killed, compared with about 300 *sectionnaires* and 90 fédérés dead or wounded. Most of the slaughter of the Swiss troops occurred after they had surrendered.[67] The French Revolution had acquired its bloody reputation.

Sans-culottes with pikes invaded the nearby National Assembly, where the king and his family were hiding. Under pressure, the deputies suspended the king and replaced him with a provisional executive council. This action of course voided the constitution with its division of power between king and assembly and the deputies directed the election of a new Constitutional Convention[68] by male universal suffrage, eliminating the distinction between active and passive citizens.

The violence during the overthrow of the French monarchy is more consistent with the social identity perspective than the ideology or rational choice paradigms. The escalation of violence on that day was remarkably similar to that of the storming of the Bastille. Mass violence broke out when the wrath of the attackers was provoked by the unexpected shots coming from the Swiss guards—a threat against some in-group members is a threat to all and calls for revenge. Ideology did not play much of a role in the developments of the day. The National Guards and especially the sans-culottes were, if anything, smugly anti-intellectual. Rational choice cannot explain the very different fates of the Swiss guards and the French troops. All Frenchmen shared a common national identity in contrast to the Swiss. The Swiss were targeted and slaughtered, while the French troops were welcomed by their compatriots and spared. As the Swiss were more disciplined and fiercer fighters than the unreliable French troops, a rational calculation would have been to try to side-step them to avoid losses in attackers' ranks. In fact, the opposite happened.

The First Terror and the Massacres of September

The six weeks between the fall of the French monarchy and the assembling of the Convention were marked by confusion and so much violence that several historians call this period the First Terror.[69] The confusion came from dual political authority, namely the Legislative Assembly Provisional Executive Council and the Insurrectional Commune, led by the Parisian radicals (which itself had voided the Paris municipal council). The Executive Council was composed of mostly Brissot allies who realized that they needed a radical figurehead to have any credibility with Parisian crowds and appointed Georges-Jacques Danton to lead them. Although he had not taken a stand between his Jacobin comrades, Robespierre and Brissot, Danton was closer to the former than the latter. His priority was defending the city against the Prussian invasion.

On the other hand, the commune was under the influence of people outraged at their friends' death during the storming of the Tuileries. Despite the fact that they had massacred most of the Swiss troops, they still wanted revenge on those that they believed supported the king, like refractory priests and aristocrats. They were convinced that Paris was full of these alleged traitors. The commune closed the gates of the city to prevent them from escaping and established its own committee of surveillance to replace the police. It closed down non-radical newspapers and demanded the arrest of the former king and his family, whom the assembly transferred to the commune for imprisonment at the Temple Prison. Newly appointed surveillance committee officers went door to door to question suspects and arrested hundreds of them, mostly refractory priests and well-known monarchists. By the end of the month, almost a thousand of these suspects were detained in improvised prisons. The regular courts could not process this huge increase of prisoners and the commune threatened to take justice into its own hands. This forced the Legislative Assembly on 17 August to establish a special court to try crimes in connection to the 10 August journée. After two weeks, only 32 suspects had been tried and 17 executed by guillotine, a new contraption designed to perform executions more humanely.[70]

The showdown between the assembly and the commune came to a head at the end of the month. The assembly, firmly under Brissotin control, tried to dissolve the commune by declaring it illegal. The commune, led by Robespierre and confident of its control of the sectional troops, responded by expanding its membership to include even more radicals, like the journalist Marat, who was calling for the blood of the royalists. The betrayal and flight abroad of La Fayette discredited his assembly allies and empowered the commune.

On 2 September 1792, the news of the fall of Verdun to the Prussians reached Paris and panicked its population, for nothing now stood between the invading army and the capital. The situation had reached a crisis point. At the Legislative Assembly, Danton declared that the situation called for "boldness, more boldness and ever more boldness to save France."[71] The commune reacted by ringing the tocsin to assemble tens of thousands of volunteers at the Champ de Mars before their departure to meet the enemy. At the same time, a rumor spread that after their departure, prisoners would break out of jail and massacre the defenseless people of Paris in collusion with the enemy. A Parisian section sent a resolution to the others urging prompt justice for all the malefactors and conspirators in prison as the only way to avoid this danger and increase the zeal of the departing volunteers.

In this panic and exasperated by the slowness of the special court, small crowds of sans-culottes, militiamen, and fédérés started to murder refractory priests and prisoners being transferred under escort in the streets of Paris. The next morning, several small crowds invaded half a dozen prisons on their own initiative and, in a parody of justice, established makeshift courts that judged and sentenced prisoners in rapid fashion. Those condemned to death were immediately butchered. In this breakdown of law and order, neither the commune nor the assembly believed it could stop the slaughter or even believed it had the jurisdiction to do so. Both Danton and the chief of the National Guards were preoccupied with the defense of Paris and totally indifferent to the fate of the prisoners. Pétion, whose position was unclear in this power conflict, went to a prison to stop the massacre. The killers listened to him respectfully but resumed their murderous mission after he left. This orgy of blood lasted for five days and killed between 1,100 and 1,400 detainees from a total prison population of about 2,800. Most of the killed were common criminals (many were counterfeiters blamed for the inflation) rather than political prisoners or priests. Among them were 37 women, who were raped before being bludgeoned to death. The massacres burned themselves out as there were fewer prisoners left to kill and the people of Paris were horrified by what had happened (to the indignation of the killers, who believed that they had performed their patriotic duty).[72]

These five days of September offered an opportunity for some radicals to eliminate their rivals. On 2 September at the Jacobin Club, Robespierre accused Brissot of having sold France to the Duke of Brunswick. Three officers of the local surveillance committee immediately came to Brissot's house, questioned him, and carefully examined his correspondence before exonerating him.[73] Marat at the commune asked for a warrant to arrest a member of the

Executive Council.[74] At the time, such an arrest might have led to the execution of the suspect: the break between the two Jacobin factions had become irreversible and their conflict would escalate to a fight to the death.

During this time of fear, Paris held its elections for the Convention. The Legislative Assembly had expanded the electorate to include all males above the age of 21 regardless of wealth. Robespierre had maneuvered to have the second round of elections held at the Jacobin Club, which he controlled. The procedure was a voice vote. He packed the audience with radicals to intimidate the electors. In this menacing atmosphere, he, Marat, and their allies from the commune were all elected to the Convention while the Brissotins had been too afraid to show up for fear of being arrested. In fact, very few people voted despite the universal franchise because of the security situation. Instead, the Brissotins were elected from the provinces. The election effectively resolved the political showdown between the commune and the assembly since most of the commune leaders were now deputies at the Convention.

A French victory against the Prussians in Valmy by General Charles-François Dumouriez was quickly followed by another against the Austrians in Lille and relieved Parisians. The Convention benefited from the prestige of these victories, as the frontier troops were under its command. It abolished the monarchy and declared France a republic on 21 September 1792. This establishment of the republic was a second revolution. At the same time, all political leaders were horrified by the September massacres and were determined to curb the power of mobs by restoring law and order. The special court was dissolved in early October. The fédérés stationed in Paris were appalled by the events and left.[75] On the other hand, the participants in the events of the summer remained armed and felt a sense of pride, importance, and power in the new political arena.

How can we explain the September massacres? During the French Revolution, they were never forgiven. Radicals, owing their power to the Parisian crowds, urged people to move on and gloss over them. They excused the massacres as people's vengeance and the necessary consequence of the events of 10 August.[76] But non-radicals were not so kind. After Robespierre's overthrow in Thermidor, its participants, the *septembriseurs*, were persecuted even after many other political crimes were absolved. The mass murder of defenseless people was inexcusable.

The ideological thesis cannot explain these excesses of violence. There was no ideologue among the perpetrators, and the leading ideologues reluctantly tolerated them. They had not trusted Parisians to support them in cracking down on the septembriseurs when the Prussians were almost at the gate and had sworn to drown Paris in blood. A few hundred at most carried out the massacres while thousands shared the septembriseurs' ideology. Even their sans-culotte friends were horrified at the monstrosity of their deeds.[77] If ideology had led the perpetrators to commit the massacres, why did the vast majority of people holding the same ideology not participate and even later condemn them?

Rational choice theory has similar trouble to explain these massacres. The perpetrators did not benefit from them, with the exception of a few who robbed their victims. But these were exceptions and the allure of personal gain cannot be the explanation. In fact, the perpetrators believed that they accomplished their civic duty for the majority and had sacrificed their pay from missing work days. In fact, they were annoyed that they did not get any recognition for their sacrifices.

A few historians rose to the challenge of explaining the massacres. One explored the mentality of the revolutionaries and postulated a trilogy of fear, defensive reaction, and punitive will as one of the keys to understanding the violence of the French Revolution.[78] The fear of an enemy plot was a constant in the first half of the revolutionary decade and increased the likelihood of defensive violence.[79] This sometimes gave way to a punitive will "either to cripple the aristocratic conspiracy, hoarders, and all enemies of the people, or to punish those enemies. From July [1789] on, this took the form of imprisonments, acts of brutality, and popular massacres . . . Punitive will provoked the massacres of 1792."[80] The moral outrage at the needless deaths of their friends on 10 August and the approaching Prussian troops bound on sacking Paris convinced a few to take violent action to defend their community and punish internal traitors. The rape of the women before being clubbed to death is indicative of this punitive will. This vindictive violence may be a variant of the black sheep effect of the social identity perspective. It punishes alleged treason by in-group members more harshly than similar action by outsiders. This punitive element is facilitated by what another historian called the *mépris de l'homme*, or contempt of man by reducing him to an abstraction.[81] As we saw in the previous chapter, this dehumanization is inherent in the process of self-categorization, conceiving out-group members not as individuals but as stereotypical members of that category (the enemy as an abstract entity). This transformation of fright into vindictive fury would benefit from additional study.[82]

Probably the main factor leading to the September massacre was another factor of the social identity model, namely the disillusionment with legitimate means of redressing political grievance. The special court was simply too slow to satisfy the radicals, afraid that some of the arrested alleged traitors were still dangerous. Therefore, a few self-selected to take justice in their own hands for the sake of their imagined community. They did not simply invade the prisons and murder indiscriminately. They set up parodies of court procedures in the prisons, where they became prosecutors, judges, juries, and executioners. They created the rough-and-ready procedures, which they believed to be legitimate in these times of great danger and lack of law and order, to address their political grievances. This pretense of legitimacy attempted to veil their raw punitive will.

The Execution of the King and the Radicalization of the Convention

The Brissotins again dominated the new assembly and wasted no time in accusing Robespierre and his allies of carrying out the September massacres. The radicals now sat high up on the left of the Convention president and were nicknamed the Montagne (Mountain). The Brissotins elected from the provinces wanted to curb the power of Paris by instituting a federal system of government with increased autonomy for the provinces. The Montagne, conscious that it owed its power to Parisian crowds, tried to impose a more centralized system of government based in Paris.

The discovery of the king's correspondence with Austrians and émigrés in a safe at the palace proving his unmistakable treason further fueled their fight. All agreed that the king was guilty: he was tried and convicted almost unanimously in December. Montagnards and Brissotins disagreed on the nature of the sentencing. The former wanted to execute him immediately. The latter wanted to involve all the people of France through a direct vote as to his sentence. After heated debates, the Convention condemned him to death by one vote. He was executed on 21 January 1793. This provoked the first prominent assassination of the Revolution. On the eve of the king's execution, one of his former bodyguards, Philippe de Pâris, recognized a nobleman, Louis-Michel Lepeletier, Marquis de Saint-Fargeau, who had voted for death, and stabbed him to death. Lepeletier was given a state funeral and declared the first martyr of the Revolution. Pâris escaped but killed himself ten days later before he could be captured.[83] Although he did not leave any documents explaining his turn to violence, one can probably assume that anger at Lepeletier's betrayal—a traitor to his aristocratic in-group—, honor, and the chance of running into him all contributed to the political murder.

The situation in France once again deteriorated on all fronts. The 1792 harvest was very poor, and shortages from the war accelerated general inflation.[84] Again these were blamed on enemies of the Revolution. Poor Parisians demanded some sort of price control, but the liberal Brissotins rejected this on the basis of their free market ideology. On 26 February 1793, a gathering of laundresses protesting the cost of soap spontaneously formed a crowd, looted food shops, and marched to the Convention to demand lower prices, but were easily scattered by the National Guards.[85] The Montagne, in order to keep the support of the crowds, reluctantly declared itself in favor of price control, or the Law of Maximum (of prices), as it was then called.

On the military front, the fruits of the victories of the fall had evaporated. The French had annexed conquered territory, and most European powers became hostile to this change of borders. Under the leadership of Brissot, the Convention declared war on England, Holland, Spain, Portugal, and the Italian states (in addition to Austria and Prussia) on 1 February 1793. At the end of the month, it ordered a mobilization of 300,000 men throughout France and delegated responsibility for this task to local municipalities. It also dispatches 82 deputies (mostly Montagnards, to decrease their presence at the Convention) on mission as special representatives with full powers all over France to ensure the implementation of its decrees.[86] This measure became a future instrument of the Terror.

By the beginning of March, the French northern army suffered defeats at Aachen and Liège, which were blamed on the treason of two generals, assumed to be part of a large counterrevolutionary plot. The Austrians and Prussians were preparing again to invade. Sans-culottes tried to spark another insurrection on 9 March, but only three or four Parisian sections responded, and the small crowd was easily dispersed.

The next day, the Convention created an Extraordinary Criminal Court to judge national enemies, loosely defined as counterrevolutionaries or "disorganizers" in the popular vocabulary of the time. The law suspended the protections guaranteed by the Declaration of the Rights of Man and the Citizen for the duration of the war and allowed the court to impose capital punishment for trivial offenses. This court was later renamed the Revolutionary Court and became another future instrument of the Terror. The Montagnards, in the minority and unable to form a government, fought to control these new legal instruments of violence allegedly targeting traitors for they potentially allowed them to legitimately eliminate their rival without having recourse to unpredictable popular uprisings to intimidate or attack them.

At this point it would be easy to blame *la force des choses* for the radicalization of the Convention. But this would reduce the deputies to simple robots responding mindlessly to circumstances and take away their free will and responsibility for their slide into the Terror. Instead, a process internal to the deputies cleared their path to violence. For the past year, the tone of their debates had steadily escalated as they stretched analogies to their extreme, inflated potential threats, and displayed increasing intolerance for differing views. Exaggerated concepts imbedded in this hyperbolic speech began to frame their understanding of reality. This extremist discourse shaped how the deputies felt about and made sense of events, thus influencing how they acted.

The debates around the creation of the new court illustrate this rhetorical escalation. A deputy argued, "Our dangers are great; prompt and severe measures must be taken. Our enemies, from without as well as within, do not wait: let's imitate them or fear the consequences of our inertia."[87] Another said, "They cut the throats of patriots in Liège without giving them a jury, and we would give one to traitors! No matter how bad this court can be, it would still be too kind for these scoundrels."[88] Danton cut to the heart of the matter, "Let's be terrible to spare the people from being so; let's organize a court . . . so that the sword of the law hovers over the head of all our enemies."[89] Robespierre wanted to include criticism of people's champions as a political crime, but another deputy protested, "Freedom of the press or death!"[90] Most deputies were reluctant to go along with the creation of the court but the revelation of the sans-culotte journée attempted the previous day moved them to pass the proposal setting an effective legal mechanism to address the crowd's political grievance and pre-empt it from taking justice in its own hands, as suggested by Danton's quote.

Extremist discourse precluded dispassionate discussions in search of just solutions to problems the deputies were facing. The deputies bear a large responsibility for the way they talked about their problems, which created a polarized atmosphere, favored extremist concepts to interpret their reality, and led to extreme solutions. In retrospect, their situation was never as calamitous as depicted in their discussions. It was this cumulative radicalization of discourse[91] rather than ideology per se that favored extreme solutions.[92] Indeed, the Convention's debate about the creation of this court was remarkably devoid of ideological references or reasoning. The deputies' concern was to punish the nation's internal and external enemies and the few protests to preserve civil rights were shouted down by Montagnards. Traitors or internal enemies were viewed as even worse than external ones, deserving the worst of punishments for their heinous betrayal undermining the meaning of the social identity of patriots.[93] Equally remarkable is the fact that no one mentioned that the Convention had created this crisis in the first place by declaring war on all its neighbors, or that its arrest warrants for suspected generals would probably force their defections to the enemy, making them traitors, a self-fulfilling prophecy.

Intense factional rivalry for leadership within the Convention drove this radicalization of discourse. The Brissotins and Montagnards fought for the allegiance of their more neutral colleagues, collectively known as the Plain for they sat in the lower section of the Convention. Since the Brissotins had declared war a year earlier, the Montagnards now exploited the deteriorating security situation to discredit their rivals in the government, rally the Plain to their side, and gain control of the Convention despite their relatively small number.

The general military conscription was very unpopular in the south and west of France and ignited violent local protests. Already upset with the ban on their local refractory priests, peasants from the Vendée armed with primitive weapons resisted attempts to conscript them and attacked local district authorities. A republican column sent to reestablish law and order in the province was ambushed on 19 March. Around the same time, General Dumouriez, suffered two major defeats in Belgium. As he had previously commanded the ambushed detachment in Vendée, some Montagnard deputies suspected widespread treason and issued a warrant for his arrest. Forewarned, Dumouriez took hostage the visiting minister of war and the Conventional special representatives on mission to his command and defected to the enemy with his prisoners. The Montagnards lumped the Vendée protests and new military defection together into one huge treasonous plot in order to discredit the Brissotin government. On 6 April, the Convention created a new Committee of Public Safety (another future instrument of the Terror) to replace the Brissotin-controlled Committee of General Defense. Popular journalists like Marat published strident defamatory accusations against the government. The Brissotins arrested Marat, now a deputy, and thereby established a precedent that deputies had not immunity. Marat defended himself eloquently and was exonerated and released on 24 April. In turn, one of the radical Paris sections demanded the arrest and trial of 22 Brissotin deputies.[94] The war between Brissotins and Montagnards factions had finally escalated into a fight to the death with the ability of the new legal means of violence to eliminate their respective rivals.

The Montagnards could also try to engineer a popular unrest against their rivals: the successful overthrow of the king had legitimized the right of insurrection in the minds of the people.[95] To protect themselves against this possibility, on 20 May, the Brissotins convinced the rest of the Convention to order the arrest of "disorganizers" calling for an insurrection. In response, the majority of Paris sections created a Central Revolutionary Committee to which they delegated command over their respective National Guard battalions. The Central Revolutionary Committee sidelined the Paris commune and appointed François Hanriot, a prominent septembriseur, as the Guards' overall commander. It sounded the tocsin at dawn on 31 May 1793, mobilizing the Guards, who surrounded the Convention and demanded the arrest of the 22 Brissotin deputies and the creation of a revolutionary army. The Convention gave in to some minor demands but put off a decision on the rest.[96]

On 2 June, the news of an insurrection in Lyon against the Convention and its massacre of 800 patriots reached Paris and outraged the sans-culottes. Since the Convention was dragging its feet about the arrest of the 22 deputies, the Central Revolutionary Committee dispatched Hanriot once again to the

Convention, this time with dozens of cannons and a mob of more than 100,000 sans-culottes, as this was a Sunday holiday. Spooked by the size of the crowd and the weaponry, the deputies handed over to Hanriot their 22 colleagues and added several more. This coup d'état changed the balance of power in the Convention in favor of the Montagne. But security for the prisoners was lax, and many escaped. Another 73 deputies protested the coup and were also arrested. Over the next week, the Central Revolutionary Committee encouraged the sections to arrest more than 1,300 people in Paris. Many cities in France rose up against this usurpation of power and mobilized into a federalist insurrection against Parisian despotism.[97] On 8 June, the Central Revolutionary Committee was officially incorporated into the commune of Paris, a move that legalized and therefore put an end to the insurrection.[98] Montagnard deputies took control of the Convention and wrote a new, more egalitarian constitution in June 1793 that legalized the right to insurrection in recognition of the role played by the sans-culottes. This Constitution of 1793 was later approved by a public plebiscite during the summer, but was immediately suspended until the end of the war emergency.

The developments of the spring of the spring of 1793 are a good illustration of group dynamics within the social identity paradigm. The high threats from out-groups had generally radicalized the Convention, and the black sheep effect explains its obsession with internal enemies. Two factions, with roughly similar ideologies, competed with each other for leadership within it and escalated the conflict, especially in the rhetoric of their mutual accusations. Indeed, ideology was rarely mentioned during the discussions surrounding these events. The multiple failures of the majority faction in terms of the conduct of internal and external war and management of the economy opened the door for the minority to mobilize support of the disgruntled masses to overthrow its rival faction by force. This coup was relatively bloodless, showing that crowd violence mostly depends on fluid contextual factors: since the mob was not provoked, it refrained from the use of actual violence and relied on intimidation.

The Sans-Culottes and the Journées Révolutionnaires

The May-June 1793 journées révolutionnaires was the apex of the sans-culottes' power. For more than a century and a half, the historiography of the French Revolution adopted the Thermidorean framework in conceptualizing them as just mob riffraff and blames the violence of the Revolution on them.[99] But who were the sans-culottes, and what led them to turn to political violence? As we saw, in the early part of the French Revolution, poor people entered the political arena through large demonstrations, but after the summer of 1792 they were given full rights as citizens (right to vote, bear arms, and hold office). After that summer, they were called sans-culottes. They were not workers, as later Marxist historians believed, but respectable craftsmen and shopkeepers well integrated into their neighborhoods. In the past half-century, historians have focused on this important group, whose interventions dramatically influenced the course of the Revolution.[100] One described their everyday life in the neighborhood of Saint Marcel and how they sporadically mobilized themselves into the journées révolutionnaires.[101]

The sans-culottes gradually evolved into a revolutionary community over time and, through their infrequent but successful interventions, became aware of their collective political power.[102] The July 1791 massacre at their peaceful demonstration at the Champ de Mars was a crucial milestone in their evolution, for it marked their rupture with the National Guards, who carried out the carnage.[103] From then on, the sans-culottes, who were too poor to vote or become National Guards, distinguished themselves from their former allies. By mid-1792, their social identity was fully formed. They called themselves sans-culottes ("without breeches") in contrast to what they were not—idle elites, recognizable by their fine clothes and breeches. Instead, these assertive anti-elitist manual workers, craftsmen, journeymen, peddlers, and shopkeepers wore practical pants. They created a counterculture in contrast to elite culture, valuing productive manual labor (in contrast to the idleness of the rich), jealous egalitarianism suspicious of any leadership (in contrast to status-conscious elites), transparency (in contrast to the secret intrigues of politicians), votes by popular acclamation (in contrast to "secret ballots in which cabals triumph"[104]), and communitarianism (in contrast to the liberal individualism). They also had their own style of dress (in contrast to refined clothes), way of talking (using the egalitarian *tu,* in contrast to the aristocratic *vous*), and way of life (living simply in small, crowded apartments on the top floors of buildings, in contrast to houses or luxurious apartments on lower floors). Former businessmen and civil servants, who lost their jobs because of the Revolution, shed their old-regime habits and appearance and adopted this countercultural lifestyle when they became sans-culottes leaders.[105] In the minds of people at the time, there was definitely a sans-culotte prototype, which was not static but changed according to the context. Others tried to emulate the appearance, habits, norms, and actions of these prototypes and adopted their attitudes and behaviors.[106]

In other words, the sans-culottes' social identity was a self-categorization activated according to their context.[107] It was foremost a politicized social identity in contrast to local elites, who originally had exclusive political power based on their exclusive right to vote, bear arms, and hold office. The sans-culottes interpreted many natural events politically and blamed their worsening economic conditions like food shortages or inflation on hoarders and aristocratic plots to starve Paris.[108] Being an imagined community,[109] this group was difficult to define precisely because its social boundaries were fluid and evolved over time according to context.[110] Because a sans-culotte was a political and cultural social identity, he is difficult to define in non-political categories, be they social, economic, psychological, or religious.

A strong sense of fraternity and pride forged in the exhilaration of participating in dangerous journées also characterized them.[111] Participation in a journée transformed and solidified their social identity. Being in an important demonstration gives participants a sense of exhilaration, of collective significance, a transcendental feeling of being part of something greater than their individual selves, of making history. The sans-culottes experienced this feeling and pride, which stayed with them even after their action ended and helped define their identity, not only to themselves but to their neighbors, who now viewed them and treated them differently. These continuous processes maintained their politicized social identity long after the journées were over.[112]

Given their politicized social identity of sans-culotte, the journées révolutionnaires[113] can be explained by the escalation of the conflict between the sans-culottes and their perceived enemies, disillusionment or lack of confidence with legal means to redress grievances, and moral outrage at dramatic threats against their community, which led them to mobilize to defend themselves against these enemies. Additional factors facilitated their mobilization. First and foremost, none of their seven effective journées were punished by the authorities.[114] On the contrary, two were retrospectively legitimized and celebrated.[115] They created a powerful precedent for future insurrections, now seen by sans-culottes as legitimate additions to their protest repertoire. Second, from the spring of 1792 to the spring of 1795, sans-culottes were allowed to carry weapons, allegedly against foreign invaders but really only used in their journées. After Thermidor, they attempted two journées that failed, the reactionary government severely repressed and disarmed them. After that, the sans-culottes effectively disappeared from history.

The sans-culottes were not inherently violent: in most journées, there was little violence; and in two, it was provoked; but one, the September massacres, showed their potential for violence in the context of a breakdown of legitimate law enforcement. This last episode violence was clearly excessive and inexcusable, and was so viewed by the general population at the time. After Thermidor, two years later, the septembriseurs were still singled out for punishment.

Ineffective legitimate law enforcement also played a role in three other journées.[116] Two were military operations led by radical Parisian sections,[117] and one was coopted by the Paris commune.[118] The context of severe food shortages or inflation and the escalation of conflict with the "enemy," real or rumored, played a prominent role in the majority of these journées.[119]

The fear of a threat from an imagined hostile out-group helped activate not only a politicized social identity but also a sense of urgency for defense against this threat. The participants in all effective journées came armed for a possible fight: they thought of themselves as soldiers, defending their group and what it stood for—reforms, early on, and later the Revolution. As soldiers, they were armed. During their first journée in July 1789, they tried to defend themselves but were without weapons and that insurrection was in essence a three day search for weapons (rather than the later myth of liberation of the Bastille). On the other hand, in most of collective protests that did not materialize into journées, the protestors were unarmed. The lack of weapons at the time showed that they had not come for a fight and indicates a lack of martial social identity at the time. Unarmed, when confronted with firm but disciplined state action to disperse, they could only comply or be killed.[120]

The activation of a martial social identity was not sufficient to trigger violence, as the majority of the journées were not violent. However, it seemed to be a necessary condition for violence. Perceived out-group threat to their in-group was conceptualized as plots[121] by aristocrats, foreigners, counterrevolutionaries, hoarders, Brissotins, fédérés, or whoever the enemy of the day was imagined to be.[122] These out-group threats had three major consequences: they activated a martial social identity in the in-group, created readiness for defensive violence, and justified or legitimated violence in the perpetrators' minds.[123]

Charlotte Corday's Assassination of Marat

The Montagnard coup of May-June 1793 divided France into several camps—Montagnard north and center; Brissotin-Fédéré west, south, and south-east; and royalist west (the Vendée)—and was the setting of the most famous assassination of the Revolution. Some Brissotin deputies had escaped to Caen, the center of the fédéré rebellion, and tried to mobilize a small army to march on to Paris. A young woman living in the city participated in some of their meetings, listened to their complaints, identified with them, shared their outrage at the Paris coup, and resolved to assassinate Marat, the most vocal of the Parisian extremists.[124] Very few documents survive about the past of Marie Anne Charlotte de Corday d'Armont, better known as Charlotte Corday, as she intentionally burned all her papers before leaving for Paris. She was single and a descendant of the classical dramatist Pierre Corneille, but her family had fallen on hard times and was hanging on the last vestige of its honorable past. Her letters to her father indicate that she was concerned about restoring the honor that her family had long lost.[125] She had been raised in a convent and was fond of the biblical story of Judith and the writings of Milton against tyranny.[126] A week after the execution of the king, she wrote to her sister about her horror and indignation. "All these men, who were supposed to give us freedom, assassinated him: they are only executioners."[127] She was inspired by the assassination of Lepeletier.

On 9 July, she left for Paris, where she arrived two days later. On 12 July, she located where Marat lived and wrote a short political will to the French people that she hoped would inspire them to rise up against the Montagne. She decried its crime and oppression, which were leading France to catastrophe. "Already the fire of discord and civil war enflame half of this vast empire. There is still a way to put it out, but it must be effective and prompt." She singled out Marat as "the vilest scoundrel . . . the face of all these crimes." She exhorted French people to stand up and march so "that the reign of laws succeed to anarchy, that peace, unity, and fraternity erase forever any idea of factionalism." She saw herself as a Brutus and concluded, "Oh, my country, your misfortunes tear my heart apart. I can only give you my life, and I thank God for the freedom that I dispose. No one will lose by my death. I will not imitate Pâris by killing myself. I want my last breath to be useful to my fellow citizens, my head to be carried about Paris [on a pike] and become a sign around which all friends of the law can rally, the wavering Montagne to see its demise written in my blood, me to be its last victim."[128]

On 13 July, Corday went to Marat's apartment, claiming that she knew the names of all the Caen conspirators. She was allowed to see him while he was soaking in his bathtub to alleviate the discomfort caused by a skin condition. He asked her about the conspirators and she gave him their names. When she asked him what he was going to do with them, he replied that he would have them all guillotined in Paris in a few days. On hearing this, she pulled out a knife hidden in her bodice and killed him with one stab to his chest. She did not try to escape and was subdued by his staff.[129] The police came, arrested her, and immediately interrogated her. When asked why she committed her crime, she replied that "civil war was on the brink of enflaming all of France and she was persuaded that Marat bore the main responsibility for this tragedy, she had preferred to sacrifice her life to save her country."[130]

At her interrogation in prison, Corday repeated that she had come to Paris only to kill Marat for his crimes. She blamed him for the September massacres, fueling civil war in France, trying to become a dictator, and depriving the people of France of their sovereignty by arresting and imprisoning Conventional deputies.[131] In a letter to her father from prison, she wrote, "I avenged many innocent victims, I prevented other disasters."[132] At her trial on 17 July, she insisted that she had acted alone and killed Marat to bring back peace to her country. She killed one man to save 100,000. When the court president asked her whether she thought she had killed all the Marats, she answered, "This one dead, the others might perhaps think twice."[133] She had formed her project since the 31 May affair. She was one of those "people who put aside their own interest and know how to sacrifice themselves for the country."[134] The jury convicted and condemned her to death. She was executed the next day.

With Corday, we have all the major themes that characterize modern political violence: self-identification with a persecuted political community, self-sacrifice in defense of this threatened community, revenge, concern with honor, attempt to strike fear in the midst of the enemy, hope that the attempt would inspire a popular uprising that would either overthrow a government or at least force it to give in to challengers' grievances, and a note left behind for the public to explain one's action.

Although she was a loner, Corday was clearly part of the political protest community in Caen, shared their outrage at the May-June 1793 coup which came after an escalation of violence in the country, and was convinced that legitimate protest was no longer enough. Barred from joining the fédérés because of her sex, she became a soldier on her own to help them overthrow the tyranny of the Montagne, like Brutus with whom she identified. The theme of honor in the plays of her ancestor probably inspired her to sacrifice herself for the nation. Ideology could not explain her actions, as she did not share the ideology of the fédérés. Her self-sacrifice is contrary to the rational choice's pursuit of self-interest. Her note lacks any reference to any ideological goals or utilitarian cost/benefit calculus.

The Terror and the Noyades of Nantes

Over the summer 1793, the situation in France continued to deteriorate. Foreign troops again advanced on French soil. Fédéré insurrections covered most of the south and west of France, including the major cities of Lyon and Marseille. The rebellion of the Vendée went from bad to worse. As it had not yet fulfilled its goal of raising 300,000 troops, the Convention again declared *la patrie en danger* on 23 August and decreed a new *levée en masse* (mass mobilization) to reach this goal. Many Parisian sans-culottes enlisted in the army. On 29 August, the port of Toulon defected and the Mediterranean French fleet surrendered to the British. The news of this new betrayal reached Paris on 2 September 1793.

We now come to the period that covers most of the second year of the new French revolutionary calendar (22 September 1793 to 21 September 1794), which French scholars referred to as *la Terreur* (the Terror, with a capital T).[135]

In the exaggerated vocabulary of the time, everyone frequently used the word *terreur*, which simply meant great fear, as in driving fear into the hearts of the enemy. In 1789, it often referred to the tendency of protest crowds, obsessed with real or imagined counterrevolutionary plots and immersed in a culture of punishment from the Ancien Régime, to dish out immediate and exemplary punishments "to sow terror in the souls of the guilty."[136] From this popular origin, the notion of terrorizing the enemy was gradually adopted first by local militants, then by the Paris commune, and finally by the political clubs. In the provinces, local revolutionaries spoke of terror to intimidate their opponents because they were more isolated from state support than their comrades in Paris.[137] At the national assemblies, before the Terror, deputies from all sides accused rivals of using systems of terror to intimidate them.[138] However, despite all this talk of terror, they had refrained from such a systematic policy of terror for fear that it might be used against them.[139] The words *terrorisme* (terrorism) and *terroriste* (terrorist) started making their appearance after the fall of Robespierre in late July 1794, but not during the period retrospectively called *la Terreur*.[140] The word *terrorism* popularized by the Thermidorean reaction was a pejorative word of abuse from the start.[141]

There is no accepted starting date for the Terror as opposed to its end on the day of the fall of Robespierre, 9 Thermidor, year II (27 July 1794). As we saw, many instruments of the Terror were created in the spring of 1793. However, many scholars use 5 September 1793, the date of a journée révolutionnaire triggered by the high price of bread and the recent betrayal in Toulon. The Paris commune and the Jacobin Club had coopted this demonstration to demand the creation of a revolutionary army to enforce the food supply to Paris.[142] Bertrand Barère, the rapporteur of the Committee of Public Safety to the Convention, responded at the assembly that enemy threats had led the committee to propose the creation of a "revolutionary army to carry out this great expression of the Paris commune: 'Make terror the order of the day' . . . against those who try to stop your revolutionary march by terror."[143] This army, composed of 6,000 Parisian patriots supported by 1,200 artillerymen, would enforce the supply of Paris once price controls were instituted.[144] Its creation and the Law of Suspects two weeks later completed the establishment of all the instruments of terror under the Committee of Public Safety dominated by Robespierre. This last law defined the legitimate targets of repression and included those refused a certificate of *civisme* (good citizenship); fired civil servants; noblemen and émigrés and their respective families.[145]

This concept of civisme was a vague wastebasket category that used a person's words or deeds as indicative of his good standing as a citizen. The surveillance committees handed out certificate of civisme on advice of local political clubs. These certificates were important for they were required for holding public office and in investigation carried out by the committees. Violent words against the enemy were indicative of civisme and protection against arrest for *incivisme*. This of course further ratcheted up the radicalization of discourse. In these paranoid times, this resulted in the disappearance of free speech because any implied criticism of the government was viewed as incivisme and made the speaker liable to arrest and execution. Leaders were able to use this concept to eliminate anyone horrified at the atrocities and criticized the Terror, and more radical rivals, who called for even more violence. But common people also used this tactic. Denunciations to committees of surveillance were seen not only as a patriotic duty but a good sign of civisme, and campaigns of political purification fueled intense local rivalries that often ended in the physical elimination of one of the competing factions.[146]

The Terror is famous for its violent excesses not in Paris but in the provinces where most of the killings occurred, especially in the Vendée in the context of a civil war, before returning to Paris in the last month of that fateful year during the short period labeled the Great Terror. Three instances stand out in terms of their notoriety and horror: the *noyades* (mass drownings) of Nantes, General Louis Turreau's neo-genocidal *colonnes infernales* (infernal columns),[147] and the *mitraillades* (executions by cannon grapeshots) of Lyon.[148] All were initiated or encouraged by Conventional representatives on mission but had not received official approval from Paris. Let's examine the noyades of Nantes, the best documented massacre, to see whether these semiofficial acts of violence might add to our understanding of the turn to political violence.

At least half of all the violent deaths of the French Revolution occurred in the Vendée rebellion. Many of the deaths can be accounted for by the general savagery and cruelty of civil wars. Each side demonized the other and reduced its enemy into a one dimensional evil stereotype. Patriots lumped the sporadic shootings by protestors against the conscriptions of March 1793 and the many killings of republican troops in the region together and imagined these incidents as attacks from a large formidable foe directed by foreign enemies like England and the émigrés. This eventually became a self-fulfilling prophecy. As republican armies proved inadequate to face these internal threats, the rhetorical talent of Convention leaders escalated the Vendée conflict to a war of annihilation.[149] On 1 August 1793, Barère convinced the Convention to pass a law directing its armies to burn the regional forests, destroy rebels' shelter and harvest, grab their cattle, and confiscate their property. Women, children, and old people of the area were ordered displaced to the interior of the country.[150] All this talk of exterminating a vaguely defined and ever expanding enemy created a hostile and permissive environment allowing and condoning the worst of atrocities.

Since March 1793, several criminal, revolutionary, and military courts had been set up to deal with the ever expanding number of prisoners, resulting in thousands of executions. These included not only alleged rebels, but also loyal revolutionaries, victims of political rivalry. In a repeat of the First Terror, suspects captured in the Vendée and Brittany were sent to Nantes, where they were crammed into small rooms as all available buildings were requisitioned and transformed into makeshift prisons. In the fall, the daily prison census in the city was around 4,000 people, almost equally divided between men and women, in addition to small children—orphans of people killed in the fighting. The prison overcrowding became a management crisis because of severe food shortage and the potential of epidemics spilling out of overcrowded prisons endangering the local population.

To straighten out this mess, the Convention sent Jean-Baptiste Carrier as its special representative on mission with full power of a proconsul. He had an abrasive personality and focused on efficiency. Being a stranger to the region, he sought the help of the most radical local sans-culottes in reorganizing the town's repressive institutions.[151] Among them was the Marat Company of the local revolutionary army,[152] which consisted of about 40 to 60 men, mostly illiterate small shopkeepers and artisans, in their thirties and married but poor enough to need the security of a soldier's pay.[153] "Two features distinguished the members of this company from the other revolutionary soldiers. One was that all or nearly all had participated in the campaign against the Chouans [more on them later], in the battalions of the Nantes National Guard; several had gathered up the mutilated corpses of their comrades, who had fallen into the hands of the peasants, and all lived in fear, knowing the fragility of the situation at Nantes, threatened on all sides by a violently counterrevolutionary countryside. In the second place, nearly all were natives of Nantes."[154] In other words, Marats self-categorized along town/country, friend/foe, revolutionary/counterrevolutionary, and republican/royalist axes.

The Marats' original mission was to arrest suspects on behalf of the local committee of surveillance, but Carrier expanded it to carry out punitive expeditions of burning farms and churches, and summary executions in the countryside. It was in this context that the noyades took place. The guillotine and even firing squads did not kill fast enough. Carrier ordered his deputies to get rid of 90 old and disabled refractory priests imprisoned on a ship because there was no more room in the prisons. Late on the night of 16 November, the Marats tasked with this mission tied up the priests and transferred them onto a barge with portholes cut out under the water line. Then the Marats opened up the portholes, sinking the barge into the Loire River. Three or four priests managed to escape and the rest drowned. The escapees were quickly recaptured and turned over to the revolutionary court. In early December, 58 more priests were transferred to Nantes. Carrier ordered the same treatment for them and bragged about it to the Convention: "58 . . . priests . . . arrived from Angers to Nantes; immediately they were held in a boat on the Loire; last night, they were all engulfed in this river. What a revolutionary torrent the Loire is!"[155] The Convention applauded the public reading of his letter.

In early December, Carrier heard about an attempted escape from the Bouffay Prison, next to the docks in Nantes. This immediately reignited the common fear of a potential large prison breakout inside the city. Carrier ordered his deputy to take care of the situation and warned him not to take half measures. At the time, the prison housed 129 detainees, including women and children, some imprisoned for minor offenses and others just awaiting trial. About 30 Marats arrived at the prison on the evening of 14 December 1793. They sat down to eat a meal, drank a lot, and joked with the female staff. After they were drunk, they tied the prisoners in pairs, humiliated them with macabre humor and vulgarity, and hinted at their fate. The prisoners had already heard rumors of the noyades and resisted. They were dragged to the docks and dumped into the hull of a specially prepared barge, which was towed to the middle of the river, where its underwater sealed panels were opened. The screams of the victims faded with their drowning. One man escaped and later testified at Carrier's trial.[156]

It is not known how many people drowned in Nantes during these months. Scholars estimate that between 2,000 and 5,000 people died this way. Neighboring towns also practiced these noyades, but Nantes got the notoriety.[157] They stopped with the disbanding of the Marat Company in late December 1793 after the Convention dissolved all these provincial units.[158] Robespierre recalled Carrier to Paris when one of his secret envoys denounced these excesses. After his recall, the killings on all sides continued in the region, especially with the punitive colonnes infernales of General Turreau. By the end of the Vendée War, in 1796, about 200,000 people had perished.[159]

Unlike the violence of the Parisian sans-culottes, historians have not focused on any explanations for the massacres in Nantes, especially on the perpetrators' side. Richard Cobb is an exception. He described the despicable acts of the Marats, some of whom robbed and raped prisoners: "All were possessed of a physical brutality unusual among the *révolutionnaires* of the Year II, and at least one of their number . . . had the courage to admit before the Thermidorean tribunal that he regretted nothing, and that if he had to do it again he would be there to cut off the hands of those trying to cling to the edge of the barges or to deliver blows with the flat of his sabre to the female prisoners." Cobb's description of the Marats show that the perpetrators were not just following orders but participated with enthusiasm in their evil deeds. Cobb blamed *la force des choses* for this brutality. "They were, however, neither criminals nor brutes. Circumstances had made them ferocious, and if [one] . . .

had reached the point where he could push old men, women and children into the water, it was due to his position as a member of a besieged terrorist minority in a town deeply hostile to the Revolution . . . They were limited individuals, made brutal by circumstances, dishonest too, but at the same time sincere revolutionaries who lived in fear . . . [and] were very far removed from the easy-going and debonair *révolutionnaires* of the departments. They operated amidst hatred and fear, brutally executing the commands of their superiors . . . and in the Year III most were released because they had 'not acted maliciously' but simply followed orders."[160]

Cobb explained the fear of a prison break in the Bouffay noyades. "The Nantes sans-culottes lived in constant fear of a concerted attack by the brigands who dominated the surrounding countryside, while their friends and relatives crammed the town's prisons. The notion of a prison plot was a real threat for these sans-culottes artisans, outsiders and a minority in the community in which they lived."[161] One Marat explained that he had been wounded by brigands and had discovered the mutilated bodies of some of his friends. When invited to participate in the noyades, "I jumped at the chance . . . the horrors I had lived through decided that."[162]

Cobb concluded, "Several elements made up this approval of the repression: a sense of preservation, a desire to punish, a thirst for revenge, class hatred, a wish to be rid of non-productive *bouches inutiles* [useless mouths], a hatred of priests, particularly refractory ones, and above all a hatred of the townsman for the countryman. Usually repression took place in areas far removed from one's own and it was easier to use extreme brutality against 'étrangers' than against neighbors. The victims of the *noyades* were only rarely Nantes people."[163]

It must be stressed that the noyades, Turreau's infernal columns, and the Lyon mitraillades were not typical even of the Terror, but some of its most extreme incidents carried out in extreme circumstances. But many members of this unit were not extremist and still participated in the massacre, as was the case in many other such military units since.[164] These excesses bring into focus the punitive element in some political violence. We already encountered this element in the summer 1792 massacres. In both August and September, the danger was past, and the massacres were just punitive cruelty. Likewise, most of the Vendée massacres as well as the Lyon mitraillades occurred when the danger had passed and seemed to be pure punitive brutality.

The noyades, infernal columns and mitraillades show that the violence of the Terror was not due to a top down system of terror but more to local initiative with tacit Committee of Public Safety and Convention approval. When these massacres surpassed people's tolerance for even very harsh justice, the Convention special representatives on mission who had initiated them were recalled to Paris to answer for their excesses. Fearing for their lives, they went on to lead the plot to overthrow Robespierre and save themselves.[165]

During the year of Terror, the Committee of Public Safety was able to reverse the insecurity of the nation and save the Revolution from internal and external enemies: the Vendée had been tamed; Lyon and Marseille were back in the fold; the harvest had been good; and foreign troops had been chased out of the country and were fleeing everywhere—but at great human cost as the Revolution consumed its some of its greatest champions. Not only were constitutional monarchists and Brissotins killed, but the Committee of Public Safety went on to get rid of Montagnard colleagues for being either too extreme or too lenient. Their support was no longer necessary to members of the committee with the gradual consolidation of power in its hands. Tens of thousands of common people also perished in the civil war. Ironically, the committee's success contributed to Robespierre's downfall. As long as there was great danger, the people rallied around him or at the very least tolerated the atrocities of the Terror as necessary for their survival. Now, the widening discrepancy between his alarmist claims justifying his extreme policies and the milder reality experienced by the rest of the population undermined his credibility and precipitated his demise.

Toward the end of the Terror, there was one clear assassination attempt and another less convincing one. Very early in the morning on 22 May 1794, 50-year-old Henri Admiral fired twice at his downstairs neighbor, Jean-Marie Collot d'Herbois, a member of the Committee of Public Safety. The two guns misfired, and Admiral was immediately arrested. The previous day, he had waited for Robespierre to come out of the committee, but when he did not see his target, he resolved to kill his neighbor instead. That same evening, 20-year-old Cécile Renault presented herself at Robespierre's residence and asked to speak to him. In the state of alert from the attempt earlier that day, his guards searched her and found two small knives hidden on her. She denied wanting to harm Robespierre and claimed she always carried them for her own protection. The authorities lumped the two attempts together and believed they had uncovered a gigantic plot on the life of their leaders. At his interrogation, Admiral admitted he had always been a royalist and had fallen on hard times, for which he blamed the revolution. In despair, he had resolved to kill Robespierre. For him, this was not "an assassination but an act of charity for the republic."[166] He denied being part of any larger plot. Despite the denial of the two suspects, the police arrested all of their acquaintances and relatives and put them on trial. The 54 defendants, including 10 women, were victims of the new speeded-up trial procedures: they were tried, convicted, and executed all on the same day, 17 June 1794.[167]

This parody of justice, which did not generate any evidence on their turn to political violence, was based on a new Law of 22 Prairial, year II (10 June 1794), which streamlined the prosecution of the "enemies of the people." It denied defendants any civil rights or due process protection, prevented them from having lawyers or even testifying on their own behalf and gave juries only the choice of death or acquittal as sentences.[168] This law ushered the seven weeks of Great Terror when more than 1,400 were executed in Paris alone, more than the total of the preceding year.[169]

The remaining Conventional deputies now feared that Robespierre might turn against them. At the top of his list of proscribed people were his former comrades, whose excesses in the provinces had forced their recall. These discredited terrorists (as people were starting to call them) feared for their lives and spread rumors that all the deputies were going to be arrested. This prompted a rebellion on the Convention floor on 9 Thermidor, year II (27 July 1794), resulting in the arrest of Robespierre and his close allies, who managed to escape later that day and took refuge at the Hôtel de Ville. The Convention declared them outlaws making them eligible to be killed on sight without any due process. That night, Robespierre's allies tried to assemble a crowd in front of the Hôtel de Ville to march on the Convention. However, by then, his policies had alienated the sans-culottes, who no longer identified with him, and were completely confused about the issues tearing the government apart. They did not know what to do when asked to intervene: they simply adopted a wait-and-see attitude and did nothing.[170]

Robespierre was recaptured by Convention forces and executed the next day along with his close allies. A few days later, the 22 Prairial Law was repealed. The expression "system of Terror" was first uttered by Barère the day after Robespierre's execution to blame all the excesses of the Terror personally on Robespierre and exonerate the rest of the Committee of Public Safety, including himself. A month later, the expression was picked up and popularized by the leaders of the Thermidorean reaction[171] to reduce the committee's concentration of executive power and eliminate the remaining policies of the Terror.[172] The new leaders condemned this whole period of Terror and indicted Carrier as a representative for the excesses of the Terror. His well-publicized prosecution ending in his execution became a show trial attempting to completely discredit Robespierre's terrorist policies.[173]

Explaining the Violence of the Terror

It is now customary to limit terrorism studies to non-state political violence. This was not always so. In fact, the field started out as an exploration of state political violence, trying to understand the terrorism of totalitarian states.[174]

The explanation of state political violence is assumed to be trivial: perpetrators are simply following orders. As we have seen, this argument protected the Marats from being persecuted during Thermidor. Although this argument is often adopted for policy reason, it is not sufficient for a scientific inquiry as Cobb's account shows that the Marats were not simple robots following orders. Their turn to violence was far more complicated. Furthermore, in both the summer of 1789 and 10 August 1792, French troops refused to follow orders and fire on crowds of compatriots. In fact, many switched sides. This issue of state agents' compliance with the use violence deserves more scrutiny.[175]

The historiography of the French Revolution explains the violence of the Terror with two major sets of arguments. Historians who view the perpetrators from the outside, as out-group members, portray them as predisposed to violence because of their personality, ideas, or inevitable group dynamics. Those who view them from the inside, as in-group members, blame circumstances—*la force des choses.*

The first set of explanations has three variants. The first of these is that the perpetrators were sans-culottes, in other words ruffians who simply acted out their nature or temperament. This is of course the thesis of conservative historians[176] who try to discredit the social, economic, and political achievements of the French Revolution. The problem with this argument is that the duration of the sans-culotte phenomenon was about three years. After 1795, they completely disappeared from history. If they existed because of innate characteristics, how do we explain their disappearance?

A second variant blames the violence on ideological indoctrination and assumes that strong ideas propelled sans-culottes into action.[177] There are two problems with this explanation. The political violence during the Revolution was not one-sided: it included sans-culotte and Montagnard violence but also royalist (in the Vendée) and conservative violence during the Thermidorean reaction, which almost equaled the Terror. In fact, the conservatives had their own journée révolutionnaire in October 1795. Needless to say, these two opposite sets of groups did not share the same ideology. However, the major problem with this explanation is that the perpetrators were not intellectuals but very pragmatic people with a strong distaste for abstract ideas. They certainly had strong views about such ideas as personal freedom, equality, right to subsistence, or communitarianism, but these were more guidelines for their everyday life than rigid doctrines. There is no doubt that these ideas and values helped them to self-categorize into a group in contrast to others, but the ideas themselves were not what drove them to violence.

A third variant came a century after the Terror, which it blamed on crowd dynamics.[178] Gustave Le Bon built on the first variant's denigration of revolutionary crowds and argued that people in crowds regress to a mental state where they become vulnerable to suggestion or hypnosis by charismatic leaders (Great Men of History) who manipulate them into violence. Despite its popularity with the lay public, most academic historians of the French Revolution have ignored this argument.[179]

The second set of explanation takes the perspective of the actor and, like him or her, blames the turn to violence on circumstances, especially radicalization by internal and external wars. Threatened by enemies everywhere, "patriots" lashed out indiscriminately from desperation and for survival. In terms of the factors leading to violence, these historians focus on historical contingencies such as the dynamics of events and structural constraints.[180] The problem with this argument is that, as mentioned, most of the greatest atrocities of the Revolution were committed when the perpetrators were no longer in danger.[181] As a result, these historians have been accused of trying to whitewash the perpetrators' guilt in carrying out the horrors of the Terror.[182]

The major problem with all these explanations is that they confuse the violence of the Terror with that of the sans-culottes' journées révolutionnaires. Montagnards certainly used the threat of journées' violence for their own ends as they did not control the Convention. However, they did so reluctantly and were weary of uncontrollable mobs. We already saw that during the First Terror they refrained from interfering in the massacres. They used the journées to overthrow their rivals at the Convention in the spring of 1793 but the violence during the Terror did not rely on crowds. In fact, except for the September 1793 journée, which was authorized by the Convention and carefully choreographed by the Paris commune and Jacobin Club (it was more like a legalized peaceful demonstration), there were no journées during the Terror. The violence of the Terror was ordered and directed by elected notables, state instruments, local militias, and revolutionary military units, not by unruly mobs of sans-culottes.

The Committee of Public Safety was deeply suspicious of mobs because it could not fully control them. One of the major factors mobilizing sans-culottes into journées was the lack of legitimized means to redress their political grievances. To eliminate this factor and pre-empt future journées, the Convention created legitimized instruments of violence to channel the sans-culottes' potential violence into more controllable institutions: the special Convention representatives on mission with full power, the Committee of Public Safety, the Committee for General Security, the Revolutionary Court, local committees of surveillance, the revolutionary army, the Law of Suspects, and finally the Law of 22 Prairial. Montagnards used the Convention deputies' fear of mob violence to create these instruments. Robespierre and his followers were careful to incorporate sans-culottes into these instruments when it was appropriate: local assemblies, committees of surveillance, and of course the revolutionary army. Now, instead of using violence to redress their grievances, sans-culottes could simply denounce the ones they blamed for them to surveillance committees for further investigation. These instruments enabled anyone to eliminate rivals legally on the flimsiest excuse. Arrests from tipoffs by committees of surveillance could lead to rapid conviction by the Revolutionary Court and eventual execution. These instruments carried out the violence of the Terror.

At the same time, to further avoid the danger of unruly mobs, the Committee of Public Safety gradually weakened the Parisian sans-culottes by encouraging them to enlist in French armies fighting foreign invaders at the border or sending them as the revolutionary army to put down rebellions in the provinces. When the sans-culottes were gone, the Committee of Public Safety cracked down on their leaders in Paris in the second half of the year of Terror.

The violence of the Terror required the perpetrators' identification with the Revolution. Simply being a state agent was not enough. Aristocratic officers defected to foreign royalists. French troops refused orders to fire on the crowd in the summers of 1789 and 1792. Here we must distinguish between the nation and the Revolution. The regular French armies fought enemy invaders and identified with the nation of France. Generally, they did not commit the excessive massacres of the Terror. On the other hand, the revolutionary armies were composed of sans-culotte volunteers fighting for the survival of the revolution itself against internal enemies. They identified with the Montagnard leaders of the Convention and the Committee of Public Safety. They were the ones that carried out the horrors of the Terror.

This identification was the result of a long evolution of political self-categorization. The above narrative shows that activists' social identity was not static in the five years between the storming of the Bastille to the fall of Robespierre. It evolved according to its context and the people against whom they defined themselves: member of the Third Estate v. Aristocrat; patriot v. royalist; republican v. constitutional monarchist; Montagnard v. Brissotin; Jacobin v. fédéré; revolutionary v. counterrevolutionary . . . This evolution of self-categorization makes it hard to make a linear prediction of what kind of rivalry and conflict will occur later on as these are so dependent on their unpredictable context. For instance, the Brissotins did their utmost to generate a war to unify the country behind them and against monarchists, their main rivals at the time, but the war ended up discrediting them and played in the hands of unanticipated new rivals, the Montagnards, a year later.

Parallel to this evolution of social identity was the gradual expansion of out-group enemies, who became legitimate targets for political violence. This was temporarily codified into the Law of Suspects that included not only all previous out-group members, namely aristocrats, monarchists, émigrés, fédérés, fired civil servants, and their respective families but added the crime of incivisme. Although this law greatly expanded the category of the legitimate targets of political violence, it was originally designed to limit them by the publication of a formal list of them. Contrary to the common conception of the Terror, political violence during its time was not indiscriminate but focused on an ever expanding out-group against whom its leaders self-categorized.

The Terror was also the culmination of a long escalation of conflict between rival groups vying for control of the state, which became a fight to the death. As one historian describes this escalation of retaliatory violence, "Thus threatened, provoked and desperate, the Revolution each day gained in audacity. It rose ever higher as danger gathered around it; the day came when some started to see these retaliations born from *la force des choses* as a system. They began to maintain the French nation in this state of exaltation as long as there were obstacles to overcome."[183] After the failed flight of the king, the tone of the debates in the Legislative Assembly kept rising. The war accelerated this process of escalation and eventually led to the overthrow of the monarchists. During the First Terror, Robespierre and Marat tried to eliminate some of their enemies by suggesting they were traitors (to be arrested and perhaps killed in prison at the time of the September massacres). Within a year, the Convention tore itself apart by allowing the arrest of some of their deputies and enacting laws creating the instruments of Terror. Each escalation from one group was experienced as a moral outrage by its rival, fueling the process leading to ever increasing violence, resulting in the Terror.

Contributing to this process was a rhetorical escalation that reached unprecedented heights, with constant talks of extermination of the enemy. The language of the Revolution became a language of violence. This was a fight for leadership at the national and local levels of government as prominent militants outdid each other in increasingly violent verbal jousts to attract a greater following. The verbal extremism was not confined to competing leaders. The requirement of certificate of civisme for many common people artificially inflated rhetorical violence. These dynamics created a hostile and permissive climate allowing and condoning the worst atrocities. This oratorical extremism was not sufficient for the turn to political violence, as many did not take the bait and remained nonviolent, but it gave cover to the few terrorists, as they started to be called. Verbal extremism had a strong influence on the turn to political violence, not because any ideological reasoning directly compelled people to violence, but because radical discourse legitimized or justified violence in the minds of the perpetrators, and sometimes the authorities.

The above analysis shows the similarity of the processes of turning to political violence by both state and non-state actors. The major difference between the Terror's violence and the journées's violence is the existence or absence of legal means of redressing political grievances. The disillusionment with the lack of ability these means was a major contributing factor to the sans-culottes' violence. On the other hand, their existence facilitated the violence of state agents and gave them cover for some of the worst atrocities committed in French history. While the Terror was the result of the creation of these legal tools to defend the severely threatened Revolution, state agents' compliance with orders to use these instruments against their own unarmed population requires additional factors specific to the social identity perspective: self-categorization in contrast to enemies of the Revolution which dehumanized them into hostile stereotypes; difficult living conditions blamed on out-group enemies (severe food shortages and inflation); strong in-group fear of enemy plots; expansion of the boundaries of out-group members as legitimate targets of violence; influential violent in-group prototypes escalating the stakes into a deadly fight for control of the Revolution in the context of total war; a discursive Manichaeism and lexicon of extermination; black sheep effect against perceived group traitors driving a punitive will; and moral outrage at each step of escalation of out-group aggression including credible out-group lethal threats.[184] There was no need for a martial self-categorization in defense of one's group since the perpetrators had already volunteered as soldiers or state agents defending the threatened Revolution. This perspective preserves the actors' personal responsibility but takes into account the importance of contexts.

Thermidor, the White Terror and the End of the Sans-Culottes

Thermidor triggered a reactionary White Terror during which victims of the original Terror or their allies got even with their former tormentors. Many of these murders were private affairs, no longer involving instruments of the state, and were rarely punished by authorities. The White Terror lasted about a year and almost matched the horrors of the Terror.[185] Many of these new massacres were carried out by gangs of the *jeunesse dôrée* (golden youth) espousing a reactionary ideology.

The worsening economic conditions caused by a harsh winter and abolition of price controls dictated by the new economic liberalism sparked two more sans-culotte journées in the spring of 1795. But by then, the Thermidorean Convention had dismantled the Parisian sections, closed down revolutionary clubs, and arrested leftist anti-government leaders, thereby effectively eliminating any opposition leadership. When the shortage of bread reached famine level in the early spring, local protests spontaneously coalesced into a crowd of mostly women who invaded the Convention on 12 Germinal, year III

(1 April 1795), and asked for "bread and the Constitution of 1793."[186] But without any leader or plan of action, the crowd was easily dispersed by detachments of National Guards and groups of jeunesse dôrée. The government immediately imposed a state of siege in Paris and arrested more radical leaders, including some that had helped orchestrate Thermidor but were now denounced as terrorists, like Barère and Collot d'Herbois.

The measures passed by the Convention failed to alleviate the bread shortage, and new protests exploded seven weeks later despite the increased repression. On the morning of 1 Prairial, year III (20 May 1795), women from poor neighborhoods rang the tocsin at dawn and invaded their local assemblies to mobilize their menfolk, who grabbed their pikes and guns, and followed the women to the Convention. The mob took it over and intimidated the deputies to ensure an affordable food supply to the capital, release prisoners, and implement the Constitution of 1793. The insurrection continued the next day as many National Guards deserted and joined the protestors. On the third day, regular army units were called in to supplement loyal National Guards and groups of jeunesse dôrée. The next day, these units launched coordinated assaults on rebellious neighborhoods, which surrendered at the news of a full regular army marching on Paris. The government conducted wide sweeps of prominent protestors and completely disarmed the poor Parisian sections.[187] As many sans-culottes had enlisted in the armies fighting on the border, the elimination of about 6,000 activists, the disarming of poor Parisians, and police surveillance completely deactivated the sans-culotte movement. The continuing White Terror gave it the coup de grace.

Leftist revolutionaries did not have a monopoly on nongovernmental political violence. Conservatives also mobilized for their own bloody journée on 13 Vendémiaire, year IV (5 October 1795), to destroy the republic and restore the monarchy. During the summer of 1795, the Convention had written a new constitution reinstated the restriction of active citizenship (right to vote, bear arms, and hold office) to the propertied few and established two legislative bodies, which in turn elected an executive committee of five directors, the Directorate. The new constitution was overwhelmingly adopted on 23 September 1795. However, conservative sections of Paris were upset by its election rules that kept two thirds of the sitting deputies. This ensured the continuation of non-monarchist policies within the new assembly. The conservatives talked of insurrection. Now that the government was no longer protected by armed citizens, it ordered some army units into the capital and released from prison some of the leftists imprisoned the previous spring. This backfired, as conservatives convinced themselves that a mob of terrorists would come and massacre them. Many armed conservatives, who had protected the Convention the previous spring, took over their respective sections and threatened to march on the Convention. Former sans-culottes, despite suffering from continued bread shortages and lack of weapons, supported the government, for they saw these conservatives as their bigger enemies. During the night, the government ordered more troops into Paris, and the artillery chief of the detachment, a relatively unknown General Napoleon Bonaparte, protected the Convention with cannons. When the conservative crowd marched on the Convention, he did not hesitate to fire his famous "whiff of grape-shot" into the crowd.[188] After two days of fighting, the army subdued the conservative mob at the cost of hundreds of fatalities on both sides.[189]

In contrast to the aftermath of the leftist spring journées, the ensuing crackdown was relatively mild, as the government treated the conservatives as misguided citizens rather than fanatic enemies. And before disbanding itself, on 26 October 1795, the Convention granted a general amnesty to all political prisoners who had no blood on their hands. This resulted in a release of many former terrorists. This event inspired Edmund Burke to write, "Thousands of those Hell-hounds called Terrorists . . . are let loose on the people."[190] This quote was later picked up in the *Oxford English Dictionary* as allegedly the first English usage of the word *terrorist*.[191]

Babeuf's Conspiracy for Equality

Burke may have been right to be suspicious of the amnestied terrorists, because they became the nucleus of a conspiracy against the Directorate, known as the Conspiracy for Equality, a precursor of communism, or simply Babeuf's conspiracy, after its most prominent publicist. Although the conspiracy had little impact at the time, the Directorate used its trial to discredit terrorists forever. It might have been forgotten had not one of its survivors written an account of it about three decades later that became required reading for both policemen and revolutionaries as a manual for conspirators. Babeuf was retrospectively enshrined as one of the first communists, and his conspiracy became the prototype of a terrorist conspiracy, in the modern sense of the term. This conspiracy illustrates the dramatic transformation of the political arena by the French Revolution, whose greatest significance is simply the fact that it happened. That, by itself, was enough to inspire generations of dreamers to believe that they could change the world for the benefit of the people.

François-Noël "Gracchus" Babeuf was a product of the Revolution and the first in a long line of revolutionaries who tried to spark an insurrection based on the model of the successful journées révolutionnaires that overthrew the government, monarchy and Brissotins. His strategy was to create an incident that would trigger an uprising and harness the power of the crowd to overthrow the government. He attributed the failure of the two journées of spring 1795 to a lack of leadership and concluded that a successful general insurrection could only come from the leadership of a small group of dedicated full-time conspirators.

Babeuf could not have been more miscast as the leader of a conspiracy. He was 36-year-old at the time, came from a poor background and had worked as an agent for feudal landlords in asserting their rights over peasants. He later used this knowledge to champion agrarian land reforms and egalitarianism. He married a rather inarticulate woman, with whom he had five children. He was never emotionally close to his wife despite her devotion to him. He was a loner who never had any close friends but grew close to his two sons when they reached the age of ten. His lack of friends was probably due to an inability to understand people. His frequent failures to gauge his interlocutors' feelings resulting in disastrous social faux pas (insulting potential and actual benefactors) at crucial points of his life[192] and his inability to feel his emotions and reason them out in a given situation, make me suspect that he may have suffered from an autism spectrum disorder. In any case, his lack of social skills clearly hindered the later conspiracy.

Babeuf caught the spirit of the Revolution and went to Paris, where he showed talent as a pamphleteer. His sans-culotte views earned him the nickname "Marat of the Somme."[193] He did not take part in the Terror, as he was imprisoned for a local squabble in his home village. He was released a few days before the fall of Robespierre and first used his rhetorical skills to condemn Carrier and the terrorists. But, with the worsening of the economic situation, he changed his mind. The excesses of the Terror had been replaced by the blatant social and economic inequalities of the Thermidorean reaction: corrupt rich bourgeois exploiting the new regime's liberalism were feasting and spending fortunes on entertainment while he and most people in Paris were starving. Babeuf launched personal attacks on the new Convention leaders and even called for an insurrection. He was arrested in February 1795 and imprisoned during the two failed sans-culottes journées of spring 1795.[194]

During his nine-month incarceration, Babeuf further developed his political ideas in discussions with another inmate, Charles Germain, a 25-year-old former military officer convicted for fighting with a conservative spectator in the gallery of the Convention.[195] On reading about the failure of the Prairial journée, they explored ways to ensure the success of future ones. Germain suggested a surprise uprising prepared by careful organization and propaganda. Babeuf rejected this idea and suggested instead that insurgents establish a "center of population" in a supportive region, an experimental "republican Vendée." Its fame would spread to adjacent regions, which would adopt, extend, and consolidate the social revolution.[196] In prison, Babeuf also met future conspirators, including Philippe Buonarroti, a 34-year-old radical conspirator from Tuscany who had been granted honorary French citizenship:[197] "Like-minded people, burning with patriotism, inflamed by persecution and strengthened in their shared feelings by extensive and frequent communication, found themselves naturally predisposed to try everything to revive the revolution and reach their goals. The prisons of these times were the cradles of democratic conspiracies."[198] This description implies that a sense of shared social identity emerged among some of these prisoners, who later got in touch after their release during the general amnesty and established a network of likeminded people. Germain felt that this identity was akin to belonging to a political sect, a fraternity of equals.[199]

Babeuf and his fellow political prisoners were released in October 1795. My reconstruction of the Conspiracy for Equality is limited by the surviving archival material. A large number of documents were captured with the arrest of Babeuf, but they mostly dealt with utopian projects, ideological justifications, and general calls for insurrection. The police informant and later main witness for the prosecution, Charles Grisel, turned out to be an unreliable witness on cross-examination. The defendants had been such inept conspirators that, at trial, they were able to deny with great plausibility that there had ever been a plot. But 30 years later, Buonarroti confirmed the existence of a plot by writing an idealized version of it that reads like a well-planned military operation.[200] On balance, the contemporary sources show evidence of a conspiracy so sloppy that it bears little resemblance to Buonarroti's embellished recollection. The following is based on my interpretation of this mixed evidence, much of which was presented at court. Incidentally, this was the first trial whose full proceedings were transcribed by stenographers.[201]

After his release from prison, Babeuf resumed publication of his newspaper *Tribun du Peuple*, excoriating the new Directorate and openly advocating insurrection against it. Building on his prior reputation, the paper did well and had several hundred subscribers all over the country. It did not take long for Babeuf to cross the line with the censors, and a warrant was issued for his arrest in early December, less than six weeks after his release. Babeuf lived as a fugitive until his arrest five months later. He took refuge with Augustin Darthé, a 31-year-old veteran of the Bastille storming where he was severely injured, later appointed prosecutor for the Revolutionary Court and imprisoned during the Thermidorean reaction.[202]

After their release from prison, the revolutionaries vented their frustrations and grievances in cafés. These small discussions rapidly expanded into larger meetings, taking place discreetly near the Pantheon, "in a vast cellar, where the pallor of torches, the buzzing of voices and the uncomfortable position of the participants, standing or sitting on the ground, reminded them of the grandeur and danger of their enterprise, as well as the courage and prudence that they needed."[203] The discussions were passionate, expressed a common hatred of the Directorate but reflected a wide diversity of political views and solutions. These meetings became known as the Pantheon Society and grew to more than a thousand participants. They discussed Babeuf's articles and talked about organizing a mass movement around the demand of going back to the Montagnard Constitution of 1793. Buonarroti, Darthé, and Germain each presided over some of its meetings, which the fugitive Babeuf could not attend. The society's verbal attacks on the Directorate and appeals to the army to set up a more egalitarian government went too far. On 27 February 1796, General Bonaparte, as commander of the Army of the Interior, came with a large number of cavalry to personally close down the society.[204]

Forced underground, the society broke up into multiple clandestine cabals, each with its own fantasy of overthrowing the government. They sorted themselves according to common backgrounds: former Convention deputies, former military men, and former prisoners.[205] This fracturing of the movement depressed some of the militants.[206] In addition, many were issued warrants for their arrests and had to hide. Germain, Buonarroti, and Darthé continued their militancy, but now in a clandestine setting. Babeuf was not part of this group at first, but Germain and Darthé invited their respective friend and roommate to join it as its publicist. By the end of March, they gave themselves the pompous title of the Secret Committee of Public Safety, or the Insurrectional Committee. They dreamed of organizing an insurrection but they were not true organizers. Instead, they were propagandists, who spent all their time writing down manifestos of their programs, developing elaborate plans for carrying them out, and drawing up lists of potential supporters.[207]

The limits of the evidence prevent us from tracing their progression to violence, as the captured documents focused on ideological programs and exhortations rather than the evolution of their insurrection. Nevertheless, they complained about the government's aggression in closing down the Pantheon Society.[208] In addition, Buonarroti, Germain, and Darthé—and of course Babeuf, already under an arrest warrant—felt a sense of moral outrage for having been issued warrants because police spies allegedly saw them reading posters about the closing of the Pantheon Society.[209] This state persecution gave credibility to floating rumors that royalists and émigrés had come back to carry out a coup against the government and eliminate the true patriots. The government's lenient attitude toward the October 1795 journée conservatives and White Terror murderers reinforced this belief. They feared that their life was in danger.[210] There was also a sense of betrayal as the 1795 Constitution (approved by only 900,000 votes) had erased the egalitarian sections of the 1793 Constitution (approved by 4,800,000 votes).[211] Believing that the new

Directorate had usurped the sovereignty of the people, the conspirators wanted to restore the Constitution of 1793.[212] As if in response, new laws were passed in mid-April 1796 that prohibited public assemblies and punished by death any demand of the restoration of the 1793 Constitution.[213] The conspirators stated that they wanted to "live free or die."[214]

Riding a wave of popular disappointment with the Directorate because of hyperinflation and widespread corruption, the conspirators decided to start their insurrection. Their plan was based on the model of the successful journées.[215] The Insurrectional Committee tried to establish links with the twelve reorganized *arrondissements* in Paris through principal agents, and with military units stationed in Paris through military agents. These intermediaries were in charge of mobilizing their respective institutions. For support in the provinces, they counted on the subscribers of the *Tribun du Peuple*. The committee was also preparing the ground through propaganda work, through Babeuf's *Tribun du Peuple*, pamphlets and placards posted all around Paris.[216] However, Paris in 1796 was no longer the Paris of 1792–94: the sans-culottes had been disarmed; many had left for the army at the front; the consolidated Paris local assemblies were controlled by royalists or moderates even in the former sans-culottes districts;[217] the National Guards had been reorganized and were more conservative; and their radical former cannon unit commanders were under tight police surveillance.[218] Furthermore, the transparent culture of former sans-culottes was not compatible with a clandestine conspiracy.[219] The insurrection might have looked good on paper but it did not generate much enthusiasm: only half of the designated would-be principal agents showed up at the crucial final preparation meeting.[220] The wide gap between wishful thinking and reality might be best illustrated in the trajectory of the person who became the main police informant.

Charles-Jacques-Georges Grisel, a 31-year-old former tailor, had volunteered for the army in 1791 and was a captain stationed in the Grenelle garrison in Paris. On 10 April 1796, an acquaintance ran into him in the street and invited him for a drink. In their conversation, this acquaintance talked about the White Terror's persecution of patriots in the south and the government's exploitation of soldiers.[221] Such talk about out-group offenses makes salient the common social identity of speakers and sets the stage for a recruitment pitch based on this commonality: the potential recruit as member of this imagined in-group should join it against its out-group enemy. If the potential recruit agrees with the complaints, he is self-categorizing as member of this in-group and receptive to accepting a more active role against the out-group.

The acquaintance showed Grisel a copy of the *Tribun du Peuple*, encouraging soldiers to rise up and restore the 1793 Constitution, and asked him what he thought of it. Grisel read the piece and opined that the writer did not understand anything about soldiers. The appeal to abstractions like common happiness would not resonate with them. Grisel suggested instead appealing to their homesickness, economic situation (as they were paid in worthless paper money), and desire for food, drink, and women. The acquaintance took him to a well-known revolutionary café, where he introduced Grisel to Darthé, who immediately revealed to Grisel the existence of a secret insurrectional committee and commissioned him to write a pamphlet addressed to soldiers. The next day, Grisel returned to the café and gave Darthé his address. Darthé liked it and had it printed the next day. On 13 April, he gave dozens of copies to Grisel to distribute at his garrison. Two days later, Darthé introduced Grisel to Germain to discuss the conspiracy. Finally, on 17 April, Buonarroti took Grisel to meet Babeuf and the rest of the committee at Babeuf's hiding place. So, in about a week's time, Grisel, a total outsider, was introduced to the whole Insurrectional Committee without ever being vetted. At his trial testimony, Grisel said that he notified his chain of command, but no evidence supported this claim. This unbelievable breach of clandestine tradecraft shows the ineptitude of the conspirators and their desperate need for active-duty soldiers.

Grisel could not meet with the conspirators for the next two weeks. He resumed contact on 1 May, when he was made a member of the just created military committee, which also included Germain (a former soldier, now constantly dressed as a captain). They were to be the agents in contact with the military and police to get access to weapons and encourage troops to rebel. The committee was issued no money; in fact, there never was any money at all for the conspiracy. The next day, Grisel wrote to Lazare Carnot, the director most hated by these revolutionaries and least likely to be part of the conspiracy. They met on 4 May, and Grisel revealed the plot to Carnot, who encouraged him to stay in place. Later on a tip by Grisel, Carnot sent a large detachment of police to raid an important conspiratorial meeting on the evening of 7 May, but the police misunderstood the time and arrived two hours too late. On 10 May, the police raided the homes of most of the conspirators, arresting more than 100 people, including all of the members of the Insurrectional Committee along with their compromising archives.

Overall, the conspirators seemed incompetent and fantasized a lot. One later testified: "I believed that all of this only existed in Babeuf's head. I'm telling you in good faith, I've seen Babeuf completely sick, run in his room, jump and say: 'We are in insurrection!' It's the truth, it happened several times when we were alone."[222] In any case, the conspiracy leaders seemed out of touch, as their forced clandestine existence cut them off from the people, who, they naïvely hoped, would spontaneously rise up upon reading posters calling them to do so and overthrow the unpopular Directorate. In the testimonies and captured documents, there was very little explicit reference to violence.

There was talk about killing individuals standing in the way of the people, but there was no plan for any specific violent operation. If the planned journée could be bloodless, like the May–June 1793 overthrow of the Brissotins, so much the better. If not, it could have been a bloodbath.

The government was determined to have a show trial to discredit once and for all these leftist conspirators, especially in the context of an upcoming election. It used the excuse that one of the conspirators, Drouet, the man who had stopped Louis XVI at Varennes, was a sitting deputy to convene a special High Court of Justice—even though Drouet had escaped and was at large. On 20 February 1797, the court tried 64 defendants, 47 present in the courtroom and the rest in absentia. The trial backfired on the government; their witnesses gave poor performances on the stand, and some members of the jury were sympathetic to the defendants. Most of the proceedings focused on Babeuf, Germain, and Buonarroti, with Darthé refusing to cooperate, saying he did not recognize the legitimacy of the court. In the end, on 27 May 1797, only nine defendants were convicted and the rest acquitted. Buonarroti, Germain, and five other defendants were convicted and deported to a penal colony. Babeuf and Darthé were condemned to death for advocating the restoration of the 1793 Constitution. They tried to stab each other to death when they heard the sentence. As inept as usual, they just managed to wound each other and were executed the next day.[223]

At first blush, this seems to be an ideologically driven conspiracy. However, on closer look, there was much ideological disagreement among the conspirators, as noted by Buonarroti, and they only agreed on the overthrow of the Directorate and restoration of the 1793 Constitution. As the main conspirators found out, conspiracy to overthrow a very repressive government is a high-risk enterprise with a very high likelihood of punishment and a very low probability of reward, inconsistent with rational calculation. On the other hand, the conspirators formed a political protest community that became outraged at the escalation of the government's repression with the issuance of warrants for their arrests. They had realized that protest was useless and decided to trigger an uprising before they could be arrested. Like the sans-culottes they were emulating, they thought of themselves as soldiers defending their community and the vanishing sans-culottes.

La Machine Infernale: The First Vehicular Bomb

In the violent decade of the French Revolution, the very small number of assassination attempts on major political leaders is surprising, given the intermittent periods of general lack of law and order. People seem to have used denunciations and legitimate means to get rid of rivals through committees of surveillance and revolutionary courts.[224] The lack of access to these instruments firmly in the hands of Montagnards contributed to the actions of Corday and Admiral. Outside of Paris, especially during the White Terror, assassinations were common to get even with local rivals during a time when the state could not impose a monopoly on violence.

In terms of achieving political change, assassinations are generally not effective in a government ruled by collective power. Although Robespierre has gone down in history as a tyrant, the actual political power during the Terror was vested in the Committee of Public Safety and not in his person alone. The entire collective government had to be changed, which could be done only through large-scale insurrections (journées). To spark one was the strategy of the Conspiracy for Equality. This dramatically changed with Napoleon Bonaparte's coup in 1799. He replaced the Directorate with his Consulate, concentrating power in his own person. In this context, any violent attempt to overthrow the Consulate had to focus on his elimination.

Bonaparte's military victory at Marengo in June 1800 consolidated his power and started to bring a semblance of political and economic stability to France. Within six months, it also spawned a series of personal *attentats,* or violent political attacks, against him. Former revolutionary Dominique Demerville summarized the situation: "What are we waiting for before hitting this new Caesar? We no longer need popular masses; a few brave people are enough to free the country!"[225] On 10 October 1800, someone denounced him to the military authorities on suspicion that he was planning an attentat because he had told a friend not to go to the opera that evening. The chief of military police went to the opera that evening, did not notice anything unusual, and returned to his office.[226] Nevertheless, the regular police arrested Giuseppe Ceracchi and Joseph Diana as alleged assassins, and about 50 more in the next few days in what became known as the conspiracy of the daggers.[227] They were well-known revolutionaries, and the police accused them of attempting to stab Bonaparte to death during the performance. Although this conspiracy has mostly disappeared from the history books, it might be one of the first to have used a police agent provocateur, who claimed that Demerville and the others had tried to recruit him to kill Bonaparte.[228] At trial, Demerville, who had been bedridden for two months prior to his arrest and had confessed during the investigation, testified that the confession was beaten out of him in his weakened state.[229] All the other defendants denied there had been a conspiracy.[230] Supporting their claim of innocence was the fact that the two alleged assassins were unarmed when arrested at the opera.

In November 1800, while the investigation into the conspiracy of the daggers was unfolding, another incident took place. There is very little surviving evidence about the Chevalier affair. Alexandre Chevalier, one of the survivors of an extreme faction of sans-culottes was a former navy artillery man and chemist who invented a new device to kill Bonaparte. When the police arrested him and an accomplice, they found a *machine infernale* at the place, consisting of a reinforced barrel filled with scrap iron, gravel, and eight pounds of gunpowder, wrapped with paper with nails glued to it. The detonator was a sawed-off shotgun shooting into the barrel. Pulling on a string attached to its trigger activated the mechanism. A police expert stated that the device was not designed to kill a specific person, but to maim or kill indiscriminately a large number of people in its vicinity. This type of device had been used in naval fighting to disable ships. It could be very lethal if used in a confined space filled with people.[231] Chevalier had tested his device the previous month, causing a frightful explosion. After the success of the test, the conspirators were making plans for an insurrection to follow their attentat and for a new government to take over and restore the 1793 Constitution.[232]

The plots against Bonaparte did not come only from republican extremists. The Vendée insurgency in the West had given way to the Chouans in Brittany, a group that conducted a sort of guerilla warfare (the expression did not appear until two decades later) which waxed and waned over seven years.[233] It was supported by émigré aristocrats and at times the British government. By 1800, its leader was Georges Cadoudal, or simply Georges, as both friends and enemies called him. Bonaparte's new strategy of pacification succeeded in progressively isolating the Chouans from their local popular support, and the Chouans degenerated into local brigands robbing, kidnapping or killing their enemies. As part of his strategy, Bonaparte even met with Georges in March 1800 and offered him a position of general in his army. Georges turned him down, but, no longer able to continue his guerilla war in Brittany, he took refuge in England, where he met with the new King Louis XVIII, his brother the Comte D'Artois, and British Prime Minister William Pitt.[234]

After Marengo, Cadoudal had also concluded that any popular uprising had to start with the elimination of Bonaparte himself. He therefore decided to expand his theater of operation to the capital where he dispatched two of his lieutenants, Pierre Robinault de Saint-Réjant and Joseph Picot de Limoëlan. Saint-Réjant (also spelled Saint-Réjeant or Saint-Régent), a 32-year-old former naval artillery officer who had gained a reputation as one of the most aggressive Chouan fighters, was in charge of the military operation. Limoëlan, a 31-year-old rich aristocratic former military officer, had fought with the émigré army. He had joined Cadoudal's Chouans relatively late, but quickly gained his boss's trust and was in charge of funds and logistics for the operation. As soon as he arrived in Paris, he ran into an acquaintance, Jean Carbon, a 44-year-old former ship surgeon, and a Chouan, who was living in Paris with his sister. Limoëlan recruited him as his assistant.[235]

At trial, all the defendants denied their participation in the bombing, so it is difficult to trace their turn to violence from the transcripts. Nevertheless, all were already seasoned Chouans, some fighting for years in Cadoudal's army. They were simply soldiers sent on a perilous mission behind enemy lines to carry out an attentat on Bonaparte's life. Cadoudal's nephew later claimed that the operation was just an attempt to kidnap the first consul.[236] There is some evidence that Cadoudal originally thought about a kidnapping in June 1800.[237] But by the fall, he seems to have changed his mind because he sent only four people to Paris, an insufficient number to carry out a kidnapping of a person constantly protected by two dozen elite troops. Apparently, the plan for eliminating the first consul was left to the initiative of the field commanders, given the difficulty of communicating with Georges.[238]

The evidence shows that Saint-Réjant and Limoëlan experimented with several ways of eliminating the consul. The conspirators drifted into Paris separately, using false identities. They were immediately detected by police spies infiltrated among Chouan sympathizers in Paris. One, named Desgrée, reported regularly on them to the police chief. On 25 November, he reported that the conspirators had bought some guns and had gone for target practice in the Bois de Boulogne. On 2 December, Saint-Réjant and Limoëlan told Desgrée that they would try to assassinate the first consul at the theater, inspired by the conspiracy of daggers reported in the press, but using guns instead of daggers. The next day, Saint-Réjant asked Desgrée to take a letter to Cadoudal in Brittany.[239] It is not clear when the conspirators discovered the treason, but Cadoudal had Desgrée shot on arrival.[240]

The conspirators then disappeared from police monitoring. It is not known whether they had staged their gun practice to deceive the police. Nor do we know how they got the idea to use Chevalier's idea of a machine infernale. The papers had carried details about the Chevalier affair, and they may also have communicated with him as he was freely discussing his machine in prison at the time.[241] According to the investigation, Carbon bought a horse and cart on 17 December. The conspirators built an explosive device larger than Chevalier's and activated it with a fuse instead of a gun. Through experiments the day before the attack, Saint-Réjant calculated the length of fuse to use.

The attack was simple. On Christmas Eve 1800 (3 Nivôse, year IX) Bonaparte and his family left the Tuileries Palace for the opera. At a narrowing in the rue Saint-Nicaise along the way, a horse drawn cart with a large barrel mounted on it partially blocked the way. The barrel was full of powder, gravel, and scrap iron and Saint-Réjant was waiting by it. Limoëlan was posted ahead to signal the first consul's carriage turn into the rue Saint-Nicaise from the palace. The plan was for Saint-Réjant to immediately light the fuse, timed precisely to explode as the carriage went by. However, it seems that Limoëlan failed to signal, and Saint-Réjant had to improvise and shorten the fuse. The device exploded too late, missing the consul's carriage by seconds. Bonaparte felt the shock but was unhurt. Saint-Réjant tried to get away from the blast but suffered a concussion and injuries to his ears, nose, and throat, causing profuse bleeding. The explosion caused great damage: 4 to 10 people were killed, including a little girl, and 28 to 60 people injured.[242] Detached limbs and blood were everywhere. Buildings adjacent to the bomb were destroyed, and most of the buildings in the neighborhood sustained some damage. Roof tiles rained on people in the street. To my knowledge, this was the first vehicle-borne improvised explosive device, the ancestor of the modern car and truck bombs.[243]

This was also the first act of political violence that blindly killed innocent civilians through an intentional and indiscriminate explosion.[244] The horror of the act was such that no one ever claimed responsibility for it. It elicited all the horror and social response characteristic of any act of modern terrorism. The press and the authorities described the unknown perpetrators as monsters, whose motivation could only be fanaticism that resisted any rational reasoning.[245] This perspective of course obscures and denies the political dimension of this violence and reduces it to pure barbarism, which can be countered only by its complete elimination. Because of the similarity between Chevalier's machine infernale and the 3 Nivôse device,[246] people, including Bonaparte, jumped to the conviction that this was carried out by "terrorists, septembriseurs and anarchists."[247] Police reports showed that the public rallied around the first consul, whose popularity climbed to its peak. The people temporarily forgot about their everyday misery in their outrage at this new danger that threatened the whole of society, and wanted prompt punishment of the alleged perpetrators. A crowd applauded a detachment of dragoons escorting suspects to prison because it thought they were going to be tortured.[248] A newspaper noted, "Each attentat . . . tightens the bonds that tie French people to their first magistrate."[249] The aggression against the nation's leader was felt as a personal aggression against all Frenchmen.

This hardening of the popular mood against enemies of the nation gave Bonaparte the opportunity to eliminate his other internal threats. Believing that the bombing was the result of revolutionaries, he rounded up more than one hundred of them and quickly deported them to the Seychelles, a French colony, without any trial. Most of them died there.[250] Eight defendants in the conspiracy of daggers went on trial. Despite the weak evidence, four, including Demerville and Ceracchi, were convicted and executed.[251] The rest were acquitted but kept in detention for deportation. A few days later, a military commission tried, convicted and executed Chevalier all in one day, like in the days of the Great Terror.[252] Several days later, three other former sans-culottes who had written pamphlets advocating Bonaparte's assassination suffered the same fate at the hands of another military commission. When it became clear that the bombing was the work of the Chouans, Bonaparte gave the green light for his troops to murder Cadoudal on sight, without any trial.[253] All of the perpetrators were eventually caught and executed, except for Limoëlan, who became a saintly Catholic priest in America, where he died two and a half decades later. He changed his name to Father Joseph Pierre Picot de Clorivière, and was buried at a chapel in Georgetown, now part of Washington, D.C.[254]

Everyone rejected this indiscriminate attentat: Louis XVIII was outraged when he heard about it. Cadoudal claimed to his dying day that he had approved only the kidnapping of the first consul, and not an assassination by a machine infernale.[255] The widespread popular identification with the victims also led to immediate state compensation for them, including some without physical injury but whose fright prevented them from working for a week.[256] The cart bomb against Bonaparte can be viewed as the first instance of the type of modern political violence in terms of both the behaviors of the perpetrators, who hoped to spark a popular insurrection through a deliberate and indiscriminate bombing, and the psychological, social, political, and judicial reactions it spawned. In terms of our study, since none of the perpetrators, not even the repentant Father Clorivière, left a confession behind, there is no evidence to help us trace the process leading them to use a machine infernale as opposed to more traditional methods of assassination. But it was clear that they were Chouans, soldiers fighting for their comrades and cause. Their royalist ideology did not explain this use of explosive vehicles.

Conclusions

The instances of political violence examined in this chapter—Corday, the journées révolutionnaires, the Terror, the Babeuf conspiracy, and Saint-Nicaise—followed the same pattern: they all emerged from a political protest community and, in the context of escalation of conflict with their rivals, and moral outrage, they self-categorized as soldiers fighting for their community, consistent with the social identity perspective. The non-state violence also involved disillusionment with legal means of redress of their grievances. Even in such ideologically driven times, ideology cannot explain their turn to violence. Nor can rational choice.

People often distinguish between political violence carried out by a small number of conspirators like the Saint-Nicaise bombing and political assassinations like Corday's killing of Marat. The French lump them together as *attentats politiques,* political acts of aggression. The word *attentat* is often translated into English as "attempt," but this does not capture the complex, ambiguous, and evolving nuances of the word,[257] which may be more appropriately translated as "act of aggression" or "intention to harm." In French, both traditional regicide and modern terrorist acts are political attentats. As members of a nation see their head of state as their most prominent group prototype, any act of aggression against him or her is experienced as an aggression against all members of the nation. Until his failed flight abroad, Louis XVI was still seen as the prototype of the French nation and even revolutionaries would have considered any attentat on his life as one of lèse-nation, one against their self-conceptualized national identity.[258] The meaning of *attentat* was later extended to include any attack on any member of the nation. Other group members now experienced such an act of aggression as a personal attack, which activated their group social identity. This perspective may help explain why attentats or terrorist acts, in their modern sense,[259] are psychologically experienced quite differently from ordinary crimes, leading to psychological, social, political, and judicial reactions qualitatively different from those of normal crimes.

The French Revolution provided a precedent and a model for future violent political actors to follow. It democratized political violence from palace coups to truly popular events by greatly expanding the political arena. At first, such non-state political violence was within the context of mass uprisings. It later shifted to small group conspiracies trying to spark such insurrections to produce political changes. The concentration of political power into the hands of a head of state like Bonaparte brought back the popularity of attentats against heads of state (regicides, if the head of state is a king). But unlike previous regicides, these were no longer personal affairs carried out by a small palace, elite or by insane individuals but popular attempts against a tyrant to trigger or inspire mass uprising and bring about political change.

Political Violence from the Restoration
to the Paris Commune

The half century between the fall of Napoleon Bonaparte and that of his nephew Louis Napoleon in France was crucial in the development of modern political violence with the entry of the working class to foment a social revolution and the progressive turn to explosives to compensate for the challengers' weakness vis-à-vis the state. Yet, except for a few French scholars,[1] historians of terrorism have neglected this critical period in the history of political violence. By the end of this period, political violence completed its evolution to what might be easily recognizable as terrorism.

Punishment of Traitors to the Nation

Bonaparte, who became Napoleon, was overthrown after fifteen years in power and the monarchy was restored in 1815. The new king, Louis XVIII, wisely accepted some of the social developments of the French Revolution and enshrined them in a National Charter, guaranteeing some of its liberal measures. Nevertheless, after a quarter century of national glory, the French political arena had become a confusing battlefield on which the combatants included moderate monarchists (partisans of the new king), ultra-royalists (partisans of his brother, Comte d'Artois), constitutional monarchists (advocates of the British system), Bonapartists, conservative republicans (like the Thermidorean reactionaries), egalitarian republicans (like the Jacobins), politically self-conscious workers, and various other groups. For the next half century, no government earned the loyalty of all the French people, as some political factions would not consider it legitimate. This unstable situation led to constant intrigue and fighting to establish one's preferred political system, and many of the plots included violence to install the preferred political system. Any challenge to a reigning government faced a sophisticated police force, which was constantly vigilant against and cynically manipulated popular dissent. It did not hesitate to resort to sting operations, in which entrepreneurial police agent provocateurs pushed and provoked political malcontents, without funds or means to do any damage, to go far beyond what they would have done on their own.[2]

Despite the revolutionary rhetoric about liberty, equality, and fraternity, the French had been all too willing to sacrifice liberty and equality for national fraternity during the Napoleonic period. While the glory of Napoleon's Grande Armée consolidated French national social identity, its devastations abroad stirred the hearts of foreign patriots and inadvertently spread nationalism in opposition to the French invaders. The murder of August von Kotzebue by 24-year-old Karl-Ludwig Sand on 23 March 1819 caused a sensation at the time and is a good example of these nascent national identities. The killing led to the Carlsbad Decrees, which tried but failed to suppress German nationalism, as Sand continued to be a source of inspiration for it. From our perspective, this case is instructive because Sand left behind a diary tracing his evolution to political violence.

Sand had volunteered as a patriot for the army that defeated Napoleon at Waterloo in 1815. When he returned home, his diary shows that he was searching for a great cause that could give his life some transcendental meaning. His hope for a united German republic was crushed when divided German princes reasserted their authority. He and his best friend joined a nationalistic secret German student brotherhood, which fought student associations rejecting unification. In June 1817, his friend accidentally drowned, and Sand found solace in redoubling his efforts on behalf of their cause, German freedom and unification.[3] At the time, the focus of nationalist students' anger was August von Kotzebue, a well-known German playwright and polemicist who had fled to Russia before the French army and returned to Germany as a Russian consul general. He promoted Russia's interests and actively discouraged a united Germany, a threat to his Russian patron, through a prolific outburst of pamphlets attacking the idea of a German republic. In November 1817, Sand wrote in his journal, "While crossing the marketplace, we heard Kotzebue's new poisoned insult. What rage does this man possess against the brotherhoods and all who love Germany?"[4] His 1818 New Year's resolution was to sacrifice himself for the German nation. "Lord, give strength to the idea that I conceived for the deliverance of humanity by the saintly sacrifice of your Son. Make me a Christ for Germany and, like Jesus, strong and patient against pain." In May, he wrote, "Lord, why then this melancholic anxiety that has again taken hold of me? But a firm and constant will overcomes everything, and the idea of the fatherland gives joy and courage to the saddest and weakest . . . I'm always amazed that there has not been one among us who has enough courage to thrust a knife into Kotzebue's or any other traitor's throat."[5]

His desire to sacrifice himself for the German nation came from his complete identification with it. "Man is nothing compared to a people; it's one compared to billions; it's a minute compared to a century. Man, whom nothing precedes or follows, is born, lives and dies in a more or less large time, but which lasts the duration of lightning relative to eternity. On the contrary, a people is eternal."[6] On New Year's Eve, he reviewed his diary and realized that he let the year go by without fulfilling his resolution. He was now determined to act. "If something must come out of my efforts; if the cause of humanity must triumph in our fatherland; if, in the midst of this faithless time, some generous sentiments can be reborn and live; it can only be on condition that the miserable, the traitor, the seducer of youth, the notorious Kotzebue must fall. I am convinced of this, and as long as I have not accomplished the task I had resolved to do, I will have no rest. Lord, You, who know that I have devoted my life to this great act, which has now taken over my mind, give me real spiritual strength and courage."[7] This was the last entry in his journal.

Over the next two and a half months, Sand displayed a certain serenity and affection, according to his friends. Meanwhile, he secretly planned his attack. On 7 March 1819, he threw a big party for his friends and told them he was leaving. He arrived in Mannheim on 23 March, went to Kotzebue's house, and stabbed him in the heart, killing him instantly. Responding to the noise, the victim's six-year-old daughter ran into the room and threw herself on her father's body. At this sight, Sand stabbed himself in the chest but survived. Tsar Alexander demanded justice for his dead adviser. When Sand was strong enough to be tried, the Mannheim Court of Justice convicted him of murder and sentenced him to death on 5 May 1820. He was beheaded five days later. The 20,000 people who came to see the execution were crying, as was his escort.[8] Sand had become a hero for his imagined national community.

I do not know whether Sand's sacrifice fortified Louis Pierre Louvel's resolve to assassinate the Duc de Berry, but there was a great deal of discussion about Sand's act of assassination in France at the time. Louvel did not leave a diary behind, so we must rely on his statements after the crime during his interrogation and trial to trace his evolution to political violence. The 37-year-old saddle maker was a loner and honest, diligent worker who liked to read in his spare time. He had volunteered for the army in 1813 when foreigners invaded France and was posted at Metz, where the invading Russian army was led by the Comte d'Artois. He was outraged at this betrayal and swore to himself to avenge his dying comrades. Over the next six years, he pursued his mission. He commissioned a special knife in 1815, which he always carried with him in case he got the opportunity. He found work in the king's stables and tracked his prey. Instead of Artois, he determined to kill his son, the Duc de Berry, who was the last in line of this branch of the royal family—the king and Artois (the future Charles X) were too old to have any more children; Artois's first son had no children from his marriage; and therefore the Duc de Berry, who already had a daughter, was the last hope for succession. The duke also belonged to his father's ultra-royalist faction that wanted to turn the clock back to absolute monarchy. On the evening of 13 February 1820, Louvel saw the duke enter his carriage, approached, pulled out his knife, and fatally stabbed the duke.[9]

Louvel was immediately apprehended and interrogated in the room of the dying duke. He stated he had acted alone to extinguish the branch of the royal family because they were traitors to the nation. He denied that he acted out for any ideological reason and instead explained, "It's at Metz that I conceived of the project that I just executed, when I learned that Monsieur [Artois] was at Nancy, where the white [king's] flag was raised. I knew that I would lose my life over it but the Bourbons [king's family name] were too guilty for me to abandon the project."[10] He struck the duke as a patriot and hoped it would be a lesson for those who thought about betraying their country. Asked whether he was a Bonapartist, he answered that he had sympathy for the emperor, but did not like servitude. In prison, he was calm and friendly, and even looked forward to his punishment.

At his trial on 6 June 1820, Louvel read a prepared statement to explain himself: "You must see in me only a Frenchman devoted to self-sacrifice in order to destroy the greatest enemies of the fatherland . . . Even the worst of French governments has always punished those who betrayed France or who took arms against her. I believe that when foreign armies threaten our border, interior squabbles must cease and all parties of the nation must rally and fight as one against the enemy. Any Frenchman, who does not rally to the common cause, is guilty. A Frenchman, forced to leave France because of duty or government injustice, should be pitied. But, if this same Frenchman in a foreign land harms France or takes arms against it, he is guilty and cannot come back as a French citizen." Louvel believed that France had lost at Waterloo because of the betrayal of followers of Artois. "I believe that the Bourbons are guilty and the French nation is being dishonored by their rule."[11]

Louvel was convicted and sentenced to death right after his statement. Some 200,000 people attended his execution the next day.[12] Thus, both Sand and Louvel, who self-categorized as members of a nation, murdered to punish leading traitors to their respective nations. Although both acted alone, each was a member of a political community and focused his hatred on a former leader who had betrayed it. The vast crowds that came to their executions seemed supportive of them. Indeed, it is difficult to gauge the magnitude of the hatred for the Bourbon family at the time, because contemporaneous documents were produced under state censorship and police surveillance. The hatred comes through in memoirs written after their fall.[13] This black sheep effect of outrage and disproportionate punishment of in-group traitors is a common feature of self-categorization.

The Republican Attentats

The Other Machine Infernale

The aftermath of the duke's assassination brought the ultra-royalists to power and the threat of a White Terror. In reaction, republicans, liberals, and Bonapartists spontaneously formed small clandestine opposition groups all over France, calling themselves Carbonaris like their Italian predecessors.[14] About a third were mid-level military officers; lawyers, students, and small businessmen dominated the rest of the membership. They gave rise to over a dozen military-civilian attempts to overthrow the government over the next two years, including nine in the first half of 1822. The conspirators were convinced that people would rally to them as soon as an army unit would mutiny and defy authorities. However, when loyal units were sent to quash them, they displayed a strong reluctance to use violence against their colleagues. Most of these conspiracies failed because of internal disputes, lack of cohesion and trust, betrayals, and fear of triggering an uncontrollable spiral of violence, like the Terror. The government's response was measured, and only eleven conspiratorial leaders were executed. After the failure to turn the army against the government in 1823, the Carbonari movement in France faded away.[15] Nevertheless, this brief upsurge of political violence had long-term consequences, for it spooked conservative continental European monarchies haunted by the French Revolution. They protected themselves against the specter of secret subversive political societies by building political police surveillance systems that became the model for modern political repression worldwide.[16]

The Comte d'Artois succeeded his brother as Charles X in 1824 and tried to reinstate an absolute monarchy. In the summer of 1830, he abolished the National Charter, which immediately triggered a spontaneous three-day journée, known as the Trois Glorieuses (the three glorious ones), at the end of July in Paris, and he was overthrown. As the opposition was not organized, the Duc d'Orléans stepped in as King Louis-Philippe, supported by the conservative bourgeois of Paris. Because Louis-Philippe was the son of the revolutionary Duc d'Orléans, who had voted for the death of Louis XVI in 1793, he was also hated by the hardcore royalists, who called themselves *légitimistes*. This inaugurated almost two decades of continuous political unrest punctuated by large insurrections and over a dozen attentats against the king from all sides of the political spectrum.[17]

There were two large urban insurrections at the beginning of the reign of Louis-Philippe. In June 1832, popular disappointment with Louis-Philippe's failure to live up to the promise of the Trois Glorieuses, combined with a cholera outbreak, escalated into a riot, which was severely repressed. The result was about 70 deaths and 330 wounded on the government side and about 80 deaths and 200 wounded on the insurgent side. About 1,500 insurgents were arrested, and about half a dozen were condemned to death.[18] The first large-scale working-class insurrection in France was probably the Canut silk workers' rebellion in Lyon, which spread into a nationwide insurgency in April 1834, provoking a repression even more severe than the one that followed the previous insurrection. Hundreds of civilians were killed, and thousands were arrested and brought to Paris for a gigantic trial scheduled for May 1835. This severe repression discouraged the vast majority of activists from trying to organize another insurrection, but, as the chief of police at the time realized, "the failures gave to some incurable imaginations the courage of despair. We no longer feared general insurrection: the time of riots and battles was past. We entered into another period, that of isolated crimes."[19] In other words, aggressive police surveillance and repression, which easily detected any planning for mass insurrections, shifted political violence to attentats by a small number of conspirators.

The most notorious attentat in this wave of political violence was a new machine infernale conspiracy on 28 July 1835, the fifth anniversary of the Trois Glorieuses. The central character of this conspiracy was Giuseppe Fieschi, who invented and built the new machine infernale, and was the only one at the trial to confess his role in the conspiracy. However, he did not initiate this attack, which was carried out on behalf of his republican friends. The following account is based on his perspective.

Fieschi was a 45-year-old Corsican goatherd who in 1808 had volunteered for the Grande Armée, where he learned how to read and write. He participated in campaigns in Italy and Russia and was decorated for his bravery. After Napoleon's defeat, he returned to his native Corsica, where he took a cow from his sister as part of his inheritance, but his sister accused him of theft. He was arrested, and a royalist court convicted and sentenced him to ten years in prison because of his reputation as a fanatic Bonapartist. He was a model prisoner, learning weaving in prison, and was discharged at the end of his sentence. During his last year in detention, he fell in love with a female prisoner, Laurence Petit. After his release, he practiced his new trade and kept out of trouble. The July uprising opened up new opportunities for him. He moved to

Paris, was reintegrated in the army as a noncommissioned officer, and falsified some documents to get benefits as a former political prisoner. With this new status, he obtained the position of guardian of a small mill in Paris and supplemented his income as a weaver and bayonet instructor. Petit and her small daughter Nina Lassave came to live with him. At the time, Fieschi felt grateful to the new government and volunteered as a police informant on several occasions. He even fought on the side of the police and National Guards against the republican crowds during the 1832 and 1834 uprisings. He had only scorn for politics and ideology: he seemed only interested in money and had a taste for the thrill of adventure. He thought of himself as a Bonapartist, hated republicans, and volunteered to infiltrate their secret societies.

By early 1834, Fieschi's relationship with Petit had deteriorated, and he raped his fifteen-year-old stepdaughter, Nina, who became his regular lover. When Petit found out, she moved out of the home and put her daughter in a home for destitute girls. Fieschi gambled away some money that had been entrusted to him, and as a result of an investigation, his forgery was discovered and he lost his benefits and positions. A warrant for his arrest was issued in October 1834. His past conviction made him a recidivist and so he fled. A fugitive, destitute and homeless, Fieschi found refuge with a neighbor, Pierre Morey.[20]

Morey, a 60-year-old saddle maker, had been in the artillery of Napoleon's Grande Armée for ten years, where he became an expert on firearms and an excellent shot. After the foreign invasion of 1815, he killed an Austrian soldier in Dijon and was arrested. At his trial, he explained to the jury that he had killed the foreigner to prevent him from raping a young French girl. The jury acquitted him, and he went to Paris to practice his trade. He got married, became a fervent republican, and participated in the Trois Glorieuses and was stunned at Louis-Philippe's usurpation of power. He joined the secret republican Society of the Rights of Man and became one of its section chiefs. During the insurrections of 1832 and 1834, he helped wounded comrades. He lived near Fieschi, and the two had first met in 1831. Soon, they found out that they shared the same love for guns and went to target practice together. As they socialized, Morey often cursed the king, but Fieschi just humored his friend without any other response.

At his trial, Fieschi testified that he had acted not out of ideology or politics, but to avenge the injustice done to him by the government. He felt that he had received his earlier severe sentence because of his Bonapartism and should have been eligible for benefits like former political prisoners. He blamed government persecution for his social downturn. "I was fired, unable to find work, and abandoned by my common-law wife. I bonded with some people whom I believed were firm and courageous: they encouraged me in my resolution and provided me with the means to execute it. This is when I conceived of this machine: I was desperate."[21] While hiding at Morey's around January 1835, he occupied his time devising military tactics to use in various military situations. "I was pondering the following problem: if I were in a fortress with 300 men and an epidemic killed half of them, how would I defend it with so few people? I then got this idea to create this machine that would use 90 guns stacked in rows. I realized that with a cannon in the middle of it, I could destroy a whole regiment with very few men. I drew the model when Morey's wife interrupted me and told her husband, 'Morey, come and see what Fieschi has created.' I did not know what she told him. When he came, he asked me what I was doing. I told him that it was a machine. I explained it to him, saying that it could have demolished Charles X and his family." Morey thought about it and said, "This could be useful for Louis-Philippe. I said nothing: I did not have this idea in mind. He put the draft of the model in his pocket and did not tell me what he wanted to do with it. Two or three days later, he introduced me to Pepin. I was on the lam, without resources."[22]

Théodore Pepin, a relatively prosperous 35-year-old grocer, was also a section leader of the Society of the Rights of Man. He was almost killed in the 1832 riots; he was arrested for his participation but later acquitted. He also participated in the April 1834 insurrection. Morey briefed Pepin on Fieschi's ideas, and Pepin invited the two of them for lunch, when they discussed using Fieschi's machine to get rid of the government. Pepin invited Fieschi to live with him for about a week and asked his new friend to build a model of his contraption. Two weeks later, Fieschi showed his model to Pepin, who examined it and asked how much it would cost to produce. Fieschi estimated about 500 francs, and Pepin and Morey agreed to raise the money. The coming of the huge trial of the 1834 insurrectionists solidified Pepin and Morey's determination to carry out their attack. Many of their friends were defendants at the mass trial, and the two conspirators were in a hurry to get rid of the present government.[23] At first, the plan was to use the weapon against the king on 1 May, the king's feast. The conspirators then looked for a place to use the machine. Fieschi found an apartment on the third floor of a small house on the Boulevard du Temple on the path usually taken by royal processions. With Pepin's money and using a false identity, Fieschi moved in there around the end of February 1835 and resumed his relationship with the teenager Nina Lassave, who regularly came to the apartment.

The 1 May parade was canceled, and the fallback plan was to attack the king on the celebration of the Trois Glorieuses on 28 July. This gave the conspirators time to test the machine's firing mechanism. Fieschi commissioned a carpenter to build its framework, bought 25 gun barrels with Pepin's money, and had them delivered to his apartment in a trunk on 25 July. He inserted two iron bars into the wooden frame to support a row of 25 gun barrels, inclined downward and facing the target. He was putting his *machine infernale* together when his young mistress came to visit him on 26 July. When she asked about the contraption, he replied that he was building a cotton gin. She wanted to come the next day, but he told her not to.[24] Morey spent the next day with Fieschi helping him finish assembling the machine, loading the guns, and placing them in position. Morey loaded each barrel by pouring powder inside and shoving a round and buckshot all the way down to form a tight seal with the powder. He then handed each armed barrel to Fieschi, who carefully laid them on the frame in the direction of the target. They were done in early evening. Pepin was supposed to come on his horse and ride around across the street, where the king and his escort would be the next day, in order to allow Fieschi to aim the guns. Instead, Pepin sent an employee to perform that task. The armed guns were aimed, and Morey left. Fieschi was to trigger the firing mechanism alone the next day.[25]

The *attentat* against the king and his family was part of a larger plan to overthrow the monarchy and replace it with a republic. Morey and Pepin had told Fieschi that the new government would reward him, but he rejected the idea. "I'm a soldier. I'll put myself at the head of one or two hundred men. I have no ambition except for glory. I'll tell these two hundred men: this is what I've done as those who served the great Napoleon can attest. If one of them proves more competent than me, I'll gladly give up my role. Otherwise, I'll take command."[26]

On 28 July 1835, the king and his parade appeared on the Boulevard du Temple. When he was in sight, Fieschi fired his *machine infernale*. Apparently, three guns misfired and exploded, fracturing Fieschi's skull and wounding his face and hand. The projectiles missed the king (he suffered a scratch), but killed 19 people, including two general officers, and wounded 23 others.[27] Fieschi regained consciousness and escaped from the house, but a National Guard chased and arrested him. At first, Fieschi did not break cover, maintaining that he had acted alone. Lassave realized that her lover had probably carried out the *attentat* and went to Morey's home to talk about it. They both assumed that he had died in the explosion—the news of his survival and arrest had not yet been made public. Morey told Lassave that Fieschi had been a fool. Morey claimed he had loaded all the guns except the three that had exploded, and so Fieschi had caused his own death.[28] Eventually the police tracked Lassave down and discovered her just as she was about to commit suicide. She confessed what she knew and Morey was arrested.

When Fieschi was told what Morey had told Lassave, he immediately realized that he had been double-crossed by his fellow conspirators, for Morey had loaded all the guns including the three that had misfired. Morey was an expert gunman and knew how to load a gun. He had intentionally not pushed some of the rounds all the way down, leaving a space, knowing that it would cause the barrels to blow up and kill Fieschi.[29] Fieschi also assumed that Pepin had decided to protect himself and had asked an innocent employee to go to the scene the night before the attentat. He was outraged and denounced his accomplices to the police, who otherwise had very little evidence on Pepin. From then on, Fieschi fully cooperated with the police.[30] Pepin and Morey denied their participation in the attentat throughout the trial.

All three defendants were tried, convicted, and sentenced to death on 15 February 1836. They were executed four days later. While Morey and Pepin were republican militants, previously involved in uprisings against Louis-Philippe, Fieschi had participated for revenge because he felt he had been mistreated by the government after his sacrifices for the glory of France. He bonded with Morey and Pepin, shared their hatred of the government, agreed to help them as part of the group, and eventually got carried away with the thrill of adventure. As a Bonapartist, he did not share their republican ideology, but became part of their political protest community when he felt betrayed by the government with which he had previously sympathized. He clearly believed he was a soldier carrying out his duty. When he felt betrayed by his co-conspirators, he did not hesitate to turn around and make sure they would share his fate. He was apologetic at trial about the attentat and saw himself as the assassin of 40 people. He felt he deserved the guillotine and went to it without hesitation.

Since the other conspirators denied their involvement, it is more difficult to trace their paths to violence. They were veterans of two insurgencies against the government and saw the upcoming trial of their comrades from the 1834 uprising as a deadline to overthrow the government and save them. Republicans hated Fieschi for his betrayal but crowned Pepin and Morey as heroes for the republican cause. Laure Grouvelle, the 34-year-old daughter of a famous revolutionary journalist-writer, treated them like religious saints. She had grown up in the shadow of her father's reputation and was moved by the misery of poor people from an early age. At the age of fifteen, she vowed to dedicate her life to helping the poor. She later joined several republican societies. During the Trois Glorieuses, she spent her time visiting the sick, indigents, and prisoners. She became a volunteer nurse during the 1832 cholera epidemic, during which she helped bury the dead and earned the nickname of Our Lady of Good Assistance.[31] She also ran a society giving help to prisoners, former prisoners, and political refugees.[32] After Pepin and Morey's execution, she collected shreds of their clothing still impregnated with their blood, hair locks, and even pieces of the rope tying their hands on the scaffold and kept them like religious relics.[33] Pepin and Morey had become models for republican extremists to emulate.

Fieschi's machine infernale made further history. Just before World War II, two Soviet artillery officers saw a picture of Fieschi's device in a magazine. The idea of multiple launchers inspired them. They replaced the gun barrels with rocket launchers and developed the BM-13 Katyusha Rocket Launcher system (called "Stalin's organs" by the Germans). This device became the staple of Soviet artillery during World War II, and their four-inch rockets standard weapons for insurgents ever since, like the Afghan mujahedin during the Soviet-Afghan war of the 1980s.

Soldiers for Persecuted People

Another attentat using a strange weapon was carried out on 25 June 1836. Twenty-six-year-old Louis Alibaud was a poor and handsome southerner who had received a good education. In 1829, he joined the army and was stationed in Paris during the Trois Glorieuses, but he could not bring himself to fire on the people. He deserted and joined the barricades, but could not bring himself to fire at his former comrades, either. He suffered an arm wound and spent a month at a military hospital. He was soon promoted to corporal and then to quartermaster sergeant three years later. He had a good reputation, but the insurrection of June 1832 turned him against the monarchy. "As a republican, I hate all royalty because kings are for themselves and not for the people. Nevertheless, before 6 June [1832], I never thought about assassinating Louis-Philippe. But, since then, there was no longer any representative government: only the king governed. He outlawed the Charter. His ministers said that the king did everything. If the king is all, then . . . it is from him that all evil flowed. This is why, hating evil, that is, tyranny, the massacres that dishonored Paris and the bloody executions in Lyon, I resolved to cut evil at its root."[34] He wanted to kill the king since "the massacre of the citizens in the streets of Lyon and the cloisters of Saint-Méry [6 June 1832]."[35]

After Alibaud was promoted, he got into a scuffle and was court-martialed. He retained his rank because of his previous good conduct but would not be promoted for two more years. In early 1834, his request for a medical discharge for his previous arm injury was granted, and he returned to live with his parents in Perpignan, in the south of France. At the time, Barcelona rebelled to establish a republic in Spain, and he joined European revolutionaries going there to help out. He arrived in September 1835, but the rebels were defeated and he returned home after a few weeks. "I had not totally decided [to kill the king] when I left Spain, but when I arrived in France, I was sure. It was the departure of the Duc d'Orléans for Africa that convinced me to come to Paris . . . The king dead and the duke absent, this would have been a great opportunity for the revolution."[36]

Alibaud arrived in the capital in mid-November, found an inexpensive hotel, paid for the first month, and succeeded in staying for another one on credit.[37] He went to reconnoiter the king's palace and the Tuileries Gardens, where the king took occasional walks when the weather was nice. He also looked for a weapon, saw an ad in the paper for a cane gun, went to visit the shop owned by a gunsmith, Louis François Devisme, and tried out the weapon. He said that he was a traveling salesman from the south and could sell guns there. Devisme gave him a case with three cane guns to take with him and demonstrate on the road. After two weeks, Devisme got a note from Alibaud, who claimed to be sick but would soon get to work. After another month, Devisme got worried and went to Alibaud's place to get his guns back. When he arrived at Alibaud's place, Alibaud was with a woman he had just picked up on the street. Embarrassed, Devisme left. The next morning, a friend of Alibaud brought the case back with a gun missing. A note explained that it had been stolen, but Alibaud promised to pay for it later.[38]

With the darkness of winter and the king indoors, Alibaud got depressed. In mid-January 1836, he asked the hotel manager to deliver several pounds of coal to his room. The manager became suspicious and confronted Alibaud, who confessed he wanted to asphyxiate himself. The manager convinced Alibaud to give up his suicide scheme.[39] Alibaud was destitute, living on credit, but found shelter with the brother of his childhood best friend. He stayed with him for a few weeks, until he found a job as a bookkeeper at a wine shop for a decent salary with room and board. He lived there until the weather got better and the king started to come outside again. Alibaud began to spend so much time away from work to stalk his prey that his boss fired him for his long absences.[40]

Alibaud moved to a cheap hotel room and again lived on credit, claiming to be a civil servant paid at the end of the month. He also found a restaurant to feed him on credit. A republican saw him reading the newspapers there and asked him whether he was interested in joining one of the secret republican societies, where he could find some comrades ready for the good fight. He answered, "No, you are too slow to act."[41]

Alibaud spent all his days watching the king's movements, waiting for the right time to strike. He saw the royal carriage pass several times, but he did not want to shoot the king when other passengers were present. On 25 June, he again aborted his attack on the royal carriage when saw some ladies in it, deciding to wait for the king's return at the end of the afternoon. He went for lunch, walked around, went back to the Tuileries, and spent half an hour talking to a National Guard on duty until the king's carriage returned. He waited until it came within six feet of him, raised his cane gun, aimed at the king, and fired. It is not clear whether someone interfered with his aim, but he just missed the king, who had nodded his head in salute to the guards. He was immediately subdued and not able to pull his dagger to kill himself. He was beaten and dragged to the local National Guard command post, where the sergeant on duty was none other than Devisme, the gunsmith, who immediately recognized him and the weapon he had made. From the time of his arrest, Alibaud was very calm, forthcoming about his attentat and his reasons for it, and only regretted his failure in his mission and in taking his life. "One who gives up on his life holds that of his enemy in his hands. If I failed it was due to a cause independent of my will: I was disrupted. Therefore, my affair is clear and I've accepted my fate."[42]

The government-controlled press went on an all-out smear campaign on Alibaud, portraying him as a vain scoundrel. The government rushed him to trial on 9–10 July before the Court of Peers to deny the defense time to prepare adequately. Nevertheless, Alibaud justified his action: "It is in the nature of men to rebel against domination, injustice and arbitrariness. Each man has a personal right to fight against tyranny. When a prince violates the constitution of a country, when he puts himself above the law, men are not obligated but forced to obey. Then force pushes back with force. With respect to Philippe I, I had the same right as Brutus used against Caesar . . . A governing king is responsible for all the acts that flow from his power . . . Regicide is the right of men who can only get justice by their own hand."[43]

In his closing argument, Alibaud rejected killing in general. "To kill one's own is against nature, one must feel an irresistible push to carry it out. I had to feel burdened by deep misfortune and also the country's ugly plights. The actions of Philippe's government have transformed a virtuous man into a regicide . . . I tried to use all sorts of honest means to live an honorable life. I have done everything in my power to come to the help of my parents, but the century's corruption is so great that a good man is always a fool for swindlers. I wanted to go back to the source of my misfortunes and found it in large part in the king who governs France. Corruption in a ruler is the worst of all evils, it flows from the throne and spreads among people."[44] The president of the court stopped the speech for good at this point and the court tried in vain to prevent its publication in the newspapers.

Alibaud was convicted and sentenced to death on 10 July 1836. His sentence was carried out hours later, in the middle of the night, to prevent his execution from becoming a mass political protest. His calm and dignity for the two weeks between his arrest and execution were noticed by all despite the state's attempt to smear his image. He also became a hero for republicans.

Grouvelle dipped a handkerchief in his blood after his execution and brought fresh flowers to his grave, as well as to those of Morey and Pepin.

Alibaud is in the line of Corday, Sand (whom he mentioned at one point), and Louvel and anticipates the French anarchists more than half a century later. His crime was in the name of the common people of France. He thought of himself as a soldier, not for the king but for his imagined community of ordinary Frenchmen, whom he felt the king had betrayed when his government slaughtered common people. His dual social identities as a soldier and Frenchman came into conflict, and he was forced to choose during the journées of July 1830 and June 1832. His meeting and fighting alongside international revolutionaries in Barcelona hardened his determination to go back and sacrifice himself for his people at home, and he hoped that killing the king would spark a revolution. From then on, he pursued his prey relentlessly, despite momentary despair in the middle of the winter when he contemplated suicide. The coming spring gave him energy and opportunity to carry out his act of political violence, which triggered the usual state repression.

The republican underground press saluted the attentats of Morey, Pepin, and Alibaud. "The clubs, riots and insurrections have failed. The attentat has come to cut the Gordian knot of the future . . . Because Louis-Philippe cannot be tried before a new Convention, convicted and legally executed, and because it is impossible to attack him overtly, there is only the *attentat* left to give justice."[45] Alibaud's attentat inspired further republican ones during Louis-Philippe's reign.[46] Given the very aggressive preventive police tactics, it is difficult in retrospect to gauge what was real from what was just feared. Dozens of plots were allegedly interrupted, but the absence of concrete acts in furtherance makes them unconvincing, based on prison snitches, rumors, and fears. There was a real plot by a mechanic named Champion, who built a small model of a complex machine infernale, with three rows of ten cannon barrels, springing into position, but he hung himself in jail and did not leave behind any evidence about his motivation.[47]

A new machine infernale was the center of another plot, involving Grouvelle. Here, again, the main characters all denied their involvement at trial, and their state of mind can only be reconstructed from fragments of letters or notes that survived. During Grouvelle's visits to political prisoners, she met Louis Hubert, a 31-year-old Alsatian bilingual in French and German. He had come to Paris as a teenager to work for a wine-merchant uncle. He joined the secret Society for the Rights of Man and was associated with an alleged republican plot to kill the king, but the police had preemptively arrested the conspirators in June 1835. Because of his strong defiance against the authorities, he was sentenced to five years in prison. He was there during Alibaud's short incarceration and wrote him a note saying, "Stay calm, Alibaud, be courageous and don't let these people intimidate you."[48] Apparently, Grouvelle got wind of it, visited Huber in prison, and became infatuated with him, as she felt he was cast from the same mold as Alibaud and Morey.[49]

A general amnesty released Huber from prison in May 1837. He immediately went to see Grouvelle, and they intended to get married. A few weeks after his release, Huber noticed in the common room of his shelter a young man reading a book of French grammar. The man was 21-year-old Jacob Steuble, a Swiss man who spoke only German. Huber talked to him in his native language. Steuble's father was a metal mechanic who had invented a war weapon that he had tried to sell to Russia, England, and France. It had multiple guns that could shoot at a high rate of fire and would allow four soldiers to hold off 10,000 troops.[50] He had come with his son to Paris to sell his weapon to France. The son and father got into a fight, and the father left when the French government turned him down; the son, who had also worked on the invention, was left behind, alone and destitute.

At the end of June, Huber took Steuble to meet Grouvelle, who gave him some money. Huber asked Steuble whether he was familiar enough with his father's invention to reproduce it. Steuble answered that he believed he could, but asked Huber what would be the use of the weapon. Huber answered with a question, "What is your political preference?" Steuble said, "I prefer that of my country, a republic." Huber said, "Well, would you build it to reestablish a republic?" Steuble replied, "Yes, why not?" He observed that his weapon could be very useful in a revolution and its efficiency could quickly put an end to widespread carnage.[51] The weapon consisted of two superimposed racks of eight gun barrels each, assembled around an iron pole that allowed them to swivel. The whole contraption was mounted on a two-wheel platform for mobility.[52] Believing it would be safer to design and build it abroad, Huber and Steuble left for London on 31 July with money given them by Grouvelle. In London, Steuble made drafts of various aspects of the weapon, while Huber returned to Paris to raise more money and work out the details of the operation against the king. According to a note recovered during the investigation, "We will rent an apartment near the Chamber of Deputies, with a stable and a place to put some wood on the ground floor. This is where we will put the material to build two engines, which would be assembled on the eve of the opening of the Chamber. When the king arrives, we will suddenly wheel the machines onto the street to pulverize the general staff and all around it. I am certain of success in three minutes. During this operation, two men located on a roof will fire Congreve rockets at the roof of the Chamber of Deputies, which will catch fire in five minutes."[53]

When Huber came back to London in early October, he quarreled with Steuble and grabbed the plans from his accomplice. Unbeknownst to Steuble,

Huber left London and returned to Paris to have the weapons built there from the stolen drafts, not knowing that Steuble had prudently withheld the draft of a crucial piece of the machinery. After his return to Calais in early December, Huber wrote to an accomplice. "We can, if circumstances are right, strike the big blow. But let's think carefully about it, let's not recklessly compromise the security of the people . . . and see whether the people can achieve happiness without bloodshed. I don't believe this is possible . . . The people need to be rid of human-faced vultures that want to devour all that are not like them. If, in the worst case, we die in the fight, we would suffer the fate of martyrs: we will gladly drink the poison and die with a good conscience regardless of public opinion. As to our co-religionists, there are so few pure ones—most preach virtue but are only selfish, ambitious, intransigent and political jugglers . . . I adore the republic but abhor false republicans."[54]

However, Huber lost his briefcase with the above letter in it. Someone picked it up, read it, and gave it to the police, who rounded up the conspirators. They went on trial in Paris on 7 May 1838 and stubbornly denied that there was a plot. Nevertheless, on 25 May, the jury convicted them and sentenced Huber to deportation and Grouvelle and Steuble to five years in prison. Upon hearing the sentence, Huber protested that Grouvelle was innocent and tried to stab himself with a pocket knife. The guards and Grouvelle intervened before he could hurt himself, and she hugged him. The guards had trouble separating them. Huber left the courtroom screaming, "The blood of Morey will be avenged . . . corrupt people, you have condemned virtue."[55] Steuble slit his throat and died in prison shortly thereafter.[56]

It is clear that Grouvelle and Huber belonged to the same political protest community as Morey, Pepin, and Alibaud. Huber had already been involved in violence, and the other two supported him when it seemed that he had come upon a chance opportunity to carry out an operation against the government. The near success of Fieschi's attentat had demonstrated that this type of operation could be successful. Steuble was a foreign republican and did not feel he belonged to his comrades' political group. When a dispute arose with Huber, he had no problem abandoning his co-conspirators.

Communist Political Violence

After the severe repression of the 1834 insurrection, workers distanced themselves from their liberal and republican bourgeois colleagues, who were progressively adopting legal methods of political protest. Auguste Blanqui, Armand Barbès, and Martin Bernard joined the new Société des Familles, formed from a combination of extremist republicans (Blanqui), students

(Barbès), and workers (Bernard). They appreciated the need for workers to arm themselves in case of a conflict with authorities and started to manufacture gunpowder. When a factory was discovered in Paris in 1836, Barbès and Blanqui were arrested, but they were freed in the general amnesty of May 1837. All three reorganized their society under a new name, Société des Saisons (Society of the Seasons), which grew to about 1,000 members by May 1839. This was a strictly secret, disciplined, hierarchical, and compartmentalized organization based on the Buonarroti blueprint described for Babeuf's conspiracy and headed by a secret committee of Blanqui, Barbès, and Bernard. It rehearsed for an eventual insurrection, secretly buying ammunition. The strategy was to capture a symbolic piece of territory in the capital and invite the population to join the insurrection, overthrow the government, and spark a social revolution to improve the conditions of the working class. The government and public called these new organizations communist or socialist.[57]

It is hard to reconstruct the motivation of the leaders of this insurrection because they refused to cooperate at their respective trials.[58] In fact, when Barbès was challenged by the presiding judge, he said, "When an Indian is defeated, when fate made him fall under the power of his enemy, he does not think about defending himself. He does not engage in pointless words. He gives up and presents his head for scalping. I do like the Indian: I give you my head."[59] When the judge interpreted this comment to mean that Barbès took part in an act of savagery, Barbès replied and turned it around by stressing the savagery of the state: "When I compared myself to a savage who presented his head when he was defeated by his enemy and did not expect any mercy from him, I did not approve of the pitilessness of the scalper."[60] The communist leaflets accused the governments of not only carrying on wars and their human massacres but also creating famines. But they also rejected exploitation that condemned men to humiliation and poverty.[61] Their program was clearly social revolution, not just political reform.

The militants were showing signs of impatience, tired of promises and rehearsals. Even Barbès gave up and returned home to the southwest of France. Fearing a mass desertion, Blanqui decided to act. He had carefully prepared his insurrection to take advantage of political opportunities. During the spring of 1839, the government was facing a crisis, with the posts of ministers of interior and war vacant. Blanqui recalled Barbès to Paris; suspecting the reason for this summon, Barbès reluctantly returned to the capital. He wrote a letter to a friend explaining his reasons for joining the planned insurrection despite no longer believing in it. "I don't know if the affair fails or is aborted whether people will blame me by accusing me of deserting my post." It is clear that he felt that he could not let his colleagues and friends down. He continued his jeremiad, "I leave, my heart tortured and tormented by sad premonitions because there may not even be a real showdown. More likely, there will be one done with the remnants of my past friends and at the cost of my freedom. But God's will be done! I am tired of fighting against my fate . . . In some royal jail, I will not be unhappier than I am now . . . There are people whose destiny is to suffer all the ills of the motherland. Oppression and tyranny creates certain victims, and like birds mesmerized by snakes, they must accomplish their fate. No doubt, I am one of these cursed beings." So Barbès returned to Paris without any illusion of what awaited him.

Blanqui chose Sunday, 12 May, to carry out his insurrection because the chief of police and many of the officers of the National Guards were away at the races. About 600 members answered his call. They stormed a large gun shop, and Blanqui distributed the stored ammunition. The insurgents wanted to know the names of their leaders, the secret committee. When told they were Blanqui, Barbès, and Bernard, half of them hesitated to continue because of the lack of prominent leaders to guarantee that the insurrection was serious. They faded away but were careful to keep the expensive stolen rifles. In the end, Barbès led about 300 people to the police prefecture. The insurgents shot the outside guards, but those inside closed it down and returned fire. Discouraged, the insurgents stormed the unprotected Hôtel de Ville. As National Guards appeared, however, they retreated to local barricades, where they were easily captured by the growing government forces. The final toll was more than 80 killed and 50 wounded among the insurgents, and 30 killed and 60 wounded on the government's side. A large wave of arrests wiped out the Société des Saisons. Barbès was wounded and immediately arrested, and Blanqui and Bernard fled when it became clear to them that things had turned against them. Blanqui's apparent abandonment of his followers created a breach between him and Barbès that plagued French radical politics for the next 30 years. At their respective trials, Barbès, Blanqui, and Bernard were condemned to death, but their sentence was commuted to life imprisonment.[62]

The failed insurrection showed that, in the absence of polls or elections, it was difficult to gauge the popularity of a political cause. The insurgent leaders had obviously overestimated the willingness of the population to rise up against an unpopular king and regime. This disastrous uprising also demonstrated the paradox of secrecy: while it allowed the conspiracy to proceed within a hostile environment, it prevented the leaders from preparing the population to support them. The population did not know them (even many of the Société members did not know them), so it simply watched the fight without engaging itself on either side.

A former Société member, Maris Darmès, carried out an attentat on 15 October 1840 when he shot at the king with a carbine. Overloaded, it exploded, severely injuring Darmès and missing the king. Darmès refused to cooperate at the trial, leaving us with very little evidence for our study from it. In May 1841, he was convicted, sentenced to death, and executed.

Another attentat credited to a progeny of the Société des Saisons was the tragicomic incident against the king's oldest son, the Duc d'Aumale, on 13 September 1841. The shooter in this incident was 27-year-old François Quenisset. He had joined the army at age eighteen, but was court-martialed three years later for insulting his officer and sentenced to five years' detention. He escaped from prison, took on a false identity, and went to Paris, where he became an excellent sawyer day laborer. He moved in with a laundress, and the couple just managed to make ends meet.[63]

In January 1840, Quenisset got into a fight in a tavern and was arrested. In the jail, he met some political prisoners, with whom he bonded. They introduced him to a lawyer, who offered his services for free, helping him get off after only a six-month detention. They talked to Quenisset about republican doctrines, but he was not interested in politics. Nevertheless, they saw him as a reliable man of action who could be very useful to the cause.[64] After his discharge, Quenisset returned home to his common-law wife and his work. When they had a daughter in July 1841, Quenisset decided to legitimize his status. He was still a deserter, so he asked his father, who was old and sick, to get a certificate from the mayor of his village that would allow him to apply for leave from the army. The mayor refused, and Quenisset, still living under a false name, was devastated. Just then, on the street he ran into one of the political prisoners he had met, who was with a friend. The former prisoner introduced Quenisset, saying, "Here is a good comrade, a man whom we can count on."[65]

About two weeks later, Quenisset ran into the friend, who bought him drinks and invited him to the same local tavern on the following Monday evening. Quenisset came with a friend from work, Jean-Marie Boucheron. About half a dozen republicans and half a dozen newcomers were present. After dinner and many glasses of wine, the militants closed the door. One of them addressed the newcomers, explaining that they were workers and egalitarian revolutionaries and wanted to take over the government and create national workshops and schools. There would be work for everyone, and the pay would be much better than they had. Schools would teach their children for free. The inebriated guests approved. The speaker concluded that for this to happen, they had to use force and overthrow the throne. He asked whether the newcomers wanted to join their group. The guests shouted "yes!"[66]

Quenisset and Boucheron were taken to an adjacent room, where they were blindfolded. The local chief, Just Brazier, told them that they were joining revolutionaries. The Société des Travailleurs Égalitaires (Society of Egalitarian Workers) swore them to secrecy and warned them not to tell their wives.

Brazier made them swear to abandon everything, their wives and children, to join the comrades at the first call to fight their enemies, and not to fear death or prison. When Quenisset came home late, and drunk, his wife accused him of having been with women. He endured her jealousy rather than tell her the truth. Over the next few weeks, Quenisset occasionally stopped by the tavern for some drink and companionship. But when meetings were called, he preferred to stay home and play with his daughter.[67]

On 13 September 1841, Quenisset got up at five in the morning as usual to search for day work. He had come too late, but an acquaintance bought him a glass of wine for breakfast. He continued his search elsewhere when he saw a commotion at the neighborhood tavern. A dozen militants were debating whether to fight or stay put. Quenisset joined them for some more wine and asked what was going on. Brazier replied that the revolution had come. The 17th Regiment was coming home on parade to celebrate its victories in Algeria. Brazier said that this was their opportunity, but they were short of weapons. One of them said that the regiment had weapons, and they could take them from the parading soldiers. They would only shoot at officers in the hope that the soldiers would join them. As Quenisset did not have a weapon, Brazier gave him a pair of pistols to share with Boucheron. Quenisset met his friend at another tavern, where they drank some more wine while waiting for the regiment. They had lunch and drank some more. Quenisset then joined his revolutionary comrades gathered on a sidewalk. By then, Quenisset had had about 30 glasses of wine and nine glasses of eau-de-vie.[68] About 60 members of the Society were screaming, "Long live the 17th! Down with Louis-Philippe! Down with the Royal Family and the Princes!" Brazier told Quenisset to attack and shoot in the middle of the group of parading officers. Quenisset took out his gun and fired. One horse was hit, but the shot scared off his comrades, who immediately dropped their weapons and ran away, leaving him alone to face the police and soldiers.[69]

Quenisset was accused of trying to assassinate the Duc d'Aumale, who was riding at the head of his regiment. He defended himself by saying he did not know that the duke was there. "We wanted to make a revolution to overthrow the throne . . . I will explain to you that I don't know what a revolution is; but in the situation I was in, being a deserter for the last four years, these people did not have any trouble in recruiting me. When they made me swear the oath, I told them I was a deserter. They answered that the revolution would take care of my situation. I went there like a sheep, in the hope of changing my situation, which was unbearable because each night I was afraid that two policemen would come to take me away. I can prove that I did not want to make a revolution . . . I was thinking about returning to my regiment. I asked my father to request from the mayor a certificate that my father was over 70 and invalid. This would have helped me get my leave. . . . My father let me know that the mayor refused. Without this news, I would never have joined these societies."[70]

The police arrested most of the members of the Society as well as the tavern owner and tried them in December 1841. On 23 December, the court convicted them, sentencing Quenisset, Brazier, and the tavern owner to death and Boucheron to ten years in prison. The king commuted the death sentences to life in prison, and Quenisset was eventually deported to New Orleans.

Quessinet was not motivated by ideology or even politics. He simply befriended a group of activists who had helped him in prison. He joined their group out of loyalty and just happened to have been the first one to shoot in their attempt at revolution. Feeling betrayed by his friends, he no longer felt any loyalty toward them and denounced them to the police.

Nonpolitical Violence with Political Implications

The above attentats were clearly political and contrast with more traditional regicides, which are often not political in motivation but have tremendous political implications. To appreciate the difference, let us look at two such attentats carried out around that time. They both involved loners with mental disorders.

The first one involved 48-year-old Pierre Lecomte, a loner who never liked to socialize with anyone and had no friends or relationships. On the other hand, he had a highly developed sense of honor and could not stand to suffer any slight. He had volunteered for the cavalry at 17 and displayed such bravery that he received the Légion d'Honneur. When the Greeks rose up against the Turks, he volunteered for the insurgents, who noticed his courage and promoted him to captain. When the war was over, he returned to Paris and became a guard for the Duc d'Orléans's estate just before the duke became king. His 14 years of service were irreproachable, and he was promoted six times. The only complaint was that he was unduly harsh toward his subordinates and aloof to the world. Around 1844, Lecomte got very sick; he had to stay in bed and asked for a month for convalescence. He was docked some money for time lost and told that if he did not report after the month, he would be fired. The estate administrator also tried to make him more responsive to his subordinates by withholding the small sum of 20 francs from his yearly bonus. Lecomte took this combination of events as a great insult and immediately resigned. The administrator calculated his pension for 15 years of service. Lecomte was enraged because he felt he was due a pension for 25 years of service (including his ten years in the army) and claimed that he had turned down returning to the army twice when he was told that his army time would count for his pension.

Upset, Lecomte went to see his employer, now the king, but his secretary suggested that Lecomte put his request in writing. Lecomte did so and sent the letter to the king. There was no response. He waited a few weeks and then sent another letter, which also got no response. Finally, he sent a third one, and to make sure it was received, he went again to see the king's secretary, who told Lecomte that he had forwarded the letter to the administration. Lecomte went to the administration, which told him that it had received the letter with an unfavorable recommendation. Lecomte was devastated. By now, he had sold his horse, his uniform, most of his weapons, and his furniture and was becoming destitute.

On 15 April 1846, Lecomte was eating his lunch at a café near the Tuileries Palace when he heard three of the king's servants say that the king would go to Fontainebleau for a promenade the next day.[71] "At this time, the idea came to me. It came to me clearly and horribly . . . I came home, in my room, in my miserable room, without furniture. I stayed there for three hours. I thought, I dreamt, I was unhappy. My project always came back. And the rain started again. It was dark outside, very windy and the sky was almost black. I felt like a crazy man. All of a sudden, I got up. It was over. I decided to do it."[72]

When the prosecutor observed that the crime had no motive, Lecomte protested: "How so? I wrote to the king. One time, two times, three times. The king did not answer me."[73] Lecomte got his shotgun, hid it under his overcoat, and went to Fontainebleau. He knew the path the king would take and waited the next day for the king to come by in his carriage. When the king came, surrounded by his family and guests, Lecomte fired two shots at him from a short distance, but missed both times. He was apprehended. During the investigation, he denied having any accomplices and admitted he had acted only out of resentment. He admitted being very sensitive about his honor and felt the injustices against him were very great.

At the trial at the Court of Peers in June 1846, Victor Hugo, the writer who had been become a Peer of France, recalled that the peers almost unanimously believed Lecomte was sane and deserved the death penalty. But Hugo was one of the three who voted against it. "I read, reread and studied all the evidence of the trial; during the debates, I studied the attitude, the physiognomy, the gestures and scrutinized the soul of the defendant . . . a solitary man. Solitude is good for great minds but bad for small ones. Solitude troubles brains that it does not illuminate . . . An attentat on the king, an attentat on a father . . . surrounded by his family! An attentat on a group of women and children . . . It is monstrous. Now, let's examine the motive. Here it is: twenty francs withheld from an annual bonus, a resignation accepted, three letters without an answer.

How can we not be struck by such a link and such an abyss . . . the greatest crime and the most trifling motive, it is evident for me that reason is lacking, that the mind, which makes such a link and crosses such an abyss, is not lucid. This guilty man . . . may not be insane for a physician, but he certainly is insane for a moralist."[74] Lecomte was sentenced to death and executed on 8 June 1846.

Victor Hugo has a point. Lecomte was not insane in the clinical or even the legal sense. But there was something wrong with him given the disparity between the offense he felt and the crime he tried to commit. His lifelong inability to get along with people and understand their intent suggests that he may have suffered from a mild form of autism spectrum disorder. One thing seems certain: his motivation had no political dimension despite its political consequences.

Lecomte had a deep sense of honor whose meaning seems to have been lost in modern Western society. People in the past felt they could not live with any explicit or implicit insult to their reputation. Regaining a lost sense of honor contributed to Billon's suicide bombing, the assassinations by Pâris and Corday, and Fieschi's participation in his attentat. Honor also prevented the Chouans from claiming credit for the Saint Nicaise attentat, which killed and maimed innocent civilians. Sand, Louvel, and Alibaud showed the same honor-based behavior at their respective trials. It is difficult for us, with our modern sensibilities, to understand the importance of this element in the historical genesis of political violence.

Shortly after Lecomte's execution, 52-year-old Joseph Henry fired two pistol shots at the king from very far away on 29 July 1846. He seems to have wanted to be executed for his crime, a sort of suicide by law. He was tried, but his insanity seemed pretty obvious to the peers, and the king's life was never in danger because of the distance of the shots. He was sentenced to life in prison. After his conviction, it was discovered that the fired bullets were blanks.[75]

A New Era of Explosives and International Terror

A popular insurgency overthrew Louis-Philippe in early 1848 and established the second French republic. Since it ushered a period of months of unrest and general lawlessness, I shall not examine each violent incident. An attempted workers' coup failed in May due to the mutual hostility of Barbès and Blanqui. A June workers' insurrection was drowned in a bloodbath: about 1,000 soldiers were killed, as well as 3,000 to 5,000 workers in addition to 1,500 shot without trial and more than 10,000 deported.[76] The harsh repression legitimized by the male universal suffrage election of the government was a harsh blow against collective working-class violence.[77] In December, Louis Napoleon Bonaparte, the nephew of the emperor, was elected president of the republic. In Italy, an insurrection declared a Roman Republic under the leadership of Giuseppe Mazzini in February 1849. As Austrian troops invaded to restore the papacy, the French Republic sent troops to protect the Roman republicans. Later, after French and Roman troops clashed, the French crushed the Roman Republic in July 1849 and restored the papacy. Eventually, French troops would stay in Rome for the next 20 years propping up the pope. The overthrow of the Roman Republic and the presence of French troops in Rome earned Bonaparte the lasting enmity of Italian republican nationalists, many of whom found refuge in London.

Meanwhile, in France, Bonaparte overthrew the National Assembly on 2 December 1851 and easily defeated an attempted Parisian insurrection in defense of the republic. Fleeing the repression, French republicans found refuge in Belgium and London. On the first anniversary of his coup d'état, Bonaparte was crowned Napoleon III, emperor of the French. The first decade of his reign saw new developments in political violence. Insurgents aware of their weakness facing government troops were looking for weapons to even the playing field and found them in new developments in explosives technology. At the same time, the efficacy of domestic political policing forced dissidents to leave their country, resulting in the emergence of an international revolutionary diaspora centered in England, Switzerland, and Belgium carrying out attentats in one country to influence events in another.

The French political exiles showered France with pamphlets, articles, and letters denouncing the emperor and calling for insurrection. There were mass arrests in Paris and Marseille when the police discovered partially built weapons for alleged use against the emperor or authorities. Several dozen workers, linked with the Société des Saisons, and half a dozen students were arrested for planning to kill the emperor during a visit to the Hippodrome on 7 June and to the Opéra-Comique on 5 July 1853. The police had them under surveillance and made sure they never had a chance of coming close to the emperor. The conspirators went on trial in November, and 21 were convicted and sentenced to prison or banishment. All the defendants denied any plot or their involvement in it,[78] which does not help our investigation.

On 11 September 1854, near the village of Pérenchies in northern France, a railway worker discovered two cylinders about eight inches long and four inches in diameter, buried two feet under a rail, from which came two copper wires. The wires were connected to a battery, hidden about 100 feet away. The cylindrical tubes were filled with five pounds of mercury fulminate, an explosive substance. The emperor had been scheduled to travel on that line the next day. The police arrested three socialist republicans for laying the mine under the railway, but none of them had the technical expertise to build the device. The investigation identified the militant Jacquin brothers, who had fled to Belgium in December 1851, as its builders. Nicolas-Jules Jacquin, age 29, was a civil engineer who conducted experiments in physics and chemistry at his workshop in Brussels. His older brother, Célestin-Nicolas, age 34, was a mechanic and probably put the device together. They had been seen buying the required materials at various shops in Brussels. Five defendants, who denied their involvement, were tried in August 1855. The Jacquin brothers were convicted and sentenced to death in absentia, as they were still in Belgium. The Belgium government refused to extradite them because this was a political and not a criminal charge.[79]

The use of mercury fulminate was a qualitative leap in the development of explosive devices because it had 20 times the explosive power by weight of gunpowder. It is still used today in detonators and blasting caps. The compound was invented by Edward Howard in England in 1800. Apparently, an exiled socialist French journalist and a former artillery officer in Brussels commissioned a famous weapon maker in Liège to make eight balls filled with Howard's compound. The manufacturer did so openly in his workshop and shipped them to his clients by train. On 11 August 1854, the Belgian police got wind of the shipment, arrested the commissioners on the charge of making new machines infernales, which were "weapons prohibited by law." The mercury fulminate–based explosive devices were put on public display and may have inspired the Jacquin brothers to build their own. In October 1855, these defendants were tried in Belgium, convicted, and sentenced to six months in prison.[80]

This was the temporary end of French domestic attacks on the emperor. The reign of Napoleon III was blessed with an unprecedented quarter-century of constant economic growth, which industrialized France from above, created an efficient infrastructure for communication, linking Paris to the provinces, and transformed Paris through the efforts of Baron Georges Eugène Haussmann. Workers had enough work to keep them busy through this period. Political calm was also due to the exile of political leaders and the efficiency of the imperial French police, which constantly monitored popular neighborhoods through an extensive system of informants. In the second decade of this reign, the emperor enacted more liberal laws, giving workers the right to strike. All these factors resulted in about 15 years of domestic political calm in France. During this time, political violence in France came from the outside, imported by a nationalist Italian diaspora.

Italian Nationalist Attentats Against the Emperor

First Round

Nationalist Italians sought revenge on Napoleon III for betraying the Roman Republic and preventing Italian unification. Giovani Pianori, a 28-year-old Roman shoemaker, was the first one to try to kill the emperor. During the brief Roman Republic, he had joined Garibaldi's army to defend it against the French in 1849. Afterwards, he drifted to Piedmont, Corsica, Marseille, Lyon, and finally Paris, which he reached around August 1854. According to his landlady, he was a hardworking and outgoing shoemaker during that stay. In early December 1854, he went to London, where he hung out with Italian refugees and allegedly acquired enough money to buy himself nice clothes and two luxury two-shot pistols. At his trial, he claimed to have made the money by working, but his expenses and lifestyle were disproportionate to the income of a shoemaker. He returned to Paris in late March 1855, and his landlady later testified that he was a changed man. He no longer worked, and he seemed morose and preoccupied all the time. Three days before the attentat, he moved to another hotel room, and on 28 April 1855, he approached the emperor, who was riding his horse unescorted on the Champs-Élysées. Pianori took a pistol out and shot twice at the emperor but missed. He was pulling his second pistol out when a passerby wrestled him to the ground, and he was arrested. When asked his motive, he replied that he had been thinking about it for a long time because the French expedition of 1849 had ruined his country and chased his family out of Rome. He was tried nine days later and denied plotting with Italian republicans or revolutionaries in London, to the skepticism of the prosecutor and presiding judge. He was convicted, sentenced to death, and executed on 14 May 1855. His last words were, "Long live the republic!"[81]

Second Round

A second Italian plot was led by Giuseppe Mazzini. He was born in 1805 in Genoa, became an Italian Carbonari, and was arrested in 1827. Upon his release three and a half years later, he migrated to Marseille and created Young Italy, a secret society promoting Italian unification. He became involved in multiple failed insurrections from abroad and returned to Rome in early 1849 when it became a republic. He was elected the leader of the short-lived government, but had to flee again when French troops overthrew the republic. He eventually settled in London and Switzerland, whence he attempted multiple invasions and insurrections all over Italy. He never forgave Napoleon and openly advocated his assassination. In June 1857, he wrote this to lieutenants in London: "Carrying out attentats is vital for Italy . . . The Paris affair has become more urgent than ever."[82] Three of his letters transited through Paris, where the police intercepted them. They suggested that there were two assassins in Paris ready to kill the emperor and gave the address of the leader. The police immediately went there and arrested Paolo Tibaldi, Giuseppe Bartolotti, and Paolo Grilli. At their residence, the police discovered a trunk containing 16 handguns and five daggers, all from England.

Tibaldi, a 30-year-old sculptor from Piedmont, had come to France in 1850. He went to London for a year around 1852, but returned to Paris and became an optician. He returned to London for about three weeks in January 1857, when he sent the above-mentioned trunk to his landlady. Bartolotti was a 34-year-old shoemaker from the Roman state. He enlisted in the Anglo-Italian legion, but after he left it, he lived in York, penniless, with his mistress. In April 1857, he ran into Gaetano Massarenti, Mazzini's lieutenant, who told him that he could make a lot of money with Mazzini. Bartolotti was tempted, and Massarenti took him to London to meet with Mazzini. When they arrived, Mazzini was with Alexandre-Auguste Ledru-Rollin, an exiled republican French politician, opposed to the emperor. He had placed a distant third to Bonaparte during the 1848 presidential election. In London, he became a leader of the French opposition and, with Mazzini, one of the leaders of the community of European revolutionaries. He was later accused of financing the plot. The next day, Bartolotti returned to Mazzini's home and first met Grilli, who was in the same situation as him. Grilli, a 28-year-old carpenter, was also from the Roman state, which he left in 1854. He drifted to Genoa, Marseille, and finally London. He was destitute when he met Massarenti, who told him that Mazzini would pay 50 gold napoleons to kill the emperor. Grilli thought about the offer for three days before accepting: "Misery forced me to accept."[83] Massarenti took him to meet Mazzini and Bartolotti. Mazzini gave them both about 250 francs, and they left for Paris three days later, in late April. Tibaldi welcomed them to the city and found lodging for them.

The plan was to conduct surveillance on the emperor to determine the best opportunity to kill him. However, the emperor was spending his time in Fontainebleau, and Bartolotti returned to England for a while. Massarenti tracked him down and reprimanded him for leaving his post, so Bartolotti returned to Paris in early June. During the investigation, Tibaldi denied everything, while his accomplices admitted that they did it for the money. They did not have any sympathy for the emperor after his role in the overthrow of the Roman Republic. Their trial was held in August 1857. They were all convicted, as well as Mazzini, Massarenti, and Ledru-Rollin in absentia. Tibaldi was deported, while Bartolotti and Gilli were sentenced to 15 years in prison.[84]

Third Round: Orsini's Bombs

The third Italian plot was by far the most famous: Orsini's attentat against Napoleon III on 14 January 1858. Felice Orsini was a larger-than-life adventurer
who was already very well known before he committed his attentat. His memoirs and testimony at trial give us a window into what led his turn to political
violence.

At the time, Orsini was a 39-year-old from Romagna, the son of a military
man. He had studied law, and joined Mazzini's Young Italy before getting his
degree. "Love of my country was uppermost in my mind."[85] He also studied
military tactics in the hope of using them one day. He and his father were arrested for participating in an insurrection in 1844: the son received a life sentence but was amnestied two years later, allowing him to get married. He
distinguished himself in the First Italian War of Independence against Austria
in 1848 and was elected a deputy to the Assembly of the new Roman Republic
in 1849. He fought alongside Garibaldi against the French troops. "I was proud
to hear that Rome . . . was not prepared to cede her rights or to bow to the
Gallic arms, which . . . have often oppressed the nations and riveted the chains
of servitude. France . . . [shed] Italian blood and wantonly and immorally destroyed the Roman Republic."[86] With the fall of the republic, he fled abroad to
become a full-time conspirator and insurrectionist with Mazzini.[87]

In the early 1850s, Orsini was involved in various schemes to infiltrate
Italy and spark insurrections. When he was in London, he was constantly so-
cializing and plotting with other European conspirators. In honor of Washington's Birthday in 1854, the U.S. consul general in London invited him to dinner
with Mazzini, Garibaldi, Herzen, Ledru-Rollin, and other well-known revolutionaries. Upon returning to the continent, he was arrested in Austria in December 1854 and sent to the Mantua Fortress, which had the reputation of
being the most impregnable prison in Europe.[88] On 30 March 1856, he carried
out a spectacular escape and reached London two months later. His exploits
made him famous all over Europe.[89]

His long time in prison made Orsini rethink Mazzini's strategy of sending
young nationalists to Italy because they were invariably caught and shot, resulting in needless wasted lives, while the Italian population seemed indifferent to their sacrifice. When Orsini arrived in London, he discovered that
Mazzini had not done anything to get him out of prison. As usual, differences
in strategy melded with personal disappointment, and their relationship
soured in mutual recriminations and, worse, ridicule. Capitalizing on his
fame, Orsini wrote a best-selling book about his escape and went on a popular
speaking tour. He followed up by writing his memoirs, which were mocked by
Mazzini's followers. Humiliated, Orsini turned away from Mazzini and, in-

stead, contacted his great rival, the Count of Cavour, Prime Minister of Piedmont, who had brought his kingdom to a position of prominence in Europe
and openly advocated Italian unity as a constitutional kingdom under the
Piedmont king. Orsini would have preferred a republic, but realized that Cavour's strategy was the most likely to establish a united and independent Italian nation. Although Cavour had sympathy toward Orsini, he did not answer
the adventurer's letters because he was already involved in delicate negotiations with Napoleon III at the time. Orsini took the lack of response as a rejection and looked for a different strategy to unite Italy.[90]

It was then that, disappointed with both Italian leaders at the time, Orsini
began hanging out with Simon Bernard, a 40-year-old French former naval
surgeon who became a socialist during his commission and returned home to
take the editorship of a socialist newspaper in southern France. He came to
Paris right after the revolution of 1848 and opened up a political club, where
he harangued about 4,000 people nightly with his revolutionary ideas. By February 1849, the police had closed down his club, and he sought refuge in London in 1851, where he opened up a clinic specializing in speech impediments.[91]
He continued his political activism and also became a keen amateur chemist.
He met Orsini in 1856 and became his manager, booking his appearances,
managing his finances, tutoring him on political theory and arranging for the
publication of Orsini's memoirs in English.

Bernard focused Orsini on Napoleon as the main obstacle to Italian re-
unification and revolution in Europe in general.[92] In his memoirs, Orsini
wrote, "Italy finds herself at the present moment in the most deplorable condition that can be imagined: this state of things, however, will not last long, because all depends upon Napoleon, and this man will not be tolerated long,
with his government based upon despotism and treason . . . This system . . .
must be constantly propped up anew. When these means fail, it will fall, dragging along with it others in its ruins. But why does everything depend upon
Napoleon? Because he has a large army at his disposal, which united with that
of another despotic power of Europe, would cause the scale to lean to their
side . . . *A war of independence in Italy; a revolution in Paris; a war of principles
and republicanism in continental Europe*; these are the three great events which
would rapidly follow each other."[93]

Orsini was already a soldier for Italian nationalism, and his personal history demonstrates his willingness to sacrifice his life in the context of an honorable battle. But assassination is another matter, and Orsini hesitated for a
whole year before carrying one out. He kept silent about this incubation period in London at his trial, but at his interrogation, he revealed, "It was during
the last year that Pierri and I started to talk about this project. We were convinced that the surest way to make a revolution in Italy was to produce one in

France, and that the surest way to make this revolution in France was to kill the emperor. We did not immediately decide to execute this project: we thought about it for many months and we spoke about it to Allsop and Simon Bernard."[94]

Giuseppe Pierri, a 50-year-old Tuscan, had participated in an insurrection in 1831 and had to leave Italy for France as a political refugee. He joined the French Foreign Legion in 1843 for two years. His landlord later testified that he was always involved in republican propaganda.[95] He fought on the barricades in Paris in February 1848, but returned to Italy to join the insurrection. He was the chief of a 900-man military unit that terrorized a region on pretense of punishing royalists. After the restoration in Italy, he returned to France, but had to flee again after the Bonapartist coup d'état and settled in Birmingham as a language teacher. His maid and lover recalled at his trial that she saw Orsini come to their home about three times around April 1857. They talked in a very agitated way about Napoleon III: "If he were dead, I would return to Italy."[96]

In June 1857, Antonio Gomez came to see Pierri in Birmingham looking for work. Gomez, a 29-year-old born in Naples, had fought in Lombardy in 1848 and, like Pierri, had joined the French Foreign Legion. After his discharge, he worked on the docks of Marseille for years before coming to London. He asked people in the Italian émigré community for a job and was referred to Pierri. Pierri told him to return to London and gave him a letter for Orsini.

In the fall of 1857, Orsini asked for a visa from the state of Piedmont to come and visit his wife, but the request was refused. From then on, events accelerated. On 15 October, Gomez ran into Orsini walking with Bernard on the streets of London. Orsini invited Gomez to come by his house the next morning. "During this visit, Orsini told him [Gomez] that the *prophet* (that is how he called Mazzini) was losing all his men and that his enterprises only ended in needless executions. Orsini then invited Gomez to join his own plan to carry out an uprising in Italy."[97] Gomez agreed, and Orsini put him on a retainer. However, shortly thereafter, he saw Gomez come out of a police station, so he sent him to Birmingham for Pierri to assess his loyalty.[98]

On 16 October, Thomas Allsop, a 60-year-old English barrister with strong socialist leanings and support for Italian independence, came to Birmingham. He had met Orsini in 1851 and was an intimate of Bernard's. He commissioned a metallurgic engineer in that town to cast 12 half-spheres to build six grenades. Each half-sphere had a dozen holes through which metallic spikes stood out. The inside tips of these spikes contained capsules that could detonate the explosive substance filling the grenades.[99] The same day, Bernard enquired about an armorer in Belgium who could do the same thing.

On 29 October, when Orsini came to give a lecture in Birmingham, he and Pierri bought two handguns from a gun shop there. On 4 November, Bernard bought eight pounds of alcohol and ten pounds of nitric acid at one pharmacy, and a pound of mercury at another. This yielded about two pounds of mercury fulminate. On 23 November, Allsop returned to Birmingham to pick up and pay for the metallic half-spheres. On 26 November, Orsini retrieved a large sum of money from the Bank of England and got visas for Belgium and France under Allsop's identity, which he assumed from then on. He left England on 28 November with two pounds of the explosive powder in a container, which he kept humidifying throughout the trip to stabilize it.

On 3 December, Bernard sent the half-spheres via couriers to Paris, where they were delivered on 11 December to "Allsop." Bernard bought more chemical ingredients to make enough mercury sulfate to fill three more grenades. He and the real Allsop tapped George Jacob Holyoake to test three bombs. Holyoake was Allsop's best friend, who had known Bernard since his arrival in London and Orsini for about a year. Bernard and Allsop gave him the grenades and explained to him that "Mazzini thought they might be useful in the unequal warfare carried on in Italy, where the insurgent forces of liberty were almost armless."[100] Holyoake dropped one into a deep quarry and it exploded. He was then told to throw the other two from a normal human height on the street to test them. Holyoke tried one on a dirt road, but it did not explode. He retrieved it and tried again on a hard surface with success with both remaining grenades. He notified Bernard, "Leniency of treatment was quite thrown away upon our two companions. As a man makes his bed, so he must lie upon it; still out of consideration, we wished it to be not absolutely hard. But that did just no good whatever. The harder treatment had to be tried; and I am glad to say it proved entirely successful. But nothing otherwise would do."[101]

Meanwhile, Orsini had rented an apartment in Paris. Bernard shipped the two guns purchased with Pierri to him. Pierri and Gomez were getting ready to come to Paris to help Orsini carry out his plan when Pierri received a letter from 23-year-old Count Carlo de Rudio, from an old Venetian aristocratic family,[102] who was living in utmost poverty with his wife and child in London. He had fought in the war of 1848 as a teenager and later tried to scrape out a living in Marseille. He eventually went to England at the end of 1855. He could not find a job, but he impregnated a 15-year-old girl and had to marry her. Orsini, who had fought alongside his father, heard about his plight through the grapevine and sent a friend to locate him when he had doubted Gomez's loyalty. When Rudio heard that the famous Orsini was asking about him, he wrote Orsini a letter at Pierri's address, saying he was "always ready for your orders, at whatever time, in whatever place, for whatever purpose they may be."[103] Pierri notified Bernard, who came to visit the couple and gave them money. The doctor assessed the young man and, when he was satisfied, told him that he could join the cause and meet Orsini in Paris. Bernard promised to take care of his pregnant teenage wife with money.

Meanwhile, Pierri and Gomez, armed with a gun, left England under false identities and arrived in Paris on 7 January 1858. Rudio arrived two days later. Orsini recognized his resemblance to his father. The next day, all four dined together, and Orsini and Pierri told their two accomplices their plan to throw the bombs at the emperor. Gomez, who had in effect become a domestic servant to Pierri and Orsini, said at the trial that the servant had to obey the master. Rudio also later said he felt he could not back out. Pierri was constantly with him, shared his hotel room, and never left him out of his sight to ensure he would go through with the plan.[104] In order to have a gun for everyone, Orsini went to Devisme's shop to buy a revolver. This was the same Devisme of Alibaud fame 20 years earlier, by now one of the most famous gunsmiths in Paris.

Over the next two days, Orsini and Gomez assembled their grenades. On 13 January, they read in the paper that the emperor planned to attend the theater the next evening, and everything now seemed set. On the evening of 14 January, each of the conspirators had a bomb, a handgun, and a large sum of money in case they were separated, with the exception of Orsini, who had two bombs. They proceeded to the theater and waited for the imperial cortege. By coincidence, a policeman on duty recognized Pierri from his days in Paris and took him to the nearest police station for questioning. They discovered the bomb, gun, knife, and large amount of money in his coat. Around eight-thirty in the evening, the imperial carriage slowed down at the entrance of the theater. Gomez threw the first bomb, which exploded, causing a great deal of injury and blowing out the street gaslights. Orsini directed Rudio to throw the second one, which exploded about ten seconds after the first one. Finally, Orsini threw one of his bombs; he was injured in the process when shrapnel hit his temple. The emperor and his wife sustained only scratches and were able to proceed to the theater to listen to the performance.[105] The police managed to arrest all four conspirators before daybreak. The bombing killed eight and wounded 156 people, including 21 women, 11 children, 13 soldiers, 11 guards, and 31 policemen.[106] The French government demanded that the British government arrest the other conspirators as the investigation revealed their role. Bernard was arrested on 14 February, and Allsop went missing. No one knew of Holyoake's role until he wrote his memoirs half a century later.

The four suspects in Paris were tried in late February. They were charged not with the murder of eight people but with the attentat on the emperor's life. Rudio and Gomez tried to minimize their roles. Orsini fully admitted his role, but strangely claimed to have given his bomb to another Italian, who threw it.

He now said that he was wrong to have tried to kill Napoleon III and tried to justify himself. He told the jury how much he had admired the French until the day that they crushed the Roman Republic. "Since the fall of Rome, I was convinced that Napoleon would not help us; I told myself: this man must be killed. I wanted to act alone; but seeing that it was impossible to approach him, I took some accomplices. I had at first resolved not to talk about them; but when I was arrested I saw that I was betrayed by those who had reached their hand out to help and who I believed were my brothers. I drifted to an idea of vengeance."[107]

Orsini tried to exonerate his friends Bernard and Allsop by saying he told them that the bombs were for use in an insurrection in Italy. "During one of my voyages in Belgium, I saw in a museum some bombs that were the subject of a trial some years ago."[108] However, a review of his travels shows that he had been in Brussels in March 1854, five months before the arrest of the inventor of the mercury sulfate bombs and could not have seen the display that opened to the public after the inventor's arrest.[109] On the other hand, Bernard knew the conspirators in Belgium. But Orsini, or more likely Bernard, may have come across the bombs in his research at the British Museum and perfected their design. The government again called upon Devisme to study the two recovered bombs and testify at the trial.[110] During his closing arguments, Orsini's lawyer revealed that his client had sent a letter to the emperor in which he admitted his role in the attentat and welcomed his deserved death but begged the emperor to help win independence for his unhappy country. "Do I ask that French blood be shed for Italian freedom? I would not go so far. Italy just asks that France does not intervene against it. It demands that France not allow Germany to support Austria in the fight that will soon come. And, it is precisely what Your Majesty can do, if He wants it. From Your will depends the wellbeing or unhappiness of my country, the life or death of a nation to whom Europe owes much of its civilization . . . I beg Your Majesty to give Italy the independence that its children lost in 1849 because of the same French people. Remember, Your Majesty, that the Italians, in the midst of whom was my father, shed their blood for Napoleon the Great wherever it pleased him to lead them. Remember that they were loyal to him until his fall."[111]

The letter and Orsini's dignity at the trial impressed the public. The jury convicted all four defendants and sentenced Orsini, Pierri, and Rudio to death and Gomez to life in the Guyana penal colony. During the appeal, the emperor and his wife were moved by Orsini and leaned toward commuting his sentence. His cabinet thought this would be a terrible precedent, and a compromise was reached to commute only Rudio's sentence to life because of his age and subordinate role. Orsini and Pierri were guillotined on 13 March 1858.[112]

Across the channel, Simon Bernard went on trial at the Old Bailey in April

1858 for accessory to murder of one of the soldiers who died in the *attentat*. The Crown put on a very compelling case over the six-day trial, but the defendant kept silent. In his closing argument, Bernard's barrister Edwin James turned the tables and put Napoleon on trial, playing on English nationalism to resist French calls to punish Bernard. He concluded that he had discharged his duties "as an English advocate in an English court of justice and before an English jury [which] should discharge it, fearlessly and conscientiously . . . with courage and intrepidity." He then went on to denigrate France for its lack of press freedom and Napoleonic despotism, which had forced England to bring charges against his client and was trying to intimidate the jury "into giving a verdict which you may hereafter regret, and with which your children hereafter may upbraid you." He urged the jury to send a message to the despot. "Tell him that no threats of mighty armaments—no insane dread of foreign invasion—will for one instant intimidate you. Tell him that the jury box is the sanctuary of English liberty . . . Tell him that on this very spot your predecessors have not quailed before the arbitrary power of the Crown, backed by the influence of Crown-serving and time-serving judges. Tell him that, under every difficulty and danger, your predecessors have maintained inviolate the liberties of the people. Tell him that the verdicts of English juries are based upon the eternal and immutable principles of justice. Tell him that, panoplied in this armor, you will return a verdict which your own hearts and consciences will sanctify and approve. Tell him that you will acquit the prisoner—and that though 600,000 French bayonets glittered in your sight; though the roar of French cannon thundered in your ears, your verdict will be firmly and courageously given—careless whether that verdict pleases or displeases a French despot, or secures or shatters forever the throne which a tyrant has built upon the ruins of the liberty of a once free and still mighty people."[113]

The record noted the reaction of the public. "A vehement burst of applause, which could not be controlled, followed the . . . learned counsel's speech . . . delivered with the greatest oratorical power, and had a thrilling effect upon the audience."[114] Despite the judge's damning summation of the evidence, the jury returned a verdict of not guilty. The *Times* of London notes, "On the announcement of this decision, a scene occurred unexampled perhaps in an English tribunal . . . a shout of exultation. Vainly did the Lord Chief Justice endeavor, by voice and gesture to still the tumult, and as powerless were the stentorian lungs of Mr. Harker . . . the verdict had reached the ears of the crowd assembled outside the Old Bailey, and the rapturous cheer which they raised, and afterwards repeated, could be heard within the court . . . spontaneous ebullition of popular feeling."[115] Pride in one's social identity is not a monopoly of politically violent people.

Orsini became a legend among revolutionary circles and a model for others to imitate. His portable bombs, thereafter referred to as Orsini bombs, also became a standard tool for non-state political violence. Later, Holyoake wrote about Bernard's "lamentable end. A bewitching angelic traitor was sent as a spy to beguile him, and to her, in fatal confidence, he spoke of his friends. When he found that they were seized one by one and shot, he realized his irremediable error, lost his reason, and so died."[116]

Fourth and Final Round

Ironically, Napoleon III did just what Orsini had asked him to do—and more—as he shed French blood for Italian independence. He and Cavour reached an agreement six months after Orsini's execution, and together they repelled the Austrians from northern Italy. But Napoleon had to withdraw from the fight when Prussia massed troops at France's eastern borders. This was seen as a betrayal by the Italians. Meanwhile, Garibaldi with 1,000 volunteers conquered Sicily and southern Italy for the Piedmont kingdom. In 1862, Garibaldi moved unilaterally to free Rome from the French, but the Piedmont authorities opposed him for fear that foreign armies would return to Italy in defense of the papacy and negate some of the gains of unification. Two Italian armies faced each other at Aspromonte on 28 August 1862. Shots were fired, but Garibaldi forbade his troops to fire at other Italians. Garibaldi was wounded, and many of his companions were taken prisoner. They fled abroad again, but swore revenge—not on fellow Italians, but on Napoleon, who was still propping up the papal state.

One of these men was 28-year-old Pascale Greco from Calabria, who had fought with Garibaldi at Aspromonte. Greco was in contact with Mazzini, who was in Lugano, Switzerland, planning another insurrection, to be instigated by the assassination of his old enemy, Napoleon. He decided to send Greco to Paris to determine the best place and method to carry out the attentat, and execute it if possible.[117] Greco left for Paris in May 1863, but, finding that the emperor had gone to his summer residence, he returned to Mazzini. On a mission to Milan, he met 32-year-old Natale-Agostino Imperatori, a veteran of Garibaldi's volunteers in Sicily. They socialized and talked about their love of the nation and hate for Napoleon. Greco revealed that he was part of a plot against the emperor, and Imperatori begged to join him. Greco asked Imperatori to prove his commitment to the cause. Imperatori wrote a letter to Mazzini: "After telling several times your friend G . . . , of my desire and firm resolution to go to Paris to try to kill N., I did not find him eager to support my enterprise and firm determination. I therefore took the liberty to write you in the certainty of your support of my firm intention."[118] Mazzini agreed to bring him on board, as the letter would prevent him from backing out. In October, Mazzini left for London, and from there his followers shipped unloaded bombs, explosive powder, guns, and knives to Greco.

On one of his trips to Genoa to pick up these shipments, Greco ran into Raffaël Trabucco, a 40-year-old horn player who had joined Garibaldi's army as a lieutenant and fought in Sicily, Naples, and Aspromonte. "Ah, what a sad affair! I saw Garibaldi, my poor general, wounded. I myself was shot in the chest. I saw my general dragged in prisons . . . True patriots were treated like rebels."[119] Trabucco told Greco he was planning to throw bombs in Turin at one of Garibaldi's rivals. Greco told him about his plot, and Trabucco volunteered to join. Greco accepted and returned to Lugano with his shipment.

As the conspirators were getting ready to go to France in late December 1863, Imperatori said that he had another volunteer for the plot. It was 21-year-old Angelo Scaglioni from Pavia, who had also fought at Aspromonte and had stayed with his wounded chief rather than flee the field. He had come to Lugano to see his fellow veteran Imperatori, who had told him about the project. Scaglioni insisted on being part of it and was accepted by Greco.

All four conspirators, each carrying money and armed with two bombs, a handgun, and a knife, together crossed the border to France on 24 December. A border patrol officer (mistakenly) recognized one of their names as that of a former conspirator and notified the police in Paris, who discreetly followed them when they arrived by train the next morning. The conspirators went around checking appropriate sites and decided to load the explosive powder into the bomb shells on 2 January 1864 in preparation for their attentat. The police arrested them the next day with eight loaded bombs. They confessed and were tried in late February 1864. Devisme testified again as an expert. He reported that all the guns were worthless, but he had also tested the bomb shells with the spines screwed in, and they went off every time in 20 trials. He then exploded two loaded bombs; they caused devastating damage as they broke up into 40 or 50 fragments. All four defendants were convicted. Greco and Trabucco were sentenced to deportation to a penal colony and Imperatori and Scaglioni to 20 years' detention.

All the conspirators in this wave of political violence were former soldiers in Garibaldi's nationalist army that had tried to unify Italy. They were part of the Italian political diaspora, devoted to the cause, and thought of themselves as soldiers for their nation. Their attentats were simply a continuation of their mission. Mazzini was the common link in three attentats, and the fourth was done in competition with him. As soldiers for a united Italy, they were receptive to Mazzini's ideas and eager to accomplish them.

This was the end of the Italian nationalist attacks on Napoleon III. In 1866, Italy gained Venice when Austria was defeated by Prussia, which was allied with the Italian kingdom at the time. In 1870, during its war with Prussia, France removed its troops from Rome, allowing the Italians to take the city, the final missing piece needed for unification. The nationalist dream of a united Italy was finally achieved. Ironically, Mazzini was still banned from his country, because as a staunch republican he rejected the new kingdom of Italy under the Piedmont crown.

Personal Revenge and the Emergent Working-Class Political Community

The end of the reign of Napoleon III saw a resurgence of homegrown political violence. The bitterly contested elections of June 1869 politicized France again. Most of the large cities voted against the government, and with relaxation of censorship, new radical publications whipped up the working masses against the empire. The situation deteriorated rapidly when soldiers shot into a crowd of peaceful strikers on 8 October 1869, killing 14 and wounding about 50 workers. Militants started meeting, talked about revolution, and advocated arming themselves for self-protection. Radical intellectuals were also pushing the envelope of what the government could tolerate. Henri Rochefort, a popular 39-year-old polemicist, protected by his immunity as an elected deputy to the National Assembly, published a newspaper, *La Marseillaise*, and hired 31-year-old Gustave Flourens and 21-year-old Victor Noir for its staff. Flourens, a biologist fired from his academic position for his extreme views, had earlier fought with Cretan insurrectionists against the Ottoman Empire. He became the newspaper's military editor and started organizing French troops for the republican cause. The newspaper was very critical of the government and especially Napoleon's family. Prince Pierre-Napoleon Bonaparte, first cousin of the emperor, defended his family and responded in kind. Rochefort, who had a very brittle temperament and fought in dozens of duels, took offense and sent Noir and another staffer on the evening of 10 January 1870 to Bonaparte's palace to demand a retraction of the prince's statement or a duel to clear the offense. Pierre Bonaparte was himself a violent man with a very short temper, to the point that his imperial cousin avoided him. At Bonaparte's house, the prince fired five shots and killed the unarmed young journalist. Noir's companion accused Bonaparte of unprovoked murder, and this news outraged republicans. The government thought it prudent to respectfully arrest the prince.

Noir became a martyr for the republican cause. "The blood of Victor Noir cries for vengeance before the nation!" All the opposition resolved to meet at the funeral "of the child of the people assassinated by a prince of the Bonaparte family."[120] Flourens tried to rally the workers for an insurrection:

"Tomorrow we must win or die. It is not a riot but a revolution that we must make . . . '48 started out with a death, we have Victor Noir."[121] A supporter remembered, "We agreed to meet the next day at the funeral home and that we would be armed. Bad weather and the crowd prevented us from carrying out our plan."[122] A very agitated crowd numbering between 100,000 and 200,000 people gathered on 12 January but Rochefort persuaded it to honor the wishes of Noir's family and bury him in their cemetery plot in a suburb of Paris rather than march to the center of the city and confront government troops blocking their path.[123] He rejected Flourens's urging as premature, as there was no organized leadership to sustain a revolutionary journée.

Flourens had previously recruited two soldiers to the republican cause, Corporal Fayolle and Camille Beaury, a 21-year-old malcontent who had already twice tried to desert. Beaury went to the funeral in uniform and then, afraid of having been noticed at the demonstration, deserted once again. Fayolle and a comrade had volunteered for guard duty and waited for the funeral crowd to come by to open the doors of their garrison to it. They were ready to cut the telegraph wire linking the garrison to army headquarters, but the crowd did not come and they deserted their post.[124] Beaury fled to Brussels, where he went to see François Hugo, the son of the famous writer, who gave him money and found a place for him to stay. Beaury later testified that Hugo told him, "I would gladly give one thousand francs to be rid of Bonaparte. There could only be a lasting republic in France if the emperor were killed." Beaury claimed that this was the source of his idea to kill the emperor.[125] He also wrote to the staff of *La Marseillaise* to solicit money: "I left my regiment, preferring exile to slavery . . . I am now safe from the claws of despotism. But I am now lost in a city that I don't know, barely dressed, with only 5.80 francs left, and I am forced to pay cash. My situation is unbearable . . . I am starving . . . If my request is not answered, I will prefer a voluntary death to the sad fate of being arrested as a vagabond or falling into the hands of the enemy."[126]

Meanwhile in Paris, at a 21 January banquet celebrating the execution of Louis XVI, workers glorified the regicide, booed Rochefort's timidity, and acclaimed Flourens's efforts. As the drinking progressed, they bragged about defeating the authorities with Orsinian bombs and nitroglycerine. They resolved to establish a revolutionary committee to organize the masses in military units and acquire weapons. A week later, a militant named Verdier betrayed his friends to the police and wrote a long report on the meetings and their participants.[127] The police immediately put them all under surveillance.

On 7 February, the National Assembly, after a long debate, stripped Rochefort's immunity for his incendiary writings, and a warrant went out for the arrest of the whole staff of *La Marseillaise*. Most of them were arrested, but Flourens escaped and called for an immediate insurrection. For the first time in nearly two decades, half a dozen barricades went up in mostly poor neighborhoods. But the population did not follow the militants, and the police were easily able to put down the small insurrection. Flourens fled to Belgium. The police rounded up all the other suspects denounced by the traitor. One named Mégy resisted when they barged into his home; he shot a policeman dead, and was immediately apprehended.[128]

From Brussels, Beaury was following the developments in France with an increasing sense of outrage: "I find it impossible to keep silent in the presence of such blatant injustice."[129] On 21 March, Pierre Bonaparte was tried for the murder of Victor Noir. Bonaparte claimed that Noir had slapped him with his glove and he had simply defended himself. However, the autopsy report indicated that Noir's body still had both gloves on. A medical expert testified that he had noted a bruise on Bonaparte's face, undoubtedly caused by the slap. This was enough of an excuse for the jury of peers to acquit Bonaparte. However, it made him civilly responsible for Noir's death and ordered him to pay 25,000 francs to the family of the victim as well as the court's cost. The acquittal further outraged republicans, and when the expert resumed his lectures at his medical school, students screamed that he was a defender of assassins. The authorities closed down the school for the rest of the academic year.[130] To add insult to injury, the same high court found Rochefort guilty of slander and sentenced him to six months in prison.

Beaury, Fayolle, and Flourens linked up in Brussels. Beaury told Flourens about the idea of killing the emperor, and Flourens actively encouraged him. The three went to London to a banquet in honor of Paolo Tibaldi, who had been amnestied and arrived in London on 2 April 1870. Tibaldi had not changed and intended to repeat his attempt to kill the emperor. Flourens invited the two soldiers and Tibaldi for lunch the next day. Beaury later testified, "After the meal, we retired to Flourens's room to discuss the means to get rid of the emperor. Florens and Tibaldi said they would go together to Paris to kill him. Fayolle and I had the same intention. So we decided to draw lots. I came first and Fayolle second. We decided that I would leave immediately and Fayolle would follow if I failed. Flourens and Tibaldi would then come together if Fayolle failed."[131]

Beaury left the next evening and got in touch with one of Flourens's contacts for support. He intended to wear his military uniform so that he might approach the emperor closely enough to take out his revolver and shoot him. But the contact was under police surveillance, and Beaury was arrested on 29 April. At the same time, the police conducted a comprehensive sweep of other militants loosely connected to Flourens's contacts and were surprised to find 21 bombs based on a mixture of potassium chlorate, sulfur, and potassium prussiate in one of the apartments. They lumped together all 72 militants arrested in the past two months and charged them in the same dual plots to threaten the life of the emperor and public safety.[132] The French émigré press doubted the existence of this second plot and accused the government of trying to influence the upcoming May 1870 plebiscite on a new constitution.[133]

The trial started in Blois on 18 July 1870, the day France declared war on Prussia. The disastrous start of the war quickly displaced the trial from the front pages of the newspapers. Some of the lawyers asked for a postponement to allow jurors to rejoin their battalions. Half of the defendants were tried for manning barricades in February. Verdier and Beaury, who had flipped to avoid the death penalty, provided the most incriminating testimony against their fellow defendants. On 8 August, the court convicted 17 defendants present and acquitted 38. Mégy and Beaury were sentenced to 20 years of forced labor and detention, respectively. The rest of the sentences ranged from three to 15 years of detention.

The French prosecutors conflated two different phenomena at the trial: one was an old-fashioned attentat on emperor's life and the other was the reemergence of a working-class political protest community. The attentat itself was the product of an escalation in the conflict between republicans and Bonapartists and their police agents. The outrage at the unprovoked murder of a member of their political community led to a call for an insurrection. When it failed, some of the soldiers for the community decided to carry out an attentat against the emperor. The 1870 Beaury attentat was the only exception to the 40-year lull in homegrown parricide in France, which lasted from 1855 to 1894. Political violence had shifted to a different strategy.

The other phenomenon was the reemergence of working-class organizations. In 1864 and 1866, the government had granted workers the right to strike and form associations, respectively. Some of these associations linked up with the newly created International Workingmen's Association (IWA) in London in 1864 and exercised a strong influence in France. The electoral campaign of 1869 and the 1870 plebiscite further politicized workers, and when they were faced with police threats, many decided to arm themselves for protection. The discovery of 21 grenades in late April 1870 was probably part of this phenomenon and separate from Beaury's attentat.

In the summer of 1870, the disastrous French defeats accelerated the radicalization of the French working-class. On 2 September 1870, Napoleon III abdicated his throne, and two days later the Assembly proclaimed the Third French Republic. Political prisoners like Rochefort were freed, and many of the émigrés, including Victor Hugo and Flourens, returned to France. The return of the most militant socialists increased demands for a new, more egalitarian constitution and effective government in the face of the German enemy, which had laid siege to Paris, resulting in widespread food shortages and starvation for the poor inhabitants. There were half a dozen attempted insurrections, but the people did not follow the militants' efforts until 18 March 1871, which inaugurated the two-month large-scale insurrection quickly labeled the Paris Commune. Other large cities in France, like Lyon and Marseille, had similar but milder insurrections at the same time. The people took power in the capital and created a chaotic, but more egalitarian, political system.

However, the new conservative government formed outside of Paris could not tolerate this form of sedition in its midst and proceeded to systematically crush the rebellion. The regular armies, freed by the Prussians, did not have much trouble defeating the untrained amateurs defending their city. They disarmed the combatants and slaughtered them, using newly invented machine guns, without the pretense of a judicial hearing. The estimates of the number of murdered citizens during the "Bloody Week" at the end of May 1871 ranged from 17,000 to 30,000 people killed. This did not count the considerable number of people who died of starvation during the siege and the several thousand who died fighting. The authorities then went from house to house to arrest militants and deported them to penal colonies overseas.[134]

I shall not analyze the Paris Commune in this book focused on political violence in peacetime. Political violence in peacetime is analytically very different from that in wartime or during time of widespread general political unrest. It has very different meaning for participants, and their respective paths to violence may be quite different. Mixing them together may obscure some of the mechanisms leading to peacetime political violence. This should not detract from the fact that the Paris Commune and its martyrs have become a central point of reference for socialists around the world from then on. Its starting date, 18 March, was commemorated as a worker holiday for decades. The scale of the French government massacre of the Communards and its deportation of survivors completely eradicated the French labor movement in the capital. For the next decade and a half, it became unable to mount much political protest, let alone violent protests.

Conclusions

Comparing the decade of the French Revolution with the first three quarters of the nineteenth century, there was a shift in the nature of political violence from insurrectional uprisings to attentats. I counted 18 insurrections and five attentats during that decade, while the nineteenth-century period included 12 insurrectional uprisings[135] and 19 attentats.[136] The nineteenth-century insurrections clustered around times of political instability (1789–95, 1830–34, 1848–51, 1870–71), while the attentats, on the contrary, occurred during relatively stable times. During mass political unrest, governments were unable to use usual methods of repression, and political challengers were able to organize insurrections to try to capture state power. However, when they miscalculated, the result could be a bloodbath, as happened in 1832, 1834, and June 1848. Indeed, as police prefect Gisquet noted, the inability to mount insurrections shifted political violence to attentats.

Many attentats conspirators had previously participated in insurrections or were former nationalistic soldiers targeting their enemies. Some of these attentats can be lumped into campaigns of political violence emerging out of the same political protest community. Pepin-Morey, Alibaud, and Huber-Grouvelle were part of a militant republican community that had participated in the popular insurrections of the early 1830s. Darmès and Brazier-Martin were members of socialist societies connected with the failed insurrection of 1839. The Jacquin brothers and Dr. Bernard were part of the anti-Bonapartist republican opposition forced into exile in the early 1850s. The Italian attentats emerged from the diaspora Italian nationalist community. None of these conspirators suffered from a mental disorder. However, of the eight loners (Pâris, Corday, Louvel, Alibaud, Meunier, Lecomte, Henry, and Bellemare), half had a mental disorder, but none showed any signs of psychopathy, while the other half clearly identified with a political protest community. So, with the exception of the four *attentateurs* (as they were called in nineteenth-century Europe) with mental disorders, all the other lone perpetrators had self-categorized themselves as part of a political protest community, and they volunteered to commit their acts of political violence in its name.

The political violence during this period ranged from narrowly targeted to more indiscriminate. Alibaud aborted his attentat against the king when he saw some ladies in his carriage but carried it out later in the day when he saw the king riding by himself. But the technology of violence and especially the conspirators' fascination with machines infernales made violence more indiscriminate. These devices were at first variants of multi-barreled guns (Fieschi and Steuble) and finally powerful mercury fulminate explosive devices pioneered by the Jacquin brothers and modified by Dr. Bernard. The inventors of the two complex guns were not part of the political protest community, but were commissioned to build their weapons on behalf of the conspirators. They felt no loyalty to this community and testified against their fellow conspirators. On the other hand, the manufacture of bombs is simpler than such complex weapons. This allowed for in-house expertise within the political community, like the Jacquin brothers, Dr. Bernard, and Orsini, who taught themselves chemistry—alchemists of the revolution. These simpler weapons became favorites among violent political actors for, although indiscriminate, they had a chance of killing a well-defended target. For the first time, a few could kill many, and the odds of success were improved when targeting well-defended objectives. There was no longer a need to penetrate the various protective rings around such a target or to be in intimate contact with it to carry out an attack. The sphere of fire emanating from these devices allowed the perpetrators to kill from greater distances, or even at times when they were not present, like the Pérenchies attentat. Most of the latest attentats in our chronology involved some sort of explosives.

The results of political violence were mixed. Overall, the journées révolutionnaires seem to have been more successful in their aim to overthrow a government; but if they failed, they triggered very severe and bloody state repression like that of the Paris Commune. They were high-risk, high-cost, but high-reward tactics. On the other hand, all the attentats failed: even when they succeeded in killing their targets, as Corday and Louvel did, they failed in their goal. There were near misses, as with Fieschi et al., Alibaud, and Orsini et al., but these conspiracies only increased police repression of their political protest communities. The loners did not have much impact except for perhaps rallying society around the monarch.[137]

Besides killing off political violence in France for a decade, the slaughter of the Communards had also a profound effect on socialists of all kinds. To those who did not believe in the necessity of any form of authority—anarchist in the new and specific meaning of the term—it symbolized the horrors of authoritarianism. The IWA broke up over this issue. Anarchists, led by Mikhail Bakunin, objected to Karl Marx's strong-handed hierarchical tactics and accused him of being no better than any autocrats. The split created two major branches of the socialist labor movement: a hierarchical and disciplined movement and one preaching variants on the idea of anarchism, each with its own kind of political violence. Russia took the first model, as discussed in the next chapter, while anarchists in the United States and France took the second, as seen in the following chapter.

C h a p t e r   4

The Professionalization of Terroristic Violence in Russia

In the second half of the nineteenth century, political violence reached the Russian empire after a half-century absence. The cost of that political peace was a frozen society, which was rapidly falling behind as the rest of Europe was industrializing. Russian people lacked education and were unaware of different social and political possibilities. To catch up, Russia began educating its gifted youth, opening up the social horizons of its students. Some of them realized the inherent injustices of their society and tried to change it, at first peacefully and then violently, calling themselves terrorists—not in our modern sense of the term, but as followers of Robespierre. Their relentlessness succeeded in the first popular killing of a major head of state in peacetime, constituting a crucial precedent in the history of political violence. In fact, most historiographies of terrorism start with them[1] but ignore their path to political violence.[2] Because of the size of this political protest community and the richness of its material left behind, this long chapter gives us a unique window into this tragic collective transformation of peaceful activists to violent terrorists.

Russian Nihilism

Russian political violence was a response to the disillusionment with Tsar Alexander II's liberal reforms. The Crimean War of the 1850s exposed Russia's social, economic, cultural, and military backwardness after 30 years of repressive reactionary rule. Liberals viewed their government as a moral and political monstrosity—"obsolete, barbarous, stupid and odious."[3] The accession of Alexander II to the throne prompted an emotional "Russian Spring"[4] as the new tsar declared his intention to do away with serfdom, open up universities, and reform the legal system. Modernization requires the creation of an educated elite. Universities expanded and were free for poor students: enrollment tripled in six years. New freedoms allowed students to organize their own libraries and associations to discuss new books. New publications proliferated throughout the country, and opposition newspapers abroad gave the new tsar the benefit of the doubt.

On 19 February 1861,[5] Alexander II signed the Emancipation Statute, which abolished serfdom, emancipated over a third of the population, and granted peasants equal protection under the law. However, the new law forced peasants to compensate their former masters for the often substandard lands they were allocated. This put them in never-ending debt, making their physical survival precarious. This replacement of legal bondage with an economic one deeply disappointed peasants and liberals. Unrest broke out across the land, and in April 1861, troops shot into a crowd of protesting peasants, killing 91 and wounding another 300.[6] The honeymoon was over.

Students grew bolder and more vocal under their new freedoms. About two-thirds still came from the nobility, and they were not afraid to complain about the irrelevance of their studies and challenge old tyrannical methods of teaching. They grew bored and disruptive in class and openly confronted their professors. The faculty felt that things had gone too far and convinced the government to ban unauthorized student associations, allow the faculty to supervise them and their libraries, and cut scholarships for poor students.[7] When school started again in the fall, students protested and demonstrated to restore the scholarships and their right of free associations. They engaged in "passionate discussions . . . which became the decisive factor that formed their group consciousness and gave them the feeling of a common mission to fulfill."[8] The minister of education closed down the universities and ordered the police and Cossacks to conduct brutal mass arrests of the mutinous students. This repression politicized the students, who had no common ideology,[9] around their emergent hatred of the regime. Returning from his summer vacation, the tsar was appalled at the brutal crackdown and replaced his reactionary administrators with liberals, who released the incarcerated students in December 1861 and restored their freedoms. But the damage was done. Prison was a new experience for the progeny of the nobility and upper middle class, and created a new social identity for the militants in comparison to the state and their peers not committed enough to have earned this badge of courage. This new political community became the nucleus of radical agitation from then on.[10]

Some student study circles became political, like the one around Nikolai Chernyshevsky, the main contributor to the literary magazine *The Contemporary*. The 39-year-old son of a priest had come to study in St. Petersburg at age 18 but poverty excluded him from the capital's upper social stratum. He adopted utopian socialism[11] and, as a prolific writer, corresponded with exiled writers, like the revolutionary Alexander Herzen and the novelist Ivan

Turgenev. Herzen, a rich dissident nobleman, had fled Russia in 1847 for London, where he was joined by his close friend Nicholas Ogarev, and the two friends founded *The Bell*. Published abroad, *The Bell* was free of censorship and became the most widely read and influential Russian magazine of the time. Despite its being officially banned, censors looked the other way, and tsarist officials eagerly read it to discover what was truly happening within their own office. Even the tsar was rumored to read it regularly.[12]

By 1861, the disappointment with Alexander II's reforms turned both magazines against the tsar. In June, *The Bell* declared, "The tsar has cheated the people,"[13] concluding that a just and healthy society could come only through the violent overthrow of the status quo. Because of government censorship, *The Contemporary*, published in St. Petersburg, could not explicitly endorse this solution, but it made its points through metaphors, analogies, and allusions. Informal literary circles formed to discuss *The Bell* and decipher the meaning of the more cryptic *The Contemporary*. Dissidents came to believe that the peasants, aware of the deception of the Emancipation Statute, would rebel. They expected that the outbreak of the anticipated Polish nationalist secessionist movement would trigger widespread peasant unrest, escalating into a revolution in 1863.[14] A few suggested creating a political underground to guide the upcoming revolution. Ogarev suggested calling this projected organization "Land and Liberty," from his own answer to the question "What do the people need?"[15]

This strategy appealed to the students released from jail.[16] Land and Liberty was basically a loose collection of different circles emerging from the network of correspondents and readers of *The Contemporary* and *The Bell* in contact with each other.[17] Each circle had its own local norms and goals. Their activities and vitality varied greatly, and there was no coordinating central authority. The regime unknowingly destroyed the Land and Liberty project before it had a chance to develop into a formal organization by carrying out a wave of arrests in the summer of 1862. It intercepted some letters from Herzen to Chernyshevsky, who was arrested on 7 July 1862 on charges of sedition and illegal contacts with Herzen. He was sentenced to 12 years at hard labor, followed by exile for life in Siberia. The government had inadvertently produced a martyr for the revolutionary cause.[18]

Poland revolted as expected, but the anticipated widespread peasant unrest never took place. At first, Russian radicals seemed encouraged by the revolt, but as violence escalated, Polish rebels fought back against the brutality of the Russian military and shed Russian blood. This created a bind for Russian radicals, as their dual social identity split into a divided one: Russians or radicals? From his exile, Herzen felt more radical than Russian and supported the Polish rebels. But in Russia itself, nationalism trumped revolution. It was one thing to support Poles demanding independence, and another to support Poles killing Russians. The officer corps, which had been expected to rebel, remained loyal. Only a few officers of Polish descent refused to fight in Poland. The anti-Russian stance of *The Bell* discredited it among Russian radicals. Within months, the hope of Land and Liberty faded away, as continuing local discussion circles dissociated themselves from this project.

These circles also discussed novels with political implications, especially Turgenev's recent *Fathers and Sons*, which captured the generational conflict in Russia between liberal fathers, romantics rejecting revolution as an elusive dream, and their radical sons, determined to bring about real change. One of his characters, Eugene Barazov, became a source of inspiration for young radicals. But the novel emphasized the negative aspects of this "nihilist"[19] generation, namely its rejection of Russia's hypocritical and despotic norms, including religion, rather than its new values, built on a foundation of science rather than religion. From his prison cell, Chernyshevsky countered by writing a novel, *What Is to Be Done?*[20] stressing the new positive values. Smuggled out of prison, the book caught the imagination of the radical circles and became the most influential book in nineteenth-century Russia.[21]

The novel describes several characters who lived by a strict materialist individualism that gave them freedom of thought, movement, and activity, including sex. It argued that each person pursuing his or her own self-interest would result in happiness for all. From these fundamental principles, its characters defied conventions, built communes, enjoyed life to the fullest, and became new people through self-understanding. The novel articulated a socialist utopia based on complete equality of gender, opportunity, means, and pleasure. Its most memorable character was Rakhmetov, from an old and wealthy noble family, who became a monk of the revolution, denying himself any pleasure, such as wine, women, sugar, or white bread. He ate only what the poor could afford and slept on a thin bag of straw and nails to toughen himself up. He was totally dedicated to the revolution, always scheming and preparing for it, which the novel implied was about to come in three years' time.[22]

These characters fired the imagination of young romantics, who had no real-life models to guide them. Rakhmetovan cooperatives or communes flourished all over Russia, and "new men" who were students or former students tried to live by the novel's positive nihilist utopian values. This imagined community modeled around fictional prototypes flourished into a counterculture against "the conventional lies of civilized mankind," a rebellion of aristocratic sons (and daughters) against their authoritarian fathers. Nihilists carried their love of absolute sincerity into the smallest details of everyday life and gave up "superstitions, prejudices, habits, and customs which their reason would not justify." Men dressed in old, worn plaid shirts and let their hair grow long, while women cut their hair and wore simple woolen dresses. Both men and women sported blue-tinged glasses and neglected their hygiene, for they believed that time spent in the bathroom was vanity and better used for reading. They worshiped reason and were scientific materialists. They rejected outward politeness as hypocrisy, expressing themselves in a blunt and terse way, thus projecting a certain external roughness. They prized individual freedom, rejected imposed social constraints, and preached gender equality, revolting against the subjugation of women. "Marriage without love, and familiarity without friendship, were equally repudiated. The nihilist girl, compelled by her parents to be a doll in a Doll's House, and to marry for property's sake, preferred to abandon her house and her silk dresses . . . Nihilism, with its affirmation of the rights of the individual and its negation of all hypocrisy, was but a first step toward a higher type of men and women, who are equally free, but live for a great cause."[23]

As nihilism later became misunderstood outside Russia, Peter Kropotkin felt compelled to defend it. "In the press . . . nihilism is continually confused with terrorism. The revolutionary disturbance which broke out in Russia toward the close of the reign of Alexander II, and ended in the tragic death of the Tsar, is constantly described as nihilism. This is however a mistake . . . Terrorism was called into existence by certain special conditions of the political struggle at a given historical moment. It has lived, and has died. It may revive and die out again. But nihilism has impressed its stamp upon the whole of the life of the educated classes of Russia, and that stamp will be retained for many years to come."[24]

In Search of Hell

Chernyshevsky's admirers, organized in informal circles, were leaderless and scattered around university towns, meeting in the evenings for revolutionary talks and drinking. There was a lot of scheming but no action.[25] The assassination of U.S. President Abraham Lincoln in April 1865 was widely discussed. Although Chernyshevsky's followers were on the side of the North and against slavery, John Wilkes Booth's cry, "Sic Semper Tyrannis," resonated with them and inspired widespread discussions of political assassination of heads of state.[26]

On 4 April 1866, Dmitry Karakozov, a 26-year-old former student of minor nobility, carried out an attentat on the tsar. The tsar was walking in a public park in St. Petersburg, as was his custom, when Karakozov made his way through the crowd, pulled out his gun, fired, and missed. He tried to flee but was immediately captured.[27] The inquest report became the main basis of the historiography of the Karakozov affair.[28] It depicted a vast conspiracy of a secret society of students called "The Organization," poised to overthrow the government through revolution, proselytizing among peasants that the land belonged to them and building libraries and cooperatives to subvert people. At the core of "The Organization" was "Hell." "Its members took an oath to murder whomever obstructed the path—including the disobedient inside 'The Organization'—and designated one among them as tsaricide. The tsaricide was obliged to sever all personal ties and delve into an underworld of debauched vagabondage so as to divert attention from his political activities . . . Upon execution of the crime, the tsaricide had to immediately commit suicide by poisoning himself, leaving behind an explanatory proclamation. And so Karakozov set off for Petersburg."[29] The report blamed ideology— illegal books, revolutionary literature, and illusionary ideas of equality and unlimited personal freedom, perverting traditions—for this crime, which was intended to unleash general unrest and revolution.

The report contained a kernel of truth. Nicholas Ishutin, Karakozov's slightly older first cousin, had gathered around him a circle of students and dropouts from the University of Moscow to emulate Rakhmetov's ascetic rejection of convention and self-sacrificial dedication to the cause. "All Russia read in astonishment . . . that these young men, owners of considerable fortunes, used to live three or four in the same room, never spending more than five dollars apiece a month for all their needs, and giving at the same time their fortunes for starting cooperative associations, cooperative workshops."[30] Its members spread propaganda through Sunday schools and convinced themselves that the peasants were about to rebel against the sham of the Emancipation Statute.

The police arrested and tried 36 people in connection to "The Organization" and "Hell." The court found that "as far back as 1863, a circle of young people infected with socialist ideas formed in Moscow . . . [were building] schools and various associations, a bookbinding institution, and a clothing company . . . societies of translators and of mutual aid."[31] With time, members of this circle held infrequent discussions about unleashing a social revolution and freeing their idol Chernyshevsky. "In a small circle there were discussions about whether it would be worthwhile . . . to permit tsaricides and the extermination of governments in general as one of the means toward a general revolution . . . Some rejected [tsaricide] outright, others postponed it for an indefinite time, except Karakozov."[32] Allegedly, eight people, including Karakozov and Ishutin, of course, had participated in this discussion. Four of the participants had known about Karakozov's criminal intentions. Members of "The Organization"[33] were aware that its goals were illegal, but some had rarely come to meetings, did not understand abstract thought, and had only participated in hope of gaining some material advantage from it. Karakozov, who was denied a mental health defense at trial, pled guilty to attempted tsaricide and claimed to have acted alone. The court sentenced him and Ishutin to death. Karakozov was executed on 2 September 1866,[34] but Ishutin's sentence was commuted to life.[35] The other six defendants who had participated in the discussion were sentenced to hard labor,[36] while the rest received a variety of smaller sentences.

Although the defendants were extensively questioned about "Hell," the verdict never mentions it. Ishutin testified, "'Hell' did not exist; it was no more, no less than some stupid speeches made under the influence of wine . . . [Karakozov] was not a member of the circle 'Hell,' since 'Hell' itself did not exist, but he was there during our talks, though in his morbid condition he did not participate at all."[37] An anonymous informant had revealed its alleged existence to the police during the investigation, was paid 1,000 rubles, and disappeared. All the alleged conspirators denied its existence.[38] Its Rakhmetovan myth persisted over time: "A member of Hell must live under a false name and break all family ties; he must not marry; he must give up his friends; and in general he must live with one single, exclusive aim: an infinite love and devotion for his country and its good. For his country, he must give up all personal satisfaction and in exchange he must feel hatred for hatred, ill-will for ill-will, concentrating these emotions within himself."[39]

Karakozov acted on his own in his attentat. He was a member of a subversive Moscow circle but decided to do this alone. A few of his closest friends knew about his intention and tried to dissuade him, but they did not report him, hoping it was just talk. So what was his motivation? Ishutin cited his cousin's "morbid condition."[40] Karakozov was suffering from nine years of alcohol dependence, drinking half a bottle of spirits a day; gonorrhea for about two years; bloody diarrhea for about six months; typhus; fatigue; and depression. He was hospitalized from November 1865 to January 1866 with fever, insomnia, and lack of appetite. In the hospital, he asked for opium—apparently to kill himself rather than stop his diarrhea. He was discharged when his fever broke, and a note mentioned that he also suffered from hypochondria and depression. After his discharge, he was reclusive, sat silently in a separate room, hiding his face with his hand, and slept almost all day. Ishutin testified, "It was his sick condition, his sense that the illness was incurable, his nervous condition—this put the idea in his head that he would definitely die; for days he lay by himself in his room and did not participate in any of our discussion."[41]

In late January, Karakozov disappeared for three days and later said that he had wandered about aimlessly contemplating suicide. He probably heard the discussion about regicide around that time. Then he went to St. Petersburg for treatment at a prestigious medical clinic. After the failure of an initial treatment, the head of the clinic diagnosed him as a hypochondriac and repeated the same treatment. At a third visit, Karakozov was prescribed morphine. At his next visit, he asked to be hospitalized, but this was not possible as he was not a legal resident of St. Petersburg. Instead, he received electrical therapy and given an appointment for another session.[42] He was now obsessed about dying and wanted his death to be useful for the people. He wrote a manifesto for workers, explaining his decision to kill the tsar. "Brothers, I have long been tortured by the thought and given no rest by my doubts as to why my beloved simple Russian people has to suffer so much! . . . Why next to the eternal simple peasant and the laborer in his factory and workshop are there people who do nothing—idle nobles, a horde of officials and other wealthy people, all living in shining houses? . . . The man really responsible is the Tsar . . . who . . . gradually built up the organization of the State, and the army . . . handed out the land to the nobles . . . He is the people's worst enemy . . . I have felt the grief and burden of seeing my beloved people die in this way; and so I have decided to destroy the evil Tsar, and to die myself for my beloved people."[43] Karakozov sealed the manifesto in an envelope and gave it to a stranger with instructions to open it in one week and circulate it among the students at the university. Instead, the stranger looked inside, read it, and forwarded it to the governor-general of St. Petersburg's office, where it languished three weeks on a desk.[44]

During that time, Karakozov returned to Moscow and told his friends about his plan to kill the tsar. They tried to talk him out of it. After a week, he returned to the St. Petersburg clinic, where he took some strychnine and potassium sulfate that was lying around. From 2 April to the morning of 4 April, he wandered around town and drank vodka. "When I lay down to sleep I already thought I would not wake up again. My head burned like fire. I have no words to describe the sick, tortuous condition in which I found myself."[45] On the morning of 4 April, he became obsessed with the thought "that I have to die, that all attempts, all hopes for the fruition of my efforts to bring good to the people . . . are lost. And under the influence of those ideas I decided to commit the crime, and the idea was executed that same day."[46]

At first, after his arrest, Karakozov gave only the political rationale for his act.[47] But he soon became erratic. He tried to bite through the arteries of his wrists, and then to starve himself, but he was force fed. After another suicide attempt, he finally admitted the influence of his illness on his crime: "that disturbed, heavy mood of the soul, that illness, this spawned the idea that I was no longer capable of doing anything for the cause of the people, and that I did not have much longer to live. All that could have brought me to suicide and, consequently, to the crime I committed; I thought by committing the crime I would sacrifice myself and be useful to the people."[48]

The Karakozov affair grew into the myth of a heroic freedom fighter whose plot became a precedent for subsequent assassination attempts against the tsar. Conservatives, denying any political reasons for the crime, naturally blamed it on ideology poisoning the perpetrator's mind. However, the reality is far more complex. Karakozov was certainly part of an imagined nihilist community. When he believed he was dying, he tried to give meaning to his miserable life by volunteering to kill the tsar to punish him for his persecution of his imagined community. Mental illness contributed to his attempted tsaricide.[49]

The affair put an end to the liberal experiment in Russia. The tsar appointed reactionaries as ministers, who reinstated the old university regulations, withdrew scholarships for poor students, and canceled plans for modern high schools, replacing them with two-year schools teaching religion, reading, and writing. The tsar also dramatically expanded his own personal political police, the Third Section of His Majesty's Chancery. He appointed General Fyodor Trepov, who had shown great zeal in putting down the Polish uprising, as the St. Petersburg chief of police. What became known as the "white terror" of the next two years effectively put an end to the subversive activity of any study circles.[50]

A Polish Nationalist Attentat on the Tsar

The next year, Antoine Berezowski, a 20-year-old Pole, carried out an attentat against the tsar when he was visiting France.[51] He had joined the Polish insurrection in 1863 despite the opposition of his father. Russia had been very brutal in crushing the insurrection with massacres of the local population, executions of hundreds of prisoners, and exile of tens of thousands to Siberia. At Berezowski's trial, his former regimental commander testified that Berezowski had been "one of the best soldiers of my regiment . . . loved by his peers and superiors. I took special care of him because he was the youngest of my soldiers and he was passionate about the Polish cause. When the insurrection was crushed, he cried like a Christian who had lost his mother . . . His behavior and his studies converged on one thing: the welfare of Poland. To finish his education, he found a way to save 185 francs on a salary of five francs [a week]. He eagerly read everything that fell under his hand, especially everything consistent with his patriotic sentiments."[52] Another soldier added, "I met him when he joined our insurrection when he was sixteen. After the campaign, we went to Galicia. . . . He was still a child. He was crushed by the painful events in our country . . . When we tried to distract him by showing him some local monuments, he said, 'Who cares! They are not in our country. If Poland were free, we would have as many of them.'"[53]

When the regiment disbanded, Berezowski went to Belgium and worked in a factory. His commander recommended him for work as a mechanic in a train factory in Paris in February 1865. With his savings and the help of the Parisian Polish community, he continued his education in July 1865. The school director later testified that he left the school when he ran out of money. "By perhaps exaggerated scruples, he did not want to ask to stay: he was very obedient, hardworking, religious, sincere, and especially an excellent comrade."[54] He returned to his previous job and left on 30 April 1867 allegedly because of sickness. He read a lot, especially about the campaigns of Napoleon I, and had about 30 books, mostly on philosophy and history. Of interest was a Jesuit justification of regicide earmarked at short narratives of previous regicides.[55]

Newspapers announced that the tsar would visit Paris in June. Berezowski went to see the tsar arrive at the train station and watched him come out of the Opera House three days later. He was surprised that on both occasions he was able to get close to the tsar. The tsar and the emperor were scheduled to be at a military review at Bois de Boulogne on 6 June, and he resolved to take his chance then. He confided in no one, for fear of being betrayed. On 5 June, he bought a double-barreled handgun, capsules, and rounds. As he was loading his gun in his room, he saw that the caliber of the rounds was too small for the gun, so he jerry-rigged two bullets and jammed them into the barrel. In the morning, he stopped at a local café owned by a compatriot, drank a glass of vermouth on credit, and left his coat there as collateral. In its pocket was a book on the history of Poland earmarked at the oath of Jan Kilinski, a leader of the 1794 Polish insurrection against Russia: "I commit myself to do all I can for the success of the insurrection and vengeance against the enemy for all the misfortunes befalling our own . . . May it please God and his martyred son to help me!"[56]

At the Bois de Boulogne, he got close to the carriage carrying both Alexander II and Napoleon III, drew his pistol, and discharged it at the tsar. The gun exploded in his hand, however, injuring him instead of the tsar. He was immediately subdued by the crowd and yelled, "Long live Poland!" The arresting officer testified that "[Berezowski said] he did his duty in fulfilling an oath he swore to himself at the age of 16. War between Poland and Russia had not stopped: this gave him permission to do what he did and he regretted his failure. If he could do it again, he was ready to do so. He added that he was guilty of betraying the hospitality of France and not respecting his host sovereign."[57] When asked whether he had any accomplices, he replied, "My country."[58] He justified himself by saying, "Poland and Russia are still at war and I kill my enemy where I find him."[59] When it was pointed out to him that he could have injured the emperor, he protested, "A Polish bullet could only hit a tyrant. The Emperor of the French is a friend of Poland."[60]

Berezowski was tried on 15 July 1867 amid a great deal of public sympathy. His defense attorney played on the brutality of Russian repression in Poland to good effect, sparing him the death penalty. He was found guilty and sentenced to life at hard labor in New Caledonia.[61] Although Berezowski was a loner, he viewed himself as a soldier fighting for Poland, as he had been four years earlier, and his attempted tsaricide was a continuation of his war.

Catechism of the Revolutionary

Back in Russia, the white terror could not eradicate subversion. Escaping the hopelessness and boredom of the provinces, students continued to form secret Rakhmetovan circles and were joined by young women looking to evade their destiny of becoming wives to boring small civil servants or merchants. The following four trajectories capture the emerging scene in the capital in 1869.

Peter Tkachev, the oldest of these students, a 25-year-old son of a poor nobleman, had been swept up in the wave of arrests in St. Petersburg in 1861. He converted to economic materialism after reading Marx. A romantic, he viewed history as made by great men like Rakhmetov, whose "distinctive badge lies in the fact that all their activity, their whole way of life is dominated by one ambition, one passionate idea: to make the majority of men happy and to invite as many to the banquet of life. The bringing about of this idea becomes the only purpose of their activity, because this idea is completely fused into their conception of personal happiness. Everything is subordinated to this idea, everything is sacrificed—if one can even use the word sacrifice."[62] His writings and activities earned him two more stays in prison, which led him to use clandestine conspiratorial tactics to survive. He embraced Babeuf's egalitarianism and Buonarroti's conspiratorial strategy and came around to the idea that the revolution in Russia could come only when an organization of such dedicated revolutionaries would capture the state and impose it on society. This strategy of revolutionary takeover of the state was called Jacobin by Russian revolutionaries and later historians.[63]

In the capital, Tkachev ran into 22-year-old Sergei Nechaev. Born into a modest family, Nechaev had left home in 1865 as a bored, resentful, and arrogant teenager to teach Bible studies at a parochial school in St. Petersburg. Over the next three years, he read a lot and became fascinated by Karakozov, the Carbonaris, and Babeuf's conspiracy. He audited classes at the university and attended local student radical meetings, where he hoped to recruit followers for his dream of becoming the leader of the Russian revolution. He modeled himself on Rakhmetov.[64] He and Tkachev shared similar ideas, which they elaborated in their *Program of Revolutionary Action*.[65]

Vera Zasulich, a 20-year-old born into poor nobility, grew up with her two sisters, Alexandra and Ekaterina, dreaming about a meaningful life, inspired by Chernyshevsky's ideas. When forced to go to school to become a governess at 17, she ran away to avoid living in subservience on some wealthy estate caring for spoiled children. She joined her two sisters, who were living around Moscow, and they set up a Rakhmetovan sewing cooperative. At first, it seemed idyllic, with enough money, picnics, and hikes as in the novel, but then the better seamstresses left for better wages and the cooperative collapsed. Alexandra stayed in Moscow and married Peter Uspensky, who was working in a bookstore that clandestinely distributed subversive material. In August 1868, Vera and Ekaterina left for St. Petersburg, where Vera worked in a bookbinding cooperative, and they started hanging out with radical students.[66] One evening in the fall, she ran into Nechaev at a student discussion, and they began seeing each other over the next few weeks.

Mark Natanson, the 18-year-old son of a Jewish merchant in Kovno, had witnessed and been revolted by the harsh suppression of the 1863 Polish rebellion. He came to St. Petersburg to study medicine in 1868, became involved in the student circles, and met Nechaev in early 1869.[67] Nechaev was convinced that the revolution would start on 19 February 1870, the date when the Emancipation Statute required the peasants to either give land back to landowners or continue paying compensation. He believed that an organization of "revolutionary prototypes"[68] was needed to raise society's consciousness for the necessity of revolution and guide it. He had a two-part strategy: first, radicalized students should fan out to the countryside; second, the assassination of the tsar would trigger the revolution.[69]

Nechaev tried to recruit students for his Revolutionary Committee by inviting promising candidates and, in front of portraits of Robespierre and Saint Just, telling them about Babeuf's tactics and Tkachev's and his Jacobin program. On 31 January 1869, he tried to recruit Vera Zasulich. She had a crush on him, but hesitated. "Serving the revolution, this was the supreme happiness, of which I could only dream." When Nechaev then told her, "I have fallen in love with you," she replied, "I value your friendship, but I do not love you."[70]

Nechaev also secretly tried to transform his followers into hardened revolutionaries by betraying them to the police and letting them taste the regime's persecution. He hoped that they would start hating the regime and nurture this hate into revolution. However, by the beginning of 1869, rumors started circulating about him and his fantasies in St. Petersburg. He realized it was time to leave, as too many people were onto his lies. A few days later, Zasulich received a short note from him saying, "I am being taken to a fortress. Tell our comrades."[71] She showed it to friends, who protested to the university administration. They were stunned to hear that he was not a student there, or

arrested, and assumed the administration was lying. Nechaev had gone to
Moscow, where Uspensky was able to get him a passport allowing him to sail
to Europe and Geneva to meet Mikhail Bakunin.[72] Back in St. Petersburg, the
authorities cracked down on a series of student disturbances and arrested Natanson and Tkachev, among others.[73]

At that time, Bakunin was perhaps the most celebrated revolutionary in
the world. He knew Pierre-Joseph Proudhon and Karl Marx and had participated in some of the rebellions in 1848, for which he was arrested in Germany
and extradited back to Russia. He was exiled to Siberia, from which he escaped in June 1861. Six months later, he arrived in London and joined Herzen's
The Bell. At the outbreak of the Polish uprising, he chartered a boat to bring
weapons to the Poles, but got stuck in Scandinavia. He then left for Italy before
moving to Geneva, where he joined the IWA. Nechaev found him there in
April 1869 and claimed to be the leader of a vast underground movement, led
by his Revolutionary Committee, and that revolution in Russia would start
next February with the tsar's assassination.

For Bakunin, this was a dream come true. He had been out of Russia for
about two decades and lost touch with its revolutionaries. He was convinced
of the peasants' revolutionary potential on the model of the large peasant uprisings of Stenka Razin and Yemelyan Pugachev in the seventeenth and eighteenth centuries, respectively. Razin and Pugachev had been Cossacks from
the southern or eastern frontier who had rebelled against tsarist incursions
into their territories. Starting out as bandits, they had success that transformed
them into rebels and Bakunin's heroes.[74] At the time of Nechaev's visit, Bakunin believed, "The times of Stenka Razin are drawing near . . . Now as then,
the Russia of peasants and workers are rising."[75] He exhorted students to go to
the people.[76] If need be, they might even ally themselves with brigands, like
Razin and Pugachev.

Bakunin's wishful thinking blinded him to Nechaev's deception: "I have
here with me one of those young fanatics who know no doubts, who fear
nothing . . . They are magnificent, these young fanatics, believers without
God, heroes without rhetoric."[77] He helped Nechaev raise funds for the upcoming revolution. Nechaev continued his secret denunciations of his acquaintances in Russia by sending them letters and revolutionary leaflets,
knowing that the Third Section was closely monitoring all the mail from Geneva. He compromised about 400 people, including Vera Zasulich, and she
and her sister Ekaterina were arrested at the beginning of May 1869.[78] Vera
later commented that Nechaev, "if he did not actually detest the young people
who were attracted to him, he certainly did not feel the least sympathy toward
them, not a shade of pity, but much contempt."[79]

Nechaev returned to Russia in August with money, a certificate stating

"The carrier of this is one of the confidential representatives of the Russian section of the World Revolutionary Alliance, no. 2771,"[80] and a small pamphlet, *Catechism of the Revolutionary*, elaborating the practical rules of conduct of his "prototype of a revolutionary."[81] "The revolutionary is a doomed man. He has no interest of his own, no affairs, no feelings, no attachments, no belongings, not even a name. Everything in him is absorbed by a single exclusive interest, a single thought, a single passion—the revolution . . . He has broken every tie with the civil order . . . He knows only one science, the science of destruction. To this end, and this end alone, he will study mechanics, physics, chemistry, and perhaps medicine. To this end, he will study day and night the living science: people, their characters and circumstances and all the features of the present social order at all possible levels . . . For him, everything is moral which assists the triumph of revolution . . . Night and day, he must have but one thought, one aim—merciless destruction." Everything is subordinated to the revolution. "The extent of his friendship, devotion, and other obligations towards his comrades is determined only by their degree of usefulness in the practical work of total revolutionary destruction. The need for solidarity among revolutionaries is self-evident. In it lies the whole strength of revolutionary work . . . He is not a revolutionary if he feels pity for anything in this world. If he is able to, he must face the annihilation of a situation, of a relationship, or of any person who is a part of this world—everything and everyone must be equally odious to him. All the worse for him if he has family, friends, and loved ones in this world; he is no revolutionary if they can stay his hand. Aiming at merciless destruction, the revolutionary can and sometimes even must live within society while pretending to be quite other than what he is."[82]

Nechaev also outlined the structure of his revolutionary organization, based on Buonarrotian strict hierarchy, compartmentalization, and need to know. At the top was a cell of five people, each of whom headed another cell of five people, each of whom led a subordinate cell, and so on. Each was responsible for the recruitment of four people in his cell. Each cell was independent from the others, and members of each cell were bound together by loyalty and secrecy.[83]

Nechaev arrived in Moscow in September 1869 and appointed Uspensky his lieutenant in his new organization, the People's Justice.[84] Their goal was to recruit as many people as possible to carry out a series of high-profile assassinations that would trigger the revolution come February. In less than three months, they managed to get 70 to 80 people at various stages of recruitment. When someone named Ivanov became suspicious of Nechaev's fantasies and challenged his statements at meetings, Nechaev denounced him to his top cell members as a police spy who had to be eliminated. They killed him and dumped his body in a pond, but the body resurfaced; on it, the police discovered a card for Uspensky's bookstore.[85]

Nechaev realized it was time to leave Russia for good. He asked Uspensky's wife Alexandra (Vera's sister) to leave her husband and accompany him abroad. She was overjoyed—"I could never dream of such happiness"[86]—but could not travel, as she was nine months pregnant. He left for St. Petersburg alone. On 26 November, the police raided Uspensky's apartment and discovered Nechaev's catechism, minutes from meetings, and a list of assassination targets. Uspensky was arrested and confessed to everything.[87] The police arrested 152 people for complicity in the affair, but Nechaev slipped through their hands. He left Russia on 15 December with a much older woman with a long radical history, who had abandoned her husband, lover, and child to follow him but returned, disappointed, a month later: "I could not get his attention; he would not talk, do, or even think about anything except his enterprise . . . He drinks but little . . . and [even in his sleep] mumbles incoherent words concerning his business."[88] Nechaev returned to Geneva to see Bakunin, who, unaware of the above events, welcomed him back. However, as the predicted uprisings did not take place, Bakunin grew disillusioned with his protégé and finally broke with him in June 1870, when rumors of the murder and deceptions reached Geneva.[89]

Meanwhile, Zasulich, who was in prison during Nechaev's return, avoided implication in the affair but was administratively exiled in April 1871.[90] The defendants in the Nechaev affair were tried in June 1871. Only half of the defendants were found guilty, and they received fairly lenient sentences. Uspensky was sentenced to 15 years of forced labor in exile, where his wife and son followed him.[91] Tkachev was convicted only of writing a seditious pamphlet and exiled to Siberia.[92] The story of Nechaev's perfidy discredited him among the Russian émigrés. He was eventually arrested in Zurich in August 1872 and extradited to Russia. He was tried in January 1873, convicted of Ivanov's murder, and sentenced to 20 years at hard labor, which he served in the Peter Paul Fortress until his death in November 1882.[93]

Nechaev may have been one of the few psychopaths in the history of modern political violence. He self-categorized into a political protest community against the tsarist state but did not seem to display the usual cognitive consequences of this self-categorization, such as bias toward in-group members. Indeed, his antisocial tendency may have prevented him from experiencing these pro-social biases and feelings. Instead, he did not respond to in-group norms and coldly harmed in-group members by denouncing them to their enemies for some bizarre justification. This antisocial element is the essence of psychopathy. His catechism of a revolutionary reflects this psychopathic element of discarding in-group companions in favor of antisocial individualism moved by abstraction. This caricature of a revolutionary continues to fascinate precisely because of the horror of these psychopathic features but is in fact the very opposite of a politically violent person, as the present inquiry demonstrates.[94] Nevertheless, it conforms so well to the out-group prejudice of dehumanizing evil imputed to politically violent people that counterterrorism experts seldom fail to cite it when describing terrorists.[95]

The Saintly Circle

After his release from jail in May 1869, Mark Natanson founded an urban student commune in the capital. In the evenings, friends came and debated Nechaev's Jacobinism and Peter Lavrov's romantic moralism. Lavrov, a former professor of mathematics arrested in the wake of the Karakozov affair in 1866, argued from his Siberian exile in *Historical Letters* that students had a duty to work for the improvement of society. "Every comfort which I enjoy, every thought which I had the leisure to acquire or work out was purchased by blood, by the suffering or labor of millions. I cannot correct the past . . . Evil has to be righted insofar as possible, and it has to be done during one's lifetime . . . I am obliged to do and it is quite an easy duty, since it coincides with that which is a source of pleasure for me—searching for and disseminating greater truth, clarifying for myself the fairest social order."[96]

Lavrov's ideas gained fluency as Nechaev's immorality, pseudoscientific coldness, and deceptive intrigues horrified students, discredited political violence, and probably postponed its outbreak by at least half a decade.[97] From Geneva, Nechaev kept sending poisoned letters to acquaintances, including Natanson, who was rearrested on Christmas 1869. He protested that he opposed Nechaev, cooperated with the police in this matter, and was released shortly thereafter. However, this second arrest precluded him from pursuing his medical studies, and Natanson instead became a full-time political organizer.[98]

German Lopatin, a 25-year-old former member of Ishutin's circle and recent disciple of Karl Marx, helped Lavrov escape from his exile in February 1870. Lavrov fled to Europe and became the editor of a new journal, *Forward!* in which he urged students to undertake a period of preparation of intense scientific self-education and then go educate peasants. This duty of self-sacrifice and devotion to the masses caught the imagination of the students, reared on Christian values of the nobility of self-sacrifice and redemption. The idea of noblesse oblige especially appealed to young aristocrats and children of clergymen, who together constituted the vast majority of what later became known as populists because they carried out Lavrov's pilgrimage to the people.

Numbers help gauge the significance of this student movement. Around 1870, Russia had a population of about 80 million people, but there were only about 5,000 university students entire in the country. Gymnasiums[99] contributed an additional 50,000 male and 27,000 female students. A few elite women succeeded in auditing university courses in Russia but were not allowed to take a degree. So, in addition to the above, there were 104 Russian women studying at university in Zurich. More than 90 percent of the student populists of the 1870s came from university centers in St. Petersburg, Moscow, Kiev, Kharkov, Odessa, and Zurich.[100]

Lavrov's new emphasis on the ethical dimension of the struggle appealed to many newcomers to the movement. Circles formed at universities and engaged in moral self-discovery through study, mutual support, and free discussions of socialist texts. "The circle accepted as members only persons who were well known and had been tested in various circumstances, and of whom it was felt that they could be trusted absolutely. Before a new member was received, his character was discussed with the frankness and seriousness which were characteristic of the nihilist. The slightest token of insincerity or conceit would have barred the way to admission."[101] They were not doctrinaire; they discussed every aspect of their lives and spent most of their time together. Their dedication to the group and self-understanding became the central aspect of their lives and forged a strong sense of shared social identity. "What united us was the intensity of subjective feeling, not one or another revolutionary doctrine."[102] Natanson's best friend Nikolai Tchaikovsky stressed this social bond: "We must be as clean and clear as a mirror. We must know each other so well that, should there arise difficult times of persecution and struggle, we are in a position to know *a priori* how each of us will behave."[103]

Despite their nonviolence, populists knew that their activity was subversive and had consciously joined in the spirit of self-sacrifice. "About ourselves, we were always pessimistic: we would all perish; they would persecute us, lock us up, send us into exile and hard labor (we didn't even think about capital punishment then!) . . . If not for the persecution, I'm not at all certain that I would have become a socialist at that time."[104] Each new member accepted the serious implication of joining: "Giving my consent I of course knew that in doing so I left my Rubicon behind, that there would be no retreat and that from now on all my modest energies must inevitably be placed in the service of the circle, and that the fate awaiting me would not be a crown of laurels but prison and exile."[105]

These communes did not have a formal leader; all major decisions had to be unanimous, and minor ones required a simple majority.[106] In St. Petersburg, the group under the influence of Natanson, "a man of great energy and initiative and rare organizing ability,"[107] became a prototype for other circles to emulate. Natanson had established links with publishers who allowed him to buy books at a steep discount and distribute them at cost to other circles with which he had established contacts. Thus they were able to discuss similar social, economic, and political books. He invited members from other circles in and out of the capital to come and participate in the commune's discussions. They came to visit, establishing links, which created an informal network throughout the country.

One of the local circles was composed exclusively of rich and aristocratic young women who were taking classes at a local gymnasium, the first to offer classes to women in Russia. The group included Alexandra Kornilova, Anna Korba, Sofia Leshern von Gershfeld, Olga Shleysner, and Sofia Perovskaya. The 17-year-old daughter of the governor-general of St. Petersburg who had been fired in the wake of the Karakozov affair, Perovskaya had rebelled against her father. These feminists rejected their preprogrammed social trajectory in favor of a life of self-discovery and education in order to help Russia and promote women's emancipation.[108] They were suspicious of men and initially refused an invitation to join Natanson's circle for fear of becoming subordinated to the more knowledgeable men. However, Shleysner became a frequent visitor to Natanson's circle and orchestrated multiple discussions between the two groups, which reassured the women and led to a merger in the summer of 1871.[109] The merged circle discussed socialist thinkers, current events, including the Paris Commune, and the Nechaev affair. The self-sacrifice of the Communards canonized them in the eyes of the circle, while Nechaev showed them what to avoid. "The negative attitude toward *nechaevshchina* called forth the urge to build an organization on opposing principles, founded on close acquaintanceship, sympathy, complete belief in the equality of all members, and above all—on a high level of moral development."[110]

The merged circle organized a nationwide friendship-based network of distribution of subversive literature such as Lavrov's *Forward!* It organized a printing operation abroad, then smuggled and distributed scientific and revolutionary literature to other university cities. It corresponded with circles in the country and Zurich, and conducted local propaganda among newly formed local circles of workers. As the prototype for all such circles, its moral atmosphere became the norm for the others. Despite its strong influence on the entire movement, its total membership over its five-year existence was not more than 30 members and about 15 associates, linked together more by friendship and common ideals than by formal rules or common ideology.[111]

Police Crackdown on the Tchaikovsky Circle

How did a group of people consciously self-selected on the basis of high ethical standards and explicit rejection of violence become over time one of the most dedicated, persistent, and ferocious group of terrorists the world has ever known? This enigma is the major focus of the rest of this chapter.

The police monitored the circle's activities and let it be while it was merely engaging in discussions. But as its proselytizing activities spread to local workers, the police cracked down and arrested Natanson in November 1871 for conspiring to distribute subversive literature. He was administratively exiled to Archangel, and Olga Shleysner married him in early 1872 in order to go with him. Tchaikovsky hosted the remainder of the circle, which took on his name, becoming the Tchaikovsky circle. The group continued to thrive and attract new recruits. Lopatin, who had helped Lavrov escape and was translating Marx's *Capital*, joined it and was preparing Chernyshevsky's escape when he himself was arrested and exiled. Another newcomer was Sergei Kravchinsky, a 20-year-old cadet nobleman at the Artillery School. He had converted to the populist cause and was fascinated by the French Revolution, whose success he attributed to the energy of its individual heroes. In 1871, he resigned his commission and joined the circle full time. "All his energies were directed to developing his own mind, to preparing itself for that revolutionary function which even then he knew was to be his lot. He already read many languages and had an excellent memory."[112]

Another recruit was Peter Kropotkin, a bit older than the rest at age 30. He was born a full prince but had dropped his title as a teenager. He had been an imperial page before joining the army, where he developed an interest in geography, geology, and socialism and became a secretary of the Russian Geographical Society. In 1872, he went to Switzerland to learn more about socialism, and he became a member of the IWA and converted to anarchism. He returned to St. Petersburg with a trunk full of banned books on politics. He was then invited to join the Tchaikovsky circle, with which he shared his books and his impressions of the IWA and the anarchists. "The two years that I worked in the Circle of Tchaikovsky . . . left a deep impression upon all my subsequent life and thought. During these two years it was life under high pressure,—that exuberance of life when one feels at every moment the full throbbing of all the fibres of the inner self, and when life is really worth living. I was in a family of men and women so closely united by their common object, and so broadly and delicately humane in their mutual relations, that I cannot now recall a single moment of even temporary friction marring the life of our circle."[113]

Given the intimacy of the circle, the police had trouble penetrating it, but its proselytism made its members vulnerable to identification and arrest. In

November 1873, Perovskaya and three other members were arrested and the rest of its members left the capital.[114] Kropotkin had to stay because he was the secretary of the Geographical Society in the capital. An informant denounced his proselytism among workers, and he was arrested in March 1874. His arrest marks the end of Tchaikovsky's circle in St. Petersburg, but its Moscow affiliate survived.[115]

Another influential populist circle was composed of young Russian women who had gone to Zurich to escape their prescribed boring and loveless gender trajectory in favor of studying trades like engineering and medicine useful for the development of Russia. They formed around 1872 and became known as the Fritschis, named after the manager of their boarding house. Their political discussions transformed them into dedicated socialist revolutionaries. The Fritsche circle, dominated by 19-year-old Sophia Bardina, included the Figner and the Liubatovich sisters.[116] Vera Figner, a 20-year-old with a very happy childhood, had been blissfully unaware of the misery around her until her gymnasium graduation, when she first realized "that not everyone lived under such happy conditions as I." She felt a duty to bring the "blessings of civilization" to the "uneducated masses, who lived from day to day, submerged in manual toil, and deprived of all those things."[117] She decided to be a physician for them, went to Zurich for medical school, and met the other rebels. The women concluded it was necessary to go to the people, share their "plain living, to engage in physical labor, to drink, eat, and dress as the people did, renouncing all the habits and needs of the cultured classes," to avoid being an exploiter, earn their trust, and conduct successful propaganda. In its discussions, "the Fritsche circle was tolerant of the individual opinions of its members. It is true that many of them held the most extreme views and—as if showing off for each other—we all chose as our heroes the most irreconcilable leaders of the great French Revolution. Some were enthralled by Robespierre, while others would settle for no less than Marat, the 'friend of the people' who demanded millions of heads."[118]

Going to the People: The Russian Populist Pilgrimage

The summer of 1874 saw a widespread movement of populists invading the countryside. There was no real triggering event, and some had previously tried to proselytize in the countryside. The "pilgrimage to the people" was uncoordinated, but it was quite deliberate, for most of the participants had prepared themselves by learning a trade in the spring. In October 1873, Kravchinsky, who knew the New Testament by heart, traveled with a friend through the countryside as a religious preacher, attempting through biblical quotes to persuade peasants to start a revolution. The peasants treated them as apostles; their fame spread rapidly—and came to the attention of the local gendarmes, who arrested them. As they were being transferred to a city, friendly peasants got the gendarmes drunk at a rest stop, and the two daredevils escaped to Moscow, where they integrated with its Tchaikovsky circle.[119]

Kravchinsky's trip was widely discussed among populist circles, which shared Chernyshevsky's romanticism, Lavrov's moralism, and Bakunin's optimism. The news of his exploits fell on fertile minds; impatient youths, tired of endless discussions and immersed in Lavrovian self-sacrificing Christian theology, felt ready.[120] Most of the pilgrims went to the land of Razin and Pugachev, guided by Bakunin's hope of awakening its peasants' revolutionary potential. They were eager to tell the peasants and workers the truth. The pilgrimage was mostly a bandwagon effect, as news of a pilgrimage elsewhere inspired other circles to join the moving train. Young people, self-categorized into a political protest community, acted out their shared social identity.

However, things did not go as expected: the chaotic pilgrimage turned out to be a complete disaster. In the countryside, peasants and workers were not receptive to the "flying propaganda," so called because students kept moving to spread their message. Peasants did not identify with or trust the obviously well-off outsiders, who did not have the strength or stamina to work in the fields and seemed to stir up trouble for them. They also had a deep loyalty to the tsar, whom they viewed as a liberator, and blamed all their troubles only on local landowners and bureaucrats, who, they assumed, were persecuting them behind the tsar's back. They believed that if the tsar knew, he would come to their rescue—the "Myth of the Good Tsar."[121] They were indifferent to these traveling propagandists and often beat up these pampered children of the elite or, worse, denounced them to the police, who arrested them.

Most of the pilgrims were quickly discouraged and gave up within weeks. The most perseverant lasted only months. It is hard to estimate the number of these repentant noblemen, the vast majority of whom were children of the nobility and gentry and the rest of clergymen. Most estimates are based on the archives of the Third Section, which indicate 1,665 participants. They were young: 27.5 percent were younger than 21 years; 38.4 percent were between 21 and 25 years; and another 21 percent were between 26 and 30 years.[122] This was about a third of Russia's tiny university student population. A Ministry of Justice memorandum at the end of the year summarized the events of the "mad summer." People arrested and handed over to his ministry numbered 770, of whom 612 were men and 158 women. Of those arrested, 265 had been kept in prison, while 452 had been granted bail and were monitored. Another 53 escaped. The Minister of Justice triumphantly reported that the movement had been crushed.[123]

The pilgrimage had one immediate effect on the government. This movement's size and distribution across the country were unprecedented and surprised the government, which, like any government facing a similarly mystifying event, eagerly connected imaginary dots and suspected that it was coordinated by an umbrella organization, probably directed from abroad. However, no evidence has ever surfaced supporting such wide conspiracy or even any form of leadership.[124] Fearing that it was facing an existential threat to the regime, the government dramatically increased its persecution of populists and arrested not only anyone who was involved in subversive activities but also anyone associated with them. These arrests escalated the conflict between the populists and the state. The regime's overreaction and mounting repression helped create the very enemy it feared, in a vicious self-fulfilling prophecy.

The government's fear of a revolutionary organization found some partial support in the short-lived All Russian Social Revolutionary Organization in Moscow, or simply the Moscow Organization, which was a small mixture of Georgian aristocrats, Fritschis, and workers.[125] The government had been alarmed by the radical evolution of the Fritschis in Zurich and issued an edict that all Russian students should leave the city by January 1874. Many returned, but the most dedicated continued their studies elsewhere in Europe. They followed the developments of the pilgrimage to the people and met with a small group of Georgians attending a congress of Caucasian intellectuals in Geneva in August 1874. They concluded that part of the failure of the summer was due to a lack of organization, and decided to return to Russia to form a group focusing on workers instead of peasants. The leading members were Ivan Dzhabadari and his close friend Prince Alexander Tsitsianov. On his way to Moscow, Dzhabadari convinced a few workers from the capital to join them. All of them converged in Moscow, where at the beginning of 1875, many of the Fritschis got jobs in large textile factories and tried to organize the women there. Gesia Gelfman, a 20-year-old daughter of a Jewish businessman who wanted to marry her off to a family friend, had run away and drifted to Moscow, where she met Fritschi Olga Liubatovich, who invited her to join the organization. However, most of the women factory workers were not like her and seemed interested only in clothes, romantic adventures, and malicious gossip. Faced with this political apathy and hard work, most of the Fritschis did not last a fortnight in the factories.

The Moscow Organization was clandestine to protect itself against state persecution. To counter the government's increased aggressiveness against them, its members agreed to use more confrontational "disorganizational" tactics, including the use of armed resistance against arrests. This type of violence was "permitted only in the most serious and unavoidable circumstances, not to be squandered on insignificant trifles, which could only deprive that mode of activity of all moral support."[126] The organization did not practice good tradecraft in its meetings with workers, whose mistresses became jealous of the presence of so many pretty, young women at the meetings, and denounced the group to the police. This triggered a wave of raids throughout the spring and summer of 1875, which eradicated the organization.[127] During one of these raids, Prince Tsitsianov put these disorganizational tactics into practice as he pulled out a gun and shot but missed a policeman at close range, while the diminutive Liubatovich tried to choke one of the officers.[128] This was probably the first instance of political violence among the populists. The Moscow Organization defendants were tried in the winter of 1877 in what is known as the Trial of the 50.

Many of the arrests were based on quite flimsy grounds: "Mere suspicion led to arrest. An address; a letter from a friend who had gone 'among the people;' a word let fall by a lad of twelve who, from excess of fear, knew not what to reply, were sufficient to cast the suspected person into prison."[129] Prison became a transformative experience. Later memoirs imply that prison experience was the main contributing factor to their later turn to political violence. Take Andrei Zhelyabov, born in 1850, the son of a house serf. A brilliant student and excellent speaker, he was expelled from the University of Odessa in 1871 for participation in a student demonstration against a professor. He gravitated to an Odessa populist circle and was arrested in 1874 for subversive activities but released on bail. However, the local police report did not satisfy St. Petersburg, which ordered his rearrest in November. "It was then that I became a revolutionary."[130] He was again released on a bail of 3,000 rubles paid by his father-in-law in March 1875. Under heavy police surveillance, he refrained from any political activities but took a course on the chemistry of explosives during that time. He also learned more from fishermen, who used dynamite to fish.[131] He was summoned back to jail in September 1877 and later transferred to St. Petersburg as part of the famous Trial of the 193, when he was acquitted of all charges.[132]

Another example was Nikolai Kibalchich, born in 1853 into a family of priests. An excellent student, he studied the chemistry of explosives for two years at the Institute of Transportation Engineers. Around 1873, he became a populist and switched to medicine because he thought he might be able to contribute more directly to people's well-being as a physician. After a pilgrimage in the Ukraine, he was arrested in October 1875 in a raid on his residence when the police discovered some subversive leaflets that a friend had asked him to keep. "If not for the arrest, if not for the severe measures of the ruling powers toward those activists who did go to the people, I would have gone to the people and would still be there among them to this day. The goals, which I set for myself, would have been of a cultural character, partly socialistic, but precisely to elevate the intellectual and moral level of the masses."[133] Kibalchich was transferred to a jail in Kiev for investigation of his propaganda activities in the Ukraine. Although he was eligible for bail, he could not raise the money. He languished in jail until his trial on 1 May 1878, when he was sentenced to one month in prison. In other words, he had endured jail for 969 days for an infraction that the court later determined to be worth 30 days! "Prison confinement, more or less prolonged, has always on the not-yet-fixed personality one of two possible influences. For some people—those of wavering and weak nature—it scares them and forces them to change their course for the future; others, on the other hand, it steels them and increases the seriousness of their resolve to continue on the path which, in their eyes, leads to the goal of their life. I belonged to the second group."[134] Many people who knew him before and after his prison experience testified to his transformation.[135]

The disproportionate repression demoralized the young militants, who resented being in jail: all they had done was sacrifice themselves to enlighten the peasants and workers by distributing leaflets and talking to them. They had avoided any confrontation with the state. Their imprisonment had no end in sight, as the government did not know what to do about them. Those who had escaped arrest were upset over the fate of their friends. Vera Figner, who returned to Russia in late 1875, wrote, "I myself was in such a mood, that I longed to die."[136]

Land and Liberty

The disaster of the peaceful pilgrimage to the people and the ensuing harsh tsarist repression disillusioned young Russian idealists, who started to question their assumptions about the effectiveness of peaceful proselytism. "The Russian government has no pity with respect to its enemies: Russian socialists should feel the same with respect to this government; and as long as they limit themselves to just propaganda, their cause will gain nothing or very little in these conditions . . . Why should he [the revolutionary] limit himself to propaganda? We will necessarily come to this question and we will answer it in the sense that we must come to the aid of every strike and riot, even provoke them, and do so well armed. To die while defending our ideas is in every case better than to commit suicide resulting from poor treatments."[137]

Revenge against government injustice was a common theme in the later accounts of violent militants. They languished in prison for years without being told of the charge against them, and their eventual acquittals did not soften the bitterness of harsh prison years. Dozens either went mad, committed suicide, or died of other causes in prison.[138] The central prison of Kharkov was nick-named the House of Horrors by its prisoners.[139] While this argument for the turn to violence has obvious merit, it is too simplistic. The vast majority of po-litical prisoners still rejected violence. Even a few who tried to kill people after their prison stay later rejected the systematic terrorism of People's Will.[140] On the other hand, some of the most zealous champions of violence never experi-enced prison.[141] The turn to political violence requires more nuance than an argument based solely on revenge for unjust imprisonment.

The tsarist government tried to regain the trust of the intelligentsia, which was generally sympathetic to these young idealists, by discrediting them with the same tactic that had been so successful against Nechaev. It would expose the true nature of these dangerous rebels through evidence presented at public trials and drive a wedge between populists and the public. The Ministry of Justice tried to build as strong a case as possible against this subversion, and this was the main reason for delaying the great trials until 1877.[142]

Meanwhile, new adherents to populism as well as veterans hiding from the police drew their own conclusions from the disaster of the pilgrimage. Again, the critical impetus for this new phase of the struggle came from Na-tanson, who had escaped from exile with his wife in late summer 1875 to pick up the pieces of the movement. He traveled throughout Russia and abroad to convince disillusioned militants to return to the movement. The failure of semi-random flying propaganda pointed to the necessity of a national organi-zation to transform society. State persecution pushed it underground for self-protection. The new group's security measures earned its members the nickname of "troglodytes"—because they concealed their names and ad-dresses, it was as if they lived in secret caves. Not in on the joke and informed of the existence of such a group in the capital, the police confabulated the meaning of the name in a report to the tsar: "Troglodyte was the name given in ancient times to wild Ethiopian tribes... These tribes lived in herds. Women and children were shared. Today, in Africa, the name 'troglodytes' is given to races of chimpanzees, extremely intelligent and so well-trained that they can sometimes replace servants, but also extremely irritable, changing quickly from high spirits to ferocity."[143]

In addition to propaganda, Natanson favored new measures such as demonstrations and adoption of protective disorganizational tactics such as the elimination of police spies and rescue of imprisoned comrades. Support of these prisoners was especially popular among militants. In the spring of 1876, a populist student had died of consumption after being jailed for three years. Natanson organized a funeral procession for his burial. The large crowd in March 1876, composed of the liberal intelligentsia, became the first political demonstration in St. Petersburg in over a decade and reassured populists that public opinion was still behind them.[144] He also organized the spectacular escape of Peter Kropotkin, who had become sick in prison and been transferred to a military hospital in St. Petersburg. With the help of the staff, Kropotkin ran away on 30 June 1876 into a cabriolet pulled by a champion racehorse called Barbarian. After celebrating his escape with Natanson at the fanciest restaurant in St. Petersburg that evening, Kropotkin was exfiltrated to western Europe, where he spent the rest of his days in exile and became a leading authority on anarchism.[145]

Around the country, populists polarized into Lavrovian pacifists preaching propaganda and Bakunian insurrectionists trying to foment peasant uprisings. The latter seemed more prominent in the south, especially the Kiev commune. Ekaterina Breshko-Breshkovskaya, a 32-year-old former member of the Tchaikovsky circle from a rich and liberal aristocratic family, came to Kiev and started the commune, which included Jacob Stefanovich and Maria (Masha) Kolenkina. They performed their pilgrimage together, but Breshkovskaya was arrested in the fall.[146] The other two regrouped the commune. By 1876, its core included Stefanovich, Kolenkina, Lev Deich, and Zasulich. Jacob Stefanovich, the 22-year-old son of a priest, and Lev Deich,[147] the 21-year-old old son of a Jewish merchant, were best friends from high school. Deich had participated in helping a comrade escape and had been arrested in 1875. He escaped by himself and came to live at the commune. In exile, Zasulich's request to study midwifery had been granted, and she enrolled at the Kharkov Midwives' Institute in January 1874. There she met Kolenkina; they became close friends, left the school, and joined the Kiev commune. Its members lived together in a small apartment as illegals,[148] rejected abstract ideas, and were itching for action. They swore that they would not allow themselves to be captured like sheep and would put up armed resistance if necessary.[149] They were joined by former student Michael Frolenko, the 27-year-old son of an army sergeant-major who had become an illegal two years earlier.[150] "In 1876 I found myself in the circle of the Kiev rebels. Here the propaganda phase was definitely over and everything was directed toward organizing an armed group so once the peasants would rise we would join them and lead the rebellion."[151] He raised 500 rubles to buy about 20 revolvers.[152]

In the spring of 1876, with just their weapons, the members of the commune dressed as peasants and moved to Elizabethgrad, where they hoped to resurrect the spirit of Razin and Pugachev. They went from village to village to convince the peasants to rise up for their rights, but in vain. Kolenkina and Zasulich traveled together, and, anticipating the upcoming revolt, they practiced shooting with their weapons. After a fruitless few months, the conspirators regrouped at Elizabethgrad. Stefanovich decided to try a more deceptive approach and exploit the Myth of the Good Tsar. He had heard that peasants in Chigirin had believed in the myth and started a local insurrection in his name to seize land from local gentry, which was quickly put down by force. Stefanovich made contact with the remnant of the rebellion and told them that he would himself go to the tsar to find support. Stefanovich explained to Deich his plan to repeat the scenario of the insurrection. They commissioned another member of the commune to go to Switzerland to print an impressive-looking Secret Imperial Charter, ordering the peasants to organize an insurrection against the treasonous nobles and officials, then to seize and redistribute the land.[153]

At Elizabethgrad, a 20-year-old former pilgrim named Nicholas Gorinovich showed up and tried to join the commune. As he acted very strangely, the others assumed that he was a police spy. Deich and an accomplice, Victor Malinka, beat him to unconsciousness, poured acid on his face to render him unrecognizable, put a sign on him stating "This is the fate of all spies," and left him for dead.[154] This horrible crime, similar to Nechaev's, drew no criticism from the populists. They distinguished it from Nechaev's acting out for his own benefit to eliminate a rival and understood that these new disorganizational tactics protected the group. "These acts were at first called 'self-defense' or 'self-protective' in the south and 'disorganization of the state' in the north."[155]

By the fall of 1876, the Elizabethgrad commune split up. Zasulich went to hide with her sister Ekaterina. Frolenko returned to Odessa: "Activity among the peasants becomes impossible . . . We shall try in the cities. We are all armed. We decide on individual struggle against the government, armed resistance to arrest; we shall liquidate spies, traitors . . . officials."[156] In November, Stefanovich, Deich, and Ivan Bokhanovsky went to Chigirin as "emissaries of the Tsar," armed with the charter adorned with an impressive imperial stamp, and convinced initially suspicious peasants of its authenticity. They told the peasants to keep it secret, even from their priests, who were spies for the gentry, and to stay united. The peasants were to receive the land free, without compensation. Over almost a year, the three conspirators organized about 1,000 peasants in twelve districts. The insurrection was scheduled for October 1877, but it was discovered the month before and hundreds of peasants were thrown in jail. Stefanovich, Deich, and Bokhanovsky were arrested in September 1877 and transferred to the Kiev prison for trial.[157]

Zasulich and Kolenkina heard news about the failed uprising and the arrest of their friends. The women had mixed emotions. They were upset that their friends were imprisoned but also angry at them for excluding them from the Chigirin expedition. Zasulich borrowed money from her sister and sent it to Kiev to help fund possible escape attempts for their friends. However, she and Kolenkina discussed their sense of betrayal by their male comrades. Zasulich felt especially betrayed. She trusted Deich like no one else because she felt that he accepted her for what she was and they had become lovers. In fact, she had spent her last night with him talking, but Deich had not trusted her enough to share his plans with her. He had excluded them because he was "convinced they would have served no function that would have justified the enormous risks they would have to face."[158]

During the summer of 1876, Natanson gathered around him a new generation impatient for activity. One was 19-year-old George Plekhanov, born into the gentry, who came to St. Petersburg to attend university. After his disappointment with the pilgrimage, he had returned to the capital to proselytize among workers, who seemed more receptive. He identified the most gifted workers and trained them to organize their colleagues in their own language and according to their own priorities.[159] Another was 22-year-old Alexander Mikhailov from Kursk who had been passionate about politics since gymnasium. He was expelled from university for his involvement in student protests and went to Kiev, where he witnessed pointless disputes between idealistic students lacking revolutionary fire and Kiev commune illegals preaching action over theory. He was convinced that only a strong organization in the capital could eliminate these divisions.[160] He joined Natanson's organization in August 1876 and developed a crush on Natanson's wife. "I met for the first time a woman to whom I became deeply attached. This was the unforgettable Olga Natanson. But she loved her husband passionately, and I for myself liked and respected Mark . . . Hence my feelings for Olga never passed the bounds of closest friendship."[161] Instead, Mikhailov sublimated his emotion into absolute devotion to the organization.

Other new recruits included Osip Aptekman and Alexei Emelianov. Aptekman was born Jewish but got caught up in the religious atmosphere of the pilgrimage to the people and had converted to Orthodox Christianity.[162] He had survived the repression in Kharkov, where Natanson met him. Emelianov, better known to history under his alias Bogoliubov, was the son of a Cossack soldier. Too sensitive to follow in his father's footsteps, he came instead to the capital to organize workers after the disappointment of his pilgrimage to the people.

In the fall of 1876, Natanson named his organization Land and Liberty, in memory of the project of the previous decade. It aimed to "prepare the people for the struggle to obtain what the State has seized from it in past centuries . . . As history shows, the people has always lacked organization, unity, and the ability to carry on the struggle . . . The creation of such an opposition must be the essential aim of the Populists."[163] Its program was the transfer of all land to the peasants, the breakup of the Russian empire according to local desires and the transfer of all political functions to self-administered traditional communes. It recognized that only a violent revolution could bring about its demands. Its strategy was "(1) *Agitation*—to be carried out both by word and above all by deed—aimed at organizing the revolutionary forces and developing revolutionary feelings (revolts, strikes; in general, action is in itself the best way to organize revolutionary forces), (2) *The disorganization of the State.*"[164] The term *disorganization* was undefined and open to interpretation.

Plekhanov was making inroads into the working class in St. Petersburg, but Natanson wanted to increase the pace of propaganda by organizing a demonstration on the model of the March 1876 funeral. The project was also meant to invigorate militants who were quickly growing tired of theoretical argument: they needed to do something. The demonstration took place at Kazan Square on 6 December 1876. The turnout from the workers was disappointing; the crowd numbered about 200 to 300, mostly students and intellectuals.[165] Plekhanov gave a speech decrying the oppression of peasants, concluding with: "Death to the Tsar! Long live freedom!" A young boy holding a red banner with the Land and Liberty emblem was hoisted up.[166] The police dashed to break up the crowd, and local janitors and small shopkeepers rushed into the ensuing brawl to beat up those dressed up like nihilists. The police arrested 32 people, including Emelianov, but the organizers got away.[167]

The Great Trials of 1877

The great trials of 1877, designed to influence public opinion and prevent the intelligentsia from identifying with their populist children, took place in reverse chronological order with respect to the arrests. To better control the message, the government set up special political courts, with hand-picked judges, and limited potential sympathizers in the audience by requiring special passes. The regime edited the proceedings of the trials and published them in its own journal.[168]

The trial of the Kazan Square demonstrators, which became known as the Trial of the 21 (defendants), took place in late January 1877. Most had played a peripheral role but were still convicted. The sentences were especially harsh: three were sentenced to 15 years at hard labor; two were sentenced to 10 years at hard labor; and ten were sentenced to indefinite Siberian exile.[169] Emelianov was sentenced to a prison term. The severity of the punishments for teenagers for a street brawl that usually drew a fine or a few weeks' detention at most shocked the public and blew back against the government: far from driving a wedge between the intelligentsia and the revolutionaries, it made the public sympathize with them.

The Trial of the 21 was just a prelude. The Trial of the 50, which involved the Moscow Organization, opened in late February in Moscow. The defendants used a strategy suggested by Lavrov: since this kangaroo court would convict them no matter what, they should use it to profess their socialist faith and dramatize their martyrdom to inspire new recruits. "Your martyrdom is, perhaps, your final weapon."[170] The defendants put on a show. They shed their defiant and rebellious attitudes, softened their rhetoric, and eliminated any reference to anger and violence. They tossed away their nihilist clothes and dressed in fashionable and elegant attire. They appeared clean, well groomed, polite, respectable—and innocent. They were all under 30 and looked even younger. The pride and dignity of the defendants on the first day surprised and impressed the curious audience. Kravchinsky recalled, "Even those who could not but consider such men as enemies were bewildered at the sight of so much self-sacrifice. 'They are saints.' Such was the exclamation, repeated in a broken voice, by those who were present."[171] The women created a sensation: they were so young and pretty, and yet they were just as steadfast as the men.[172] Turgenev and two other prominent poets each dedicated a poem to them.[173] Mikhailov from St. Petersburg and Valerian Osinsky from Kiev came to have a look at "the 'Moscow Amazons,' who had grown up in baronial mansions, sampled all the charms of free intellectual work in the universities of Europe, and then, with such courageous simplicity, entered the filthy factories of Moscow as ordinary workers."[174] Osinsky, the 24-year-old son of a wealthy noble landowner from Rostov-on-the-Don, had studied engineering in the capital and been appointed secretary of the Rostov municipality in 1873. His comrades had dissuaded him from going on the pilgrimage because he could help them better from his position of authority. When his true loyalty was discovered, he moved to Kiev to become more politically active.[175]

The government case rested mainly on informants and subversive material discovered with the defendants. These prosecution witnesses did not project much credibility during their testimony: they were illiterate, could not identify the subversive documents, and were ignorant of the meanings of fancy words like revolution. They were easily discredited, and most retracted their incriminating statements. There was no evidence of any secret umbrella organization, and the prosecution could not substantiate its accusation that the Fritschis were "emissaries from abroad"—agents of Bakunin or Lavrov.[176]

On the other hand, the defendants presented themselves with good manners and decorum. They represented themselves and chose Sophia Bardina and Peter Alexeev to plead their defense. The two rehearsed their speeches for hours to make sure that they had the right tone, appealing to the public while condemning the regime. Of course, they stressed their complete dedication and self-sacrifice for justice. Alexeev, a worker from St. Petersburg, who had come to join the Moscow Organization, went first and described the worker's plight: no education, working 17 hours a day from the age of ten in filthy factories, too tired to learn or read, insufficient food, sleeping on the floor, and earning a pittance—no better than animals. Only the revolutionaries had tried to help them. "They alone will accompany us, unswervingly, until the muscular arm of the million working people is raised and the yoke of despotism, guarded by soldiers' bayonets, blows away like ashes!"[177] The presiding judge tried to interrupt several times, but Alexeev kept on with his strong voice. This was the first time that an ordinary worker's voice was heard in public, and it created a furor.

Bardina followed: "If the ideal society of which we dream could be brought into being without any violent revolution, we would be happy in the depths of our souls. I only think that in certain circumstances violent revolution is an inevitable evil."[178] She concluded, "Go on persecuting us, physical force is still on your side; but moral force and the force of historical progress is on ours; ours is the power of ideas, and ideas—you may regret it—cannot be impaled on the points of bayonets."[179]

Despite the defiance, the judges were moved by these charming young idealists, ready to suffer for the sake of their beliefs, and convicted only 15 defendants. Prince Tsitsianov and Alexeev were sentenced to 10 years at hard labor; Sophia Bardina and Olga Liubatovich were sentenced to 9 years at hard labor.[180] However, on appeal, all the sentences were reduced and converted to exile. The government strategy again had backfired. The speeches were published in the underground press, generating sympathy for the defendants and proselytizing their cause.

Meanwhile, Land and Liberty consolidated its central position in the socialist movement. It invited revolutionary leaders in other parts of the country to join its organization: Osinsky in Kiev, Frolenko in Odessa, Alexander Barannikov in Astrakhan, and Alexander Kviatkovsky in Nizhny Novgorod. Barannikov, a 19-year-old from the Kursk gentry, had been a cadet but left the military the previous year to become a revolutionary. Kviatkovsky, a 24-year-old from the Tomsk gentry, had been arrested in 1874 for possession of banned books and went underground when he was provisionally released.

Building on its network of militants around the country, Land and Liberty led a second movement to the countryside by establishing six or seven settlements of about ten members each, in the lands of Razin and Pugachev, under guidance of its central group in St. Petersburg. This second pilgrimage to the people was different from the previous one in that the new pilgrims avoided flying propaganda and hoped to influence peasants through long interactions with them by living in stationary communes and providing needed skills to them as teachers, physician assistants, or midwives. The Natanson couple, Plekhanov, and Mikhailov went to Saratov; Barannikov to Astrakhan; and Kviatkovsky to Nizhny Novgorod.[181] During a brief return to the capital,

Natanson was arrested in early June 1877 by the police, who were still looking for the organizers of the Kazan Square demonstration. A worker had denounced him, but he paid for his treachery when two disorganization section members murdered him in July 1877.[182] The two went on to murder another police informant three months later.[183] Severe punishment of in-group traitors—the black sheep phenomenon—is often how political protest groups cross the threshold of fatal violence. Natanson was administratively exiled, but this time, his wife Olga stayed behind to help run the organization.[184]

Though not formally part of Land and Liberty, Vera Figner and Alexander Soloviev went to the Samara settlement in August 1877. Soloviev, the 31-year-old son of a government official, had resigned his teaching post three years earlier to become a populist. Figner had qualified as a physician assistant and took care of twelve villages. She felt overwhelmed, lonely, and helpless, unprepared for the "abyss of poverty and grief" she saw. "One could not look with equanimity at the filthy and emaciated patients. Most of their ailments were of a long standing . . . endless sores and wounds, and all this under conditions of such unimaginable filth of dwelling and clothes, of such unhealthful and insufficient food, that one asked oneself in stupor: was that the life of animals or human beings? Tears often flowed in a stream from my eyes as I prepared medicine for these unfortunates." She felt desperate at the futility of her efforts and unable to talk to them. "Would it not be irony to speak of resistance, of struggle, to people completely crushed by their physical privations? For three months, day after day, I saw the same picture . . . These three months were a terrible experience for me, confined to the material side of the people's life. I had hardly a chance to look into their souls; my mouth could not open for propaganda."[185] The government discovered and cracked down on this smaller second pilgrimage.

By summer 1877, the government was getting ready to try the remaining imprisoned populists. It recalled people out on bail and transferred them to the House of Preliminary Detention in St. Petersburg. On 13 July, St. Petersburg Governor-General Fyodor Trepov came for a surprise inspection. Trepov was stunned at the lax discipline. Regulations prohibited defendants in pretrial detention from communicating with each other, but prisoners were walking around the courtyard in groups, and others leaned out of windows conversing with one another. Enraged, Trepov picked one prisoner at random and shouted at him: "How dare you stand in front of me with your hat on?" This was Emelianov/Bogoliubov, who was still there after his conviction awaiting transfer to another prison. Before Emelianov could explain that the communication ban did not apply to him because he had already been tried and convicted, Trepov knocked the cap from his head, screaming, "Hat off!" Other prisoners thought that Trepov had slapped Emelianov in the face and started screaming, "Butcher! Bastard! Get out of here, you wretch!" Surprised by the defiance, Trepov then ordered that "Bogoliubov" be taken away and flogged that afternoon. Prisoners started to destroy whatever they could.[186] The flogging that took place was a grave breach of protocol. The uprising continued, and more than 100 policemen had to be called the next day to put it down.

Corporal punishment had a long and humiliating history in Russia. In 1863, Alexander II abolished all forms of corporal punishment in Russia, except for soldiers and sailors. Overnight, corporal punishment completely disappeared, and by the time Trepov ordered it for Emelianov, it was deemed utterly unacceptable and an insult to a person's dignity. This physical and symbolic aggression was shocking and personally felt by all the populists, in or out of prison. Its news quickly spread outside: "One had to see the fury on everyone's face, hear their expressions of indignation and anger, and hear their oaths to stand up for the honor and human dignity, so horribly desecrated in the case of Bogoliubov."[187] The flogging was interpreted as a deliberate aggression against all revolutionaries, who identified with Emelianov, and demanded a response. To many, this was the last straw; violence now needed to be answered with violence. In view of the upcoming Trial of the 193, Land and Liberty put out the word not to do anything that could prejudice the judges against the defendants. The response to the in-group moral outrage would have to wait until after the verdict.

The assembly of all the defendants in the Trial of the 193 consolidated their esprit de corps. Up to that point they had been physically isolated from each other in the countryside and later in separate prisons, but now they were able to communicate with each other, through talks during walks in the courtyard, shouting from their cells, tapping messages on walls, receiving visits not only from relatives but also from fellow revolutionaries in disguise.[188] Those who could not communicate in prison did so in the courtroom. They discovered they had much in common, especially in terms of their opposition to the government and a shared fate. They felt outraged at the unfair repression. They established strong personal bonds with new comrades. As with Babeuf's conspirators, bringing them together allowed them to communicate and negotiate a common shared social identity. Their previously imagined community now felt all too real. The Trial of 193 started in October 1877 and was held in camera, with only a few selected members of the public allowed to attend,[189] a compromise designed to prevent another revolutionary propaganda victory and still maintain a semblance of legitimacy for public opinion. However, the public had heard about the deliberate humiliation to a member of the intelligentsia by General Trepov and was sympathetic to the young militants about to go to trial. In a wider context, the trial started as the Russian public was trying to digest the news of a disaster during the siege of Plevna during the

Russo-Turkish War, resulting in about 20,000 Russian fatalities, which was seen as more evidence of the government's incompetence.

The prosecutor again tried to show that the pilgrimage campaign had been the result of a coordinated large-scale conspiracy, directed from abroad, but lacked evidence of any overall glue linking individual acts together. He had issued a very long indictment just days before the opening of the trial so as not to allow the defendants, with their diverse interests, enough time to present a common defense. The trial opened in complete chaos, as all 193 were assembled and led to the courtroom. Many friends who had not seen each other for years greeted each other in delight and started catching up on news. They continued to talk in the courtroom and paid no attention to the proceedings. They noticed the absence of the public in the galleries, protested that this violated their right to a public trial, and refused to recognize the court and participate in the sham. Pandemonium broke out, and the judge cleared the court. The next day, when the judge declared he would divide the proceedings into 17 smaller trials, the defendants again protested and hurled insults at the prosecutor and judge, who again cleared the court. About 150 defendants boycotted the proceeding. The court dragged some into the courtroom to testify, but the spectacle became so odious that the judge allowed them to stay away.[190] This situation divided the defendants into a hard-core group that protested the legitimacy of the proceedings and refused to cooperate, and a more compliant group that tried to influence their potential sentences through cooperation.

During the trial, on 7 December 1877, an explosion in a gunpowder factory killed six workers and injured scores more. The negligence of the factory owner angered the workers, but the police effort to break up the large funeral outraged them even more, and made them more receptive to Land and Liberty's message. Out of this crisis emerged a remarkable worker, 19-year-old Stephan Khalturin, who had left school to find work and eventually drifted to St. Petersburg, where he found work at a factory. A born leader and talented organizer, he encountered Land and Liberty at the funeral and became the bridge between it and the workers.[191]

The trial proceeded with the prosecution presenting its weak case to a relatively empty room. The defendants secretly decided to have one of them, Ipolit Myshkin, present their defense in a speech. Myshkin was the 29-year-old son of a simple soldier and became a legal shorthand reporter. He had joined the populists and started a small press for the Moscow Tchaikovsky circle in 1873. Two years later, he tried to rescue Chernyshevsky from Siberia, but was caught and resisted arrest by firing at two Cossacks.[192] When his turn came, he surprised the judges with his willingness to address the court. He forecast an inevitable revolution, and when they realized it was just propaganda and tried to interrupt him, Myshkin refused and finished in defiance of the judges.[193] Sheriffs rushed the witness stand to interrupt him, but his fellow defendants blocked them, resulting in a brawl. Gendarmes from the outside stormed the court and dragged Myshkin away. The speech gained wide circulation in the public and inspired defense attorneys to aggressively discredit the government's claim of a vast conspiracy and protest the multiple examples of police and prison brutality, made more credible by Trepov's well-known gesture.

In the end, the judges rejected the prosecution's claims but convicted defendants who had clearly engaged in serious revolutionary activities or violently resisted arrests. On 23 January 1878, they convicted 103 defendants and acquitted 90. Of those convicted, 61 were sentenced to time served or house arrest. Five people, Myshkin and remnants of the original Tchaikovsky circle, were sentenced to ten years at hard labor; ten were sentenced to nine years at hard labor; three were sentenced to five years; and all of these sentences were followed by banishment to Siberia. In addition to these lenient sentences, 151 defendants were immediately released, bringing an atmosphere of joy and celebration among revolutionary circles in the capital.[194]

Among the released were Perovskaya, Zhelyabov, Lev Tikhomirov, Anna Yakimova, and Nikolai Morozov. After her prominent father paid her bail, Perovskaya had spent her time at her family estate in Crimea under strict police surveillance, volunteering as a nurse at a Simferopol hospital. She returned to the capital for the trial.[195] She grew fond of Tikhomirov, a 25-year-old former member of the Tchaikovsky circle who had been arrested in 1873. Yakimova was the 22-year-old daughter of a priest arrested for subversive activities at a teacher's training school. Nikolai Morozov, the 23-year-old son of a wealthy landowner descendant of Peter I and a serf, had joined the Moscow Tchaikovsky circle in early 1874. He was particularly taken with the daring exploits of Kravchinsky, with whom he shared the romantic notion that history was made by a few great men. After two short failed pilgrimages, he was tasked to go abroad and start a journal intended solely for workers. He went to Switzerland in late 1874, where he met with Tkachev, who had escaped from his exile. He read extensively during his stay abroad and became fascinated with Friedrich von Schiller's *William Tell*.[196] He shared with both Tkachev and Kravchinsky the same elitist concept of a revolutionary and became a convert to the necessity of Jacobinism, the takeover of the state by a group of dedicated revolutionaries to change society. He worked on his newspaper with Grigory Goldenberg, the 19-year-old son of a Jewish merchant near Kiev, who shared their perspective that history was made by great men. Morozov returned to Russia in the spring of 1875 but was arrested at the border.[197]

Both the defense and prosecution appealed these sentences to the tsar.

The Legitimation of Zasulich's *Podvig*

The day after the verdicts were announced, Vera Zasulich shot General Trepov. There had been several separate plots to avenge Emelianov and kill Trepov. Osinsky and Frolenko had come up from the south and rented an apartment across the street from Trepov's office to spy on his movements.[198] Zasulich had read about the Bogoliubov affair in a newspaper while she was resting in Penza and was still smarting from her rejection in the Chigirin affair. She got in touch with her friend Kolenkina, and they decided to prove that they could be as aggressive as their male comrades in avenging Trepov's insult. They returned to St. Petersburg to show that they fully belonged to the in-group of revolutionaries. In the capital, the two friends rented an apartment with two other women, and it quickly became a meeting place for local revolutionaries.[199]

The women soon learned about the men's plot and decided not only to beat them to the punch but trump them by also assassinating the prosecutor at the Trial of 193. They threw dice: Zasulich got Trepov, and Kolenkina the prosecutor.[200] "We decided to turn to terror, and our decision, once made, was irrevocable."[201] To beat their competition, they determined to carry out their plan at the earliest possible moment. Their plan was simplicity itself and took advantage of the very fact that they were women. They would dress up, assume the identity of petitioners, meet both officials, and shoot them at the same time. Neither woman made a plan of escape: like Karakozov, they wanted to be caught and become heroes for the cause, an inspiration for their comrades and potential recruits.[202]

Early on the morning of 24 January 1878, Vera Zasulich went to Trepov's office hours. When she came face to face with him, she pulled out a pistol, shot him twice, dropped the weapon, and waited.[203] She was immediately beaten by the staff and arrested. When asked why she had shot Trepov, she simply replied, "For Bogoliubov."[204] Kolenkina went to the prosecutor's home, but he was not there. She returned home, inconsolable that she had not been able to share her best friend's fate.[205]

The news of the assassination attempt spread quickly throughout the radical community, Russia, and the world. The novelty of a young woman's apparently unprovoked attack against a high official piqued the public's curiosity. For her comrades, the news of her gesture was at first eclipsed by their celebration of the release of their friends from prison. Many, including Figner, had converged from all over Russia on St. Petersburg for the verdict. "People thronged their apartments from morning to night. It was an uninterrupted session of a revolutionary club, where ninety to a hundred visitors attended in a day; friends brought with them strangers who wished to shake hands with those whom they looked upon as buried alive."[206] New bonds were established:

Figner first met Perovskaya, who also first met Zhelyabov. However, the celebrations were short lived. On advice of Third Section chief General Mezentsev, the tsar, very upset at the leniency of the verdicts, annulled the verdicts and issued an order to administratively exile the newly released prisoners to Siberia. About 40 of them went underground, most with the help of Land and Liberty, and quickly rose to prominent positions in the organization.[207] Hunted by the police, the remaining Land and Liberty members also went underground, isolating themselves from the rest of the world. They lived hidden in the apartments of trusted colleagues, rarely coming out. They interacted only with other illegal members, who shared their views, narrowing their cognitive horizons.[208]

The revolutionaries believed that they would never again get the sort of leniency granted in the verdicts of the Trial of the 193. This increased their resolve not to be arrested without a fight. "The watchword of the revolutionists became 'self-defense:' self-defense against the spies who introduced themselves into the circles under the mask of friendship and denounced members right and left, simply because they would not be paid if they did not accuse large numbers of persons; self-defense against those who ill-treated prisoners; self-defense against the omnipotent chiefs of the state police."[209]

Violent resistance to arrest came within a week in Odessa. Ivan Kovalsky had been arrested in 1874 for going to the people and released on bail. Influenced by Tkachev's Jacobinism, he formed his own group with a small printing press in 1877. Inspired by the execution of a local bandit, the group circulated a manifesto raising the following question: if execution was the punishment for someone who had killed for robbery, what should be the punishment for those who robbed and oppressed the people? On 30 January 1878, a strong contingent of police raided their refuge. Kovalsky kept the police at bay by shooting at them while his comrades burned compromising papers. When his gun jammed, he attacked them with a knife and wounded an officer. Finally, the police overwhelmed and arrested the group.[210] Valerian Osinsky, frustrated at having been denied the fame of assassinating Trepov, discussed with Mikhailov, a fellow member of Land and Liberty's disorganization section, a possible expansion of their section's activities. He suggested an escalation from simple self-defense to more offensive actions emulating Zasulich's feat, such as the elimination of high government officials who had been particularly cruel to their imprisoned comrades. Mikhailov was not sure how the organization would react, and the two friends decided that Osinsky should test the waters in the south, which was generally more violent than the north.

Before carrying out this campaign of violence, Osinsky stopped in his hometown of Rostov-on-the-Don to get rid of a well-known police informant,

Akim Nikonov. Two of his comrades carried out the assassination on 1 February and posted the following warning around the town: "Last year Nikonov betrayed to the authorities some thirty of his and our comrades. We regard murder as a terrible counter-measure. But the Administration in its oppression of the Russian People is attacking us, the People's defenders, as if we were wild beasts. Thousands of our martyrs lie dying in prison through the treachery of spies. We are now determined to defend ourselves. Those who follow the example of Nikonov will share his fate. The Administration has left us no choice."[211] The posters bore an oval stamp, in the center of which were superimposed a crossed axe, revolver, and dagger, and around which were the words "Executive Committee of the Social Revolutionary Party."

This fictitious "Executive Committee" was composed only of Osinsky, Frolenko, and their small group in Kiev. They decided to inaugurate their new strategy by carrying out an attentat on the prosecutor in charge of the cases of the Chigirin conspirators. Deich and Stefanovich were in contact with Osinsky from prison and tried to dissuade him, but Osinsky persisted. On 23 February, backed by two comrades, he ambushed the prosecutor, shot him six times at point-blank range, left him for dead, and ran away. He later found out that the prosecutor was not even wounded; his thick fur coat had stopped the bullets.[212]

At the same time, Osinsky was organizing an escape of his imprisoned friends, and Frolenko got a job as a prison guard. At the prison, Deich had befriended Kibalchich, who was still waiting for his trial. Deich became very excited when he found out that Kibalchich had studied explosives and told him about the planned escape attempt. Kibalchich and Osinsky had also been classmates in the capital. Deich talked about Kibalchich to Frolenko, who found out that Kibalchich was eligible for bail and suggested that they simply free him on bail, as money was not a problem.[213] Osinsky was very close to Dmitri Lizogub, a 28-year-old wealthy noble landowner who had grown up in France and become a populist at St. Petersburg University in the early 1870s. He had pledged his entire fortune to Land and Liberty and started the liquidation of his lands to get cash.[214] He put up the 500 rubles for bail, but the money had to come from a family member or someone that could vouch for the prisoner. Frolenko suggested that Kibalchich marry one of his former girlfriends, who would then put up the bail money. The authorities refused permission for Kibalchich to marry and instead transferred him to the capital in early March for his trial.[215]

In St. Petersburg, the Ministry of Justice decided to try Zasulich in a civilian rather than a political court. Conscious of its failure at the large political trials and the unpopularity of General Trepov, the government believed that Zasulich would be convicted in a simple attempted murder trial, with no political connotation. The trial on 31 March 1878 shaped up as the entertainment event of the year. Tickets were snatched up weeks in advance, and the size of the crowd gathered in front of the courtroom was unprecedented. Ladies came dressed in elegant gowns, the men in tailcoats and black ties.

The prosecutor presented the facts of the murder attempts simply, without going into any details about the backgrounds of Trepov and Zasulich. Trepov refused to come to testify on his own behalf. The public knew very little about Zasulich's background, which allowed her lawyer, Peter Alexandrov, to stage-manage the trial in favor of his client. As a true nihilist, Zasulich had an unkempt appearance and never combed her hair. Alexandrov dressed her up in a black silk dress and had her hair parted in the middle, with two long braids hanging down her back, imitating the image of a saint. In the courtroom, she sat up straight and looked at the floor in apparent humility. Alexandrov begged her not to mention her past or political beliefs and to simply say that her lawyer would tell it to the court. When she took the stand, she explained in a hushed voice that when she learned of the beating of "Bogoliubov," she remembered from her experience the punishment dished out to other prisoners.[216] "I waited for some response, but everyone remained silent. There was nothing to stop Trepov, or someone just as powerful as he, from repeating the same violence over and over. I resolved at that point, even if it cost my life, to prove that no one who abused a human being that way could be sure of getting away with it. I couldn't find another way of drawing attention to what had happened. I saw no other way. . . . It's terrible to have to lift a hand against another person, but I felt that it had to be done."[217]

This theatrical and self-sacrificing testimony set up Alexandrov's closing statement, which shifted the focus and put Trepov on trial instead of his client. He painted a portrait of his client as a saintly person who had sacrificed herself for someone she did not know for the sake of higher principles. The general hostility to Trepov, whose career was defined by brutality and cruelty, played into his hand. He gave a fictitious description of Zasulich's life: a happy childhood, meeting Nechaev at the age of 17, the wasting of her best years in prison, and "a selfless love for everyone who, like herself, was forced to drag out the miserable existence of a political suspect." He stressed she had never known or seen Bogoliubov. He was simply a political prisoner to her. "A political prisoner meant for Zasulich her own self, her bitter past, her own story, the story of irretrievably ruined years, the best and dearest in the life of every man who is not afflicted by a fate similar to that of Zasulich." When no one stood up for his insulted honor, his client realized she had to. "'If I commit a crime,' Zasulich thought, 'the silenced question about Bogoliubov's punishment will arise; my crime will provoke a public trial, and Russia, in the person of her people's representatives, the jury, will be compelled to pronounce a verdict not on me alone . . . in the sight of Europe, this Europe which likes to call us a barbarian state, in which the attribute of the government is a knout.'" He stressed that she had no personal interest in her crime, concluding, "Indeed, she may leave this court condemned, but not disgraced."[218] Applause from the audience interrupted Alexandrov several times. The jury did not deliberate very long and declared Zasulich not guilty—to a standing ovation from the public, jurors, and even judges.[219]

Zasulich was released from the House of Preliminary Detention that evening at the insistence of a crowd that had gathered there to cheer her on. Despite the legitimacy of the verdict and the approval of the crowd, the tsar's unhappiness with the soft handling of the revolutionaries led him to fire his Minister of Justice and issue a warrant to detain Zasulich. She immediately went into hiding, frustrating the intense police search for her. She hid at various apartments and was visited by revolutionary admirers. Kravchinsky rushed back from Switzerland to meet her. "Zassulic was not a terrorist. She was the angel of vengeance, and not of terror. She was a victim who voluntarily threw herself into the jaws of the monster in order to cleanse the honor of the party from a mortal outrage . . . Yet this occurrence gave to the Terrorism a most powerful impulse. It illuminated it with its divine aureole, and gave to it the sanction of sacrifice and of public opinion."[220] Finally, she was smuggled out to Switzerland in late May 1878.

As previously mentioned, many historians trace modern terrorism back to Zasulich's heroic deed (*podvig* in Russian).[221] But it was preceded by almost a century of attentats in France alone and the assassination of a half dozen spies in Russia. Although her podvig was the first instance of a campaign of offensive attentats in Russia, its unique feature was its legitimation through her trial's verdict. The reception of this verdict in the court of popular opinion in Russia and western Europe indicated that it was legitimate, and perhaps necessary, to resort to violence to fight against the state in some circumstances. Alexandrov's fictitious portrait of Zasulich transformed her into the prototype of the selfless and virtuous assassin legitimizing and inspiring political activists disillusioned with peaceful protest to follow her lead.

Zasulich had not known the victim of Trepov's barbarity, but the fact that he was a fellow in-group member was enough for her to feel outraged by the state aggression against him and want to seek revenge for him. Now the state took the gloves off and threatened even greater persecution against the group, ignoring the restraints of its own laws. The emerging stories of police and prison brutality showed that social revolutionaries could no longer expect to receive the genteel treatment accorded to children of the elite. Indeed, revolutionaries felt a much stronger and violent threat from the new aggressiveness of state agents. This convinced all to take defensive action against these agents and some to take the initiative to punish some of the most odious agents.

The public legitimation of Zasulich's podvig cannot be underestimated in the Russian turn to political violence. But Zasulich knew the truth and had just wanted to become a martyr for the group. When she unexpectedly failed, she became depressed and later resisted any attempt by her friends or the international community to celebrate her act. She became a strong opponent of political violence in general. She was always distressed at the news of an assassination attempt, feeling a large degree of responsibility with her precedent.[222]

Nevertheless, her podvig became a source of inspiration for others.[223] Podvig based on revenge rather than a strategy of fomenting terror in the population or change/overthrow of the government is what drove the early Russian terrorists, and those who championed such tactics now called themselves terrorists, adopting the name of Robespierre's followers.

Debates over Terrorist Violence

Zasulich's podvig opened the floodgate for a series of domestic and international copycats. Within months of the verdict, four attentats on crowned heads of state took place. Emil Hödel and Karl Nobiling fired shots at Kaiser Wilhelm I on 11 May and 2 June, respectively.[224] Although both said they were inspired by Orsini, their timing points to some influence by Zasulich. Juan Oliva Moncusi fired at King Alfonso XII of Spain on 25 October[225] and Giovanni Passannante tried to stab King Umberto I of Italy on 17 November 1878.[226] Only Nobiling was able to hit his target, severely wounding the kaiser.

With these four attempts in quick succession, most of the governments in Europe assumed that there was a worldwide conspiracy guiding these assassination attempts. They lay the blame on the Jura Federation and the IWA. Swiss authorities expelled prominent foreign anarchist leaders and closed down their newspaper. This opened the door for relatively unknown Peter Kropotkin to rise to prominence as he started publishing *Le Révolté* to succeed the banned newspapers. Kropotkin claimed all his life that this worldwide conspiracy was groundless.[227] The historical evidence supports him.

In Russia, revolutionaries endured escalating government repression. "What government was this, which acted so insolently against all the laws of the country? . . . Against such a government everything is permitted. It is no longer a guardian of the will of the people, or of the majority of the people. It is organized injustice. A citizen is no more bound to respect it, than to respect a band of highwaymen . . . Thus arose the Terrorism. Conceived in hatred, nurtured by patriotism and by hope, it grew up in the electrical atmosphere, impregnated with the enthusiasm awakened by an act of heroism."[228]

Osinsky's group in Kiev continued its campaign of assassination of cruel

government officials, who were moved by fear to improve the prison conditions of the Chigirin conspirators.[229] Its next target was the Kiev chief of police, Baron Heiking, whose efficient team was eradicating local revolutionary
networks. Since he had not been particularly cruel, when Deich and Stefanovich learned about it, they strongly protested. Nevertheless, Osinsky convinced a reluctant comrade to carry out the execution. On 24 May, he killed
Heiking, and during his getaway killed one policeman and seriously wounded
another.[230] The finality of the murder woke up some of the conspirators to the
grim reality of what they were doing. "It made it clear to me that I myself was
no use for terrorist work. It was odd. I had, naturally, never imagined that a
revolution would be bloodless—on the contrary I had always thought that
streams of blood would flow. But the whole streams of bloodshed in a popular
rising did not seem to me nearly as terrible as the few stains I saw on the pave-
ment the next day."[231] Heiking's deputy, George Sudeikin, replaced his less effective boss and would eventually bring the downfall of the terrorists.

Osinsky and Frolenko succeeded in freeing the imprisoned Chigirin conspirators. Frolenko smuggled in some soldiers' uniforms for Stefanovich,
Deich, and Bokhanovsky, and in the early morning of 27 May, they all walked
out together through the front gate and vanished.[232] Ironically, the liberation
of Stefanovich and Deich tipped the scales against Osinsky within the group,
as they added their voices to the opponents of assassination within his group.
"Such actions only compromise the revolutionaries and do not frighten anybody."[233] Heiking's assassination was the last one carried out by Osinsky and
his group.[234]

The increasing efficacy of the repression was taking a toll on Land and
Liberty. Out-group state aggression had a transformative effect on some in-
group revolutionaries. "The views of Alexander Mikhailov underwent
change . . . The mood for war overtook even those who used to stand to the
side of the revolutionary movement. Mikhailov, as a member of the central
group, constantly participated in activities that the group planned and executed. These acts of war, no doubt, transformed him, while the possibility of
continuing the work 'in the people' faded and grew distant."[235] He now believed that the need for self-protection required a more centralized and disciplined organizational structure. In May 1878, Land and Liberty published its
program. Its introduction admitted a preference for anarchism, but the security situation forced it to adopt a hierarchical structure. It proclaimed itself to
be an organization of "men closely united to each other . . . [ready to give] all
their forces, means, bonds, sympathies and dislikes, and indeed their very
lives" to the organization. This "fundamental circle" became in effect a party of
clandestine full-time revolutionaries, whose strong sense of secrecy and responsibility was made necessary by state repression.[236] Admission to the group

required a rigid appraisal of the candidate's personality and background, guaranteed by five members and agreement by two-thirds of the fundamental group. Private property was pooled in common. Its constituent local groups enjoyed autonomy in their local and internal affairs, but were obligated to follow the overall program and to collaborate in the activities of the umbrella organization. An administration consisting of three to five individuals elected by a two-thirds majority was indefinitely set up to coordinate all activities.[237] The organization's major function was to recruit people with "religious-revolutionary natures . . . hostile to the state," lead peasant groups, connect with groups of workers, and establish relations with liberals so as to exploit them. Its minor function was to disorganize the forces of the state, which involved recruitment of army officers and government employees to interfere with the state's fight against the revolutionaries, and the systematic annihilation of the most dangerous and important government elements.[238] Mikhailov became the head of the disorganization section and earned the nickname of *dvornik*, meaning doorman or gatekeeper in the sense of maintaining and protecting a building. Only he knew the complete organizational chart of Land and Liberty and kept it memorized, not daring to commit anything to paper.

This function of disorganization was open to interpretation. Plekhanov interpreted it narrowly as defensive violence against state aggression, while romantics like Osinsky, Kravchinsky, and Morozov saw it as permission to carry out their fantasies of revolution. Kravchinsky had been mesmerized by Zasulich's attempt on Trepov and dreamed of a series of assassinations of the worst government officials without any attempt to escape to achieve fame and glory, followed by pamphlets explaining the reasons for the executions. He believed that the public would love them as they had loved her podvig. He saw this new tactic of terrorism as a noble, beautiful sacrifice for the people's sake and volunteered to inaugurate it on General Mezentsev, who had prevailed on the tsar to annul the acquittals of the Trial of the 193. "If time were consumed in killing a vile spy, why allow the gendarme to live on with impunity who sent him forth, or the procurator who from the information of the spy obtained materials for ordering the arrest, or the head of the police who directed everything? The logic of life could not but compel the Revolutionaries to mount these steps by degrees, and it cannot be doubted that they would have done so, for the Russian may be wanting in many things, but not in the courage to be logical."[239] He announced to his shocked friends that he would go to General Mezentsev's reception room, kill him, and wait to be arrested. Deich insisted on a more detailed plan of action. Kravchinsky suggested killing Mezentsev in a duel, but his friends dissuaded him by arguing that he was far too valuable to the movement to sacrifice himself so needlessly. With the help of Mikhailov and Barannikov, a former cadet like himself, he came up with a more suitable plan.[240]

Whatever qualms Land and Liberty had in carrying out their assassinations were settled by the execution of Ivan Kovalsky. The death penalty had been abolished in Russia for common criminals and only attempts on the tsar, high treason, were punishable by death. Resisting arrest was simply defined as criminal in a civilian court. So, the government tried Kovalsky under martial law (distinguishing political from common crime) in a *military* court, which condemned him to death. There was a large mass protest in the streets of Odessa on his behalf, prompting the authorities to open fire, killing two people. His comrades tried several times to free him, but in vain; he was executed on 2 August 1878. This first execution of a revolutionary for simply resisting arrest[241] deeply shocked the revolutionaries. Two days later, on 4 August, elegantly dressed Kravchinsky and Barannikov walked up to Mezentsev, taking his usual stroll with an aide. Kravchinsky pulled out a dagger and plunged it into Mezentsev. His aide tried to grab Kravchinsky, but Barannikov shot him. The two assassins then jumped into a waiting cabriolet, and the racehorse Barbarian once again galloped them to safety.[242]

A few days later, Kravchinsky published a short pamphlet, *A Death for a Death,* explaining his action. The rationale was *lex talionis,* the retaliation of an eye for an eye. Killing was deplorable, but revolutionaries were dying a slow, tortured death in prison or exile, and the time had come for them to fight back. It adopted the government's new definition of criminal acts carried out by revolutionaries as political and announced that every persecution and especially execution of a revolutionary would now be met with a terrorist act.[243]

The tsar was personally moved by the murder of his confidant Mezentsev. He immediately replaced him with General Alexander Drenteln and issued an edict transferring the jurisdiction of all political crimes to military courts with their curtailed rules of evidence, confirming the death penalty as a possible punishment, and urging the execution of the verdicts without delay. It stated that "the patience of the government is now exhausted"[244] and attributed the series of assassinations to "a circle of criminal conspirators [who] reject any social order, private property, the sanctity of marriage vows, and even faith in God."[245] It also appealed to the Russian public for help in countering them.[246]

While the public did not react with the enthusiasm Kravchinsky expected, the revolutionaries celebrated. They gathered at Sofia Leshern's place, where Olga Liubatovich had just arrived and was hiding after her escape from Siberia by faking her suicide by drowning. Osinsky entertained them with the story of the escape of the Chigirin conspirators, and Kravchinsky, while not confessing his role, described the assassination of Mezentsev earlier that day.[247] A few days later, Kravchinsky returned with Morozov, who fell in love with Liubatovich. Terrorism resonated with Morozov's romanticism about great men like William Tell making history. "He became an apostle of terror; the ideal he preached was of an equal duel between the forces of revolution and the state. This rich fantasy created rather fantastic plans for this struggle, plans limited on occasion by poetic inventions."[248] A week later, Kolenkina came and, during that visit, Perovskaya showed up. After the Trial of the 193, she had gone to Kharkov and tried in vain to organize the escape of Myshkin. She was arrested during a visit to her mother and administratively exiled, but during her transit, her two police escorts fell asleep and she escaped.[249] The news of Perovskaya's escape was of course another reason for celebration. Kravchinsky came and read a pamphlet written by the Kharkov prisoners documenting their humiliations and atrocities in the "House of Horrors." Perovskaya immediately wanted to return to Kharkov, but she lacked false identification. Her friends prevailed on her to wait until she was better prepared. Instead, Kravchinsky showed his disregard for the authorities by taking the young women out for walks in full daytime, and even took them to the opera.[250]

The tsar issued another edict prohibiting people who had been convicted of political crimes from residing in the capital. This drove some of them, like Kibalchich, who had just been released on 7 June, to go underground. He resumed his studies of explosives. "Foreseeing that the party in its terrorist struggle would want to apply such substances as dynamite, I decided to study the preparation and use of explosives. With this goal in mind I . . . occupied myself with practical chemistry, reading all the literature on explosive substances I could obtain. After this I began amassing in my room a sizeable amount of the chemical precursors, setting about to prove that I could, on my own and with substances ordinarily available to me, produce nitroglycerine and dynamite."[251] Friends introduced him to Kviatkovsky, whose disappointment with his experience of the second pilgrimage had convinced him of the necessity for more violent protest against the tsar. Kviatkovsky became a close friend and ally of Mikhailov.[252]

Tsarist repression continued. In August, the financier of the organization, Dmitri Lizogub, was arrested in Kiev. He anticipated a long detention and turned over control of his assets to an old friend, Vladimir Drigo, to fund Osinsky's operations.[253] In October, a series of mass arrests struck Land and Liberty, netting Olga Natanson and Kolenkina. Kolenkina put up resistance and shot at the police, but was still apprehended. Mikhailov barely escaped the sweep and rebuilt the organization on a more secure basis. He invited freed revolutionaries to join the fundamental circle and set up a system of strict compartmentalization and a network of hiding places in St. Petersburg. He also eliminated flamboyant displays of gallantry that put people in danger. Many people left St. Petersburg, which was becoming dangerous: Liubatovich, Deich, Stefanovich, and Kravchinsky left for Switzerland, and Perovskaya for Kharkov.

Land and Liberty acquired a printing press thanks to Aaron Zundelevich, the 23-year-old son of a Jewish merchant. He had become a populist around 1875 and fled to Switzerland to avoid arrest. There he befriended Kravchinsky, with whom he secretly returned to the capital to express admiration for Zasulich. With his Jewish connections, Zundelevich was able to smuggle anything within Russia and from outside. With the press, the organization published its first newsletter, *Land and Liberty*, in November 1878. Mikhailov recognized its propaganda value: "The important thing is that some clandestine review should come out. The police looks for it and is unable to find it—that's what strikes the public. It's of no importance what's written inside. I think that the ideal review would be one which had nothing at all printed in it. But unfortunately that's not possible."[254]

The same month, Nikolai Kletochnikov, a 31-year-old minor bank official, came to St. Petersburg. "Up till the age of thirty I lived in the provinces and consorted with other officials. We spent our time drinking and running after women . . . I wished for something better. So I came to Petersburg. But the general moral standard in Petersburg seemed no higher."[255] He asked around to meet revolutionaries, and someone introduced him to Mikhailov, who decided to test him. He asked Kletochnikov to check on possible police connections of a woman renting apartments where aspiring revolutionaries invariably were arrested. Kletochnikov rented a room from her, and she grew to like him. When he hinted he had to leave to find a job, she told him she could help him find one. A secret police officer friend came, interviewed him, and offered him a job for one month as an outside agent. At the end of the trial period, Kletochnikov had made a good impression, and the Third Section offered him a position as a confidential clerk. He immediately showed his worth to the revolutionaries.

The fall of 1878 had seen a renewal of student unrest across the country, especially in St. Petersburg, Kiev, and Kharkov. The government immediately put them down with great brutality. Hundreds of students were beaten, flogged, arrested, and deported. At the same time, Land and Liberty, especially through Plekhanov and Michael Popov, helped to organize workers of St. Petersburg. There were an unprecedented 26 labor strikes between 1877 and 1879 to protest against poor working conditions. In December 1878, the Northern Union of Russian Workers was formally established, with Khalturin as one of its leaders, but it was short-lived as police spies infiltrated it and betrayed most of its leaders, who were arrested. Kletochnikov warned Mikhailov about an upcoming police raid on the union and identified its spy, Nikolai Reinstein. Mikhailov alerted Khalturin, who went underground. Mikhailov then dispatched Popov to track down and kill the spy, which Popov accomplished in Moscow in late February 1879.[256] Working inside the Third Section as a mole,

Kletochnikov became the guardian angel of Land and Liberty and later People's Will for the next two years.

Soloviev's Attempt on the Tsar

In the south, the whole network of revolutionaries was swept up by police chief Sudeikin. There were about half a dozen raids from December 1878 to February 1879 that captured about two dozen people. True to their words, most of the rebels resisted arrest and fired back at the police, knowing that they would face the death penalty. On 24 January 1879, Osinsky and his lover Leshern were captured while resisting arrest.[257] Three weeks later the remnants of the southern network vanished with a new wave of arrests.

However, shortly before his capture, Osinsky had planned with Goldenberg the assassination of Kharkov Governor-General Prince Dmitri Kropotkin, a cousin of Peter Kropotkin, in retaliation for the flogging of students at the House of Horrors. Goldenberg, who had been arrested and exiled upon his return from Switzerland, escaped and returned to Kiev in June 1878. He joined Osinsky, who provided him with money and a revolver to carry out the plot. On 9 February 1879, Goldenberg fired at Kropotkin, killed him, and escaped.[258]

The eradication of the southern network discouraged the revolutionaries, but the fact that many of their imprisoned comrades faced execution led some to escalate to violence. There were 15 executions of revolutionaries by hanging in 1879.[259] At the same time, the failure of the second pilgrimage to improve peasants' well-being deeply discouraged the pilgrims. "We already saw clearly that our work among the people was of no avail. In our persons the revolutionary party had suffered a second defeat . . . The trouble was merely in the lack of political freedom . . . The situation becomes unendurable, all the indignation of society centers itself on the man who expresses and represents that imperial authority . . . who has declared himself to be responsible for the life, well-being, and happiness of the nation . . . If all means of convincing him have been tried and alike found fruitless, then there remains for the revolutionist only physical violence: the dagger, the revolver, and dynamite."[260]

Alexander Soloviev took up the revolver. After discussions with Figner at their commune in early 1879, he came to the capital to kill the tsar. Land and Liberty's fundamental circle was becoming polarized around this issue of central terrorism. The majority die-hard populists led by Plekhanov, Deich, Stefanovich, and Popov rejected terrorism focused on the tsar, despite the fact that Deich and Stefanovich had tried to spark an insurrection and Popov had already killed. Mikhailov, Frolenko, Zundelevich, Morozov, and Tikhomirov were its advocates. These last two had taken over editorship of *Land and*

Liberty after the other editors had left. Although never sharing Morozov's romantic fantasies about pure terrorism, Tikhomirov was becoming convinced of the necessity of central terrorism in addition to organizing the people. Leon Mirsky's attentat against General Drenteln on 13 March 1879 drove the two factions further apart.

Mirsky, an immature 19-year-old nobleman of Polish origin, was trying to impress a beautiful lady who had told him how much she admired the bold freedom fighter who had killed Mezentsev. She had allegedly acted on behalf of Mikhailov, whom Mirsky immediately contacted and volunteered to dispatch Drenteln. He got a horse and a pistol, galloped up to Drenteln's carriage, and shot at him, but missed. He was spirited out of St. Petersburg, but he then bragged to everyone about his exploit. He was arrested four months later, but was spared the death penalty on account of his youth.[261]

Immediately after the attentat, the police searched everywhere for the perpetrator and detained dozens of people. Plekhanov protested to Mikhailov that such attempts backfired and would destroy their organization. But Morozov supported them, and since he could not officially engage the organization, he published a separate and complementary leaflet on 25 March, the *Bulletin of Land and Liberty*, expressing his views. His article "On Political Killings" was signed by "The Revolutionary Committee of the Social Revolutionary Party," Osinsky's fictitious entity. "Political killing is, above all, an act of vengeance . . . the only means of self-defense in present conditions, and one of the best ways of agitating. By striking at the very center of the government organization it shakes the whole system . . . and disrupts all its functions. When the advocates of freedom are few in number, they always shut themselves up in secret societies. This secrecy . . . has given mere handfuls of daring men the ability to fight millions of organized but overt enemies . . . [With] political killing . . . such people will become truly terrible to their enemies. The latter will live in constant fear of their lives . . . Political killing is the realization of the revolution in the present."[262]

This article outraged Plekhanov, who now insisted that a general conference be held in the near future to determine the course of Land and Liberty. But the escalation of political assassinations reached its logical conclusion with the targeting of the tsar. Three members of Land and Liberty had come to St. Petersburg with the intention of killing him: Soloviev, Goldenberg, and a Pole. Mikhailov discouraged the last two because any attentat on the tsar by a Jew or a Pole would trigger a pogrom or a similar effect on Poland. It had to be carried out by a pure Russian—like Soloviev. When Mikhailov informed the fundamental circle of Soloviev's intent, the discussion became extremely heated, with members of the rival factions threatening to denounce or kill each other. At the end, the Land and Liberty leadership rejected endorsement of Soloviev's attentat.[263] Nevertheless, Mikhailov told Soloviev that he personally would help with weapons and means of escape. Soloviev accepted a revolver, ammunition, and poison and refused any other help. They stayed together the night before the attentat.[264] On 2 April 1879, Soloviev approached the tsar on his regular morning walk. He pulled out a gun and shot at him four times, but the tsar successfully evaded the bullets. Soloviev was immediately apprehended and unable to swallow the poison. He was tried on 25 May, convicted, sentenced to death, and executed three days later.[265]

After the attentat, the two revolutionary factions aired their differences publicly. Plekhanov reaffirmed Land and Liberty's traditional priority on populist agitation in a lead article in *Land and Liberty*. This could be done by organizing protests, avenging victims of state abuses, and forming armed bands—in short, the type of countryside defensive terrorism that had already been considered and rejected as ineffective by second-wave pilgrims like Figner. On the other hand, the *Bulletin* declared on behalf of the "Executive Committee" that the tsar's performance over the past 24 years fully deserved a death sentence. The upcoming congress would resolve this issue that divided Land and Liberty.

The government reacted to the attentat by imposing a state of siege in threatened provinces, where military men were installed as governors-general: Kharkov went to General Count Mikhail Loris-Melikov and Odessa to General Totleben. Their powers now extended to every aspect of civil administration, including public order. In Kiev and Odessa, their first task was to eradicate the rebels' activities in their jurisdiction. The revolutionaries arrested in the first part of the year were tried and convicted. Those who had resisted arrest were sentenced to death, while all the others received long sentences, followed by exile to Siberia. In Kiev, Osinsky and two comrades were executed on 14 May 1879, followed by three other executions on 18 June.

History Needs a Push: The Split in Land and Liberty

The anger at the execution of their southern comrades shifted influence within Land and Liberty to its more belligerent faction: Mikhailov, Kviatkovsky, Zundelevich, Morozov, and Stepan Shiraev. Shiraev, a 22-year-old son of a serf, had gone to fight in Herzegovina and then to Switzerland, where he hung out with the Russian émigrés. There, he learned about "propaganda by the deed" and returned to St. Petersburg to preach its virtues.[266] In May, Tikhomirov joined this faction. He represented the theoretical mixture of social revolution and political violence bridging populism and terrorism that was shared by most of the companions. This created some friction with Morozov, who advocated straightforward political violence, like his heroes William Tell and Charlotte Corday, without the larger social program.[267]

This terrorist faction wanted to create a larger organization but was held back by their loyalty to the overall organization and their friends in it. Mikhailov believed that although the government repression had thinned the ranks of Land and Liberty, those who remained had "a remarkable unity of spirit and aims. Everywhere the majority had only one desire; a bloody fight with the government. But there are people who are more influenced by theory than by the logic of events, and they did not share this state of mind. These people had their representatives in the Populist organization, and so this organization . . . could not change direction without the problem being discussed collectively."[268] Both factions agreed to hold a congress on 21 June in the center of the country at Tambov, to facilitate attendance for members scattered around the empire. Mikhailov set about to round up potential allies outside the capital and invite them to a pre-congress meeting in Lipetsk to coordinate their ideas and present a united front at the congress. He asked Frolenko for advice. Frolenko suggested Nikolai Kolotkevich, Barannikov, and his wife Maria Oshanina. Kolotkevich, the 28-year-old son of a noble landowner, had been part of the Kiev commune and participated in the Chigirin conspiracy. Oshanina was a Russian Jacobin in the Tkachev mold. They all agreed to come to Lipetsk.

After returning to Odessa, Frolenko decided to also sound out Zhelyabov, who had returned home after the Trial of the 193. He had shied away from Osinsky because he disliked Osinsky's aristocratic, condescending attitude toward him and dismissed Osinsky's flamboyance as amateurish, seeking attention, and lacking methodology.[269] But he had reached the conclusion that organized violence against the state should complement social activism. "History moves too slowly. It needs a push."[270] Notified, Mikhailov took a trip to Odessa to check him out and extended an invitation to Lipetsk. Zhelyabov agreed to participate in an attentat against the tsar, but he reserved the right to leave the group afterward.[271] He and Mikhailov became fast friends.

The reason for Mikhailov's trip to Odessa was to meet with Drigo, who still controlled Lizogub's wealth. Although Land and Liberty still got small contributions from sympathizers across the country, Lizogub had been by far its largest financier. After Lizogub's arrest, Drigo was in touch with Osinsky, but this link was broken with Osinsky's arrest. Zundelevich reestablished contact but received only 3,000 rubles from Drigo, who afterward avoided him. Mikhailov met Drigo and demanded 10,000 rubles in cash immediately and 60,000 more in promissory notes. Hoping to keep his friend's money, Drigo ran to the police, who set a trap, but Mikhailov, with his usual caution, eluded capture. So Drigo was arrested instead and sent to St. Petersburg to be questioned by the Third Section. Drigo promised to identify and help arrest members of Land and Liberty if he could keep part of Lizogub's fortune. The police released him, but the mole Kletochnikov alerted Mikhailov to the plan.[272]

On 17 June, Mikhailov, Shiraev, Tikhomirov, Morozov, Kviatkovsky, Frolenko, Zhelyabov, Kolodkevich, Barannikov, and Oshashina converged in Lipetsk. So did Goldenberg, who saw himself as the hero of the terrorists. He had not been invited because of his irritating boasting about his assassination of Prince Kropotkin. Morozov opened the meeting by presenting his program of pure political violence: "In view of existing social conditions in Russia, we see that no activity aimed at the good of the people is possible, given the despotism and violence, which here reign supreme. There is no freedom of speech or freedom of the press, which would allow us to act by means of persuasion. And so any man who wants to go in for progressive social work must, before anything else, put an end to the existing regime. To fight against this regime is impossible without arms. And so we will fight with the means employed by William Tell until we achieve those free institutions which will make it possible to discuss without hindrance, in the press and in public meetings, all social and political problems, and solve them through free representatives of the people."[273]

While most of the conspirators thought this program too narrow without a concomitant program to organize peasants and workers, they did not want to start on a negative note and reluctantly approved Morozov's program. Zhelyabov was elected secretary to facilitate the meeting. Tsarist repression forced them to abandon their cherished egalitarian anarchism and adopt a centralized and disciplined hierarchy. In a gesture to Osinsky, they adopted the name "Executive Committee" for their organization. The members agreed to sacrifice everything for the committee—all for one and one for all—and an administrative team was elected: Mikhailov, Frolenko, and Tikhomirov. Morozov and Goldenberg were very disappointed that they had not been chosen. Goldenberg privately complained that none of these leaders had carried out any terrorist acts. However, the group had rejected Morozov because of his too-narrow focus on violence and Goldenberg because of his immaturity. Tikhomirov and Morozov became editors of the official organ of the Executive Committee. After three days, Mikhailov closed the meeting with a summary of the career of Tsar Alexander II and asked: "Must we forgive, because of two good deeds carried out at the beginning of his reign, all the evil that he has since done and will do in the future?" Everyone present answered with the single cry of "No."[274]

The ten members of the Executive Committee (minus Goldenberg) then went on to attend the congress, which had been moved to Voronezh at the last minute. Plekhanov had also invited his allies like Perovskaya and Figner in the

countryside and those in Switzerland. Deich, Zasulich, Stefanovich, and Liubatovich were smuggled back in by Zundelevich's contacts but did not make
it in time for its 24 June opening. Kravchinsky had to stay behind because his
wife was about to give birth.[275] So about 21 delegates in total attended at the
start, and half of them were part of the Executive Committee. Mikhailov set
the emotional tone of the congress by reading Osinsky's last letter that had
been smuggled out of prison. During his last night, Osinsky had shouted his
will in cypher through his window across the yard to Leshern, who wrote it
down. "Dear Friends and Comrades! . . . I embrace you and ask you not to
think badly of me . . . We have no regret at having to die. We die for an idea,
and if we do have any regret it is only that . . . before our death we have not
done what we wanted to do. I send you wishes, my dear friends, for a more
profitable death than ours. This is the only, the best of all wishes that we can
give you . . . Do not throw away your precious blood in vain."[276]

They discussed the incredible news that Lizogub, who had only contributed money and never been involved in any violent act, might be facing the
death penalty. The vast majority of the delegates were aware of their internal
division but, faced with the immediacy and finality of a separation, could not
bring themselves to go through with it and tried to gloss over their differences. Plekhanov was the only one who had come seeking a confrontation
with his rivals, but when no one else supported him, he left the meeting saying, "There's nothing more for me to do here."[277] Figner tried to hold him
back, but Mikhailov signaled her to let him go. His departure lifted the danger of an immediate split.

The rest of the delegates reaffirmed the 1878 program of Land and Liberty
but modified the disorganization clause to allow more offensive action, opening the door for a repeat of Soloviev's attentat. Angry at the execution of their
southern comrades, they agreed in principle to plan the assassination of the
tsar, with the details to be worked out later. Funds for terrorist activities were
increased to a third of the total budget, with the rest still assigned to work
among people in the countryside to reflect their priority. They rejected Zhelyabov's suggestion to establish a constitutional assembly, which, to them,
merely replaced one set of oligarchs with another—politicians and financiers.
Finally, they elected Mikhailov, Frolenko, and a populist as their administrative group and Tikhomirov, Morozov, and the same populist as editors of *Land
and Liberty*.[278] Stefanovich, Deich, and Zasulich, finally caught up with their
peers for the last day, insisted on the primacy of agitations and organization of
the people, but did not reject the use of violence—in fact, all three newcomers
had already used it. Revenge, self-protection, and even central disorganization
were legitimate reasons to use it, but they rejected the concentration of all resources to target the tsar. At the end, each faction seemed to have gotten

something: the terrorists had modified the program to allow targeting of the tsar, while the populist maintained the budgetary priority of work in the countryside. The meeting ended with the organization still intact, as they simply could not bring themselves to end close relationships that had been forged in such harsh conditions over the years.

However, these differences were too serious to be ignored for long. What divided them was not an ideological dispute, for they basically shared the same one and even agreed on the necessity of defensive violence. Internal spies not only physically endangered in-group members but also undermined the meaning of membership, accounting for its severe punishment—the black sheep effect. Getting back at abusive officials was still self-defense. What they disagreed on was the progression to offensive political violence, such as attentats against high government officials and the tsar. The populists rejected this form of violence as counterproductive and favored instead insurrectional violence through urban factories and rural uprisings.[279] They even tried to resurrect the plan for an uprising in Chigirin as an alternative to centralized terrorism. Popov went there for reconnaissance, but increased police vigilance and peasant disinterest discouraged them and they gave up on the plan.[280] The terrorists, on the other hand, believed that the populists' low level of violence was a waste of time and believed that only a concentration of violence on the tsar itself had a chance to succeed and generate reforms. As groups they were very different. The terrorists had a strong sense of shared social identities forged at Lipetsk, while the populists were individualists who had not coalesced together. During the Voronezh meeting, each member stayed loyal to his or her own faction, and no one defected to the other. Back home in St. Petersburg, they continued their discussions to reach a compromise that might keep their organization intact, but in vain as each faction pursued its own goals.

Meanwhile, Mikhailov was losing faith in the use of firearms and was thinking about using explosives. Kviatkovsky had informed him about Kibalchich, who had worked in June and July in a large fireworks factory to learn new techniques and have access to their library. They decided to set up a technical cell for the production of explosive materials and devices. They rented an apartment to turn it into a bomb factory and put Kibalchich in charge of the cell, assisted by Shiraev, who had some experience with electrical devices and worked on detonators, and 22-year-old Grigory Isaev, who had dropped out of medical school. Kibalchich lived in the apartment and directed the others to get him supplies. They tested their devices in deserted areas outside the city.[281]

On 10 August 1879, Lizogub was executed by hanging in Odessa, along with two other rebels. His death sentence was contrary to the law, as he had not been involved in any violent actions or resisted arrest.[282] Lizogub refused to defend himself in court. The verdict shocked everyone: "No one expected a severer punishment for Lisogub than transportation to Siberia, or perhaps some few years at hard labor; for nothing else was laid to his charge than that of having spent his own money . . . Amid universal consternation, Demetrius Lisogub was condemned to death . . . After hearing his sentence, his jaw fell, so great was his astonishment. He scornfully refused the proposal made to him to save his life by petitioning for pardon."[283] Governor-General Totleben approved the sentence, and Lizogub died in an exemplary way: "Those who saw him pass, say that not only was he calm and peaceful, but that his pleasant smile played upon his lips when he addressed cheering words to his companions. At last he could satisfy his ardent desire to sacrifice himself for his cause. It was perhaps the happiest moment of his unhappy life . . . Lisogub was the Saint."[284] In the social identity perspective, he was a martyr for the group.

The day after the three executions in Odessa, two more revolutionaries were executed in Nikolaev.[285] The hanging of Lizogub made such a strong impression on the public that it compelled the government to cancel the right of governors-general to confirm death sentences, which henceforth had to be countersigned in St. Petersburg.[286]

People's Will and the Bombing Frenzy

The outrage at Lizogub's unjust hanging and the execution of four other rebels in the middle of August strengthened the resolve of the Executive Committee to get on with its mission and shifted influence within Land and Liberty to the terrorists. All the later memoirs of the surviving members of People's Will mention the fact that from the middle of 1878 to the end of 1879, there were almost 20 executions of revolutionaries. "My past experience had convinced me that the only way to change the existing order was by force. If any group in our society had shown me a path other than violence, perhaps I would have followed it; at the very least, I would have tried it out. But, as you know, we don't have a free press in our country, and so ideas cannot be spread by the written word . . . And so I concluded that violence was the only solution. I could not follow the peaceful path."[287] The terrorists felt that they were ready to act, and this meant separating themselves from their populist comrades.

The split with the populists was amicably reached a few days after Lizogub's execution. The two factions of Land and Liberty promised to collaborate in the future and decided to split material, money, and their name down the middle: the populist took the Land and the terrorist Liberty.[288] The populists called themselves Black Partition to refer to their program of partitioning equally the fertile black land of Russia. The terrorists chose People's Will to keep the Russian word *Volya* (meaning both will and liberty) in their name. Members sorted themselves out after appeasing their conscience about leaving their friends. Ironically, some of the most violent ones, including Popov, Deich, Stefanovich, and Zasulich, went with Black Partition, while others with no blood on their hands joined People's Will, including Zhelyabov, Zundelev-ich, Anna Yakimova, Perovskaya, and Figner.[289] "Sofia Perovskaya and I, who had not taken a definite stand at Voronezh in our efforts to preserve the unity of the organization, no longer objected when the time had come for action, and our comrades from St. Petersburg showed us that all the means by which the attempt was to be made were in readiness."[290] Faced with the impossibility of rescuing her comrades from prison, Perovskaya joined in: "I simply seek vengeance for my dear friends dead or dying on the scaffolds and in fortress casemates."[291] In-group loyalty motivated her to stay in Russia and fight: "I will remain here to perish along with my struggling comrades."[292] Later she also stressed increased state aggression against her community for her decision. To the peaceful settlements in the countryside, "the government responded with frightful repressions and a series of measures" making their proselytism among the people impossible. Then "a series of hangings and other mea-sures . . . forced the party to resolutely pass over to the path of struggle with the government, in which terrorist acts were one of the significant means."[293] Like Zhelyabov, Perovskaya set the condition that this was a one-shot deal: after the tsar's assassination, she would not feel bound to continue terrorist tactics.[294]

Black Partition did not get off to a good start, and its members were plagued by organizational problems. A few members were arrested, and they lost their printing press. Within five months, all the leaders, including Plekha-nov, Deich, Stefanovich, and Zasulich, immigrated to Switzerland, where they continued their revolutionary propaganda. With their departure, the influ-ence of Black Partition vanished in Russia.

The Executive Committee now became the Executive Committee of the People's Will and moved on with its major business by formally condemning Alexander II to death at its meeting on 26 August 1879. By now, it had 25 mem-bers, and, thanks to the technical cell's effort, possessed about 216 pounds of explosive substance.[295] Mikhailov and Zhelyabov were in charge of the execu-tion of the sentence. They determined that the easiest way to strike the tsar was in transit from his annual fall retreat with his mistress at Livadia in the Crimea. The Committee decided on a three-pronged attack by mining the railroad in three places along the expected route. It organized three teams of about half a dozen each to conduct attacks around Odessa, Kharkov, and Moscow with Fro-lenko, Zhelyabov, and Mikhailov, respectively, in charge of each team. The rest would stay in St. Petersburg and continue to conduct propaganda and organize students, workers, and military officers. The tsar left St. Petersburg for Livadia in mid-September 1879, setting the plans in motion.

The mood of the conspirators is captured in Figner's disappointment at not being initially selected to participate: "I was not among those assigned to carry out the assassination. However, the prospect of bearing only moral responsibility for an act that I had endorsed, of having no material role in a crime that threatened my confederates with the gravest punishment, was intolerable to me, and so I made every effort to get the organization to give me a role in implementing the plan. After being reprimanded for seeking personal satisfaction instead of placing my resources at the disposal of the organization, to use as it thought best, I was sent to Odessa, where a woman was needed."[296] She brought along the dynamite and joined Kibalchich there. Frolenko got a job as a railroad guard at a small station, from where the group dug a tunnel and eventually placed a mine under the railroad.[297]

Around Kharkov, Zhelyabov bought a plot of land near the railroad track at Alexandrovsk. Soon others arrived with the dynamite. Goldenberg came uninvited and helped in the manufacture of the mines, but Zhelyabov did not trust him and kept him at arm's length. Instead, he recruited local 21-year-old carpenter and sympathizer Ivan Okladsky. The team dug a tunnel to the railroad line in horrible weather conditions that caused constant flooding, but they eventually succeeded in placing a mine there just before the imperial train was to arrive.[298]

A similar scenario unfolded near Moscow, this time starring Mikhailov, Perovskaya, Shiraev, and others. As in Alexandrovsk, the weather conditions were horrible and the tunnel collapsed several times, but they managed to place a mine under the rails just in time. Goldenberg also showed up uninvited in Moscow to see whether he could be selected for the honor of triggering the detonation.[299]

Back in St. Petersburg, Khalturin, the former union leader, found a job in the Winter Palace in September 1879. He came to Plekhanov volunteering to kill the tsar, but Plekhanov wanted nothing to do with this and instead put him in touch with Yakimova and Kviatkovsky, who had stayed behind. Yakimova came from the same town as Khalturin, and may have known him from back home. The three agreed to blow up the Winter Palace in case the tsar ever returned to the capital. Kviatkovsky, assisted by Yakimova, went to the bomb factory, brought some of the explosive material to his apartment, and parceled it into packages small enough for Khalturin to smuggle into the palace. This operation was so sensitive that they kept it from anyone but Mikhailov.[300]

While these four plots were progressing simultaneously, Zundelevich got hold of a printing machine and published 3,000 copies of *People's Will* starting on 1 October 1879. Written mostly by Tikhomirov, the newsletter developed a sophisticated analysis of Russian society and economy. It noted that the situation had changed in the past two years, when a simple flogging almost caused a revolution, while at present beatings, shootings, and hangings took place regularly without much reaction. Since the masses could not rebel spontaneously, it was necessary for a small, dedicated, and resolute revolutionary party, like a Jacobin party, to initiate a political revolution. Economically, it was imperative to act immediately and grab power for the people before the tsar had an opportunity to pass it on to the bourgeoisie. The articles were a call to arms and glorification of fearless fighters and the sacrifice of revolutionary activities. They also presented an extensive social program calling for a constitutional assembly as a necessary intermediary stage before the masses could assume power directly.[301]

Under the pressure of events, ideology gave way to practical concerns and action. Indeed, the major participants in this violent campaign, Mikhailov, Zhelyabov, Khalturin, Kviatkovsky, Perovskaya, and Figner, were not ideologues. "The most essential part of the program . . . was the annihilation of the autocratic form of government. I really ascribe no practical importance to the question whether our program advocates a republic or a constitutional monarchy."[302] They did not contribute any articles to *People's Will*. With the exception of Kibalchich, who wrote an article for its last issue, the field leaders did not seem to get involved in theoretical issues, which interested only ideologues. Morozov, the author of the party's program approved at Lipetsk, was upset that his program was now rejected because it lacked a parallel social program. Miffed, in January 1880, he and his lover Liubatovich left in protest for Switzerland. With his departure, People's Will was rid of its last romantic, like Kravchinsky, Osinsky, and Goldenberg, who saw themselves as great heroes moving history and had been a powerful voice in the group's turn to violence. Ironically, People's Will's obsession with the assassination of the tsar to the exclusion of almost everything else forced it carry out Morozov's program rather than its own.[303]

In mid-November 1879, the tsar returned to his capital but bypassed Odessa. Since the explosive was no longer needed there, Goldenberg was dispatched to bring it to Moscow. He was arrested on his way back at Elizabethgrad on 14 November 1879 when a policeman saw him acting suspiciously and an inspection of his heavy trunk revealed 50 pounds of explosives.[304] On November 18, the imperial train passed through Alexandrovsk: Zhelyabov pressed the switch closing the electrical circuit just as the tsar's car passed over the mine, but nothing happened.[305] In Moscow, Shiraev pressed the switch when the second train of the imperial convoy went over the mine. A huge explosion took place and eight cars derailed, but there were no casualties. This was the supply train, which had developed mechanical problems, prompting the tsar, who usually traveled in the second train, to move his train to the lead. He arrived safely in St. Petersburg. Nevertheless, four days later, a leaflet signed by the Executive Committee of People's Will took credit for the Moscow near-miss: "We once more assert Alexander II to be . . . the person who is chiefly to blame for the judicial murders; fourteen executions rest on his conscience, the hundreds of people tortured to death and the thousands now suffering cry out for revenge. He deserves the death penalty for all the blood he has shed, for all the torments he has caused. But our concern is not with him alone. Our aim is the freedom of the people and the good of the people. If Alexander were to recognize the evil he has done to Russia, if he were to hand over his power to a General Assembly chosen by the free vote of the people, then we for our part, would leave him in peace and forgive his past misdeeds. But, till then, implacable war."[306]

Of course, nothing was mentioned about the two other failed attentats. Despite the failures, the Moscow explosion had a strong effect on the government and was widely covered in the Russian and world press.[307] This was a qualitatively different type of attentat from that of a lone gunman or even a small number of conspirators. People realized that it required meticulous preparation, difficult-to-obtain explosives, money, manpower, and organization that had not been seen before.

Poor tradecraft took a toll on the revolutionaries in the fall and winter of 1879–80. On 24 November, Kviatkovsky was arrested, and in his apartment the police found a plan of the Winter Palace with a cross marking the tsar's dining room.[308] Zundelevich was next, and with him went the knowledge of all the smuggling routes to the West. On 4 December, it was Shiraev's turn. Finally, on 17 January 1880, the police raided the press. The typesetters resisted arrest, firing at the police while they destroyed compromising documents.[309]

With Kviatkovsky's arrest, Mikhailov introduced Khalturin to Zhelyabov to be his contact man. They stood down for a while as the police investigated the marked Winter Palace map. The Third Section conducted a brief inspection of the palace and let it go at that. The conspirators also had to wait for Kibalchich's return from Odessa, where three more revolutionaries were executed. Figner stayed behind to organize local people and plan revenge on the bloody governor-general Totleben and his chief of chancellery Panyutin.[310]

Kibalchich came back to a new bomb factory and resumed making explosive material. Up to that point, Khalturin had managed to bring in only about 70 pounds of explosive substance, which he stored in a trunk under his bed in the basement of the palace. He slept on top of the chemicals and was feeling their effect on his health: severe, constant headaches; inability to sleep; loss of appetite and hair; fainting spells; and lack of concentration. Despite these difficulties, he relentlessly pursued his mission throughout the winter. Zhelyabov noticed Khalturin's rapidly declining health and urged him to carry out the operation as soon as possible because of it. Khalturin protested that there was not enough explosive and was determined to smuggle in more. Finally, they decided to carry out the attack during the visit of the tsar's cousin on 5 February. Khalturin dragged his trunk, filled with about 280 pounds of explosives, to the room below the dining room, set the fuse, and left the palace. However, terrible weather had delayed the guest's train and the dinner. The explosive device detonated when the tsar and his cousin were starting on their way to the dining room, so they escaped injury. The explosion destroyed the dining room, blew out part of the wall of the palace, killed 11 people, and wounded another 56, mostly members of the tsar's guards.[311]

When Khalturin heard the news that the tsar was safe, he was furious at Zhelyabov and accused him of sabotaging the operation by not allowing him to smuggle in enough explosives for the operation. People's Will got Khalturin out of St. Petersburg to Moscow.[312] On 7 February, People's Will published a leaflet claiming credit for the explosion. It noted that the plot failed because "Alexander the Hangman" had been late for his dinner by half an hour and regretted the loss of the lives of the unfortunate soldiers. It again declared that it was in the midst of a war with the tsar, put the blame for the attack on the tsar's repression, and again promised to cease the attacks if the tsar abdicated and allowed the free election of a national assembly.[313]

The tsar was shocked by the near-miss at his own residence. After immediately imposing a state of siege on St. Petersburg, with soldiers patrolling the streets for weeks, he realized that he had to do something different to counter this invisible threat. No one knew who or where the terrorists were. The explosion caused a great deal of admiration among the youth, who now wanted to become part of People's Will, since at least it was doing something. This enthusiastic response provided a sense of validation to the terrorists disappointed by their latest failure. "Society, at any rate its more intelligent element, greeted our activity with great enthusiasm, and offered us sympathetic aid and ardent approval. From this point of view we had a right to speak in the name of society. We constituted to a marked degree the front rank of a part of that society. Knowing that this group sympathized with us, we did not feel ourselves a sect, isolated from all the other elements of the empire."[314]

Fighting the Dictatorship of the Heart

The tsar decided to change tack and appointed his best administrator, Count Mikhail Loris-Melikov, the governor-general of Kharkov, to head a Supreme Commission with virtual dictatorial power. Loris-Melikov had the reputation of being a liberal and a proven track record in suppressing political unrest through a combination of focused repression against troublemakers and good public relations that isolated them from their potential constituency. He replaced the reactionary minister of education with a liberal, to the delight of the students, and stabilized the price of bread in the capital.[315] Liberals hoped that he might be the person to guide the government to pass and implement the long-awaited reforms. On the counterterrorism side, Loris-Melikov reformed the political police and introduced modern police methods. He transferred the Third Section from the Tsar's Chancellery to the Ministry of the Interior, where it became the Department for Protecting the Public Security and Order, abbreviated to its well-known name Okhrana. It recruited all the janitors of St. Petersburg to be its eyes and ears on the ground, co-opted photography shops to report any individual with suspicious requests for photographs that might be used for propaganda, and required chemical salesmen to report the sale of any chemical precursors of explosives. Finally, all the major political police stations and government offices were linked with a new invention: the telephone.[316]

About ten days after Loris-Melikov's accession to power, a student named Ippolit Mlodetski fired at him and missed. As public opinion supported Loris-Melikov, People's Will was careful to distance itself from this attentat: "It is a fact that Mlodetski offered his services to the Committee for some terrorist act. But he was unwilling to await a decision and he proceeded to carry through his attempt without the knowledge and without the assistance of the Executive Committee . . . Had Loris been sentenced to death, the Executive Committee would have found more efficient means of putting the sentence into effect."[317]

Revolutionaries were not under any illusion about Loris-Melikov. They were familiar with his ruthlessness in pursuing them combined with his public relations campaign in Kharkov. They feared that his "dictatorship of the heart"[318] would win over the support of the intelligentsia and leave them bereft of its support. In this race against time, they decided to continue their attentats but intensify their organizing among the intelligentsia, students, workers, and military officers. In March, Kletochnikov informed Mikhailov that Goldenberg was telling all he knew about People's Will to the Odessa prosecutor. This caused surprise, for despite his vanity, Goldenberg was considered too brave and loyal to betray his comrades. Panic spread in People's Will because he knew so much about the organization and its members. In a sense, Goldenberg was a victim of Loris-Melikov's dictatorship of the heart. During his incarceration, he had fallen for prosecutor Dobrzhinsky's bluff that he knew all about People's Will and just needed a few small details about the organization to prevent unnecessary bloodshed. Dobrzhinsky portrayed himself as a liberal in the Loris-Melikov mold, who wanted to bring the same reforms to Russia demanded by the revolutionaries but in a nonviolent way. He flattered Goldenberg by telling him that fate had put them in a position where only they could save Russia from a bloodbath. Loris-Melikov played along with this charade and visited Goldenberg in his cell. Blinded by his vanity, Goldenberg fell for the trick and revealed all he knew after assurances that his comrades would not be harmed. Kletochnikov found out about it in early March 1880, and Mikhailov tried to mitigate the damages. However, the police now knew the terrorists' identities and the nature and extent of the threat it was facing.[319] Despite Mikhailov's efforts, the police arrested several distant accomplices, including Okladsky from Alexandrovsk.[320] Some of them resisted arrest and fired back, killing an officer and wounding another.

Mikhailov and Zhelyabov decided to carry out another attentat in Odessa on the tsar's way to Livadia in May. Perovskaya, Isaev, and a few others were dispatched there with explosives to meet up with Figner, still there organizing an attentat against Panyutin, to avenge the executions of so many comrades. "Panyutin was the terror of the citizens of Odessa . . . He took measures for a thorough purging of the city . . . [seizing] a few of the city duma members; arrests of teachers, writers, students, officials and workingmen followed; vast numbers of people were exiled in a most arbitrary and revolting fashion. He was rough and coarse in his treatment of people, and the relatives of the exiles had to undergo humiliating scenes in his chancellery."[321] But the plot against the tsar took precedence, and the conspirators rented a shop from which they started digging a tunnel under a road the tsar was expected to take. However, the tsar's wife died and he canceled his trip. The Committee called the conspirators back. After the transfer of the governor and his deputy elsewhere, all the conspirators, including Figner, returned to St. Petersburg.[322]

At the end of May 1880, 11 members of Land and Liberty, including Olga Natanson and Maria Kolenkina, were put on trial, convicted, and given long sentences at hard labor. Most of them eventually died in prison or exile. Meanwhile, as all the members of People's Will were back in the capital, they planned another attentat. This time, they decided to blow up Kamenni Bridge on the way from the Winter Palace to the train station. It took Kibalchich about three months to manufacture the 360 pounds of explosive substance required to blow up the bridge and destroy anything on it. The substance was packaged in rubber bags and sunk to the bottom of the canal at the base of the bridge's stone support. The attentat failed on 17 August, when the stableman taking care of the horse Barbarian overslept and failed to bring the wires and detonator to set off the charges in time as the tsar passed over the bridge.[323]

During the beautiful summer, the conspirators paired off romantically: Mikhailov with Anna Korba, and Zhelyabov with Perovskaya. "In the last year of Sofia's life she fell in love for the first time. It was Zhelyabov. She had always been a strong feminist and maintained that men were the inferior sex. She had real respect for very few of them. But Zhelyabov was up to her caliber. She was utterly in love with him, in a way I never thought could happen to her with any man."[324]

People's Will's proselytism among the students, intelligentsia, workers, and military was more successful. At the end of August, it acquired a printing press and resumed publication of *People's Will* after an eight-month absence. Tikhomirov and Kibalchich also wrote anonymous articles in the liberal press as Loris-Melikov's policies had partially lifted censorship. Some members attended liberal salons under false identities[325] and met with students, still awed by the Moscow and Winter Palace bombings.[326] They organized workers in St. Petersburg and, by the end of the year, had recruited about 20 of them and had another 250 sympathizers, divided into cells at various factories. They helped workers to print their own newspaper, the *Worker's Gazette*,[327] and to publish a comprehensive *Program of the Working Class Members of the People's Will* at the end of the year.[328] They also made inroads within the Russian army and navy through the efforts of Zhelyabov, Perovskaya, and Kolotkevich. In retrospect, their most significant recruit was Sergei Degaev, a 23-year-old retired captain studying at the Institute of Transport Engineers. The number of officers attracted to People's Will was large enough that a Military Circle of People's Will was created in the fall of 1880.[329]

Around that time, Morozov in Switzerland elaborated on his Lipetsk program in a pamphlet called *The Terrorist Struggle*, which still advocated only terrorism without any accompanying social program.[330] Up to that point, he and other members of People's Will had generally avoided the terms *terrorism* and *terrorist* in print. However, by then usage of the word *terror* was deeply rooted in the public consciousness, and Morozov adopted it in his pamphlet.[331] His open advocacy for a permanent system of political assassinations embarrassed the leadership of People's Will.[332] "As a Party we disapprove of the line of argument, and we have asked our émigré friends abroad, so long as they are abroad, not to express views on the tasks of the Party in Russia. Now apparently we are to be held responsible for the views of Morozov because at one time in the past certain members of the Party, like Goldenberg, took up the attitude that our whole task was to clear our way by a series of political murders. At present terrorism is only one among a whole row of other means designed to secure the amelioration of our national life."[333]

The Trial of the 16, which included Kviatkovsky, Shiraev, Zundelevich, Evgenia Figner, and Okladsky, among others, opened on 25 October 1880. Six days later, all were convicted. Kviatkovsky and another defendant, who had killed a policeman, were sentenced to death. The tsar and Loris-Melikov could not forgive Kviatkovsky, whose marked map showed that he had been involved in the Winter Palace bombing, and he was executed by hanging on 4 November 1880. Shiraev, Zundelevich, and Okladsky were sentenced to life at hard labor, and the rest received lesser sentences followed by exile to Siberia. Okladsky's proceedings were a charade, as he had broken down and was providing information on his comrades that helped in their convictions. He was secretly released after the trial and became a police informant.[334]

The Assassination of Alexander II

The execution of Kviatkovsky showed the limits of Loris-Melikov's liberalism. The Executive Committee had not ordered any new attentat against the tsar after the Kamenni Bridge failure and had moved on to social organizing. However, the executions of their comrades outraged them and reset their focus on the tsar. At a hectic meeting of the Executive Committee, "There was a good deal of argument over the renewal of terrorist activity. It was clear that it would mean that our other activities would suffer: we would have to devote all our resources to terrorism. Mikhailov took pains to emphasize the importance of the other sides of our work. So did Zhelyabov. He realized the difficulties we were up against better than anyone else. Tikhomirov as usual agreed with the majority. Perovskaya was all out for terrorism, whatever the cost. So was Yakimova."[335] Kibalchich remarked, "Our girls are fiercer than our men." Zhelyabov conceded, "The honor of the Party demands that the Emperor be killed."[336]

Mikhailov wanted to publish a special leaflet in honor of the executed comrades with their photographs on it. He went to a photography shop to have photos made from negatives and was arrested on 28 November when he returned to pick them up. He was carrying false identification, but Okladsky identified him. At his apartment, the police found 70 pounds of explosives.[337] Kolotkevich and Barannikov took over handling Kletochnikov for the Executive Committee. The loss of Mikhailov accelerated the demise of People's Will, as he had been responsible for its security. Within four months, People's Will ceased to exist as an effective organization.

At an emergency meeting of the Executive Committee to discuss Mikhailov's arrest, Zhelyabov once again tried to push Mikhailov's and his previous suggestion of taking advantage of the recent crop failure and famine in the countryside to organize a peasant revolt. He proposed to postpone any attentat on the tsar as the Committee was not able to pursue both goals at the same time. But everyone else feared that postponement meant cancellation. Angered at the execution of their comrades and shocked at Mikhailov's arrest, they greeted this proposal with silence, indicating of their disapproval. Zhelyabov understood and did not even put his proposal to a vote.[338] People's Will resumed its active war against the tsar.

The terrorists identified a small street that the tsar drove through on Sundays on his way to review the honor guard at a riding school. They repeated the Odessa scenario by renting a shop on the street and digging a tunnel from it to the middle of the road. In addition, Kibalchich said he could also make hand-carried bombs, which he and Zhelyabov had successfully tested in a deserted forest. So, the attentat had three contingencies: the first was to detonate the mine under the street if the tsar traveled that way; the second was to use hand-carried bombs if the tsar chose the route along the Catherine Canal; and if these two options failed, Zhelyabov would stand by, charge the tsar's carriage, and stab him to death. On 3 December 1880, the terrorists started digging their tunnel, and Kibalchich started working on the various explosive devices.

The wave of arrests continued in January 1881. In the middle of the month, the stableman was arrested and the horse Barbarian was confiscated. On information provided by Okladsky, Barannikov and Kolotkevich were arrested, as was Kletochnikov. Kletochnikov had come to warn them, but a delay had caused him to walk into the apartment when the police were already there. With his arrest at the end of January, People's Will was no longer protected from the Okhrana.

Zhelyabov called a meeting of the Executive Committee and told them that in his opinion, the only option was to continue their plot. Of course, it would be physical suicide, but to stop would be moral suicide, the negation of all that the party stood for. They might go down, but others would come to take their places.[339] After the meeting, he took Oshanina aside. She had come from Moscow, where she was organizing on behalf of the party. In her memoirs, she wrote, "I think he felt that some of our people were getting off the rails . . . He mentioned . . . the bad attribute of terrorism: it was apt so to dominate people's minds as to affect their freedom of judgment . . . Zhelyabov did not count on its forcing the Government to grant any important political concessions. The most he hoped for was that the prestige we would gain would make it easier for us to . . . broaden our basis of support in all sections of society. But that, of course, would only be possible if there survived a sufficient number of really capable members to carry on the Party's work . . . He was hoping . . . to build up a new Executive Committee in Moscow if the old one were wiped out."[340]

As the police were closing in on them, the terrorists decided to carry out their attentat on 1 March. The tunnel was almost ready, and there were enough explosives. Kibalchich was perfecting the hand-carried bombs. Zhelyabov had recruited four people to be the bomb-throwers from their workers section: Ivan Emilianov and Nikolas Rysakov, both 19 years of age; 21-year-old Timothy Mikhailov, who was intellectually impaired; and 24-year-old Ignat Grinevitsky, of Polish origin. They first met as a group on 20 February, and two days later Zhelyabov took them to a deserted spot in a local park where they practiced bomb throwing at dummies.[341]

With their numbers rapidly dwindling, Zhelyabov recalled comrades to the capital: a friend came from Odessa, and Morozov came back from Switzerland but was arrested at the border on 28 February.[342] Okladsky identified Zhelyabov's friend from Odessa, and police went to his residence the evening of 27 February, just as Zhelyabov came to visit. They were both arrested, and the prosecutor Dobrzhinsky, now in the capital, immediately recognized Zhelyabov from Odessa.[343] The next day Okladsky confirmed his identity, and Loris-Melikov informed the tsar of the arrest of the head of People's Will.

That morning, the Executive Committee held an emergency meeting. Perovskaya was in despair over the arrest of her lover, but she was resolved to go through and finish Zhelyabov's plot. The Committee reviewed the situation: the mine was not yet in place; the shop was under suspicion; the hand-carried bombs were not yet made, it was uncertain whether they would work at all; and they had lost their operational leader. But they all agreed with one voice: "Act! Whatever happens, act tomorrow! The mine *must* be laid. The bombs *must* be loaded by morning and put into action."[344] Perovskaya assumed Zhelyabov's role, Isaev was dispatched to lay the mine, and Kibalchich worked through the night to finish all the hand-carried bombs. Frolenko was in charge of detonating the mine at the shop, and Perovskaya was to lead the foot bombers along the Catherine Canal.[345]

Of the bomb-throwers, only Grinevitsky knew the full extent of the plot. That sleepless night he believed that the next day would be his last and wrote a note: "Alexander II must die . . . And we, his assassins will die with him . . . Our dear and unhappy country [Poland] will require many more victims to become free . . . The near future will show whether it is for me or another to strike the final blow. But he will die and with him we shall die, his enemies and executioners. What of the future? I, with one foot already in the grave, am afflicted by the thought that after me there will be many further victims. It will not be my lot to take part in the final battle. Fate has allotted me an early death. I shall not see one day, not one hour of our triumph. But I believe that by my death I am doing all that I have in my power to do."[346]

On 1 March 1881, the tsar went to review the troops and then visited his cousin. On the way back, he chose to ride along the Catherine Canal. Perovskaya spotted his convoy and signaled her four bombers. Timothy Mikhailov got cold feet and left. Rysakov was next, and threw his bomb a little late. It exploded at the back of the tsar's carriage, damaging the back axle and seriously wounding a Cossack and a boy who had stopped to watch the convoy, but the tsar was untouched. He stopped his carriage and walked back to check on the wounded. Grinevitsky, who was leaning against the parapet of the canal, waited until the tsar came close to him to throw the bomb down at their feet. The second explosion fatally wounded both the tsar and the bomber. The tsar was loaded into the escort police sleigh pulled by Barbarian, who had been hitched to it at the police stable that morning. Both the tsar and Grinevitsky expired a few hours later.[347]

In her memoirs, Figner recalled that bittersweet moment: "I rushed home. The streets hummed with talk, and there was evident excitement . . . I was so agitated that I could hardly utter the words announcing the death of the Tsar. I wept, and many of us wept; that heavy nightmare, which for ten years had strangled young Russia before our very eyes, had been brought to an end; the horrors of prison and exile, the violence, executions, and atrocities inflicted on hundreds and thousands of our adherents, the blood of our martyrs, all were atoned for by this blood of the Tsar, shed by our hands . . . In this solemn moment, all our thoughts centered in the hope for a better future for our country."[348] Perovskaya came and cried. She refused the congratulations and wanted the Party to devote all its resources to rescue Zhelyabov. A People's Will leaflet the next day took credit for the assassination of "Alexander the Tyrant . . . The police maltreated the people and he rewarded them instead of punishing them. He hanged or exiled any who stood out on behalf of the people or on behalf of justice."[349]

Rysakov had been arrested at the site of the bombing and started talking. The apartment of Gelfman and her lover was raided the next night. They resisted; her lover killed himself with his last round, but she was arrested. Timothy Mikhailov was arrested the next day. When Zhelyabov heard about the successful assassination, he wrote a letter to the prosecutor claiming responsibility for the deed and demanded to be tried with those arrested in the attentat.

Many members of the Executive Committee left St. Petersburg and urged Perovskaya to do the same, but she would not hear of it. She was devastated by Zhelyabov's claim of responsibility. "Up until then it had been possible to hope that he would not be implicated. Of course there was a good deal against him in his police dossier, but there could not have been any evidence as regards the actual assassination. But it was clear from the paper that now his fate was definitely sealed. It was a terrible moment for Perovskaya. She did not lose her self-control. She walked on slowly with her head bent and the paper dangling from one hand. She said nothing and I did not want to speak. I knew she was in love with Zhelyabov. At last she said something. I asked: 'Why did he do it?' She said, 'He is right. It was necessary.'"[350]

St. Petersburg was in a state of siege. Police and Cossacks were patrolling everywhere. On 10 March, Perovskaya was recognized in the street and arrested. It was unclear whether she had wished to join her lover's fate. With information from Rysakov and Okladsky, the police arrested Kibalchich at his apartment. Frolenko was also there, but since neither informant knew him, he was not included in the group of tsaricides.

On the day of Perovskaya's arrest, the Executive Committee wrote a letter to the new tsar. "In the course of ten years we have seen the fact that the government of the late Emperor sacrificed everything, freedom, the interests of all classes, the interests of industry and even its own dignity, everything, unconditionally, in its attempt to suppress the revolutionary movement, that movement has nevertheless tenaciously grown and spread . . . They have hanged our followers, both guilty and innocent; they have filled the prisons and distant provinces with exiles. Whole dozens of our leaders have been seized and hanged. They have died with the courage and calmness of martyrs, but the movement has not been suppressed, it has grown and gained in strength."[351] The letter gave a choice to Alexander III: reform from the top or revolution. It then listed the types of reform that might stop further political violence. This letter implies that People's Will expected the new tsar to be receptive to liberal reforms despite his reactionary reputation. Figner confirmed this incredible expectation: "To be sure, it did expect concessions, a relaxation of the rigid regime, the cessation of reaction, partial liberty, which would have made existence endurable and peaceful activity possible. This expectation proved to be a mistake, a very sad and unfortunate mistake . . . unfortunate because it involved new catastrophes in the future, new social and political disturbances."[352]

On 26 March 1881, a special court tried Rysakov, Timothy Mikhailov, Gelfman, Kibalchich, Perovskaya, and Zhelyabov for tsaricide. Zhelyabov chose to represent himself and summarized his evolution from populism to terrorism: "The Russian People's Party did not always use bombs . . . We chose . . . peaceful propagation of peaceful ideas. This surely was harmless. What happened? Those concerned were imprisoned or sent into exile. An entire peaceful movement, opposed to violence, opposed to revolution, was crushed . . . In 1875, I was not a revolutionary . . . My aim was to work for the good of the people by the spread of socialist ideas. I did not approve of violence, I was not concerned with political matters—my companions even less so. In 1874, as far as we had political ideas, we were anarchists . . . I say that all I wished to do was to work in a peaceful manner among the people. I was put in prison. There I became a revolutionary."

Zhelyabov went on to describe the failure of the pilgrimage to the people as the government made it impossible for them to spread their ideas by this means. "We took to deeds, not words. Action meant some use of force. But force was not used to any great extent. So things went on up to 1878 . . . a transitional year, as can be seen from the pamphlet *A Death for a Death* . . . Circumstances were forcing me, among others, to declare war against the existing political structure. All the same I spent the summer of 1878 in a village, propagandizing peacefully." He described the failure of their simple reliance on individual initiative, with perhaps the exception of the distribution of banned literature. At the Lipetsk conference, they decided to bring about revolution through a social revolutionary party. "But once we had set ourselves the task of carrying out an armed revolution it was obviously necessary to establish a strong, centralized machine, and we—myself included—devoted vastly more time and effort to this work than to preparing assassinations . . . I devoted all my powers to the creation of a strong centralized organization . . . I tried first to do this by peaceful means. Later on I was forced to turn to violence." He then admitted his participation in multiple attentats against the tsar but concluded, "I would willingly abandon violence if there were the possibility of serving my ideals by peaceful means—of peacefully expounding my views and organizing those of my way of thinking. I repeat again as my last word, to avoid any misunderstanding, a peaceful solution is possible. I myself would at once abandon terrorist activity if the conditions [were right]."[353]

So, like French revolutionaries, Zhelyabov used *la force des choses* to explain his turn to political violence, namely the state's disproportionate aggression against his peaceful political protest community. Kibalchich shared his analysis: "I am by character drawn to peaceful social action . . . I was not able to resist that historical course of flow that pushed an entire group of people into the terrorist struggle . . . The continuous persecutions and hindrances to its [the party's] actions among the people forced it to take the terrorist actions in the first place."[354]

After three days of proceedings, all six defendants were convicted and sentenced to death. Gelfman's sentence was commuted to life in prison because she was pregnant. On 3 April 1881, Timothy Mikhailov, Kibalchich, Rysakov, Perovskaya, and Zhelyabov were executed by hanging. Gelfman gave birth in October, but her daughter was taken from her three months later. Gelfman died of "depression" six days later, on 31 January 1882, and the baby died seven months later.[355]

The Demise of People's Will

The assassination of Tsar Alexander II was the high point of People's Will. Contrary to its hope, the new tsar, Alexander III, replaced his liberal ministers with well-known reactionaries. Sudeikin was appointed head of all secret police activity across the empire and rounded up hundreds of young people trying to emulate the tsaricides. A wave of reaction engulfed the country, and pogroms erupted in the Pale as Gelfman's presence among the tsaricides was taken as a sign of a Jewish conspiracy. The authorities encouraged local hooligans to go on rampage. The remnants of the Executive Committee, including Tikhomirov and Oshanina, went to Moscow to hide, and Figner went to Odessa to organize new local groups.

Despite its murder of Alexander II, People's Will did not approve of assassinations in general. Figner condemned President James Garfield's assassination in the United States in a statement released on behalf of the Executive Committee on 10 September 1881: "The Executive Committee regards it as its duty to declare in the name of the Russian revolutionists its protest against such acts of violence as that of Guiteau. In a land where personal freedom gives an opportunity for an honest conflict of ideas, where the free will of the people determines not only the law but also the personality of the ruler, in such a land political murder as a means of struggle presents a manifestation of that despotic spirit which we aim to destroy in Russia. Personal despotism is as condemnable as group despotism, and violence may be justified only when it is directed against violence."[356]

The trial of 20 People's Will members, including Mikhailov, Morozov, and Yakimova, took place in February 1882. They were all convicted, and ten of them were sentenced to death. All but Mikhailov had their sentences commuted; he was executed on 18 March 1882. On the same day, Khalturin, who had returned to the struggle, together with a student who longed to sacrifice his life for the cause, shot and killed the governor of Odessa. They were arrested, tried, convicted, and executed within three days.[357]

Sudeikin's dragnet was closing in on the Executive Committee during the spring and summer of 1882. Oshanina and Tikhomirov went abroad, leaving Figner as its only surviving member in Russia.[358] Degaev was arrested in Odessa, and Sudeikin used with him the same ploy that had been so successful with Goldenberg. Sudeikin convinced Degaev that the two of them were the only hope to save Russia from a bloodbath. After being released in a fake escape, Degaev led Sudeikin to Figner, who was arrested on 10 February 1883, eliminating the leadership of People's Will in Russia. She was tried and sentenced to 20 years in prison. Degaev became the new leader of the followers of People's Will and provided Sudeikin with information about hundreds of followers, virtually wiping out their network in Russia during the spring of 1883. Sudeikin then sent his agent abroad to meet with the émigré Executive Committee, but Degaev confessed his treason to Tikhomirov, who tasked him to return to Russia and kill Sudeikin. Degaev went back and killed Sudeikin on 16 December 1883.[359]

Peter Iakubovich, a popular poet and philosopher, tried to pick up the pieces of the revolutionary network and organized the Union of Youth of People's Will. The Executive Committee sent German Lopatin back to St. Petersburg in March 1884 to help him. The two established a close working relationship, expanded their circles, and resumed publication of *People's Will*. However, on 4 October 1884, Lopatin was arrested while carrying a comprehensive list of all the members of the network throughout the empire, leading to the arrests of approximately 500 people over the next two months. These two blows, Degaev's betrayal and Lopatin's carelessness, completely severed any ties between the rebellious youth in Russia and the émigrés of the Executive Committee of the People's Will[360] and eradicated People's Will from the country.

People's Will has gone down as one of the first and most important terrorist groups in modern history. Yet it was very small. From its inception to its demise five years later, it had no more than four dozen members and never more than 30 at any one time because arrests outnumbered recruitments afterward.[361] In fact, it was small enough for the Russian government to wipe them out. But, as government repression and the social, political, and economic backwardness of Russia persisted, the history of People's Will became a precedent and an inspiration for new politicized generations to emulate.

Within a short time, its members' self-sacrificing struggle and redemptive suffering made them warrior-saints for Russian students. They inspired another attentat on the tsar six years later by a new group that called itself the Terrorist Faction of People's Will to emphasize its continuity with the original group. Tsarist repression had brought about a calm at St. Petersburg universities that masked a strong hatred for the government, which was expressed in a large funeral demonstration marking the anniversary of a nihilist poet on 17 November 1886. Mounted policemen and Cossacks humiliated the more than 1,000 students by trapping them in the cold rain for hours and went on to arrest several nihilistic-looking students. Outraged students wrote a letter of protest—"We counterpose to the brute force that supports the government another force . . . of the organized and united consciousness of our spiritual solidarity"[362]—but got no response. In this politicized atmosphere, three radical student leaders—23-year-old Peter Shevyrov, probably suffering from bipolar affective disorder and tuberculosis;[363] 23-year-old Pole Joseph Lukashevich, whose hero was Kibalchich;[364] and 24-year-old Cossack Vasily Osipanov, who dreamed of being Rakhmetov[365]—convinced half a dozen of their irate friends to join them in seeking revenge. The new recruits included 22-year-old Orest Govorukhin and 20-year-old Alexander Ulyanov, whose father was an academic administrator and whose younger brother Vladimir would become famous as Lenin. "After long and heated discussions of the

matter of systematic terror with Lukashevich and Shevyrov . . . Alexander Ily-
ich [Ulyanov] and I decided to help their cause, although we didn't decisively
commit ourselves to the group. Little by little we were drawn into the work,
fulfilling Shevyrov's commissions."[366] They finally agreed to help out. Osipanov
recruited five friends, two of whom were macho Cossacks who worshipped
Razin and Pugachev and wanted to be bomb-throwers.

All participants took their predecessors as models. A few had already determined to emulate their heroes, and the seemingly trivial insult to their
honor by the police intervention at the demonstration was enough to convince the others to participate. All were already politicized, so the insult fell on
fertile ground. The disillusionment with the lack of response to their protest
helped convince the more reluctant participants that violence was their only
resort. The conspirators sorted themselves according to their social identities.
The scientists made the bombs, and those who identified with their family's
martial background became the bomb-throwers. Ideology seemed to have
been an afterthought, as Ulyanov wrote their manifesto on the eve of the attentat.[367] Rational choice theory cannot explain the participants' self-sacrifice
contrary to their self-interest.

The plot was basically a repeat of the Perovskaya prong of the 1881 attentat
when the tsar would travel to celebrate mass for the sixth anniversary of his
father's assassination on 1 March 1887. But poor tradecraft revealed the plot to
the police, which had no trouble rounding everyone up the day before the
scheduled attentat. The conspirators were tried and convicted in mid-April
1887. On May 8, Ulyanov, Shevyrov, Osipanov, and the other two would-be
bomb throwers were executed. Lukashevich got a life sentence, and the other
conspirators received heavy sentences.[368]

This attentat was the last significant instance of targeted political violence
in Russia for about 14 years. Some plots were conceived by Russian émigré
revolutionaries from the safety of their Western asylum, but they did not reach
Russia. Of course, grievances against the state did not disappear and would
explode again in the early twentieth century.

Conclusions

This account for the turn to political violence resulting in the creation of People's Will and its determination to kill the tsar to spark a revolution shows that
it is a collective story and not a collection of individual stories. Individual
members' travel along the path of violence cannot be understood outside this
collective trend adopting terrorism as a last resort. As suggested by the social
identity perspective, this detailed history from nihilists to People's Will through

populism and Land and Liberty illustrates the double self-categorization first into a political protest community and then into soldiers for the revolution. At first, students were politicized by police brutality and formed an imagined political protest community, which became militantly nonviolent, horrified by the self-promoting manipulation and deception of one of their members. They became disillusioned with their failure to arouse the people through their peaceful pilgrimages to the people and increasingly outraged by the disproportionate violent state repression of their community. The state initiated violence against the peaceful pilgrims and steadily escalated it by introducing the death penalty for violent political crimes. This escalation of conflict between them and the state, along with the radicalization of their discourse and outrage at the judicial murder of some of their peaceful members, shifted influence to a vocal minority advocating violence for self-protection and further social change. The result was the creation of a determined, tight-knit group of dedicated terrorists who persevered for almost two years to achieve their goals despite multiple failures that could have discouraged them.

The ideological argument for this turn to violence fails with the fact that members of People's Will were generally not concerned about ideology, but simply wanted to get rid of the tsars. In fact, their ideology kept changing according to the circumstances of the militants, which transformed them from zealous peace advocates to some of the most determined practitioners of violence. Rational choice theory also has trouble explaining the ubiquitous self-sacrifice of its members, who did not expect to survive to see the revolution and benefit from it.

Most histories of terrorism start with Zasulich's podvig. However, some colleagues from her imagined political protest community had already crossed the threshold of violence. Zasulich was just part of this nascent wave of political violence. Its emergence in Russia cannot be understood without this incubation period, and ignoring this evolution by starting the narrative in the middle suggests that political violence came out of nowhere and obfuscates the collective path that peaceful populists took to become some of the most relentless of terrorists.

Historians cannot be blamed for focusing on People's Will, for there seems to have been something qualitatively different about it than previous conspiracies of political violence. This was the first time a political organization became totally dedicated to violence by going underground; following the model of Rakhmetov, its members abandoned jobs, family, and former friends to focus exclusively on this violence. This may have been the first instance of what can be called the professionalization of political violence.

Chapter 5

Anarchism and the Expansion of Political Violence

The end of the nineteenth century saw two major developments in the history of political violence. The first was a change in its meaning with the concept of propaganda by the deed. Violence was no longer just revenge or the elimination of a tyrant. The violence itself became propaganda to inspire masses to rise up and make the revolution. It became a spectacle to spread one's message. The second was an expansion of political violence to the point that it no longer targeted selected state officials but became more indiscriminate, mostly as a result of the use of explosives, which are an indiscriminate weapon. At first the ideological justification for indiscriminate political violence was proposed by rogue members of the anarchist community, which universally rejected it. But with time, the notion that there are no innocent members of a nation foreshadowed the massacres of the twenty-first century.

Propaganda by the Deed

Some historians trace modern terrorism to the rise of anarchism and propaganda by the deed.[1] In the previous chapter, we saw that Stepan Shiraev had brought back the concept of propaganda by the deed from Switzerland and preached its virtues to his comrades in Land and Liberty. This concept emerged from the Italian anarchist context. The 1873 depression in Europe hit its southern region especially hard and triggered mass unrest in Italy in 1874. Bakunin believed in unleashing the revolutionary potential of the peasants by spreading revolutionary principles "not with words *but with deeds, for this is the most popular, the most potent, and the most irresistible form of propaganda.*"[2] This resonated with Italian anarchists competing against domestic rivals, who could tap into the glory of the Risorgimento: "Violent action . . . was considered a necessity. Having no other means at hand that corresponded with the Garibaldian and Mazzinian revolutionary Italian traditions of the people, recently emerged from the revolutionary period, we needed an affirmation—propaganda of the deed—to pose the problem."[3] In other words, given the insurrectional background of the Italian left, anarchists had to do something spectacular just to get any attention from their colleagues.

Errico Malatesta captured his companions' naïve optimism: "We put our hopes in general discontent, and because the misery that afflicted the masses was so insufferable, we believed it was enough to give an example, launching with arms in hand the cry of 'down with the masters,' in order for the working masses to fling themselves against the bourgeoisie and take possession of the land, the factories, and all that they produced with their toil and that had been stolen from them."[4] The Italian anarchists, funded by Carlo Cafiero, tried to spark an insurrection in July 1874, but the police had been forewarned and arrested most of the prominent anarchists throughout the country. Only 21-year-old Malatesta and half a dozen companions were able to carry out a small-scale insurrection in Puglia in mid-August. They tried to convert the peasants in tiny villages to their cause: the peasants listened but did not move. A large force of *carabinieri* finally arrested the insurrectionists a few days later before they did any harm.[5] At their trial, prosecutors tried to exaggerate their deeds and even manufactured evidence against them. This was easily refuted, and the failed insurgents were acquitted in August 1875. The jurors even congratulated the defendants, who left the courtroom to the acclaims of an awaiting crowd outside. The well-publicized trials mesmerized Italy, giving a boost to their cause. This unexpected publicity was not lost on the anarchists. "Oh, if only the government would multiply these trials! They would cost some of us a few years in prison, but they would immensely benefit our cause."[6] This success reinforced their belief in this strategy: "The insurrectionary deed . . . is the most effective means of propaganda and the only one which . . . can penetrate to the deepest social strata and attract the living forces of humanity into the struggle."[7]

In April 1877, two dozen Italian anarchists tried to repeat their earlier adventure and roamed around the Matese mountain range near Naples preaching anarchism and insurrection. They seized a village town hall and burned all the official documents, including tax registrations and property records, to the delight of the on-looking peasants. Malatesta and Cafiero, the only insurrectionists able to speak the Matese dialect, harangued the peasants about the benefits of anarchy and urged them to take weapons against their masters. The insurrectionists then moved to another town, where they repeated their revolutionary activities. The peasants applauded them and cheered them as they departed, but returned to their daily routines. Suspicion and fear trumped their revolutionary potential. The insurrectionists, including Sergei Kravchinsky, who was resting in Naples at the time when Malatesta invited him to join

them, were arrested after a six-day campaign. A small skirmish with the cara-
binieris resulted in one death and one injury.[8] Despite its failure, the short-
lived insurrection captured national and international attention for a few
weeks. Over the next eighteen months, new recruits flocked to the ranks of the
anarchists.[9]

In June 1877, Andrea Costa, another Italian anarchist, gave a conference
in Geneva on *propagande par le fait* (translated as propaganda by the deed),
and its announcement in the 3 June 1877 *Bulletin de la Fédération Jurassienne*
was the first time the expression appeared in print. Two months later, Paul
Brousse argued that propaganda by the deed was a powerful way to awake
popular consciousness, as it brought to life the ideas of anarchism in an article
entitled "La Propagande par le fait" in the same bulletin.[10] The two failed Italian insurrections were generally peaceful, and the shooting of the two cara-
binieris was accidental.[11] Costa, Cafiero, Malatesta, and Brousse rejected
assassinations and other violent acts throughout their careers.[12] Propaganda
by the deed is often confused with violence and modern terrorism, but its
original meaning was a relatively peaceful spectacular act meant to awaken
the political consciousness of the masses.

In 1881, the success of People's Will influenced revolutionary discussions
in western Europe and the United States. Social revolutionaries tried to resurrect the dormant International Workingmen's Association. On 14 July 1881, 31
prominent anarchist delegates, including Kropotkin, Malatesta, Cafiero,
French Communards, and even Tchaikovsky, gathered in London for six days
to adopt a common program in what became known as the International
Working People's Association (IWPA) to distinguish it from the first IWA.
There was a wide divergence in perspectives; the anarchists agreed only on the
absolute autonomy of all groups.[13] Although some delegates wanted to create
an international revolutionary organization, most objected, and a slim majority at the congress agreed only on the establishment of a correspondence bureau based in London—which never got off the ground. Nevertheless, the
myth of the "Black International," which was to haunt most police forces of the
western world for the next four decades, was born. In its final resolution, the
delegates recognized "the necessity to join propaganda by the deed to spoken
and written propaganda" and recommended to members "to give great weight
to the study and applications of technical and chemical sciences that have already shown their usefulness to the revolutionary cause and will be called to
do more so in the future, as a means of defense and attack."[14] This study was a
euphemism for the manufacture of dynamite. These minimal suggestions
were all that libertarian anarchists could agree on at the congress, but they
were united in their common indignation at the injustice of Johann Most's
trial that had taken place in London two months earlier.

Most was a 35-year-old German socialist firebrand, a former deputy of the German Reichstag who had previously been imprisoned for political agitation. In the widespread crackdown after the two 1878 attentats on Wilhelm I, Most lost his Reichstag seat and was forced into exile. He arrived in London, where, taking full advantage of British liberal laws, he started publication of a newspaper called *Freiheit* (freedom) in January 1879. His newspaper and fiery speeches made him popular among the radical left in Europe. Most celebrated the tsar's assassination in *Freiheit*. "Triumph! Triumph! . . . One of the most abominable tyrants of Europe . . . who caused innumerable heroes and heroines of the Russian people to be destroyed or imprisoned—the Tsar of Russia is no more."[15] The article encouraged others to follow suit. Most was arrested and tried at the Old Bailey for libel justifying assassination and intent to incite persons to conspire against the lives of sovereigns of Europe. He was convicted on 26 May 1881 and sentenced to 16 months of hard labor. Overnight, Most became a martyr of the socialist movement in Europe.[16] Pledges of support and contributions came from Europe and America. But Most could not communicate with his followers from prison. *Freiheit* ceased to exist, and the indignation at his conviction gradually faded.

What had convinced British authorities to crack down on Most's call for violence was the sustained campaign of bombings Britain was experiencing at the time. The Fenian Skirmishing Campaign, from January 1881 to January 1885, was conducted from New York and involved about two dozen bombings with much material damage. It eventually ended because of lack of support for the campaign in Ireland, poor tradecraft by the skirmishers, and extensive British infiltration of their organization in the United States—indeed, with so many British agents of influence within the Skirmisher leadership, it is difficult to untangle what was inherent to the Skirmishers and what was state entrapment.[17]

Like the Italian diaspora campaigning against Napoleon III, the bombers felt part of a very small vanguard and considered themselves soldiers for Ireland. As soldiers, they followed a martial code of conduct. "I was determined and quite ready to sacrifice my life if necessary . . . I have acted right, confident that I have committed no wrong, outrage or crime whatsoever, and that I have cast no disgrace."[18] During their operations, they carefully avoided injuring people as much as possible, while causing the maximum material damage. They even hesitated to shoot unarmed policemen apprehending them. Despite causing a great deal of damage to buildings over four years, their campaign of violence killed only one person. However, their bombs wounded about 100 people. At their trial, they kept a military-like bearing. But despite this honorable demeanor, Irish people in Ireland never embraced them. They were simply unwelcome strangers from America needlessly complicating an already complex situation at a particularly sensitive time.[19]

The Haymarket Martyrs

The 1881 London congress was a sign of the growing popularity of anarchism, in its specific ideological sense, from the theories of Max Stirner, Pierre-Joseph Proudhon, Mikhail Bakunin, and Peter Kropotkin. Like nihilism, anarchism is not synonymous with political violence or terrorism. Before the word acquired this specific philosophical meaning in the second half of the nineteenth century, it just meant being against authority. People called violent political challengers "anarchists" in the general sense of the term. Only in the first half of the twentieth century did the word *terrorist* become more popular and replace *anarchist* to refer to politically violent people.

Philosophical anarchism preaches social change, but most versions of anarchism advocate peaceful change. Its anti-hierarchical message resonated with workers, and the industrialization in the West dramatically increased their numbers, resulting in an explosion of anarchists in the last third of the nineteenth century. As strong individualists, they lacked the discipline of an overall organization to prevent rogue members from engaging in violence. A few anarchists self-categorized with workers and appointed themselves as defenders or avengers of working-class martyrs—usually over the opposition of most workers. If we discount the intense but brief blood orgies in April 1834, June 1848, and May 1871 in France and the bloody repression of workers' demonstrations in Russia in 1903–1906, which were more than simple class warfare, this labor struggle was probably far bloodier in the United States than in all countries of Europe combined.[20]

In the United States, labor violence was stimulated by a desire for self-defense against predatory aggression of industrialists. Indeed, the victims of state and industrialist violence greatly outnumbered those of workers' violence, but the latter got all the attention of the hostile press. The present focus on anarchist violence should not be interpreted as blaming the anarchists for this violence, as industrialists or the state usually initiated it. However, since the industrialists influenced the state to carry out much of this violence on their behalf, this book on non-state political violence needs to focus on anarchist violence. This exploration of the anarchists' turn to political violence is hindered by the relative lack of reliable primary sources. The trials of alleged perpetrators were full of prosecutorial (and judicial) malfeasance, including perjury of state witnesses amounting to frame-ups. The alleged perpetrators usually denied their role in the violence—and rightly so, as later evidence exonerated them. One of the few well-documented cases was Alexander Berkman's attentat on Henry Frick during the Homestead strike. To understand his turn to violence, we need to trace the evolution of the American anarchist community.

A series of murders was committed in the context of coal miner organizing in Pennsylvania in the 1870s, and it was feared that they were secretly coordinated by a group called the "Molly Maguires." Based on such flimsy evidence that, to this day, it is still not clear whether this organization even existed, 20 labor organizers were tried, convicted, and hanged in 1877.[21] They became the first martyrs of American labor. A few weeks after their execution, a 10 percent decrease in wages sparked the Great Railroad Strike of 1877, which rapidly spread to 17 states and was put down with force by police, local militias, and the U.S. Army. About 100 workers were killed and countless wounded.[22] The violence of the state suppression of the strike shocked workers to their core but provided a blueprint for industrialists on how to deal with labor unrest. The few strikes in the next few years were similarly and brutally put down by the police, militia, and hired gunmen, such as the Pinkertons.[23] At this point, workers' violence was considered criminal and not yet political.

Labor leaders tried to address their grievances through the political system by trying to get some friendly candidates elected, but soon lost faith in the ballot box as a means to improve the workers' conditions. The evolution of labor in the United States was not conducive to the development of a collective identity among workers. Immigrants poured in from Europe—5.5 million in the 1880s alone—and sorted themselves into different national, cultural, and linguistic communities. To make matters worse, they competed for the same jobs, hired themselves out as strikebreakers, and undermined any real efforts at larger organizing.[24] The Revolutionary Socialist Party, an umbrella association formed in Chicago in October 1881, could not overcome this fragmentation, which prevented the emergence of a transcending social identity. The party was an amalgam of revolutionaries united by their opposition to authority, whether the state, business owners, or church, but divided by different ideologies and concerns about events in their home countries. They disagreed about tactics and strategies. The arrival of Johann Most in America provided them with a unifying prototype.

After his release from prison in Britain, Most continued to be harassed by authorities and accepted an invitation to come to America for a lecture tour. He arrived in New York in December 1882 to a cheering crowd. Over the next six months, he delivered 200 speeches all over the country and became one of America's best-known faces. He stayed and resumed publishing *Freiheit*, still in German, mixing articles about theory for intellectuals and exhortations in more colloquial language for workers. By mid-1883, he was the indisputable

voice for anarchy in the United States and re-energized disillusioned anarchists.[25] At a congress in Pittsburgh in October 1883, they tried to consolidate
their faction. They distanced themselves from the Socialist Labor Party, which
was advocating a constitutional strategy, and called themselves the International Working People's Association in the spirit of the London congress. Its
"Pittsburgh Proclamation" gave it a common platform and declared that the
American economic "system is unjust, insane and murderous. It is therefore
necessary to totally destroy it with and by all means, and with the greatest energy on the part of everyone who suffers by it."[26] It warned not to expect "that
the capitalists of this age will give up their rulership without being forced to do
it . . . They will not resign their privileges voluntarily . . . There remains but
one recourse—FORCE! . . . What we would achieve is, therefore, plainly and
simply . . . destruction of the existing class rule, by all means, i.e., by energetic,
relentless, revolutionary, and international action . . . Peaceful education and
voluntary conspiracy . . . can and ought to run in parallel lines."[27] This clear
political platform moved its advocated violence from the criminal to the political arena, both for the anarchists as well as for the rest of society.

The depression of 1883–1886 created severe distress in workers, who
flocked to the new IWPA. Resistance to the imposition of harsh discipline in
new industrial factories contributed to the popularity of anarchist ideas rejecting such organizational structure. The failure of political action and trade
unionism gave the IWPA's violent rhetoric credibility and shifted social influence to its champions among politicized workers. Continued violent repression by industrialists convinced many to arm themselves for self-protection.
Paramilitary Lehr und Wehr Verein (Education and Defense Society) units
became popular and regularly conducted drills in large cities. However, they
still organized themselves along lines of national origin or language, preventing the fractured IWPA from becoming a unified and effective force. As the
economic situation deteriorated, most IWPA members believed that revolution was imminent and anticipated that owners would enlist troops with firearms and new Gatling guns against them in the upcoming fight. To counter
this great disparity in weaponry, IWPA leaders preached the acquisition of
dynamite, which had already been used against property to intimidate owners
in labor disputes. Most became the high priest of the cult of dynamite: "Today,
the importance of explosives as an instrument for carrying out revolutions
oriented to social justice is obvious. Anyone can see that these materials will
be the decisive factor in the next period of world history. It therefore makes
sense for revolutionaries in all countries to acquire explosives and to learn the
skills needed to use them in real situations."[28]

Most had clandestinely worked in a dynamite factory for a few months to
get practical skills in its manufacture. He serialized specific recipes for making

explosives and other weapons in *Freiheit*: "We have already pointed out that the cheapest way to get explosives is to buy them ready-made, or confiscate them. For those who have absolutely no other choice than to make everything themselves, we shall now provide the necessary instructions. We shall avoid scientific and technical jargon and specialized expressions that impede understanding by the layman."[29] He collected his articles in an 1885 pamphlet, *Science of Revolutionary Warfare: A Handbook of Instruction regarding the Use and Manufacture of Nitroglycerine, Dynamite, Gun-Cotton, Fulminating Mercury, Bombs, Arsons, Poisons, etc.* The pamphlet became an instant bestseller among anarchists. It was widely praised in IWPA newspapers. "Dynamite! Of all the good stuff, that is the stuff! . . . In giving dynamite to the downtrodden millions of the globe science has done its best work. The dear stuff can be carried in the pocket without danger, while it is a formidable weapon against any force of militia, police, or detectives that may want to stifle the cry for justice that goes forth from the plundered slaves. It is . . . exceedingly useful. It can be used against persons and things. It is better to use it against the former than against bricks and masonry . . . It brings terror and fear to the robbers."[30]

IWPA's enthusiasm for dynamite and violence was such that its opponents started calling its members anarchists, as a derogative term. However, IWPA members adopted it as a sign of pride. "We began to allude to ourselves as anarchists and that name, which was at first imputed to us as a dishonor, we came to cherish and defend with pride."[31] By 1885, most IWPA journals had the term *anarchist* in their subtitles. Their talk about violence was about retaliatory violence, self-protection, and angry refusal to submit, as had happened in 1877. For all their posturing, IWPA leaders, including Most, remained men of words rather than deeds: they had never been personally violent. The gap between the advocacy of violence to destroy the capitalist system and its actual practice was very wide.[32] But far from deterring their enemies, this war of words of course alarmed and unified capitalists, the middle class, and the state, who came to fear that anarchists were conspiring to launch a preventive and comprehensive all-out attack on them. Similar to the run-up to the Terror in France, this cumulative radicalization of discourse created the conditions that triggered the Haymarket incident.

Workers gave an ultimatum to factory owners to implement an eight-hour working day by 1 May 1886 or face a general strike, which the anarchists hoped might spark their long-awaited insurrection.[33] At the same time, the authorities were ready to suppress the radical movement once and for all. "The public mind was in a state of fear and suspense, not knowing the direction whence threatened devastation and destruction might appear."[34] On 1 May 1886, about 40,000 workers walked out on strike in Chicago, while another 45,000 were granted an eight-hour day. A peaceful demonstration of 80,000

people walked through the center of town. Two days later, there were altercations at a factory lockout between dismissed workers and scabs protected by
Pinkerton agents and the police. The police shot into the crowd, killing two
protestors and wounding dozens. Outraged IWPA leaders called for a large
demonstration at Haymarket Square on the next evening, 4 May. The turnout
was a disappointing 3,000 workers. By the time the last speech was ending,
most of them had gone home, and about 300 workers were still left when the
police came marching in formation to disband the meeting. A bomb thrown
at the police exploded, killing one policeman and wounding two dozen others.
The police panicked and started shooting in all directions, killing six of their
colleagues and wounding another three dozen. The civilian toll was estimated
at a similar level of casualties since there was no official count. This is what the
forensics later reported, but at the time, the press and the police believed that
the fatalities and casualties were all due to the explosion and fire from anarchists in the crowd.[35]

The Haymarket explosion triggered the first "red scare" in American history. The feared antipersonnel use of dynamite had occurred, and panic ran
deep. The press screamed for blood and fueled the hysteria for months.[36]
"Some of the prominent police officials, in their zeal, not only terrorized ignorant men by throwing them into prison and threatening them with torture if
they refused to swear to anything desired, but they offered money and employment to those who would consent to do this. Further . . . they deliberately
planned to have fictitious conspiracies formed in order that they might get the
glory of discovering them."[37] A state reign of terror descended on Chicago for
about eight weeks as the bombing was believed to be part of a vast anarchist
conspiracy.[38] Even Johann Most in New York was arrested because ten days
prior to the bombing he had brandished a rifle before an audience in New
York to demonstrate his seriousness. "To arm is not hard. Buy these, steal revolvers, make bombs, and when you have enough, rise and seize what is yours.
Take the city by force and capitalists by the throat. Shoot or be shot!" He was
tried on charges of inciting a riot and disturbing the peace, convicted, and
sentenced to a year at hard labor.[39]

In Chicago, all the detained anarchists were eventually released, except for
eight leaders: Alfred Parsons, August Spies, George Engel, Adolph Fischer,
Louis Lingg, Oscar Neebe, Michael Schwab, and Samuel Fielden. Only Fielden
had been present at Haymarket Square at the time of the bombing. He had just
concluded a speech and was coming down from the podium, surrounded by
journalists. The "Chicago Eight" were indicted for the murder of the only policeman definitely killed by the bomb. Their trial started in July 1886, when the
city was still in the midst of unprecedented hysteria. The judge allowed the
jury to be packed with people clearly prejudiced against the defendants,

conducted it with "malicious ferocity" in blatant partiality for the prosecution, and attempted to influence the jury in its favor.[40] The prosecution admitted it had not caught the bomb-thrower and argued that the defendants formed a conspiracy resulting in the bombing, but all defendants had airtight alibis. In his later review of the affair, Illinois Governor John Altgeld concluded: "The facts tend to show that the bomb was thrown as an act of personal revenge, and . . . the prosecution has never discovered who threw it, and the evidence utterly fails to show that the man who did throw it ever heard or read a word coming from the defendants; consequently it fails to show that he acted on any advice given by them."[41] Indeed, Altgeld blamed the police for the incident.[42] At the end of the trial, the judge instructed the jury that if the defendants "by print or speech advised, or encouraged the commission of murder, without designating time, place or occasion at which it should be done, . . . and induced by such advice and encouragement, murder was committed, then all of such conspirators are guilty of such murder, whether the person who perpetrated such murder can be identified or not."[43] Altgeld found this interpretation of the law contrary to all the precedents he reviewed.[44]

After a few hours of deliberation, the jury convicted all eight defendants. The verdict was universally acclaimed in the popular press, which viewed the anarchists guilty as a group because they had promoted the cult of dynamite and urged resistance to the police and the end of the existing order. Other socialists and labor leaders also distanced themselves from anarchists. This near universal backlash silenced all anarchist talk of violence for a time. But the episode inexorably linked anarchism with bombings in the public's mind. Anarchists became typical terrorists, in the modern usage of the term. This stereotype of a terrorist—wild-haired, bushy-bearded, crazed-eyed, black-dressed, foreign-looking fanatic, with dynamite in one hand, a pistol or a blood-soaked dagger in the other—has persisted to this day despite the facts that the words *terrorism* or *terrorist* were never used at the time and the actual bomb-thrower was never identified.

The sentencing hearing was held in October 1886. All the defendants remained defiant, especially 21-year-old Lingg, who had just come from Germany and had been building bombs, but of a different type than the one that was thrown: "If they use cannons against us, we shall use dynamite against them . . . I am the enemy of the 'order' of today, and . . . with all my powers, so long as breath remains in me, I shall combat it . . . I am in favor of using force . . . You laugh! . . . I die happy on the gallows, so confident am I that the hundreds and thousands to whom I have spoken will remember my words; and when you shall have hanged us, then—mark my words—they will do the bomb-throwing! In this hope do I say to you: I despise you. I despise your order, your laws, your force-propped authority. Hang me for it!"[45] All the defendants were sentenced to death by hanging except for Neebe, who received 15 years at hard labor.

The sentences generated strong indignation among liberals and socialists worldwide. Even in despotic Russia, terrorists were spared death if they had no blood directly on their hands.[46] As the hysteria against anarchists calmed down, the misconduct of the trial was there for all to see. The defendants appealed in vain to the U.S. Supreme Court. Lingg blew himself up with a small explosive device smuggled into his cell. Only Schwab and Fielden appealed for clemency to Governor Richard Oglesby, who commuted their sentences to life in prison. Spies, Parsons, Fischer, and Engel were executed by hanging on 11 November 1887.[47] This day became a worldwide anarchist commemoration of the Chicago Five martyrs, the first true anarchist martyrs, on par with the victims of the Paris Commune.[48]

The Homestead Strike Incident

American anarchists were forced to keep a low profile during the backlash of the Haymarket bombing, but the martyrdom of the Chicago Five became a source of inspiration for the next generation of anarchists. Russian-born 17-year-old Emma Goldman, who had just come to Rochester, New York, with her older sister to escape an unhappy family situation, followed the trial in *Freiheit* and learned about anarchism. "The reports in the Rochester newspapers irritated, confused and upset us by their evident prejudice. The violence of the press, the bitter denunciation of the accused, the attacks on all foreigners, turned our sympathies to the Haymarket victims."[49] She was devastated by its eventual outcome: "The innocent blood of the Haymarket martyrs was calling for revenge . . . I was in a stupor; a feeling of numbness came over me, something too horrible even for tears . . . I was entirely absorbed in what I felt as my own loss . . . The next morning I woke as from a long illness, but free from the numbness and the depression of those harrowing weeks of waiting, ending with the final shock. I had a distinct sensation that something new and wonderful had been born in my soul. A great ideal, a burning faith, a determination to dedicate myself to the memory of my martyred comrades, to make their cause my own, to make known to the world their beautiful lives and heroic deaths."[50]

Goldman decided to ask Johann Most in New York to help her in her new mission. She arrived in August 1889 and hoped to set up a Rakhmetovan sewing cooperative.[51] An acquaintance took her to Sachs's Café to meet the Minkin sisters, who were looking for a roommate. There she was also introduced to 19-year-old Alexander (Sasha) Berkman, a nephew of Mark Natanson, who was his role model. Berkman had immigrated to New York the previous year after his parents' death.[52] He had read *Freiheit* in Vilnius and looked up its office when he landed in New York. He became a typesetter for the newspaper and hung around Most's group of anarchists. He patterned himself on Rakhmetov and Nechaev's portrait of a revolutionary—everything had to be dedicated to the cause of revolution.[53] The next day, Berkman took Goldman to the *Freiheit* office to meet Most, who immediately took an interest in the bright and attractive young woman. Goldman and Berkman spent the rest of the day together, discussing politics and their conviction that America had become as despotic as Russia with the hanging of the Chicago martyrs. Berkman said, "Someday I will avenge our dead." She replied, "I too . . . their death gave me life. It now belongs to their memory—to their work." Berkman suggested, "We are comrades. Let us be friends, too—let us work together."[54] They also quickly became lovers.

About a week later, Berkman introduced Goldman to his cousin Modest (Modska) Aronstam, who shared their beliefs but not Berkman's single-mindedness.[55] They all hung out with the Minkin sisters. Lingg was their idol: "In our eyes he stood out as the sublime hero among the eight. His unbending spirit, his utter contempt for his accusers and judges, his will-power, which made him rob his enemies of their prey and die by his own hand—everything about that boy of twenty-two lent romance and beauty to his personality. He became the beacon of our lives."[56] Modska was an artist and Goldman posed nude for him. They also became lovers.

Like some of their comrades, they mimicked Lingg's physical appearance and were nicknamed "Lingg."[57] Soon, Berkman, Aronstam, Goldman, and Helen Minkin moved into an apartment, where they embraced the Rakhmetovan arrangement and shared everything. Most also started dating Goldman and opened new cultural horizons for her. "His own rich personality meant far more to me—the alternating heights and depths of his spirit, his hatred of the capitalist system, his vision of a new society of beauty and joy for all. Most became my idol. I worshipped him."[58] He spotted her talent as a speaker and convinced her to go on a speaking tour in early 1890. Romance reinforced politics: Goldman was sexually involved with all three men, and Most also became involved with Helen Minkin. As anarchists, they believed that love should not be possessive.

Sasha, Emma, and Modska gradually drifted away from Most. They viewed him as too authoritarian, no longer an active revolutionary, and even perhaps sexually jealous. The trio moved to Worcester, Massachusetts, to raise money for the cause. They again lived together and opened a restaurant there. The young anarchists stayed abreast of anarchist news and followed the unfolding attentats in France.

In May 1892, labor tension arose at the Carnegie Steel Company in Homestead, Pennsylvania. Its chairman, Henry Clay Frick, wanted to roll back some gains won by the workers and completely eliminate their union. On 29 June, he locked them out of his factories and planned to bring in replacements protected by the Pinkerton Agency. Even the most conservative members of the press condemned his arbitrary and drastic methods.[59] The young Worcester anarchists followed these developments. "We became so absorbed in the news that we would not permit ourselves enough time even for sleep. At daybreak one of the boys would be off to get the first editions of the papers. We saturated ourselves with the events in Homestead to the exclusion of everything else. Entire nights we would sit up discussing the various phases of the situation, almost engulfed by the possibilities of the gigantic struggle."[60]

In early July, Goldman read that sheriffs evicted the families of strikers from company houses. She took the paper back to her two lovers. Berkman said that he must go to Homestead. "I flung my arms around him, crying out his name. I, too, would go. 'We must go tonight,' he said; 'the great moment has come at last!' Being internationalist, he added . . . we must bring them our great message and help them see that it was not only for the moment that they must strike, but for all time, for a free life, for anarchism. Russia had many heroic men and women, but who was there in America?"[61]

The three companions left for New York early the next morning. Their plan was to write a manifesto to the workers, translate it into English, print the two texts in New York, and take them to Pittsburgh, where, with the help of local comrades, Goldman could address them.[62] Berkman later remembered: "I could no longer remain indifferent. The moment was urgent. The toilers of Homestead . . . were awakening. But as yet the steelworkers were only blindly rebellious. The vision of Anarchism alone could imbue the discontent with conscious revolutionary purpose; it alone could lend wings to the aspirations of labor. The dissemination of our ideas among the proletariat of Homestead would illuminate the great struggle, help to clarify the issues, and point the way to complete ultimate emancipation."[63]

On 6 July, Goldman and Berkman read that the Pinkertons had shot at the strikers and killed women and children.[64] "We were stunned. We saw at once that the time for our manifesto had passed. Words had lost their meanings in the face of the innocent blood spilled . . . Sasha broke the silence. 'Frick is the responsible factor in this crime,' he said; 'he must be made to stand the consequences.' It was the psychological moment for an *Attentat*; the whole country was aroused, everybody was considering Frick the perpetrator of a cold-blooded murder. A blow aimed at Frick would re-echo in the poorest hovel, would call the attention of the whole world to the real cause behind the

Homestead struggle. It would also strike terror in the enemy's ranks and make them realize that the proletariat of America had its avengers."[65]

Berkman later explained his attentat on Frick. To him, tyrants had stolen what belonged to the people. In his moral logic, "The removal of a tyrant is not merely justifiable; it is the highest duty of every true revolutionist. Human life is, indeed, sacred and inviolate. But the killing of a tyrant, of an enemy of the People, is in no way to be considered as the taking of a life. A revolutionist would rather perish a thousand times than be guilty of what is ordinarily called murder. In truth, murder and *attentat* are to me opposite terms. To re-move a tyrant is an act of liberation, the giving of life and opportunity to an oppressed people." This unpleasant act became the test or even pride of a true revolutionary, "to sacrifice all merely human feelings at the call of the People's Cause. If the latter demand his life, so much the better." He felt he was such a revolutionary and not a hero. "It merely means a revolutionist who does his duty. There is no heroism in that: it is neither more nor less than a revolution-ist should do ... I am simply a revolutionist, a terrorist by conviction, an in-strument for furthering the cause of humanity; in short a Rakhmetov. Indeed, I shall assume that name upon my arrival in Pittsburgh."[66]

It is clear from the above that Berkman believed that in carrying out his attentat, he was simply acting as a soldier for the revolution. Attentats are what revolutionary soldiers do. The three conspirators got bomb-making material and tried the recipes in Most's *Science of Revolutionary Warfare,* but their test bomb failed to explode. Goldman and Aronstam insisted they go with Berk-man, who would not hear of it: it would be unnecessary and even criminal to waste three lives on one man. Berkman expected to be condemned to death and wanted to die proudly in the assurance that he gave his life for the people. "But I will die by my own hand, like Lingg. Never will I permit our enemies to kill me."[67] He would kill Frick not as a man, but as the enemy of labor.[68] Gold-man still insisted on going and dying with him, citing Perovskaya, who had let herself be captured and die on the scaffold with her love Zhelyabov.[69] Berkman left by train, and Goldman was to wire him $20 so he could buy a decent suit and a gun and knife to kill Frick, copying Zasulich's attentat on General Trepov. Goldman even tried to raise money through prostitution but was so inept at it that a potential customer just took her out for a drink, gave her $10 for effort, and advised her to quit this line of work. She got the rest of the money from her sister in Rochester and wired it to Berkman.[70]

On 23 July 1892, Berkman went to Frick's private office and shot him three times.[71] He was tackled by the staff before he could kill himself and arrested. The press and socialists immediately condemned the attentat. The strikers dis-tanced themselves from it as well, as it was discrediting their simple demands to maintain their work conditions. Indeed, it may have undermined their cause, as the press, which had so far been sympathetic, turned against them because of their alleged association with anarchists. The Carnegie negotiators stiffened their position, and the workers returned to work in November under the terms dictated by Frick, who had recovered from his wounds.[72]

Goldman felt elated by the act and was supported by her circle of friends. She organized a mass meeting of well-known anarchists in support of Berkman. But in *Freiheit*, Most, released from prison, wrote that Berkman's act was a failure, a mistake, misguided and feckless. He criticized attentats, which were futile in a country without proletarian consciousness because workers could not understand them. Unlike countries where they were the only way to make a statement, in America propaganda by the word was possible and should be used instead.[73] Most's argument repudiated everything that he had promoted for the past ten years. Goldman was furious, for it betrayed Berkman at the time when he most needed support. She defended the attentat in a rival journal with the romantic argument that the vital thing was the motive rather than the success of the act and demanded an explanation for Most's abrupt reversal.[74] As Most ignored her, she went to his next lecture and sat in the front row. When Most came to the podium, she loudly asked for explanations. When Most mumbled something about hysterical women, she jumped onto the podium, pulled out a horsewhip, lashed him across the face and neck, then broke the whip and threw the pieces at him.[75] Berkman's attentat, Most's condemnation, and Goldman's defense of it generated intense discussions among American anarchists. The older generation believed in building support among workers, while the younger one supported Berkman and Goldman in their radicalism.[76]

Like his Russian predecessors, Berkman hoped to use his trial for propaganda purposes. He represented himself and carefully prepared a statement in German explaining his action. But the authorities were equally determined not to allow proselytism in the courtroom. At his trial on 19 September 1892, Berkman brought his statement to be read in court and asked for an interpreter. The court granted him one—but he was blind and could not read. When Berkman read it, his statements were poorly translated, and the judge limited him to five minutes. The jury found him guilty on all counts, and the judge sentenced him to 22 years in prison.[77]

Berkman and Goldman never became the leaders and inspiration of the American labor movement that they had dreamed of. At a time when labor was still uneasy with the example of the Chicago martyrs, they self-categorized with these martyrs (along with their Russian revolutionary heroes) and especially with the most extreme one, Lingg, whom they took as their prototype. Their disillusionment with legal methods of protest and their outrage at the Pinkerton atrocities pushed them over the edge to violence on behalf of their

imagined community of workers. But, like Russian peasants with the populists, workers rejected them because they were obviously not part of the strikers who were unfamiliar with their strange abstract principles. The workers
simply wanted to maintain their hard-won material gains and collective bar-
gaining. Berkman was just an outsider and did not even speak their language.
Like many self-appointed champions of a cause, Berkman and Goldman were
living in their fantasies.

The attentat on Frick was the end of an era. After it, police vigilance and a
strategy to earn the trust of workers forced American anarchists to stop advocating violence in their newspapers and speeches. Many channeled their energy into more active roles in trade unions for the next two decades.

Reprises Individuelles

Our narrative on the evolution of indiscriminate political violence returns to
France. Up to this point, political violence had focused on specific targets—a
responsible head of state, a brutal state agent, an obstacle to social change—
and tried to minimize collateral damage to distinguish itself from criminal
violence. Developments in late nineteenth-century France blurred this distinction and led to the justification of indiscriminate violence as rogue anarchists argued that no one in their out-group was innocent as its members
perpetuated the social system of persecution against them. The rest of this
chapter examines this expansion of the anarchists' targeted out-group to the
bourgeoisie, leading to more indiscriminate political violence.

Anarchism also became popular in France, especially after the general
amnesty of 1880 allowed condemned Communards to return from exile.
Informal groups of anarchists sprang up almost overnight, especially in industrial places. They subscribed to anarchist newspapers and through their
communications and occasional meetings formed an informal network of
people sharing a similar social identity.[78] The names they chose for
themselves—"partisan of dynamite," "insurgents," "revolver in hand," "social war," or simply "dynamite"[79]—seem to have been a conscious attempt to
intimidate industrialists and authorities in the context of labor disputes,
which inevitably led to violence.

In March 1882, 19-year-old Pierre Fournier spontaneously shot and
slightly injured an industrialist during a lockout in despair and revenge for his
inability to find any other work.[80] In August, near Lyon, a group of armed
miners called the "Black Band" dynamited several crosses and religious stat-
ues, and pillaged and burned a chapel in protest of the firing of atheist miners
denounced by its priest.[81] Authorities arrested 23 anarchists, who denied their

involvement or the existence of the Black Band at their October 1883 trial. The trial was interrupted and postponed due to death threats against the judge and jury and linked to a series of explosions in Lyon.[82]

Lyon anarchists had tried to rescue their "soldiers"[83] by intimidation, backed up by a bombing at a restaurant, Bellecour, that killed one person and wounded half a dozen in the early morning of 23 October 1882. Later on the same day, a second bomb went off at a military recruitment center and caused only material damages.[84] This aggression against the social order in general transformed a criminal incident into a political one. The police suspected that a "Black International" was coordinating this series of explosions and arrested all the prominent anarchists of the region, including Kropotkin, who was living nearby, close to the Swiss border. Charged with belonging to an international association for disturbing the peace, 66 defendants went on trial in January 1883. They were convicted and sentenced to prison terms—Kropotkin got five years.[85] The police arrested another local anarchist, 22-year-old Antoine Cyvoct, for the Bellecour explosion. He was tried, convicted despite his denials, and sentenced to death.[86] Cyvoct became another martyr for the anarchists. During the summer and fall of 1883, local anarchists carried out a dozen bombings of industrialists in the region, resulting in about a dozen wounded. They were captured, tried, and convicted to prison terms.[87]

Belief in the necessity of violence separated anarchists from their comrades on the left. During the 1880s, this violence was mostly for intimidation, with incendiary devices exploding near police stations, prisons, labor placement bureaus, and military recruitment centers. They were carefully timed to detonate so as to cause the maximum material damage with minimum human harm.[88] French Marxists criticized the lack of efficacy of these tactics. "Let's not preach personal war but class war: the first only results in individual punishments while the second tries to transform the economic system."[89] The mainstream press sharply criticized anarchists for these explosions and denounced them as ruffians, simple outlaws, and thieves.

In the middle of the decade, illegalism, a variant of anarchism, emerged. In October 1887, Clément Duval and an accomplice burglarized and tried to set fire to the townhouse of an art collector. Two weeks later, the police caught up with Duval, who resisted arrest and stabbed one of the policemen. He claimed to be an anarchist, and the mainstream press immediately picked up on his past criminal record and denounced him and other anarchists as thieves. Duval protested in a letter to *La Révolte*, the flagship anarchist newspaper. He had been wounded in the war of 1870 and required medications for the rest of his life. He had a wife and two children, and when he was laid off in 1878, he had no choice but to steal 80 francs for his expensive medication and the survival of his family. He proclaimed his anarchist beliefs and pride in his past condemnation. "When society refuses one the right of existence, one must take it and not hold out his hand, which would be cowardice."[90] But was this a case of a thief hiding behind the pretense of anarchism and discrediting the movement, or was it an anarchist "expropriating bourgeois property" (as anarchists termed theft)? Illegalism expanded legitimate targets of anarchism to all propertied bourgeois. The editors of *La Révolte* reserved judgment and promised to closely monitor the trial.[91] More radical anarchist papers defended Duval against the mainstream press.

At the February 1888 trial, Duval said that his accomplice set fire to the residence when he was disappointed with the take. He rejected the charge of attempted murder on the policeman. "The officer arrested me in the name of the law; I struck him in the name of liberty!"[92] In front of an audience packed with his friends, he turned the tables on his prosecutor. "I am not a thief, but a rebel. I have to tell you why I am an anarchist . . . Theft for us is a restitution! When I looted the townhouse . . . I acted as an anarchist. I gave people a lesson of propaganda by the deed. You are persecuting me because of my political opinions. I do not recognize people's right to judge me; I do not recognize your law. I am not a defendant, I am an avenger . . . Long live anarchy! Long live the social revolution. You are lucky! I will blow you up, I only robbed to better blow you up!"[93] The audience echoed, "Long live anarchy! Long live the social revolution!" Duval was taken away in a straitjacket, and in his absence, the jury convicted him and condemned him to death. Given the unexpected harshness of the sentence, the president of the republic commuted it to life at hard labor.[94]

Duval's straight demeanor at trial, his bellicose defense of anarchic principles, and probably the approval of his companions in the audience convinced the editors of *La Révolte*. "For us, Duval is a perfectly honest man. He illustrates anarchist morality . . . He has shown us what all the disinherited ones must do on the day of the revolution. We do not recognize individual property. Let us show it by our actions as well as our words."[95] All the anarchist press closed ranks behind their flagship journal and criticized the mainstream press as "guard dogs of bourgeois property." Anarchists organized demonstrations protesting the harshness of his sentence. Anarchists often used the proceeds of their robberies to fund their press and give money to their needy companions. This Robin Hood principle of robbing the rich to give to the poor, called *reprises individuelles*,[96] was again a source of polemical exchanges during the trial of Vittorio Pini in 1889.[97]

Support for reprises individuelles became a second distinction between anarchists and socialists. Although socialists understood the necessity of stealing as a last measure to feed oneself, they did not consider theft as a revolutionary act furthering the revolution. Jean Grave, editor-in-chief of *La Révolte*, shared their concerns. While he allowed his staff to support reprises individu-elles, he refused to allow them to glorify these illegal acts, like all the other anarchist newspapers. He feared that such acts would pollute the purity of anarchy with non-revolutionary criminal appetites that might discredit the movement.[98]

By the late 1880s, French anarchists were organized into small, tight groups loosely linked with one another. Unlike their American counterparts, they shared the same language, cultural background, and sense of shared so-cial identity. They called themselves companions and often met in the eve-nings, usually with their families, to socialize, eat, drink, sing, and discuss politics. They spontaneously helped other companions. Hospitality for a needy comrade—feeding him, sheltering him, and helping him find work—became a sacred duty. They contributed to mutual aid funds for those struck by adver-sity. They appropriated many symbols of France for themselves: they believed themselves the true descendants of the French Revolution and sang the *Mar-seillaise* at their meetings before this song became the French national anthem—when it did, they replaced it with the *Internationale*. They con-structed their shared social identity around their adoptions of certain martyrs, like the victims of the Paris Commune, the executed Russian revolutionaries, and of course the Chicago Five. And they shared a vague utopia, where people were free and equal, without any exploitation or domination.[99]

A very active press, ranging from the highbrow *La Révolte* to the collo-quial *Le Père Peinard* or *L'Endehors,* united them in a discursive political pro-test community despite their diversity. At the height of anarchism's popularity, there were about 250 of these newspapers circulating around France, influenc-ing about 100,000 people.[100] Anarchists refused to register for the draft and abstained from voting, which they believed legitimized the government. A few of them also engaged in illegal acts, such as counterfeiting money, carrying out reprises individuelles and setting up explosions against property—propaganda by the deed.[101]

Ravachol's Martyrdom

The Chicago Five provided the anarchist movement with its first internation-ally accepted martyrs. The Second Socialist International met in Paris in July 1889 and passed a resolution to adopt 1 May, May Day, as an international an-nual labor holiday to commemorate the martyrs and promote the eight-hour day. The first May Day took place in various parts of France and Spain in 1890, when workers left their jobs to celebrate the holiday, with some minor clashes with the police.[102] Its 1891 celebration became the triggering event for the subsequent wave of political violence that terrorized France for more than two years.

In the northern town of Fourmies, factory owners refused to allow their workers to take the day off, and its mayor called the police and army in anticipation of trouble. Workers who took the day off confronted those who did not, and the police arrested four protestors. A crowd asked for their release and threw rocks at the soldiers. Their commander warned the crowd and then ordered his troops to shoot. Ten people, half of them children and young women, were killed and about three dozen wounded. Two labor leaders were arrested for inciting the crowd and later sentenced to short prison terms.[103] On the same day, about 20 anarchists celebrating May Day in the Parisian suburb of Clichy stopped to drink at a wine shop. Three policemen tried to grab their red flag. An altercation escalated to a firefight, wounding a policeman and an anarchist. Three anarchists were arrested, charged with resisting arrest and drawing blood from law enforcement officers, a charge potentially carrying a death sentence. They were severely beaten, and their jailors refused to give them any medical help despite the fact that they had open wounds. When an investigating judge came the next day, he spent all his time giving them first aid. At the time, the incident was barely noticed as the massacre in Fourmies monopolized news headlines.

When the three anarchists came to trial on 28 August 1891, they pled self-defense and claimed that the police officers had assaulted them. They described at length the beatings they experienced before and after their arrests. The prosecutor Bulot argued that their attack on the police was deliberate and asked for the death penalty, which elicited screams from the wife of defendant Henri Decamps in the audience.[104] The jury convicted Decamps and another defendant on the lesser charge and suggested leniency. The judge Benoit rejected this recommendation and sentenced them to the maximum of five years for Decamps and three years for his companion.[105] Anarchists packing the courtroom swore revenge.[106] They resented the unpunished police brutality, and the insistence of Bulot and Benoit on a severe sentence for a trivial fight. These severe sentences stood in sharp contrast with the also unpunished police massacre at Fourmies. The perceived impunity of the police brutality and the unjust court severity became a cause célèbre in anarchist circles.[107] To them, their companions were punished just for being anarchists—an aggression against all anarchists.

Decamps's wife sought comfort at the home of her best friend, whose husband was Charles Chaumentin (also written as Chaumartin), a 35-year-old trade school instructor and a prominent local anarchist.[108] At the time of the trial, Chaumentin was sheltering a 32-year-old companion calling himself Léon Léger, who was facing a murder charge under his real name, François

Koenigstein, in the Loire district, where he was known by his mother's maiden name, Ravachol. Ravachol came from a very poor family and had worked as a shepherd at the age of seven to support his mother and three younger siblings. As a teenager he became a worker, attracted first to socialism, then anarchism.[109] During times of unemployment, he discreetly took evening classes in chemistry and started experimenting with explosives. His various employers fired him when they discovered his political views and activism.[110] Destitute and unemployable, Ravachol turned to stealing chickens to feed his starving mother and siblings. He relocated to Saint-Etienne for anonymity, and when he found some work, his mother and brother came to join him. When he was out of work, he made bootleg alcohol and counterfeit coins to make ends meet. Around 1890, he fell in love with Madeleine Labret, who was unhappily married to someone 20 years her senior. Ravachol and Labret became lovers, and he tried to convert her to anarchism, but she had no interest in politics. When his mother tried to break up the relationship, Ravachol left her and moved in with his mistress.

Ravachol's income from his low-level illegal activities was not enough, so in March 1891, he robbed a wealthy individual's unoccupied house but found no money. He heard about a local woman buried with her jewelry; he robbed her grave, but found nothing. He then heard about an isolated 92-year-old hermit who had accumulated in his isolated house in Chambles a lot of money from 50 years of alms. Ravachol hesitated but finally went to rob the hermit's house on 18 June, expecting the house to be empty, and was surprised to see the hermit in bed. When the latter turned hostile, Ravachol strangled him. Throughout the night, he collected the large quantity of gold and silver coins scattered throughout the house and buried them near a road outside the house, making half a dozen trips in the middle of the night, before returning home in Saint-Etienne at daybreak with part of the money. The next night, he hired a coach, returned to his hiding place, filled up two suitcases, and returned home with them in the early morning. He had garnered about 35,000 francs.[111] On 21 June, the body of the hermit was discovered. Ravachol rented a new apartment, hid some of the money in the basement of his lover's house, and returned to his old apartment to make sure it was clean. When he arrived, he was arrested by the police, who had been tipped off by the coachman. On the way to the police station, he managed to escape.[112] He still had about 8,000 francs on him. To elude the police search for him under his name of Koenigstein, he faked his own suicide by throwing his clothes in the Rhone River along with a suicide note.[113] Labret and some of his anarchist friends were arrested.

Ravachol temporarily hid at the home of a companion, Joseph Béala, and his girlfriend Rosalie Soubert, who found him shelter with one of their anarchist acquaintances, Charles Chaumentin, in Saint-Denis, near Paris. Ravachol moved there at the end of July 1891. Chaumentin helped him find another apartment on the Ile Saint-Louis, in the center of Paris, but "Léon Léger" spent so much time with Chaumentin that his host's children called him "Cousin Léon." Shortly after Léger came, Chaumentin traveled to Saint-Etienne to pick up 3,000 francs from Béala and returned it to Ravachol, who gave some of it to needy companions, including Decamps's wife, and bought clothes for her children. Chaumentin introduced his new guest to the local anarchist groups. The focus of most anarchist conversations at the time was of course the Clichy Three trial. During that time, Ravachol was transforming his Ile-Saint-Louis apartment into a bomb factory and bought both equipment and material from nearby chemical shops.[114]

On 11 December 1891, Ravachol's lover Labret, her husband, and two anarchist companions, who had helped Ravachol in his bootlegging and counterfeiting business, went on trial for the murder of the hermit of Chambles. Labret was convicted and sentenced to seven years' hard labor for receipt of stolen property, her husband was acquitted, and the companions received lesser sentences. The trial was widely debated among anarchists who suspected that Ravachol's unlikely escape was due to the fact that he was on the police payroll and had acted as an agent provocateur. Even champions of reprises individuelles rejected his crime, and *La Révolte* editorialized that the case did not reflect anarchist ideals. Ravachol's friends from Saint-Etienne protested that he had been dedicated to the cause and the crimes were not for personal gain. *La Révolte* responded, "We do not know Ravachol, but the trial did not paint him in a sympathetic light."[115]

The trial revived the debate about reprises individuelles. Jean Grave wrote that people "did not like being robbed in the name of equality, cheated in the name of liberty, and given counterfeit money in the name of solidarity. Such actions might seem right in some groups, but the people have too much common sense to fall for it . . . We are a party of the revolution. And because of it, we are not going to perpetuate stealing, lying, cheating, murdering, which are the essence of the society that we want to destroy."[116] Kropotkin and Malatesta in London supported his position. They rejected Ravachol's acts as just bourgeois crimes and not propaganda by the deed.

Perhaps Ravachol felt the need to redeem his sullied reputation by avenging the Clichy Three. His new Paris companions did not know who Léon Léger really was, but Chaumentin, Béala, and Soubert did. At the end of January 1892, Chaumentin gave shelter to Charles Simon, a frail 18-year-old known as "Biscuit" who had been in the audience during the Clichy Three trial and had vowed to avenge them. He probably discussed the trial with Ravachol.[117] In mid-February, Faugoux, a 26-year-old anarchist on the run because he had been sentenced in absentia to two years in prison for publicly approving the murder of an informant, came to spend the evening at the Chaumentin house-hold.[118] Ravachol was also there, and the conversation drifted to the necessity of obtaining good-quality dynamite. Faugoux said that he knew about a quarry in a southern suburb of Paris where dynamite was very loosely secured, and added that he had two friends who could help them steal a large amount. A few nights later, Ravachol, Faugoux, and his friends, one of whom was named Drouet, stole 360 sticks of dynamite, 3 kilos of black powder, 100 meters of fuse cord, and 1,400 blasting capsules.[119] Ravachol kept most of the dynamite, but Drouet took over 150 sticks himself (more on this later).[120] Faugoux was arrested shortly thereafter when an informant reported him to the police but kept the theft of the dynamite secret.[121]

Shortly after this theft, the couple Béala and Soubert moved to Saint-Denis and also brought 120 sticks of a different kind of dynamite for Rav-achol.[122] At his apartment, Ravachol, assisted by Simon, made simple bombs consisting of pressure cookers containing dynamite and iron shards. Ravachol, Simon, and Béala first tried to bomb the Clichy police station. On the evening of 7 March, they took a bomb there, but a sentry posted in front of it made them abort their mission. Béala urged them to continue: "It's not enough to talk, we must act!"[123]

They settled on the assassination of Benoit, the presiding judge of the Clichy Three trial. They found his address on boulevard Saint-Germain in a tele-phone directory but not his apartment number. Chaumentin wanted to participate in the operation, but his accomplices refused because he had a family to support. On the evening of 11 March 1892, Ravachol, Simon, Béala, and Soubert boarded a trolley going to the boulevard Saint-Germain, and Soubert hid the bomb under her skirt as the trolley crossed Paris. As they ap-proached their target, Ravachol, Simon, and Béala took the bomb and exited the trolley. Ravachol, who had dressed well for the occasion, went in Benoit's building alone with the bomb, while Simon and Béala acted as lookouts. Shortly after Ravachol exited the building, the bomb exploded, causing a great deal of damage but injuring only one person. Benoit, on the fifth floor, was not injured, but his apartment was severely damaged.[124] Two days later, at his apartment, Ravachol made a more powerful bomb with the assistance of Simon, Béala, and Chaumentin.[125]

Meanwhile, Drouet gave the dynamite he had kept to a friend for safe-keeping because he was afraid that the police would come and search his home. This friend gave it to another companion, who gave it to another, until it fell into the hands of Théodule Meunier, who made a bomb, which exploded at 1:30 a.m. on 15 March near the Lobau barracks, in Paris. It greatly damaged the empty building but injured no one.[126] The same day, Mrs. Chaumentin confided to a close female friend that the boulevard Saint-Germain bombing was the work of her husband and their cousin Léon. This friend was a police informant, and Chaumentin was arrested the next day.[127] Simon was arrested a week later on an unrelated charge. Ravachol quickly changed apartments, took his powerful explosive device with him, and decided to continue alone. He tracked down where the prosecutor Bulot lived in the rue de Clichy and, on the morning of 27 March, left the bomb in the building. It destroyed the central staircase of the building, caused extensive damage, and injured five people. Bulot, however, was not injured at all.[128]

Ravachol then went to have lunch at the restaurant Véry, where he spoke to the waiter, Lhérot. The waiter was about to do his mandatory military service and complained about the military. Ravachol tried to convert him to anarchism and mentioned a new explosion in the rue de Clichy. After Ravachol left, Lhérot read the press description of the suspect in the bombing and realized that it must have been his customer. When Ravachol returned on 30 March, Lhérot recognized him and informed his boss, who alerted the police. Ravachol was arrested after a big scuffle and was taken away, screaming, "Long live Anarchy!"[129]

Meunier read about the arrest in the press and was incensed at the betrayal of the waiter. He decided to avenge this companion he did not know by bombing the restaurant and killing Lhérot. He made another explosive device and, on 24 April, went to the restaurant, dressed in a nice suit and a top hat. He placed his suitcase bomb under the bar counter, paid for his drink, and left. The explosion killed two people, including Véry, the owner and Lhérot's brother-in-law, and injured dozens of others. Meunier returned home and bragged about the bombing to his girlfriend.[130]

Ravachol was upset at the press mischaracterization of his acts as cowardice and accusing him of attacking women, children, and servants. He wrote a short autobiographical statement explaining himself and claimed that he did it for anarchy, not for personal gain.[131] The trial of Ravachol, Simon, Chaumentin, Béala, and Soubert opened on 26 April 1892. Ravachol explained that he had targeted the judge Benoit for his prejudice and severity at the trial of the Clichy Three and the prosecutor Bulot for his request of the death penalty. "I wanted those that carry out these sentences to understand that they have to be kinder."[132] Ravachol said he regretted causing the injury to innocent victims and the fact that he had dragged into this plot people whose only crime was to know him. "I acted in the name of anarchy, which is the big family where everyone eats as much as he needs. I wanted to terrorize, to bring attention to us and in order for people to understand who we are, the defendants of the oppressed."[133] Both Ravachol and Simon were convicted and sentenced to life at hard labor, while Chaumentin, Béala, and Soubert were acquitted. Ravachol and Simon welcomed their sentence with "Long live Anarchy!"[134]

Ravachol, Béala, and Soubert were then transferred to stand trial for the murder of the Chambles hermit. The trial took place in June 1892. Ravachol defended himself with dignity and admitted his crime against the hermit, but denied participation in four other unsolved murders. "I have sacrificed my person. If I still fight, it's for the idea of anarchism. If I am condemned, it's of no importance. I'll be avenged."[135] The jury convicted Ravachol in the murder of the hermit and sentenced him to death. Béala and his lover were acquitted.[136] Ravachol was guillotined on 10 July 1892.[137] His dignified acceptance of his fate impressed even his guardians.

While both the mainstream press and the socialist press excoriated Ravachol as a common criminal, anarchists rallied around him. What impressed them was the fact that Ravachol could have just faded away and lived off the money he stole from the hermit, but instead, he gave it away to the needy and then decided to sacrifice his life for the cause. "I know of very few men that surpass him in generosity."[138] His calm and dignity at his trials and especially at his execution rehabilitated his image among anarchists, and he became their hero and model. Some compared his sacrifice to that of Christ and beatified him as "Ravachol-Jesus."[139] Even the cautious *La Révolte* felt obligated to defend him. "We had disavowed Ravachol during the Chambles affair when all the evidence seemed that he had acted in his own interest, but his later actions show us another angle and force us to change our appreciation of him."[140] After his second conviction, *La Révolte* closed ranks with other anarchists: "As to Ravachol, he was . . . calm, without boasting, taking sole responsibility for his actions in a simple way and trying to spare his comrades. This man . . . is not at all the criminal that the bourgeoisie and the so-called socialists have tried to make us believe. We even believed this ourselves at the time when we did not understand his action and saw him as a vulgar criminal . . . He sacrificed his life for an idea and to avenge an injustice against some comrades he did not know. Despite being almost illiterate and without education, he found in the energy of his conviction to answer back and embarrass his judges. This man is above the insults of bourgeois and pseudo-socialist writers."[141]

The Era of the Attentats

Through his trial and exemplary death, Ravachol became the prototype for anarchists to emulate. Anonymous notes signed "followers of Ravachol," "avengers of Ravachol," or simply "Dynamite" threatened landlords or employers.[142] His example converted some hesitant anarchists to violence. Émile Henry, an assistant editor at *L'Endehors*, had been skeptical of the benefits of reprises individuelles and violence. "We should put an end to these people who dishonor our party; robbers are too cowardly ever to become revolutionaries; they want to exploit others and live comfortably in bourgeois style, they don't think of sacrificing their lives for ideas."[143] He disapproved of Ravachol's March bombings: "Such acts do us the greatest harm with the masses, who . . . only know what the ordinary newspapers say. A real anarchist . . . goes and strikes his particular enemy down; he does not dynamite houses where there are women, children, workmen, and domestic servants."[144]

La Révolte also urged anarchists not to rely on violence but to reconnect with the masses, participate in trade unions, and use strikes as a weapon to advance the revolution. *Le Père Peinard,* on the other hand, continued to glorify individual violence to the extent that press freedom allowed it. The companions were divided. From London, Malatesta and Kropotkin continued their criticism of such actions. In *L'Endehors*, Malatesta wrote that he understood acts of vengeance, but did not approve of them. "These are not the acts that we can accept, encourage or imitate . . . Hate does not beget love; the world cannot be renewed from hate. And the revolution of hate, either would fail completely or would produce a new oppression . . . and would not fail to yield the same effects that all oppression produce."[145] This rubbed Émile Henry the wrong way. Although he had espoused this position in March, five months later he had changed his mind and rejected it, coming from an outsider. As an editor of the paper, Henry felt compelled to reply. "Should the future Ravachols before joining the fight submit their projects for acceptance to the Malatestas self-appointed as grand jury to judge the appropriateness of these acts?" He asserted the efficacy of brutal revolt that "wakes up the masses, violently whips them into shape and shows them the vulnerability of the bourgeoisie, which trembles when the rebel walks to the scaffold."[146]

Who was this Émile Henry, and what had changed his mind? He was the 20-year-old son of a prominent Communard whose family had returned home to a suburb of Paris in 1882 after the amnesty. He was an excellent student; he passed the written exam for the prestigious École Polytechnique but failed the oral one. He then moved in with his brother, Fortuné Henry, in Paris in late 1890. He was shocked by the poverty around him and the general hypocrisy of society.[147] Fortuné, an anarchist, introduced his brother to his companions in mid-1891. "First of all, the character of these people attracted me. I appreciated their great sincerity, their absolute frankness, their deep contempt of all prejudices, and I wanted to understand the ideas behind such people so different from any other I had previously known."[148] The fact that Henry also fell in love with one of the married women in this circle may have deepened his commitment to anarchism.[149] He moved into a working-class neighborhood in Paris and in early 1892 showed up at the office of *L'Endehors* asking to work for anarchism. With his boundless energy, Henry soon became one of the most dedicated members of this group of anarchists.[150]

In the wake of the 1892 bombings, the police cracked down on anarchists. As many were arrested and others fled to London, Henry became the acting managing editor of *L'Endehors* because of this attrition of more senior editors. He was arrested and interrogated on 31 May 1892, but was released. The arrest prompted his boss to fire him from his day job. After his departure, his boss found a manual for the manufacture and use of dynamite in Henry's desk. In the summer of 1892, he left his volunteer position at the newspaper, for he had other plans. A convert to the use of dynamite, he raised money for Meunier, now a refugee in London, and began experimenting with unstable and corrosive chemicals. In September, he worked as an apprentice to a watchmaker to sharpen his skills as a bomb-maker.[151] At that time, he became obsessed with the strike at the Carmaux mines in the south of France, which was polarizing France. "The first news filled me with joy: the miners seemed willing to give up their peaceful and useless strike . . . On 15 August 1892, they stormed the buildings of the mine when the scared ones interfered . . . who . . . pushed people to accept all kinds of misery and try to cash in on the sufferings of strikers, so that they can get elected. I am talking about socialist chiefs, who took over the leadership of the strike . . . The strike lasted to the point when the strikers were starving, and two months later, they returned defeated to their mines . . . The company, more powerful than ever, resumed its exploitation of the workers to the joy of the stockholders."[152]

The strike's failure convinced Henry of the futility of legal trade unionism. "I wanted to show to the miners that there is only one category of people, anarchists, who sincerely feel their suffering and are ready to avenge them. These men do not sit in Parliament [like the socialists] but march to the guillotine. Therefore, I prepared a pot of dynamite. I then remembered the accusation against Ravachol: what about the innocent victims? *The building* that housed the headquarters of the Carmaux Company *only housed bourgeois. There were not going to be any innocent victims. All of the bourgeoisie lives off the exploitation of the poor and therefore must atone for its crimes.* So, with the absolute certitude of the legitimacy of my act, I set down the bomb in front of the office of the company . . . In case the device was discovered before it exploded, it would blow up at the police station, also targeting my enemies."[153]

This excerpt from Henry's testimony at this trial clearly indicates that he shared the miners' identity and miseries. He appointed himself as their avenger after his disillusionment with socialist unionist tactics and the outrage of their betrayal of the strikers. His expansion of the boundaries of the enemy outgroup for the first time justified indiscriminate political violence—there were no innocent bourgeois. His attentat finally became terrorism in the modern sense of the term.

After the strikers at Carmaux surrendered on 3 November, Henry went to case the headquarters of the company on avenue de l'Opéra. On 8 November 1892, he set his explosive device near its office front door and returned to work. One of the office workers discovered the device and notified the police, who took it to the police station at the rue des Bons-Enfants, where it exploded, killing five people outright and injuring another, who later died of his injuries. Henry fled to London and stayed there for a year, leaving behind an unsolved crime.[154]

After the ensuing severe crackdown on anarchists and the departures of the bombers to London, there were no bombings in the French capital for about a year. Instead, gangs of anarchists pulled off spectacular robberies in Paris and fenced the stolen goods in London, where there was a thriving international anarchist community as Henry, Malatesta, and Meunier comingled with hardened practitioners of reprises individuelles. The French population and police believed that the anarchist crimes in Paris were orchestrated by an anarchist cabal in London, the Black International.[155] Although there was no formal umbrella organization orchestrating attentats worldwide, anarchists did form a loose imagined political protest community with a presence in England, France, Switzerland, Belgium, Spain, Italy, and the United States. They met informally and knew each other, but being anarchists they would not tolerate the discipline necessary to form a structured hierarchical organization.

The reputation of the anarchists became such that even petty criminals pretended to be anarchists, sometimes with tragic consequences for them. In early 1893, two thieves broke into a courtyard to steal some rabbits and got caught by the police. One of them, named Forêt, resisted arrest by shooting back and grazing a policeman's arm. When they went to trial, Forêt's accomplice kept quiet and got two years in prison.[156] Forêt, on the other hand, upped the ante and declared, "I am an anarchist. The reprise individuelle is my right. I completely agree with all the anarchist theories. I am for dynamite. Ravachol did well and I applaud the explosion of the rue des Bons-Enfants. I only regret one thing in my life: it is that I've never blown up anyone."[157] Despite the triviality of his offense, he received the death penalty![158] The severity of this punishment shows the hysterical fear that anarchists inspired at the time.

In 1893, the focus of anarchist attention shifted to the escalating cycle of violence in Spain. Four well-known anarchists were garroted (strangled with a rope) in the town of Jerez on 16 February 1892 for participating in a large demonstration of vineyard workers to free imprisoned militants, which degenerated into a riot, in which two people were killed. The four men died defiantly, shouting, "Viva la anarquia!" One of them called to the silent crowd,

"Let no one say we die as cowards. It is your task to avenge us against this new Inquisition!"[159] The cry for revenge was answered a year later on 24 September 1893 when Paulino Pallas threw a bomb at the military governor of Catalonia, General Arsenio Martinez-Campos. The bomb missed the general, but killed one of his escorts and severely injured several others. Pallas made no attempt to flee and instead threw his cap in the air, shouting, "Viva l'Anarquia!" The authorities arrested him and found at his home a lithograph of the Haymarket martyrs. At his trial, Pallas testified that his act was revenge for the Jerez martyrs. He was condemned to death and shot on 6 October 1893.[160] On 7 November 1893, Santiago Salvador Franch threw two homemade bombs into the audience at the Theater Liceu of Barcelona during a performance, killing 22 people and wounding 35. He said that he did this to avenge his friend Pallas.[161] This indiscriminate bombing caused by far the largest number of casualties at the time and was the talk of Europe, especially in anarchist circles.[162] In London, "the bombs of Barcelona hypnotized" Henry.[163]

The Dawn of Indiscriminate Murder

Anarchist companions did not embrace every crime committed in their name. Léon-Jules Léauthier, a 19-year-old shoemaker from Marseille, had started reading *Le Père Peinard, La Révolte,* and other anarchist weeklies at an early age and became a strong supporter of propaganda by the deed. He experimented with explosive devices, but without success. He wanted to go to Paris, where the action was. In April 1893, came to the capital, where he immediately found a job as a shoemaker. He continued to read anarchist literature and praised the action of Pallas in Barcelona. On 11 November, he left a letter for prominent anarchist Sébastien Faure,[164] telling him that he was destitute and about to be kicked out of his apartment, which would leave him the stark choice of starvation or suicide: "Well, no, I will choose neither one nor the other: the first one because food is not lacking in the shops, and the second because I will not suffer the shame of being a coward or innocent . . . As for me, I am an anarchist since the age of sixteen . . . [and] the time has come for me to show that a revolutionary must not be either scared or faint-hearted toward an executioner. This is why I have firmly resolved to seek vengeance. I will avenge myself as I can, not having the means to make a big splash like the sublime companion Ravachol. My weapon will be my working knife . . . I would like to be able to choose among others a magistrate . . . *But I will not strike an innocent when I strike the first bourgeois I meet.*"[165]

The next day, he went to a nice restaurant, ordered a very expensive meal with champagne, and at the end of it confessed he had no money. He was thrown out. A day later, 13 November, he repeated his action at another nice restaurant in the evening, slowly ate another sumptuous meal, and at the end stabbed a well-dressed customer sitting near him, severely wounding him. The victim was the Serbian ambassador to France. Léauthier escaped in the ensuing confusion but, after roaming in the streets for an hour, simply gave himself up at a police station. At his later trial, he declared, "I cry in front of a child, I tremble before a lizard, but I will go smiling to the guillotine shouting: 'Hurray for the social revolution! Long live anarchy!'" When he received a sentence of life at hard labor, Léauthier yelled, "Long live anarchy!" and twirled his bowler hat for the benefit of sympathizers in the audience.[166]

Léauthier's immature self-glorification did not fool anarchists, and the case did not have much impact. They rejected his justification, and Faure, who had been sympathetic to Ravachol, immediately forwarded his letter to the mainstream press when Léauthier was arrested. While the companions dismissed both Forêt and Léauthier as bizarre and unrepresentative, they completely embraced Auguste Vaillant's attentat.

Vaillant was a 32-year-old who had been born in such abject poverty that his parents had been forced to abandon him, and he grew up a street urchin in Paris from the age of 12. He was arrested a few times for begging and petty theft and worked at odd jobs. He turned to socialism in his early twenties, becoming secretary of a socialist circle in Montmartre, and he married and had a daughter. He gradually became an anarchist, socialized with other companions, and dabbled in chemistry. He went to Argentina in 1890 to make his fortune, and although he received land and cattle, he became homesick and estranged from his wife. He spent his solitude reading extensively on politics and philosophy. In the spring of 1893, he returned to France with his daughter and moved to Choisy-le-Roi with his wife's first cousin, Mrs. Marchal, who left her husband for him. He found a job as a salesperson but continued to live in abject poverty, as his income did not match his expenses. He became despondent: he later testified that his inability to provide for his family was the final impetus that led to his decision to bomb those responsible for all this social suffering.[167]

Remarkably, Vaillant left a diary of his last days before the bombing.[168] It tells a different story. On 20 November 1893, he wrote, "I've decided! I am determined to commit a revolutionary act. It's true I might lose my head, but can I stay indifferent when every day I see many comrades fall? Can I continue this life of cowardice and lies, dragging my miserable life like a convict's ball and chain? . . . Every week, I am forced to see my [common-law] wife and daughter suffer from not being able to have decent clothes or enough to eat, while others do not know what to do with their money and burst with indigestion."[169] He quit his job and went to Paris to try to raise some money for this project.

He did not expect to survive his mission, so he decided to record his thoughts for posterity. In his diary, he noted that after he came back from Argentina, he simply wanted to find a decent job, proselytize his views, and encourage the study of science, which he felt was the future. He convinced some companions to start a study circle in Choisy-le-Roi. He wanted to teach them about evolution but the lack of money brought a halt to this activity because he could not afford to spend anything outside his household. He traced the idea of throwing a bomb in Parliament to mid-November. "One day I felt a horrible chest constriction, surely resulting from these painful thoughts that filled my life. I believed that I would suffocate for a few minutes, but these attacks became more and more frequent and longer to the point that I had to stay in bed for three or four days. I put a mustard poultice under my left breast, and the pain has now gone. But during these few days, I was afraid that death would come suddenly before allowing me to finish the work for which I had expanded so much energy and vital strength. The idea to act took root in me and never left. After thinking about it, I resolved to go to the Chamber of Deputies and, like our comrades in Barcelona, to throw bombs on the politicians from the public galleries. *At least, people will not complain that we hit some innocents.*"[170]

These episodes seem to be either panic attacks or a myocardial infarction. His description of two such attacks waking him up on 28 November are more consistent with panic disorder.[171] It appears that fear of a meaningless death precipitated Vaillant's attentat despite the intellectual justifications he later provided at his trial. The above excerpt reveals that his decision to carry it out was not the result of deep deliberation but the apparent consequence of panic attacks and the fear of dying without having done anything meaningful in his life.[172]

On 26 November, a companion gave Vaillant 100 francs, and the next day he rented a room in Paris and shopped for material to build his device. Two days later, he spent his first night alone in Paris and awakened twice in panic by nightmares of police surrounding and arresting him. He printed some fake business cards to allow him to gain entrance at the Chamber of Deputies. By 1 December, he finished making his explosive powder. On 3 December, he took his common-law wife to the theater to make her happy before their final separation. He spent the next two or three days at home in Choisy-le-Roi, nursing a bad foot that prevented him from walking. "The more I'm coming to the end, the more I'm becoming impatient and the more I'm afraid to fail."[173] He received an additional 20 francs from a companion. On 8 December, he wrote, "Tomorrow is probably my last day of freedom. The end is near. As much time as I'm analyzing my feelings, I don't feel any hatred against those that will fall tomorrow. What I'll do, I'll do in cold blood . . . I anticipate my death with tranquility: isn't it the refuge of disillusionment? But at least, I will die with the satisfaction of having done what I could to speed up the birth of a new era. I only ask one thing: it is that in the breaking up of my body, all my molecules should spread to the whole of humanity and transmit the virus of anarchy in order to activate the coming of the future society."[174]

On the morning of 9 December, "This morning when I left my companion and my daughter, my heart was aching with a poignant emotion, but I had the strength to hide my troubles from them. Poor cute ones, what will happen to them?" Later, "It's noon. I'm going with the device to the Chamber of the Deputies. On the way, I'll mail this diary to the comrades . . . Long live Anarchy!"[175] Vaillant went to the public gallery, and around 4:00 p.m., while the Chamber was in session, he threw his bomb on the deputies below. The bomb exploded high and lightly injured about 50 people, including Vaillant. He was arrested at the hospital the next morning and confessed. The Chamber of Deputies bombing triggered another large wave of arrests and general harassment of anarchists. The deputies rushed to pass the "Scoundrel Laws," limiting freedom of speech and associations. They banned any professed sympathy for anarchist criminals, allowed the closing of newspapers and preventive arrests, and banned associations of "evildoers" conspiring against society.[176] Hundreds of anarchists were arrested in late December, and all their newspapers were closed down and their sale banned. People suspected of anarchist sympathy were persecuted by multiple police raids looking for anarchist propaganda or bomb material. The status of being an anarchist was essentially a crime.

The government rushed Vaillant to trial. The right-wing press asked for the death penalty, stating, "There is no discussion with a beast, one kills it."[177] At his trial on 10 January 1894, Vaillant claimed that he wanted only to injure the deputies, not to kill them. He had the choice of putting large or small pieces of shrapnel in his small bomb and chose small pieces in order to maim, not kill. He also had chosen a less powerful explosive substance than nitroglycerine or dynamite for the same reason.[178] He justified his action in the name of social injustice.[179] He was convicted, and his reaction to his death penalty was, "Long live Anarchy!"

His demeanor at trial, his apparent selflessness, the unpopularity of the deputies mired in multiple scandals, and the lack of fatalities seem to have swayed the public to leniency. Only the President Sadi Carnot could commute his sentence, and many people petitioned him to do that. One journalist wrote, "Now our wretched society is putting the life of one man into the hands of another. It allows Carnot to be an assassin or a man. Which role will he choose? We don't know. But if he decides for death in cold blood, there won't be a person in France to take pity on him if one day he finds his wooden carcass broken by a bomb." Under the new law, this journalist was sentenced to two years in prison and fined 1,000 francs.[180] *Le Figaro*, which had energetically campaigned for the death penalty before the trial, changed its mind. Some of the wounded deputies petitioned the president to spare Vaillant's life.[181] Vaillant refused to appeal the verdict, and Carnot did not do anything. Vaillant was guillotined on 5 February 1894, shouting, "Death to bourgeois society and Long live Anarchy!" His tomb immediately became a center of pilgrimage. Every day, long lines of visitors brought enough flowers to completely cover his tomb.[182]

Government repression of any form of dissent became intense. People were sentenced to years in prison for just suggesting that maybe Vaillant was right. Jean Grave, who had rejected *reprises individuelles* and violent action, was sentenced to two years just for reprinting a book describing an anarchist utopia.[183] Public opinion swung against the government.

Meanwhile, Émile Henry returned to Paris as Émile Dubois in mid-December 1893. "I had come back to Paris during the Vaillant affair. I saw the formidable repression that followed his bombing. I witnessed the draconian measures that the government took against anarchists. Everywhere, there were spies, raids, arrests. A lot of individuals were randomly taken from their families and thrown in jail. What was happening to our comrades' wives and children during their incarceration? No one cared about them. Anarchists were no longer human: they were tracked like wild beasts. The liberal press, the vile slaves of state power, was asking for their extermination. At the same time, all the libertarian newspapers and pamphlets were seized, and the right of assembly was prohibited."[184] Henry was outraged at the Scoundrel Laws and the death sentence against Vaillant, who had killed no one. His decision to bomb a restaurant was a response to this "challenge thrown at the anarchists." He justified the indiscriminate nature of his violence on bourgeois reduction of anarchists to a stereotype. "But why, you may ask, should we target peaceful customers, who listened to music and are not magistrates, deputies or public servants? Why? It's simple. The bourgeois reduce anarchists to one category. One man, Vaillant, threw a bomb; nine tenths of the companions did not even know him. It did not matter. You persecuted blindly. Anyone who had any connection to anarchists was hunted down. Well, if you hold a whole party responsible for the act of one man and you strike indiscriminately, we too will strike indiscriminately."[185] This fascinating example of mutual self-categorization, trading one stereotypical target for another, expanded a few anarchists' out-group to the bourgeoisie in general, which became a legitimate target of *attentats*. The vast majority of anarchists rejected his logic.

There was an intense wave of bombings throughout France in the wake of Vaillant's execution, but they either failed to go off or damaged only property. Henry manufactured a bomb in his room. A close friend tried to dissuade him from carrying out an *attentat* but failed.[186] Exactly a week after Vaillant's execution, on 12 February 1894, Henry searched for a full café, walked into the Café

Terminus, and threw his bomb. He tried to flee but was caught. The explosion wounded about two dozen people, one of whom eventually died. Henry held out for three days to give some of his friends the opportunity to clean out his place and then confessed everything to the police.[187]

On 20 February, two more bombs went off in the center of Paris, on rue du Faubourg Saint Martin and rue Saint Jacques. The first caused no human casualty, while the second killed an old woman and injured a policeman. On 15 March, another bomb went off at the Church of La Madeleine. The perpetrator, Joseph Pauwels, had accidentally dropped it, causing a premature explosion that killed only him. He had a letter from Émile Henry and a picture of Ravachol in his wallet. Some speculated that he was one of those who emptied Henry's apartment after his arrest, took some explosive material, and was responsible for all three bombings.[188] Pauwels and Henry used to hang out together in London. One of their companions, Martial Bourdin, also had accidentally killed himself in London in Greenwich Park on 15 February when he tripped and his bomb detonated prematurely. This bombing alarmed Scotland Yard, which raided and closed down the main anarchist hangouts the next day.[189] On 4 April, a bomb exploded at the restaurant Foyot, injuring several guests.[190] This partial list does not include the many bombings and attentats outside of Paris at that time.[191]

When information about Henry was disseminated, people were surprised by the fact that this was a relatively privileged man with a solid education and shocked at his indiscriminate targeting. Unlike Vaillant, Henry "wanted to kill as many people as possible. I was hoping for about 15 dead and 20 wounded."[192] The indiscriminate nature of the act made many anarchists uneasy. One of them wrote, "A mortal enemy of anarchy could not have done better than this Émile Henry when he threw his incomprehensible bomb in the midst of peaceful and anonymous people who had come to drink a mug in a café before going to sleep . . . (perhaps a police provocation). I prefer to believe that this Émile Henry was only acting on the advice of his own folly. Émile Henry insists he is an anarchist. It's possible. But anarchy has broad shoulders . . . Today, it's the fashion among criminals to claim to be anarchists, especially when they strike it rich . . . Each party has its own criminals and his madmen."[193] Even Henry's friends echoed this sentiment: "Despite the fact that Émile Henry is a very intelligent and courageous anarchist, his act mostly struck anarchy . . . I approve all violence that strikes obstacles and the enemy, not one that strikes indiscriminately."[194] Of course, it was difficult for anarchists to debate this issue since the closure of their papers had robbed the partisans of terror of their voice.

Henry's cold-blooded and defiant attitude throughout his detention, well documented in the mainstream press, elicited little sympathy from the companions. Henry was not surprise: "I don't have any illusion. I know that my actions won't be well understood by unprepared masses. Influenced by your newspapers, even some workers, for whom I have done this, believe that I am their enemy . . . I don't ignore the fact that there are some individuals who call themselves anarchists but disavow propaganda by the deed. They try to establish a subtle distinction between theorists and terrorists. Too scared to risk their lives, they renounce those who act . . . In this war without pity that we have declared against the bourgeoisie, we ask for no pity. We give death and we know how to submit to it . . . You have hanged in Chicago, decapitated in Germany, garroted in Jerez, fired in Barcelona, guillotined in Montbrison and in Paris, but you will never be able to destroy anarchy . . . it will end up killing you."[195] Henry was convicted and sentenced to death on 28 April 1894. He called out, "Courage comrades, long live Anarchy!"[196] Unlike jurors in many previous anarchist trials, those at his trial did not receive death threats. He was executed on 21 May 1894.

Anarchists plotting revenge rarely mentioned either Léauthier or Henry. Vaillant remained the martyr-saint most cited. Informal circles of anarchists talked about avenging him. In the French Mediterranean port of Sète, Sante Caserio mourned him as well as Ravachol, Pallas, and the Chicago Five. A 21-year-old Italian apprentice baker, he had become an anarchist three years earlier in reaction to an anarchist trial in Rome. He was arrested in April 1892 for distributing anarchist propaganda to soldiers but fled Italy after posting bail and went to Switzerland, Lyon, and finally Sète, where he worked in a bakery and hung out with anarchists at local cafés.[197]

In mid-June, Caserio read that President Sadi Carnot would come to Lyon for a celebration. On 23 June, he left Sète, bought a dagger, and arrived in Lyon the evening of 24 June 1894. He followed the crowd and arrived at the main road, on which the president was traveling. He rushed the carriage and stabbed the president, yelling, "Long live Anarchy. Long live the Revolution." He was immediately arrested.[198] Caserio was tried in early August 1894. He explained his action: "Vaillant . . . did not kill anyone, just wounded a few; but bourgeois justice condemned him to death. And not satisfied with this death, it pursued anarchists, and arrested not only those who knew Vaillant, but also those who just went to anarchist lectures. The government never thought about their wives and children . . . The government searched private homes, opened private letters, banned lectures and meetings, and practiced the most wretched oppression against us. Even today, hundreds of anarchists are arrested for writing an article in a journal or giving an opinion in public." Caserio explained further, "We respond to governments with dynamite, bombs, stilettos, and daggers. In a word, we must do our best to destroy the bourgeoisie and governments. Gentlemen of the jury, as members of the bourgeoisie, if you want my head, take it. But don't believe that in doing so, you are stopping the anarchist movement. Be on your guards: man reaps what he sows."[199] The jury deliberated for a short period before convicting and sentencing him to death. He was guillotined on 16 August 1894. This essentially concluded the wave of attentats in France in the period of 1892–1894.

After its extensive sweep of anarchist circles, the government attempted to convince the public that all the anarchist robberies and attentats were part of a vast conspiracy headquartered in Paris and London. It lumped together 19 intellectual leaders with 11 reprises individuelles practitioners and tried them for being part of an association of evildoers under the new laws. The intellectuals included Jean Grave, Félix Fénéon, and Sébastien Faure. They were accused of glorifying terrorist acts and being part of a grand conspiracy. The prosecution, which had strong evidence against the "thieves," implied that these crimes were committed at the direction of the intellectuals.

The Trial of the 30 took place in August 1894.[200] The prosecution categorized all the defendants as "beasts" and "miserable ones," while the defendants called each other companions.[201] Given the lack of evidence for a conspiracy, the intellectual defendants easily ridiculed the prosecution's allegations. Since the companions constituted a network of friends, the government had no trouble showing that the defendants met and knew each other, but could not pin anything more on them. But as each intellectual's relationship with a robber was shown to be insignificant, one of the intellectual defendants pointed out, "You can add as many of these zeros as you like, you still won't get a total of one."[202] At the end of six days of intense questioning, the prosecutor hinted that the case against the intellectuals was not very strong, but he still counted on the anger of the jury against all the attentats of the past few months to convict them. The jury did not. On 12 August, it acquitted all the defendants except for three thieves sentenced to hard labor.

The mainstream press cried foul and blamed the ineptitude of the prosecutors and the naïve jury, but the public welcomed the verdict with joy. The jurors explained to the press that they rejected the new Scoundrel Laws: "We don't like anarchists. But we did not like to be dragged into something we didn't agree with. They showed us that the thieves stole: we convicted them. They showed us people who were not associated with anything: we acquitted them."[203]

The acquittal of the anarchist writers finally broke the cycle of violence between the government and anarchists. A legal correspondent commented, "If the wave of anarchist attentats came to an end, it has to be at least partly attributed to the verdict's wisdom. To acquit was to eliminate in advance the potential avengers by not creating new martyrs."[204] The exoneration of the intellectual leaders of the movement calmed people down. What had started out as an attempt to punish police brutality and injustice in the Clichy Three case got out of hand and escalated into a cycle of violence, fueled by a hysterical the press. The violence degenerated from narrowly targeted violence against the judge and prosecutor of the Clichy Three into the indiscriminate bombings of Henry.

Most of the attentats in this wave were carried out by loners. It is clear that although they were physical loners in the commission of political violence, they were deeply imbedded in the anarchist community. Outraged at government persecution of their companions and disillusioned with legal means to address their grievances, they volunteered to act out in defense of their companions and avenge their martyrs. The fact that they were loners in the commission of their act implies no particular distinction from others who carried out such acts collectively.

By the time of the Trial of the 30, anarchist leaders also realized that the attentats had distanced them from their constituency, the working class, and had gotten them nothing in terms of advancing their cause. In fact, they were worse off, as the bombings prevented propaganda when the government closed down their papers.[205] French anarchists pulled back from indiscriminate violence to advance their goals through the trade union movement.

International Assassinations of Heads of State

The end of the era of attentats in France did not end the wave of anarchist violence in the world. On 10 September 1898, 25-year-old Luigi Lucheni, born in Paris but raised in Italy, stabbed and killed the Austrian empress Elizabeth who was vacationing in Geneva. It is difficult to trace his turn to violence because, while Lucheni admitted his crime at his trial, he was very evasive. Two years later, a psychiatrist interviewed him at length and noted that, although part of an anarchist circle in Lausanne, Lucheni had come to anarchism just months prior to his crime. He became obsessed with assassinating a head of state and went to Geneva in early September to do it. Empress Elizabeth was in town and he killed her.[206] He was sentenced to life in prison.

On 29 July 1900, 30-year-old Gaetano Bresci shot and killed King Umberto I of Italy in Monza. Bresci was a silk weaver who had immigrated to Paterson, New Jersey, when he could find no work in Italy. He was very active in anarchist circles in that city.[207] He read about a massacre at a demonstration protesting the high cost of bread in Milan, killing between 100 and 400 people and wounding thousands. Outraged that King Umberto had decorated the general responsible for ordering the shootings into the peaceful crowd, Bresci returned to Italy to kill the king. He was tried a month later and sentenced to life in prison.

Bresci inspired another anarchist assassin: Leon Czolgosz, who carried in his pocket a newspaper clipping about his hero.[208] Czolgosz, the 28-year-old son of eastern European immigrants to the United States, worked at a mill until 1898. He quit his job, became a recluse on his parents' ranch, displayed strange behavior, and developed a superficial interest in anarchy. Apparently, the news of Bresci's regicide inspired him to do the same in America. He shot and eventually killed President William McKinley on 6 September 1901 at the Pan-American Exposition in Buffalo, New York. He was immediately arrested and confessed to the police that he had also been inspired by an Emma Goldman lecture a few months before. "She set me on fire. Her doctrine that all rulers should be exterminated was what set me to thinking so that my head nearly split with the pain. Miss Goldman's words went right through me, and when I left the lecture I had made up my mind that I would have to do something heroic for the cause I loved."[209] He wrote a confession: "I made my plans 3 or 4 days ago to shoot the President. When I shot him I intended to kill him and the reason for my intention in killing was because I did not believe in presidents above us. I was willing to sacrifice myself and the president for the benefit of the Country. I felt I had more courage than the average man in killing president and was willing to put my own life at stake in order to do it."[210] He remained silent at his trial, about a month later. He was convicted and sentenced to die. He was executed on 29 October 1901. There was an academic debate about Czolgosz's mental condition.[211]

The reaction against anarchists was swift: Most and Goldman were arrested.[212] She later recalled, "The country was in a panic . . . The people of the United States and not Czolgosz . . . had gone mad. Not since 1887 had there been evidenced such lust for blood, such savagery of vengeance. 'Anarchists must be exterminated!' the papers raved; 'they should be dumped in the sea; there is no place for the vultures under our flag.' "[213] Leading the charge against anarchists was the new president Theodore Roosevelt, in a speech to Congress that anticipated that of his successor a century later: "President McKinley was killed by an utterly depraved criminal belonging to that body of criminals who object to all governments, good and bad alike, who are against any form of popular liberty if it is guaranteed by even the most just and liberal laws." He blamed anarchism for appealing to "the dark and evil spirits of malice and greed, envy and sullen hatred. The wind is sowed by the men who preach such doctrines." He rejected their protest against "inequalities in the social order." On the contrary, he argued, "The man who advocates anarchy directly or indirectly, in any shape or fashion, or the man who apologizes for anarchists and their deeds, makes himself morally accessory to murder before the fact. The anarchist is a criminal whose perverted instincts lead him to prefer confusion and chaos to the most beneficent form of social order." The president equated anarchist advocates and practitioners with ordinary murderers. "He is not the victim of social or political injustice. There are no wrongs to remedy in his case. The cause of his criminality is to be found in his own evil passion and in the evil conduct of those who urge him on, not in any failure by others or by the State to do justice to him or his. He is a malefactor and nothing else. He is in no sense, in no shape or way, a 'product of social conditions' . . . Anarchistic speeches, writings, and meetings are essentially seditious and treasonable."[214]

Anti-anarchist laws were passed by the states: meetings, lectures, and recreational events by anarchists were prohibited or subjected to intimidation. Answering the president's urging, Congress passed the Immigration Act of 1903 barring them entry into the United States.[215]

Conclusion

The early anarchist wave of political violence is consistent with the outlined model of acquisition of a politicized social identity, which forms an imagined political protest community. As conflict with the state escalated along with their verbal accusation, some members became disillusioned with peaceful protest, and moral outrage at disproportionate state aggression tipped them into volunteering as soldiers protecting their community. A few rogue elements expanded the category of their enemies to include people not directly involved in the aggression against them, leading to indiscriminate killings. Conservatives blamed these attentats on ideology, but this ignores the fact that most leaders of the anarchist community rejected the violence of the attentats as counterproductive to bring about the revolution. These leaders shared the same ideology as the perpetrators but were not violent. Therefore, ideology by itself cannot be an adequate explanation for the violence. Likewise, rational choice theory is not consistent with the fact that the self-sacrifice of the perpetrators was so contrary to their self-interest.

Chapter 6

The Specialized Terrorist Organization

The PSR Combat Unit, 1902–1908

At the beginning of the twentieth century, another milestone in the history of political violence was reached when a large political party created a department of professional terrorists dedicated to carrying out the violent part of its political program. People's Will had earlier tried to do this but had to choose between its peaceful organizational program and its violent program because it was simply too small to do both. The formation of the Russian Socialist Revolutionary Party (PSR in Russian) at the turn of the century implemented their predecessor's parallel programs and provided a model for systemic political violence for future political parties. The story of the PSR Combat Unit was all the more remarkable because for most of its life it was led by a state agent. Indeed, given matching political police developments, penetration of the Combat Unit was simply a foreshadowing of modern counterterrorism tactics.

The Progeny of People's Will

In Russia, militant political dissent continued into the twentieth century. Nicholas II ascended to the throne but changed little in the political arena. The famine and cholera epidemic of the early 1890s brought attention to the urgent need for economic and social reform to improve the lot of the peasants. The spiritual heirs of People's Will were scattered throughout Russia and the Russian diaspora communities in western Europe. Three trends had changed the political protest community.

The first was the gradual adoption of Marxism as a framework for the revolutionaries. The progeny of Black Partition had embraced a literal interpretation of Marx, believed that Russia needed to pass through a capitalist stage before a proletarian revolution could succeed, and championed the working class to the relative neglect of the peasantry. An attempt to consolidate these scattered groups into one umbrella organization, the Russian Social Democratic Labor Party (RSDRP in Russian), took place in Minsk in March 1898, but most of the delegates who came were arrested. Some members fled to Germany and rallied around their organ, *Iskra* (the Spark). Prominent members of this group included former members of Black Partition—Plekhanov,[1] Axelrod,[2] Deich, Zasulich—and newcomers like Vladimir Ulyanov (Lenin).

A second trend was the rise of nationalism among minorities in the empire, especially Poles, Jews, Baltic minorities, and southern minorities. The Polish Socialist Party (PPS) was created in Paris in 1892, and its branches spread to the western and northern parts of the empire. Its political platform was independence, equal rights, freedom of the press, progressive taxation, eight-hour workday, minimum wage, free education, and workmen insurance. The PPS was involved in generally peaceful labor agitation until 1904. Likewise, secular Jews trying to escape the strictures of traditional Jewish orthodoxy, tsarist persecution, and violent societal racism formed the General Jewish Bund in Russia and Poland in October 1897 in Vilna. It rejected Zionism, the movement to establish a homeland in Palestine, as a form of escapism and instead sought to establish democracy and socialism in Russia.

A third trend was the return from exile of former People's Will members, who inspired and educated a new generation of militants into their brand of populism. In contrast to the RSDRP, these new populists believed in the possibility of a socialist revolution without waiting for the development of capitalism. With their adoption of Marxist concepts, they were now called neo-populists. The most prominent returning exile was the indefatigable Mark Natanson, who settled in Saratov and invited about 20 activists to a meeting there in September 1893. They adopted a program creating the Social Revolutionary Party of People's Rights, advocating political freedom, representative institutions, and people's rights to the satisfaction of their material needs. While terrorism, the glory of People's Will, was not specifically mentioned in the program, it was widely interpreted as being included in the notion of people's needs. The Okhrana arrested Natanson and most of the leaders of the new party on the night of 21 April 1894. Natanson was sent back to Siberia,[3] but the party's ideas lived on through a new generation of militants. One of Natanson's recruits, Victor Chernov, a 21-year-old former law student and civil servant from Saratov, was arrested in April 1894 and exiled in central Russia. In 1899, he left for Zurich, where he published a series of theoretical philosophical and political articles.[4]

Another prominent returnee was Breshkovskaya, who had been convicted at the Trial of the 193 and came back from exile in 1896. She settled in Minsk and resumed her proselytism. She became very popular among the younger generation of militants who affectionately nicknamed her the "babushka [grandmother] of the revolution."[5] Among this new generation was 28-year-old Gregory Gershuni, a previously arrested pharmacist who opened a laboratory in Minsk upon his release in 1898. He resumed his political work and organized the youth Breshkovskaya was attracting. They established the Workers Party for the Political Emancipation of Russia in Minsk, but police persecution forced them to find refuge in Switzerland in 1900.[6]

Under the influence of the returning exiles, multiple circles of "socialist revolutionaries" sprang up around Russia. They rejected the social democrats' conclusion that agrarian Russia was not ripe for a revolution and instead tried to trigger one through the strategy of People's Will. In 1898, in Moscow, 32-year-old Andrei Argunov tried to regroup the remnants of Natanson's party into an umbrella organization, the Northern Union of Socialist Revolutionaries, and published its platform, which adopted a modified program of the original People's Will, including political terrorism as an effective means to advance the revolutionary struggle.[7] Two years later, another group in the south, the Socialist Revolutionary Party, adopted a similar platform that focused on industrial workers, who were assumed to be more receptive to revolutionary and socialist influence, but did not mention the issue of terrorism.[8]

Student Unrest at the Turn of the Century

In the winters of 1899 and 1901, student unrest triggered a wave of political violence and generated future recruits for the socialist revolutionary movement. As usual, a trivial incident sparked the conflict. Students at St. Petersburg University had gotten into the habit of celebrating the anniversary of the founding of their university with alcoholic binges and raucous behavior. Its rector, determined to eradicate this unseemly behavior, warned the students at an address of the student body during the ceremonies on 8 February 1899 and was booed. When the students left the auditorium, a detachment of mounted police charged them and whipped them on their heads. A later investigation showed that the police nursed resentment toward the students and had welcomed the chance to settle scores with them. Whips had been deliberately issued to the police the previous evening.

This police brutality shocked the students and intelligentsia alike—how could the sons of society's elite of be treated like mere peasants?[9] The students lumped the police and school administration together as enemies who had attacked and humiliated them. This unprovoked police brutality unified the students in protest: the next day they went on strike, demanding publication of police procedures for handling crowds, official investigation of the incident, and confirmation of the principle of inviolability of a person already enshrined in Russian law.[10] The strike spread to other university towns, but instead of appeasing the students, the police escalated the conflict by arresting hundreds of them, especially in Moscow, Kiev, and Warsaw.

The tsar hesitated, and on the advice of his finance minister, Sergei Witte, commissioned reactionary General Vannovsky to investigate the incident. This partial concession to the students temporarily defused the situation. An assembly of St. Petersburg University students ended their strike on 1 March, followed by Moscow students four days later, despite the fact that many students were still under arrest.[11] Some students felt betrayed by the cowardice of the assembly, which had avoided addressing the main issue behind police brutality, namely the fundamental incompatibility of autocracy and student demands for fairness. These still angry students identified with the beaten-up and arrested fellow students. They looked at the police, and especially the police chief in St. Petersburg, Nicholas Kleigels, as their main enemy. A student later recalled, "We were not just protesting against the 8 February beating. The latter was just a particular manifestation of the present Russian system, a system based on arbitrariness, secrecy and the total . . . absence of the most necessary . . . sacred rights essential for the development of the human personality."[12]

General Vannovsky's report concluded that the students were defending the honor of their uniform or their comrades sitting in provincial jails. Kleigels protested that the report was biased against the police. Nevertheless, jailed students in St. Petersburg and Moscow were released, while police repression continued in Kiev and Warsaw. The news from the provinces disturbed the St. Petersburg students enough to call for a new assembly, which on 17 March voted to resume the strike in solidarity with their provincial colleagues. The Moscow students followed suit. The administration responded by closing down the universities and unleashed the Okhrana, which arrested prominent strikers—about a third of the student body—and expelled them from Moscow and St. Petersburg.[13] In the summer, the government revamped its higher education policies. It expanded the faculties, built more dormitories, and forced students to attend the university closest to their residence. It also issued the 1899 Temporary Rules ordering the conscription of disorderly students into the military for long periods of service.[14] The government allowed the remaining students to resume their studies, and the next school year was relatively calm.

The student unrest of 1901 started in Kiev. In mid-November 1900, a small student assembly met to protest against a professor's bad lectures. Inspectors took the names of the students present, and a university court sentenced them to the university jail, a traditional punishment. Two students, including Alexis Pokotilov, refused to comply and were expelled, causing an uproar in the student body. On 7 December, a large assembly of students demanded the return of their expelled classmates and the abolition of the jail. When the students refused to disperse, the governor-general of Kiev sent in the army. The students left, but the authorities took the names of about 400 students present. During the Christmas holidays, a special disciplinary board sentenced 183 to immediate military service based on the Temporary Rules and the rest to less severe punishment.[15]

When the students returned to class in January 1901, they were torn between solidarity for fellow students and their own fear of conscription if they protested. By the end of the month, student assemblies at Kharkov, Kiev, St. Petersburg, and Moscow called for strikes, but most students ignored them and attended classes. In St. Petersburg, the administration sentenced 28 leaders to immediate military service, and one of them committed suicide.[16] Pokotilov came to St. Petersburg in January to enlist support for his Kiev comrades. He had come with another expelled student, Peter Karpovich. Unbeknown to the other, each had secretly decided to kill Minister of Education Nicholas Bogolepov.[17] Pokotilov tried to get support from student groups in the capital, but did not make a good impression: he was described as an alcoholic whose face was heavily scarred with eczema. He had no clear political views except for an obsession to support his comrades. At one of his meetings, he took strong exception to some who felt that the student movement was finished and jumped on a chair screaming, "We need a demonstration!" He then fell off the chair in hysterics.[18]

Meanwhile, on 14 February, Karpovich showed up for an appointment with Bogolepov and shot him in the neck. Bogolepov died two weeks later. Karpovich was arrested, convicted, and sentenced to 20 years in exile. After the attentat, some students in St. Petersburg called for a demonstration on 19 February, the anniversary of the Emancipation Act, and all of them were arrested. Not knowing whether the demonstration was canceled, most students stayed home; only about 400 turned out at the demonstration in Kazan Square, which turned riotous. The police arrested 244 people: 128 female and 71 male students, and 45 onlookers.[19] On the same day, in Kharkov, mounted Cossacks encircled a small crowd of students marching to the university and beat them up. The whole student body went on strike as a protest and demanded repeal of the Temporary Rules.

In Moscow, a large student assembly convened on 23 February. Cheered by a large crowd of students, relatives, and friends, they hung a large banner demanding, "Down with the Temporary Rules!" The police asked them to leave and, when they refused, stormed in. When the students were escorted out of the building, the surrounding crowd broke through the police line to join their trapped comrades. They took over a large exhibition hall just outside the university and partied all night. The police slowly evacuated the building, transferred 358 male students to prison, and released the women. Two days later, on Sunday, 25 February, a huge crowd assembled in front of Moscow Governor-General Grand Duke Sergei's residence in support of the students' grievances and marched for hours, singing songs. A strike was averted when the administration appointed a commission to look at the grievances.[20]

Public opinion had swung to the students' side. St. Petersburg students issued an appeal to the public at large to defend basic human rights, join forces with them, and come to a demonstration in front of the Kazan Cathedral the next Sunday. The response was one of the largest street demonstrations the capital had ever seen. The crowd of mostly young people completely overflowed the square. The atmosphere was jubilant until unprovoked Cossacks charged the crowd and beat the demonstrators. About 775 men and women were arrested. The atmosphere in the prison was very relaxed, with the authorities allowing the students liberal visitations from friends and relatives, shipments of cigarettes, and general celebration with songs, shouts, and laughter. A week later, the students were released. They were expelled from their universities and temporarily forbidden to return.[21]

By then, the tsar had gauged the public's mood and come to his senses. He appointed General Vannovsky as minister of education and suggested educational reforms. During the summer of 1901, most of the conscripted students were discharged from the military, and expelled students were allowed to resume their studies.[22] The students felt they had won, but Nicholas Kleigels and Grand Duke Sergei had earned their undying enmity.

The Creation of the Socialist Revolutionary Party and Its Combat Unit

In Moscow, Argunov continued his efforts to consolidate the socialist revolutionists and established a printing press just across the border in Finland. The first issue of the Northern Union of Socialist Revolutionaries' official organ, *Revolutionary Russia*, came out in January 1901. The journal attempted to unite all potential audiences—workers, peasants, intelligentsia, and national minorities—and glossed over any controversial parts of Argunov's original program. The result was so bland that it did not inspire much. Nevertheless, the widespread publication of a clandestine newspaper was seen as a major victory.[23]

A rising star in Argunov's Northern Union was Evno Azef, an engineer who had been active in revolutionary student activism abroad. Azef was the 31-year-old son of a poor tailor in Rostov-on-the-Don who had embezzled money from an employer and used the proceeds to finance his education. He studied electrical engineering in Germany, where he joined émigré revolutionary circles. He secretly volunteered his services to the Okhrana in 1893 and kept a low profile. Over the next 15 years, he would play a double game with both the Okhrana and the revolutionaries. Unfortunately, he did not leave any memoirs or confession behind.[24] He was not ideologically oriented, claiming to be a man of action, and therefore stayed mostly quiet in discussion groups. Given his double game, he of course never fully confided in anyone. This lack of firsthand information has posed a challenge for his biographers, including this author, who tried to make sense of his puzzling and inconsistent behavior.

Azef traveled around Europe on behalf of the Okhrana and met most of the leaders of the Russian revolutionary community abroad. He married Luba Menkina, a fellow militant from the University of Berne, who bore him a child in 1895. After getting his graduate degree, Azef got a job with a Berlin engineering firm, but the Okhrana called him back to Moscow. In the fall of 1899, the Azef family returned to Moscow, where his handler was Sergei Zubatov, the innovative chief of the Moscow Okhrana. Zubatov's strategy consisted of painstakingly identifying all the members of a dissident network and then arresting them all in one blow.[25] He immediately directed Azef to target Argunov's Northern Union. After Russian émigrés vouched for his *bona fides*, Azef became a confidant of Argunov and made himself indispensable. He soon got to know most of Northern Union's members in Russia and provided this information to his handler. Zubatov wanted to move the Union's printing press to a place where he could reach and destroy it, eliminate the Union's activities in Russia, and drive them abroad. He increased obvious police surveillance on the Union printing press in Finland, forcing it to relocate to a new secret place in Tomsk, Siberia. Just before the printing of the third issue of *Revolutionary Russia*, the police raided the site of the new press betrayed by Azef. At the same time, Zubatov increased police harassment of the Union members in Russia. Fearing arrest, Argunov tasked Azef to go abroad and negotiate the consolidation of all the socialist revolutionary parties as his emissary. "Like a dying man, we entrusted everything to Azef. We told him all our passwords, all our connections (literary and organizational), the names and addresses of our associates, and we recommended him warmly to all our friends. He was . . . enjoying our full confidence as the representative of the 'Union.' We looked upon him as a comrade, even, perhaps, as a friend. In those days of misfortune his active participation drew him closer to us."[26] Azef left Moscow for Geneva with his family in November 1901. After a decent interval to protect its star agent, the Okhrana rolled up the whole Northern Union in Russia.[27]

Over the next two months, as Argunov's representative, Azef negotiated with Chernov, Gershuni, and Michael Gotz in Paris, Geneva, and Berlin. Gotz, the 35-year-old son of a Moscow tea millionaire, had joined and financed the Moscow People's Will in 1884 while at the University of Moscow. He was arrested in 1886, sent to Siberia, and released in 1899. He emigrated, first to Paris and later Geneva. He had an attractive personality, agile mind, and inexhaustible energy, despite suffering from a spinal injury sustained during his incarceration, which left him in constant pain. He liked to keep away from the limelight but was one of the largest financial contributors to revolutionary activities and acted as their coordinator.[28]

The negotiations were successful, and the major socialist revolutionary parties merged into the Socialist Revolutionary Party (PSR). Its program emphasized agitation in the countryside and factories and, as the heir to People's Will, advocated the use of terroristic tactics as part of its overall political strategy. It was ruled by a central committee that elected its executive trio: Chernov, Gotz, and Gershuni. Azef and Breshkovskaya were elected members of the Central Committee.[29] Azef resumed the publication of *Revolutionary Russia* from Europe, which became the official periodical of the PSR under the editorship of Chernov and Gotz.[30]

The PSR leadership wanted to complement political activism with a campaign of terrorism, in the People's Will sense of the term—namely, a campaign of assassination of senior tsarist civil servants—but held back on the tsar himself because of his continued popularity with the peasants. The popular approval of Karpovich's assassination of Bogolepov the previous year had brought the issue of terrorism back to the forefront. The executive committee tasked Gershuni with the creation of a clandestine combat unit (*boevaia organizatsiia*)[31] of the PSR to carry out this campaign. Because of the reluctance of some members of the Central Committee to embark on a terrorist campaign, the executive committee decided to conceal the existence of the unit until a successful assassination allowed it to present the hesitant members with a fait accompli. Gershuni, the head of the Combat Unit, agreed with the strategy. He was a practical organizer and had little patience for theoretical disputes, which he viewed as "bookworms' war of ink."[32]

Gershuni began his campaign of terrorism by planning an ambitious double assassination of the leaders who had suppressed the student uprising, Minister of the Interior Dmitry Sipiagin and the Holy Synod procurator Konstantin Pobedonostsev, the tsar's reactionary adviser. In the wake of the student uprisings, Sipiagin had threatened to "wash St. Petersburg in blood" if the students tried again to demonstrate.[33] Gershuni enlisted his close friends Pavel Kraft and Michael Melnikov into the unit, and they planned the double murder from Finland. Gershuni did not like meticulous planning, preferring to improvise and take advantage of opportunities. Stepan Balmashev, a 21-year-old former student at the University of Kiev and a close friend of Pokotilov, volunteered for the assassination of Sipiagin. Balmashev had participated in the university unrest, and had been arrested and conscripted. He was discharged from the military when the government eased its repression and became a member of the Kiev PSR group, through which he met Breshkovskaya and Gershuni.[34] On 2 April 1902, Balmashev took a train from Finland, dressed as an aide-de-camp for Grand Duke Sergei. He arrived at the Ministry of the Interior and asked to speak with Sipiagin. He was taken to the minister, to whom he gave a sealed envelope. While Sipiagin read his death sentence from the PSR Combat Unit, Balmashev took out a pistol and said, "This is how to act with the enemies of the people."[35] He fired twice and killed the minister. He was immediately arrested. It is unclear why the second prong of the plan failed.[36]

On 3 April 1902, the PSR Combat Unit announced its existence to the world: "They wanted it and they got it . . . Robbed of every chance of responding to its crimes in a peaceful manner and despite all the horror that we feel for the following way of fighting, we, the conscious minority, hold it to be not only our right but our holy duty to respond with force and avenge the spilling of the people's blood with the blood of its oppressors . . . There is only one possible peaceful resolution: allow the people to check the state's arbitrary attitude by peaceful and civilized means."[37]

The story of a young lieutenant, Michael Grigoriev, and his fiancée, Zoe Yurkovskaya, gives us an insight into the "recruitment" into the Combat Unit. Gershuni had left his luggage with them in St. Petersburg, as they were PSR sympathizers, and came back to fetch it the day after the assassination. Grigoriev congratulated Gershuni, but Yurkovskaya was very upset that Gershuni had not trusted them enough to include them in the action. She told him that she had made it very clear that she had wanted to carry it out herself. She now told him that she was resolved to accomplish a terrorist act, with or without Gershuni's help. Gershuni asked Grigoriev what he thought, and Grigoriev supported his fiancée: they would do it together. Gershuni tried to talk them out of it, but finally relented. They agreed to kill Pobedonostsev and Police Chief Kleigels at Sipiagin's funeral, the next day. Grigoriev would don his uniform, get close to Pobedonostsev, and shoot him. Yurkovskaya, dressed as a high school student, would shoot Kleigels during the confusion. However, Pobedonostsev was "prudent enough not to attend the funeral,"[38] which aborted their plans.[39]

Balmashev was convicted at a court-martial and sentenced to death.

When asked who his accomplices were, he replied, "The rulers, headed by the tsar. Let's get them here next to me on the bench."[40] He was executed on 3 May 1902. For Gershuni, the assassination of the hated minister of the interior was a resounding success. The intelligentsia welcomed the demise of the despised minister, and hundreds of youthful volunteers got in touch with PSR in order to join the Combat Unit. Gershuni was overjoyed by his success: "It is only the beginning. The Gordian knot has been cut; the terror has justified itself. It has begun; all discussion is now superfluous . . . It is time for the youth to come forward. Time does not wait; we must act at once."[41]

The general public approval of Balmashev's shot immediately propelled the popularity of the PSR higher than that of its rival RSDRP and silenced its potential critics. Lenin and Plekhanov at first claimed that Balmashev was a member of the RSDRP, but Gershuni had no problem refuting this claim. Up to Sipiagin's assassination, the social democrats had been friendly to their new rivals and welcomed them in the ranks of the revolutionaries. However, with the popularity of the rival's new tactics, they viewed the upstart PSR as a strong competitor for its constituency. In order to draw sharp boundaries between the two parties, they highlighted their differences, especially their attitudes toward terrorism.[42] Lenin adopted the traditional Marxist critique that history was made by large forces, like the working-class, and individual action, like single combat, was irrelevant to that process. He complained that "the organization of terroristic acts by the party distracts our very scanty organizational forces from their difficult and by no means completed task of organizing a revolutionary *workers'* party; that *in practice* the terrorism of the Social Revolutionaries is nothing else than *single combat*, a method that has been wholly condemned by the experience of history."[43]

Chernov replied that the PSR's objective was not individual terror but the activation of the dormant revolutionary potential of the masses through agitation and propaganda by the deed. Therefore, this tactic was to complement other political work such as organizing the masses and not to substitute for it. Violence could awaken the population and be the spark that sets fire to the revolution. In addition, the Combat Unit was useful for protecting the movement from informants and bringing fear and disorganization into the ranks of the government.[44]

Gershuni's Arrest

The theoretical disputes about the proper role of terror were confined to ideologues. Young militants on the ground sided with the new PSR, and Gershuni's Combat Unit acquired immense popularity, far beyond that of a typical party unit. Terrorism, as Gershuni conceived it, stressed its moral dimension and became a matter of honor for every true revolutionary: the duty to defend one's own dignity, which was constantly attacked by state persecution in everyday life, justified the violent act. Terrorist revolutionaries were heroes avenging the spilled blood of the peasants. As practiced within these limits, terrorism was an act of redemption, carried out in the spirit of sacrifice. A Combat Unit member was more than just a soldier for the revolution because he was willing to give his life for the revolution. His self-sacrifice justified the violence that every revolution requires. These themes of redemption and penance for one's sins were core elements of Russian Orthodox Christianity. It was ironic that Jewish atheists (most members of the Combat Unit, including its leaders Gershuni and Azef, were Jewish)[45] used these Christian themes to argue that they redeemed the sins that every revolutionary committed in the course of his activity and did penance for these sins through the sacrifice of their lives. Self-sacrifice justified murder.[46]

The Combat Unit was responsible for only one of several forms of political agitation for the PSR, but given its popularity and the continued lack of receptiveness of the masses for other forms of propaganda, it acquired priority within the party. Gershuni, supported by Gotz, rolled over any opposition to terroristic attacks within it. As a member of the executive committee, Gershuni did not require supervision from the committee and enjoyed a high degree of independence and wide latitude of action. His next targets were the new Minister of the Interior Viacheslav von Plehve, probably the most despised politician in Russia; the governor-general of Kharkov, Ivan Obolensky, who had crushed a peasant uprising by mass flogging; and Zubatov, the very effective Moscow chief of the Okhrana. Von Plehve was a reactionary without scruples and had destroyed numerous revolutionary groups when he was in charge of the Okhrana. He was well protected against simple terrorist attacks, but Gershuni believed that these counterterrorist measures could be defeated with dynamite. He wanted to establish a dynamite workshop in Switzerland and recruited Azef for this task. Azef was indeed trying to get close to Gershuni to get information about the Combat Unit, but at the time police agents were prohibited from taking part in terrorist activities. Therefore, instead of accepting this task, he accepted the executive committee appointment of PSR representative in St. Petersburg, in charge of all party activities in the capital, most of which consisted of organizing students and workers and smuggling subversive material.

Obolensky seemed an easier target than von Plehve. A worker, 27-year-old Foma Kachura, volunteered for the task. He had been a socialist for half a dozen years and participated in a May 1901 workers' demonstration in Ekaterinoslav, which Cossacks dispersed with whips. Shortly thereafter, he quit

work and announced to his comrades that he would go and kill Pobedonostsev as revenge. Gershuni was notified and through an intermediary convinced
Kachura to stay put in return for a promise to admit him into the Combat
Unit. Another candidate for the unit became impatient and decided to kill a
government official, but mistook another man for him and stabbed this innocent victim to death.[47] To prevent another such mistake, Gershuni admitted
Kachura into his unit after graphically describing to him what would happen
after his capture. Kachura accepted the task of killing Obolensky. The evening
of 22 July 1902, the governor-general was taking a walk with a lady, followed
by a police contingent. Kachura approached them, but in trying to avoid the
woman, he missed his first shot. Then the woman grabbed his arm and made
him miss again. By this time, the police had caught up to him. He shot again
and wounded the police chief. He was arrested and incarcerated in St. Petersburg. After a year of interrogation, he broke down and provided information
on his comrades.[48]

After von Plehve took over as minister of the interior, Zubatov told him
about Azef and his opportunity to infiltrate the Combat Unit, which needed
the minister's authorization to override the prohibition of agents from participating in violent acts. The minister gave them a green light and Azef joined
the PSR Combat Unit. Gershuni called a meeting of the leadership of the
Combat Unit, which now included Melnikov, Kraft, and Azef, in October 1902
in Kiev. Gershuni told them he, along with Grigoriev and Yurkovskaya, intended to kill von Plehve. Azef of course reported this to Zubatov, who put all
the conspirators under close surveillance. Finally, at the beginning of the new
year, Zubatov conducted a nationwide sweep of PSR militants, effectively cutting off communications between the local PSR branches and the Central
Committee in Switzerland. Melnikov, Grigoriev, and Yurkovskaya got caught
in the dragnet but Gershuni managed to avoid arrest.

At the end of March 1903, Gershuni met with Azef in Moscow. Perhaps
sensing the net closing in on him and trying to establish the continuity of the
Combat Unit, he designated Azef as his deputy and successor to the executive
committee in case anything happened to him. He ordered Azef to go back to
Switzerland and interview potential candidates for the unit. Gershuni would
stay and take care of Ufa Governor-General Nicholas Bogdanovich, who was
next on his target list. Bogdanovich had just suppressed a strike earlier that
month at a factory by firing into a crowd of strikers, killing 69 and wounding
about 250 people. Scores more were arrested.[49] Azef was preparing to move
abroad with his family when the Kishinev pogrom took place on Easter Sunday, 16 April 1903. After communion, baited by von Plehve, a notorious anti-
Semite, gangs of hooligans converged on the Kishinev Jewish community and
attacked. They killed 45 people, injured more than 600, raped countless

women, castrated a few men, and looted and destroyed more than 1,300 shops and homes. Azef was outraged and complained about von Plehve to Zubatov before leaving for Switzerland. According to Zubatov's recollection, Azef "shook with fury and hate in speaking of Plehve, whom he considered responsible."[50]

In Ufa, Gershuni found that the local PSR was already planning to kill Bogdanovich. Two members had volunteered for the job: 24-year-old Igor Dulebov and another, nicknamed "the Apostle." Dulebov had been expelled from the University of Moscow for radical activities and become a locksmith at a railroad workshop. Gershuni agreed to use him as a potential assassin because of his sense of dedication. The night before the attentat, Dulebov wrote a long letter justifying his action, stating that he had prayed all his life for an opportunity to do some good for his fellow men, and was thankful for the privilege of carrying out the operation.[51] On 6 May 1903, the two assassins came up to the governor-general in the middle of his usual midday stroll, emptied their revolvers into him, and disappeared into the nearby woods. After this success, Gershuni returned to Kiev, where he was betrayed by a local police informant and arrested on 13 May 1903.[52] He was tried before a military court along with Melnikov, Kachura, Grigoriev, and Yurkovskaya, among others, in February 1904. He was convicted and condemned to death, but his sentence was commuted to life at hard labor.[53]

The Forging of a Tight Combat Unit

When Azef arrived in Switzerland in June 1903, Gotz and Chernov greeted him as the new chief of the Combat Unit.[54] He had to rebuild it after the wave of arrests, partly due to his information to the police, and change the tactics of the unit now that their targets had adopted special precautions against lone assassins. He also held von Plehve responsible for the Kishinev pogrom, and was determined to kill him for it, but needed to do it in a way that would not jeopardize his relationship with the Okhrana. Organizationally, he reported to Gotz, who provided him with political guidance and money but gave him complete independence in terms of personnel and tactics. The people he recruited were almost exclusively from the large reservoir of former university students expelled for their political activities and victims of state repression. He returned to the tactics used by People's Will, including the use of explosives (he took time to study this technology of destruction during his stay in Europe) and careful study of the routines of his targets using a team of observers, who could map out the target's movements in order to find the most favorable time and place to carry out an attentat. These observers would be disguised as cabbies and peddlers to give them a reason to be on the street spotting their target. At the same time, a team of explosives specialists would prepare the bombs and hand them off to an execution team. Just before the attentat, only the essential members of the team would stay in the area, while the others would leave.[55]

Azef recruited Pokotilov, the Kiev student and would-be assassin of Minister Bogolepov, and sent him for an intense course on bomb making. He also relied on recommendations from Gotz, Breshkovskaya, his own network of acquaintances, and those of members of the unit. His most important recruit was 24-year-old Boris Savinkov, the son of a judge in Warsaw. Savinkov grew up in Warsaw and went to gymnasium with Ivan Kaliaev, who became his best friend. Kaliaev was two years older than his friend. He was the son of a small Russian landowner and army officer and a Polish beauty, who was a humanitarian and devoted Polish nationalist. She had told her son about the 1860s Polish uprising against the tsar and its bloody repression. After gymnasium, the two friends became active in student politics. Kaliaev joined the Polish Socialist Party (PPS) at Moscow University, where he studied Polish and Russian literature and regarded himself as a poet. In the fall of 1898, he transferred to the University of St. Petersburg, where he joined Savinkov who was studying law. They were very active during the student unrest of 1899 and were expelled from the university.

After his expulsion from the University of St. Petersburg, Savinkov got married, had a child and went to study at universities in Berlin and Heidelberg. However, he disliked Germany and returned to St. Petersburg after a few months to resume his political activism. Both Savinkov and Kaliaev worked with the St. Petersburg Social Democrats. However, they participated in the riotous demonstration in Kazan Square in the aftermath of Bogolepov's assassination. They were both arrested and Savinkov received a bad cut on the head from a Cossack's saber. Kaliaev was exiled to Ekaterinoslav in southern Russia, where its governor, Count Keller, had resorted to draconian measures in his repression of a peasant demonstration. Strongly impressed by the Combat Unit's assassination of Sipiagin, Kaliaev decided to kill Keller but gave up when he got no support for his plan. He came to conceive of himself as a terrorist.[56]

After a few months in prison, Savinkov was freed on bail and awaited the disposition of his case in Vologda. Breshkovskaya came twice to Vologda on recruiting missions for the PSR and talked to Savinkov. Savinkov told her that the killing of Sipiagin had capped his spiritual conversion to the PSR and terrorism. She told him that his best friend Kaliaev had already done so and in fact had recommended Savinkov to her. Savinkov was sentenced to exile but the news of Gershuni's arrest made him determined to join the Combat Unit.

He escaped and arrived in Geneva in July 1903. He went to see Gotz and told him that he wanted to join the Combat Unit. "I regarded terror as of decisive significance, but I was entirely at the disposal of the Central Committee."[57]

In August, on Gotz's recommendation, Azef came to visit Savinkov and listened while Savinkov told him that he considered the assassination of von Plehve the most important task of the moment. Two weeks later, Azef welcomed Savinkov into the Combat Unit, explained his overall strategy, and appointed Savinkov coordinator of the information from the observation team in St. Petersburg. Savinkov was to establish a new identity and cover story for his return to Russia. Azef also asked him for possible recommendations for the unit, and Savinkov suggested Joseph and Ignat Matzevsky, university friends of his who were now in Geneva, and Kaliaev. Azef recruited the Matzevsky brothers and sent them back to Savinkov to explain tactics to them. Kaliaev was another story. He also escaped from Russia in the fall of 1903 and reconnected with Savinkov in Berlin. Savinkov introduced him to Azef, who was not impressed by the frail young poet.[58]

Another recruit for the Combat Unit was 24-year-old Igor Sazonov, son of a rich merchant in Ufa, who had studied medicine at the University of Moscow to become a country doctor. At the time, he was a monarchist and deeply religious but was caught up in the student strike in early 1901, flogged by mounted Cossacks, arrested, and expelled from school. He spent a year and a half in prison in Moscow, where he was first exposed to revolutionary literature. "My friends know well with what difficulty I have reached my present conclusion. It is not easy to reject the fundamental laws of humanity, but I have been forced to it. From now on I dedicate myself to open warfare with the government and I know that once decided upon my course, I shall go on to the end."[59] When Sazonov returned to his native Ufa, he organized socialist study circles, which included Dulebov, the future assassin of Bogdanovich. Sazonov was arrested in 1902 and exiled to Irkutsk, but the next year made his way to Switzerland. He contacted Gotz, who referred him to Azef, whose usual interview was to test the resolve of potential candidates. Azef tried to talk them out of joining the unit, pointing out all the inherent problems of a life underground. Those not put off by his portrait of a life of constant paranoia and tedium, interspersed with occasional panic, but willing to embrace it, were accepted. Sazonov passed the test.

Another Gotz referral was Maximilian "Marc" Schweitzer, the 22-year-old son of a Jewish merchant in Smolensk. After taking part in revolutionary activities in his local gymnasium, he went to study physics and mathematics at Moscow University. He was very congenial, calm, happy, and well balanced. Caught up in the student unrest of 1899, he was arrested, expelled from school, and exiled to Yakutsk, where he started studying the chemistry of explosives.

After the end of his exile in 1903, he went to Geneva and contacted Gotz. Azef welcomed him and encouraged him to continue studying explosives and bomb making.[60]

In terms of their paths to political violence, each of the members of the Combat Unit, with the exception of Azef, was a volunteer who had joined for his own personal reason. It was a bottom-up process of joining, much like enlisting in an army, to fight the oppression of the state. Indeed, the unit was uniquely set up as a battalion with a strict hierarchy, and its members thought of themselves as soldiers for the revolution. None had any military training or background of violence.

Meanwhile, Azef's situation with both the Okhrana and the PSR was changing. In Russia, von Plehve, who had never trusted Zubatov, dismissed him when an Okhrana-controlled conservative trade union, created to prevent workers from joining more radical ones, asked for real concessions.[61] The Okhrana Paris chief, Leonid Rataev, now became Azef's case officer.[62] At the PSR, Gershuni's arrest and the consequent disappearance of his authority allowed some Central Committee members to criticize the Combat Unit's monopoly on terrorist attacks. They tasked one of their favorites, Serafima Klichoglu, to assassinate von Plehve as well. Azef protested and even tried to dissuade Klichoglu from her pursuit, but in vain. So, he denounced her to Rataev. In early February 1904, the Okhrana raided Klichoglu and her associates, arrested 58 people throughout Russia and seized six printing presses. These arrests happened soon after Azef's meeting with her, and he became afraid that he might be suspected of betrayal. To protect himself, Azef's strategy was to denounce people with whom he had no connection to keep in the clear. The Okhrana's apparent disregard for his protection upset him to the point that he threatened to break his contact with it. Rataev tried to correct its mistake by deflecting suspicion onto someone else.[63]

Meanwhile, Savinkov and the Matzevsky brothers had arrived in St. Petersburg in November 1903 to start the casing of von Plehve. They got nervous and felt that the police were zeroing in on them. Not receiving any word from Azef, they panicked and dispersed throughout Russia. Savinkov went to Kiev, where, in a PSR safe house, he met Dulebov, who was planning to leave Russia. They left together and went to meet with Gotz, who was convalescing in Nice. Gotz told Savinkov about the addition of Pokotilov, Sazonov, and Schweitzer to the Combat Unit. He urged Savinkov to go back, meet Azef in Moscow, and take his friend Kaliaev as well. When Azef finally caught up with Savinkov in January 1904, he berated his subordinate for having abandoned his post and sent Savinkov back to St. Petersburg to meet the growing team and coordinate their activities. Back in the capital, Savinkov reconnected with Joseph Matzevsky—his brother had dropped out—and met Schweitzer and Pokotilov, who was becoming impatient. "You know I wanted to kill Bogolepov. Karpo-vich anticipated me . . . then Balmashev . . . I said I could not wait any more, that the very next assassination would be my work. Gershuni came to Poltava. It was decided I would kill Obolensky. I began preparing for this. Suddenly, I learn that not I but Katchura . . . Katchura was a worker. They preferred him. And now von Plehve. I will not yield to anybody. The first bomb will be mine. I have been waiting too long. This is my right. I have absolute faith in our suc-cess . . . Von Plehve will be killed. Only it's difficult to wait. I have been in Moscow a long time, taking care of the dynamite. It is impossible to live thus, always waiting. I can't."[64]

Azef came to St. Petersburg to meet his team in the second half of Febru-ary: Savinkov was the coordinator; Sazonov and Matzevsky cabdrivers; Poko-tilov and Kaliaev peddlers; Schweitzer the bomb maker; and a newcomer, Abram Borishansky, a Jewish worker from Bialystok, was to bring explosive material from Geneva. By mid-March, the team felt it had enough informa-tion on von Plehve's pattern of movement to attempt the bombing. On 16 March, Azef returned to St. Petersburg. He was skeptical about its readiness, but Savinkov told him that the team was running out of patience. Azef reluc-tantly agreed, gave them the green light to proceed with an attack on 18 March, and left town. Schweitzer worked through the night and built five bombs. Pokotilov and Borishansky each got two four-pound bombs, and Sazonov got a large seven-pound bomb to hide under his cover in his lap. Kaliaev, who was the signal person, complained that he had no bomb: "There is no bomb for me. Why for Borishansky and not for me? . . . I do not want to take fewer chances than the others."[65] Shortly before von Plehve's carriage was to appear, Borishansky suddenly left his post. Pokotilov noticed it and immediately went to notify Savinkov. While he was out of position, von Plehve's carriage went by at great speed, and he did not have time to return to his position. Sazonov, who had positioned his carriage against the grain of the traffic to be able to see von Plehve's oncoming carriage, was being harassed by the other cabbies for being pointed in the wrong way. He noticed von Plehve's speeding carriage too late to grab his bomb. The attempt was a complete failure.

Borishansky later explained that he had left because he thought he was being surrounded by police spies. The group dispersed and waited for Azef's return. When they did not get any news from him, they believed he had been arrested and agreed to regroup in Kiev. Savinkov took control over the dispir-ited members there. He split the group in two: Schweitzer, Kaliaev, and he would stay in Kiev to kill Governor General Kleigels, the former St. Petersburg police chief; Borishansky, Pokotilov, Sazonov, and Matzevsky would return to St. Petersburg and try again to kill von Plehve. The St. Petersburg group took most of the explosive material, leaving the Kiev group with enough for one bomb. On 30 March, Pokotilov worked through the night to arm the bombs for the anticipated attentat, but something went wrong and he blew himself up in his hotel room.[66]

Azef gathered his demoralized troops and took them to a place near Kharkov, where they could rest and regain their composure. He told them that they should concentrate only on von Plehve and abort the attempt on General Kleigels. Savinkov later remembered, "Azef's firm insistence upon action, his calmness and self-assurance, buttressed our spirits, so much so that I could not understand how I ever ventured to liquidate the von Plehve enterprise and embark upon the provincial, politically unimportant undertaking to assassinate Kleigels."[67]

With the chance to rest together, the Combat Unit bonded in a relaxed atmosphere. Dulebov joined the group at this time, as did Dora Brilliant, Pokotilov's beautiful lover, who was determined to continue his work. She was the 23-year-old daughter of a prosperous Jewish merchant who had run away from her family to study obstetrics at Yuriev University, where she participated in student unrest. She was exiled to Poltava, where she met Breshkovskaya and Gershuni. Their influence turned her into a determined revolutionary. She joined the party in 1902 and went to Kiev, where she met Pokotilov.[68] As Savinkov recalled, "The silent, modest and shy Dora lived only by one thing—her faith in terror. Loving the revolution, tortured by its failures, recognizing the necessity of killing von Plehve, she nevertheless feared this killing. She could not compromise with the spilling of blood. It was easier for her to die than to kill. And yet her constant request was to be given a bomb and to be permitted to be one of those who were actually to do the killing. The key to this enigma, in my opinion, was, first, that she could not separate herself from her comrades, or play a lighter, less dangerous role, leaving to them the more perilous part of the undertaking and, secondly, that she considered it her duty to cross the threshold to that region where actual participation in the enterprise began." Terror for Brilliant and Kaliaev was only justified by their own sacrifice. "Questions of program did not interest her. She may have, perhaps, emerged dissatisfied to a certain extent from her committee work . . . Terror for her personified the revolution, and her entire world was embodied in the Terrorist Brigade."[69] In his memoirs, Savinkov was careful to neglect mentioning that he promptly took advantage of her vulnerable state and fragile beauty by seducing her and taking her as his mistress.[70]

Savinkov also grew to appreciate Sazonov, "a true descendant of People's Will, a fanatic of the revolution who refused to see or recognize anything outside of it. In his passionate faith in people and in his love for them was his strength . . . Sazonov was young, healthy and strong . . . For him, too, terror was, above all, a matter of personal sacrifice, of heroic deed . . . Von Plehve's death was necessary for Russia, for the revolution, for the triumph of social-ism. Before this necessity all moral questions on the theme 'Thou shalt not kill' paled into insignificance."[71]

Sazonov once told Savinkov, "You know, I used to think terror was neces-sary, but that it was not all-important. I see now that we must concentrate all our forces on terror; only thus can we win. And so does the 'poet' think, too."[72] The poet, Kaliaev, also believed that terror was the keystone of the revolution. Of course, he understood the importance of peaceful activity, but he found it difficult to engage in propaganda and agitation. He dreamed of future terror and its decisive influence in the revolution. "You know, I would like to live long enough to see the day when we will be another Macedonia. There terror is a mass phenomenon; every revolutionist is a terrorist. And with us? Five, six persons, that's all. The rest engages in peaceful work. But can a Socialist Revo-lutionist work peacefully? A Socialist Revolutionist without a bomb is no lon-ger a Socialist Revolutionist. And is it possible to speak of terror without taking part in it? Oh, I know: there will be a conflagration that will sweep the whole of Russia. We shall have our own Macedonia. The peasant will seize bombs. And then—the revolution."[73]

At the same time, Schweitzer was making explosive material from locally purchased chemicals. During that month of rest and relaxation in Kharkov, the Combat Unit forged an esprit de corps, regaining enthusiasm and confi-dence. Its members understood their mistakes and now knew how to correct them. The combatants were ready to resume their fight. As Savinkov remarked, "Without exaggeration, one might say that Azef revived our organization. We went to work with faith and determination to kill von Plehve, no matter what the cost."[74]

The Assassination of von Plehve

In May 1904, the group returned to St. Petersburg with a slight change of sce-nario. Savinkov came as a rich English businessman with Dora Brilliant as his mistress. They moved into a large, fashionable apartment. Sazonov pretended to be their butler, and a new member, Praskovia Ivanovskaya, their cook. She was the 51-year-old daughter of a priest, who had a long history of revolu-tionary activities. Her brother, a follower of Nechaev, gave her subversive ma-terial to distribute when she was still in school. He was arrested and a defendant in the Trial of the 50 in 1877. She helped him escape from prison and later linked up with Osinsky in Odessa and became one of the original members of People's Will. She was arrested in September 1882 and sentenced to death at the Trial of the 17 in 1883, but her sentence was commuted to 15 years at hard labor and exile in Siberia. She escaped in 1903 and joined the PSR Combat Unit.[75] Matzevsky and Dulebov were cabbies, while Kaliaev and Borishansky were peddlers. Schweitzer made about 40 pounds of explosive material and brought it to St. Petersburg in June.[76] The conspirators used Savinkov's apartment as their main meeting place, where even Azef was able to spend ten days unnoticed at the end of May. The easy and enthusiastic atmosphere of Kharkov continued to prevail. "By this time all members of the organization had not only renewed their acquaintance but had grown closer to each other. There were strong ties of comradeship—the failure of 18 March and Pokotilov's death. Both the old and new members of the organization felt this strong bond of union, and the line of division between the older and the younger among us, between the workers and intellectuals had become obliterated. We were one fraternity, living by one idea, by one aim. Sazonov was right when later . . . he said: 'Our band, our knightly order was animated by a spirit in which the word "brother" expressed but inadequately the reality of our relations.' This fraternal bond was felt by all of us and filled us with assurance in inevitable victory."[77]

The observers determined von Plehve's pattern and, by late June, the team was ready for the operation. Savinkov, Sazonov, and Kaliaev traveled to Moscow to meet with Azef to put the final touches on the plot. Azef had the deciding voice.[78] The plan called for four bombers, spaced 40 paces apart. Borishansky would let the carriage through and block its way back in case it did a U-turn. Sazonov with the largest bomb was the designated killer, and Kaliaev was there if Sazonov missed. Finally, Borishansky had suggested a 20-year-old friend from Bialystok, Schmil Sikorsky, as a fourth bomber in case Kaliaev missed as well. Sikorsky, a leather worker, had joined the PSR and hated the tsar as a Pole and von Plehve as a Jew. The conspirators agreed to this plan. Kaliaev suggested he could throw himself under the horses' feet to slow down the speeding carriage, but Azef pointed out to him he would be killed. Kaliaev replied, "Of course," but Azef said it would not be necessary.[79] The time and place were set for 8 July near the Warsaw Station. After the meeting, Savinkov and Sazonov went for a walk. Savinkov asked his friend how he would feel after the killing. Sazonov replied, "Pride and joy . . . [and] only that."[80] The St. Petersburg apartment was vacated, leaving only personnel essential to the execution of the plot in the capital. Ivanovskaya and Azef went to Vilna to wait for the result of the operation. Brilliant objected that she had not been selected as a bomber, but Savinkov, being a male chauvinist, believed that there was no reason for women to throw bombs as long as men were available. In addition, he was convinced that his lover was too unstable to throw a bomb and rejected her plea.[81]

The night before the attempt, Schweitzer manufactured four bombs.

However, in the morning, Sazonov was late getting to the rendezvous, and the attempt had to be postponed for a week. Sazonov was very upset with himself, but the failure was treated as a practice run. On 15 July 1904, everything went according to plan. Sazonov got the twelve-pound bomb, while the other three bombers got six-pound bombs. When von Plehve's carriage came, Sazonov got close enough to throw his bomb, which exploded as planned. The carriage was destroyed, and von Plehve and his coachman died on the spot. Sazonov was severely wounded. The others got away as planned except for Sikorsky, who panicked and threw his bomb into the river. A boatman took him to the police station.[82] Only the wounded Sazonov and the inexperienced Sikorsky were arrested.

When Azef heard about the assassination of von Plehve, he took the first train to Paris and, on the way, wired Rataev in Paris his sorrow and surprise at the assassination. When he arrived, he met with his case officer, who had just been recalled to St. Petersburg to explain how he had failed to protect the minister, who was his boss. Azef complained about the incompetence of the police, as he claimed to have reported all he knew to Rataev, and this should have been enough for the Okhrana in St. Petersburg to unravel the plot. Azef hoped that this excuse would save him from the police. It turned out that von Plehve had been so unpopular that the investigation into his death was mostly a pro forma affair: everyone seemed relieved to be rid of him, even the police. "Hated during his lifetime, Plehve went to his grave deserted by all."[83]

To understand this indifference to his murder, one must appreciate the consequences of the Russo-Japanese War. On 26 January 1904, the Japanese conducted a successful attack on the Russian fleet at Port Arthur. This was followed by defeat after defeat, which exposed governmental and military incompetence and irresponsibility. One commentator at the time captured the mood of the country: "Impatience, feelings of resentment, indignation—these grew everywhere and became stronger. With each new defeat, with each new retreat to 'previously prepared positions' in 'accordance to prior plans,' indignation grew more intense and there took shape a mood of protest. There was no malicious joy. Oh no! There was a feeling of burning shame and undeserved injury."[84]

The war also precipitated an economic crisis and widespread hardships, as war logistics were given priority over transporting economic goods. The government was blamed for the catastrophe, especially von Plehve. The Austrian ambassador in St. Petersburg noted that his assassination did not even raise the usual degree of human compassion for a victim: "Not a trace of this is to be found. Up to now I have found only totally indifferent people or people so cynical that they say that no other outcome was to be expected."[85]

The news of the assassination reached a meeting of the PSR Central

Committee in Geneva. "For several minutes, pandemonium reigned. Several men and women became hysterical. Most of those present embraced each other. On every side there were shouts of joy. I can still see N.: he was standing a little apart; he dashed a glass of water on the floor and, gnashing his teeth, shouted, 'That's for Kishinev!' "[86]

The party endorsed the success of the Combat Unit as its own victory and triumph, and Azef became the hero of the day. His authority, which had been challenged by several on the Central Committee, became reinforced. When he arrived in Geneva, Breshkovskaya greeted him in the old Russian fashion of bowing almost to the ground to express her gratitude. Azef became a high priest of terrorism in the PSR pantheon, on a par with Zhelyabov and Gershuni. Gotz remarked, referring to Gershuni, "Formerly we were led by a romantic, now we have a realist. He is not a talker, but he will carry out his plans with a ruthless energy which nothing can withstand."[87]

The PSR Central Committee issued a proclamation in French from Paris: "More than any others we condemn publicly, as did our heroic predecessors of the People's Will, the use of terror as a measure of systematic warfare in free countries. But in Russia, where despotism precludes any open political struggle and knows only lawlessness, where there is no protection against irresponsible authority, absolutist in all aspects of its bureaucratic structure, we are compelled to interpose the law of revolution against the law of tyranny."[88] A special edition of *Revolutionary Russia* explained von Plehve's assassination. "Who ruined the country, who submerged it in torrents of blood? Who carried us back to the Middle Ages with his ghetto, with the slaughter in Kishinev and the decomposed corpse of St. Seraphim? Who strangled the Finns for the sole reason that they were Finns, the Jews for the sole reason that they were Jews, the Armenians because of Armenia, the Poles because of Poland? Who fired on us, starving and unarmed, who violated our women and dispossessed us of our remaining good? . . . Who? Always he, the unlimited master of Russia, the old man in the gold-bedecked uniform, blessed by the czar and cursed by the people."[89]

The remainder of the Combat Unit traveled to Geneva except for Matzevsky, who left the unit to join the Polish underground. Its triumph had quieted Azef's critics, at least temporarily. Azef also enjoyed the loyalty of his subordinates, whom he had personally recruited and forged into a very tight group. Now, Azef exploited his triumph by formalizing his informal understanding with Gotz in terms of complete operational autonomy. He wrote a set of by-laws for the unit,[90] summarized in *Revolutionary Russia*: "The Terrorist Brigade is to receive from the party, though its central organ, general instructions concerning the initiation or cessation of any militant activities and of particular persons against whom these activities are to be directed. Concerning everything else it is to enjoy the widest possible powers and autonomy. It is to be connected with the party only through the party's central organ and is quite independent of any local committees. It is to have its own organization, composed of picked members (very limited in number, due to its peculiar nature), its own treasury and its own source of income."[91] It was directed by its own executive committee, elected by its own members. This executive committee was headed by a director, who was the ultimate deciding voice in case of disagreements and the only intermediary with the PSR Central Committee. This executive committee would admit new members and exclude old ones, elaborate new operational plans, and publish statements in the name of the unit. Gotz approved these by-laws on his own authority. The unit elected Azef as its director, Savinkov as his alternate, and Schweitzer as the third member of the executive committee.[92]

The Triumph of the Combat Unit

Azef consolidated his position within the PSR Central Committee, despite the fact that he was not a believer in the party's ideology or even a socialist, but just a fellow traveler. He freely admitted that he would leave the party as soon as political freedom was achieved.[93] Chernov later recalled, "He had no belief whatsoever in the masses or mass movements as an independent revolutionary force. His only immediate reality was the struggle for political freedom, and his only revolutionary means, the terror. He would seem to have regarded propaganda work, agitation, and mass organization with contempt as mere educational work, and recognized as 'Revolution' only the active fighting done by the few members of a secret organization."[94] He was a "liberal terrorist" who viewed terrorism as the only way to achieve political freedom.

Flush with success after the assassination of von Plehve, the Combat Unit became extremely popular and people wanted to join this mysterious entity. Boris Moiseyenko, who had been in exile in Vologda with Savinkov and had also wanted to kill von Plehve at the time, contacted his friend in Geneva to join the unit. Savinkov introduced his friend to Azef, who admitted him.[95] Azef expanded the unit further by admitting his younger brother, Vladimir Azef, a German-trained chemist; Jacob Borishansky, Abram's younger brother; and Tatiana Leontyeva, the daughter of the vice-governor of Yakutsk and a relative of Moscow police Chief General Dmitry Trepov. She was extremely well connected in the St. Petersburg aristocracy and a lady-in-waiting to the tsarina. She had come to Geneva and offered her services to Breshkovskaya, who had referred her to Azef.[96] Savinkov became immediately infatuated with her and made every effort to seduce her. This caused a break-off with Dora Brilliant, who became more depressed, on the verge of an emotional collapse.[97]

During the summer, Azef moved to Paris, where he installed his family in a comfortable apartment and set up a bomb factory for Schweitzer to teach the business of explosives to other members of the unit. Savinkov, Brilliant, Kaliaev, Dulebov, Borishansky, Moiseyenko, and Vladimir Azef took his classes. The relaxed atmosphere of Paris helped to integrate the new members into the unit and consolidate their esprit de corps. Azef's indifference to the PSR program was shared by his subordinates. None was a true believer and none followed the socialist revolutionary line. Savinkov criticized the Central Committee as a pack of gutless chatterboxes who understood nothing about revolution. To him, "A socialist revolutionary without a bomb is not a socialist revolutionary." He disregarded party discipline and orders when he disagreed with them. He was more of an individualist anarchist, dedicated to the idea of revolution but contemptuous of peasants and workers. His loyalty was to his comrades in the unit. When once asked why he served the Revolution, he replied, "The sense of comradeship, love and respect for the comrades is the cause. Everything that the comrades want, must be provided." Like them, he was willing to kill for the cause, but unlike many of them, he was not interested in dying for it.[98]

Schweitzer was a political moderate who believed in Parliament and that "terror was the most important task of the moment, that, compared with this, all other tasks paled into insignificance, that the success of all other undertakings might well be sacrificed to the success of terror, that the Terrorist Brigade, being a part of the Party of Socialist Revolutionists, sharing its aims and tendencies, was in reality performing a task beyond mere party aims and serving not this or that particular party program but the cause of the Russian revolution as a whole. I must add, however, that neither Kaliaev nor any of us believed we had the right to express this view publicly, before a court, for by joining the party we assumed the obligation to pursue the strictly party line."[99]

Kaliaev elaborated on this: "I do not know what I would do had I been born a Frenchman, Englishman or German. In all probability, I would not manufacture bombs, and, most probably, I would not be interested in politics at all. But why should we, the Party of the Socialist-Revolutionists, i.e., the party of terror, throw stones at Italian and French terrorists? Why should we dissociate ourselves from . . . Ravachol? Why this hurry? Why this fear of European public opinion? It is not for us to fear—we must be feared and respected. Terror is power. It is not for us to proclaim our lack of respect for it . . . I believe more in terror than in all the parliaments in the world. I will not throw a bomb into a café, but it is not for me to judge Ravachol. He is more of a comrade to me than those to whom this proclamation is addressed."[100]

Moiseyenko agreed with Kaliaev. At this point, it appears that most members of the Combat Unit shared their leader's liberalism, which was to be achieved through violence. They were not socialists, but asked for civil liberties, the rule of liberal democratic law, and the creation of a legislative body with a strong voice in shaping the laws of the empire.[101] On the other hand, Dulebov and Borishansky, being workers, were far more radical, as they approved all methods of struggle against the most dangerous element in the enemy's camp—the bourgeoisie. Brilliant agreed with them. In effect, the repressive autocracy in Russia united liberals and radicals in their use of violence against the regime. Indeed, within the Combat Unit, political "differences had little effect . . . upon our relations with one another. The same spirit of mutual love and friendship continued to prevail in the organization."[102]

On 26 August 1904, the tsar appointed Prince Peter Sviatopolk-Mirsky, a liberal, as minister of the interior. Known to favor reforms, Mirsky relaxed press censorship, dismissed the most notorious reactionaries from his ministry, and restored full rights to political prisoners and exiles. His liberalism emboldened many people to express their disappointment with conditions in Russia. Defying the ban on assembly, people everywhere held political meetings and demanded a constitution with a representative assembly. Students at all major universities clamored for democratic reforms but were again violently put down by Cossacks. The tsar seemed to vacillate, promising reforms to petitioners but reassuring reactionaries that he would never give in to reformers. By the end of the year, even Mirsky was losing heart.[103]

In this period of political agitation, Azef became invaluable to the Okhrana in his reporting on the rapid developments among radical émigrés. His production in the second half of 1904 was the most prolific and significant of his career as an informant, and went a long way to redeem his reputation with the Okhrana after his apparent failure to prevent von Plehve's assassination. Most of his reporting involved his rivals within the PSR and other revolutionary organizations, which led to their arrests when they tried to return to Russia.[104]

In mid-November 1904, Azef mustered his troops in Paris to discuss their upcoming campaign. Ivanovskaya and Leontyeva came from Geneva for the general meeting, as all the others were already in Paris. They decided to strike a blow against the reactionary forces of the empire by simultaneously eliminating the tsar's two uncles—his closest and most influential advisers and pillars of reaction: Grand Dukes Sergei in Moscow and Vladimir in St. Petersburg. There also arose the question of what to do about General Kleigels, and the group decided to include him in a three-pronged attack. The Combat Unit would send three teams to assassinate these targets. The largest team, led by Schweitzer, would go to St. Petersburg and included Dulebov, Ivanovskaya, and Leontyeva, who had access to the court, and would be augmented with some of Leontyeva's comrades. The second team, led by Savinkov, would go to Moscow and included Kaliaev, Moiseyenko, and Brilliant, with possibly another member to be recruited in Russia. Borishansky would go to Kiev and recruit some help locally. Schweitzer divided the manufactured explosive material accordingly, and the three groups left for Russia later that month.[105]

In St. Petersburg, Sazonov and Sikorsky went on trial on 30 November 1904 after Sazonov's recovery and interrogation. He had managed to smuggle a letter to his comrades in which he apologized for revealing his identity when he was delirious in the hospital, and his inability to explain the PSR program to the court—a failure he of course shared with his comrades. "As you know, my conception of terror springs from the People's Will and so to some extent I disagree with the program of the Terrorist Brigade. When I appeared before the court I felt I was in a false position. I should not have spoken of my personal views. I should have spoken exclusively of the views of the Brigade. Did I commit a sin against the Brigade? Please forgive me. Tell the party to announce my errors publicly, tell them to say they are not responsible for the words spoken by individual members, especially one who is ill. I have still not recovered. The blow on my head was too strong. So I am weighed down with a sense of sin, and I want to confess my errors to you, my dear comrades. And if I am the only one who has wronged our cause, let this too be known. I have tried so consciously to lessen the importance of my errors."[106]

The defendants' deed had been applauded throughout Russia, and as their lawyer stated, "The bomb was loaded not with dynamite but with the tears and sufferings of the people."[107] At the trial, the judges treated Sazonov with respect and allowed him to explain himself. "I wish to explain that our party . . . is by its very nature inimical to every kind of violence . . . We are not forcing our ideals upon the people: we wish only to speak the truth . . . We hate and despise violence, and we are convinced that violence is powerless against ideals. But all our attempts at peaceful activity have been met by ruthless prosecution on the part of the government. We are subjected to the humiliation of corporal punishment, beaten by knouts, trodden upon by horses, and shot down as soon as we declare our desires and our purposes. We are deprived of the protection of the law and declared to be enemies of the people . . . Yes, the government made me a revolutionist and a terrorist, though originally I prayed only for peace . . . Since I began to understand the work of the Ministers of Russia, I felt I had no right to enjoy a peaceful and happy life. So in killing von Plehve I acted according to the dictates of my conscience."[108]

The defendants were convicted: Sazonov was sentenced to life at hard labor, and Sikorsky to 15 years at hard labor. A year later, Sazonov smuggled out another letter, describing his sense of shared social identity with his comrades. "Dear comrades! A year and a half has passed since I was removed from your ranks, but though physically separated from you, I have not for a moment ceased to live with you in my thoughts . . . With what exaltation have I greeted your victories, and with what sorrow have I grieved over your failures . . . I cannot refrain from telling you, brothers-comrades, how happy I have been to recall you to my mind, your loving, purely fraternal attitude toward me, the confidence you placed in me when you entrusted me with such a responsible task as that of July 15. For me, it would have been a thousand times worse than death to defile your love, to prove myself beneath your confidence, to becloud in any way the work of the Terrorist Brigade, the whole greatness of which I am the first to recognize and before which I stand in awe . . . I feel the need to repeat again and again that there must be no misunderstanding between me and those who may one day be called upon to sacrifice themselves. It is absolutely necessary for my happiness to feel identified with you on all matters pertaining to the life and the program of our party."[109]

The Start of the Russian Revolution of 1905 and the Assassination of Grand Duke Sergei

The three Combat Unit teams set up in their respective cities. Azef stayed behind in Paris, partly because he was afraid he might be arrested in the wake of von Plehve's assassination. In St. Petersburg, Schweitzer did not have any trouble recruiting at least eight militants for his team, but now most of his team was inexperienced. However, serious unrest would soon break out in the capital, which would change the pattern of activities of his target. In Kiev, Borishansky managed to recruit only a couple, and he was facing some difficulties as well.

In Moscow, Savinkov was more efficient in implementing his scheme. Kaliaev and Moiseyenko tracked Grand Duke Sergei's ducal carriage and movements despite the fact that he slept in three different palaces. Brilliant kept the explosives and the detonators in Nizhni-Novgorod until the observation team finished its work. Savinkov realized that they needed a second bomber to ensure that any attack would be fatal. He went to Baku to comfort Sazonov's distraught fiancée by seducing her and she told him about a schoolteacher and former student, Peter Kulikovsky, who was dedicated to the PSR and had pleaded with her to recommend him for the unit. Savinkov interviewed him and took him to Moscow to join the team.[110]

When Savinkov returned to Moscow, everything seemed changed. There had been student demonstrations on 5 and 6 December, and Grand Duke Sergei and his police chief General Dmitry Trepov—the son of Fyodor Trepov

(Vera Zasulich's victim) and Leontyeva's relative—had put them down with his usual cruelty. Outraged, the local Moscow PSR committee had issued a death threat against the grand duke and the police chief. Because of the threat, the grand duke moved into the Kremlin and changed his pattern of travel, thus negating a month's worth of careful observations by the Moscow team. The local committee did not know about the presence of the Combat Unit or its mission, as the unit usually avoided contact with local PSR groups for fear of being detected by police spies who might have infiltrated them. Savinkov had to meet with the leader of this local committee to get it to stand down. The day after the meeting, this leader was arrested, and Savinkov ordered a temporary stand-down in case he had been detected.[111]

Meanwhile, revolution was brewing in St. Petersburg. Labor unrest, led by Father Gregory Gapon, was coming to a boil. The 34-year-old son of a clerk, he had become a priest and devoted himself to missionary work among poor workers and beggars in St. Petersburg. With former Okhrana chief Zubatov's encouragement to create a conservative labor union, he formed the St. Petersburg Assembly of the Russian Factory and Mill Workers in 1903. It did not get involved in labor disputes or political demands but concentrated on the organization of dances, concerts, and lectures and projects for self-improvement. It quickly grew to about 5,000 to 20,000 members by January 1905. Unbeknownst to his police handlers, Gapon had great ambition and believed he could convince the tsar to grant better economic and political conditions to the workers, such as eight-hour days, the right to form trade unions, and workers' insurance. When four union members were fired in December 1904, the Assembly unanimously voted to go on strike until their reinstatement, and by 7 January, some 100,000 workers at 382 enterprises, about two-thirds of St. Petersburg's factory labor force, walked off their jobs. Gapon declared his intention to present the tsar on the following Sunday with a petition asking for economic and political reforms.[112] However, the tsar gave orders not to permit marching workers to enter the center of the city and recalled about 12,000 troops to protect him. On Sunday, 9 January 1905, between 50,000 and 100,000 people gathered and peacefully marched to the Winter Palace, singing religious hymns. When they reached the gate of the palace, the soldiers opened fire into the crowd without warning. Officially, there were 130 killed and 299 seriously wounded, but the foreign press reported that the fatalities numbered in the thousands. "Bloody Sunday" instantly and forever killed the Myth of the Good Tsar, who had enjoyed the affection and loyalty of the workers because of their belief in his benevolence. Gapon, up to then a loyal servant of the tsar, was now heard shouting, "There is no God any longer! There is no Tsar!" The fury of the crowd was directed at the government: "Murderers! Bloodsuckers! Hangmen! You run away from the Japanese, but shoot at your own people!"

Gapon escaped with the help of a close friend, worker Peter Rutenberg, and went underground.[113]

All segments of society condemned the authorities, and particularly the tsar, for Bloody Sunday. Workers throughout the empire went on strike, which led to clashes with the authorities, resulting in dozens of deaths. To reestablish order in St. Petersburg, the tsar appointed General Dmitry Trepov of Moscow as governor-general of St. Petersburg. He assumed command on 11 January with almost unlimited power.

The widespread unrest disrupted the planning of the Combat Unit teams. Their targets moved to different palaces, and in St. Petersburg, Trepov effectively imposed a state of siege, with troops posted everywhere in the streets. Rutenberg, a PSR member and friend of Savinkov's from their university activism, came to Moscow and asked Savinkov to come to help in the St. Petersburg uprising. Savinkov traveled to the capital on 12 January and learned that Leontyeva had volunteered to kill the tsar. She had been selected to be a flower girl at a court ball on 20 January, which the tsar was expected to attend. Without approval from the Central Committee or Azef, Schweitzer had approved the plan. Savinkov did not like it because of his general reluctance to use female assassins but did not veto it. At the end, the ball was canceled and the plan came to naught.

Schweitzer informed Savinkov that they could no longer track Grand Duke Vladimir, but had found the trail of Minister of Justice Nikolai Muraviev, and suggested assassinating him. The arrival of Trepov in St. Petersburg and his history of harsh repression also earned him a position as a target on par with the grand duke. Before returning to Moscow on 15 January, Savinkov recalled Borishansky to the capital, as General Kleigels was no longer an important target. The attempt against Muraviev was carried out on 19 January. The first bomber got cold feet and fled, while the second was inadvertently prevented from coming closer to the minister by other cab drivers. Later that day, unaware that he had survived an attentat, a demoralized Muraviev tendered his resignation to the tsar. Since he was no longer in the government, the Combat Unit aborted any further plotting against him.[114]

Back in Moscow, Savinkov resumed the plot against Grand Duke Sergei. "I can say without exaggeration that all members of the Moscow division . . . were one close, well-knit family. Our differences of character and opinion did not interfere with this. Perhaps, the individual characteristics of each of us only helped to strengthen it. I am inclined to attribute the success of the Moscow assassination to this very close association of the members of our organization . . . Moiseyenko was a man of independent and original opinions. From the party point of view he was a heretic on many questions. He attached little significance to peace work, and could ill conceal his contempt for conferences, meetings and other party assemblages. He believed only in terror."[115]

Indeed, the team's collective identity extended to the rest of the Combat Unit. Kaliaev told Savinkov: "As you know, I do not recognize the past. I know only the present. For me Alexis [Pokotilov] is not dead. For me Yegor [Sazonov] is not in Schluesselburg. They are with us. Don't you feel their presence?"[116] The tedious observation work allowed the team to figure out the new habits of the grand duke and anticipate that he would attend the Bolshoi Theater on 2 February. Brilliant came to Moscow, stayed at an elegant hotel, and armed two bombs, one for Kaliaev and another for Kulikovsky. Dressed as peasants, they positioned themselves along the two possible routes for the grand duke to take to the theater. The grand duke came via Kaliaev's road. Kaliaev saw the carriage, dashed forward, and raised his hand to hurl his bomb. He looked inside the carriage and saw there, in addition to Grand Duke Sergei, his wife, Grand Duchess Elizabeth, and the children of Grand Duke Paul—Marie and Dmitri. He let his hand down and withdrew in the dark. No one had noticed him, and the carriage proceeded to the theater.[117]

Kaliaev later asked Savinkov, "I think I have done properly. How can one kill children?"[118] Savinkov applauded him. Kaliaev said that, if Savinkov insisted, they still had the opportunity to kill the grand duke and the whole family on their return from the theater, but Savinkov replied that this was quite out of the question. They waited until the end of the performance to see whether the grand duke would travel by himself, but he returned accompanied by his family. Savinkov brought back the bombs to Dora Brilliant, who approved: "The 'poet' did as he should have done."[119] They resolved to try again two days later.

Savinkov, Kaliaev, and Kulikovsky went to a restaurant for the rest of the night to drink and talk. Kaliaev and Kulikovsky left Moscow in the morning to rest in a suburb, planning to return the next morning. On Friday, 4 February, Brilliant again armed two explosive devices and gave them to Savinkov. Moiseyenko picked him up in his sleigh to meet the bombers and informed him that Kulikovsky had left because he was not sure he was cut out for terrorist activities.[120] They were now down to one bomber. They picked up Kaliaev, and Savinkov said that he was postponing the attentat once again until either Moiseyenko or he could take part as the second bomber. Before doing so, Moiseyenko had to get rid of his documents as a cabby lest the police catch on to their tactics, and Savinkov had to get rid of his British passport so as not to get its true owner in trouble. This decision meant that Brilliant would have to disarm the bombs again—the insertion and extraction of the detonator was a particularly dangerous procedure, as attested by Pokotilov's accidental death. Kaliaev refused: "Not under any circumstances. We can't subject Dora again to this danger. I take everything upon myself."[121] He would kill Sergei and then kill himself, like a "brave Japanese."[122] He seemed so confident and enthusiastic that Savinkov relented and agreed to carry on with just one bomb. Kaliaev waited for the ducal carriage near a Kremlin gate, and when the carriage passed, he ran to it and hurled his bomb, blowing up the carriage, Grand Duke Sergei, and his coachman into unrecognizable pieces. Kaliaev suffered minor injuries, and was immediately arrested. He shouted, "Down with the Damned Tsar! Long live freedom! Down with the accursed government! Long live the Socialist Revolutionary Party!" He was so drained that he fell into a deep sleep when he arrived at the police station.[123]

Moiseyenko picked up Brilliant and Savinkov in his cab. When they heard that the grand duke was dead, Brilliant collapsed, her head fell on Savinkov's shoulder, and she broke out weeping, "I killed the grand duke."[124] The next evening, the grand duchess came to visit Kaliaev in his cell. Kaliaev told her, "When I was a boy, I thought of all the tears that are shed in the world, and all the lies that are told, and sometimes it seemed to me that if I could, I would shed enough tears for everyone, and then the evil would be destroyed! But what could I do? If I went to the Grand Duke and showed him all the evil he had done, the misery of the people, why, he would have sent me to a madhouse or—and this is much more likely—thrown me in prison, like thousands of others who have suffered for their convictions. Why didn't they let the people speak?"[125]

Then he talked about Bloody Sunday. "Do you really believe such things could go unpunished? Then there is this terrible war which the people hate so violently. Well, you have declared war on the people, and we have accepted the challenge! As for myself I would give a thousand lives, not one, if only Russia could be free!"[126] The widow gave him an icon and told him she would pray for him. Kaliaev accepted the gift. "My conscience is clear, I am sorry I have caused you so great a sorrow. I acted with a deep sense of my responsibility, and if I had a thousand lives, I would give them all, not only one. And now again I will say how sorry I am for you, but still I did my duty and I'll do it again to the very end, whatever happens."[127]

In the next few days, Kaliaev wrote to his friends, "I often think of the last moment: I should like to die immediately. It is an enviable fate. But there is a still greater happiness—to die on the scaffold. Between the act and the scaffold there lies a whole eternity. It is perhaps the supreme happiness of man. Only then does one know and feel the whole strength and beauty of the Idea. To commit the deed and later to die on the scaffold—it is like sacrificing one's life twice."[128]

A few days later, he wrote to them again: "I am happy in the knowledge that I have fulfilled my duty towards Russia now lying in a pool of flowing blood . . . I have given myself wholly to the fight for the freedom of working people, and for me there can never be any concession to autocracy . . . To die for one's conviction—what is this but a call to battle? Whatever the sacrifices needed to liquidate autocracy, I firmly believe that our generation will put an end to it forever ... With all my heart I am with you, my beloved, dear and unforgettable ones. You held me up when times were hard: we shared together our joys and troubles; and when one day the people celebrate their triumph, then remember me, and let all my labor as a revolutionist be regarded as no more than the expression of inspired love for the people and profound respect for you. Take my work then as a tribute of deep devotion to the party, the bearer of the testament of *The People's Will* in all its immensity. My whole life seems as strange as a fairy story, as though everything that ever happened to me was already foreseen in the days of my childhood, coming to birth within the secret recesses of my heart until it burst into a flame of hatred and revenge for all. I should like to name for the last time all those who are close to my heart and infinitely dear to me, but let my last breath be my final greeting and a fierce clarion-call summoning you to victory. I embrace and kiss you all."[129]

Back in St. Petersburg, a memorial mass was to be celebrated on 1 March at the Peter and Paul Cathedral to commemorate the death of Alexander II. Expected at the memorial was the entire government, including Grand Duke Vladimir and Governor-General Trepov. This was the perfect opportunity to blow up the whole lot. Schweitzer's team had been augmented by Brilliant, Moiseyenko, and Borishansky—Savinkov had returned to Geneva after the assassination of the grand duke—and now numbered about 20 members. The attacks were to take place as officials were making their way to the service. To prepare the required number of bombs for this ambitious project, Schweitzer worked around the clock, forgoing sleep. Fatigue caught up to him late in the night of 26 February: something went wrong as he was inserting the detonating mechanisms in the explosive devices. An enormous explosion at the Hotel Bristol killed him and shook the city.

Azef sent word to the remaining members of the St. Petersburg team to avenge the death of their leader by focusing exclusively on killing General Trepov instead of the grand duke since he was now in charge of the repression. The team reoriented itself to the new task, but on 16 and 17 March, the Okhrana conducted lightning raids against the team and succeeded in arresting all its members, including Moiseyenko, Borishansky, Ivanovskaya, Dulebov, and Leontyeva. Only Brilliant somehow escaped the dragnet. This almost wiped out the Combat Unit. Since Azef had not betrayed his team, he was convinced that another spy had penetrated the PSR.[130]

Meanwhile, in Moscow, Kaliaev's trial started on 5 April 1905. He was allowed to explain himself: "I am not a defendant here, I am your prisoner. We are two warring camps. You—the representatives of the imperial government, the hired servants of capital and oppression. I—one of the avengers of the people, a socialist and a revolutionist. Mountains of corpses divide us, hundreds of thousands of broken human lives and a whole sea of blood and tears covering the country in horror and resentment. You have declared war upon the people. We have accepted your challenge ... Between you and me there can be no reconciliation, as it cannot be between absolutism and the people ... I recognize neither you nor your law."[131]

Kaliaev admitted to killing the grand duke, but, to him, this was no crime. The man he killed was a prominent leader of the reactionary party now ruling Russia and had made himself liable to revolutionary punishment with many crimes. "First, as governor-general of Moscow ... he made the city his own feudal principality, interfered with all cultural work, suppressed educational organizations, tyrannized over poor Jews, attempted to pervert the workers, and prosecuted all the opponents of the existing order ... Secondly, as one occupying a high position in the governmental machine, he stood at the head of the reactionary party, the inspirer of its most repressive measures, and the patron of the chief protagonists of a policy of violent suppression of all popular and social movements ... Finally, there was his personal influence on the Czar. The 'friend and uncle of the Czar' acted always as the most merciless and unbending upholder of the interests of the monarchy. Against him the revolutionary organization decided to fight, and indeed it had no other alternative."[132]

Kaliaev concluded, "I am glad, I am proud to die for her [a new Russia] in the consciousness of having done my duty." He was convicted and sentenced to die. He responded, "I rejoice at your verdict."[133] He refused to appeal and was hanged in the early morning of 10 May 1905.

In retrospect, the assassination of the grand duke was the zenith of the Combat Unit's glory and effectiveness. The execution of Kaliaev and the comprehensive wave of arrests in St. Petersburg in March effectively ended its second and heroic phase. Only the Azef brothers, Savinkov, and Brilliant survived. They went to Switzerland and France to recover and rebuild. A dramatic spike in labor unrest in the cities, peasant unrest in the countryside, and the continued catastrophic defeats in the war against Japan—especially the February defeat of Mukden, where Russia lost 90,000 soldiers, and the May disaster of the Battle of Tsushima Straits, which virtually wiped out the Russian Fleet—affected the PSR Central Committee, which was now focusing on preparing for a mass uprising. Therefore, it authorized the formation of local combat units attached to local PSR committees. In the process, it abolished the Combat Unit's monopoly on violence. The goal now was to foment mass political unrest and help rebellious nationalities, such as the Polish, Baltic, and Caucasian nationalists. Savinkov was outraged that the Central Committee had bypassed the Combat Unit, but to sweeten the pill, the Central Committee elected him to its membership. Azef sent him to the south of France to rebuild the Combat Unit with new members recruited by Azef and Gotz. Azef went on a tour of Russia to evaluate how local PSR committees were organizing mass terror and to recruit for the Combat Unit. Unhappy with this strategy to disseminate violence, which undermined his influence within the PSR, Azef did his best to denounce to Rataev these local combat units and their attempts to import weapons to Russia from the west.

Meanwhile, the assassination of Grand Duke Sergei and the countrywide unrest resulted in another swing to the right and the replacement of ineffective police and Okhrana officers. Peter Rachkovsky replaced Alexei Lopukhin as chief of police, and Colonel Alexander Gerasimov became the chief of the St. Petersburg Okhrana. Rataev in Paris was the last holdover of the Zubatov protégés at the Okhrana. His position was very precarious, and he was forced to pressure Azef to be more productive.

General Breakdown of Law and Order and the First Disbanding of the Combat Unit

After the eradication of the unit, Savinkov went on a recruiting campaign. Leo Zilberberg was the outstanding recruit of this class, reminding both Azef and Savinkov of the dead Schweitzer. He was a 25-year-old former physics and mathematics student from Moscow University, who had been arrested in 1902 during some student unrest and exiled to Yakutsk and benefited from a general student amnesty. He joined the PSR and in the spring of 1905, he and his wife Zenia Pamfilova volunteered for the Combat Unit. Aron Shpaizman, a 30-year-old bookbinder and his wife Mania Shkolnik, a 21-year-old seamstress, constituted a second couple of recruits. They had been arrested together in 1903 for operating a revolutionary print shop. They were tried and exiled to Siberia, from where they had escaped together. Savinkov had met them and recruited them together. Rachel Luriye, the 21-year-old daughter of a well-to-do Jewish parents, who had first joined the Jewish Bund before switching to the PSR in 1904, completed the new class.[134]

The new members of the unit trained in a relaxed setting in the south of France. Savinkov medicated his exhaustion with opiates and became addicted. He also believed that the drug enhanced his sexual powers. His romantic attention fell on Zilberberg's sister, Eugenia Somova, who had accompanied her brother as a distraction from her recent separation from her husband. This was the start of a lifelong affair, which even produced a son.[135] At this point in time, all the members of the Combat Unit were Jewish except for Savinkov. This probably reflected the anger and desire of Jews for vengeance in the wake of the pogroms in the Pale. In the last four months of 1904, there were 33 pogroms against Jews, many of them staged by soldiers and government officials, and nationalist reactionary gangs like the Black Hundreds. In April 1905, there was a pogrom in Zhitomir, supported by the army and the police, which lasted for three days, killed 29 Jews, and destroyed an enormous amount of property.[136]

Law and order vanished in Russia in the summer of 1905. Pogroms continued to break out with regularity. On 10 July, 100 Jews were murdered in Kiev, and on 1 August, about 60 more in Bialystok. Jews and the Bund organized small self-protective units. At the same time, the police force became demoralized because it had become the target of small groups of belligerents. It stopped patrolling and left society open to mass robberies and murders. Cities organized local militias to defend themselves. Outlaws formed their own fighting groups, further spreading the violence. As the U.S. ambassador in St. Petersburg reported that summer, "Murder, pillage, massacre and riots are rife in different parts of the country." One of his consular officers elaborated, "The whole country is simply permeated with sedition and reeking with revolution, racial hatred and warfare, murder, incendiarism, brigandage, robbery and crime of every kind . . . As far as can be seen we are on the high road to complete anarchy and social chaos . . . One of the worst signs is that the public under this long reign of anarchy and crime is growing callous and the news of the murder of an acquaintance or friend is . . . received with indifference while cases of brigandage are looked upon as being quite in the ordinary course of events."[137]

Unrest was especially widespread in Poland, the Pale, and the Baltic and Caucasian states. Peasants stopped paying taxes and rents, and the army and navy were again soundly defeated by Japan. The tsar sent Count Sergei Witte to negotiate a peace treaty in Portsmouth, Maine. A mutiny broke out on the battleship *Potemkin* in mid-June, which triggered a riot in its home port of Odessa. The troops fired into the crowd indiscriminately, killing about 2,000 people and seriously wounding another 3,000.[138]

Azef and Savinkov tried to save their funding from the Central Committee by carrying out a high-profile assassination on General Kleigels in Kiev. They repeated their modus operandi, but it soon became apparent that the observation team was useless. Nevertheless, Savinkov believed he had enough information for an attentat, but twice the bomber did not show up. Disgusted, Savinkov called off the operation in July, and on further investigation Shkolnik confessed that her husband Shpaizman (the designed bomber) did not want her to have anything to do with the assassination and threatened to use force to prevent her from participating. Savinkov and Azef expelled the couple from the Combat Unit.[139]

Azef and Savinkov continued their recruitment drive inside Russia. A worker, Fedor Nazarov, whom Savinkov first met in a restaurant, drinking beer and listening to music, told him in a calm, almost lazy manner, "Clean them all out with bombs . . . There is no justice in the world. Look at how many they've killed in the uprising. Children begging for bread. Are we to tolerate this much longer? Well, be patient if you can. I can't!"[140] Savinkov described the source of Nazarov's contempt for ideology: "Having experienced the Sormov barricades, demonstrations of workers under the red flag and parades by the same workers under the patriotic, national colors, he developed a contempt for the masses, their vacillations and lack of courage. He did not believe in their creative capacity, and lacking such a faith he was inevitably driven to the theory of destruction. This theory was in harmony with his emotions. His words and actions glowed with hatred for the well-fed and the oppressors rather than with love for the hungry and the injured. By temperament he was an anarchist and far removed from acceptance of any party program. From his experience he developed an original philosophy of his own, in the spirit of individualist anarchism. He excelled all others in daring and quiet courage. His love for the organization and every one of its members was as great as his contempt for the masses and his hatred for the government and bourgeoisie."[141]

On the other hand, another recruit, Boris Vnorovsky, who had previously met Savinkov in Vologda, told Savinkov at his interview, "I am a socialist-revolutionist. I believe in terror. That's reason enough."[142] Vnorovsky later left an autobiographical note explaining his involvement in political violence. His parents, after taking part in revolutionary activities in December 1881, had been exiled to Kostroma, where he grew up a red diaper baby. "I first learned of socialism from my mother when I was six years old. I never had to struggle with religious doubts, and I remember, even before I entered the gymnasium, how I preached atheism to a childhood friend . . . The conversations of family friends, most of them former exiles, who discussed social questions, the tales of my own parents of their own former activities, and good selection of books helped to lay the foundations of the future revolutionist, and instilled in me the ideals of religious tolerance, nationalism (my father was a Pole), and anti-militarism. These ideals became so close to me that I never ventured to question them." He had been involved in the student unrest at the University of Moscow. "I read Social-Democratic literature, which failed however, to arouse my sympathy. The shot fired by Karpovich produced a profound impression on me . . . Historical materialism failed to satisfy me. I always sympathized with terror."[143] He was invited to join the Combat Unit in January 1905, but after Bloody Sunday, he favored a mass insurrection. "It seemed to me it was necessary to prepare immediately for an armed uprising and that such an uprising should be attempted even if we had only one hundred resolute men in

Moscow. I maintained that even if all these were to perish, their sacrifice would be an inspiration to others."[144] He tried to establish a bomb factory for workers when he received another invitation to join the Combat Unit, which he now hesitantly accepted. "I felt I was bound to ignore the fact that I did not consider myself called upon to kill human beings (I always detested hunting, regarding it as brutal) or that my own life was perhaps dear to me. I knew I would be able to die like a good soldier."[145]

By the end of the summer, Azef and Savinkov had managed to rebuild their unit in St. Petersburg to conduct another attentat on Governor-General Trepov. On 21 August 1905, at a safe house, Rataev, who had been fired, turned Azef over to his replacement, the new director of the Okhrana, Peter Rachkovsky. After Rataev left, Rachkovsky congratulated Azef for all his years of work for the police, raised his monthly salary, and insisted that Azef had to be of greater assistance than in the past. Rachkovsky asked Azef to identify photographs of suspected terrorists. Up to then, Azef had only reported on his rivals within the PSR and spared his own unit. However, this was now impossible: the first picture was Savinkov. Azef accurately identified him and revealed his address in St. Petersburg. Azef also identified Breshkovskaya and revealed the address of some bomb factories in Moscow and Saratov. Some detectives were dispatched to arrest Savinkov, who immediately detected them and left the country. The increased police surveillance in the capital made the team stand down on its attempt on Trepov.[146]

Not everything went well during the police reorganization. On 8 September, a disgruntled protégé of Zubatov wrote an anonymous note to a member of the St. Petersburg PSR Committee naming Azef and Nikolai Tatarov as traitors in their midst. Tatarov, the son of a high priest in Warsaw, had been a revolutionary for ten years. He was in contact with members of the Combat Unit during the March 1905 wave of arrests and was a candidate for the PSR Central Committee. By chance, Azef was with the recipient of the note when it was delivered. He complained to Rachkovsky about the leak that very evening and decided to stand down from his police work until further notice. He left Russia, feeling confident that his past successes as chief of the Combat Unit would shield him against the denunciation.

Spontaneous violence continued to increase in Russia. The insurgents felt that the indiscriminate shootings into crowds of people had severed the bonds between them and the authorities and no longer saw any reason to follow their rules. They simply took the law into their own hands. Even the Social Democrats, who had earlier condemned such violence in their rivalry with the PSR, no longer discouraged it. Most of it was carried out by anarchists and criminals who hated the authorities and justified their acts as "political." To anarchists, society was divided into two categories: those that supported the regime and the rest. To them, supporters were legitimate targets of violence without the need for any further reason. They called their form of violence "terror without motive" (*bezmotivnyi terror*).[147] Many of them were just teenagers, and, in the field, there was a lot of cooperation among various leftist groups: local PSR committees' combat units, social democrats, Bundists, anarchists, or simply criminals. The general insurrection in Russia was moving toward civil war. In October 1905, the country was completely paralyzed by a general strike involving transportation, energy, and food. Governor-General Trepov issued an order to the army and the police to put down any disturbance by force, but these two agencies of law and order ignored him.

To break the deadlock, the tsar appointed Count Witte as prime minister when he returned from his successful negotiation of the 29 August Treaty of Portsmouth ending the Russo-Japanese War. The tsar also issued the Manifesto of 17 October, which granted the population civil rights in the form of freedom of speech and assembly, and promised the formation of a popularly elected Duma, which had to approve all laws. Prime Minister Witte issued an amnesty for most political prisoners. Some former members returned to the Combat Unit, while others got involved with some other violent leftist groups.[148] The measures worked: workers returned to work.[149]

Meanwhile, in Geneva, the Central Committee started investigating the allegation of treason against Tatarov. The more they learned about him, the more the evidence pointed to his guilt. The release of many Combat Unit members arrested in March 1905 by the October amnesty compounded the evidence against him: some of them had seen him come to the Okhrana headquarters to identify them. With this conclusive evidence, the Central Committee secretly condemned Tatarov to death and ordered the Combat Unit to carry out the execution.[150]

The concessions of the Manifesto called into question the PSR campaign of violence targeting high-level government officials, as the original aims of the campaign had been to wrestle these concessions from the government. The Central Committee held a general meeting in St. Petersburg in early November to decide what to do. This short period following the proclamation of the Manifesto, known as the "Days of Liberty,"[151] had de facto instituted freedom of the press and civil liberties. One of the Central Committee members argued that "the most important problem before the party was the solution to the agrarian question . . . that now, with the achievement of political liberty, the entire strength of the party should be concentrated upon this aim; that terrorist struggle had outgrown its usefulness; that the sacrifices in men and money it would entail would only weaken the party and interfere with the realization of its economic program in all its aspects."[152]

Chernov, Gotz, and Azef agreed and voted to stop the campaign of violence. Savinkov polled the members of the Combat Unit: all were against stopping. Nevertheless, the vote of the Central Committee was overwhelmingly for stopping Combat Unit operations and dissolving it. Savinkov commented, "We were faced with the alternative of bowing to the will of the Central Committee or entering into conflict with the party. We chose the first as lesser of the two evils. Moreover, it would have been impossible for us at that time to act independently: the organization was weak, without means of its own, and we could not count upon public support in the optimistic atmosphere prevailing at that time."[153] The Combat Unit was dissolved in November 1905 and its members dispersed across Russia.

Continued General Unrest and the Second Round of Centralized Terrorism

It is ironic that centrally organized political violence ceased to exist at a time when political violence was exploding throughout the country. The Black Hundreds organized mobs against opponents of the old order. Anti-Jewish pogroms broke out throughout the country, about 690 by one count. The worst seems to have taken place in Odessa, where more than 500 people were killed.[154] Jews were not the only victims: students, workers, and intelligentsia were also targeted by roving gangs of Black Hundreds. On 22 October, a "day of terror and infamy" occurred in Moscow, where gangs committed "brutal murders and tortured people, mainly students but also workers and other people who appeared suspicious to the crowds or aroused hostile feelings among them."[155] This provoked a dramatic increase in the ranks of both revolutionaries and criminals, and the situation rapidly deteriorated into general insurgency. Many of the most outrageous acts of violence, such as the 14 November 1905 twin bombings of the Hotel Bristol Café in Warsaw and the 17 December 1905 Libman Café bombing in Odessa, were carried out by local anarchist gangs, many of which consisted of anti-intellectual teenagers.[156] At a time when the Combat Unit's professionalism was limiting its violence on its respective targets, the significance of the lack of discrimination of these bombings—a further step toward modern terrorism—was lost in the midst of general lawlessness. Not only did the government lose its monopoly of violence within its territory, but the national revolutionary organizations had also completely lost control over it—it had simply become plain criminality. PSR, social democrats, and even anarchists like Kropotkin abroad condemned this unrestrained local violence. Violence in periods of no law and order often loses its political meaning.

On 3 December, the newly appointed Acting Minister of the Interior Peter

Durnovo tried to put an end to the breakdown of law and order in the capital by ordering the arrest of a citywide council (Soviet) executive committee and its deputies. This effectively ended the Days of Liberty that had started with the 17 October Manifesto. A protest general strike was called in St. Petersburg, but the workers there were too exhausted and did not respond. However, in Moscow many workers answered the call and started an insurrection by seizing local police stations. The tsar had just appointed Admiral Fyodor Dubasov as governor-general of Moscow. He was a well-known reactionary who had suppressed several insurrections. When Dubasov arrived in Moscow in early December, he felt he did not have enough troops to confront the workers' insurrection. He prevailed on the tsar to send him a regiment from the capital under the command of Colonel Min, who had no scruples about using his field artillery to shell rebel buildings and barricades. The result was a bloodbath: 1,059 people were killed, most of them civilians, including 137 women and 86 children. The insurgents gave up in a day. In St. Petersburg, Colonel Gerasimov conducted comprehensive sweeps of revolutionaries: his forces conducted 350 searches in one day, closed down three bomb factories and several printing presses, and confiscated 400 bombs. He also temporarily closed down liberal newspapers and reapplied censorship to the others.[157]

Although the tsar confirmed his promise of election for a Duma, his crackdown on liberals and the left called for a new response from the revolutionaries. The Socialist Revolutionary Party held its Founding Congress in Imatra, Finland, in late December 1905 and early 1906 to discuss its strategy for the developing situation. Mark Natanson, returned from exile, had joined the PSR Central Committee. The Congress decided to boycott the election, which it assumed would be a sham by the government. Chernov, Argunov, and Natanson convinced the Congress to initiate a "partisan war" against the state, by which they meant general attacks on policemen and other government officials, jails holding political prisoners, government institutions, and military barracks.[158] It also voted to reestablish the Combat Unit and directed Azef to regroup it and conduct operations before the opening of the Duma, which was scheduled for 27 April 1906. His deputies were Savinkov and Moiseyenko. Their principal assigned targets were Minister of the Interior Durnovo and Moscow Governor-General Dubasov for their roles in the bloody repression of the December 1905 uprising; secondary targets were Colonels Min and Riman for their roles in the Moscow suppression and Admiral Chuchnin for his role in the brutal crushing of the naval mutiny.[159]

Up to this point, the term *terrorism* meant targeted violence against high government officials. It was viewed as righteous violence in the cause of political change, against a corrupt and unjust autocracy on behalf of a helpless and oppressed people. Terrorists were then heroes, fighting for virtue against the vices of the state, and carrying out podvig—heroic deeds. Zasulich, Kravchin-sky, Zhelyabov, Perovskaya, Ulyanov, Gershuni, Sazonov, Kaliaev, Savinkov, and Azef (as people were not yet aware of his treason) were prototypes of these moral and virtuous characters. However, with the generalization of violence in 1905 and its degradation to the point that some violence had little redeeming value—terror without motive—the words *terrorism* and *terrorist* acquired a pejorative connotation even for the Russians. One of the last acts of such self-less violence was the Spiridonova case, which at the time, helped by journalistic spin, rapidly became a legend.

On 16 January 1906, Maria Spiridonova, a member of the local Tambov PSR committee, shot and fatally wounded Tambov Vice Governor Gavrila Lu-zhenovsky. Spiridonova was a 20-year-old clerk who became involved in local revolutionary activities, during which she met Vladimir Volsky, the married local PSR leader, and became his lover.[160] She was arrested and imprisoned for three weeks in March 1905 for participating in a student demonstration, and the arrest led to the rejection of her application to a school for medical assistants a little later. The local PSR committee had condemned Luzhenovsky to death for his repression of peasant unrest in 1905. Spiridonova volunteered for the job, stalked her prey for several days, and shot him. She was arrested, beaten by Luzhenovsky's guards, and sexually harassed during her overnight transportation back to the Tambov police station. From the police station, she wrote her comrades: "I wanted to kill Luzhenovsky according to a resolution by the Tambov SR committee, for his criminal flogging to death and excessive torturing of peasants during the agrarian and political disorders and, after that, in the districts where Luzhenovsky was present; for Luzhenovsky's mur-derous adventures in Borisoglebsk as security chief; for his organization of the Black Hundreds in Tambov; as a response to the introduction of martial law and the increase of police authority in Tambov and other districts . . . I took it on myself to carry out this sentence."[161]

A month after her arrest, Spiridonova also wrote a letter to a liberal St. Petersburg newspaper, where she detailed her beating by Cossacks and im-plied that she had been sexually abused. The newspaper published the letter, which triggered national indignation at her post-arrest treatment. It sent one of its reporters to investigate. The reporter embellished and sensationalized the story and published it in a series of articles: it became the story of a virgin, just emerging from childhood, abused for her beauty, youth, and gender by government agents. The reporter completely ignored Spiridonova's politics and the reasons for the assassination and made up a story of rape, which, he alleged, gave her syphilis. The minister of justice ordered the Tambov prosecu-tor to investigate. He found that she had been beaten and verbally sexually harassed, but not raped, and that the syphilis story was unfounded. Both

Spiridonova and the local socialist revolutionary committee were horrified by the articles and wrote a pamphlet condemning them as pulp literature and for not telling about the political reasons for her action. It appears that all parties entered into a conspiracy to omit the fact that she was not a virgin and indeed was living with a married man.[162] On 11 March, a court martial convicted and condemned her to death, but nine days later the Moscow military governor commuted her sentence to life imprisonment. Her alleged rapist was assassinated on 2 April 1906. She became the woman martyr of the revolution, the "SR Blessed Virgin."[163]

During the Spiridonova affair, Azef, Savinkov, and Moiseyenko called up their old comrades and their siblings to reconstitute the Combat Unit. Another volunteer for the reconstituted Combat Unit was Michael Sokolov, "the Bear," who had already made a name for himself for his unlimited radicalism, known as Maximalism. He was a young peasant from Saratov and part of the impatient younger generation of PSR members, who advocated the use of local violence against rural landlords and urban factory owners: agrarian or economic terrorism. "Strike at the tsarist civil servants, the capitalists, and the noble landowners! Strike ever more strongly and demand land and freedom."[164] The PSR Central Committee had rejected these indiscriminate "pogrom-like" tactics and called him to come to Switzerland to answer for his deviations from the party strategy. Sokolov complied and confirmed his desire to stay in the party. He returned to Russia, where he was arrested and then released in the October amnesty, and he became a leader of the Moscow December 1905 uprising. He went to Finland to gather support for his Maximalist program of wresting concessions from the state through local violence. Sokolov, a strong believer in terrorism, at first agreed to become part of the revived Combat Unit but changed his mind in mid-February 1906, saying, "Your method of work has outgrown its usefulness. You can't do much by sitting six months on a coach box. Only guerilla warfare will do. I am quitting the organization." Savinkov tried to dissuade him—assassination of important targets required preparation and patience.[165]

Altogether, the new Combat Unit had 33 members, including its leaders. Savinkov believed this was too many and would hurt the organization, but Azef overrode him. They chose Finland as their base of operations, and their first order of business was the execution of the traitor Tatarov. Moiseyenko had tracked him back to Warsaw, where he lived with his parents. They tried to lure him away from his parents' apartment, but Tatarov was not fooled. Nazarov volunteered for the task. On 22 March 1906, he went to the apartment, fought off the aged parents, and shot and stabbed Tatarov to death.[166]

At this point, Azef told his two lieutenants he wanted to leave the Combat Unit out of weariness. Disappointed that the 17 October Manifesto had not fulfilled its promise, he felt tired and depressed. Savinkov and Moiseyenko talked him out of it. They plotted the twin assassinations of Durnovo and Dubasov using the same scenario as the previous plots. While he was helping plan the assassinations, Azef received a visit from Rutenberg, the companion of Father Gapon, the hero of Bloody Sunday. Gapon had escaped Russia and toured western Europe, where he sank to drinking, partying, and debauchery after various revolutionary parties had rejected him as their leader. When Gapon returned to Russia, Rachkovsky called on him as an old Okhrana agent, and he agreed to spy on the PSR and especially its Combat Unit. Since Gapon did not personally have access to the unit, he tried to recruit Rutenberg, who was stunned, but played along. Rutenberg notified Azef about the betrayal at the beginning of February 1906. Azef appreciated the delicacy of the situation because people still worshipped Gapon for leading the demonstration on Bloody Sunday. The only solution was to catch Gapon *en flagrant délit* of betrayal—when he was meeting with Rachkovsky—and execute them both. Rutenberg told Gapon he wanted to meet with the police chief, and a meeting was set in a restaurant's private room. Rachkovsky notified Gerasimov about the planned meeting, but Gerasimov warned him not to go alone to meet with revolutionaries, who would love to avenge themselves for his role against them. Rachkovsky aborted the meeting.

Meanwhile, evidence was mounting against Gapon for his embezzlement of money entrusted to him by some workers' organizations. Nevertheless, the PSR Central Committee ruled that, because of his prominence, only a general meeting of all revolutionaries could decide his fate. Azef did not inform Rutenberg about this decision. Azef also covered his tracks with his case officer Rachkovsky after the failure of the plot against him by informing him about a vague plot against him. He also urged Rutenberg to invite Gapon to an isolated cabin on the Finnish border, where half of dozen of Gapon's most devoted companions would listen to their conversation in an adjacent room. There on 28 March, Gapon chided Rutenberg for his hesitancy to betray the PSR and offered him a large sum of money to do so. Gapon's companions then came out of the adjacent room and hanged him. After the murder, Rutenberg found out that it had not been sanctioned by the Central Committee, and Azef denied that he had given Rutenberg permission to execute Gapon. Disgusted, Rutenberg resigned from the PSR and completely gave up politics.[167]

Meanwhile, in Moscow, a Combat Unit team was having a hard time setting up Dubasov's assassination because he was suspicious that he was a target and frequently changed his patterns of travel. The team tried to ambush Dubasov several times throughout March when he returned from his regular trips to the capital. The terrorists waited with their bombs in the freezing cold on his expected routes, but Dubasov kept changing his schedule and routes of travel. At the beginning of April, they aborted another attack when the bombers felt they were under surveillance. In mid-April, the bomb-maker blew off the fingers of both hands when she was arming a bomb. She went to the hospital, where the police arrested her. At the apartment, the police found most of the explosive material for the Moscow team. When Moiseyenko, who had fallen in love with her, came to her aid, he was arrested in turn.[168]

In St. Petersburg, Azef was in charge of the assassination attempt on Prime Minister Durnovo, and, as usual, positioned observers pretending to be cab drivers. The Okhrana, now familiar with the tactic, detected one of the observers. The police followed him to a restaurant, where he met with a stranger whom one of the veteran policeman recognized as a police undercover agent. They notified Gerasimov, who ordered the policemen to arrest the mysterious man at the next opportunity. They did so on 15 April 1906 and took Azef to meet with Gerasimov. Azef did not break cover and pretended to be an innocent engineer. Gerasimov laughed, told Azef he was in no hurry and put him back in a cell to think things over. After a day or so, Azef let Gerasimov know that he worked for Rachkovsky and that he would talk only in the presence of his case officer. Gerasimov called the assistant minister of the interior, who immediately came over to Gerasimov's private office.

At the meeting, Rachkovsky greeted Azef, who immediately cursed him, complaining that Rachkovsky had abandoned him. They had not met since September 1905, as Rachkovsky had refused to respond to Azef's letters. Azef accused him of ingratitude for saving his life when Azef had notified him (after the fact) of Rutenberg's plot against him. Rachkovsky apologized and agreed to pay Azef his back salary. Azef then went on to tell them about the plot against Durnovo, being careful to betray only the three cabbies that he realized the police had detected. He told them about plots against Generals Min and Riman along scenarios similar to Balmashev's assassination of Sipiagin. He also informed them that Father Gapon's body was hanging from a hook at a cabin on the Finnish border. Azef was reinstated as a secret Okhrana agent, and Gerasimov took over his case, under Rachkovsky's nominal supervision. Significantly, Azef played down his role in the Combat Unit, claiming that he was working under the leadership of Savinkov and held back his knowledge of the plot against Dubasov in Moscow.[169]

Azef was released before anyone noticed his short absence. Now that Gerasimov was forewarned about the plot on Durnovo, he doubled the police protection, harassed the observation team, and changed the minister's pattern of activities, precluding any further attentats against him. The three detected cabbies were quietly arrested and sentenced to long terms in prison. Generals Min and Riman were also notified of plots against them. Police protection was increased, and no one was allowed to see them except after a thorough bodily search. A few days later, the police discovered Father Gapon's body on Azef's information.[170]

After his release, Azef realized that his influence within the PSR was rapidly waning. The initiative had passed to local PSR combat units. In addition to Spiridonova's assassination, a Sebastopol PSR member fired several shots at Admiral Chuchnin on 22 January 1906. He was wounded, but she was killed by his guards. On 22 March, a bomb killed the Tver governor. In Moscow and elsewhere, Sokolov's group staged several spectacular bank robberies that netted over a million rubles for the revolutionaries. With the exception of its executions of Tatarov and Gapon, the Combat Unit had no success to its credit and was in danger of becoming irrelevant. Azef needed some sort of success: without informing Gerasimov, he went to Moscow to help Savinkov. They guessed that Admiral Dubasov would attend a religious service on 23 April at the Kremlin celebrating Empress Alexandra's birthday. They posted Vnorovsky and two bombers to cover each of the three possible routes from the governor's residence to the Kremlin. Vnorovsky hurled his bomb at the governor-general's carriage, and the explosion instantly killed him and Dubasov's aide-de-camp but only wounded Dubasov. Although Dubasov survived, his long rehabilitation prevented him from ever returning to public life.[171] At his apartment, Vnorovsky had left a note explaining his motive. "Before my own conscience and in the face of death, which I am about to go forward to meet, I may say that I have completely overcome any fear of death. I shall kill myself without any hesitation if my bomb fails to explode. I shall do this without the twitch of a muscle, and with complete equanimity. I shall mount the scaffold calmly in the event of success. This will not be the result of any deliberate effort over myself, of a last outburst of strength and will power, but the quite natural consequence of what I have experienced. Until October 17, I worked in the Terrorist Brigade, when I temporarily ceased my activity, and when the government's subsequent policy had been revealed I resumed the organization of terrorist acts by an independent flying detachment. My greetings to the comrades who worked under my leadership! When the Terrorist Brigade resumed its activity I asked to be sent to Moscow. Only two days remain now before I am to go forward into action. I am calm. I am happy."[172]

The attentat on Dubasov was greeted with public approval,[173] and the Combat Unit issued a proclamation taking credit for the near miss, which rehabilitated Azef's reputation within the PSR Central Committee.[174] It had neutralized most of the main targets before the opening ceremony of the Duma: Durnovo had been dismissed; Dubasov was wounded and permanently out of public life; Generals Min and Riman were isolated in their homes. Only Admiral Chuchnin, who had also been wounded, was still active. However, this was the end of the Combat Unit's effectiveness against high-value targets. It had sustained severe losses, and its demise was the result of Azef's betrayal to his new case officer Gerasimov.

Azef's Treason and the Demise of the Combat Unit

Azef's presence in Moscow during the attentat on Dubasov was duly reported to St. Petersburg. Rachkovsky and Gerasimov confronted him when he returned to the capital, but he protested his innocence and instead accused Zinaida Zhutchenko of organizing the plot. Zhutchenko was a local PSR member who had befriended members of the Combat Unit. Azef guessed that she was also an important Okhrana informant in Moscow.[175] She had reported that Azef was in charge of the attentat. Both police officers were confused by this cross-accusation of their star informants, but Gerasimov decided to believe his own agent.[176] To show his absolute loyalty to the police, Azef betrayed his friend and faithful deputy Savinkov. He told them that Savinkov was on his way to Sebastopol to try to kill Admiral Chuchnin. The Okhrana wasted no time in establishing discreet surveillance on Savinkov on his trip to Sebastopol. As a result, Savinkov and Nazarov were arrested.[177] Although Savinkov managed to escape with the help of his Combat Unit colleagues, the unit was disbanded for a second time with the convocation of the Duma. "The decision of the party council ran so greatly counter to the opinion of the majority of my comrades that it is difficult to say what they would have done had they learned of the council's action in time. This calling off of terrorist activity for the second time seemed to us a great political mistake and was a great blow to the Terrorist Brigade, which had just begun to regain its old strength. We might have perhaps declined to submit to the Central Committee in this instance and entered upon an open breach with the party."[178]

As expected, the Duma and the government, which included Peter Stolypin as minister of the interior,[179] quickly found themselves at loggerheads and paralyzed the country. By May 1906, Russia erupted in a new wave of unrest, marked by general lawlessness, similar to that seen six months earlier. Local revolutionaries assassinated local officials. Gangs of Black Hundreds roamed free in various cities as policemen disappeared. Once again, there was a surge of pogroms: on 1 June, 82 Jews were killed and 700 more injured in Bialystok, and three-quarters of its population fled the city. On 5 June, 50 more Jews were murdered in a city nearby. The Bialystok police chief had encouraged the crowds, and an investigation showed that a peasant in the procession had been paid a lot of money to shoot at Jews and provoke the riot. A Duma investigation blamed the police, and further investigation discovered that Ministry of the Interior officials had played a decisive role in fomenting pogroms throughout 1905 and 1906. This forced Stolypin to clean up the ministry and get rid of Rachkovsky, who was strongly implicated in them.

Stolypin relied on Gerasimov for general security, and as a result Gerasimov became effectively in charge of both police and Okhrana affairs as other officers communicated directly with him.[180] On Stolypin's advice, the tsar dissolved the Duma on 8 July 1906, set the date of the next Duma to 20 February 1907, and appointed Stolypin as prime minister in addition to minister of the interior. Stolypin and Gerasimov imposed an effective state of siege on St. Petersburg to prevent the outbreak of any mass protest against the dissolution of the Duma. The Stolypin era had begun.[181]

The dissolution of the Duma led to scattered disturbances directed at the government throughout the empire. On 2 August 1906, "Bloody Wednesday," the Polish Socialist Party combat organization, carried out 100 attacks in 20 Polish cities targeting Russian government officials and policemen. By noon, 26 policemen and soldiers had been killed. The estimated casualties ranged from 20 to 80 killed and 40 to 70 injured.[182] The imperial army imposed a state of siege and terrorized rebellious districts in Warsaw and Lodz, and government-sponsored gangs carried out the Siedlce pogrom three weeks later. Black Hundreds and revolutionaries fought each other and robbed banks and civilians as well. The state rounded up revolutionaries in a massive sweep of arrests. On 12 August 1906, three of Sokolov's Maximalists carried out a suicide bombing of Stolypin's weekend dacha on Aptekarsky, killing 27 other people, including four high-level officials, and seriously wounding 70 people, including two of Stolypin's daughters. The tsar invited Stolypin and his family to move into the Winter Palace, which was more secure than the prime minister's residence. The next day, a local PSR member assassinated General Min, and the following day, the governor-general of Warsaw was shot to death.[183]

Stolypin ordered the convening of field courts-martial to try captured revolutionaries, which sped up the process from capture to execution to four days. For the next seven and a half months, 1,144 men were executed; 772 were sentenced to prison terms; 7 more were sentenced to simple exile; and only 71 of the accused were acquitted. This unprecedented number of hangings led people to call a hanging noose a "Stolypin necktie." During 1906, over 100,000 people were arrested, leftist sympathizers were persecuted, and the crackdown on the press resumed.[184]

The dissolution of the Duma led the PSR Central Committee to reconstitute the Combat Unit for a third time, with Stolypin as its main target. However, Azef's information to Gerasimov allowed the policeman to thwart all planned attentats, which demoralized the Combat Unit. At a conference to discuss this issue, the Central Committee dissolved the unit once more, accepted the resignations of Azef and Savinkov, and created three new units directly responsible to the Central Committee. Azef and Savinkov went to relax on the French Riviera.[185] Many of the original unit members simply left centralized political violence to join local groups.[186] Without Azef to betray them, they achieved some success: they killed the commandant of St. Petersburg General von Launitz on 21 December 1906,[187] the St. Petersburg chief prosecutor Pavlov five days later, and St. Petersburg prison governor Gudima on 17 January 1907. Gerasimov was in a panic that he could no longer protect all high government officials in the capital and wrote to Azef for help. Azef reported that his successor Zilberberg and his team stayed at the Tourist Hotel in Finland. Gerasimov sent a pair of spies to the hotel, and they were able to identify him there. Zilberberg came to St. Petersburg on 9 February 1907, where he was arrested. He was court-martialed, convicted, and eventually hanged on 16 July 1907.[188]

The second Duma of February 1907 disappointed Stolypin, as the left won an even more impressive victory than it had the first time despite his attempts to rig the elections.[189] At the urging of Gerasimov, Azef returned to Finland to take part in the second congress of the PSR. Gershuni was back, having escaped from Siberian exile by hiding in a cabbage keg.[190] He was elected to the PSR Central Committee along with Natanson, Chernov, and Azef, who kept Gerasimov updated on these developments.[191] Although no longer directly involved in terrorist activities, Azef got wind of a plot against the tsar and informed Gerasimov, who arrested the whole group of plotters on the night of 31 March 1907. Tsar Nicholas II promoted Gerasimov to the rank of general. Azef's case officer was very grateful to his agent for this promotion.[192]

On 3 June 1907, Stolypin dissolved the Duma a second time on the pretext of a leftist plot to carry out a military uprising against the government. Within three days, 600 leftist politicians, including Duma members, who lost their immunity with its dissolution, were in custody.[193] Stolypin reinstated the field courts-martial to curb the sharp rise in violence during that spring. Some historians lump all these crimes, which are really indicators of a general breakdown of law and order, into the category of revolutionary terrorism, and imply that the revolutionaries were the main instigator.[194] This seems rather one-sided as the breakdown of law and order was far more general and largely due to a perceived lack of legitimacy of the government after the Revolution of 1905. There is little evidence that the PSR had much influence on what was happening locally, and its very few attacks, although spectacular, were drowned in the overall number of violent incidents. This general state of lawlessness seems to have ended mainly because of public weariness with it. It took time for the lawlessness to fade away, but the masses were discouraged and eventually returned to the everyday business of making a living. The left refused to take part in further elections, and the succeeding Dumas became far more compliant with the government.[195]

After the dissolution of the second Duma, Gershuni strongly campaigned for the revival of the Combat Unit, whose target was now the tsar himself. The Central Committee unanimously decided to reconvene the Combat Unit under the control of Gershuni, with Azef in charge of all targeted political violence commissioned by the party. Azef tried to recruit his old deputy Savinkov, but the latter had lost faith in the unit's methodology and declined. Gershuni succumbed to tuberculosis and died a few months later, leaving Azef once again in control of all PSR central terrorist activities. He continued to keep Gerasimov informed about developments within the PSR, but seems to have withheld from his case officer the fact that he was the chief of the unit. Some of his PSR rivals no longer trusted him because of growing rumors that he was a double agent for the Okhrana and did not keep him informed about their operations. They killed the chief of the central prison administration on 28 October and the courts-martial general prosecutor on 27 December 1907. Gerasimov became alarmed at this new trend and demanded that Azef help him put an end to it. Azef indicated where his rivals met in Finland, and Gerasimov was able to follow them and arrest them when they crossed back to Russia in February 1908. They were tried, sentenced to death, and executed.[196]

During this period, the spy and the case officer developed a close bond through working together, and the policeman respected Azef's withholding of some unimportant information for his self-protection. Gerasimov became a very strong advocate for his agent within the Ministry of the Interior, especially with his boss Stolypin, and was careful to let Azef know how valuable the prime minister considered his information on the political developments within the PSR and on other attempts. Gerasimov also doubled Azef's salary after the "conspiracy against the tsar" affair. Given his bond with his case officer and his dislike of his rival Trauberg, it is not difficult to understand Azef's complete betrayal of his rivals.

By winter and spring 1908, Azef kept Gerasimov informed about several plots of his units, but did not betray any of his members. It seems he was losing heart in terrorism and the spying game as his mind was now consumed with something else: he had fallen in love with a cabaret performer and spent much of his time with her on long trips throughout western Europe in the first half of 1908. As a good case officer, Gerasimov warned his agent that his behavior was now attracting too much attention from everyone, but Azef no longer cared. By June 1908, he retired from the Okhrana with the blessings of Gerasimov, who promised to continue his salary in guise of a pension. He also retired from the Combat Unit after the PSR congress in London in July 1908, which he attended with his mistress.

By then Azef had come under suspicion of being an Okhrana mole in the PSR. Vladimir Burtzev, acting on information from his sources within the police and his own research, overtly accused Azef during the London PSR congress. To finally settle this nagging issue, Chernov and Natanson convened a revolutionary tribunal to try Burtzev for defamation of Azef's reputation and invited Peter Kropotkin, Vera Figner, and German Lopatin to act as impartial judges. Chernov, Natanson, and Savinkov acted as prosecutors against Burtzev. Figner had had her sentence commuted to 20 years and was allowed to leave Russia for western Europe in 1906, and Lopatin had been freed during the 1905 revolution. For weeks, they listened to Burtzev's evidence and checked it by inviting testimony from various witnesses. The most damning evidence was from a former chief of police who confirmed Azef's status as an Okhrana spy. Before condemning Azef, they wanted to hear what he had to say in his defense and asked him to come explain himself. Instead, Azef vanished from his Paris apartment in the early morning of 6 January 1909. He went straight to Germany, where he collected his mistress, and they disappeared. They lived together in Berlin, where he died of renal failure on 24 April 1918.[197]

The Azef affair had a devastating effect on PSR morale, and a later resurrection of the Combat Unit, under the leadership of Savinkov, was mostly ineffective. In its prime, the Combat Unit was a specialized terrorist unit. It was a military unit under the command of its parent organization, the PSR, receiving funding, direction, and leadership from it. The volunteer members composing the unit were, in essence, professional soldiers for the revolution, just like any soldiers fighting for their nation. They shared a strong esprit de corps, carried out terrorist activities for each other and the greater cause, and were careful not to let their buddies down. For instance, a bomber might refuse to abort an attentat to spare the bomb maker the danger of disarming the bombs, or members might ask to be chosen as bombers.

Conclusion

As the narrative clearly demonstrates, a social identity paradigm is a more fruitful perspective to understand the PSR Combat Unit than either rational choice theory or the ideological argument. The unit clearly refutes the ideological thesis of the turn to political violence. For the most part, its members, including its leaders Azef and Savinkov, did not share their party's ideology: they were not socialists but constitutional liberals or anarchists. Some, like Sazonov, apologized for not being able to represent the party's ideology at their trials. Combat Unit members even defied the PSR Central Committee twice when they were ordered to disband, before finally doing so reluctantly. In essence, the unit was a vehicle for all kinds of politicized protesters to volunteer and become soldiers to fight against their common enemy, the tsarist regime. Nor is the history of the unit compatible with the rational choice theory perspective on the turn to political violence. The types of sacrifice for the group and the cause demonstrated by Combat Unit members cannot be reconciled with a utilitarian perspective without distorting the meaning of utilitarianism beyond recognition.

What kind of perspective can we use to understand Azef's confusing behavior during his leadership of the Combat Unit? Azef's apparent fluctuations of loyalty between the Combat Unit and the Okhrana have puzzled his biographers. Clearly the ideological argument fails as all witnesses and later commentators agree that Azef was definitely not ideologically motivated. Nikolajewsky provides the most complete account of Azef, but it suffers from a lack of any attempt to understand his subject and adopts a utilitarian rational choice theory perspective by attributing Azef's behavior to his overwhelming greed. His only comment on the psychology of Azef was to publish a private letter from Zubatov: "Azef was a purely mercenary nature . . . looking at everything from the point of view of profit, working for the revolution for the sake of personal gain, and for the government out of no conviction but also for the sake of personal profit."[198] This reduction to a one-dimensional stereotype for an out-group enemy is not consistent with Azef's role in the murders of von Plehve, Grand Duke Sergei, and Gapon, and withholding information from his various case officers, for which Azef received no benefits.

Geifman frames her narrative with a 1951 popular but outdated and discredited work on fear,[199] and claims that fear was what drove Azef. This frame forces her to neglect or dispute facts asserted by every other biographer and contemporaneous witness. She accepts the claim in Gerasimov's book that Azef was not the head of the PSR Combat Unit while he was Gerasimov's agent, from 1906 onward. She projects this assertion backward to claim that he was never the head of the unit, despite testimony to the contrary by Azef's superiors in the PSR, his subordinates within the Combat Unit, his former police handlers, and the multiple official investigators into the Azef affair. Her reasoning, based on his actual operational absence during the various attentats, betrays ignorance of how clandestine groups operate in the field. She claims that Savinkov was the chief of the Combat Unit, which is contrary to Savinkov's description in his memoirs of his recruitment by Azef[200] and Azef's leadership with the unit throughout his book.[201]

Rubenstein, admitting that the documents he reviewed lacked psychological insight, found inspiration in a popular novel about a double agent.[202]

His attempt to explain Azef's psychological dynamics degenerates into psychobabble that makes no sense to me, as either a psychiatrist or a former intelligence officer.

An agent's loyalty varies according to circumstances, one of which is the bonding between agent and case officer. This bonding is at the core of effective spying. Azef felt strong solidarity with his original companions of the Combat Unit from 1903 to 1906, when he was caught in the attempted assassination of Dubasov and had to betray Savinkov. This closeness was based on a sense of shared social identity with people with whom one works in close contact. In general, it appears that Azef's sympathies were with the revolutionaries, and he did not hesitate to kill Minister of the Interior von Plehve, Grand Duke Sergei, and Admiral Dubasov, whom he clearly saw as enemies for their indiscriminate persecution of his friends and for their anti-Semitism. He did not respect Rataev, whom he played effortlessly, and disliked Rachkovsky, whom he tried to kill. However, he seems to have bonded with Gerasimov, who went out of his way to protect his agent and be his champion within the Okhrana bureaucracy and with Prime Minister Stolypin. In effect, he and Gerasimov self-categorized into a duo of themselves against the rest of the world. This may explain the betrayals of Azef's rivals, whom he never considered part of his own group and from whom Azef felt strong hostility.

Azef's betrayal of Savinkov was really forced on him when the Okhrana was about to arrest him.[203] After Savinkov's escape and return to the Combat Unit, Azef protected him again, and they both left the unit together. Azef's betrayal of another deputy, Leo Zilberberg, is more difficult to explain. Perhaps Azef felt betrayed by him in the fall of 1906 when Azef and Savinkov walked out on the PSR Central Committee but Zilberberg chose to break solidarity with his chiefs and stayed on. In any case, he betrayed his deputy by giving Gerasimov a small hint of where he and his group were staying in Finland, a place where he was unreachable. In a sense, the deputy's arrest in St. Petersburg was mostly the result of good police work by Gerasimov, allowing Azef to maintain a fig leaf of self-deception vis-à-vis his arrest. Otherwise, Azef mostly betrayed his rivals in the PSR. He never valued the internal debates within the party and had no trouble informing his case officer about them.

The Azef affair spanned most of the first decade of the twentieth century. During this period, the concept of terrorism degenerated from a virtuous self-sacrificial rebellion against cruel government persecution, as practiced by the PSR Combat Unit—Camus's delicate or fastidious murderers—to a criminal free-for-all that combined pointless criminality with a very thin veneer of self-serving political justification. The next chapter will examine the justification for this degradation of anarchist political violence.

Elsewhere in the world, the various insurrections against the Ottoman Empire in the Balkans and in India also were also labeled as terrorism. Indeed, this period up to the Great War has been called the Golden Age of Terrorism,[204] as the use of bombs and targeted political violence became increasingly common. Against this backdrop, the assassination of Archduke Franz Ferdinand of Austria and his wife triggered the Great War, profoundly changing the course of history. This will also be a subject of the next chapter.

C h a p t e r 7

Banditry, the End of a World,
and Indiscriminate Political Violence

With the illegalist deviance of anarchism in France, political violence continued to degenerate into a state of banditry. In Sarajevo, the most notorious attentat of all, the assassination of Archduke Franz Ferdinand, essentially ended
the old regime in Europe. Meanwhile, in the United States, a series of indiscriminate bombings—the 1910 Los Angeles Times, 1916 Preparedness Day,
and 1920 Wall Street bombings—continued the trend to indiscriminate murder. These bombings were no longer in the tradition of regicide, nor were they
aimed at public officials. Rather, they specifically targeted civilians and became a precedent for the type of indiscriminate political violence that gained
prominence in the second half of the twentieth century and continues to this
day. This final empirical chapter examines these three sets of events, focusing
on the turn to violence of these political groups.

Illegalist Political Violence

Illegalism and the Night Workers

The repression of anarchists in France continued into the twentieth century.
Many were denied jobs because of their beliefs. The continuous entry into the
labor market of young people who then could not find jobs worsened their
precarious economic situation. The absence of newspapers able to explain anarchism made Clément Duval's illegalist simplistic variant of anarchism popular among these newcomers.[1] The spectacular career of Alexandre Marius
Jacob furthered the appeal of this approach.[2]

Jacob, born in 1879 in Marseille, dropped out of school at the age of 11 to
sail the South Seas as a shipboy and read the classics of anarchist literature

during his trips. At the age of 17, he returned to Marseille and worked on an anarchist newspaper.[3] In August 1897, the French president came to visit Marseille, and the police rounded up all the militants, including Jacob, in a sting operation before his visit to avoid a repeat of Caserio's attentat. Jacob was released six months later, but the police alerted potential employers about his political views, preventing him from getting a job. The police pressured him to become an informant by conducting destructive searches of his family home on a weekly basis. "All this made me bitter and revolted me. This is when I started my open war against authorities."[4] Without any alternative, Jacob and some comrades turned to low-level burglaries.[5] They carried out a spectacular daytime robbery of a jewelry store in Marseille by pretending to be policemen investigating receipt of stolen jewels. They confiscated as evidence all the jewels, amounting to a value of 400,000 francs, and left the owner at the office of an unsuspecting investigative magistrate. Jacob went on a spree of robberies for several weeks until his arrest. He acted bizarrely and was transferred to a psychiatric hospital, from which he escaped in April 1900.[6]

Jacob then recruited a network of about three dozen anarchists, the "night workers," and organized them into professional teams: target spotters, burglars using the latest technology and techniques of robbery, and a disposition team that would melt precious metals and sell the booty. They committed more than 150 burglaries throughout France in the next three years, with proceeds totaling millions of francs, and gave 10 percent to anarchist causes. They burglarized only their class enemies—the bourgeoisie, nobility, civil servants, and clergy—and Jacob left his business card, "Attila," behind. If he realized that his victim was in great debt or not an enemy—a writer, for example—he left a note apologizing and money to repair the damages.[7]

The police finally caught up with Jacob and his gang in April 1903. Some resisted arrest and a policeman was killed in a firefight. In March 1905, 23 defendants went on trial under heavy police and military protection. Jacob completely dominated the proceedings, with his witty replies and total defiance. He took sole responsibility for all the crimes to exonerate his co-defendants and used the trial to defend illegalism and reprises individuelles: "Those who make everything have nothing, and those who make nothing have everything. This state of affairs can only result in the antagonism between the working class and the owning class, or the lazy class. The fight emerges and hate dominates . . . Society only grants three means to live: work, beg or steal. I like work and don't find it repugnant . . . What I find offensive is to sweat blood and tears for the favor of a salary and create wealth denied to me. In other words, I find it offensive to give in to the prostitution of work. Begging is degrading, the negation of dignity. Anyone has the right to the feast of life. Man cannot beg for the right to live. He must take it. Theft is restitution, taking back property . . . As soon as I became aware, I stole without any scruples." Jacob said he stole as a matter of principle to keep his dignity as a man. "I preferred to rob rather than be robbed. Of course, I too condemn any action that helps a man violently and cunningly grab the fruits of someone else's labor. But it's precisely for this that I have made war on the rich, thieves of the goods of the poor. I too would like to live in a society where theft is banned. I approve of and have used theft only as just a means of revolt to fight the most unfair of all thefts: individual property."[8] On 22 March 1905, the jury convicted 16 defendants and sentenced Jacob to life in a penal colony.[9] He later received an additional 20 years for having shot at a policeman during one of his getaways.[10]

The trial resurrected the discussion of theft as a revolutionary act. As expected, the mainstream press condemned the burglaries but enjoyed the entertainment of Jacob's obvious intelligence and wit.[11] Socialist and communist papers also condemned such theft, but they understood its temptation. Mainstream anarchist ideologues rejected Jacob's arguments and no longer gave illegalism space in their newsletters. Jacob replied full of sarcasm, "I can clearly see that I was wrong. I should not have acted without asking for the Pope's authorization beforehand. That's my error. Mea Culpa! The next time I'll ask these gentlemen to meet and give their opinion. And I will not act until I will be sure that I won't cross the principles they hold."[12] Other newsletters glorified his acts, applauding his support of needy anarchists and their propaganda.[13]

The Milieu Around l'anarchie

Jacob became a hero to many young anarchists. He was a frequent topic of informal discussion in the popular universities and *causeries populaires* (popular talks) in working-class neighborhoods. This popular educational movement took off at the end of the 1890s and faded at the start of the Great War. Craftsmen and specialized workers flocked by the tens of thousands to these evening universities and lectures to understand the great strides of natural sciences and engineering and the promises of the social sciences. The sessions were interactive, with strong audience participation.[14] Together these various milieus formed a countercultural network composed of young people questioning the way society functioned.

One of the most prominent members of this counterculture was Albert Libertad, a paraplegic orphan born in 1875 who came to Paris to participate in anarchist activities. He was a very gifted debater and soon acquired a following at the causeries populaires. He established the newsletter *l'anarchie*[15] to propagate his views that anarchy was not just a theory but a lifestyle, the joy of life, experienced to its fullest sensual and esthetic pleasures. In order to live such a life, individualist or libertarian anarchists had to free themselves from internal prejudices fostered by their religious and bourgeois education and external constraints imposed on them by political, social, and economic structures. In effect, they rejected all authority, especially the norms imposed on them by mainstream culture, constraints by state laws, and capitalistic exploitation, as well as religious and bourgeois prejudice and education. They tried to use "pure reason and science" as a guide for their lives.[16]

Libertad pushed the glorification of the individual or "ego"[17] much further than Jacob did. Libertad and his followers self-categorized in comparison to society in general and scorned people who lived resigned to social norms. "I hate the fatalists . . . I hate all those, who, by fear or resignation, give up part of their human power through the weight of their collaboration and idiotic inertia and are crushed and crush me and those I love . . . I spit on your idols; I spit on God; I spit on the fatherland; I spit on Christ; I spit on the flag; I spit on capital and the golden calf; I spit on laws and codes, on symbols and religions . . . Let's live! Fatalism is death."[18] In order words, Libertad and those who shared his social identity saw themselves as egoists in contrast to the rest of society. This inclusion of all of society in their out-group would reach its logical conclusion in political violence that degenerated in indiscriminate antisocial banditry.

Education was a central preoccupation. Indeed, several of Libertad's main collaborators were female teachers, with whom he fathered children.[19] They believed that through self-education free from bourgeois and religious concepts, they could change the mentality of people and bring about a better world. Without this evolution in people's consciousness, revolution was an illusion, and its attendant violence, built on hatred and revenge, would lead to a regime of terror that would again exploit people.[20] *L'anarchie* attracted around it many individualist anarchists. Rirette Maîtrejean, born Anna Henriette (Rirette) Estorges in 1887, ran off to Paris in 1904 and attended the causeries populaires, where she was taken by Libertad's ideas.[21] She got married to Louis Maîtrejean but fell in love with Mauricius, a writer for *l'anarchie*, and moved in with him in the fall of 1907.[22]

On May Day 1908, the workers at a quarry at Vigneux-Draveil went on strike for a wage increase, ten-hour workday, a weekly day of rest, and recognition of their union. The company replaced them with scabs, intensifying the crisis. Rirette Maîtrejean, who lived nearby, brought food to the strikers. On 2 June, the gendarmes shot and killed two strikers known to her and wounded nine others in an unprovoked skirmish.[23] The death of her comrades shocked her. On 27 July, two leading strikers were arrested. A large demonstration was called for 30 July, and thousands of Parisian workers came in a show of

support. A demonstrator fired at soldiers, who charged into the crowd, resulting in 4 dead and 200 wounded civilians. Maîtrejean was wounded by a deep
saber cut to her leg, while Libertad jumped in a river to escape even though he
could not swim. Government repression broke the strike and blamed anarchists for having provoked the troops.[24]

In the fall, after she recovered from her wound, Maitrejean returned to
Paris and *l'anarchie* a hardened militant. Libertad died in November and, in
the summer of 1909, an anarchist intellectual André Lorulot took over the
journal, joined by a new group of young Belgian anarchists.

The Belgian Group

One of the newcomers was 19-year-old Victor Kibaltchiche, born in Brussels
to Russian revolutionary émigrés and a relative of the tsaricide Nikolai Kibalchich. He was homeschooled and at the age of 12 met Raymond Callemin,
who was six months older, roaming the streets. The two became very close,
and in 1905, they met Jean de Boë, who was an orphan one year older and an
assistant sculptor. The three friends became inseparable. They joined the socialist party as young guards but quickly grew disillusioned.[25] "We had yearned
for a passionate pure Socialism. We had satisfied ourselves with a Socialism of
battle, and it was the great age of reformism . . . What could become of us with
this need for the absolute, this yearning for battle, this blind desire, against all
obstacles to escape from the city and the life from which there was no escape? . . . We had to have an absolute, only one of liberty (without unnecessary
metaphysics); a principle of life, only unselfish and ardent; a principle of action, only not to win a place in this stifling world . . . but to try, however des-
perately, to escape from it since it was impossible to destroy it . . . in this calm
moment of abundance before the great war."[26] De Boë also recalled the wonderful friendships, their thirst for knowledge, and their passion for reading.
"We were very close, sharing similar interests that put us in opposition to the
mass of young guards. After having read sociology, physiology and philosophy, I dove into literature, which pushed me toward romanticism . . . What are
were going to do? In the Party, they called us anarchists, which gave us a lively
desire to become conspirators . . . We then went to find a famous anarchist,
who talked to us several times and eight days later, we formed an anarchist
group."[27]

The friends met anarchists from a commune in a forest, "The Experiment," which they joined in 1907 for two years. Kibaltchiche and de Boë later
recalled their time there as idyllic.[28] They worked on its paper and learned all
the skills to run it. They read about the Vigneux-Draveil strike. "I remember

our anger when we learnt of these shootings. That same evening a hundred of us youngsters showed the red flag in the neighborhood of the Government buildings, willingly battling with the police. We felt ourselves close to all the victims and rebels in the world; we would have fought joyfully for the men executed in the prisons of Montjuich or Alcalla del Valle, whose sufferings we recalled each day. We felt the growth within us of a wonderful and formidable collective awareness."[29]

Kibaltchiche felt a strong sense of solidarity with anarchists, even those who practiced the reprise individuelle. In one of his first articles, he defended illegalists breaking the law for political reasons.[30] Around this time, Édouard Carouy showed up at the commune. He was half a dozen years older than the three friends and had worked as a car mechanic, in a railroad factory and steel mill, bending steel. He became interested in anarchism, drifted to the commune around 1908, and soon became part of the close circle of friends. "Anarchism swept us away completely because it demanded and offered us everything. There was no remotest corner of life that it failed to illuminate; at least so it seemed to us . . . Anarchism demanded, before anything else, harmony between deeds and words . . . That is why we adopted what was (at that moment) the most extreme variety, which by vigorous dialectic had succeeded, through the logic of its revolutionism, in discarding the necessity for revolution."[31] Their hero was Albert Libertad and his group at *l'anarchie*.

On 23 January 1909, two anarchist Jewish immigrants from Russia carried out an armed robbery in Tottenham, just north of London, and were discovered by the police. During a two-hour chase, they shot back at their pursuers, killed three people, and wounded another two dozen. They killed themselves instead of surrendering in what the press labeled the "Tottenham Outrage." Kibaltchiche defended them in their weekly newsletter, *Le Révolté*. "The London 'bandits' were at one with us! . . . In the current society we are the vanguard of a barbarous army. We have no respect for what constitutes virtue, morality, honesty: we are outside of laws and regulations. They oppress, persecute and pursue us. Rebels constantly find themselves before a sad alternative: submit, that is, give up their will and return to the miserable herd of the exploited, or accept combat against the entire social organism. We prefer combat." He refused to have any remorse for the dead and wounded, who "by their criminal weakness perpetuate oppression. Enemies!"[32] Here Kibaltchiche adopted Libertad's ideas and his self-categorization in contrast to mainstream society.

Kibaltchiche and his friends also defended another killer anarchist closer to home. At the end of 1908, they met a 21-year-old Jewish Russian immigrant, Alexander Sokolov, who had fled to Argentina a few steps ahead of the police. There, he continued his political activities, and the police accused him of trying to blow up the central Buenos Aires electricity factory. He fled again to Belgium, where he demanded 3,000 francs from a rich furrier and anarchist sympathizer, threatening to blow up his building with a bomb that he carried. The furrier wrote him a check and left town, not wanting to denounce a fellow anarchist. Sokolov discarded his bomb nearby, and it was discovered by someone, who alerted the police. The police finally traced it back to Sokolov, who was hiding in Ghent. When the police came on 15 February 1909, he resisted arrest, shooting and killing two policemen.[33]

Kibaltchiche and his companions defended him publicly and in court. "Anarchists do not surrender . . . We are in permanent insurrection."[34] At Sokolov's trial in June 1909, Kibaltchiche testified for the defense, which brought police harassment onto the group of friends. "It became impossible for me to find any work, even as a semi-skilled typographer, and I was not alone. We felt like we were in a vacuum and did not know who to turn to. We refused to understand this city, one where we could not have changed anything even by getting ourselves killed on the streets."[35] Sokolov was convicted and sentenced to life in prison.

Kibaltchiche, not being a citizen, was expelled from Belgium shortly thereafter. In Lille, France, he went to a talk by Mauricius, who was accompanied by his lover. Kibaltchiche and Maîtrejean made bad initial impressions on each other. In August, he arrived in Paris, which was rich in revolutionary history, the center of anarchism and the Russian émigré revolutionary community. Callemin, de Boë, and Carouy stayed behind and continued to publish *Le Révolté*.

Growing Popular Anger at the Police and the State

In Paris, Kibaltchiche occasionally dropped by *l'anarchie* and attended the causeries populaires, where he met with Lorulot, Mauricius, and Rirette Maîtrejean. At first she dismissed him as an "intellectual," but when they sat down to talk, they found out they shared a love of poetry, literature, and music.[36] As she later recalled, "Then, one grey autumn day, while we read and commented on the poetry of François Villon in my quiet apartment, love came . . . From this moment on, my life was changed."[37] She moved in with Kibaltchiche, who lived with a philosopher friend.[38]

Kibaltchiche supported himself by means of translations and lessons in the Russian émigré community, which did not interfere with his political activities in his neighborhood. He participated in demonstrations like the one called in protest of Francisco Ferrer's execution at Montjuich, Barcelona, in October 1909. Ferrer had used his fortune to establish an anarchist modern school, a publishing house, and a popular university. He was accused of being behind a Barcelona uprising in the summer of 1909 despite the fact that he was away at the time. He was tried, convicted, and sentenced to death. As the news of his execution reached Paris, hundreds of thousands came to protest at the Spanish Embassy, and the crowd degenerated into a riot, damaging property and killing a policeman.[39]

In January 1910, Kibaltchiche met René Valet at a local leftist tavern, and they quickly became very close friends. Valet was his age and a trade mechanic who was inspired by revolutionary and anarchic literature.[40] That winter they became drawn into the Liabeuf affair. Jean Liabeuf, a 24-year-old shoemaker, had been infatuated with a prostitute, and someone falsely denounced him as her pimp. Despite his protests of innocence, he was arrested, tried, and convicted on the false testimony of his arresting officers. During his three months in prison, he swore revenge at this blemish on his honor and miscarriage of justice. When he got out, he made two leather patches to cover his forearms and studded them with sharpened nails like a porcupine to prevent anyone from grabbing his arms. He got a knife and revolver. He tried to track down his accusers, who had been forewarned and disappeared. On 8 January, other policemen tried to arrest him because he was violating his banishment from the city. He resisted arrest, killed a policeman, and wounded half a dozen others. Liabeuf was wounded, arrested, and taken to the hospital.[41]

Most newspapers treated this incident as an "apache" story. Apaches were gangs of young hoodlums roaming poor sections of Paris, which were in a state of lawlessness reminiscent of that portrayed in the old American West.[42] They numbered about 34,000 at the time and terrorized Paris. Liabeuf's crime revived the debates about what to do with apaches.[43] However, Gustave Hervé, the combative editor of *La Guerre Sociale*, investigated and got the story of the miscarriage of justice that had motivated Liabeuf. He published a front-page editorial defending Liabeuf and blamed the vice squad for a miscarriage of justice: "To us, revolutionaries, he has shown us a beautiful example. Every day, there are honest workers who are victims of police brutality, shameful beatings, undeserved condemnations, and gross miscarriages of justice: did any of them avenge themselves? . . . Listen, honest people! Give to this apache half of your virtue and ask him in exchange a quarter of his energy and courage."[44] Further inquiry confirmed this account. Nevertheless, he was arrested and tried for incitement to murder and apology for a crime. At his trial, Hervé apologized only for having called Liabeuf an apache when he was a gainfully employed worker. The jury convicted and sentenced Hervé to four years in prison.[45]

Hervé might have been convicted in a court of law, but he won in the court of public opinion. As expected, the left-leaning press strongly protested

against the outrageously harsh penalty and crowned Hervé a martyr for freedom of the press. Meetings sprang up everywhere in his support. Writing for
l'anarchie, Kibaltchiche supported Hervé and noted that Liabeuf was a "good
example" who took down four policemen by himself, while it took hundreds
for the avengers of Ferrer to get rid of just one. "I find this Liabeuf likeable for
having done such a good job . . . [He] behaved like a man, in a situation where
all—including revolutionaries and anarchists—usually behave like
cowards."[46]

Liabeuf's trial took place in May and was anticlimactic. He admitted the
charges, but obsessively denied that he had ever been a pimp. He regretted
having killed a policeman, who had not been involved in his case, and claimed
he was defending his honor. The jury convicted him, and the judge sentenced
him to death. Liabeuf reacted, "You are condemning me to death, fine. I will
go to the scaffold if need be, but I swear to the last drop of my blood that last
August I was a victim of a miscarriage of justice. I was never a pimp!"[47] He
refused to appeal his sentence.

The left-wing press protested the severity of the sentence. Petitions for
commutation of the sentences of both Hervé and Liabeuf flooded the office of
the French president. On the street, apaches attacked policemen in the name
of Liabeuf. During a labor strike, the police struck a worker, who died a few
days later. Tens of thousands came to his funeral at the end of June, and several
serious altercations broke out between the mourners and the police. Shots
were fired at the police. An unknown number of marchers and 41 policemen
were injured.[48]

Fearing a continued escalation of violence, the police kept the time of Liabeuf's execution secret. On the evening of 1 July, people heard that the execution would take place in a few hours, and "assorted crowds, from all the
faubourgs, from all those slums stalked by crime and misery, converged" on
the prison. Kibaltchiche "had come with Rirette, with René the Angry . . .
Shouts and angry scuffles broke out when the guillotine wagon arrived, escorted by a squad of cavalry. For some hours there was a battle on the spot, the
police charges forcing us ineffectively, because of the darkness, into the side
streets from which sections of the crowd would disgorge once again the next
minute . . . There was plenty of violence and a little bloodshed—one policeman killed. At dawn, exhaustion quietened the crowd, and at the instant when
the blade fell upon a raging head still yelling its innocence, a baffled frenzy
gripped the twenty or thirty thousand demonstrators, and found its outlet in a
long-drawn cry: 'Murderers!' "[49] Valet was livid with anger, and "all that night
his hand had been closed upon the chill blackness of a Browning revolver.
Fight, fight, what else was there to do? And if it meant death, no matter. René
rushed into mortal danger out of his sense of solidarity with his defeated

mates, out of his need for battle, and, at the heart of it, out of despair. These 'conscious egoists' were going to get themselves slaughtered for friendship's sake."[50]

Kibaltchiche later concluded, "After the fight for Ferrer the philosopher, the battle for Liabeuf the desperado demonstrated (although we could not see it) the seriousness of the blind alley in which the revolutionary movement of Paris was, all tendencies included."[51] Attacks on policemen in Paris in the name of Liabeuf lasted about three months.

The Commune of Romainville or "Anarchy in Anarchy"

Back in Belgium, Callemin, Carouy, and de Boë continued their political activism and supplemented their income through petty theft. Callemin and de Boë reached the age for mandatory military conscription and left the country to avoid it. Callemin traveled to Germany and Switzerland, where he lived in poverty but continued reading popular science and became a champion of the scientist faction of individualist anarchists. De Boë fell in love with an 18-year-old woman, with whom he spent a few idyllic months in Switzerland before his political activities forced him to leave. With his friends gone, Carouy drifted to Paris, where he found work at a car factory.

Scuffles with other anarchists resulted in a death and forced Lorulot and *l'anarchie* to relocate to a large pavilion with a nice garden in the Paris suburb of Romainville in June 1910. Maîtrejean and Kibaltchiche stayed out of the skirmishes and remained in Paris. They met André Soudy, a frail and sentimental 18-year-old grocer's assistant and anarchist with tuberculosis, who babysat Maîtrejean's daughters.[52] Carouy occasionally went back to Belgium to commit some burglaries around Charleroi, and there he met three young French draft dodgers: Étienne Monier, Marius Metge, and Octave Garnier, all around 21 years of age. Garnier already had a history of political activism and *reprises individuelles*. The anarchists committed a few burglaries together and returned to Paris in the winter of 1911, when the police were closing in on them.[53] They converged on the Romainville Pavilion, where Lorulot was living with the "Red Venus," who had left her husband to move in with him (individualist anarchism espoused free love).[54]

De Boë and his girlfriend had already joined the Lorulot couple in late 1910, and Raymond Callemin arrived, by himself, in February 1911. Monier, who knew Lorulot from his prior political activities, introduced him to his companions from Belgium, and they moved in around April. Carouy then came with his girlfriend, who was married to another imprisoned companion.[55] René Valet moved in with his lover as de Boë and his girlfriend returned to Switzerland. Maîtrejean and Kibaltchiche, who still contributed to the weekly, were frequent visitors there. The six couples (Lorulot, Garnier, Metge, Carouy, Kibaltchiche, and Valet) and Callemin with a few other staffers formed a commune, where they shared work, income, and ideas—de Boë called it "anarchy in anarchy."[56] They followed a strict "scientific" lifestyle and diet. They celebrated the cult of the self, based on Max Stirner's *The Ego and Its Own*. They were against any form of authority or law and did not recognize anything above the self. They obviously believed in free love—four of the women were legally married to other men—and drifted into illegalism, harmonizing their beliefs with their criminal activities. "Illegalism transforms what common mortals find in practice reprehensible into something good, healthy and virtuous. This is how fraud becomes a right, burglary a duty, and counterfeiting a sacred mission. The anarchist must before and above all 'scheme or manage' [*se débrouiller*]. Illegalism is the triumph of 'scheming' [*la combine*] . . . Above all, one must live, but, as salaried work is an abomination to any self-respecting anarchist, the choices of means of subsistence are limited."[57]

At first, the atmosphere at *l'arnarchie* was one of joy. Everyone had a nickname, given to them as a sign of intimacy and friendship. The lodgers shared their meals, and their diets derived from their scientific views of what was natural and good for them. Callemin always started his explanations with the phrase "science says," which earned him the nickname "Science." They were especially inspired by popular scientific accounts, now totally forgotten, and were very serious about their diet: no stimulants, no alcohol, no tea, no coffee, only water; strict vegetarianism, no meat, no fish; and no salt, no pepper, no vinegar.[58] They lived a healthy lifestyle with regular exercise in the morning and did not smoke. Parties in the garden were held almost every other Sunday, as spring flowed into summer. There were passionate discussions, poetry recitations, and singing of revolutionary and other popular songs. Group excursions and picnics were common. "Each does his own task. Callemin keeps the books. Valet does the typography. Garnier and Carouy manually turn the printing machine. Kibaltchiche writes articles . . . and Lorulot looks on . . . At *l'anarchie* the salaries of all the collaborators are the same. Each has a right to room, board and laundry. There is no money. If you want some, perhaps to buy clothing or underwear, you have to manage. Kibaltchiche and I, we manage by doing translations."[59] Others, like Carouy, turned to theft, burglary, and counterfeiting.

More sinister were their long sessions of target practice at the end of their enclosed garden. No self-respecting illegalist would ever be caught without his comrade "Browning" pistol. It was more of a fashion statement than anything else, but Garnier's scorn for social norms stretched to violence. "I give no one the right to impose his will under any circumstances: I do not see why I should not have the right to eat raisins or apples because they are owned by Mr. X . . . What did he do more than me for him to consume them by himself? . . . I have a right to consume them according to my needs, and if he tries to stop me by force, I will rebel; and against his force, I will use mine because, being attacked, I will defend myself with any means." He did not want to wait for death to enjoy life and was ready to "defend myself against oppressors with all the means at my disposal."[60] Although Kibaltchiche and Maîtrejean publicly defended their companions who had crossed this line, they rejected this extreme position. "Illegalism admits everything except threat to human life. If one crosses this line, one goes way beyond the boundaries of illegalism and falls into banditry. This is the big exception. The anarchist might not be a good citizen, but he is not necessarily a bad guy."[61]

Discussions about these differences grew very animated. Kibaltchiche and Maîtrejean were philosophical supporters of illegalism, but Callemin and Carouy reprimanded them for being pure intellectuals and argued for more consistent activity such as theft and murder. Soon these disagreements turned into hostility and threats.[62] This strong advocacy of criminality frightened Lorulot, a talker and not a doer, and he moved out of Romainville to start another weekly elsewhere. Maîtrejean, with the help of Kibaltchiche, took over *l'anarchie* to return to more traditional political activism. Kibaltchiche did not like where their friends were going: "They were intoxicated with their 'scientific' algebraic formulae . . . invoking only 'scientific reason' and 'conscious egoism.' I could see clearly that their childish intoxication with 'scientism' contained much more ignorance than knowledge, and an intense desire to *live differently* at all costs . . . They were already, or were becoming, outlaws."[63]

Kibaltchiche and Maîtrejean moved in to the Romainville pavilion in mid-July 1911 and set about recruiting their own staff for the weekly because, with time, their disagreements about illegalism between them and their friends threatened to turn violent. Kibaltchiche told them what they did was simply stupid and would just land them in prison. On 23 August, a burglary ended in a firefight with the police. Two burglars were arrested, but Carouy got away. He was scared that his accomplices might talk, and he left the pavilion two days later, along with his girlfriend. A week later, at the beginning of September, the exodus began. Sensing that the police were closing in on them, Callemin, Garnier, Valet, and Metge scattered to several apartments in the north of Paris and its suburbs and moved from one to the other depending on the security situation. Rent for the pavilion was paid for the summer, and *l'anarchie* stayed there on credit during the fall. To avoid paying the overdue rent, Maîtrejean and Kibaltchiche surreptitiously moved the printing press back to Paris at night in mid-October 1911 with the help of friends and staff. Only Metge and Soudy came to visit the new site. Soudy was so sick from tuberculosis that he had to go to a hospital and then to a convalescent home for a few months.

Enter Bonnot: The Tragic Bandits

That fall, the illegals, in various combinations, carried out a dozen burglaries, which netted them little as the takes were small and they had to provide for the families of imprisoned comrades. Garnier dreamed of larger burglaries with getaway cars—they were on foot and carried everything on their person, including their heavy burglar tools. But he did not know how to drive—it was a rare skill then—and was looking for an associate who could. Enter Jules Bonnot.[64]

At 35, Bonnot was more than a decade older than the others. He came from a town near the Swiss border and had a violent temper, which had led his wife and son to leave him and earned him two short prison terms. He was a mechanic in a car factory who adopted anarchist views and lost his job when he got involved in a strike. The jobless Bonnot turned to reprises individuelles. He got his driver's license, specialized in the theft of cars, and, with two accomplices, carried out burglaries using stolen cars. By November 1911, a police investigation was catching up with the burglars, and they fled to Paris in a stolen car. On 28 November 1911, Bonnot and an accomplice were on the road when the accomplice was killed. Bonnot later claimed that his accomplice accidentally shot himself in the head while playing with his gun. Since he was dying, Bonnot finished him with a second shot, left the corpse on the side of the road (after going through his pockets), and departed. When he arrived in Paris, it was rumored that he had killed his companion for his share of the money. Bonnot called a meeting of Paris anarchists to explain his side of the story and prevent them from turning on him.[65]

Every illegalist came to the meeting. Kibaltchiche was skeptical of Bonnot's story,[66] but Garnier and Callemin thought that Bonnot with his driving skills was the answer to their problem. They were tired of "this miserable life from the meager income of small burglaries, the sale of bicycles stolen from the sidewalk, counterfeiting money or the insultingly small salary from a factory, so painfully earned under the vigilance of a supervisor, the guard dog of the owner?"[67] In anticipation of a big job, Bonnot, Garnier, and Callemin stole a large luxury car on the evening of 13 December, and Garnier bought a large acetylene torch. "For this job, there were two safes to penetrate. As I knew how to use the torch and Bonnot was a good driver, we decided to carry out the operation as soon as possible in consultation with our other comrades."[68] The burglary required the darkness of night to hide the car and strong rain to mask the noise from the torch. They looked at alternatives in case these conditions were not met. Someone had told them about a bank courier coming to a local branch every morning at the same time, carrying money and stocks. He could be robbed if the robbers could get away from the pursuing crowd. Bonnot and Garnier went to case the place and confirmed that a car would solve this get-away problem. Their aggressiveness dragged their companions into disaster.

Garnier, Callemin, Bonnot, and a fourth companion (unknown) picked up the stolen car the evening of 20 December and drove around Paris waiting for rain, which did not come. Around three-thirty in the morning, they opted for the alternative. They stayed up all night and parked the car on the rue Ordener along the path of the messenger boy. When they saw him, Garnier and Callemin got out of the car, and Garnier pulled out his revolver and shot the courier twice. Callemin grabbed the bag and Garnier fired at the crowd as they got away in the car.[69] The courier was wounded but survived. They got about 5,000 francs in cash and a large sum in stocks, which could be traced back to them. Split four ways, this was a very disappointing take.

This brazen daytime crime started a police chase around France that lasted almost five months. But a few nights after the crime, Garnier and Callemin came to see Kibaltchiche and Maîtrejean at their apartment. Garnier confessed, "What a stupid story! . . . We were going to do another job, easy and relaxing. Unfortunately, it didn't not work out. Bonnot said: 'In G-d's name, we are not going to come empty handed' and he drove to the rue Ordener. He had a tip and he had cased it well." Callemin continued, "We were four in the car, but one would never have come had he known that there could be a killing." Garnier vented his rage at "this savage crowd, this ferocious crowd that gave us chase. What business is it to all these imbeciles that we had to 'explain' ourselves with a messenger boy! If I could have, I would have killed a quarter of them."[70]

Kibaltchiche asked his childhood friend how they ever got into this mess. Callemin answered, "We had enough . . . We could no longer live like that. We digested theories, principles and axioms. The promised easy life seemed so far away. We wanted to get it all at once."[71]

Two gun shops were robbed in late December and early January, and weapons from these shops were later found among most of the companions, including at *l'anarchie*, implicating Kibaltchiche and Maitrejean in receiving stolen goods. On the night of 3 January 1912, there was a double-murder burglary at Thiais, and the fingerprints of Carouy and Metge were found all over the place. Several car thefts took place around France. On 27 February, a traffic policeman tried to stop a car in Paris and was apparently shot by Garnier. On 25 March, Garnier, Bonnot, Callemin, Soudy, Valet, and Monier stopped a car, killed the chauffeur, and seriously wounded another person. Bonnot later wrote that this murder was not premeditated. When the robbers signaled him to stop, the chauffeur went for his gun and they had to shoot him. Bonnot regretted the chauffeur's death because he was a worker like them, a slave of bourgeois society. "It was his gesture that was fatal . . . Should I regret what I have done? Yes . . . perhaps . . . But if I must continue, despite my regrets, I will continue . . . I must live my life . . . I have the right to live. Everyone has the right to live, and if your imbecilic and criminal society dares to forbid me from doing so, well, too bad for it, too bad for all of you."[72]

The six criminals then took the victim's car to hold up a bank, where they killed two employees and seriously wounded a third. On 24 April, in a raid, the police unexpectedly found Bonnot, who killed the deputy chief of police, seriously wounded an agent, and got away. The police caught up with him four days later. Hundreds of policemen laid siege to his refuge and blew it up with dynamite, killing Bonnot. On 14 May 1912, the police discovered Garnier and Valet's refuge. Another gun battle and siege ensued during the night, and the police called up the army. More than 700 policemen and soldiers sprayed the outlaws' small house with machine gun fire and blew it up, killing the two fugitives. The rest of the illegals were arrested through good police work and denunciations, as the bank put up a 100,000-franc reward for information leading to the perpetrators' arrests. After the arrests, some comrades avenged their friends by killing the informants.[73] Bonnot and Garnier had left behind notes exonerating innocent companions arrested on suspicion of having participated in the various murders.

On 3 February 1913, 22 people, who became known as the "tragic bandits," went on trial for these crimes. Seven were facing capital murder charges, including Callemin, Monier, Soudy, Carouy, and Metge. Maîtrejean and Kibaltchiche were tried as the ideologues of the gang and recipients of stolen goods—the guns found at *l'anarchie*. Despite the celebrity of the case, the proceedings were anticlimactic. The defendants denied the charges. On 27 February, a jury convicted 17 and acquitted 5, including Maîtrejean. Callemin, Monier, and Soudy were sentenced to death, Carouy and Metge to life at hard labor, and Kibaltchiche to five years in prison. Callemin admitted that he and Garnier were the rue Ordener assassins. Later that day, Carouy, who could not bear to be in prison, committed suicide with some cyanide he had hidden in the heel of his shoe.[74] On 21 April 1913, Callemin, Monier, and Soudy were guillotined.[75]

Apaches or Anarchists?

The tragic bandits' affair sparked a vigorous debate about illegalism in France. Kibaltchiche supported his friends out of solidarity. To critics who called for respect for the laws, "These laws that they respect, I know they're aimed at garroting the weakest, sanctioning their enslavement by brute force." As for respect for human life, he saw this as an excuse to kill through hunger, work, subjection, and prison. "I'm not afraid to admit it: I'm with the bandits. I find their role to be noble and I see the men in them. Elsewhere, I see only fools and puppets. The bandits show strength, daring, and their firm determination to live . . . They kill. Probably. Is it their fault? Did they want their fate? Many just sinned for wanting to be men, and not citizens, wage-earners, or soldiers. Some dreamt to work freely in a world without masters. But the choice given them was only between servitude and crime. Vigorous and valiant, they chose to fight—crime."[76] No doubt this apology earned Kibaltchiche the venom of the police and the jury. He was convicted of the same crime of which his lover Maîtrejean was acquitted.

At first, prominent libertarian anarchists condemned the tragic bandits. "Such acts have nothing to do with anarchism. They are purely and simply bourgeois. . . . Illegal bandits, perhaps, but bandits nevertheless and also bourgeois."[77] Likewise, most socialists and syndicalists condemned them, even distinguishing them from the attentats perpetrators 20 years earlier. By late April and May, after the heroic stands of Bonnot, Garnier, and Valet against hundreds of soldiers and policemen, and their behavior in court, the left nuanced its rejection and objected to the use of the army and dynamite to fight off single anarchists armed with handguns. In *l'anarchie*, Mauricius wrote: "When this life, this death, go together with gestures that would make a Spartan proud, when Bonnot, hunted by a regiment and targeted by five hundred rifles, his shed destroyed by dynamite, wounded and perhaps dying, he took out a pencil and [exonerated his friends], . . . when a man carries out such acts, he reaches at that moment the height of moral beauty."[78] Provoked by this editorial, the authorities closed down *l'anarchie* and took out a warrant against Mauricius for glorifying political violence. This effectively silenced support for the tragic bandits.

Kibaltchiche supported his friends purely out of solidarity: "If the prosecution holds me solidary with acts that are repugnant (yes, it's the right word) to me, I will have to explain myself. But I will do it in a way that won't allow the prosecution to use my words against my co-defendants . . . I am . . . disgusted, sorry to see that some comrades—comrades that I loved from the time of their first and beautiful enthusiasm—could have done such deplorable things."[79] He blamed himself for not having kept his young protégés Valet and Soudy out of trouble.

Before his execution, Callemin also disavowed illegalism and refused to appeal his death sentence. He blamed his behavior on illegalist theories and now strongly raised his voice against all the writers who, in *l'anarchie* and elsewhere, incited their readers to murder and pillage. He bitterly noticed that these "advisers, no matter how guilty they are, are never there to pay." He was an example to all those who were tempted by these theorists' seductive arguments. Instead, he recommended the study of proper scientific and philosophical works.[80] "The anarchist loses his quality of disciple of Reclus and Kropotkin as soon as he drifts into illegalism, as soon as he steals and kills. This was my case. I stopped being an anarchist when I became a thief and assassin."[81]

The illegalist political violence ended with the execution of the tragic bandits. Years later, Kibaltchiche tried to make sense of it: "Out of solidarity they rushed into this squalid, doomed struggle with their little revolvers and their petty, trigger-happy arguments . . . and against them towered Money—100,000 francs' reward for the first informer. They were wandering in the city without escape, ready to be killed somewhere, anywhere, in a tram or a café, content to feel utterly cornered, expendable, alone in defiance of a horrible world. Out of solidarity, simply to share this bitter joy of trying to be killed, without any illusions about the struggle (as a good many told me when I met them in prison afterwards), others joined the first few such as red-haired René (he too was a restless spirit) and poor little André Soudy."[82]

Kibaltchiche explained that the outlaw status of the tragic bandits—most were draft dodgers and petty criminals barred from getting a decent job by their political activities—isolated them from the rest of society and narrowed their cognitive horizons. "The most immediate cause of their revolt and ruin seemed to me to lie in their isolation from human contacts. They were living in no company but their own, divorced from the world, living in one where they were nearly always subject to some confining and second-rate milieu. What had preserved me from their one-dimensional thinking, from their bitter anger, from their pitiless view of society, had been the fact that since childhood I had been exposed to a world full of enduring hope, rich in human values, that of the Russians."[83]

Kibaltchiche linked the two waves of anarchist violence in France. "So ended the second explosion of anarchism in France. The first, equally hopeless, was that of 1891–94, signaled by the outrages of Ravachol, Émile Henry, Vaillant, and Caserio. The same psychological features and the same social factors were present in both phases, the same exacting idealism, in the breasts of uncomplicated men whose energy could find no outlet in achieving a higher dignity or sensibility, because any such outlet was physically denied to them.

Conscious of their frustrations, they battled like madmen and were beaten down."[84] He stressed that the harsh conditions of workers led to squalor and degradation: "crime, class struggles and their trail of bloody strikes, and frenzied battles of One against All."[85]

Individualist anarchists developed their sense of social identity in comparison to other anarchists and despised the general population, which they saw as a herd of sheep. They developed strong hostility to the police because of its crackdowns during strikes and because of injustices, such as their exclusion from decent jobs, and miscarriages of justices like the Liabeuf case. Of course, they were disillusioned with the effectiveness of demonstrations to influence the political system, as shown by the various protests in which they had participated. There did not seem to be a moral outrage trigger to precipitate their wave of killing. With their disdain for society and its laws, it was easy for them to drift into illegalism, namely burglaries. With the police closing in on them, they now felt they had little to lose, and it did not take much for Garnier to shoot the messenger and Carouy and Metge to kill two old people in a burglary. The rest were resisting arrest and shared a sense of fatalism. Until the very end, they hid in plain sight, went to restaurants and the opera. When they could, they went down in a blaze of fire. Those who survived gave up their beliefs but accepted the consequences of their actions. Their illegalist deviation of anarchism has now largely been forgotten. The perpetrators blamed their ideology for their drift into banditry, while Kibaltchiche and Maîtrejean blamed their group solidarity. In fact, this incident is equally consistent with the social identity perspective adopted in the narrative, the ideological thesis, and rational choice theory, as their ideology was based on extreme rational self-interest.

The Assassination of Archduke Franz Ferdinand

As political challengers kept expanding the boundaries of out-group enemies from specific state agents (in France and Russia) or industrialists (in the United States) to the allegedly complicit population as legitimate target of violence, an old-fashioned regicidal attentat in the Balkans triggered a political cataclysm that became the Great War, or World War I, which changed the face of the world by eliminating the traditional political structure in central and eastern Europe.

In the Balkans, the defeated and retreating Ottoman Empire left behind a political vacuum that led a variety of ethnic and confessional groups jockeying for power and self-determination in the abandoned territory. However, the great European powers resisted these local political and social demands lest they upset the delicate balance of power and challenge their privileges. Their interferences against the hopes of native Balkan populations led to worldwide catastrophe.

In its rearguard defense against Western advancement, the Ottoman Empire spent more on military expenditure and its costs fell on poor villagers, who paid taxes in cash to the state in addition to their taxes to their Muslim feudal landlords. The Turks had established a feudal system with themselves as lords and the Serbs as serfs. Many Serb landowners converted to Islam and became the staunchest oppressors of the predominantly Serbian serfs. They discriminated against the starving Orthodox peasant majority and kept them ignorant to maintain their absolute power, preventing any modernization through reform and education. This untenable situation inevitably led to multiple uprisings, during which Serbia gained its independence in the early nineteenth century.

A new wave of uprisings in the mid-1870s drew support from Serbia and resulted in a stalemate as Ottoman troops were unable to cope with the rebels' guerilla tactics. This situation suddenly became a crisis in 1878 when Russia joined the war against the Ottomans and threatened to reach the Mediterranean Sea via the Balkans. To block this potential access that might upset the delicate balance of power in Europe, the great Western powers quickly convened a congress in Berlin and, after Byzantine negotiations, agreed to allow Austria-Hungary to temporarily occupy Bosnia and Hercegovina after Ottoman withdrawal to stabilize the situation. The ensuing occupation was a very bloody affair with street-to-street fighting in Sarajevo, but the modern Austro-Hungarian troops prevailed. They ruled with an iron fist and brutally suppressed a general strike in 1906 and a large peasant uprising in 1910. The new masters were careful to maintain the Ottoman caste system and favored their co-religionists, Catholic Croats, and even the Muslim elite over the majority Orthodox villagers—all three confessional groups were ethnically Slavs. In the Balkans, social conflicts blended with confessional ones.[86]

Young Bosnia

By the turn of the twentieth century, a pan-Slavic independence movement emerged in secondary schools in Bosnia and Hercegovina—there were no universities and only 30 university graduates in these two provinces. Students of mostly peasant origin spontaneously self-organized into small secret societies, collectively called Young Bosnia. They were loosely affiliated, scattered in urban areas, and lacked any umbrella organization. Although Austrian authorities called them anarchists, they are difficult to label as they did not agree on a single political program, but instead self-categorized in contrast to what they rejected in their unsophisticated understanding of their social world. They rejected foreign occupation and rule (hoping to establish a pan-Slavic state unifying Serbs, Croats, and Muslims), injustice, and the backwardness of their society (yearning to modernize it on a more egalitarian footing, including the emancipation of women) and were suspicious of any authority—state, school, church, and family.[87] Like the Russian populists, they organized themselves into literary circles, where they discussed other Slav revolutionaries, especially Chernyshevsky, Stepniak (Kravchinsky), Bakunin, Kropotkin, Lavrov, Dostoevsky, but also Mazzini and his Young Italy.[88] This collection of informal circles amounted to a political protest community, which generated a counterculture, strongly influenced by Chernyshevsky. They preached the morality of simple life and the virtue of mutual aid, abstained from drinking, and, unlike their revolutionary predecessors, were completely ascetic and strictly chaste. They believed that the Austrian authorities were deliberately fomenting the moral corruption of their society to distract it from liberation.[89]

Young Bosnians considered themselves part of the international revolutionary community in Europe. One of them, Vladimir Gacinovic, traveled abroad to meet with their heroes and became their spiritual leader. He met with Mark Natanson in Switzerland and Victor Kibaltchiche and Leon Trotsky in Paris.[90] The Russian Socialist Revolutionary Party and its terrorist tactics became a model for Young Bosnians.[91] This of course was not indicative of the existence of an international conspiracy but simply showed that they moved in the same circles.

The formal annexation of Bosnia and Hercegovina into the Austro-Hungarian Empire in October 1908 was a setback to the aspiration of Bosnians for unification with other South Slavs, or Yugoslavs, and prompted a new wave of unrest. Young Bosnians swore that they would never recognize the annexation and lost faith in peaceful change, which distinguished them from their parents' generation, who "wanted to secure liberty from Austria in a legal way." They stated, "We do not believe in such liberty."[92] Although the future conspirators were too young to participate in these protests—they were still teenagers at the time of the assassination—this wave generated a prototype for them to emulate. They believed that Serbia, as the independent part of the Yugoslavs, had the moral duty to lead the unification and independence movement for Yugoslavia, very much like the Piedmont Kingdom had unified and gained independence for Italy.[93]

At the announcement of the annexation, Young Bosnians flocked to Serbia to join Bosnian irregular troops, the *komite*, in anticipation of the imminent war with Austria-Hungary. When the Serbian government capitulated and recognized the annexation, these volunteers became disillusioned that

Serbia or peaceful means would ever free their country. Bogdan Zerajic, then 22 years old, told a Serbian officer, "We must liberate ourselves or die."[94] He returned to Bosnia to continue his studies and activism. With time, he became depressed, dropped out of school, and spent most of his time alone. In January 1910, he confided to Gacinovic: "I am suffering from tremendous emotional torments, my feelings are extremely gloomy and I do not have the strength to tell anyone but you. I have become a skeptic, I do not trust in anything anymore . . . There is only one thing which satisfies me. I still have strength . . . [and] a deep understanding of all the difficulty of our situation." Zerajic concluded his letter with this cryptic message: "Please send my regards to . . . [a mutual friend] and tell him he should not be angry with me. He doesn't need this little thing now, since the armistice has been proclaimed, and he can be assured that it will not be wasted."[95] The "thing" referred to a pistol he had borrowed from this friend, and "armistice" meant the acceptance of annexation by Serbia. Zerajic had decided to assassinate Emperor Franz Josef, who was coming on an official tour of the two provinces to commemorate their annexation in early June.

Franz Josef's visit depressed the Young Bosnians: "Our hearts were filled with bitterness against everything. We hated even our own life."[96] During the visit, Zerajic shadowed him and came close enough to him, but, for unknown reasons, he did not shoot the emperor. His failure sank him into a state of despair. "Even those walking to the scaffold could feel no worse than I."[97] He resolved to shoot the governor of the two provinces a few days later. On 15 June 1910, he shot him five times in Sarajevo, and believing he had succeeded, he shot himself dead. All the shots were near misses; the governor survived.[98]

The Austrian authorities dismissed him as an anarchist (they found anarchist books at his home), and the mainstream press portrayed him as a lunatic. However, he became an inspiration to his comrades. "Up to that time we had only read about the terrorist exploits of the revolutionaries, which stirred our imagination, but we had never dreamed that something like that could happen in our own town . . . His act during such bleak times appeared to us something which could not be understood, something odd, and all the youths were struck by such an act of courage . . . It seemed as if the eyes of the youth had suddenly been opened. Young men passing by the Emperor's Bridge, where Zerajic killed himself . . . started to pay him homage by taking off their caps."[99] When his unmarked grave was later discovered, Young Bosnians came to pay their respect and stole flowers from other graves to decorate his. Gacinovic's glorification of Zerajic, *Death of a Hero*, became an important source of inspiration for the later conspirators.[100]

Zerajic's self-sacrifice resonated with the Bosnian youth raised on the Legend of Kosovo. On 28 June 1389, St. Vitus' Day, Sultan Murad had defeated

Serbian Prince Lazar at the Field of Blackbirds in Kosovo, putting an end to
Serbian independence and ushering in four centuries of harsh Ottoman rule
over Bosnia. Prince Lazar was killed during the battle. On the eve of the battle,
he had accused one of his followers, Milos Obilic, of treason. According to the
epic poems of the battle, an indignant Obilic replied that on the next day they
shall see "who is loyal to you and who is not."[101] History is vague about what
exactly happened, but, after the defeat, Obilic succeeded in coming close to
the sultan and stabbed him to death before being killed himself. Serbian legend transformed this military disaster into a noble defeat by Prince Lazar,
while Obilic became the symbol of resistance to oppression, self-sacrifice, and
martyrdom.[102] This whole region became famous for resisting Ottoman repression through Robin Hood–like *hajduks*, whose exploits became local folk
epics and established a tradition of resistance to foreign occupation. Zerajic's
selfless action resonated with Young Bosnians by linking their legendary heritage and regicide.

Brutal Repression of the Schoolboys' Demonstration
and Attentats Against Governors

At the elections of December 1911, a Croat-Serb coalition defeated government
parties and gained an absolute majority in the Croat Sabor (Assembly). To
counter the anticipated popular demands for autonomy, Count Slavko Cuvaj
was appointed governor of Croatia with orders to rule it with a firm hand. He
adjourned the Sabor, banned political gatherings, and formed an unelected
government. Students in Zagreb protested and the police charged them with
drawn sabers, seriously wounding some of them. High school students in the
surrounding provinces, including Bosnia, rose up in solidarity with their colleagues in Croatia. "Any terror against our comrades we shall accept as terror
against the whole of our society. We shall treat it as if it were a bomb thrown
against us, and our answer to such a bomb attack sponsored by the government will be an explosion which will destroy this bomb and its owner."[103] On
18 February 1912, a large secondary school demonstration organized by Young
Bosnia broke out in Sarajevo, and the police shot a Muslim student in the
head. Several others, including one called Gavrilo Princip, were wounded by
saber cuts. The demonstration was a remarkable show of pan-Slav unity bringing together Serbs, Croats, and Muslims despite their internal squabbling. Unable to restore peace, the authorities closed down the schools indefinitely. In
April, Cuvaj suspended the Croat constitution and ruled by decree.[104]

Many students wanted to kill Cuvaj. Luka Jukic, a 25-year-old Croat student from Bosnia, who had written the above words about student solidarity,

told his comrades, "This schoolboys' movement is not enough. It is too innocent. Other means must be applied, and Cuvaj should be removed at all costs
and I am prepared to do it, either with poison . . . or with bombs and revolvers."[105] He persuaded other students ready to kill the governor to let him get
the first try. Jukic tried to kill Cuvaj during a religious procession but backed
out for fear of wounding innocent children in the procession. His comrades
cursed his cowardice, and Jukic finally carried out his attentat on 8 June 1912:
he rushed Cuvaj's moving car and shot at him, but missed, gravely wounding
another official in the car. In the pursuit, Jukic shot and killed one policeman
and wounded two others.[106]

Jukic and eleven students accused of conspiracy went on trial. When
asked if he acted on behalf of a revolutionary organization, he answered, "A
revolutionary organization does not yet exist, but it will be organized if conditions are not changed."[107] His co-defendants cited the right of tyrannicide. The
judge convicted them and sentenced Jukic to death. Jukic shouted, "You cannot judge me, my judge is my country, Croatia."[108] Bowing to public opinion,
the sentence was commuted to life.[109]

Jukic made a deep impact on all young South Slavs. Several others picked
up the challenge. One climbed a telegraph pole opposite the governor's residence and shot at him when Cuvaj appeared at the window. He missed and
committed suicide in the tradition of Zerajic. A Croat immigrant to Wisconsin, Stjepan Dojcic, returned to Croatia to finish the deed. However, he could
not find Cuvaj, who had gone into hiding. He eventually shot and wounded
Cuvaj's replacement in August 1913. At his trial, Dojcic defended his action by
comparing freedom in the United States with its absence in Croatia.[110]

Let us return to Gavrilo Princip, the 17-year-old student who had been
wounded in the February 1912 schoolboys' demonstration. He was born to a
poor Orthodox family in the northern Bosnian mountains and came to Sarajevo in 1907 for secondary school, funded by his older brother. He rented a
room with a widow, whose son Danilo Ilic became his best friend. Princip
enrolled in a business school and did well for his first three years. He was a
voracious reader, especially of adventure novels by Alexandre Dumas, Walter
Scott, and Arthur Conan Doyle. He transferred to a gymnasium for his fourth
year and successfully passed his grade's exams in June 1911.[111]

Princip later said that 1911 was a critical year,[112] as he became politically
aware and a Young Bosnian. It is not known whether Ilic influenced him in
this evolution. Ilic, who was four years older than Princip, bridges the various
generations of Young Bosnia. He was the same age as Zerajic and Gacinovic,
with whom he corresponded, but through his consecutive attendance at two
secondary schools, he was also in contact with younger students. His father
had died when he was young, forcing his mother to wash laundry and rent out

a room in her house in Sarajevo to support her family. In 1905, Ilic graduated from the same business school that Princip later attended but could not find work. He lived for a few years as an itinerant laborer. He returned to Sarajevo, attended its teacher's college with students four years younger, and graduated in 1912. After graduation, he taught at two schools in small towns for a few months, but realized he did not like this profession. He returned home to Sarajevo, where he found a job at a bank. He was already a determined Young Bosnian, and his collection of anarchist and revolutionary books made a strong impression on young Princip,[113] who devoured everything he could get his hands on: "many anarchistic, socialistic, nationalistic pamphlets, *belles lettres* and everything."[114]

Princip's participation in the February 1912 schoolboys' demonstration changed his life because, as a result, he was expelled from school.[115] Outraged at this action, which seemed to close off future opportunities, he discussed with others who had been expelled the possibility of carrying out action against various Austrian officials: police officers, Bosnian Governor Oskar Potiorek, the minister of finance, and even the emperor himself.[116] But all of this brave talk came to nothing, and, too ashamed to tell his brother, he walked to Belgrade, Serbia, in May to continue his education. The night before his departure, he went to Zerajic's grave and swore that he would avenge him.[117] In Belgrade, Princip was completely destitute for weeks, sleeping in trashcans or empty dog kennels and accepting charity from monks. He reconciled with his brother, promising to be a good student, and his brother resumed his financial support. In June, he took his fifth-year exams at a Belgrade gymnasium, but failed.

What really interrupted the nascent campaign of attentats against Austro-Hungarian officials in the occupied provinces was the first Balkan War of 1912 between Serbia and the Ottoman Empire. When Serbia ordered mobilization, many Young Bosnians flocked over to Serbia and volunteered for the komites, headed by Major Vojislav Tankosic. In Belgrade, most of the Bosnian students also enlisted in the komites organized by Narodna Odbrana (National Defense). This organization was created during the annexation crisis to fight the Habsburg Empire by raising guerrilla volunteer units but had evolved into a cultural society, raising Yugoslav nationalist consciousness through propaganda. Through its network of affiliates in the occupied provinces, it also received information about what was happening on the ground there.[118] In 1912, it sent Bosnian volunteers, including Princip, to a border town for training. When Major Tankosic came to inspect them before incorporation into his komite, he dismissed the diminutive and frail-looking Princip with a wave of his hand: "You are too small and too weak."[119] Disappointed, Princip returned to his brother's house in Hadzici, near Sarajevo, in October to prepare for his fifth- and sixth-year exams.

Staying with his brother and visiting Sarajevo frequently, Princip heard about the exploits of his friends in the komites avenging the 1389 Kosovo defeat. Slav students throughout the provinces celebrated the victories of the Serbian army, which sometimes led to the closing of several high schools. Princip was always careful not to reveal too much about his feelings, but this did not stop amateur psychologist historians from speculating that the humiliation of his rejection pushed him to later accomplish an extraordinarily brave act to prove to his peers that he was their equal. Their main evidence was that, later, Princip allegedly said, "Wherever I went, people took me for a weakling—indeed, for a man who would be completely ruined by immoderate study of literature. And I pretended that I was a weak person, even though I was not."[120] Princip returned to Belgrade in March 1913 to take his fifth- and sixth-year exams, which he passed, and returned home.[121]

1913 Emergency Laws and Martial Rule

The unexpected success of the Serbians against the Ottomans alarmed the Habsburg, and relations between Austria-Hungary and Serbia became very tense in the spring of 1913. There was danger of an Austrian attack (until Serbia agreed to relinquish some of their gained territory), and Bosnian Governor Potiorek imposed a state of emergency in his province on 2 May 1913. He suspended the 1910 constitution of Bosnia and Hercegovina along with civil courts, imposed martial rule and banned all Serbian public, cultural, and educational societies; trade unions; and socialist organizations. All newspapers from Serbia were confiscated at the border, and the state took direct control of the administration of all secondary schools. Some Young Bosnians were arrested for organizing secret societies, and more than 200 high-treason trials were held in the first half of 1913.[122] At their later trials, all the direct participants in the future attentat mentioned the imposition of these "exceptional measures" (*iznimne mjere*) and high-treason trials as two of their major motives.[123] "In the first place, I was guided by feelings of revenge for all of the injustices which the Serbian people in Bosnia and Hercegovina had suffered, which were imposed on them, such as the 'exceptional measures,' etc."[124]

Already possessing a gun, Danilo Ilic decided to carry out an attentat against Potiorek to protest these extraordinary measures, but somehow did not carry it through. Instead, he went to Switzerland for about ten days in June. There he met with Gacinovic and Russian socialist revolutionaries. He brought some literature back to Sarajevo and started advocating that Young Bosnians should first prepare the population for revolution by building a province-wide revolutionary organization before carrying out political assassinations. At the outbreak of the Second Balkan War, pitting Bulgaria against Serbia, in July 1913, Ilic walked to Serbia to enlist. He became an ambulance driver, taking care of soldiers stricken with cholera. He might have caught the disease, because he returned sick to Sarajevo in September and required hospitalization for a month and a half.[125]

During that summer, Princip returned to Belgrade to study and take his seventh-year exam. He frequented cafés of Bosnian expatriates, both students and komite veterans. At the end of his stay, he ran into a friend, Nedejko Cabrinovic, the son of a café owner in Sarajevo suspected of being a police informer. Cabrinovic had been a classmate of Princip at the Sarajevo business school but had flunked out in 1908. He became an apprentice printer and was elected as the first president of the printer's apprentice guild the next year. Like Princip, Cabrinovic read Chernyshevsky, socialism, and anarchism. He worked several months at an anarchist publisher in Belgrade, attended evening anarchist lectures, and converted to anarchism. He became sick and returned to Sarajevo, where he worked at another printing shop, which went on strike in July 1912. He was staying with the anarchist leader of the strike when the police arrested him and banished him from Sarajevo. At his later trial, he remembered this incident as one of his motives for the assassination: "I was driven by personal motive of revenge. I began to deliberate about the assassination for the first time when I was driven from Sarajevo. I did not like it, that a foreigner who came to our land, could drive me from my home. When I was expelled I was ordered to go to the lieutenant-governor . . . I thought that he would pardon me . . . Instead, his secretary read me a moral sermon on life . . . and showed me the door. I was sorry that I didn't have weapons then, I would have blasted him with all six shots."[126]

Cabrinovic drifted around and went to Belgrade for a few months before friends and relatives succeeded in getting the ban lifted. He became sick but could not return because of lack of money. He ran into Princip, who suggesting applying to Narodna Odbrana for help. Cabrinovic got money from it and had enough left over for the purchase of anarchist literature, which he shipped home, and returned to Sarajevo. After his convalescence, Cabrinovic returned to work and was promoted to full membership in the printers' union, dominated by social democrats. As an anarchist, Cabrinovic objected to their authoritarian rule, and they accused him of being a police spy like his father. During the fall of 1912, he socialized with Princip, who had also returned home. He finally left Sarajevo in March 1913 for Trieste, where he read Mazzini's works and was inspired by Dojcic's attentat. With the outbreak of the Second Balkan War, he left for Belgrade, where he again met Princip. He arrived in October 1913, when the war was over and soldiers had come back to reclaim their jobs, leaving him unemployed. He eventually found a low-paying job at the state press.[127]

Another of Princip's friends was Trifko Grabez, the 18-year-old son of a village priest, whom he had met at gymnasium. In May 1912, Grabez transferred to the Tuzla Gymnasium, where, in November, he slapped a professor who had insulted him. Grabez was arrested, expelled from school, and banned from Tuzla. He went to Belgrade, where he passed his fifth-year exam in May 1913 and sixth-year exam in July of the same year. He stayed in Belgrade to continue his studies. He ran into Princip, and they roomed and studied together. They shared similar political views.[128]

Princip returned to Hadzici in late October and saw Ilic, still in the hospital, with whom he discussed an attentat on Potiorek. Ilic "spoke of pan-Slavist ideas, said they should first create an organization in all Bosnia and Croatia, then, when all was ready, they should make the attempt. Therefore, the plan was given up."[129] For the next few months, Ilic tried to build up this organization through written propaganda.

Announcement of the Archduke's Visit to Sarajevo and Initiation of the Plot

What happened next is in dispute and intertwined in polemics about the responsibility for the event that triggered World War I. There has been much speculation about the role of secret societies, like the Freemasons, Narodna Odbrana, or the "Black Hand." At trial, the presiding judge never missed an opportunity to try to link the defendants to these mysterious organizations, implying a Serbian conspiracy that would have retrospectively justified the Austrian invasion of Serbia that started the Great War. However, the defendants were careful to deny such links. Later conspiracy theories rely on secondary sources from people at best peripheral to the plot. In the following narrative, I rely on primary sources[130] and will comment about these speculations at the end of this section.

Princip returned to Belgrade in February/March 1914 to study and take his eighth-year exam. He moved in with Grabez and socialized with Cabrinovic. They frequently came in contact with demobilized komite veterans, hanging around cafés patronized by Bosnian expatriates. Two prominent veterans were Djulaga Bukovac and Milan Ciganovic. Bukovac was a Muslim from Hercegovina, who had been in Princip's gymnasium class and expelled with him during the schoolboys' demonstration. Bukovac joined the komite under Major Tankosic and was on the battlefield until the end of the Second Balkan War. He was a good friend of Princip. Ciganovic, six years older than

Princip, had been a student at the Sarajevo business school and had come to Serbia in 1909 to join the komite. He won a medal for bravery and became famous among Bosnian expatriates in Belgrade. Princip lived in his building when he first came to Belgrade in 1912 and had seen 12 bombs that Ciganovic had kept in a wooden box in his apartment. Ciganovic and Tankosic were close and came from the same area in the Bosnian mountains as Princip. Princip was poorly acquainted with Ciganovic or Tankosic but frequently ran into Bukovac in cafés.[131]

After the Second Balkan War, Young Bosnians resumed discussions about carrying out assassination campaigns against high-level Austro-Hungarian officials in the annexed provinces, especially Governor Potiorek. Princip later stated at his trial that he was a Yugoslav nationalist who believed in the unification of all Yugoslavs, free from Austria. He aimed to accomplish this by means of terror to sweep away the obstacles to this unification.[132] In March 1914, Princip read in the German press that Archduke Franz Ferdinand would come to Sarajevo to review military maneuvers, and he started toying with the idea of shifting his target to the archduke. Princip discussed this with his roommate Grabez, and they both agreed to carry out an assassination, whether Ferdinand or Potiorek.[133] Cabrinovic also received an anonymous newspaper clipping from Sarajevo, stating, "From Sarajevo it is announced, that the Archduke Heir Apparent with his wife will come to Sarajevo and participate in the maneuvers."[134] He showed it to Princip, who invited him for an evening stroll in a nearby park. According to Cabrinovic, Princip suggested that they carry out an assassination on the archduke. They would make every effort to spare his wife—they condemned Luigi Lucheni's 1898 assassination of Austrian Empress Elizabeth as a common crime. After initial hesitation, Cabrinovic agreed. "We gave each other our word of honor, shook hands, and left."[135] As they needed weapons and money, they discussed various options. They thought of approaching Narodna Odbrana, but Princip was upset at the group because of a recent refusal to give him money and ruled it out. Princip said that he would find the means.[136]

Apparently, Princip remembered the bombs in Ciganovic's apartment but did not know him well enough to approach him. He asked his friend Bukovac to introduce him and, once alone with Ciganovic, Princip revealed the purpose of the meeting and asked him to give him the bombs. Ciganovic "was quiet for a while and then he said, 'We'll see.' . . . After some time Ciganovic said to me that he would give me bombs. Because those bombs exploded after several seconds, success with them was not certain. I told him that we needed revolvers. He told me to take care of that ourselves."[137] Ciganovic hesitated because he wanted to check with his boss, Major Tankosic. When Ciganovic later saw Cabrinovic at a café, he informed the conspirator that he would supply them with bombs and even pistols.

In April, Princip wrote to Ilic in cipher that he intended to assassinate the archduke and had weapons. Princip asked him to find other conspirators.[138] Grabez, who had just passed his seventh-year exam, was returning home for a month for Easter. Princip asked him to check whether Ilic was truly on board.[139] Things stood still for about a month, and Princip and Cabrinovic discussed their plans further with Djuro Sarac, whom Princip had known from gymnasium. Sarac had criticized the annexation as "sheer theft of somebody else's property" and been arrested. After his release, he went to Serbia to continue his schooling. He joined a komite at the start of the Balkan Wars and distinguished himself so much that Major Tankosic, the overall chief of the komites, selected him as his personal bodyguard. After the war, Sarac was demobilized and spent most of his time hanging around cafés, where the two conspirators discussed their plans with him.[140] At the same time, Cabrinovic was working overtime to pay off debts, and Princip was studying for his eighth-year exam.[141] Grabez returned to Belgrade in May to take his eighth-year exam and met fellow conspirator Cabrinovic for the first time.

Before Ciganovic gave Princip weapons, he told Princip that Major Tankosic wanted to meet with the conspirators. Princip had no interest in meeting the man who had humiliated him and Cabrinovic was not serious enough for the meeting, so Grabez went alone. They met at Ciganovic's apartment. Tankosic asked Grabez, " 'Are you one of them, are you ready?' 'I am' 'Are you determined?' 'I am' 'Do you know how to shoot a revolver?' 'No.' 'Do you know how to handle one?' 'No.' Tankosic said to Ciganovic, 'Here is a revolver. Teach them to shoot on the firing range!' "[142] A few days later, Ciganovic took Princip and Grabez to shoot in one of the parks in Belgrade. Princip, who had learned how to shoot at the military training camp in 1912, was the better marksman.

On 26 May, Ciganovic gave the three conspirators six bombs, four pistols, and cyanide capsules for them to commit suicide afterward, as well as 150 dinars. He instructed them on how to use the bombs, but they did not have any opportunity to practice. As Princip already mentioned, these bombs were not appropriate to carry out an attentat, for they did not explode on contact, like Orsini or Kibalchich bombs. The bomber had to unscrew their caps, prime them by striking the top against a hard surface, and then wait for ten to twelve seconds until the bomb would explode. This was hard to accomplish in a crowd with the police watching. These bombs were effective in trench warfare and were used in the two Balkan Wars.

Although all three conspirators had crossed the border illegally several times, this time they were carrying weapons and could not take any risk of being stopped by border guards. Ciganovic gave them a card with his initials for a Serb officer at the border to facilitate their clandestine crossing. Armed with their weapons, Princip, Cabrinovic, and Grabez left Belgrade on 28 May 1914.

Formation of the Second Group of Conspirators

Danilo Ilic started building a local team of conspirators after he received Princip's coded letter. He met with Mehmed Mehmedbasic, a 28-year-old Muslim carpenter from Hercegovina and dedicated Young Bosnian who had previously met with Gacinovic several times abroad. He was tasked to murder Governor Potiorek and came to Sarajevo to carry this out in March, when he met Ilic, who advised him to stand down in favor of the archduke's assassination.[143] Mehmedbasic returned home and the two met again in Mostar, where they discussed the attentat against the archduke. Ilic told his friend that he could get weapons from Serbia and to be ready.[144]

Ilic then approached an acquaintance, Lazar Djukic, an 18-year-old student who had been in the same gymnasium class as Princip and participated in the schoolboys' demonstration with him.[145] Djukic had dropped out of the gymnasium and attended the teacher's college, where he was well known for his Yugoslav nationalism. Later, Ilic testified that he talked to Djukic about assassination in general, and Djukic said that it was hard to get weapons. Ilic replied that it was easy. According to Djukic, Ilic was more specific and talked about the archduke. Djukic said he would not do it himself, and Ilic asked him to inquire whether other students would. Djukic testified that he ran into Ilic several times and Ilic kept asking him whether he had found anyone.[146]

Around May 1914, Djukic got into a conversation with 17-year-old Vaso Cubrilovic, who was in the sixth year at the Sarajevo gymnasium and a member of a nationalist literary circle. When Cubrilovic learned of Franz Ferdinand's visit, he thought of an assassination. At his chance meeting with Djukic, Cubrilovic said, "Ferdinand is coming, we should lie in wait for him." Djukic replied, "If only there were people!" Cubrilovic continued, "I would be, but I don't have arms." Djukic said, "I will introduce you to a man who will give you weapons." After several days, Djukic introduced Cubrilovic to Ilic.[147] After a brief introduction, Djukic excused himself and Ilic promised Cubrilovic weapons right before the assassination. Ilic also said that they needed one more person.[148]

Around 20 May, Cubrilovic ran into a friend, 16-year-old Cvjetko Popovic, a student at the teacher's college who was nursing a desire for revenge for an unjust arrest the previous year during the "exceptional measures." Popovic later testified, "Among other things we talked about the arrival of the Heir Apparent Ferdinand in Sarajevo. He said that he wanted to lie in wait for him, to assassinate him . . . I said, 'How can we do it when there are no weapons?' He said that he knew a man who would take care of everything. Then we didn't talk about that any more. Later he said that man was Ilic and that we would accomplish the assassination with bombs and revolvers . . . I was already acquainted with Ilic. I was in the first year of the Teacher's School, and he in the fourth, but I had never been friendly with him."[149] Ilic did not meet with Popovic until the day before the assassination, but Cubrilovic informed him that he had recruited Popovic, and Ilic told him to look no further.

Popovic recorded his feelings around that time: "After I gave my word to join the plot, I spent the whole night thinking and dreaming about the assassination. In the morning I was quite a different man. Convinced that I had only until June 28 to live . . . I looked upon everything from a new angle. I left my school books, I hardly glanced at the newspapers which up to that day I read with interest. I almost failed to react to the jokes of my friends . . . Only one thought tormented me: that we might not succeed and thus make fools of ourselves."[150]

The Assassination

The three main conspirators, Princip, Cabrinovic, and Grabez, used Ciganovic's network of trusted nationalist smugglers to reach Sarajevo. On the way, Cabrinovic could not keep his mouth shut and chatted with strangers, including policemen. Princip and Grabez refused to talk with him the rest of the way and, to further protect themselves, they forced Cabrinovic to proceed separately by train and meet them in Tuzla while they took a more clandestine route with the weapons. They walked from one nationalist sympathizer to another and arrived in Tuzla on June 3. Not wanting to risk taking the weapons to Sarajevo, they left the weapons with a local sympathizer businessman. When they met Cabrinovic, they did not tell him where the weapons were, as they no longer trusted him. On the train to Sarajevo, Cabrinovic was recognized by a detective who knew his father. During some small talk, he asked the detective when the archduke was expected in Sarajevo, and the detective told him 28 June. This was how the conspirators learned the actual date of Franz Ferdinand's arrival. They arrived in Sarajevo on the morning of 4 June.[151]

Upon arrival, each of the conspirators went his own way. Princip moved back with Ilic, while the other two went home. At that point, Cabrinovic was out of the plot. Princip asked Ilic to bring back the weapons safely from Tuzla, and Ilic did so in mid-June. All conspirators hunkered down and waited for the archduke's arrival. Ilic was having reservations about the wisdom of the attentat. He argued with his roommate that no political organization had prepared the population and could take advantage of it. Princip later testified about Ilic, "He said that now was not the time for an assassination and that it would have bad consequences, that there would be persecution of the people. I thought that it would not be of such dimensions as happened after the assassination and I did not let him influence me."[152] Grabez also recalled, "I arrived in Sarajevo three days before the assassination and there I conferred with Princip. Ilic was strongly against the assassination and was urging me not to participate in any way. I told him that there was no sense in that, and that the assassination had to be carried out. Ilic thought that I would not carry out the assassination because he said that there were five people. He had his three, I did not know any of them, and he told me not to carry out the assassination. It is possible that he was convinced that I would not carry it out. I was firmly decided to carry it out."[153]

At the trial, Ilic testified, "Later I saw that the assassination would be harmful and began to prevent it. I talked with Princip as I also wanted to persuade him that there not be an assassination. I talked with him and he opposed it from the beginning, and later I said to him: let the other five do it, just you don't. Because I talked with him at length about that, he fell silent, but did not directly say: 'I won't,' but I understood he agreed. I thought that he would not do it. Then Mehmedbasic himself announced that he would not come to Sarajevo at all because the assassination would fail, but later on he came anyway, two days before the assassination. Since I already had arms he wanted me to give him some of the weapons to take [back home]. I did not say directly to Cubrilovic and Popovic that they should not perform the assassination, but I concluded that they were unfit for it. Because I had promised Princip that the other five would do it, later, if there were no assassination, I would have to prove that I was responsible that it did not take place. Therefore I gave the pair a bomb and a revolver. I figured out exactly. They wanted arms for training, because people who are not trained are probably not competent to do the assassination. I did not give them arms earlier than the eve of the assassination itself . . . Grabez and Princip told me about Cabrinovic, that he was a very naïve fellow and that he was not fit for the assassination. I too believed that he would not do it. I intended not to give him any kind of arms at all because he would not carry out the assassination."[154]

At the trial, Cubrilovic and Popovic confirmed that Ilic gave them each a bomb, a pistol, and some cyanide the day before the attentat. He instructed them on how to use the bomb and demonstrated how to shoot the pistol by firing one shot before giving it to Popovic. The teenagers were eager to carry out the assassination because they had bragged about it to their friends, and as nothing had happened, their friends were teasing them. They had to defend their honor.[155]

Ilic's reason for participating in the attentat he rejected remains unknown. Was he trying to sabotage it, as he claimed at his trial, or was he simply too devoted to Princip and afraid that someone would eventually reproach him for letting his friend down? In any case, he chose not to be a bomber himself.

In fact, most of the bombers did not know that he would not be one of them. Nevertheless, he distributed the weapons: the eve of the attentat, he met Mehmedbasic and gave him a bomb along with instructions on how to use it. He then went to Zerajic's grave before returning home. Cabrinovic also went to Zerajic's grave later in the evening. Like his two friends, Princip also went to the grave around midnight on his way home.[156]

In the morning, Ilic, Cabrinovic, and Grabez met at a café for breakfast and Princip joined them shortly after. Princip had re-invited his friend Cabrinovic to be a bomber the day before. Princip had come with two bombs, a pistol, and cyanide. He gave a bomb and some cyanide to Cabrinovic at the back of the café, while Ilic took Grabez home and gave him a bomb and a pistol. All six bombers went to the Appel Quay, along which the archduke's motorcade would be traveling. Despite the fact that they had assigned positions, the bombers, who did not know each other, simply milled around for an hour and a half. When the archduke's car drove by, Mehmedbasic did not throw his bomb because either he did not recognize the car or a gendarme was standing next to him.[157] Cubrilovic later admitted, "I did not draw the revolver because the duchess was there."[158] Popovic confessed, "I didn't have the courage. I don't know what happened to me."[159] Cabrinovic saw the motorcade approaching and unscrewed his bomb. "I held it with my hand all the time. When he approached I saw only a green cap and nothing else. I hit the bomb against the lamppost. It broke and I threw it ... I saw how the late Ferdinand turned toward me and looked at me with a cold, inflexible gaze. At that moment the bomb fell on the folded roof of the automobile, bounced off the automobile and fell on the ground. I turned around, took the poison, and jumped into the Miljacka."[160]

The bomb exploded under the next car and wounded a dozen people but did not harm anyone in the archduke's car. Cabrinovic was quickly apprehended. Standing further along the road, Princip heard the explosion and saw Cabrinovic being arrested. He thought that the attentat had succeeded until he heard shortly thereafter that it did not. By that time, it was too late for him to do anything as the motorcade, which had temporarily stopped, sped by him on the way to the city hall. Grabez also thought that the archduke was killed because the motorcade stopped for a long time. "Suddenly the first, second and third cars came. I turned. I saw that the Heir Apparent was still alive."[161]

After this first attempt, Mehmedbasic, Cubrilovic, and Popovic got rid of their weapons and disappeared, hoping that no one would denounce them. Grabez and Princip waited for the archduke's return from city hall. Princip went to a café at the corner of Appel Quay and the road to the old city, while Grabez posted himself further along the quay. At city hall, the archduke's entourage decided to modify their route: they would skip the planned trip through the old city and would take the quay so that the car could speed along the road, making it harder for bombers to hit it. However, no one bothered to tell the chauffeurs. When the first two cars turned into the city from the quay, the archduke's chauffeur started to follow them. Governor Potiorek, riding in the car, yelled at the driver to turn around and go back to the quay. The chauffeur stopped the car and started to back up right where Princip happened to stand. "I took out the revolver and I shot at Ferdinand twice from the distance of four or five paces . . . I did not know whether I had struck home. At that time I didn't even know how many shots I had fired. Because I wanted to kill myself I raised my arm but the policemen and some officers grabbed me and beat me."[162] The shots fatally wounded the archduke and his wife, who died shortly thereafter. It was as if Franz Ferdinand literally drove into the bullet through bad judgment and miscommunication.

Grabez disappeared after he heard that the archduke was killed. However, the police conducted a thorough investigation and arrested all the conspirators except Mehmedbasic, who had fled to Montenegro. The police also arrested all the peasants, the teacher, and the businessman who had helped Grabez and Princip along their return to Sarajevo. The trial of 25 people took place in mid-October 1914. The Austrian prosecutors and judges tried hard to prove a Serbian government conspiracy, but all the defendants denied it. Sixteen defendants were convicted of high treason, a crime punishable by hanging. However, Austrian law required a defendant to be 20 at the commission of the crime in order to be eligible for that sentence, and most of the defendants were still teenagers. Of the major defendants, only Ilic was sentenced to death, along with four other accomplices. Princip, Cabrinovic, and Grabez got 20-year sentences, while Cubrilovic, Popovic, and Djukic received 16, 13, and 10 years, respectively.[163]

The assassination activated the process that started World War I. Austria-Hungary sent an ultimatum to Serbia, which could not comply with one provision, and declared war on Serbia. This automatically dragged the main European powers into war, as Serbia had an alliance with Russia, which had a treaty with France and Great Britain. Austria-Hungary had a treaty with Germany. Within weeks, Europe was at war, and within a little more than four years, the empires of Russia, Germany, and Austria-Hungary had ceased to exist.

A Bunch of Violent Guys or a Top-Down Conspiracy?

Given the global consequences of this important *attentat*, its facts have been drowned in polemics as to the responsibility for the war. Conspiracy theories emerged and persist based on secondary sources from people peripheral to the plot and, until recently, the lack of access to the complete trial transcripts. Many conspiracy theories are based on the alleged role of Colonel Dragutin Dimitrijevic, nicknamed Apis, who was the head of a secret organization called Ujedinjenje ili Smrt (Union or Death), popularly known as the Black Hand. Major Tankosic was also a member of this organization. According to a member of the Black Hand Central Committee, Tankosic had informed Apis that some Young Bosnians had asked for weapons to carry out an attentat on Archduke Franz Ferdinand. Apis unreflectively agreed, as he never thought they would succeed and believed it would warn the archduke and his entourage to keep away from attacking Serbia. When he later informed the central committee of the Black Hand on 15 June of what they had done, the committee rejected this decision outright. Apis and Tankosic dispatched Sarac, who knew Princip, Cabrinovic, and Ilic, to Bosnia to try to stop the conspirators. Some historians attribute Ilic's strange change of heart about the assassination to his meeting Sarac.[164]

After the trial was over, Ilic made fun of the suggestion that the conspirators were pawns of a secret Serbian terrorist organization. "The atmosphere in which we live, the assassination attempts in Zagreb and in the monarchy, the students' nationalist newspapers . . . agitating for a revolution, revolutionary books like *Underground Russia* [by Stepniak/Kravchinsky], the glorification of the assassins in poems—all this developed such revolutionary spirit among the students that if I needed fifteen students to take part in a plot, I would find all of them ready."[165]

Ilic seems to be right. The defendants might well have wanted to protect semiofficial Serbian organizations, but their individual accounts corroborated each other's narratives, and the overall emerging account had no need for the addition of a superimposed conspiracy. The original three conspirators approached Ciganovic, an individual, whom they knew had bombs and could get some pistols. Ciganovic informed his good friend and former komite boss Tankevic. Their membership in the Black Hand suggests that it was probably informed about a possible attentat on the Archduke, but it neither originated nor drove the plot. There is some evidence that its leaders might later have wanted to prevent it, but they were without much influence on the conspirators. Of course, Ciganovic provided the conspirators with the means of conducting their attentat and helped them get back to Sarajevo. Without these weapons they would not have been able to even try to kill Franz Ferdinand, so he and his alleged masters must carry a large degree of blame for this attentat.

The collective story of the assassination of Franz Ferdinand followed the now familiar pattern of other attentats: activation of a politicized social identity; escalation of conflict between a political protest community and the state; disillusionment with the effectiveness of peaceful protest; outrage at state aggression like the extraordinary measures; activation of a martial social identity, which led a few to carry out an attentat when a good opportunity arose. The ideological argument does not explain it because the conspirators did not agree about their political ideology. They ranged from anarchists to socialists to strict nationalists but shared a rather primitive rebellious desire to get rid of their Austrian occupiers. Rational choice theory also fails because it cannot explain the bombers' self-conscious sacrifice, inimical to their self-interest.

Contrary to claims that Princip and his co-conspirators were not a bunch of guys,[166] in fact they certainly were a very loose bunch of violent guys since they barely knew each other. Princip was close to Grabez, Cabrinovic, and Ilic, respectively. However Grabez and Cabrinovic first met in mid-May 1914 and the two first met Ilic in June. Ilic knew Mehmedbasic but did not know Cubrilovic and had to be introduced by a third party. Ilic did not even meet Popovic until the day before the assassination. None of the first three conspirators, Princip, Grabez, and Cabrinovic, knew the last three conspirators, Mehmedbasic, Cubrilovic, and Popovic. The seven conspirators never formed a physical group. Up to this case, I believed that in-group love was a major motivator for carrying out an attentat,[167] but the assassination of the archduke showed that it was done for an imagined in-group, namely Young Bosnia.

At trial, the judges were shocked at the fact that Cubrilovic and Popovic joined a conspiracy of complete strangers, and they questioned them about their motivation. Cubrilovic testified, "Because I considered the Heir to be an enemy of the Slavs and in general because he was a representative of the regime which most greatly oppressed Bosnia and Hercegovina by means of the 'exceptional measures' and by all other harassments."[168] Popovic echoed that sentiment, "merely for revenge for the persecution of all the Slavs in the whole Monarchy . . . in Bosnia and Hercegovina. For instance, the 'exceptional measures.' In Croatia, the commissionership."[169]

Sixty years later, Popovic further elaborated on his joining the conspiracy. "Yes, they asked me and I instantly agreed. Look, you have to realize what it was like to live under foreigners. There we were, in our own country, and these fellows were telling us what to do. We students led the demonstrations against the Austrians. I had been in jail already for agitation . . . We were steeped in the literature of the Russian Social[ist] Revolutionaries. When we met, when we walked in the evenings in the park, we would ask each other, 'Have you read this or that book?', and if our *kolege* [buddy] hadn't, we would pass the book from hand to hand. We didn't have to spell things out. We knew instantly what each other had in mind . . . We hated them [foreigners] with burning hatred. Our ideal was Yugoslavia. Yes, I agreed instantly, and under the same circumstances I would do it again!"[170] Both teenagers were part of an imagined political protest community, and when invited to participate in an attentat, they simply grabbed the opportunity. There was no need for long processes of indoctrination or brainwashing.

Indiscriminate Violence in the United States

While the archduke's assassination belongs to the tradition of regicides, across the ocean in the United States political violence expanded to target civilians on a mass scale, which all readers would recognize as modern terrorism. There, at the turn of the past century, the private violence of the struggle between labor and capital spilled into the political arena when industrialists called on the state to protect them. In the west, where many people were armed and law enforcement was weaker than in the east, a series of strikes up and down the Rockies escalated from damaging property to targeting people when Idaho Governor Frank Steunenberg called black federal troops to quash a strike after the bombing of a mill. Striking miners were rounded up by the thousands. A union man blew up the former governor a few years later, allegedly on the orders of the union leader as revenge. The ensuing trial exonerated union leaders. This acquittal emboldened other unions to respond with violence to state intervention for capital.[171]

The Los Angeles Times Bombing

By 1910, explosions at non-union construction sites became a common union tactic to force construction industrialists to accept unionization and raise workers' salaries, which more than doubled during this three-year bombing campaign. There had been one bombing in 1906, three in 1907, and then about 200 of them until the spring of 1911. Most of these explosions, which destroyed dozens of bridges and buildings, were the work of Ortie McManigal, a 36-year-old former mine explosive expert who joined the Bridge and Structural Iron Workers Union in 1907. When first tasked by his union bosses to blow up empty construction sites, he had been reluctant, but, needing money for his family, he embarked on his dynamiter career but always took great care to avoid any human injuries. After a dozen success, he viewed his task as just a well-paying job. Ideology played no role in this bombing campaign, which was directly orchestrated by the union secretary treasurer J. J. McNamara. McNamara introduced his 27-year-old brother, J. B., to McManigal for them to team up in December 1909. They became friends and conducted further explosions both together and separately over the next year. J. B. McNamara did not share his older partner's respect for human lives and injured several night watchmen in his explosions. Construction companies were resigned to the bombings and simply factored them into the cost of doing business.[172]

One of the most rapidly developing cities in the country was Los Angeles, whose low-paying, non-unionized status risked eroding the benefits that labor had painfully gained in much larger San Francisco. In the summer of 1910, San Francisco employers announced that they were not going to renew contracts with their unions unless their wages were brought in line with those paid in Los Angeles. Union organizers descended on Los Angeles and called for a general strike to unionize the city and raise wages. Los Angeles employers, led by the *Los Angeles Times* owner, countered with the quick passage of a municipal ordinance outlawing "loitering, picketing, carrying or displaying banners." Hundreds of strikers were beaten and arrested by the police, and their trial was set for March 1911. Since the vast majority could not afford bail, they were jailed for eight months for an offense carrying a maximum sentence of fifty days! Strikebreakers, low-wage black workers shipped from Texas, were inexperienced, and dozens of sometimes fatal accidents turned public opinion against employers. To galvanize Los Angeles workers, California union leaders called J. J. McNamara for help. He sent his brother to give Los Angeles a "damned good cleaning up."[173]

When J. B. McNamara met with the outraged California union leaders in San Francisco, he suggested an escalation of his usual tactics. In addition to planting a bomb at the *Los Angeles Times* building, where staff worked all night long to publish the early editions, he would bomb the homes of its owner and of the head of the Merchants and Manufacturers Association. This meant that there would be some casualties. The leaders were reluctant, but McNamara argued that men must sometimes be sacrificed in a war. "Does a soldier worry about his act if it happens in the line of duty?"[174] The leaders agreed and McNamara set the triple bombing for 1:00 a.m. on 1 October 1910. He had opened up a gas pipe in the basement of the newspaper, and the blast of the bomb combined with the leaked gas caused the building to explode, killing at least 21 workers and injuring more than 100 more. The bombs at the two residences failed to detonate. In his careless way, J. B. McNamara had left many clues behind that eventually led to his arrest as well as that of his brother and McManigal. A remorseful McManigal turned against the brothers, who then pled guilty to avoid the death penalty.

This indiscriminate *Los Angeles Times* bombing horrified the nation and became a cause célèbre among leftists, who rallied behind the McNamara brothers and claimed they had been framed by capital. A socialist candidate for mayor of Los Angeles defended them and was leading in the polls. The brothers' confessions set back the leftist movement countrywide, and their lawyer lost the election in a landslide.

The narrative shows that the brothers' behavior was consistent with the social identity perspective. As union men, they self-categorized in contrast to capital and simply escalated their violence in response to capital's escalation in Los Angeles. Ideology did not motivate them: they were simply trade-unionists, not anarchists or even socialists. Emma Goldman dismissed them as "good Catholics and members of the conservative American Federation of Labor."[175] McManigal wrote, "McNamara and the others claimed that they were waging a war. In a sense they were. I mean that they really thought they were making real war."[176] Their behavior was also consistent with rational choice theory, for they had acted out of self-interest: increased prominence and income in their respective circles.

The Lexington Avenue Explosion

American anarchists were also starting to stir after almost two decades of quiescence. Police brutality at a peaceful anarchist demonstration on 4 April 1914 against widespread unemployment and unfair arrests fired up New York anarchists. The main victim was 30-year-old Arthur Caron, who had lost his job because of his political activities and come to New York during the previous months in search of employment. He was basically homeless, and he was beaten so badly that a judge acquitted him of all charges and urged an investigation of the police department's tactics. The mayor fired the police commissioner and replaced him with a progressive liberal.[177]

News from Ludlow, Colorado, threw fuel on this nascent fire. Trouble between coal miners and owners in the Rockies had been brewing for years. The owners paid miners only for the coal produced and not for digging tunnels or laying down tracks. Hazardous work conditions and explosions had also killed hundreds of workers. In September 1913, the miners went on strike at the Colorado Fuel and Iron Company for safer working conditions and compensation for all their work. As the miners were armed, the governor of Colorado called out the state national guards. With time, the regular units returned home to be replaced by volunteers, who were also company guards and were getting double pay. The day after Orthodox Easter—many of the miners were Greek—national guards and mercenary militia moved in on the miners' tent colony to level it and put an end to the strike. They murdered the miners' leader and, with machine guns, drove the others out of their tents. Then they proceeded to loot the tents and burn them. According to an official report,

"Hundreds of women and children were driven terror stricken into the hills . . . Others huddled for twelve hours in pits underneath their tents . . . while bullets . . . whistled overhead and kept them in constant terrors . . . Mrs. Alcarita Pedregon took refuge with her children where eleven children and two women were suffocated by smoke. She testified that she saw a militiaman set fire to the tent. Mrs. Pedregon was compelled to remain in the hole while she saw two of her children and eleven others slowly die."[178] At least 26 strikers' family members died that day.[179]

The whole country was outraged and none more than anarchists. "With machine guns trained upon the strikers, the best answer is—*dynamite*."[180] Since John Rockefeller, Jr., owned the largest proportion of shares in the Colorado Fuel and Iron Company, they picketed his office in New York. But Rockefeller stopped coming to work and stayed at his home in Tarrytown, New York. On 3 May, Caron and a handful of anarchists went to Tarrytown to picket Rockefeller's estate. They applied for a permit to picket it, but the town refused. On 30 May, Caron and eleven other anarchists, including Carl Hanson and Charles Berg, returned. Hanson and Berg were childhood friends and revolutionaries from Latvia who had recently immigrated and lived in a sixth-floor tenement apartment at 1626 Lexington Avenue, which housed a printing press and was a shelter for passing comrades. Caron often stayed there. When the anarchists tried to make speeches, the Tarrytown police arrested them. Alexander Berkman and a few other anarchists came the next day to protest their comrades' arrest, but they were assaulted and chased away by the town's inhabitants. The twelve anarchist prisoners were kept in jail for a week until Berkman raised their bail money. Their court date was set for 6 July.[181]

Sixty anarchists, including Berkman and the original protestors, returned to Tarrytown on 22 June and were met by a local crowd of about 500 people, which attacked them. Caron, who had not yet recovered from his previous beating, again sustained severe injuries. After returning home, Berkman, Caron, Hanson, and Berg plotted their revenge. According to one of the originally arrested anarchists, "It was Berkman who organized it, though the others were to carry it out, as he was on probation . . . Berkman still believed in the necessity of violence. Caron, Hanson and Berg had been collecting dynamite for Russia and storing it in the apartment." Caron, Hanson, and Berg set out with a bomb for Tarrytown after 1:00 a.m. on 4 July, just before their court date, but returned with it before dawn and crashed at the apartment. It is not known what had prevented them from setting their bomb. "It was not intended for Rockefeller's house but for some other location in Tarrytown, the newspaper office perhaps. There was no intention of harming anyone but only to set off an explosion as a gesture of protest."[182] In the morning of 4 July, a huge explosion blew the roof off the apartment building, collapsed the top

three stories and, besides the three bombers, killed at least two innocent people. The bomb had ignited the rest of the dynamite. Fortunately, the building
was mostly empty, as people had left to celebrate the national holiday. No one
was ever charged in connection to this explosion, which, at that time, was the
most devastating in the city's history.

By the end of the month, the anarchists were displaced from the headlines
by the start of the Great War in Europe. American anarchists were firmly opposed to it and viewed it as a capitalist war using workers as cannon fodder.
Their campaign against the war became increasingly unpopular and elicited
much hostility from zealous patriots itching to get into the war. Parades all
around the country were staged to show America's readiness for war. A bomb
went off on 22 July 1916 at the Preparedness Parade in San Francisco, killing 10
spectators and wounding 40 others. This indiscriminate bombing was another
milestone in the evolution of political violence, as civilians were now the
target.

Leftist radicals were immediately suspected, and Tom Mooney and his
friend Warren Billings were arrested. Mooney was a 33-year-old anarchist and
union organizer, and Billings was a 23-year-old union member. Mooney had
been tried already three times and eventually acquitted of possession of explosives. Although not an anarchist, he was a friend and confidant of Berkman,
who had moved to San Francisco. Billings had previously been convicted of
assault with a deadly weapon on a strikebreaker. The two were framed by local
authorities, convicted in separate trials despite obvious perjury and suppression of evidence, and sentenced to hang. For diplomatic reasons, President
Wilson asked the judge to commute their sentence to life in prison, which he
did. Through their frame-up, Mooney and Billings became martyrs of the left.[183]

Due to poor investigation, this bombing is still unsolved. Through interviews with undisclosed sources, however, historian Paul Avrich became convinced that it was committed by the Gruppo Anarchico Volonta, disciples of
Luigi Galleani, who later claimed at his deportation hearing that he knew who
the perpetrators were but refused to denounce them.[184]

The Luigi Galleani Group

Luigi Galleani,[185] an Italian anarchist, had immigrated to the United States at
the age of 40 in 1901. Two years later, he started the newspaper *Cronaco Sovversiva*, which preached rejection of private property and all authority, including the state and trade unions, and advocated a militant form of anarchism as
well as propaganda, by the deed if necessary, including assassinations and the
use of dynamite. He became especially popular among young Italian

immigrants, and soon his followers numbered in the thousands. Industrial strikes, like the "Bread and Roses" strike in Lawrence, Massachusetts,[186] forged a shared social identity among them. They supported spontaneous strikes and demonstrations, which spurred them to become active in furthering their collective goals. They established a strong network of local circles linked to each other through the announcements in *Cronaca Sovversiva*. Most circles met at least weekly to discuss political developments, raise money for the cause, listen to lectures from visiting anarchists, and socialize at picnics and political plays, which glorified their martyrs, modeled heroic actions, and helped establish norms for their subculture. These meetings made them believe that anarchism was real, because they were living it in their everyday lives. The mutual aid they provided for one another helped them develop a strong feeling of solidarity. These dispersed Galleani circles created a countercultural political protest community. They opposed the war in Europe, and some of them were briefly detained during antiwar demonstrations.[187]

On 6 April 1917, the United States declared war on Germany and its allies. The Selective Service Act required males between the ages of 21 and 30 to register with the draft board, but the young Galleanists refused to do so. The Espionage Act of 1917 prohibited any interference with military operations or recruitment. Entry into war unleashed a popular hysteria against anyone deemed unpatriotic. Mobs roughed up anarchists, disrupted their meetings, raided their clubhouses, demolished their equipment, and destroyed their libraries and files. Many anarchists went into hiding. On the basis of the Espionage Act, the federal government arrested anyone allegedly conspiring to interfere with the draft, including anarchists Emma Goldman and Alexander Berkman.[188]

Events in Europe like the Russian Revolution made the Galleanists believe that the revolution would spread to Italy. As young activists and idealists, they yearned to go back to Italy and make revolution. About 60 self-selected Galleanists from all over the United States left for Mexico and met in the city of Monterrey.[189] Among them were 25-year-old Ferdinando Sacco, 29-year-old Bartolomeo Vanzetti, 33-year-old Mario Buda, and 22-year-old Carlo Valdinoci, all from the Boston area. They were determined to fight as soldiers in the upcoming revolution, covering themselves with glory and emulating their heroes and martyrs. They lived communally, sharing everything. During these few weeks, they forged a special relationship, forming a core of ultra-militants, distinguished from other Galleanists.[190] After a few weeks, they realized that new developments in Italy did not favor their hoped-for revolution. They could not find work and their savings were depleted. Letters from home told them about high wages due to increased war demands and the relative ease of evading registration. They clandestinely slipped back into the United States.[191]

On 9 September 1917, in Milwaukee, an Italian Evangelical pastor gave a sermon on "loyalty" in favor of the draft. When he finished, local anarchists rushed the stage to tear down the American flag. The police fired at them, killing two and seriously injuring a third. They roughed up and arrested 11 more and charged them with instigating a riot.[192] The militants in Mexico were outraged at the persecution of their companions. For these militants, this outrage was the last straw, coming on top of Galleani's arrest in June 1917, which symbolized the persecution of their companions. To them, what was at stake was nothing less than "the right to exist," and their honor demanded that this state aggression be avenged. A conspiracy emerged based on their new self-categorization as an elite group ready to combat state repression.[193]

On 24 November 1917, a cleaning woman discovered a large pipe bomb in the basement of the pastor's church. The police were notified, and they took the bomb back to their station. In a repeat of the rue des Bons-Enfants explosion in Paris,[194] the detectives were handling the device when it exploded. The bomb killed ten detectives and a woman and seriously injured six more.[195] The Milwaukee 11, who had been in jail for two months, were tried four days later on new charges of contributing to the policemen's deaths. They were convicted after only 17 minutes of jury deliberation and sentenced to the maximum 25 years in prison.[196]

The conflict continued to escalate. Valdinoci went to Milwaukee, where he placed a bomb at the house of the presiding judge over the trial of the Milwaukee 11, but it failed to detonate.[197] The trail of clues led to *Cronaca Sovversiva*, and its offices were raided in February 1918. The police found the names of most of its subscribers and three months later conducted a large sweep of all Galleanists. The paper was banned in July 1918. In January 1919, the acting secretary of labor signed a warrant for deportation against Galleani and his followers.[198] Anonymous leaflets warned, "Deport us! *We will dynamite you!*"[199]

The year 1919 was one of violent labor unrest as soldiers flooded the labor market and workers demanded better pay—they had agreed to a voluntary pay freeze for the duration of the war. Believing that Bolsheviks were trying to take over the United States, Authorities panicked and severely suppressed strikes during this Red Scare.[200] Valdinoci and Buda decided to send parcel bombs to 30 prominent people who were especially hostile to their group and connected to deportation of undesirable immigrants. The packages were mailed to be delivered on May Day. However, two arrived early and one blew up the kitchen of the home of a former Georgia senator who had sponsored the Immigration Act, severely injuring his black maid and burning his wife. An alert postal clerk recognized the rest of the packages, which were then defused.[201]

After the failure of the May Day bombings, Valdinoci and Buda distributed nine more bombs to their companions. On the evening of 2 June 1919, the bombs went off nearly simultaneously in New York, Paterson, Philadelphia, Cleveland, Washington, Boston, and Pittsburgh. In each city, the pattern was the same. The bomb was left on the doorstep of a person connected with the prosecution of Galleanists. Despite the fact that all the bombs detonated and caused extensive damage, there were no human injuries, except for Valdinoci, who blew himself up on the steps of Attorney General Palmer's townhouse in the capital when his bomb exploded prematurely.[202]

Valdinoci's death demoralized his companions, and plans for further bombings were put on hold. A wave of repression forced the Galleanists to go underground or leave the country ahead of inevitable deportations: Sacco, Buda, and Vanzetti got Italian passports to return home.[203] The deportation proceedings accelerated: Luigi Galleani sailed back to Italy on 24 June 1919.[204] Public opinion rallied behind the government's brutal repression of radicals to reestablish order at whatever cost to civil rights. Between November 1919 and February 1920, thousands of people were brutally rounded up without warrants, based on questionable undercover informants and extorted confessions. About 3,000 aliens went through these proceedings and were denied counsel. On 21 December 1919, after two and a half years of incarceration for opposing the war, Emma Goldman and Alexander Berkman were deported back to Russia after more than 30 years in the United States. By spring 1920, cooler heads came to the fore. A new assistant secretary of labor took charge of deportation matters and, appalled by the gross injustices, canceled 2,000 warrants.[205]

After a few months, the Justice Department Bureau of Investigation tracked down the leaflets in the bombs to a print shop and arrested its workers, who were brutally beaten. On 3 May 1920, one of them fell from a 14th-floor window to his death. The papers claimed that he committed suicide because he had revealed the names of all his co-conspirators. This scared Sacco and Vanzetti, who resolved to get rid of the rest of the dynamite. They were arranging for a car to transport it when they were arrested two days later.[206] They assumed that they were being arrested for either the bombings or being anarchists, making them subject to deportation. Instead, they were charged with murdering and robbing two employees of a shoe company transporting the company payroll. A local detective suspected the murderers of being Galleanists and arrested the pair when they tried to get a car. Because of their evasiveness and lies about not being anarchists, the police became convinced that they were the murderers of the payroll couriers.[207]

Galleanists were outraged at these events. They did not believe in their companion's suicide and were convinced that the authorities had murdered him.[208] They were indignant about Sacco and Vanzetti's arrests on common criminal charges. It was acceptable and even a mark of honor to be arrested on political charges, but an insult to their honor to be facing common criminal charges. As Sacco later said, "If I was arrested because of the Idea I am glad to suffer. If I must I will die for it. But they have arrested me for a gunman job."[209]

On 11 September 1920, Sacco and Vanzetti were indicted for the double murder of the payroll couriers.[210] This was too much for Buda. He was outraged at the persecution of the "best friends I had in America"[211] and decided to strike back. He went to New York and bought a horse and wagon. He loaded a large dynamite bomb with a timer in the wagon and filled it with iron slugs. On 16 September 1920, he drove it to Wall Street, parked it next to the J. P. Morgan and Company building, and left. Around noon, the bomb exploded, killing 38 people and seriously wounding hundreds more, as well as inflicting $2 million in property damage.[212] Like the *Los Angeles Times* and Preparedness Day bombings, the Wall Street bombing indiscriminately targeted civilians. With these events, political violence reached the point of indiscriminate murder for political goals.

The wave of Galleani bombings in 1916–20 consisted of more than 40 bomb attentats in more than 20 cities, killing at least 60 people and injuring hundreds (if we include the Preparedness Day bombing). Nine anarchists died in them. After deportations or voluntary departures, the Italian anarchist movement in the United States went into a sharp decline. The task of defending Sacco and Vanzetti completely overwhelmed the few who remained. They faced great popular hostility and could no longer enjoy their large and merry get-togethers. Their children moved into mainstream society and did not join the movement. Old companions still met and reminisced about old times, but the movement was drained of its vitality and faded away.

The Galleani militants who had gone to Mexico self-categorized as soldiers for the revolution after their disillusionment with the possibility of peaceful protest against the war and draft. Their actual turn to violence followed their moral outrage at state aggression against companions in Milwaukee and was an act of revenge. As the state escalated its repression of the Galleani group, there was a parallel escalation in the group's violence, from narrowly targeted retaliation against specific aggressors against the group to more indiscriminate bombings. Neither the ideological thesis nor rational choice theory can explain this escalation.

Chapter 8

Policy Implications

At this point, the reader may wonder whether the model for the turn to political violence presented here is generalizable to other campaigns of political violence, especially the recent global neojihadi campaigns against the West, including those of al Qaeda and the Islamic State of Iraq and the Levant (ISIL). In the appendix, I test this model against an expanded sample of politically violent campaigns that include several Islamist groups and show that they conform to this model. I believe that the insights developed through this historical survey hold important implications for policy, and here I offer my recommendations for preventing or ending campaigns of political violence.

Preventing Political Violence

My main argument is that political violence emerges out of a political protest community. Under conditions of escalation of conflict between the state and this community, disillusionment with peaceful protest, and moral outrage at state aggression against this community, a few of its members self-categorize into soldiers and turn to violence to protect it. Each of these factors includes a large state component: its escalation of conflict and rhetorical extremism, its rejection of peaceful demands to redress protestors' grievances, and its disproportionate aggression against them. Therefore it is impossible to analyze non-state political violence without taking into account a state's contribution to its emergence. Political violence can be understood only in a dialectical relationship between a state and political protestors, in the context of an escalation of their conflict. This dynamic implies that the turn to political violence is not a linear process as it depends on the actions of the state, against which political protestors define themselves. The state influences historical and social contingencies that give the path to political violence a "fits and starts" pattern, with intense periods of activity when moral outrage demands quick retaliation separated by longer periods of relative calm. This study further argues that a double self-categorization in contrast to the state is at the core of the process of turning to political violence. Self-categorization is a natural and automatic process, part of human nature. As such, it is impossible to eliminate. However, it is possible to influence the content of self-categorization by changing its most important context—the behavior of the state.

The neglect of this sensitive issue of state contribution to the emergence of political violence is especially unfortunate because it prevents policy-makers from seeing a whole range of effective interventions against political violence. This is crucial because it is much easier to change state policies than to change human nature. By becoming aware of its contribution, the state can learn from past mistakes in its management of political violence and correct them. In addition, this awareness opens new horizons for new possible intervention along the path to political violence to prevent its emergence or to end it.

The following remarks are addressed to the state for three reasons. First, as just mentioned, it is easier to correct state policies than change human nature. Second, the state has control over its policies and their implementation but not over protestors' behavior. Finally, the state is responsible for the maintenance of public peace and this duty includes the promotion of policies minimizing the risk of violence. In this section, I recommend policies designed to prevent the outbreak of political violence while in the last section I address policies to end campaigns of political violence. In no way do the following remarks condone some of the despicable actions of political challengers or diminish their responsibility for the escalation to violence through hate speech, provocations, and advocacy and use of violence.

The main goal of the state is to protect its constituency through its monopoly on the use of legitimate violence within its territory. As citizens give up their ability to personally redress their grievances through violence, they expect the state to be fair and impartial in dispensing justice and to preserve their civil rights. Indeed, the essence of Western liberal democracies is enshrined in these rights, which face their most severe test in times of domestic political violence when states are tempted to suspend them. Western liberal democracies must not fall into this natural temptation, but, on the contrary, honor these rights to prevent or end the violence.

The process of turning to political violence starts with a grievance, which activates a politicized social identity in contrast to the state and perhaps society, resulting in a political protest community. This suggests that the first possible state intervention is to prevent this self-categorization in contrast to its agents. To prevent this first step, the state must respect legitimate protest. As shown in many historical illustrations, police brutality against demonstrators activates this political self-categorization. Fair and effective crowd policing according to the social identity perspective, which is gaining popularity among various police departments, is an important step in preventing violence. SIP researchers are already teaching law enforcement agencies responsible for policing large international events to effectively control the expected enormous crowds.[1] Such training should be mandatory for state agents dealing with political protest, so as not to inadvertently spark a campaign of political violence.

At the very least, the state must prevent private disputes from becoming political through unwarranted state intervention on the side of privileged institutions such as the use of police or military to quash student or labor unrest. It must stay neutral and allow protestors to voice their grievances and negotiate fairly with their respective institutions. Some grievances are political from the start, especially in a diverse constituency composed of multiple ethnic, sectarian, occupational, industrial, immigrant, and political interests. The state must ensure that each has proportional and fair representation in the political arena.

Once grievances become political, the state must take them seriously and, at the very least, listen to protestors in order to avoid their disillusionment with the political process and consolidation into a more militant political protest community. Of course, the state cannot give in to all parochial grievances, but it must make all of its constituents feel that they have a voice in the overall polity even when the ultimate decision goes against them. This can be achieved only through a fair and transparent process of decision making which prevents aggrieved citizens from becoming disillusioned by the political process.

The state must ensure that all members of a country feel included as full members by treating them equally. Recent immigrants present a special challenge as they are not yet integrated into the host society, but the state should not be perceived as discriminating against them and alienating them further from it. Once immigrants achieve citizenship, they should be treated like any other citizen. The state must craft a sense of national identity that includes all its constituent segments, embracing the diversity of a nation rather than endorsing a nativist and essentialist prototype of citizenship. If all members of a country, including those with political grievances, are made to feel that the state treats them as fully and equally entitled citizens, this will prevent the emergence of a community that self-categorizes in contrast to the state and the rest of society. Of course, individuals have disagreements, but they can still feel part of the group.

The model suggests that the cumulative radicalization of discourse by both contentious groups helps escalate tension between them to the point of violence. State agents must resist the temptation to demonize dissidents and speak about them in dehumanizing and extremist terms. The state should discourage the rest of society from using defamatory anti-protest speech and indeed even allow protestors to sue for defamation the most extreme anti-protest champions whipping up anti-protest hysteria and fear. Indeed, the state should be especially vigilant against a shift to extremism toward protestors among its own agents since this is a natural phenomenon in the face of radicalized protest speech. State agents should be trained to resist the temptation of self-categorization as champions of society against legitimate protest. The tendency to assume this role and its associated extremist speech reached its height in the Terror during the French Revolution and the various red scares throughout American history. Milder forms of extremist speech by the state were ubiquitous in the run-up to all the other campaigns of domestic political violence studied except for the unprovoked attacks of foreign diaspora communities.[2] The model predicts that elimination of anti-protest extremist speech disempowers extremists in a protest community as social influence remains with champions of cooperation.

The model also implies that out-group overt propaganda efforts on in-group members have negligible impact because they are immediately rejected as biased. Criticism of a political protest community must come from inside, from in-group prototypes, to have any credibility. The meta-contrast principle suggests that out-groups can have an indirect impact on in-group members: cooperative or belligerent speech by the state shifts social influence to corresponding prominent in-group advocates. The surest way to empower political extremists is for the state to verbally attack the group by using radical rhetoric. Instead, the state should empower moderates in the protest community by suggesting cooperative means to solve their grievances.

Once its discourse has crossed a radical threshold, the state must tone it back to a more measured one to influence protestors' speech. At first, extreme talk by challengers is mostly just talk, spoken in frustration. In contrast to absolute autocracies, liberal democracies should not treat such talk as a crime;[3] doing so would escalate tension. The acquittal of ideologues in the 1894 Trial of the 30 in France defused the escalation of violence between the state and anarchists and contributed to the end of the era of attentats.[4] In contrast, American prosecution of violent speech contributed to sustaining a campaign of violence at the turn of the past century.

American law treats a verbal agreement to carry out an illegal act as a crime, even if there is no act in furtherance. The vagueness of this conspiracy law allows threats uttered in frustration and anger to count as a felony even after tempers have cooled and nothing has happened. The prosecution of such utterances, which are ubiquitous in human emotional life, is viewed as patently unfair by protestors, who may retaliate against the state. Such threats should not go totally unpunished, as they frame further escalation of violence.

I suggest that they be treated as civil, not criminal, wrongs just like defamation. I am also skeptical about the effectiveness of criminal prosecution for "glorification of terrorism" now seen in Britain or France. This increases protestors' anger against the state, especially if this litigation is applied unfairly and exclusively against a specific segment of society—targeting Muslim extremists and not nativist extremists. These prosecutions have the potential to escalate violence and bring about the very situation the law hopes to avert. "Preachers of hate" should be tried for defamation in civil and not criminal court.

It is imperative for the state to avoid committing especially egregious acts of aggression against a political protest community, creating martyrs and triggering calls for violent retaliations, which fuels violence. It behooves the state to train its agents to be disciplined enough to avoid these outrageous violations. As violence escalates, such violations are inevitable, but when state agents transgress, the state must react aggressively to hold them responsible for their actions in a fair and transparent process. Impunity for state agents, who clearly broke the law, is bound to generate an escalation of protest, as was the case after various anarchist trials in the United States and recent police killings of unarmed African Americans in this country. When state agents murder innocent protestors or mete out capital punishment for minor offenses they must be held responsible to simmer down protestors' boiling anger. The state cannot afford to allow its agents to close ranks behind their own wrongdoers and avoid punishment. Injustice with impunity is a recipe for moral outrage and leads to political violence.

After mutual escalation of hostilities inspires a few protestors to volunteer as soldiers protecting their community and cross into violence, the state must adopt a strategy of fair protection of the population. The goal should be to prevent mass casualties while safeguarding civil rights and to prevent the emergence of a campaign of violence. This means that societal protection must be accomplished within limits, preserving protestors' civil rights as much as possible. This strategy dampens the volume of ever louder calls for increased retaliation from all sides and ratchets down violence. The opposite strategy may well lead to a campaign of violence, as martyrs created through unfair and disproportionate state tactics inspire their comrades to escalate to violence.

Ending Campaigns of Political Violence

Once a campaign of political violence has started, attempts to end it must be based on an understanding of the factors that perpetuate it. In this concluding section, I examine first the dynamics of campaigns of political violence and then policies aimed at ending them by interrupting this spiral of violence.

Dynamics of Campaigns of Violence

For most perpetrators studied in this volume, the first instance of violence was their last, as they died in the process or were arrested. These single attentats did not evolve into campaigns of violence. For the few who survived their first attentat[5] and those who inspired others to imitate them,[6] violence acquired an unintended dynamic of its own. Once its threshold is crossed, violence over-shadows all other aspects of group conflict. Revolutionary organizations ne-glect their peaceful social programs of recruiting the masses to their cause. Violence attracts just a few people in society and alienates them from the vast majority. The exception to this general rule is when the larger society is un-fairly ruled by a small minority easily distinguishable from the rest of society, like foreign imperialists or a distinctive ethnic or confessional elite. In these cases, violence and state retaliation may polarize society in support of the challengers viewed as part of the societal in-group against the ruling minority out-group. The size of this self-categorized native group eventually over-whelms the ruling minority. In cases of colonialism, this results in independence from the imperial power. In cases of ethnic or religious minority rule, this ends in majority rule.[7] However, in the vast majority of domestic political violence, although violence may be emotionally satisfying to counter disillusionment and address moral outrage, it is generally a self-defeating strategy for communities hoping to redress parochial grievances.

Violence also corrupts moral values, as all actors cut corners in pursuit of their goals. Vera Figner of People's Will described this insidious process: "It arouses ferocity, develops brutal instincts, awakens evil impulses and prompts acts of disloyalty. Humanity and magnanimity are incompatible with it . . . All methods were fair in the war with its antagonist, that here the end justifies the means. At the same time, it created a cult of dynamite and the revolver, and crowned the terrorist with a halo; murder and the scaffold acquired a mag-netic charm and attraction for the youth of the land, and . . . the more oppres-sive the life around them, the greater was their exaltation at the thought of revolutionary terror."[8]

Political challengers' violence brings about a mirror bloodlust in society and its official agents who, in this context, do not view themselves so much as guardians of the peace but as agents of retribution avenging the victims of po-litical violence (their in-group). The meta-contrast principle predicts that pro-testors' violence shifts social influence to more extreme state agents advocating intense repression and punishment against aggressors. These agents sacrifice reconciliation and potential peace for pure revenge. Their views gain popularity with the public, which undergoes a similar extremity shift. Violence polarizes the social world, hardens the respective belligerents' positions, and minimizes the possibility of political compromise. This is contrary to rational choice theory, which predicts that dissidents' use of violence or its threat should force the state to make concessions for their grievances. Instead, as the previous chapters show, violence forced the public and government agents to focus on the threat challengers posed and not their grievances.

Increased and more effective state repression supported by society drives all violent protestors, as well as those believed to be violent, underground into fugitive and clandestine trajectories, which narrows their cognitive horizons to an obsession about carrying out their violent mission at all costs, to the exclusion of everything else.[9] Obsession is the correct term here, for multiple failures, arrests, and deaths no longer deter them from continuing to the bitter end.[10] It is as if the violent goal takes control of these groups, their lives, their thoughts, their efforts, and their emotions. There are many temptations to continue to escalate and very few to scale back.

This obsession is consistent with the recent dual-processing theory of cognition.[11] Having a definite goal in mind focuses attention selectively on the goal and filters out irrelevant cues. This attentional blindness has been demonstrated in laboratories and real life for individuals, but not groups. Nevertheless, it is easy to imagine that groups of individuals sharing common identity and cognitive focus might harmonize their individual and largely unconscious cognitive mechanisms, which make it appear that their specific goal is in charge of their behavior. This reverses our intuition that our conscious executive self is in full control of these goal-oriented behaviors.[12]

The physical danger faced by both political challengers and state agents leads them to zealously support their respective comrades in the fight against their enemy. This esprit de corps, unlike any other in intensity, trumps any abstract political goals. At this stage, people fight more for their comrades than for the cause.[13] Suicide is the ultimate sacrifice for one's buddies and transforms one into an instant hero. The conflict becomes an end in itself, and violence then degenerates into banditry.[14]

An interesting empirical finding was that the completion of the military goal turned off this obsessive drive. Several campaigns of political violence ended with perpetrators' spectacular successes.[15] It seems that they had a feeling of unfinished business that prevented them from stopping until the accomplishment of their paramilitary goals. Even in the absence of any political concessions, they reached a sense of balance that quenched their lust for further violence. Having attained this intermediary military goal, they could afford to take a rest and even a step back to evaluate what they had done in the larger scheme of things and see whether more violence furthered or hindered the achievement of their larger political goals.

This dynamic of violence leads to continuous campaigns of political violence. This is especially true under the following conditions: political grievances persist; the state cannot eradicate the political protest community because it is too large; the violent protestors' active core survives; the state engages in indiscriminate repression of the protest community, with unfair harsh punishment of its members; and the state prevents nonviolent protestors from returning to normal life by declaring them outlaws—in essence making impermeable the boundaries between the protest community and society. All these measures put pressure on violent political protestors to organize into clandestine formal organizations with their own hierarchy, security, secrecy, and discipline, and to narrow their social horizons for long-term survival.[16] Violence is also sustained by internal dynamics, namely the need for leaders to foil ever more radical rivals for leadership of their paramilitary organization and to keep up the morale of their group to avoid its members' discouragement and exit.

Ending Campaigns of Political Violence in Western Liberal Democracies

This brings us to the issue of ending campaigns of political violence. There have been relatively few studies on this issue. One study reported that 43 percent of politically violent groups adopt nonviolent tactics and join the political process, 40 percent are eradicated by the police and another 7 percent by the military, and 10 percent achieve victory.[17] Another study listed five endings: decapitation of leadership; negotiations and transition to a legitimate political party; success in achieving the objective; failure in terms of implosion, provoking a backlash, or becoming marginalized; repression with force; and transitioning to another type of violence, such as banditry, insurgency, or war.[18]

These two large surveys are very insightful, but they sacrifice the details of each case for quantity. Their shortcomings emerge in the context of detailed historical descriptions. Most political violence consists of one-time events easily repressed by the police because of lack of support for violence within the protest community. But sometimes, the same community may give rise to multiple campaigns of political violence simultaneously or over time with different results and temporary interruptions, not permanent endings. For instance, the sans-culottes were temporarily successful in helping the Montagne capture power leading to the Terror, but ultimately were defeated by a reaction of police, National Guards, army, and paramilitary units systematically arresting and disarming them. However, this political protest community was not eradicated and gave rise to the Babeuf conspiracy a year later and an 1800 Enragé attentat. It reemerged 20 years later in the unsuccessful Carbonari conspiracies and 10 years later in the successful 1830 insurrection. This populist republican community suffered defeats in the 1832 and 1834 insurrections, which shifted violence from mass insurrection to smaller conspiratorial attentats that occurred over the next decade. It again found success in the insurrection of February 1848 before the French army violently put it down four months later, temporarily ending this type of political violence for two decades. It became resurrected in 1869 and especially in 1871 when this protest community ruled Paris under the Commune. The French army again destroyed it in the May 1871 "Bloody Week" and a wave of deportation. Violence from this evolving community reemerged in the 1880s, culminating in the early 1890s era of the attentats, which was ended by police repression, but also by fair trials that exonerated protestors not involved in violence, despite the notorious Scoundrel Laws. There was a brief reemergence of violence with the tragic bandits 20 years later, which the police, helped by the army, put down. This vague republican, liberal, and egalitarian political protest community, from sans-culottes to anarchists, lasted for more than 125 years until World War I.[19] The violence occasionally emerging from it had a fits-and-starts trajectory of short bursts of intense activity followed by longer periods of relative calm, some brief successes and some temporary endings through police repression, bloody army repression, and relatively fair trials in 1894 and 1913, respectively.

A similar prolonged and complicated trajectory characterized the half century of democratic and liberal opposition to the tsar. Russian populists, repressed by the police, gave rise to People's Will, which was temporarily eliminated by the state. Five years after its demise, the Terrorist Faction of People's Will appeared briefly for one attentat. Finally, the Combat Unit of the Socialist Revolutionary Party emerged again 15 years later and self-destructed with the betrayal of its leader. However, its parent party survived to be part of the coalition that overthrew the tsarist regime in 1917, a victory made possible by the state's defeat in war.

I suspect that the two surveys mentioned would break up the complex reality of the larger French campaign of political violence into seven smaller ones and the Russian campaign into five smaller ones. Reality is messier than the neat categories presented in these two surveys. In fact, the French and Russian campaigns of violence stemming from a given political protest community never fully ended: they were temporarily defeated, only to reemerge again and again. With basic grievances not addressed, unfair police repression did not succeed in completely ending political violence, because it could not prevent new volunteers from restarting a new campaign a few years later.

Nevertheless, we should not dismiss the value of these two surveys. The empirical chapters give examples of some of their endings. Success was temporarily achieved by the French sans-culottes and republican insurrections of 1830 and February 1848 and with the establishment of a Duma in 1906 in Russia. Anarchists moved into trade unions, joining the political process to deal with grievances. Bloody military repression ended the insurrections of 1795, 1832, 1834, June 1848, and 1871 in France and of December 1905 in Moscow. Failure in terms of implosion through internal rivalries leading to self-destruction occurred among French anarchists in the early twentieth century. Degeneration into banditry contributed to the end of the Chouans and the tragic bandits. General collapse of law and order into temporary failed states ended campaigns of political violence in the summer of 1792 in France and in 1905 in Russia. Eradication of a political protest community was achieved through the deportation of the Communards and Galleanists. Eradication is a high-risk strategy and works only if the protest community is small enough. If it is too large to eradicate, such efforts almost guarantee a sustained campaign of violence, as was seen in the emergence of People's Will when the tsarist state tried to eradicate Land and Liberty. Other possible endings, not included in the above categories, are the removal of grievances, such as the abolition of royal absolutism or the end of a war, as in the more recent example of the Vietnam War, whose conclusion eliminated support for the Weathermen; and political developments unconnected with the belligerent group that undermine the rationale for violence such as the popular election of a Duma in Russia, which led the PSR to dissolve its Combat Unit twice.

In addition to the above list, the historical narratives uncovered two other state strategies to end political violence, which are better understood through the prism of the social identity perspective. The first is undermining the meaning of the challengers' social identity through betrayal by a prominent leader, which disillusions the rest of the violent in-group. This was the case for the PSR Combat Unit, which never recovered from Azef's betrayal. This was also the case with the Fenian Skirmishers in the 1880s, whose leadership was completely infiltrated by British agents.[20] While a simple betrayal by a member reaffirms one's self-categorization and leads to anger against the traitor, as seen in the black sheep effect, the betrayal by a prototype is perhaps too devastating for groups to survive.

Another campaign-ending strategy is to craft an overriding social identity whose salience trumps that of the in-group. This happens most frequently in foreign wars, which force members of a nation to rally around the state. This occurred in Russia in 1863, when Russian nationalist social identity trumped that of the nihilists during the Polish insurrection, and in France in 1914, when the German danger trumped that of French capitalism and many anarchists joined the French army. Proximity to the danger was probably important; in the United States, the threat of distant Germans was too small for American anarchists to displace the salience of their anarchist social identity, in contrast to their European comrades.

Most often, campaigns of political violence are ended through enlightened state strategy breaking the cycle of violence. This involves the focused and proportional repression against actual law breakers, in essence decapitation of the protest community by the fair removal of the violent protestors; return to justice and fairness through impartial and transparent procedural justice with reasonable punishments; and procedures for valid grievances to be addressed in a legitimate way. Indeed, the SIP argues that fair and respectful treatment of all societal members, especially impartiality to its minority factions, is the defining characteristic of good national leadership, for it fosters a common social identity, holds the nation together, and encourages compliance with laws, commitment to the nation, and citizens' sacrifice for it.[21]

Mutual escalation of conflict contributes to the emergence and continuation of campaigns of violence. The key here is for the state to assess the threat accurately and not overreact. Accurate evaluation of the threat requires analysts who resist self-categorization as society's champions and good intelligence on protestors, especially potentially violent ones. The state should distinguish simple political protestors, who are generally nonviolent, from violent ones.[22] Confusion about them leads to unfair punishment of legitimate and peaceful dissent, which is often the first step to an escalation of violence.

Distinguishing between peaceful and violent protestors may be difficult. The boundary between them is generally fluid and porous, not rigid and impermeable. Activists may go back and forth between them, depending on the context. Being violent in one context does not imply violence in another, like violent Russian populists, who killed traitors within their ranks but later joined Black Partition which rejected the central terrorism of People's Will. In general, violence is quite rare in the larger political community, which is generally hostile to violence and its members who carry it out. The state should not prevent activists who have temporarily considered violence from going back to their peaceful activism. By declaring them outlaws and prosecuting such activists, by making the porous boundary between peaceful and violent protestors impermeable, the state needlessly turns temporary frustration and temptation to use violence into real violence, as targeted activists go underground and turn to violence with their fellow fugitives. Furthermore, disproportionate punishment by the state turns them into martyrs, inspiring others to become violent. This is especially true in the United States, where conspiracy laws are so vague that they allow prosecution of people who have never been violent or committed any acts of furtherance. Instead, the state should try to bring such activists tempted by violence back into the fold by encouraging them to rejoin their peaceful colleagues. This requires creative skills but is the essence of good leadership.

If the state has probable cause to believe that segments of a political protest community are turning violent, its public protection mission requires it to monitor this threat through surveillance. Intrusive measures violating citizens' civil rights and privacy should be sanctioned through due legal process by having impartial judges issue warrants for them. Systems in place throughout the West allow only law enforcement agencies to present evidence before such courts, and this one-sided process has to change, for state agents inevitably exaggerate the threat of their targets,[23] leaving judges at the mercy of biased information. Cleared public advocates must be able to secretly represent the interests of targets of such surveillance without arousing these targets' suspicion in order to counter state agencies' biases. Good surveillance does not need to be limited to electronic monitoring of suspected violent protestors but may also include infiltration of their networks. It is crucial that this monitoring be passive. State agents must be careful to remain vigilant observers and not become agents provocateurs, influencing naïve protestors to commit violence that they would never have committed on their own, and creating crimes where none would have ever emerged. Entrapment is based on the myth of predisposition to political violence.[24] The previous chapters clearly show that such predisposition is very rare. Instead, the model presented here suggests that naïve victims of entrapment emulate the agent provocateur, who presents him- or herself as a prototypical terrorist and a source of imitation for the victim.

Entrapment erodes a whole segment of society's trust in the state, for it views this tactic as a deceptive aggression against it and activates this segment's politicized self-categorization in contrast to state agents, increasing the size of a political protest community. Within it, such tactics empower extremists claiming that the state is at war against it, which escalates the violence. Indeed, so far I have found no evidence that entrapment tactics have prevented any attacks against society.[25] Without any clear benefit other than the bureaucratic imperative of bringing closure to ongoing investigations, sting operations foster distrust and disillusionment in a targeted community, increase the number of political protestors, escalate the conflict by putting naïve wannabes in prison for a very long time, and probably lead a few of its members to engage in violence. The United States is the only Western country commonly using such tactics against political protest communities. Instead, the state must retain or regain protestors' confidence that they can address their grievances through legitimate means. In its attempt to retain this trust, there is no role for deceptive practices like sting operations.

When countering real threats, and especially when arresting entrapped naïve protestors, the state must resist the temptation to indulge in gratuitous self-promotion. The media and politicians seldom pass up any opportunity to embellish and sensationalize news events and create an echo chamber fueling hysteria and panic in society over rather negligible threats.[26] Elimination of a national security threat can be accomplished without jingoistic flag waving. Self-generated frenzied alarmism not only escalates violence but also leads states to make drastic mistakes like the 2003 invasion of Iraq.

Contrary to alarmists' fears, the incidence of violence emerging from a political protest community is extremely small. The main challenge for the intelligence community is to detect the very small number of attacks from a sea of false alarms. This is especially true in this current global neojihadi threat in the West. A survey of all global neojihadi plots and attacks in the West in the post-9/11 decade shows that there were 66 attacks or serious plots involving 220 individuals.[27] If we assume a Muslim population of about 25 million in the West, this works out to less than one global neo-jihadi terrorist per million Muslims per year in the West. Since most Muslims in the West are not religious and well integrated, let us take 10 percent of the self-proclaimed most religious militants as a reference sample. This would amount to a base rate of less than 1 per 100,000 per year in this segment of the Western Muslim community, or about one-fifth of the homicide rate in the United States.[28] With such a low base rate, the rate of error of detecting a potential global neo-jihadi terrorist from this most extreme Muslim community is enormous.

This very low base rate of global neo-jihadi terrorist violence in the West makes talk of the "war on terror" particularly irresponsible by Western states. While such extremist speech encourages the majority of the public to take this metaphor seriously and enthusiastically support its politicians, especially at election time, such talk also leads it to acquiesce in the unjust and unfair treatment of Muslims in the West. This alienates some Muslims, who no longer feel part of the nation and a few may eventually seek revenge for their perceived persecution not only against the state but more indiscriminately against society.

Likewise, the present debate over national security versus civil rights conundrum is an oversimplification of the issues. There is no inherent contradiction between the two competing rights or permanent boundary dividing them. Any dividing line between them necessarily moves according to the context: in times of great danger, one must err toward national security; when the danger is past, civil rights must be reestablished. Citizens must always be on guard against governments' tendency to make alarmist statements disproportionate to the real danger to artificially maintain a state of emergency for the sake of convenience in their protective mission. This may lead to tyranny, as demonstrated by the Terror in France.

The United States is probably the most punitive Western nation, incarcerating almost 1 percent of its population. Its strategy against potentially violent protestors is likewise very punitive, in terms of not only likelihood of incarceration but duration as well. A good leader tries to prevent protestors from crossing into violence, not with the threat of punishment but by bringing them back to the national fold. The SIP implies that threatening political protestors escalates a conflict and increases the probability of violence, while reintegrating them back into the national community defuses it. This second strategy, crafting a common sense of shared national identity, would prevent wannabes from crossing into violence, for one does not attack one's buddies—except for traitors. Violent perpetrators against society do not see society as their in-group. In fact, crafting an inclusive sense of social identity is part of good leadership.

If the state is facing a foreign threat,[29] its strategy must be the proportional and focused retribution against the specific perpetrators, and containment of the threat. The state must not panic and conflate multiple local threats into a coordinated global one, like the myth of the Black [anarchist] International of the late nineteenth century. Likewise, at present, many people conflate many local insurgencies in the developing world into one gigantic al Qaeda or ISIL entity with local franchises. Instead, the state must deal with each threat in an appropriate, measured, and targeted way without missing potential international connections.[30]

Most political violence is domestic. Here the state must calibrate measures to counter the threat according to the size and imminence of the danger. When the threat is probable, the state may request an exceptional waiver from usual policing practices from special courts to use more active measures to prevent the threat. These active measures may extend to preventive detention when clear and convincing evidence of an imminent threat of mass casualties is discovered. To preserve civil rights, such measures must never be part of the normal policing repertoire and therefore must be time limited. When danger of mass casualties reaches an emergent level, the state may apply an emergency provision for the exceptional use of deadly force to stop such immediate threat. There must be a fair, independent judicial oversight of these exceptional practices, including not only law enforcement representatives but cleared impartial judges and public advocates. If state agents are wrong, they must be held accountable for their actions. Repressive measures must be proportional to the danger and focused on actual violent protestors, not their larger political community.

Once violent protestors are arrested, they should be subject to fair and transparent procedural justice with fair punishments. Judges overseeing these trials must be impartial and viewed as such, especially by the protest community. Judges should be especially vigilant against prosecutorial misconduct, such as not turning over exonerating evidence or making up inculpating evidence. Our historical illustrations show that such prosecutorial and court malfeasance was not a rarity in political cases, especially in the United States.[31] Prosecutors self-categorize as avengers of the victims of past crimes and may exceed the legal constraints of their job. Judges should be fair in ruling over pretrial motions and at trial continue their impartiality in ruling over objections. As humans, judges have a tendency to self-categorize as state agents against political protestors and rule in favor of the prosecution—they must guard against such tendency. Judicial sentences should also be fair: I am skeptical about the various terrorist enhancement sentences in various Western countries. They are examples of the black sheep effect and rightly viewed as unfair and discriminating against a political protest community. After conviction, prisoners must be treated fairly. Their unfair treatment may outrage their support groups and motivate them to go on to become future perpetrators.[32] Fair punishment of actual perpetrators does not elicit moral outrage.

In the turn to political violence, identity trumps ideology and self-interest. Once the state understands this perspective, it will know how to prevent and fight political violence. The formula boils down to good state leadership in the treatment of its multiple constituencies to prevent alienation of one of them and its activation into a political protest community; vigilance not to escalate hostilities with this community; respectful treatment of it and its grievances; prevention of egregious state aggression against it; and the fair, focused, and proportional repression of violent protestors. This will prevent the emergence of a campaign of political violence, undermine it if prevention fails, and, more important, realize the hope of a true liberal democracy.

This hope may run against nature. The social identity perspective suggests that political violence is the natural result of evolutionary mechanisms that make us identify and favor our group at the expense of strangers. This self-categorization helped small groups survive in a hostile environment during human evolution but is the source of political violence. Those most caring and self-sacrificing for the group because they identify most with their fellow members are most at peril to turn to violence. Now, this natural cognitive mechanism has the potential to annihilate the human race, as we have developed weapons of mass destruction capable of wiping us out. The last century's world wars have demonstrated our willingness to use them for nationalism—a self-categorization. The challenge for the prevention of political violence and preservation of our race is to transcend our nature at the very moment when this is most difficult: when escalation of conflict, with its verbal radicalization, disillusionment with peaceful solutions, and outrage at out-group aggression push us to retaliate with violence. Although our "better angels" might have dramatically decreased violence over the past seven centuries in the West,[33] survival now requires eternal vigilance against the demons of our nature.

Appendix

Testing the Social Identity Perspective Model
of the Turn to Political Violence

Can the model presented in this book be generalized to other, more modern and relevant campaigns of political violence? As noted in the preface, I have limited the number of cases in this study due to the necessity of analyzing them in enough detail to test our model. Let us expand our sample with other prominent cases, including the Fenian Skirmishers;[1] the military wing of the African National Congress (ANC);[2] the Algerian Front de Libération Nationale;[3] the French Organisation Armée Secrète;[4] the Weathermen;[5] the German Red Army Faction;[6] the Italian Red Brigade;[7] the Egyptian Islamists of 1979–81;[8] the Rajneeshees in Oregon;[9] the American Christian Patriots;[10] the Japanese Aum Shinrikyo;[11] the Algerian Groupe Islamique Armé, including the 1995 wave of bombings in Paris;[12] Hamas;[13] and the present wave of global neo-jihadi terrorism led by al Qaeda.[14] This increases the sample to 34 campaigns. They cover over two centuries from the French Revolution to the present, span four continents, and include various types of ethnic, sectarian (Christian, Buddhist, and Muslim), and secular violence from all over the political spectrum—republican, socialist, royalist, nationalist, anarchist, freedom fighter, militarist, liberationist, neo-fascist, and Islamist. These campaigns of political violence were conducted in agrarian, industrializing, industrialized, and post-industrial societies. They targeted absolute autocracies, dictatorships, imperialist and apartheid regimes, and liberal democracies.

To test the model, I use Charles Ragin's qualitative comparative analysis using fuzzy sets.[15] For each variable, a score of 1.0 indicates full membership in the fuzzy set defined by it. Anything less than 0.5 would indicate a less than half membership in that set and therefore would not support the model. Each estimate is a rough average of all the violent participants in each campaign of political violence. The variables constituting the model are the following:

PPC   1.0 indicates self-categorization into a **political protest community** (PPC), from which violent protestors emerge.

Esc   1.0 indicates a mutual **escalation** of conflict between the PPC and
the state.

CRD   1.0 indicates a **cumulative radicalization of discourse** reaching its
peak in using a rhetoric of total war in reference to the out-group.

Disil 1.0 indicates **disillusionment** with nonviolent tactics to redress
grievances.

MO   1.0 indicates **moral outrage** at out-group aggression that is recent,
within a year of the aggression

MS-C 1.0 indicates **martial self-categorization** into soldiers defending
their PPC.[16]

Translated into an equation, the model is:

PPC + Esc (including **CRD**) + **Disil** + **MO** ➔ **MS-C** ➔ **Political Violence**

Included in the table are also two alternative explanations for each of the
cases:

Ideas: 1.0 indicates full membership in the set of **ideological** political violence, meaning that its turn to political violence is completely explained by this thesis.

RCT: 1.0 indicates full membership in **rational choice theory** political
violence, meaning that its turn to political violence is completely
explained by this thesis. As all the cases were rational in their tactical operations, their score will not be 0.

Campaigns of Political Violence and Their Factors

Since the campaigns are of very unequal magnitude, some involving loners
while others mobilizing thousands of people, I look at the qualitative differences in these campaigns. First and foremost, the empirical evidence strongly
supports my basic argument, namely that the process of turning to political
violence involves two self-categorizations, first into a political protest community and then into soldiers defending it. Indeed, since the scores for membership in the political community were slightly higher or equal to those for
membership in martial social identity, fuzzy-set qualitative analysis indicates
that a political social identity is a necessary condition for a martial one defending this community.[17] Since the sample of campaigns was not selected

based on whether such a community existed in the first place, this finding is a strong indication that the path to collective violence is a collective process, not an individual one, and analyzing politically violent people as individuals (that is, finding personal predispositions to violence) misses this crucial milestone in the process. The only two people who were not part of such a community, Pierre Lecomte and Joseph Henry,[18] probably suffered from mental disorders, which significantly contributed to their acts. Their attentats were not political in the meaning of this study.

In terms of martial self-categorization, 91 percent of the campaigns supported the model. The few exceptions are revealing. The Russian populists were peaceful propagandists, and the few who turned to violence did so for personal or group reasons, such as resisting arrests or eliminating traitors and spies. As the violence escalated, a small faction began to think of themselves as soldiers for the revolution, self-organized into a disciplined martial structure, and became People's Will. The tragic bandits were individualists, who did not think of themselves as soldiers and engaged in violence for their own benefit. The Rajneeshees were involved in a land dispute and wanted to incapacitate the local constituency and prevent them from voting for a land board election to influence its result. Their violence was very limited, but the very few who carried it out were like soldiers for the cult. On the other hand, Aum Shinrikyo was very much militarized, with a minister of war and much of the cult geared to produce weapons of mass destruction.

The rest of the model is generally supported, but not as strongly as the two self-categorizations. There was an escalation of conflict between the political community and the state in 71 percent of the campaigns, with the exception of the Italian anarchists and the two Buddhist cults, whose campaigns of violence were unprovoked. The Italian anarchists were generally nonviolent in their insurrections. The two Buddhist cults used weapons that were difficult to detect, as they sought material benefits from their action, more consistent with rational choice theory. The state, not knowing that society had been attacked, did not repress them until it later became obvious that a violent action had taken place. The two diaspora communities conducting campaigns of violence from abroad, the Italian nationalists and the Fenian Skirmishers, did not experience much escalation as they were beyond the reach of the targeted states.[19] There was mild mutual escalation of violence in the Russian populist case, going from arrests, to resisting arrests, to eliminating traitors, to harsh sentences with death penalties and finally central terrorism. The Terrorist Faction of People's Will took a relatively minor symbolic humiliation at a funeral and jumped to an attentat against the tsar when their complaints went unheeded, modeling themselves after People's Will. The tragic bandits' violence was unprovoked, but the tension between anarchists and the state was rising

Table 1. Campaigns of Political Violence

Campaign	Date	PPC	Esc	CRD	Disil	MO	MS-C	Ideas	RCT
Sans-culottes[a]	1790s	1.0	1.0	1.0	1.0	1.0	1.0	0.4	0.2
Charlotte Corday	1793	0.8	0.6	1.0	0.8	1.0	0.6	0.4	0.2
Babeuf Conspiracy	1796	1.0	0.6	0.6	0.8	0.6	1.0	0.6	0.2
Enragés[b]	1800	1.0	0.6	1.0	0.6	0.4	1.0	0.4	0.2
Chouans[c]	1800	1.0	0.8	1.0	0.8	0.4	1.0	0.4	0.2
Nationalists[d]	1819–20, 1867	1.0	0.6	0.8	0.8	0.4	1.0	0.4	0.2
Republican riots[e]	1830–70	1.0	0.8	0.6	0.6	0.8	1.0	0.4	0.2
French Republicans[f]	1835–54	0.8	0.6	0.6	0.6	0.6	0.9	0.4	0.2
Italian Nationalists[g]	1855–64	1.0	0.2	0.8	0.8	0.4	1.0	0.4	0.4
Russian Nihilists[h]	1860s	1.0	0.6	0.6	0.4	0.4	1.0	0.5	0.2
Italian Anarchists[i]	1870s	1.0	0.2	0.2	0.4	0.2	0.8	0.6	0.4
Russian Populists[j]	1870s	1.0	0.4	0.4	0.4	0.6	0.4	0.2	0.2
People's Will	1879–82	1.0	0.8	0.6	1.0	0.8	1.0	0.4	0.2
Fenian Skirmishers	1881–85	1.0	0.2	0.6	0.4	0.4	1.0	0.4	0.2
People's Will, II[k]	1887	1.0	0.4	0.6	0.8	0.8	1.0	0.2	0.2
U.S. anarchists[l]	1886–92	1.0	0.8	1.0	0.8	1.0	1.0	0.8	0.2
French anarchists[m]	1892–94	1.0	1.0	1.0	1.0	1.0	1.0	0.4	0.2
Combat Unit of PSR[n]	1902–9	1.0	1.0	0.8	1.0	1.0	1.0	0.4	0.4
Tragic bandits[o]	1911–12	1.0	0.4	1.0	1.0	0.4	0.2	0.8	0.8
Young Bosnia[p]	1910–14	1.0	0.8	0.8	1.0	0.8	1.0	0.6	0.2
Galleani group[q]	1917–20	1.0	1.0	1.0	1.0	1.0	1.0	0.4	0.2
ANC military wing	1960s	1.0	0.4	0.4	0.4	0.6	1.0	0.2	0.4
Algerian FLN	1954–62	1.0	1.0	1.0	1.0	1.0	1.0	0.2	0.6

Campaign	Date	PPC	Esc	CRD	Disil	MO	MS-C	Ideas	RCT
French OAS[a]	1961–65	1.0	0.6	0.6	0.8	1.0	1.0	0.2	0.2
Weathermen[b]	1969–74	1.0	1.0	1.0	1.0	1.0	1.0	0.8	0.2
Red Army Faction[c]	1970s	1.0	0.8	0.8	0.6	0.6	1.0	0.8	0.2
Italian Red Brigades[d]	1970s	1.0	0.8	0.8	0.6	0.6	1.0	0.8	0.2
Egyptian Islamists[e]	1979–81	1.0	0.8	0.8	0.8	1.0	0.8	0.6	0.2
Rajneeshees[f]	1980s	1.0	0.0	0.0	0.6	0.0	0.5	0.2	0.8
Christian Patriots[g]	1980–90s	1.0	0.4	0.4	0.4	0.6	1.0	0.6	0.2
Aum Shinrikyo[h]	1990s	1.0	0.2	0.2	0.2	0.2	1.0	0.8	0.6
GIA[i]	1990s	1.0	1.0	1.0	1.0	0.6	1.0	0.2	0.2
Hamas[j]	2000–2004	1.0	1.0	1.0	1.0	1.0	1.0	0.6	0.2
Global neojihad[k]	1999–	1.0	1.0	1.0	1.0	0.8	1.0	0.6	0.2

[a] Journées révolutionnaires of the French Revolution (Chapter 2).

[b] Attentat Chevalier (Chapter 2)

[c] 3Attentat of the rue Saint-Nicaise (Chapter 2).

[d] Karl-Ludwig Sand, Louis Pierre Louvel (Chapter 3), and Antoine Berezowski (Chapter 4).

[e] Insurrections of 1830, 1832, 1834, 1839, 1848, and 1870 in France (Chapter 3).

[f] Attentats of 28 July 1835, 25 June 1836, December 1837 (Huber-Grouvelle), 13 September 1841 (Chapter 3).

[g] Four rounds of Italian nationalist attentats against Napoleon III (Chapter 3).

[h] Karakozov and Nechaev (Chapter 4).

[i] The two campaigns of propaganda by deed in Puglia, 1874, and Matese Mountains, 1877 (Chapter 5).

[j] These are the attentats of the 1870s in Russia, before the formation of People's Will (Chapter 4).

[k] Terrorist Faction of People's Will (Chapter 4).

[l] Haymarket incident, 1886, and Homestead strike, 1892 (Chapter 5).

[m] The era of Attentats, 1892–94 (Chapter 5).

[n] Combat Unit of the Socialist Revolutionary Party (Chapter 6).

[o] See Chapter 7.

[p] See Chapter 7.

[q] See Chapter 7.

after the violent repression of three demonstrations. The ANC military wing was never a bloody organization, and the American Christian Patriots have low-level skirmishes with law enforcement.

With the exception of the PSR Combat Unit, all cases showed higher scores on mutual radicalization of speech than on escalation of conflict. In these other cases, fuzzy-set qualitative analysis indicates that cumulative radicalization of discourse is a necessary condition for mutual escalation of violence and shows the importance of such violent discourse in the escalation of violence. The exception, the Combat Unit, was a specialized paramilitary unit, fighting a deliberate and long-term war against high state targets and was dependent on directives from its parent party and relatively unresponsive to its immediate environment. Its campaign of violence came from abroad after intense repression at home convinced its parent party leaders to conduct such a campaign. Once this decision was made, the campaign did not require a continued escalation of verbal violence.

Disillusionment with nonviolent protest as a major contributor to the turn to political violence is supported in about 80 percent of the cases. The big exception is Aum Shinrikyo, which completely rejected society in general and was enamored with secret, clever, and violent ways of accomplishing its goals. Three other exceptions were the Russian nihilists and populists, and Italian anarchists, or political communities that did not reach a threshold of a sustained campaign of violence. Their violence was generally spontaneous and defensive, such as resisting arrest, or due to mental disorder, like that of Karakozov or Nechaev. The last three exceptions were soldiers, the Fenian Skirmishers, the military wing of the ANC (formal soldiers for a larger political community), and American Christian patriots (self-appointed soldiers), who had long concluded that nonviolent tactics did not work and were engaged in a long-term campaign of violence to achieve their goals.

Moral outrage as a factor for political violence is supported in about 70 percent of the cases. The major exceptions were the two Buddhist cults and the Italian anarchists. Again, the two Buddhist cults were using unprovoked political violence as a method of accomplishing their goals in the context of their complete scorn for and rejection of society. The Italian anarchists were hoping to use their campaign as propaganda of the deed to get attention in a culture that was emerging from general insurrection. Their two short-lived campaigns were generally nonviolent. It is interesting to speculate whether their campaigns might have reached greater violence had moral outrage against authorities been present.

Moral outrage was less of a factor in military campaigns against the state. These military campaigns—Enragés, Chouans, nationalists, Italian nationalists, and Fenian Skirmishers—were long-term campaigns that might originally have been triggered by moral outrage—overthrow of a revolutionary government, the Terror in the Vendée, past war against their nation, the 1849 French betrayal against the Roman Republic, and the continued outrage of British occupation and its contribution to the potato famine—but continued long after these events. The protocol, which required that the outrage be within a year of the violence, downgraded these triggering events in the scoring. So, in these cases, the moral outrage was still there, but too far in the past to count in the scoring system. The final two exceptions—the Russian nihilists and the tragic bandits—are more idiosyncratic. As previously mentioned, mental disorder was a major contributor to the violence for the Russian nihilists. The tragic bandits, like the Buddhist cults, had complete scorn for society and, like them, got involved in unprovoked violence.

So, in general, the proposed model based on the social identity perspective is strongly supported in the enlarged sample of campaigns of political violence. But what about the other two perspectives, the ideological thesis and rational choice theory? The ideological thesis is supported in about 30 percent of the cases in our sample. It makes a strong case for American anarchists and the leftist wave of terrorism in the United States, Germany, and Italy in the 1970s. In each of these cases, the respective violent protestors separated and isolated themselves from their respective political protest communities and talked themselves into violence by drawing extreme conclusions of their original ideology and dreaming of being soldiers in an international revolutionary force. The tragic bandits also were heavily influenced by a bizarre extremist offshoot of anarchism. The ideological thesis is weakly supported in the cases of the Babeuf Conspiracy, the Italian anarchists, and the American Christian Patriots, whose idiosyncratic interpretation of their overall ideology contributed to their attempted attacks. Egyptian Islamists, Hamas, and the present global neojihadi terrorist wave of violence also seem to mildly support the ideological thesis in a violent political interpretation of Islam that has been rejected by mainstream Islam for almost 1,400 years.

Ideology should not be totally dismissed in the majority of the cases of political violence because political protesters often defined themselves in terms of a given ideology, such as republican, royalist, nationalist, socialist, anarchist, independence fighter, patriot, or Islamist. However, the social identity perspective provides an overall explanation that better fits the empirical data, and the various twists and turns of the process of becoming violent, than the ideological thesis. In summary, the turn to political violence is more about identity than ideology.

Rational choice theory does not fare well since it is supported in only 12 percent of the cases. Its explanation for turning to political violence is strongly supported in the case of the tragic bandits, as they killed while robbing banks partly for their own benefit. It is also strongly supported in the case of the Ra-jneeshees, as they tried to eliminate an obstacle to their building expansion blocked by a building commission. They used surreptitious violence to prevent people from voting in the commission election, as predicted by rational choice theory. Aum Shinrikyo's use of violence is also weakly consistent with rational choice theory, as it used it to eliminate enemies before using it to divert an anticipated police raid on them. The tragic bandits and the two Buddhist cults stand out in the sample, as they represent the extreme of political violence: violence that has either degenerated into banditry or is unprovoked, at the whim of a cult completely rejecting society. In these cases, the population or the state may view their violence as more criminal than political.

Rational choice theory perspective also finds weak support for the turn to violence of national liberation organizations, like the Algerian Front de Libération Nationale, which tried to increase punishment on imperialist occupiers in the hope of chasing them from their home. Despite their losses, many of these organizations became successful as colonialism lost its support in imperialist countries after World War II. However, in the vast majority of the cases, rational choice theory is not a relevant explanation in the turn to political violence. Indeed, political violence may be fascinating precisely because it violates rational choice, which guides our everyday lives.

In conclusion, this survey supports the use of the social identity model to understand the turn to political violence.

Notes

Preface

1 I call them global because they target the West instead of their own country and neojihadi because, although the perpetrators believe that they are participating in a jihad against the West, the vast majority of Muslims worldwide reject the notion that this wave of terrorism is a jihad. Since I could not come up with a better terms, I call it a neojihad, like a jihad but not a jihad.

2 This was the 17 July 2013 issue of *Rolling Stone* featuring Janet Reitman's (2013) story on Dzhokhar Tsarnaev.

3 I do not mean to condemn all newspaper reporting as unreliable. Indeed, some reporting is superb, but a scholar must be skeptical of uncritical reliance on the media, especially Internet based stories, and try to use more reliable primary sources of information.

4 Indiscriminate non-state political violence was rare until the end of the nineteenth century, but has unfortunately become a dominant trend since then.

5 States, with their disproportionate means of violence and persecution, have a potential to cause much more damage than violent political challengers and inadvertently prolong or escalate political violence through their use.

6 Della Porta, 2013, is an exception and discusses sources, methodologies, and limitations of her claims.

7 These methods are similar to the ones advocated by George and Bennett, 2005.

8 There are few exceptions for the current wave of political violence in the West. See Lorenzo Vidino, 2011; and for the new project of research at the International Center for Counter-Terrorism at The Hague, see Schuurman and Eijkman, 2013.

9 See Sageman, 2016: 89–109.

10 See the classical study by Allan Wicker, 1969.

11 Buford, 1993.

12 The aim was to achieve what Clifford Geertz, 1973: 3–30, calls "thick description," but I was rarely able to find enough detailed evidence to achieve this ideal.

13 For instance, the START database, which only provides time, place, type, number of people involved, their affiliation, and number of victims for each terrorist incident.

14 David Rapoport, 2001, convincingly argued about the importance of using terrorists' memoirs in understanding the meaning of their activities.

15 See the next chapter.

16 Elizabeth Loftus and Katherine Ketcham, 1994; Daniel Schacter, ed., 1995; Schacter, 1996, 2001.

17 See Rodney Stark and William Bainbridge, 1985: 307–424, and Eileen Barker, 1984.

18 Recent global neojihadi defendants in the West no longer use the courtroom for propaganda, as their predecessors did in the past. Instead, they repudiate their political acts in an attempt to win acquittal. This repudiation undermines the political meaning of their action.

19 This tendency is the concept of availability heuristics. See Daniel Kahneman, Paul Slovic, and Amos Tversky, eds., 1982: 163–208, and Kahneman, 2011: 129–145.

20 The missing campaigns of political violence correspond roughly to David Rapoport's (2002) second wave in his broad outline of the history of modern terrorism. However, I have included them in the Appendix to test the model generated on Western political violence.

Chapter 1

1 Bush, 2001.

2 The day after the 9/11 tragedy, the French newspaper *Le Monde* published its editorial under the title "Nous sommes tous Américains" ("We are all Americans"), defining all French people and all people in general as part of this larger category of non-terrorist victims, ready to fight the terrorists. See Colombani, 2001.

3 Moore, 2001.

4 Moore, 2001. This was the highest approval rating ever for a U.S. president, beating the previous record of 89 percent registered by his father, George H. W. Bush, at the end of hostilities in the Persian Gulf War in 1991 and 87 percent held by President Harry Truman just after the end of World War II hostilities in Europe.

5 In the sense of Kuhn, 1970.

6 See Turner, Hogg, Oakes, Reicher, and Wetherell, eds., 1987.

7 See Sageman, 2014.

8 I will define these terms more precisely within the SIP after this section. I am using them here as the lay public commonly uses them. A critique of common theories of radicalization is found in Sageman, 2016: 89–109.

9 This tendency to blame the person rather than the environment for other people's negative behavior is called the fundamental error of attribution. See Ross and Nisbett, 1991: 119–144.

10 See Taylor, 1988; Reich, ed., 1990; Crenshaw, ed., 1995; Silke, ed., 2003; Horgan, 2005: 47–106; and Sageman, 2004: 83–91, for a summary and critique of the terrorist personality approach. However, there are still some mental health professionals and amateur psychologists who, even though they have never actually examined a terrorist, believe that terrorists suffer from some sort of mental disorder on the basis of very selective anecdotal evidence. See Lankford, 2013, as a recent example.

11 The term was popularized by Hoffer, 1963.

12 See Clarke and Newman, 2006.

13 See Abella, 2008: 49–53.

14 This actor-observer bias is the other side of the fundamental error of attribution. People tend to attribute another person's negative behavior to internal predisposition but the same behavior in themselves to compelling circumstances. I suspect that this tendency can also be extended to social groups, implying that members identifying with their own group believe their in-group members' actions are forced upon them by circumstances, while those of out-group members are due to internal predispositions.

15 Alexis de Tocqueville in his *Souvenirs* (1986: 761–762) experienced the same contrast between those who live history and those who write about it.

16 Taylor and Currie, eds., 2012, call this opportunity structure affordance.

17 Post, 2007, champions this position. But also see Merari, 2010, who claims that suicide bombers have a dependent/avoidant personality. Kruglanski, Chen, Dechesne, Fishman, and Orehek, 2009, claim that terrorists search for personal significance, something that Borowitz, 2005, calls the Herostratos syndrome after the man who burned the ancient library in Alexandria to become famous.

18 Gurr, 1970.

19 Asch, 1956.

20 Milgram, 1974.

21 Zimbardo, 2007.

22 Ross and Nisbett, 1991.

23 Borum, 2004, and Moghaddam, 2005, 2006, tried to synthesize the relevant literature into very different linear mechanisms of radicalization. McCauley and Moskalenko, 2011, also combined various individual, group, and environmental mechanisms to explain this process. So did I in an earlier work (Sageman, 2008: 71–88, 125–146). See the critical review of these theories in King and Taylor, 2011. So far, these plausible theories all lack systematic empirical support.

24 See Reicher and Haslam, 2006; Smith and Haslam, eds., 2012; Reicher, Haslam, and Smith, 2012; Haslam, Reicher, and Birney, 2014.

25 Other well-known social scientific attempts to understand how the Holocaust was possible include studies about authoritarian personality (Adorno, Frenkel-Brunswik, Levinson, and Sanford, 1950), the nature of prejudice (Allport, 1954), obedience (Milgram, 1974), and the power of the situation (Zimbardo, 2007), which in turn influenced historical explanations of the Holocaust (Browning, 1992).

26 See Tajfel, 1970, and Spears and Otten, 2012.

27 See Turner, 1996; Haslam, Reicher, and Reynolds, 2012; and Hornsey, 2008.

28 See Stekelenburg and Klandermans, 2009, and Stekelenburg, 2014.

29 This is part of what cognitive psychologists call System 1; see Kahneman, 2011: 19–105.

30 See Enyo, 2009, and Habeck, 2006, for example. True scholars of Islam, whose voices were drowned in the post-9/11 hysteria, have refuted this simplistic thesis: Abou el Fadl, 2005; R. Baker, 2003; Bonney, 2004; Burgat, 2005; Cesari, 2004; Cooke, 2000; Esposito, 1999, 2002; Gerges, 2005; Hafez, 2004; Kepel, 2002; Khosrokhavar, 2002; Roy, 2004; Wickham, 2002; and Wiktorowicz, ed., 2004.

31 See Haslam, Reicher, and Platow, 2011.

32 This of course feeds the illusion that they are great men moving history. See Haslam, Reicher, and Platow, 2011: 1–19, for a critique of the "great men" theory of history.

33 Turner, 1991: 155–173.

34 For instance, see Bill Buford's (1993) description of his gradual and insidious depersonalization within a group of soccer fans, which led him to participate in crowd violence. He became a soccer hooligan without realizing it.

35 Hogg and Reid, 2006.

36 Bandura, 1990.

37 Hoffer, 1963.

38 Post, 2007: 193, seems to believe that such subordination of an individual to the group may be a pathological process.

39 Reicher, Hopkins, Levine, and Rath, 2005: 624–625.

40 Oakes, Haslam, and Turner, 1994: 96.

41 This accessibility is called availability in cognitive psychology and is subject to interesting biases lumped into the concept of availability heuristics. See Kahneman, Slovic, and Tversky, eds., 1982: 163–208, and Kahneman, 2011: 129–145.

42 Oakes, Haslam, and Turner, 1994: 116–124.

43 See Oakes, Haslam, and Turner, 1994, for further analysis on the relationship between social categories and social reality.

44 Schmid, 1983: 1.

45 Schmidle, 2009.

46 Schmid, 1983: 6.

47 This biased labeling of out-group members as terrorists has been incorporated into large academic databases, like the University of Maryland START Global Terrorism Database. For instance, none of the 1980s attacks of Afghan mujahedin against the Soviets in the 1980s are included, but all of their attacks against ISAF in the 2000s are included. The number of these incidents in wartime drowns out all meaningful instances of political violence in peacetime, severely undermining the usefulness of these tools.

48 The major exception are members of People's Will and the PSR Combat Unit, as explained in Chapters 4 and 6.

49 Schmid, 1983: 76.

50 The Rajneeshee attack in The Dalles, Oregon, in 1984 was done to incapacitate the electorate during an election for a land commission. The public did not find out about it until a year later. See Carus, 2000: 115–137; and Sageman, 2007: 9–32. Aum Shinrikyo carried out half a dozen attacks in 1993–94 to kill their enemies and make it appear that they had died of natural causes. The public found out about them a year or two later. See Danzig, Sageman, Leighton, Hough, Yuki, Kotani, and Hosford, 2011.

51 Kahneman, 2011. The set of associations with a term like *terrorist* comes easily and naturally to mind, and are part of what Kahneman calls System 1, subject to all kinds of cognitive biases and heuristics. The ability to logically analyze this term calls for much greater cognitive effort and energy, part of what he calls System 2.

52 There may be an exception, in the case of supreme emergency, as discussed by Michael Walzer, 2000: 251–268, and 2004: 33–66, especially 54.

53 Merleau-Ponty, 1947/1969: Payne, 1950; Camus, 1951. The National Association for

the Advancement of Colored People and northern scholars labeled KKK members terrorists.

54 The social scientific literature on the Holocaust has shown that the explanation of "just following orders" is too simplistic in trying to understand what led Nazi agents to carry out their genocidal orders. This study is inspired by that discipline's level of maturity and sophistication.

55 See Kirchheimer, 1961: 25–30; Ingraham, 1979: 18–26; Kittrie and Wedlock, 1998a: xxxi; Kittrie, 2000: 1–69; and Stone, 2004.

56 Kittrie and Wedlock, 1998a: xxxi; see also Kittrie, 2000: 47–48.

57 See Chapter 5.

58 Such as the START database already mentioned.

59 For example, I include attacks in St. Petersburg and Moscow by socialist revolutionaries during the Russo-Japanese War in 1905.

60 See the next chapter.

61 This is basically Benedict Anderson's 1991 argument adapted to political communities instead of nations.

62 See Marques, Abrams, Páez, and Hogg, 2003, for a review of this literature. We shall see this same phenomenon within each rebel group as they seek to punish their own betrayers or police spies.

63 This is not always the case in liberal democracies, as shown in Ingraham, 1979, but this depends on whether the rebel is viewed as legitimate or not at the time.

64 Haslam, Reicher, and Platow, 2011: 55–64.

65 See Lakoff, 1987. See also Kahneman, Slovic, and Tversky, eds., 1982: 23–98, and Gilovich, Griffin, and Kahneman, eds., 2002: 49–81, for some of the common cognitive biases deriving from this type of automatic thinking.

66 Haslam, Reicher, and Platow, 2011: 64–73. This sort of vagueness need not be an impediment to rigorous social science analysis, as shown by Ragin, 2000.

67 Haslam, Reicher, and Platow, 2011: 109–135.

68 This is especially true for anarchists, who reject even the notion of leadership (see Chapters 5 and 7). The exceptions are large, long-lasting groups that select a formal leadership, like the Weathermen, or groups created by larger political organizations, like the Combat Unit of the Russian Socialist Revolutionary Party (see Chapter 6).

69 Turner, Oakes, Haslam, and McGarty, 1994.

70 Reicher, Hopkins, Levine, and Rath, 2005; Haslam, Reicher, and Platow, 2011.

71 This is Borowitz's (2005) previously mentioned Herostratos syndrome. This single factor should not be stretched too much to explain the full complexity of violent political behavior.

72 See Ayers, 2009: 168; Rudd, 2009: 164, 167–168, 183.

73 See Stern, 2007: 151, and Alpert, 1981: 326–331.

74 Sageman, 2004: 107–112.

75 See Reicher, 2003; Drury and Reicher, 2000; and Zomeren, Postmes, and Spears, 2008.

76 This is in essence is similar to the process of cognitive dissonance (Festinger, Riecken, and Schachter, 1964; Harmon-Jones and Mills, eds., 1999).

77 See Haslam, Reicher, and Platow, 2011: 85–87, for an elegant mathematical demonstration of this dynamic.

78 For instance, see Perry and Hasisi, 2015.

79 As we shall see, this was the tactic of Nechaev in tsarist Russia and of the Weathermen in the United States.

80 There are some rare exceptions. Della Porta, 2013: 70-112; McCauley and Moskalenko, 2011: 154-160; Sommier, 2008 come to mind.

81 Haslam, Oakes, McGarty, Turner, and Onorato, 1995.

82 I wish to thank Alex Haslam and Steve Reicher for suggesting this general line of reasoning in private communication on 9 and 22 July 2013, respectively.

83 Gueniffey, 2000: 125, 230, makes a similar argument for the violence of the French Revolution. See the next chapter.

84 Zimbardo, 2007.

85 Reicher and Haslam, 2006.

86 Haslam and Reicher, 2007.

87 Olson, 1971.

88 Hirschman, 1970.

89 This escalation in the intensity of activities or increased proselytism is often seen in the cognitive dissonance literature. See Festinger, Riecken, and Schachter, 1964. I'm not sure why Hirschman did not include this doubling down of effort to redress a declining group in his possible alternatives.

90 Consistent with the SIP, state agents charged with maintaining the social order usually view people who challenge it as an out-group.

91 Chapter 5 shows this transformation in France and the United States.

92 Going back to the 9/11 analogy, it is clear from this psychological usage that I would translate the Arabic term *shahid* as hero rather than the common translation *martyr*. Traditionally, a shahid is a warrior who dies in battle for the sake of God. Such a warrior would be a hero and not a martyr because his death is perceived as fair.

93 I say generally because in very rare cases, the message of the martyr is specifically directed at followers not to engage in further violence, as in martyrs for nonviolence: for example, Jesus, Gandhi, and Martin Luther King, Jr. However, even such clear directives may later be twisted, as was the case for the Crusades in the Middle Ages.

94 Marques, Yzerbyt, and Leyens, 1988; Marques, Abrams, Páez, and Hogg, 2003.

95 Fehr and Gächter, 2002; Marlowe, Berbesque, et al., 2008.

96 See Nisbett and Cohen, 1996.

97 Nisbett and Cohen, 1996. The following chapters support the role of honor in the turn to political violence.

98 This has much weaker empirical support and is a combination of Baumeister's (1997: 128–202) arguments of threatened inflated self-esteem and group effects.

99 See Wiktorowicz, 2005: 85–98.

100 It is a result of System 1 cognition in Kahneman's (2011) two systems description of thinking.

101 See the cases of Louis Alibaud and Ivan Kaliaev in Chapters 3 and 6, respectively. Camus was fascinated with Kaliaev, who became the hero of his play *Les Justes*; Camus, 1949.

102 See Greene, 2013, and Haidt, 2012, for a popular summary of some of the new discoveries in neurocognitive moral reasoning by two of the most prominent scholars in this new field.

103 Tajfel, 1970, 1982; Tajfel and Turner, 1979; see also Spears and Otten, 2012.

104 Fanon, 1961, makes this argument for a colonial community. But his argument may be generalized to any exploited community.

105 Olson, 1971.

106 Della Porta, 2013: 252–260, has also observed this same phenomenon, which she calls "cognitive closure."

107 This type of thinking is also popularly referred to as "black-and-white" or dichotomous thinking. See Post, 2007: 15–37, for an example of such a reductionist analysis of "hatred bred into the bone."

108 See Bloom, 2005, for an example of how militant group competition facilitates political violence.

109 See Keniston, 1968.

Chapter 2

1 See Rapoport, 2008. He views mobs as the predecessors of modern terrorists.

2 De Tocqueville, 1856/1986: 893–1105.

3 See Weber, 1978: 54.

4 Pinker, 2011; Martin, 2006: 15–50.

5 Carrot, 2005: 221–222. This contrasted with other large European cities like London.

6 Notables were prominent French subjects, members of the clergy, nobility, and bourgeoisie, who had paid a certain amount in taxes for the privilege of participating in the election of the General Estates. Altogether, they amounted to less than 5 percent of the total population.

7 Bell, 2001.

8 Anderson, 1991: 4–7.

9 Sieyes, 1789/1988.

10 Sieyes, 1789/1988: 43–46; see also Furet, 2007: 15–16.

11 Martin, 2006: 52.

12 Carrot, 2005: 222.

13 See Lefebvre, 1982; Markoff, 1996; Tackett, 2004.

14 Rudé, 1959: 35–44.

15 There is of course no official start of the French Revolution. Some contemporaries dated it back to 1 May 1788, the start of the period of amnesty for all political crimes in the French Constitution of September 1791. See Martin, 2012: 146.

16 See also Aulard, 1923: 8–11. There was little advocacy for the use of violence for political change for the first three years of the French Revolution.

17 Tackett, 2006: 48–76, 100–113.

18 Tackett, 2006: 119.

19 Tackett, 2006: 119–129.

20 Germaine de Staël, quoted in Tackett, 2006: 136.

21 He was director general of finances, and Madame de Staël, previously quoted, was his daughter.

22 This is of course Jean-Jacques Rousseau's concept of *volonté générale*, see Rousseau, 2961: 244.

23 Bredin, 1988: 108–109.

24 Tackett, 2006: 138–148.

25 Quoted in Schama, 1989: 363.

26 Tackett, 2006: 149–155; Schama, 1989: 359–363.

27 Quoted in Schama, 1989: 375.

28 Tackett, 2006: 149–158; Rudé, 1959: 45–48; Carrot, 2005: 223; Schama, 1989: 364–377.

29 Carrot, 2005: 223, Schama, 1989: 378–385.

30 Rudé, 1959: 51–53; Schama, 1989: 385–388.

31 Rudé, 1959: 54–60; Schama, 1989: 399–406.

32 Tackett, 2006: 158–165; Schama, 1989: 419–425.

33 Lefebvre, 1982; Markoff, 1996: 337–426.

34 The police report of the incident read at the National Assembly on 25 July by the local deputy reflected this belief. See *Archives Parlementaires*, 1875: 276; Buchez and Roux-Lavergne, eds., 1834: 161–162.

35 M. de Mesmay was much later fully exonerated by the Parliament of Franche-Comté in 1790 after an extensive investigation. See Buchez and Roux-Lavergne, eds., 1834: 203; Estignard, ed., 1892: 246–251.

36 Tackett, 2006: 165–171.

37 Markoff, 1996: 427–435; Tackett, 2006: 172–175; Schama, 1989: 438–439.

38 Quoted in Markoff, 1996: 433.

39 Markoff, 1996: 174.

40 These are the second and fourth dimensions of effective leadership, in Haslam, Reicher, and Platow, 2011: 109–135; 165–195.

41 Rudé, 1959: 61–79; Schama, 1989: 456–471.

42 Martin, 2012: 183.

43 Although everyone else seemed to refer to them by that nickname, it was not until 21 September 1792 that the members of the club adopted it as their own. See Higonnet, 1998: 20.

44 Rapoport, 2008, is an exception. This was not true in the late nineteenth century study of anarchist violence which was seen as emerging from crowd phenomena.

45 See Tackett, 2006: 295.

46 Tackett, 2006: 236.

47 Marat, who was an influential journalist but not yet a deputy, started to advocate the use of riots and fear to intimidate enemies of the nation in November 1789. See Martin, 2006: 80.

48 Fouquier, 1865–67.

49 Edmund Burke, 1790/n.d., wrote most of his book in October 1789 and published it in early 1790 and therefore dealt with just the first five months of the Revolution.

50 *Archives Parlementaires*, 1883: 517 (session of 15 May 1790).

51 *Archives Parlementaires*, 1883: 662.

52 Cassette, 2016: 199–216; Schama, 1989: 549–561; Tackett, 2003.

53 Rudé, 1959: 80–94.

54 Burstin, 2005b: 252–268.

55 Martin, 2012: 278–285.

56 See also Tackett, 2003. Of course, royalists did not share the revolutionaries' self-conception of a nation, which still included the king as their prototypical leader. They continued to label those who had legitimately voted for his death as regicides and hunted them down as their personal enemies to their dying days, even decades later.

57 Casselle, 2016: 193–290; Martin, 2016: 73–137.

58 His faction was later called the Gironde, after Alphonse de Lamartine's 1851 large, two-volume hagiography. They were called Brissotins at the time.

59 Martin, 2012: 286–310.

60 Burstin, 2005b: 344–356.

61 Rudé, 1959: 98–100; Burstin, 2005b: 358–372; Cassette, 2016: 355–389.

62 Burstin, 2005b: 372–393.

63 Burstin, 2005b: 393–398.

64 Quoted in Robinson, ed., 1906: 445.

65 Casselle, 2016: 392–417.

66 During Bastille Day, the crowd spared the Bastille defenders. The overwhelming majority of victims belonged to the crowd.

67 Rudé, 1959: 101–108; Burstin, 2005b: 399–414; Martin, 2012: 322–329; Schama, 1989: 609–618.

68 Its name was inspired by the successful American Constitutional Convention.

69 See for instance, Furet and Richet, 2010: 168–171; Soboul, 1975: 259–262; Tackett, 2011: 192–216.

70 Schama, 1989: 619–623; Martin, 2006: 136.

71 Quoted in Bredin, 1988: 231.

72 Rudé, 1959: 109–112; Martin, 2012: 330–332; Schama, 1989: 624–639; Burstin, 2005b: 415–435; Tackett, 2011: 192– 216; Soboul, 1975: 262– 267; Bredin, 1988: 230–232; Cassette, 2016: 429–438; Wahnich, 2008: 453–479.

73 Robespierre, 1954: 457–459.

74 Cassette, 2016: 439.

75 Burstin, 2005b: 446.

76 Martin, 2016: 168–173.

77 Burstin, 2005b: 440–448.

78 Lefebvre, 1962, I: 120–122.

79 Rudé, 1959: 221–225, stressed the element of fear in the radicalization of the crowds. Soboul, 1980: 158–162, also stressed the fear of hostile conspiracy but added revenge and to a lesser degree the temperament of sans-culottes as ingredients for the violence.

80 Lefebvre, 1962, I: 122.

81 Quinet, 1865/n.d., II: 402–403.

82 See Wahnich, 2008, 2012, which I find unpersuasive as per the critique of Münch, 2010a.

83 Schama, 1989: 644–675.

84 Martin, 2012: 343.

85 Burstin, 2005b: 531–534.

86 Martin, 2012: 351–356; Burstin, 2005b: 534–535; Wallon, 1880–82, I: 47–67.

87 Cambacérès in *Archives Parlementaires*, 1901: 50.

88 Duhem in *Archives Parlementaires*, 1901: 51.

89 Danton in *Archives Parlementaires*, 1901: 63.

90 *Archives Parlementaires*, 1901: 65.

91 The expression is from Gueniffey, 2000: 230.

92 Gueniffey, 2000: 125, makes a similar argument. See also Burstin, 2013.

93 See also Gueniffey, 2000: 160–161. This of course is the black sheep effect.

94 Martin, 2014: 29–46; Martin, 2012: 352–362; Slavin, 1986: 1–22; Burstin, 2005b: 558–571.

95 This right of insurrection was soon enshrined in the 1793 Constitution a few weeks later.

96 Slavin, 1986: 47–105; Burstin, 2005b: 572–585.

97 Martin, 2012: 370–372.

98 Slavin, 1986: 151.

99 This negative description reached its height in Taine, 1904: 236–245, 309–321.

100 Rudé, 1959; Soboul, 1980; Cobb, 1970; Rose, 1983; Andrews, 1985; and now Burstin, 2005a, b.

101 Burstin, 2005b.

102 Rose, 1983.

103 Rose, 1983: 130–143; Rudé, 1959: 80–94; Burstin, 2005b: 252–268.

104 Higonnet, 1989: 395. See also Soboul, 1980: 136–144.

105 Burstin, 2005b: 284–286 (for Charles Alexander), 360–362 (for Claude Lazowski).

106 Burstin, 2005a: 85–86.

107 Burstin, 2005a: 81–82.

108 Burstin, 2005a: 24.

109 In the sense of Anderson, 1991.

110 See especially Burstin, 2005a: 92.

111 Higonnet, 1989.

112 See Burstin, 2005b.

113 See Rudé, 1959, for an overall analysis of these *journées*.

114 Rudé, 1959, lists seven *journées* as effective: July and October 1789; June, August, and September 1792; and May-June and September 1793. There were many other crowd activities during the first five years of the Revolution, like the Réveillon riot of April 1789 and the Champs de Mars demonstrations, which were drowned in blood by the authorities. Many other nascent demonstrations were easily dispersed by local authorities.

115 These were of course the 14 July 1789 and 10 August 1792 *journées*.

116 July and October 1789 and June 1792.

117 August 1792 and May-June 1793.

118 September 1793.

119 Rudé, 1959: 224.

120 Recall the massacres of the Réveillon riot or the Champ de Mars massacre.

121 Tackett, 2000, 2004.

122 Martin, 2002.

123 See also Münch, 2010b.

124 Mazeau, 2009: 219–220, 365.

125 Mazeau, 2009: 203–204.

126 Lamartine, 1851, 2: 642–663, especially 649.

127 Corday, 1864: 19.

128 Reproduced in Mazeau, 2009: 384–385.

129 Corday, 1864: 40; Defrance, 1909: 119–141; Mazeau, 2009: 54–83.

130 Transcript of the interrogation reproduced in Mazeau, 2009: 357.

131 Transcript of the interrogation reproduced in Mazeau, 2009: 361.

132 Reproduced in Mazeau, 2009: 370.

133 Quoted in Defrance, 1909: 344.

134 Mazeau, 2009: 376.

135 This has mistakenly been translated in English as the "regime of terror." See Laqueur, 1977: 6, and Hoffman, 1998: 15–16. The expression was a post hoc Thermidorean accusation against Robespierre after his execution. The historical record shows no systematic regime of terror because the policies of the state in that year were applied in a chaotic and inconsistent way, like in the six weeks of the First Terror. See Cobb, 1987: 512.

136 Gueniffey, 2000: 98.

137 Gueniffey, 2000: 99.

138 Martin, 2006: 196–197.

139 Gueniffey, 2000: 103–110.

140 A search for both terms on the search engine of the Bibliothèque Nationale de France for usage in the eighteenth century conducted on 17 July 2014 produced 139 and 224 hits, respectively. All but three documents postdated the fall of Robespierre. One was an undated poem addressing the Convention and using the word *terrorisme* in a negative sense as a synonym of *Robespierrisme*. The other two appeared in unbound collections of speeches and reports made at the Convention in early 1793. They both used the terms in an accusatory way. So, while the terms had already been invented before Thermidor, they were rarely used, and when they were, it was as an accusation.

141 In terrorism historiography, there is a myth that the word was used in a positive sense during the time of Terror. See Laqueur, 1977: 6, and Hoffman, 1998: 15. While Hoffman gives no reference, Laqueur's references and the historical record do not support this claim.

142 The petition was read by Pierre-Gaspard Chaumette, and the word *terror* did not appear in the speech. *Archives Parlementaires*, 1908: 411–412. See also Ladjouzi, 2000.

143 Barère was mistaken, as it was a Jacobin Club representative and not a commune representative, who had used the expression "Plaçons la terreur à l'ordre du jour." Barère had arrived late to the Convention and had not listened to the respective speeches. *Archives Parlementaires*, 1908: 425.

144 A few units were used in political repression, like the large detachment sent to Lyon to restore the authority of the Convention.

145 *Archives Parlementaires*, 1909: 303.

146 Burstin, 2005b: 628–666, 715–754.

147 Rolland-Boulestreau, 2015.

148 Bourdin, 2002; Cobb, 1987: 368–372; Waresquiel, 2014: 135–157.

149 See especially Martin, 2014.

150 *Archives Parlementaires*, 1906: 108.

151 Martin, 2014: 203–215. See also Waresquiel, 2014: 91–102 for Joseph Fouché's role in organizing the Nantes radicals before Carrier's arrival. Fouché was later responsible for the mitraillades of Lyon and much later Bonaparte's minister of police.

152 This local revolutionary army was not to be confused with the Parisian one decreed by the Convention. It was created through local initiative, with ambivalent legitimacy from the Convention. The Marat Company existed for less than three months.

153 Cobb, 1987: 687.

154 Cobb, 1987: 240.

155 Comte Fleury, 1897: 88–116 (quote p. 113); Lallié, 1879: 12–23 (quote p. 22); Lenotre, 1912: 29–75, 97–107 (quote p. 107).

156 Comte Fleury, 1897: 117–123; Lallié, 1879: 24–37; Lenotre, 1912: 111–141.

157 Martin, 2014: 217–224.

158 Cobb, 1987: 376.

159 Martin, 2014: 10.

160 Cobb, 1987: 240–241. Cobb uses the word *terrorist* in the Thermidorean sense of the term.

161 Cobb, 1987: 379.

162 This statement is from a 20-year-old former National Guardsman named Robin, quoted in Cobb, 1987: 386.

163 Cobb, 1987: 387.

164 See Browning (1992)'s study of a Nazi police reserve battalion, which committed similar atrocities during the Holocaust and was composed of a similar mixture of individuals. Both Cobb and Browning based their respective studies on primary sources from the trials of these units.

165 In addition to Carrier, there was Joseph Fouché, the butcher of Lyon, see Waresquiel, 2014: 171–190.

166 Lescure, 1864, June 5: 2.

167 Lescure, 1864; Wallon, 1881, IV: 1–11; Campardon, 1975: 350–370.

168 Eude, 1983; Gueniffey, 2000: 277–315.

169 Gueniffey, 2000: 277.

170 Burstin, 2005b: 830–872.

171 The word *reaction* also acquired its political meaning from Thermidor. See Brunot, 1937: 843.

172 Martin, 2006: 196–197; Clay, 2007; Mathiez, 1965: 176–197; Lefebvre, 1964: 134–147; Cobb, 1970: 131–150.

173 See Gomez-Le Chevanton, 2006.

174 For example, see Merleau-Ponty, 1947; Camus, 1951/1965; Payne, 1950.

175 See Browning, 1992, for his pioneering study on this issue.

176 Taine, 1904, 2002, comes to mind.

177 This is one of Burke's (1790/n.d.) theses, blaming the violence of the Revolution on the actualization of Rousseau's ideas—or in French, "c'est la faute de Rousseau" (it's Rousseau's fault).

178 These are, of course, the arguments of Gustave Le Bon, 1895/1963, 1912/1968.

179 Rudé, 1959: 210–231, is an exception. He recognized and rejected Le Bon's account.

180 This large group includes most French academic historians in the past century.

181 Martin, 2014: 228–233; Gueniffey, 2000: 255–267.

182 For a slightly different analysis of the historiography of the violence of the French Revolution, see Mayer, 2000: 96–99.

183 Quinet, 1865/n.d., II: 400.

184 See also Burstin, 2005a: 195–229.

185 Mathiez, 1965: 176–197; Lefebvre, 1964: 135–147; Martin, 2012: 484–487; Cobb, 1970: 131–150.

186 Rudé, 1959: 149.

187 Burstin, 2005b: 873–889; Lefebvre, 1964: 116–131; Mathiez, 1965: 156–175, 198–216; Rudé, 1959: 142–149.

188 Rudé, 1959: 173.

189 Rudé, 1959: 160–177; Lefebvre, 1964: 200–204; Mathiez, 1965: 236–257.

190 Burke, 1795/1999: 359.

191 It certainly was not. Not only did Burke's usage reflect common usage in the mid-1790s, but this specific quote came from a letter published posthumously in 1812.

192 See Rose, 1978: 27, 80, 97, 117, 118, 120, and 124–125, for some examples.

193 Rose, 1978: 7–149. The nickname is on page 111.

194 Rose, 1978: 171–184; Mathiez, 1965: 73–80.

195 *Débats du Procès Instruit par la Haute-Cour de Justice*, 1797, IV: 163–165.

196 See Rose, 1978: 195–196. This seems to be one of the earliest versions of the "ink blot" theory of spreading revolution or Che Guevara's *focos* strategy.

197 *Débats du Procès Instruit par la Haute-Cour de Justice*, 1797, III: 211–216; Robiquet, 1910: 9–36.

198 Buonarroti, 1828, I: 55–56. See also his testimony at trial, *Débats du Procès Instruit par la Haute-Cour de Justice*, 1797, III: 204.

199 *Débats du Procès Instruit par la Haute-Cour de Justice*, 1797, III: 67.

200 Buonarroti, 1828.

201 *Débats du Procès Instruit par la Haute-Cour de Justice*, 1797. The proceedings were published in serial format contemporaneously and later collected into four large volumes.

202 Rose, 1978: 205–222.

203 Buonarroti, 1828, I: 77.

204 Buonarroti, 1828, I: 76–109; Rose, 1978: 203–225.

205 Buonarroti, 1828, I: 145–146.

206 *Débats du Procès Instruit par la Haute-Cour de Justice*, 1797, III: 67–71.

207 *Débats du Procès Instruit par la Haute-Cour de Justice*, 1797, I: 284–287.

208 Babeuf in *Débats du Procès Instruit par la Haute-Cour de Justice*, 1797, I: 284; Germain in *Débats du Procès Instruit par la Haute-Cour de Justice*, 1797, III: 67; and Buonarroti in Buonarroti, 1828, I: 107.

209 *Débats du Procès Instruit par la Haute-Cour de Justice*, 1797, III: 67, 160, 242, 250; IV: 168–169.

210 See *Débats du Procès Instruit par la Haute-Cour de Justice*, 1797, III: 103–105, 280, 308–309, 316.

211 See Buonarroti's closing arguments, *Débats du Procès Instruit par la Haute-Cour de Justice*, 1797, IV: 271.

212 See Buonarroti's testimony in *Débats du Procès Instruit par la Haute-Cour de Justice*, 1797, III: 221–224, 248.

213 Buonarroti, 1828, I: 150.

214 Buonarroti, 1828, I: 151.

215 See Buonarroti, 1828, I: 133.

216 Buonarroti, 1828, I: 118–125.

217 *Débats du Procès Instruit par la Haute-Cour de Justice*, 1797, III: 308–309.

218 Cobb, 1987: 615.

219 Burstin, 2005b: 889–890.

220 Rose, 1978: 264–265.

221 *Débats du Procès Instruit par la Haute-Cour de Justice*, 1797, II: 178. The following narrative is based on Grisel's testimony at the trial, *Débats du Procès Instruit par la Haute-Cour de Justice*, 1797, II: 65–116.

222 Charles-Nicolas Pillé's testimony in *Débats du Procès Instruit par la Haute-Cour de Justice*, 1797, III: 199. Pillé's credibility was greatly damaged when he volunteered the fact that he constantly saw demons.

223 Buonarroti, 1828, II: 60–62.

224 Burstin, 2005b.

225 Desmarest, 1833: 20–21.

226 Gershoy, 1962: 310–313; *Procès Instruit par le Tribunal Criminel du Département de la Seine, Contre Demerville, Céracchi, Aréna et autres*, 1801: 110–112.

227 *Conspiration des poignards* in French.

228 *Procès Instruit par le Tribunal Criminel du Département de la Seine, Contre Demerville, Céracchi, Aréna et autres*, 1801: 33–43.

229 *Procès Instruit par le Tribunal Criminel du Département de la Seine, Contre Demerville, Céracchi, Aréna et autres*, 1801: 123–124.

230 Hue, 1909. Desmarest, 1833: 20–25, in charge of police investigations at the time, also did not believe there was a real conspiracy. His subordinate, Préfet Dubois, 1801: 15–17, believed in the reality of the plot.

231 Dubois, 1801: 19–25; Aulard, 1903, I: 789–791, 795–796.

232 Dubois, 1801: 31–36; Fouché, 1824: 207–210.

233 Dupuy, 1997: 81–142.

234 Cadoudal, 1887: 232–242.

235 Lignereux, 2012; *Procès Instruit par le Tribunal Criminel du Département de la Seine, Contre les nommés Saint-Réjant, Carbon et autres*, 1801.

236 Cadoudal, 1887.

237 Martel de Porzou, 1885: 212–213, reproduced a letter by Cadoudal dated 19 June 1800, where he clearly wrote about "getting hold of" Bonaparte.

238 The fact that he was not privy to the details of the plot is proved by his letter to Saint-Réjant, asking his subordinate for an update on his efforts. See *Procès Instruit par le Tribunal Criminel du Département de la Seine, Contre les nommés Saint-Réjant, Carbon et autres*, 1801, I: xli.

239 The reports are reproduced in Lorédan, 1924: 26–40; *Procès Instruit par le Tribunal Criminel du Département de la Seine, Contre les nommés Saint-Réjant, Carbon et autres*, 1801, I: vii–viii.

240 Desmarest, 1833: 35; Martel de Porzou, 1885: 306.

241 Fouché, 1824: 212; Desmarest, 1833.

242 Salomé, 2010a: 22. Different sources give different numbers. A few victims later died in the hospital.

243 Mike Davis's (2007) history of the car bomb crediting Mario Buda's 1920 Wall Street wagon bomb as the first car bomb starts 120 years too late. See also Chapter 7.

244 The far more devastating 1789 Senlis explosion by Billon described earlier was not really a political act.

245 See *Procès Instruit par le Tribunal Criminel du Département de la Seine, Contre les nommés Saint-Réjant, Carbon et autres*, 1801, I: 33–34.

246 Aulard, 1903, II: 83.

247 Aulard, 1903, II: 88. Of course the words *terrorists* and *anarchists* were used in the eighteenth-century meaning of the terms, meaning followers of Robespierre and disbelievers in authority.

248 Reproduced in Aulard, 1903, II: 106–107.

249 It was the *Journal du Soir des Frères Chaignieau*, 8 Nivôse, an IX, in Aulard, 1903, II: 96.

250 Destrem, 1885.

251 *Procès Instruit par le Tribunal Criminel du Département de la Seine, Contre Demerville, Céracchi, Aréna et autres*, 1801.

252 Aulard, 1903, II: 123–124.

253 Cadoudal, 1887: 235–278.

254 See Darrah, 1953.

255 Cadoudal, 1887: 279–291.

256 See Salomé, 2010a: 67. This may be one of the first instances of compensation for what is now called post-traumatic stress disorder.

257 Malandain, 2012.

258 See Mazeau, 2012.

259 For almost a century, terrorist acts meant acts carried out by followers of Robespierre. The conceptual link between terrorism and Robespierre was broken only in the 1880s with the Russian attentats against the tsar, as Chapter 4 will show. It took longer for this new meaning to drift to the West, where acts of political violence were called anarchist,

in its general sense of being against any form of authority. The word *attentat* was universally used to denote what is now called a terrorist act: the assassination of Archduke Franz Ferdinand was called an attentat. Although the French still use the term *attentat*, the English-speaking world now uses the word *terrorism*.

Chapter 3

1 Louessard, 2000; Salomé, 2010b; and Tardy, 2015.

2 For instance, the 1816 "conspiracy of patriots"; see *Procès de la Conspiration des Patriotes*, 1816; Louessard, 2000: 13–30.

3 Dumas, 1851: 31–36.

4 Quoted in Dumas, 1851: 37.

5 Quoted in Dumas, 1851: 37.

6 Quoted in Dumas, 1851: 37.

7 Quoted in Dumas, 1851: 38.

8 Dumas, 1851: 38–44.

9 Louessard, 2000: 45–65.

10 Quoted in Louessard, 2000: 65.

11 Reproduced in Louessard, 2000: 68–69. There are several versions of this speech, like in Société d'Avocats et de Publicistes, 1827b: 50–51, but I found this to be the most cohesive one.

12 The tragic irony of the Louvel assassination was that the duke's wife was in the very early stage of pregnancy at the time of her husband's death. She gave birth to a son, the "miracle child," but this baby never got to rule.

13 Malandain, 2008.

14 The French Carbonaris were different from their Italian counterparts and had very little contact with them.

15 Tardy, 2015: 45–183; Spitzer, 1971. For a summary of the various trials of these conspiracies, see Société d'Avocats et de Publicistes, 1827a (*Procès du Général Berton*; *Procès de Bories et autres*).

16 See Zamoyski, 2015.

17 The chronicles of the times by journalists Louis Blanc (1846) and Élias Regnault (1884), as well as police informant Lucien de la Hodde (1850), read like an uninterrupted series of plots, attentats, and very bloody popular insurrections.

18 Police prefect Henri Gisquet, 1840, II: 237–238.

19 Gisquet, 1840, IV: 4.

20 Louessard, 2000: 136–155.

21 *Procès Fieschi devant la Cour des Pairs*, 1836, II: 28–29, translation mine.

22 *Procès Fieschi devant la Cour des Pairs*, 1836, II: 32.

23 *Procès Fieschi devant la Cour des Pairs*, 1836, II: 35–41.

24 *Procès Fieschi devant la Cour des Pairs*, 1836, II: 242.

25 *Procès Fieschi devant la Cour des Pairs*, 1836, II: 42–78.

26 *Procès Fieschi devant la Cour des Pairs*, 1836, II: 79.

27 *Procès de Fieschi et de ses complices devant la Cour des Pairs*, 1836: 8–9.

28 *Procès Fieschi devant la Cour des Pairs*, 1836, II: 245.

29 *Procès Fieschi devant la Cour des Pairs*, 1836, II: 261–263.

30 See also Gisquet, 1840, IV: 48.

31 Cour d'Assises de la Seine, 1838: 136–137.

32 Louessard, 2000: 284–285.

33 Cour d'Assises de la Seine, 1838: 32; Gisquet, 1840, IV: 88–89.

34 *Procès de Alibaut devant la Cour des Pairs*, 1836: 143.

35 *Procès de Alibaut devant la Cour des Pairs*, 1836: 67.

36 Quoted in Louessard, 2000: 230.

37 *Procès de Alibaut devant la Cour des Pairs*, 1836: 68–71.

38 *Procès de Alibaut devant la Cour des Pairs*, 1836: 25, 65.

39 *Procès de Alibaut devant la Cour des Pairs*, 1836: 85–86.

40 *Procès de Alibaut devant la Cour des Pairs*, 1836: 87–88.

41 The story is reported in Louessard, 2000: 239.

42 Louessard, 2000: 235–239. The quote is from page 239.

43 *Procès de Alibaut devant la Cour des Pairs*, 1836: 143–144.

44 *Procès de Alibaut devant la Cour des Pairs*, 1836: 149–150.

45 Published in the clandestine *Le Moniteur Républicain* in May 1837, quoted in Tardy, 2012.

46 I am discounting the bizarre 27 December 1836 attentat by Pierre-François Meunier, a person with an intellectual disability who believed he had to carry out what was a cruel joke played on him by a relative and close friend. See Louessard, 2000: 256–274.

47 See Louessard, 2000: 279–281.

48 Cour d'Assises de la Seine, 1838: 29.

49 Cour d'Assises de la Seine, 1838: 33.

50 Cour d'Assises de la Seine, 1838: 35.

51 Cour d'Assises de la Seine, 1838: 14.

52 Cour d'Assises de la Seine, 1838: 9.

53 Cour d'Assises de la Seine, 1838: 151.

54 Cour d'Assises de la Seine, 1838: 6.

55 Cour d'Assises de la Seine, 1838: 177–180.

56 Both Huber and Grouvelle were released during the Revolution of 1848. Grouvelle had become insane and died in an asylum, while Huber resumed his political activism during the republic but retired from politics under the empire and died in 1865.

57 Tardy, 2015: 255–273; Hodde, 1850: 199–234.

58 Cour des Pairs, 1839, 1840.

59 Cour des Pairs, 1839: 115.

60 Cour des Pairs, 1839: 120–121.

61 See the evidence introduced at one of the trials reported in the *Gazette des Tribunaux* in *Journal des débats politiques et littéraires*, 12 December 1836: 3–4.

62 Hodde, 1850: 234–250.

63 Cour des Pairs, 1841: 9–11; Louessard, 2000: 326–327.

64 Cour des Pairs, 1841: 80–82.

65 Cour des Pairs, 1841: 83.

66 Cour des Pairs, 1841: 14–16.

67 Cour des Pairs, 1841: 16–17.

68 Louessard, 2000: 335.

69 Cour des Pairs, 1841: 17–22.

70 Cour des Pairs, 1841: 23.

71 Franck-Carré, 1846.

72 Quoted by one of the judging peers, Victor Hugo, 1888: 100–101.

73 Hugo, 1888: 101.

74 Hugo, 1888: 104–105.

75 Louessard, 2000: 356–368. During the revolution of 1848, he was released back to his miserable life.

76 Amann, 1975; Rapport, 2010: 187–211; Rudé, 1964: 164–178.

77 Tardy, 2015: 427–477.

78 Fermé, 1869.

79 Cour d'Assises du Nord (Douai), 1855. In 1833, Belgium had excluded political crimes from extradition. After this refusal to extradite the Jacquin brothers, France and Belgium negotiated the following diplomatic agreement in 1856: "An attentat on the life of the head of a foreign government or members of his family will not be considered a political crime." This became known as the Belgian clause and was incorporated into almost all future conventions on extraditions. See Bassiouni, ed., 1975: 476.

80 Scheler, 1855: 239–240; Considérant, 1854: 46. See also Tardy, 2015: 544.

81 Cour d'Assises de la Seine, 1855, and *Attentats et Complots contre Napoléon III*, 1870: 56–77.

82 Cour d'Assises de la Seine, 1864: 2.

83 Cour d'Assises de la Seine, 1857 (6 August 1857): 3.

84 Cour d'Assises de la Seine, 1857.

85 Orsini, 1857: 24.

86 Orsini, 1857: 93. This was published months before the attentat against Napoleon III.

87 Packe, 1957: 1–111; Orsini, 1857: 1–93.

88 Packe, 1957: 145–171.

89 Orsini, 1857: 149–184; Packe, 1957: 172–215.

90 Packe, 1957: 216–226.

91 Holyoake, 1900: 31.

92 Packe, 1957: 226–230.

93 Orsini, 1857: 190 (italics in original).

94 Cour d'Assises de la Seine, 1858: 35.

95 Cour d'Assises de la Seine, 1858: 63.

96 Cour d'Assises de la Seine, 1858: 66.

97 Cour d'Assises de la Seine, 1858: 11.

98 Packe, 1957: 233. Packe believes that a policeman had heard Bernard speak too loudly on the street and brought in Gomez to question him about it.

99 *Regina v. Bernard*, 1858: 962.

100 Holyoake, 1900: 19–25. The quote is from page 19.

101 Holyoake, 1900: 25.

102 Holyoake, 1900: 36.

103 Quoted in Packe, 1957: 247.

104 Cour d'Assises de la Seine, 1858: 28–30; see also Packe, 1957: 245–249.

105 Cour d'Assises de la Seine, 1858: 1–3.

106 Cour d'Assises de la Seine, 1858: 3. The authorities counted at least 511 wounds, as some people close to the explosions had up to 20 wounds.

107 Cour d'Assises de la Seine, 1858: 34.

108 Cour d'Assises de la Seine, 1858: 36.

109 Orsini, 1857: 111, stated it was 1853, but I believe that Packe, 1957: 145, has the correct March 1854 date.

110 Cour d'Assises de la Seine, 1858: 54–56.

111 Cour d'Assises de la Seine, 1858: 86–87.

112 Rudio and Gomez went to Guyana. Gomez eventually returned to Naples a forgotten man and died in 1908. Rudio escaped from the colony after three years, went to the United States, and joined the Union army, where he became a major. He died in San Francisco in 1913.

113 *Regina v. Bernard*, 1858: 1024.

114 *Regina v. Bernard*, 1858: 1024n.

115 *Regina v. Bernard*, 1858: 1062–1063n.

116 Holyoake, 1900: 34.

117 Cour d'Assises de la Seine, 1864, 26 February: 2.

118 Cour d'Assises de la Seine, 1864, 26 February: 2.

119 Cour d'Assises de la Seine, 1864, 26 February: 3.

120 Magen, 1878: 640.

121 Haute Cour de Justice, 1870, 19 July: 3.

122 Haute Cour de Justice, 1870, 19 July: 4.

123 Magen, 1878: 640.

124 Haute Cour de Justice, 1870, 19 July: 4; 28 July: 4.

125 Haute Cour de Justice, 1870, 21 July: 3; 1870, 29 July: 3.

126 The letter dated 18 January 1870 from Brussels was reproduced in *Le Temps*, 28 July 1870: 4.

127 Haute Cour de Justice, 1870, 19 July: 3.

128 Haute Cour de Justice, 1870, 20 July: 3.

129 Quoted in *Le Temps*, 28 July 1870: 4, from his testimony of 26 July 1870.

130 Magen, 1878: 652.

131 Haute Cour de Justice, 1870, 21 July: 4.

132 See the indictment in Haute Cour de Justice, 19–22 July 1870.

133 Magen, 1878: 666–670. After reviewing the evidence presented at the trial, I have not been convinced of the existence of the larger plot.

134 See Merriman, 2014 and Serman, 1986, for an account of the Paris Commune.

135 If we discount the multiple insurrectional attempts in the fall of 1870 after Napoleon III's abdication when political legitimacy was in flux.

136 In addition to the ones covered in this chapter, there were also the 1832 unsolved

shooting at the king at Bergeron; the 1836 attentat by Meunier, an intellectually disabled loner; the 1855 attentat by Bellemare, an insane loner; and the 1866 Berezowski attentat against the visiting tsar (see the next chapter).

137 The Italian nationalist attentats did not have much effect on French foreign policy, except in the paradoxical acceleration of Napoleon III's support for Italian independence after Orsini's attentat.

Chapter 4

1 See, for instance, Rapoport, 2002.

2 This is of course not true of historians of nineteenth-century Russia like Franco Venturi, Michael Confino, and Adam Ulam.

3 Isaiah Berlin, 1959, in his introduction to Venturi, 2001: viii.

4 Confino, 1990: 501–503.

5 Throughout this study, I have used the Julian calendar when writing about Russia, which was still using it at the time. For events in the nineteenth century, the Julian calendar was twelve days behind the Western Gregorian calendar, and for events in the early twentieth century, it was thirteen days behind the Gregorian calendar. So, in the Gregorian calendar, the Emancipation Statute was signed on 3 March 1861.

6 Confino, 1990: 503.

7 Venturi, 2001: 226.

8 Confino, 1990: 504; Venturi, 2001: 220–231.

9 Venturi, 2001: 220.

10 Ulam, 1977: 96–98.

11 Venturi, 2001: 129–150.

12 Ulam, 1977: 39; Venturi, 2001: 1–35, 90–128.

13 Quoted in Venturi, 2001: 109.

14 Ulam, 1977: 103.

15 Venturi, 2001: 260.

16 Ulam, 1977: 101–106, 115–117.

17 Venturi, 2001: 268.

18 Venturi, 2001: 176–186; Ulam, 1977: 112–114.

19 Confino, 1990: 490–492. Over the years, the pejorative meaning assigned by the critics trying to discredit the young Russian rebels of the 1860s triumphed over the more positive connotation of the term. The pejorative sense later merged with the notion of terrorism, giving rise to the now common assumption that terrorists reject all values.

20 Chernyshevsky, 1863/1989.

21 Its sales eclipsed the novels of his contemporaries Dostoyevsky and Tolstoy and continued to influence Russian radicals for half a century, as evidenced by Lenin's well-known pamphlet of the same title forty years later.

22 Chernyshevsky, 1863/1989: 271–313.

23 Kropotkin, 1899/1971: 297–299, 301. See also Confino, 1990: 505–512.

24 Kropotkin, 1899/1971: 297. Here the word *terrorism* specifically refers to the short campaign of political violence by People's Will, not the modern meaning of the word.

25 Venturi, 2001: 285–330.

26 Venturi, 2001: 344.

27 Ulam, 1977: 3–4; Verhoeven, 2009: 7.

28 See, for instance, Ulam, 1977: 148–168; Venturi, 2001: 331–350.

29 Reprinted in Verhoeven, 2009: 48.

30 Kropotkin, 1899/1971: 301.

31 Quoted in Verhoeven, 2009: 29.

32 Quoted in Verhoeven, 2009: 29–30.

33 The lack of the article "the" or "a" in Russian creates confusion. "Organization" does not have to be a formal association ("The Organization") but could be simply a meeting of people (an organization). See Verhoeven, 2009: 33–34, for discussion of this terminology.

34 Verhoeven, 2009: 27–28.

35 Venturi, 2001: 349–350.

36 Verhoeven, 2009: 30–31.

37 Quoted in Verhoeven, 2009: 35.

38 Verhoeven, 2009: 33.

39 Quoted in Venturi, 2001: 337.

40 Verhoeven, 2009: 133–134, makes a strong case for the contribution of mental illness to the attentat.

41 Quoted in Verhoeven, 2009: 139.

42 Verhoeven, 2009: 139–142.

43 Quoted in Venturi, 2001: 345–346.

44 Ulam, 1977: 2.

45 Quoted in Verhoeven, 2009: 142.

46 Quoted in Verhoeven, 2009: 142–143.

47 Verhoeven, 2009: 143.

48 Quoted in Verhoeven, 2009: 143.

49 Ulam, 1977: 164–163, calls the whole affair a story of "madness, criminality and youth's immature delusions" and the perpetrators "a handful of lunatics and a bunch of deluded adolescents who needed reform school rather than Siberia."

50 Venturi, 2001: 350.

51 This incident has been ignored by Russian historians. Even the encyclopedic Venturi, 2001, ignores him. The French contemporaneous press dealt with him extensively.

52 Cour d'Assises de la Seine, 1867, 16 July: 2.

53 Cour d'Assises de la Seine, 1867, 16 July: 2.

54 Cour d'Assises de la Seine, 1867, 16 July: 2.

55 Cour d'Assises de la Seine, 1867, 16 July: 2.

56 Cour d'Assises de la Seine, 1867, 17 July: 1.

57 Cour d'Assises de la Seine, 1867, 16 July: 1.

58 Cour d'Assises de la Seine, 1867, 17 July: 2.

59 Cour d'Assises de la Seine, 1867, 17 July: 1.

60 Cour d'Assises de la Seine, 1867, 17 July: 1.

61 About 20 years later, this was commuted to life in exile on the island. He was

pardoned in 1906, but elected to stay there in order to be left alone and read. He died there in 1916.

62 Quoted in Venturi, 2001: 408.

63 Venturi, 2001: 389–428.

64 Ulam, 1977: 176–178; Siljak, 2008: 89–92; Venturi, 2001: 360–361.

65 Venturi, 2001: 390–391.

66 Siljak, 2008.

67 Young, 1980: 65–69.

68 Quoted in Venturi, 2001: 362; Confino, 1966: 613.

69 Siljak, 2008: 93–95.

70 Quoted in Siljak, 2008: 98. Zasulich later wrote that her hesitancy was pure calculation because she felt that Nechaev was too involved in the revolution to really love someone.

71 Ulam, 1977: 180.

72 Ulam, 1977: 180–181; Siljak, 2008: 99.

73 Young, 1980: 69; Venturi, 2001: 391.

74 Avrich, 1976: 265. Bakunin cites Razin and Pugachev, among others, in his letter to Nechaev, explaining his break with him. See Confino, 1966: 647–651.

75 Quoted in Venturi, 2001: 367.

76 Venturi, 2001: 368.

77 Quoted in Venturi, 2001: 364.

78 Siljak, 2008: 100–103, 114.

79 Quoted in Gleason, 1980: 341.

80 Ulam, 1977: 186.

81 Confino, 1966, has convincingly shown that Nechaev is its author. Bakunin rejected it as a "Georgian bandit's catechism" (Confino, 1966: 633). The progression from Chernyshevsky's Rakhmetov, to Ishutin, to Tkachev's new man, and to Nechaev's revolutionary has been noted in Venturi, 2001: 365, and Confino, 1966: 616–618.

82 Nechaev, 1869/1987: 68–70. Although the portrait of the revolutionary in the catechism is later described as the prototype of a terrorist, the words *terrorist* and *terrorism* are never mentioned in it.

83 Siljak, 2008: 121–122.

84 Venturi, 2001: 370.

85 Ulam, 1977: 186–193; Siljak, 2008: 122–125; Venturi, 2001: 380–381.

86 Quoted in Siljak, 2008: 125.

87 Ulam, 1977: 193; Siljak, 2008: 125.

88 Quote in Ulam, 1977: 193. Her resentment against Nechaev was such that she volunteered to lure him to a place where the police could kidnap him and return him to Russia.

89 Confino, 1966; Avrich, 1988: 32–52.

90 Siljak, 2008: 126–128.

91 Siljak, 2008: 129–130; Ulam, 1977: 197. About ten years later, other prisoners suspected him of being a police informant and killed him.

92 Venturi, 2001: 391. He escaped to Europe in December 1873 and became a strong advocate for Russian Jacobism.

93 Ulam, 1977: 198; Siljak, 2008: 131; Venturi, 2001: 386–388.

94 Nechaev's catechism was admired by many later politically violent groups such as the Black Panthers and the Red Brigades. The Weathermen tried to fashion themselves according to this prototype, but without referring to Nechaev. This is a case of fact following fiction. See also Avrich, 1988: 32–52.

95 For instance, the media's caricature of Mohammed Atta, who led the 9/11 attack against the United States.

96 Quoted in Pomper, 1970: 106.

97 Ulam, 1977: 203–233, and Pomper, 1995: 72–75.

98 Young, 1980: 72.

99 Gymnasiums are academic high schools.

100 Pomper, 1970: 112–113.

101 Kropotkin, 1899/1971: 306.

102 Leonid Shishko, quoted in Broido, 1977: 77.

103 Quoted in Venturi, 2001: 473.

104 Figner, 1992: 20. Although she was not part of the St. Petersburg group, Vera Figner was part of a similar group in Zurich. Indeed, she seems to have recognized that it was the persecution of her political community that made its social identity salient to her.

105 Nikolai Charushin, a member of the Tchaikovsky circle, quoted in Pomper, 1970: 115.

106 Broido, 1977: 76.

107 Venturi, 2001: 472.

108 Venturi, 2001: 480–481; Elizaveta Kovolskaya in Engel and Rosenthal, eds., 1992: 212–217; Broido, 1977: 65–77.

109 Young, 1980: 130–140.

110 Alexandra Kornilova, quoted in Young, 1980: 80.

111 Venturi, 2001: 481.

112 Tchaikovsky, quoted in Venturi, 2001: 474.

113 Kropotkin, 1899/1971: 317.

114 Tchaikovsky went south but eventually immigrated to a Shaker religious commune in the United States. See Ulam, 1977: 206.

115 Kropotkin, 1899/1971: 330–337.

116 Broido, 1977: 101–118; Figner, 1991: 39–40, and 1992: 25–28; Porter, 1976: 139–142.

117 Figner, 1991: 159.

118 Figner, 1992: 26–27.

119 Kropotkin, 1899/1971: 322–323.

120 This religious dimension even struck Jews like Osip Aptekman. Other Jews, like Lev Deich, became atheists and joined the socialist movement to escape from their heritage. The populist circles and this pilgrimage to the people was the first instance of a sizable number of Jews joining a nationwide social movement in Russia.

121 See Field, 1976: 1–29.

122 Pomper, 1970: 114. Venturi, 2001: 595–596, gives similar numbers, but a different way to break them down. Ulam, 1977: 214, agrees with the official estimate, but Pomper, 1970: 125, factors in the inefficiency of the police and puts his estimate at about 2,500

participants (about half of the university student population!). I suspect that the official numbers underestimate the size of this movement, as the vast majority became discouraged, returned to their studies, moved on, faded out of history, and have been forgotten.

123 Venturi, 2001: 506; Ulam, 1977: 214.

124 Ulam, 1977: 236–237.

125 The SRSRO or Moscow Organization is not to be confused with the Moscow Tchaikovsky circle. They were two distinct groups.

126 Dzhabadari, quoted in Young, 1980: 3.

127 Broido, 1977: 99–118.

128 Ulam, 1977: 255; Broido, 1977: 118; Young, 1980: 3–4.

129 Stepniak, 1883: 33. Stepniak was Kravchinsky's nom de plume.

130 Quoted in Footman, 1968: 55. Yuri Trifonov, 1978, wrote a very accurate historical novel on Zhelyabov and People's Will, which paints the atmosphere of this period.

131 Footman, 1968: 55–56.

132 Footman, 1968: 68.

133 Quoted in Croft, 2006: 104–105. Kibalchich speculated that had the government been more understanding then, there would have been no bloodshed.

134 Quoted in Croft, 2006: 53.

135 Croft, 2006: 52.

136 Figner, 1991: 44.

137 This was published in the 14 November 1875 issue of the *Bulletin de la Fédération Jurassienne* and quoted in Maitron, 2007: 77.

138 Kropotkin, 1899/1971: 414, mentioned 21 prisoners who suffered from these conditions, while Stepniak, 1883: 33, gave a figure of 75 such prisoners.

139 Stepniak, 1883: 34.

140 Most famously, Vera Zasulich and Lev Deich, who had experienced prison and had participated in at least one assassination attempt, later rejected the strategy of People's Will.

141 Valerian Osinsky and Alexander Mikhailov come to mind.

142 See the report of the Committee of Ministers meetings of 18 and 25 March 1875 reproduced in Siljak, 2008: 195.

143 Quoted in Venturi, 2001: 562.

144 Venturi, 2001: 568.

145 See Kropotkin, 1899/1971: 365–377, and Stepniak, 1883: 149–158, for a detailed account of the escape.

146 Blackwell, ed., 1918: 1–82; Porter, 1976: 198–202.

147 Also spelled Lev or Leo Deutch, Deych, or Deuc, according to different sources.

148 They had no official papers granting them the right to live in Kiev.

149 Venturi, 2001: 571.

150 Venturi, 2001: 571.

151 Quoted in Ulam, 1977: 247.

152 Ulam, 1977: 247.

153 Field, 1976: 113–143, 172–180. In his account, Stefanovich was careful to shield his friend Deich.

154 Siljak, 2008: 162; Ulam, 1977: 260; Venturi, 2001: 581. Gorinovich survived, horribly scarred and disfigured. He had not been a police informant, but after his near-death, he told the police all he knew. Malinka and Deich were eventually arrested, tried, and convicted for this crime.

155 Deich, quoted in Young, 1980: 5.

156 Quoted in Ulam, 1977: 247. It seems that Frolenko was not aware of the Chigirin conspiracy.

157 Field, 1976: 143–163; Venturi, 2001: 582–583; Ulam, 1977: 260–261; Siljak, 2008: 163–164.

158 Quoted in Siljak, 2008: 165. Deich's decision not to take Zasulich in his confidence might also have to do with the fact that the Chigirin conspirators were afraid their companions might not approve of their deceptive tactic. However, his belief that his lover was not cut out to be a violent revolutionary is well documented.

159 Baron, 1963: 1–29; Venturi, 2001: 575.

160 Venturi, 2001: 562–568.

161 Quoted in Ulam, 1977: 292.

162 Venturi, 2001: 503–505.

163 Mikhailov, quoted in Venturi, 2001: 572.

164 Quoted in Venturi, 2001: 573–574 (italics in original).

165 Ulam, 1977: 254, cites a reliable source stating that there were at most 50 workers at the demonstration.

166 Vera Figner wrote, "I was among the initiators" of Land and Liberty (Figner, 1991: 48), but she did not formally join the organization. Though she was part of a separate circle, she still worked closely with friends at Land and Liberty.

167 Ulam, 1977: 253–254. See also Plekhanov's own account in Meadowcroft, 2011: 305–309.

168 Siljak, 2008: 197.

169 Ulam, 1977: 254.

170 Quoted in Siljak, 2008: 199.

171 Stepniak, 1883: 27.

172 Broido, 1977: 132.

173 Venturi, 2001: 586.

174 Liubatovich, 1992: 150.

175 Broido, 1977: 133.

176 Broido, 1977: 133.

177 Meadowcroft, 2011: 280.

178 Quoted in Venturi, 2001: 587.

179 Quoted in Broido, 1977: 137. For a different translation of excerpts of Bardina's speech, see Porter, 1976: 151–152. The speeches were published in the underground *Forward!*

180 Broido, 1977: 133.

181 Venturi, 2001: 579–580.

182 The informant was Nikolai Sharashkin, and the two murderers were Andrei Presniakov and Nikolai Tiutchev. Young, 1980: 113–114.

183 The victim was Kir Belanov. J. Jackson, 2012: 133. Newell, 1981: 41, gives the murder of two other police spies: Tavleev in September 1876 and Finogenov in St. Petersburg in July 1877.

    184 Venturi, 2001: 563.

    185 Figner, 1991: 50–51.

    186 This account is taken from Siljak, 2008: 180–181, which seems to be the most detailed I've seen.

    187 A populist quoted in Siljak, 2008: 186. Flogging was a traditional punishment for disobedient serfs. I wonder whether this symbolic degradation to the status of a serf was a source for the outrage of the pampered aristocrats.

    188 Ulam, 1977: 239.

    189 Broido, 1977: 138.

    190 Broido, 1977: 138–140; Siljak, 2008: 206–207.

    191 Meadowcroft, 2011: 309–312; Venturi, 2001: 542–543.

    192 Venturi, 2001: 591.

    193 Large excerpts of the speech are quoted in Footman, 1968: 70, and Venturi, 2001: 589–590.

    194 Siljak, 2008: 209; Broido, 1977: 142; Venturi, 2001: 591.

    195 Stepniak, 1883: 122–124; Young, 1980: 151–158.

    196 Schiller, 1972.

    197 Young, 1980: 186–215.

    198 Footman, 1968: 71; Siljak, 2008: 212; Venturi, 2001: 596.

    199 Siljak, 2008: 210.

    200 Porter, 1976: 216.

    201 Kolenkina quoted in Siljak, 2008: 212.

    202 Siljak, 2008: 213.

    203 In an earlier work, I wrote that Zasulich had called herself a terrorist (Sageman, 2008: 34). On further checking, this is wrong. I mistook Ulam's (1977: 269) retrospective comment that she was a terrorist but not a killer as her words. The best description of her act is in Siljak's account. Rapoport, 2002: 50, made the same error.

    204 Siljak, 2008: 8.

    205 Ironically, Zasulich, who shot Trepov, was generally against political violence and assassination. See Zasulich, 1992: 88–93. On the other hand, Kolenkina, who had failed, was a strong advocate for both. See Siljak, 2008: 301.

    206 Figner, 1991: 52.

    207 Ulam, 1977: 275–277; Stepniak, 1883: 38.

    208 Stepniak, 1883, passim.

    209 Kropotkin, 1899/1971: 427–428.

    210 Venturi, 2001: 598–600.

    211 Footman, 1968: 73.

    212 Venturi, 2001: 602; Ulam, 1977: 281.

    213 Croft, 2006: 47.

    214 Stepniak, 1883: 93–100; Venturi, 2001: 635–637.

    215 Croft, 2006: 47–48.

216 Siljak, 2008: 234.

217 Zasulich, 1992: 78.

218 Kucherov, 1952: 89–92.

219 Kucherov, 1952: 92–93.

220 Stepniak, 1883: 36. Stepniak's book was of course propaganda, and he ignored Zasulich's past.

221 For instance, see Rapoport, 2002.

222 Zasulich, 1992: 88–93.

223 Pomper, 1995: 83.

224 M. Miller, 1995: 39–40.

225 Bookchin, 1998: 94.

226 Pernicone, 2009: 149. A bomb exploded in a crowd in Pisa protesting the attempt on the king three days later and killed three people. It is unclear whether it was thrown by an anarchist or a police agent provocateur.

227 Kropotkin, 1899/1971: 416–417.

228 Stepniak, 1883: 38–39.

229 Stepniak, 1883: 159.

230 Venturi, 2001: 602; Ulam, 1977: 282–283; Footman, 1968: 75.

231 Vladimir Debogori-Mokrievich, quoted in Footman, 1968: 76.

232 Stepniak, 1883: 158–165. See also Footman, 1968: 76–79.

233 Quote in Ulam, 1977: 283, is attributed to Deich.

234 Ulam, 1977: 283; Venturi, 2001: 602.

235 Figner, quoted in McCauley and Moskalenko, 2011: 133.

236 Venturi, 2001: 612.

237 Venturi, 2001: 613–614.

238 Venturi, 2001: 615.

239 Stepniak, 1883: 35.

240 Siljak, 2008: 267; Ulam, 1977: 293–294.

241 Footman, 1968: 82.

242 Ulam, 1977: 294; Siljak, 2008: 267–268; Footman, 1968: 82.

243 Ulam, 1977: 294; Siljak, 2008: 268; Footman, 1968: 82.

244 Quoted in Venturi, 2001: 616.

245 Quoted in Ulam, 1977: 295.

246 See also Footman, 1968: 83–84.

247 Liubatovich, 1992: 146–152.

248 Liubatovich, 1992: 153, and quoted in Young, 1980: 217.

249 Liubatovich, 1992: 154; Payne, 1957: 150.

250 Liubatovich, 1992: 155–156.

251 Croft, 2006: 54.

252 Venturi, 2001: 641.

253 Ulam, 1977: 320. At the time, most revolutionaries assumed that Drigo had betrayed his friend to the police, as reported in Kravchinsky's (Stepniak's) memoirs. Archival evidence discovered in the twentieth century exonerates Drigo.

254 Quoted in Venturi, 2001: 620.

255 Quoted in Footman, 1968: 88–89.
256 Footman, 1968: 89–90; Ulam, 1977: 310–311.
257 Ulam, 1977: 284–285.
258 Footman, 1968: 91; Ulam, 1977: 308–309.
259 Butterworth, 2010: 140.
260 Figner, 1991: 59–60.
261 Ulam, 1977: 311–314.
262 Reprinted in Trifonov, 1978: 156–157.
263 Baron, 1963: 36–37.
264 Ulam, 1977: 316.
265 Ulam, 1977: 316.
266 Venturi, 2001: 821n.
267 See Venturi, 2001: 643.
268 Quoted in Venturi, 2001: 640.
269 Footman, 1968: 86.
270 Quoted in Footman, 1968: 87.
271 Footman, 1968: 95.
272 Ulam, 1977: 320.
273 Quoted in Venturi, 2001: 549–650.
274 According to Morozov's memoir, quoted in Venturi, 2001: 653.
275 Liubatovich, 1992: 163–164.
276 Croft, 2006: 59; Venturi, 2001: 628–629.
277 See Baron, 1963: 38–41; Venturi, 2001: 654.
278 Footman, 1968: 103–104; Venturi, 2001: 656.
279 See the discussion in Newell, 1981: 55–59, 99–100.
280 Young, 1980: 166–167.
281 Croft, 2006: 56–64.
282 Ulam, 1977: 321. He may have been the victim of a prison stool pigeon, who was trying to ingratiate himself with the authorities and portrayed Lizogub as not just the financier but the head of the revolutionary movement.
283 Stepniak, 1883: 99.
284 Stepniak, 1883: 100.
285 Venturi, 2001: 635.
286 Venturi, 2001: 638.
287 Figner, 1992: 43.
288 Venturi, 2001: 657.
289 Liubatovich, 1992: 166.
290 Figner, 1991: 69.
291 As told to her brother Vasily Perovsky, quoted in Young, 1980: 168.
292 Reported by Lev Tikhomirov, quoted in Young, 1980: 169.
293 Quoted in Young, 1980: 170.
294 Young, 1980: 171.
295 Croft, 2006: 64.
296 Figner, 1992: 44–45.

297 Figner, 1991: 78–80.

298 Footman, 1968: 111–115; Ulam, 1977: 337.

299 Footman, 1968: 117–120; Ulam, 1977; 338.

300 Baron, 1963: 46; Venturi, 2001: 685–686; Ulam, 1977: 340.

301 See Venturi, 2001: 665–681, for a good analysis of the content of the five issues of *People's Will* published before the assassination of the tsar.

302 Figner, 1991: 165.

303 See Liubatovich, 1992: 174–179.

304 Ulam, 1977: 339.

305 Footman, 1968: 116. Kibalchich and Shiraev investigated the cause of the malfunction but came to no conclusion. Zhelyabov might have mixed up the wires, or the rain or floods might have interfered with the mechanism.

306 Reproduced in Footman, 1968: 122–123; Trifonov, 1978: 235–238.

307 Figner, 1991: 80.

308 Croft, 2006: 69; Footman, 1968: 125.

309 Ulam, 1977: 339; Venturi, 2001: 683–685; Footman, 1968: 129–130.

310 Figner, 1991: 83.

311 Footman, 1968: 130–132.

312 He was so upset with People's Will that he left the organization for about a year. See Croft, 2006: 72.

313 The text is reproduced in Croft, 2006: 72–73.

314 Figner, 1991: 82–83. See also Ulam, 1977: 343.

315 Ulam, 1977: 341–343.

316 Croft, 2006: 75.

317 Quoted in Footman, 1968: 133, and Ulam, 1977: 343.

318 Ulam, 1977: 343; Footman, 1968: 149.

319 Footman, 1968: 134–135; Ulam, 1977: 344–345. For a fictionalized account of this strange betrayal, see Trifonov, 1978: 262–267, 322–330. In prison, Goldenberg ran into Zundelevich, who told him about the damage he had caused. Goldenberg committed suicide on 15 July 1880.

320 Venturi, 2001: 698.

321 Figner, 1991: 83.

322 Figner, 1991: 84–85.

323 Footman, 1968: 137–138; Croft, 2006: 77–78.

324 Tikhomirov, quoted in Footman, 1968: 147.

325 Venturi, 2001: 693–694.

326 Footman, 1968: 142, 152.

327 Footman, 1968: 153–154; Venturi, 2001: 705–706.

328 Venturi, 2001: 699–704.

329 Venturi, 2001: 696–698; Footman, 1968: 155–157; Figner, 1991: 88–91; Pipes, 2003: 10–12.

330 Ivianski, 2006: 81–82; Ulam, 1977: 345. Much of the pamphlet is reproduced in Morozov, 1880/1987.

331 Ivianski, 2006: 80. This is Ivianski's argument.

332 Ulam, 1977: 345–346. Many historians of terrorism conflate his pamphlet with the program of People's Will.

333 From Zhelyabov's statement at his trial, quoted in Footman, 1968: 215.

334 He later identified many of his former colleagues to the police. His role was discovered when the Bolsheviks read the Okhrana archives in 1925. He was arrested, tried, convicted, and sentenced to ten years in prison. See Footman, 1968: 142–143.

335 Maria Oshanina, quoted in Footman, 1968: 159.

336 Quoted in Footman, 1968: 159.

337 Croft, 2006: 83; Footman, 1968: 159–160; Venturi, 2001; Ulam, 1977: 350. He was tried and sentenced to death on 25 February 1882, but his sentence was commuted to life in prison, where he died in 1884.

338 Footman, 1968: 161.

339 Footman, 1968: 168.

340 Quoted in Footman, 1968: 169.

341 Ulam, 1977: 352.

342 Young, 1980.

343 Footman, 1968: 175–177; Ulam, 1977: 353–354.

344 Figner, 1991: 96, italics in the original.

345 Footman, 1968: 181.

346 Quoted in Footman, 1968: 182, and Ulam, 1977: 356.

347 Venturi, 2001: 712–713; Croft, 2006: 91–93; Ulam, 1977: 355–356; Footman, 1968: 185–218.

348 Figner, 1991: 99.

349 Footman, 1968: 190.

350 Tyrkov, quoted in Footman, 1968: 194.

351 Figner, 1991: 307–308.

352 Figner, 1991: 115.

353 Footman, 1968: 215–218.

354 Croft, 2006: 121–122.

355 Croft, 2006: 131.

356 Figner, 1991: 7.

357 Naimark, 1983: 51–52.

358 Figner, 1991: 129.

359 Naimark, 1983: 53–58; Pipes, 2003. Degaev fled the country and eventually settled in the United States, where he became a professor of mathematics at the University of South Dakota.

360 Naimark, 1983: 59–67.

361 Ulam, 1977: 327. They were very selective in terms of their recruits.

362 Pomper, 2010: 119.

363 Pomper, 2010: 102–106.

364 Pomper, 2010: 106–109.

365 Pomper, 2010: 110–112.

366 Govorukhin, quoted in Pomper, 2010: 113; see also 120.

367 Pomper, 2010: 144–151.

368 Pomper, 2010: 459–199. Govorukhin had fled earlier when the police were closing in on him.

Chapter 5

1 See Rapoport, 2002.

2 Bakunin, 1972: 195–196; emphasis in the original.

3 Costa, quoted in Pernicone, 2009: 85.

4 Quoted in Pernicone, 2009: 84.

5 Pernicone, 2009: 94.

6 Quoted in Pernicone, 2009: 98.

7 Cafiero, quoted in Maitron, 2007: 75 [translation mine]. This letter was published in the *Bulletin de la Fédération Jurassienne*, no. 49, 3 December 1876.

8 Joll, 1980:103; Pernicone, 2009: 122.

9 Pernicone, 2009: 122–128.

10 Maitron, 2007: 76–77.

11 Indeed, Cafiero, Malatesta, and their companions were found not guilty of that crime in August 1878. See Pernicone, 2009: 144.

12 See Pernicone, 2009, and Maitron, 2007: 78.

13 Bantman, 2006: 966.

14 Reprinted in Maitron, 2007: 114–115.

15 Read at the trial, *Regina v. Johann Most*, 1881.

16 Trautmann, 1980: 69.

17 McKenna, 2012: 18, 25–26, 61–63, 135–137; Whelehan, 2012: 123–125.

18 William Lomasney, quoted in Whelehan, 2012: 102.

19 An account of this campaign is not included in this book because I could not locate primary source material for it. For those interested in this campaign, see Whelehan, 2012, and McKenna, 2012.

20 As emphasized several times, this book is not a comprehensive survey of non-state political violence. It does not include the century-long bloody resistance of Native Americans to a virtual white war on them, which over time amounted to a de facto genocide against them. Nor does it include the political violence of abolitionists in the run-up to the American Civil War (see Reynolds, 2006) and that of the white supremacists in the south afterward. In the historiography of terrorism, relevant political violence is limited to that connected with the labor struggle.

21 Kenny, 1998.

22 Bruce, 1989; see also the State of Pennsylvania's *Report of the Committee Appointed to Investigate the Railroad Riots in July, 1877*, 1878.

23 Adamic, 2008: 37.

24 Zinn, 1999: 265–267.

25 Trautmann, 1980: 118–120.

26 Trautmann, 1980: 254. He reproduced the entire Pittsburgh Declaration as Appendix B in the book.

27 Trautmann, 1980: 256–257.

28 Most, 1885/1978: 1.

29 Most, 1885/1978: 30.

30 Albert Parsons's *Alarm*, quoted in Adamic, 2008: 35, and Avrich, 1984: 170.

31 Parsons, quoted in Avrich, 1984: 133.

32 Avrich, 1984: 174.

33 Avrich, 1984: 184.

34 Schaack, 1889: 139.

35 Avrich, 1984: 208–210.

36 Avrich, 1984: 216.

37 Altgeld, 1893/1986: 47. Governor of Illinois Altgeld investigated the incident half a dozen years later.

38 See, for instance, the long monograph by Chicago police captain Schaack, 1889.

39 Trautmann, 1980: 143.

40 Altgeld, 1893/1986: 34, 57.

41 Altgeld, 1893/1986: 51.

42 Altgeld, 1893/1986: 46.

43 Avrich, 1984: 277.

44 Altgeld, 1893/1986: 35.

45 Reproduced in full in Rosemont and Roediger, 2012: 47.

46 With the exception of Dmitri Lizogub, whose death sentence provoked such universal outrage.

47 Avrich, 1984: 279–380.

48 This date was later taken for the commemoration of the far greater tragedy of the tens of millions who died during World War I.

49 Emma Goldman, 1970: 7.

50 Goldman, 1970: 9–10.

51 Goldman, 1970: 26.

52 Goldman, 1970: 4–6.

53 Goldman, 1970: 46; Berkman, 1912: 13–14.

54 Goldman, 1970: 31.

55 Avrich and Avrich, 2012: 28. He is "Fedya" in Goldman's autobiography.

56 Goldman, 1970: 42.

57 Berkman, 1912: 13.

58 Goldman, 1970: 40.

59 Goldman, 1970: 84; Berkman, 1912: 10. But see also Burgoyne, 1979.

60 Goldman, 1970: 84.

61 Goldman, 1970: 85.

62 Goldman, 1970: 86.

63 Berkman, 1912: 10–11.

64 Berkman, 1912: 9, and Goldman, 1970: 86. Their versions of the events were one-sided. Workers had surrounded the plant, and Frick hired about 300 heavily armed Pinkerton men to break the siege in the middle of the night. It's unclear who fired first, but a general firefight ensued, killing two and injuring 11 workers, while the Pinkertons suffered

two dead and 12 wounded themselves. See Burgoyne, 1979: 52–64, and Krause, 1992: 19–20.

65 Goldman, 1970: 87.

66 Berkman, 1912: 13–14. Note the use of the term *terrorist,* as the term applied to his Russian childhood heroes, the martyrs of People's Will.

67 Quoted in Goldman, 1970: 87.

68 Goldman, 1970: 88.

69 Goldman, 1970: 88.

70 Goldman, 1970: 91–93.

71 Berkman, 1912: 28–29.

72 Burgoyne, 1979: 146–158.

73 Trautman, 1980: 203–204; Goyens, 2007: 131.

74 Goldman, 1970: 103.

75 Goldman, 1970: 105; Trautmann, 1980: 182.

76 Goyens, 2007: 133.

77 Berkman, 1912: 63–64.

78 Bouhey, 2008: 35–91.

79 Maitron, 2007: 123, 163.

80 Bataille, 1883: 317. Fournier was sentenced to eight years at hard labor.

81 The priest had buried a dead atheist miner in a religious ceremony despite the miner's explicit wish for a non-religious burial. Five miners who protested were fired from their jobs. See Maitron, 2007: 160–161.

82 Bataille, 1883: 321–346.

83 This was the expression used by Bataille, 1884: 282.

84 Bataille, 1883: 343–345; Maitron, 2007: 167.

85 *Le Procès des Anarchistes devant la Police Correctionnelle et la Cour d'Appel de Lyon,* 1883.

86 His sentence was commuted to life in a New Caledonia penal colony. His innocence—he was not in France at the time of the attentat—was later recognized, and he was exonerated in 1898. See Maitron, 2007: 167–170.

87 Bataille, 1885: 217–232.

88 Bouhey, 2008: 149–158.

89 Quoted in Maitron, 2007: 155.

90 The letter is reproduced in its entirety in Maitron, 2007: 184–185.

91 Bouhey, 2008: 83.

92 Quoted in Maitron, 2007: 184.

93 Bataille, 1888: 327.

94 Bataille, 1888: 329.

95 Quoted in Bouhey, 2008: 83.

96 This expression means "individual taking back," or expropriation from the rich.

97 Bouhey, 2008: 85; Maitron, 2007: 187–189.

98 Bouhey, 2008: 88–90.

99 Bouhey, 2008: 67–87.

100 Merriman, 2009: 5–58; Bouhey, 2008: 129; Maitron, 2007: 139–150. The estimate is from Maitron, 2007: 130. He estimated about 1,000 active militants, about 4,500 sympathizers buying anarchist newspapers, and about 100,000 vague sympathizers who would have voted for anarchist candidates, had they run for office.

101 Bouhey, 2008: 93–158.

102 Maitron, 2007: 196–197; Bookchin, 1998: 106.

103 Bataille, 1892: 335–346.

104 *Gazette des Tribunaux*, 29 August 1891: 3.

105 Faure, 1891: 33.

106 Varennes, 1895: 1–5; Salmon, 1959/2008: 73–78; Faure, 1891.

107 Faure, 1891.

108 Varennes, 1895: 21.

109 From Ravachol's autobiography in Maitron, 1992: 42–73.

110 Maitron, 1992: 56–57.

111 Bataille, 1893: 49.

112 Maitron, 1992: 65–73.

113 Bataille, 1893: 49.

114 Salmon, 1959/2008: 111–113.

115 Quoted in Maitron, 2007: 220–221.

116 Quoted in Maitron, 2007: 193.

117 Varennes, 1895: 18; Bataille, 1893: 24.

118 Bataille, 1893: 72; Varennes, 1895: 53–55.

119 Bataille, 1893: 70.

120 Bataille, 1894: 383.

121 Varennes, 1895: 61. Faugoux, Chévenet, Drouet, and a fence went on trial for the theft of the dynamite on 27 July 1892. They were all convicted: Faugoux was sentenced to 20 years at hard labor, Chévenet to 12 years at hard labor, Drouet to 6 years in prison, and the fence to 5 years in prison. See Bataille, 1893: 69–75.

122 Bataille, 1893: 8, 18.

123 Bataille, 1893: 10.

124 Bataille, 1893: 10–11.

125 Bataille, 1893: 11–12.

126 Bataille, 1894: 380–393, and *Gazette des Tribunaux*, 27 July 1894: 2.

127 Maitron, 2007: 459–461. Chaumentin started confessing his role on 23 March, and he betrayed his friends by testifying for the prosecution at the various trials dealing with Ravachol.

128 Bataille, 1893: 20–21.

129 Bataille, 1893: 31–32, Salmon, 1959/2008: 129.

130 *Gazette des Tribunaux*, 27 July 1894: 3, and Bataille, 1894: 379–400. Meunier fled to England, where he was arrested and extradited back to France. He was tried on 26 July 1894 and sentenced to life in prison.

131 This is reproduced in its entirety in Maitron, 1992: 42–73. See also Salmon, 1959/2008: 132.

132 Bataille, 1893: 22.

133 Bataille, 1893: 23, and Varennes, 1895: 18.

134 Bataille, 1893: 35, and Varennes, 1895: 26.

135 Quoted in Maitron, 2007: 222–223. See Bataille, 1893: 50–52, and Varennes, 1895: 28–46.

136 Bataille, 1893: 36–64. Béala and Soubert were tried a third time, on 5 July 1892 in Saint-Etienne, on the charge of helping a fugitive of justice. This time, they were convicted. Béala was sentenced to a year in prison and Soubert to six months. See *Gazette des Tribunaux*, 6 July 1892: 5; Varennes, 1895: 67–68.

137 Bataille, 1893: 65–68.

138 Elisée Reclus, quoted in Maitron, 2007: 224.

139 See Malato, 1894, and also Maitron, 2007: 224.

140 Quoted in Maitron, 2007: 221.

141 Quoted in Maitron, 2007: 222.

142 Merriman, 2009: 86.

143 Malato, 1894.

144 Malato, 1894.

145 Quoted in Maitron, 2007: 240.

146 Quoted in Maitron, 2007: 240, and dated 28 August 1892.

147 Merriman, 2009: 25–40.

148 *Gazette des Tribunaux*, 29 April 1894: 2.

149 Merriman, 2009: 36–38.

150 Merriman, 2009: 59.

151 *Gazette des Tribunaux*, 28 April 1984: 2.

152 *Gazette des Tribunaux*, 29 April 1894: 2.

153 *Gazette des Tribunaux*, 29 April 1894: 2 (italics added).

154 Merriman, 2009: 99–105.

155 Bouhey, 2008: 264–274.

156 *Gazette des Tribunaux*, 27 May 1893: 3.

157 Varennes, 1895: 96.

158 *Gazette des Tribunaux*, 27 May 1893: 3, and Varennes, 1895: 96.

159 Bookchin, 1998: 107–108.

160 Anderson, 2005: 115–116.

161 Anderson, 2005: 115–116. Salvador was tried and garroted on 21 November 1894.

162 Merriman, 2009: 126–130.

163 Malato, 1894. Of course, Henry was born in Barcelona and would have paid attention to developments there.

164 This letter was entered into evidence at his trial. See *Gazette des Tribunaux*, 24 February 1894: 2.

165 *Le Figaro*, 15 November 1893: 1 (italics mine). Henry had already used indiscriminate killing the previous year, but that bombing was still unsolved and its motive unknown.

166 *Gazette des Tribunaux*, 24 February 1894: 3.

167 See *Gazette des Tribunaux*, 11 January 1894: 1–2; Varennes, 1895: 109–123.

168 This was published in *Le Figaro*, 21 July 1894: 1. Vaillant mailed his diary to the prominent anarchist Paul Reclus on his way to the bombing. Reclus sent it to *Le Figaro*.

169 *Le Figaro*, 21 July 1894: 1.

170 Quoted in *Le Figaro*, 21 July 1894: 1 (italics added).

171 American Psychiatric Association, 2013: 208–217.

172 This fear of dying meaninglessly as motivation reminds us of Karakozov; see the previous chapter.

173 Quoted in *Le Figaro*, 21 July 1894: 1.

174 Quoted in *Le Figaro*, 21 July 1894: 1.

175 Quoted in *Le Figaro*, 21 July 1894: 1.

176 Varennes, 1895: 353–355.

177 Varennes, 1895: 123.

178 Varennes, 1895: 115–116, and *Gazette des Tribunaux*, 11 January 1894: 1.

179 Varennes, 1895: 117–120, and *Gazette des Tribunaux*, 11 January 1894: 2.

180 Varennes, 1895: 124–125.

181 Varennes, 1895: 126.

182 Varennes, 1895: 128–129.

183 Varennes, 1895: 125–164.

184 *Gazette des Tribunaux*, 29 April 1894: 2.

185 *Gazette des Tribunaux*, 29 April 1894: 2.

186 Maitron, 2007: 239, and Merriman 2009: 149.

187 Merriman, 2009: 149–161.

188 Maitron, 2007: 247, and Merriman, 2009: 174–178, believe that Pauwels is the culprit for all three bombings, but Bouhey, 2008: 292–294, disputes it. All cite contemporary police reports linking the two.

189 Merriman, 2009: 164. See also "Propaganda by Deed: The Greenwich Observatory Bomb of 1894." Bourdin was immortalized as the inspiration for the main character of Joseph Conrad's novel *The Secret Agent*.

190 Félix Fénéon, another one of Henry's anarchist companions, later confessed he had done it to a friend. See Maitron, 2007: 247, and Merriman, 2009: 172–173. See also Salmon, 1959/2008: 212–215.

191 See Varennes, 1895: 175–181, 199–207.

192 *Gazette des Tribunaux*, 28 April 1894: 2.

193 Octave Mirbeau, quoted in Maitron, 2007: 246–247.

194 Malato, quoted in Maitron, 2007: 247. Malato (1894) repeated this analysis six months later.

195 *Gazette des Tribunaux*, 29 April 1894: 2.

196 *Gazette des Tribunaux*, 29 April 1894: 2, and Varennes, 1895: 243.

197 Varennes, 1895: 256, 259–260; *Gazette des Tribunaux*, 3 August 1894: 1–2.

198 Varennes, 1894: 246–272; *Gazette des Tribunaux*, 3 August 1894: 1 and 4 August 1894: 1–2.

199 Caserio, 1894. This pleading was withheld in the newspapers at the time and in Varennes a year later because of the Scoundrel Laws.

200 Varennes, 1895: 286–345, and *Gazette des Tribunaux*, 7, 8, 9, 10, 11, 12, and 13 August 1894.

201 Varennes, 1895: ii.

202 Faure, quoted in Varennes, 1895: 306.

203 Quoted in Varennes, 1895: 346. Their acquittal gutted the essence of the Scoundrel Laws and preserved some semblance of freedom of the press and freedom of association in France.

204 Varennes, 1895: 347.

205 Maitron, 2007: 261.

206 See Ladame and Régis, 1907.

207 Goldman, 1970: 272, 289.

208 Johns, 1970: 14–15.

209 Leon Czolgosz in "The Assassin Makes a Full Confession," 1901.

210 Czolgosz, 1901.

211 Channing, 1902.

212 Goldman, 1970: 300.

213 Goldman, 1970: 304.

214 Roosevelt, 1901.

215 Kittrie and Wedlock, 1998a: 264–265.

Chapter 6

1 See Baron, 1963: 59–207.

2 See Ascher, 1972: 56–167.

3 See Naimark, 1983: 235–237.

4 Hildermeier, 2000: 45.

5 Blackwell, ed., 1918: 102–105; Hildermeier, 2000: 44.

6 Blackwell, ed., 1918: 107; Hildermeier, 2000: 42–43. Hildermeier commented that Gershuni was a born organizer and could have been the future Socialist Revolutionist Party's Lenin had he lived longer.

7 Hildermeier, 2000: 29–31.

8 Hildermeier, 2000: 31–35.

9 Kassow, 1989: 90–92.

10 Kassow, 1989: 93.

11 This was a spontaneous strike, not orchestrated from abroad. See Kassow, 1989: 104.

12 Quoted in Kassow, 1989: 105.

13 Kassow, 1989: 107–112.

14 Kassow, 1989: 114. It appears that Count Witte was behind this rule, despite the opposition of other reactionaries and the Ministry of War.

15 Kassow, 1989: 120.

16 Kassow, 1989: 123.

17 Savinkov, 1972: 11.

18 Kassow, 1989: 124–125.

19 Kassow, 1989: 126–127.

20 Kassow, 1989: 133–137.

21 Kassow, 1989: 127–131.

22 Kassow, 1989: 131, 138.

23 Hildermeier, 2000: 29–31.

24 The five major biographies of Azef are by Bernstein (1909), Longuet and Silber (1909), Boris Nikolajewsky (1934), Richard Rubenstein (1994), and Anna Geifman (2000). Of course, many people prominently mention Azef in their memoirs, including Boris Savinkov (1972), Alexander Spiridovitch (1930), and Alexander Guérassimov (1934).

25 Schleifman, 1988: 27.

26 Nikolajewsky, 1934: 41–42.

27 Nikolajewsky, 1934: 28–42; Longuet and Silber, 1909: 97–104.

28 Hildermeier, 2000: 44–45.

29 Hildermeier, 2000: 42–46. It is impossible to give a precise date of the foundation of the PSR because it arose from a series of negotiations among the representatives of various groups.

30 Bernstein, 1909: 44.

31 It is difficult to translate this expression accurately. Savinkov called it the Terrorist Brigade in translation. At the time, the word *organizatsiia* did not have the connotation of a formal group, as already mentioned in my analysis of Ishutin's "organization." As we shall see, Gershuni improvised as he went along, and his unit was more of a one-man show run out of his back pocket than anything resembling a formal entity until around the time of his arrest. CIA's Ben Fischer, 2010: 28, 48, called it the Fighting Unit and then the Combat Unit. I prefer this last expression, as it seems more colloquially appropriate in English.

32 See Hildermeier, 2000: 58.

33 Longuet and Silber, 1909: 108.

34 Spiridovitch, 1930: 150–151; Savinkov, 1972: 11.

35 Longuet and Silber, 1909: 109.

36 Gershuni, in his memoirs (Guerchouni, 1909: 72–73), wrote that an assassin dressed as a brigadier general was to kill Pobedonostsev at the exit of the Holy Synod at around the same time as Sipiagin's assassination. However, a telegram sent to the assassin never made it because of a wrong address (Longuet and Silber, 1909: 111n).

37 Quoted in Spiridovitch, 1930: 159.

38 Nikolajewsky, 1934: 50.

39 Guerchouni, 1909: 73–76. See also Longuet and Silber, 1909: 108–111. Azef was probably not involved in this planning, as indicated in a letter of his, quoted in Longuet and Silber, 1909: 114n.

40 Longuet and Silber, 1909: 110.

41 Nikolajewsky, 1934: 50–51.

42 These common disputes about very small points that distinguish various groups are just exercises in self-categorization. Often they get quite heated: "much to do about nothing." This natural tendency was poetically described by Freud as the "narcissism of small differences."

43 Lenin, 1902/1987: 210. Emphasis in the original.

44 Hildermeier, 2000: 52–54, 58–60; Geifman, 1993: 46–47.

45 Besides their outrage at government-sponsored pogroms, Jews like Gershuni also wanted to refute the myth of Jewish cowardice. See Guerchouni, 1909: 51.

46 See Hildermeier, 2000: 54–55.

47 Guerchouni, 1909: 80–82.

48 Guerchouni, 1909: 82–83; Longuet and Silber, 1909: 112–113.

49 Rubenstein, 1994: 66.

50 Nikolajewsky, 1934: 68–69; Rubenstein, 1994: 66–68.

51 Payne, 1957: 228.

52 Nikolajewsky, 1934: 65–66.

53 Guerchouni, 1909: 64–97.

54 Nikolajewsky, 1934: 67–68. Geifman (1993: 53; 2000: 55) in both of her books bizarrely claims that Savinkov took over the Combat Unit in May 1903, a time when Savinkov was still in exile (Savinkov, 1972: 10). Indeed, Savinkov's entire book clearly shows that he was subordinate to Azef, the undisputed chief of the Combat Unit.

55 Longuet and Silber, 1909: 120; Nikolajewsky, 1934: 69–70.

56 Geifman, 2000: 60.

57 Savinkov, 1972: 5–10; Spence, 1991: 8–25; Spiridovitch, 1930: 174n.

58 Payne, 1957: 289–290; Spiridovitch, 1930: 238n; Savinkov, 1972: 11, 14.

59 Quoted in Payne, 1957: 225.

60 Spiridovitch, 1930: 244; Geifman, 2000: 60; Rubenstein, 1994: 80; Savinkov, 1972: 128.

61 Ascher, 1988: 24–25.

62 Fischer, 2010: 26–28, questions the competence of Rataev as an administrator and case officer.

63 Rubenstein, 1994: 84–87; Nikolajewsky, 1934: 72–76.

64 Pokotilov quoted in Savinkov, 1972: 22.

65 Savinkov, 1972: 28.

66 Savinkov, 1972: 30–36. For a slightly different version of these events, see Spence, 1991: 32–36.

67 Savinkov, 1972: 36.

68 Savinkov, 1972: 189.

69 Savinkov, 1972: 42–43.

70 Spence, 1991: 36.

71 Savinkov, 1972: 38, 43.

72 Quoted in Savinkov, 1972: 39.

73 Quoted in Savinkov, 1972: 39. Macedonia around that time was experiencing a nationalistic insurrection against its Turkish rulers.

74 Savinkov, 1972: 40.

75 Ivanovskia, 1992.

76 Savinkov, 1972: 37.

77 Savinkov, 1972: 47. This portrait of the group describes their sense of shared social identities.

78 Savinkov, 1972: 48.

79 Savinkov, 1972: 48.

80 Savinkov, 1972: 49. However, later from prison, Sazonov wrote, "The consciousness of guilt never left me." Savinkov commented, "To the feeling of pride and joy was added another, a feeling we did not know then."

81 Spence, 1991: 37.

82 Savinkov, 1972: 54–63.

83 Nikolajewsky, 1934: 92–95. The quote is from page 94.

84 Quoted in Ascher, 1988: 43.

85 Quoted in Ascher, 1988: 54.

86 Stepan Sletov, quoted in Nikolajewsky, 1934: 88.

87 Quoted in Nikolajewsky, 1934: 90.

88 Reprinted in Savinkov, 1972: 78.

89 Reprinted in Rubenstein, 1994: 110.

90 See Spiridovitch, 1930: 188, for a complete copy of the unit's new statutes.

91 Reprinted in Savinkov, 1972: 75.

92 Nikolajewsky, 1934: 96; Savinkov, 1972: 75.

93 Nikolajewsky, 1934: 97.

94 Quoted in Nikolajewsky, 1934: 97.

95 Savinkov, 1972: 74.

96 Spiridovitch, 1930: 245; Savinkov, 1972: 79.

97 Spence, 1991: 41. Needless to say, Savinkov did not spend too much time with his wife and son.

98 Spence, 1991: 37, 40–41, 56.

99 Savinkov, 1972: 77–78.

100 Quoted in Savinkov, 1972: 78. Kaliaev obviously confused Ravachol with Henry.

101 See Ascher, 1988: 30, 31–35, for a description of Russian liberals at the turn of the century.

102 Savinkov, 1972: 79.

103 Ascher, 1988: 53–73.

104 Nikolajewsky, 1934: 95.

105 Savinkov, 1972: 79–81.

106 Payne, 1957: 249–250.

107 Quoted in Payne, 1957: 251.

108 Quoted in Payne, 1957: 252.

109 Reprinted in Payne, 1957: 255–256, and Savinkov, 1972: 66–67.

110 Spence, 1991: 44.

111 Rubenstein, 1994: 126.

112 The petition was very deferential to the tsar, believing him to be a benevolent ruler, but asked for far-reaching political demands. The entire petition is reproduced in Ascher, 1988: 87–89.

113 Ascher, 1988: 74–92. The quotes are from pages 91 and 92, respectively.

114 Savinkov, 1972: 91–93.

115 Savinkov, 1972: 96.

116 Savinkov, 1972: 97.

117 Savinkov, 1972: 99. This incident became famous in Camus's long essay on rebellion (1951) and his play *Les Justes* (1949). He called members of Savinkov's Moscow team "delicate murderers" (1951: 571–579).

118 Savinkov, 1972: 99.

119 Savinkov, 1972: 101.

120 This is the version in Savinkov, 1972: 102–103. Spence (1991: 45) claims that Kulikovsky deserted the group because he was fed up with the constant delays and was physically exhausted. Later events are more consistent with the latter than the former version. On 28 June 1905, Kulikovsky appeared at a reception for the mayor of Moscow, Count Schuvalov, where he shot him with a revolver and killed him. He was arrested, convicted, and given a death sentence, which was commuted to life at hard labor.

121 Savinkov, 1972: 104. Spence (191: 45) added that Brilliant was now a nervous wreck and confined to the hotel room. She might not have been capable of loading the bomb a third time.

122 Spence, 1991: 45.

123 Payne, 1957: 310–312; Savinkov, 1972: 107.

124 Savinkov, 1972: 105; Payne, 1957: 314.

125 Quoted in Payne, 1957: 319–320.

126 Quoted in Payne, 1957: 320.

127 Quoted in Payne, 1957: 322.

128 Reprinted in Payne, 1957: 323.

129 Reprinted in Payne, 1957: 323–324.

130 Nikolajewsky, 1934: 107–113; Rubenstein, 1994: 146–153; Savinkov, 1972: 131.

131 Quoted in Savinkov, 1972: 112–113.

132 Quoted in Payne, 1957: 332.

133 Quoted in Payne, 1957: 333.

134 Savinkov, 1972: 122, 305, 307.

135 Spence, 1991: 46, 66, 85, 99. Savinkov's incessant need for new sexual conquests helped the Okhrana, which was kept informed of some of his activities by jilted lovers. His frequent seduction of female subordinates led to accusations that he sexually exploited them and then sacrificed them when he grew tired of them. See Spence, 1991; 86.

136 See Ascher, 1988: 130.

137 Quoted in Ascher, 1988: 132.

138 Ascher, 1988: 127–174.

139 This was Rubenstein's (1994: 158–159) version. Spence (1991: 47) wrote that they grew weary of delays and simply deserted. Later events are more consistent with Spence's version: in January 1906, they threw two bombs at the governor of Chenigov, seriously wounding him. They were arrested: the husband was condemned to death and executed, and his wife was sentenced to 20 years at hard labor in Siberia.

140 Savinkov, 1972: 199.

141 Savinkov, 1972: 198–199.

142 Savinkov, 1972: 147.

143 Quoted in Savinkov, 1972: 217–219.

144 Quoted in Savinkov, 1972: 219–220.

145 Quoted in Savinkov, 1972: 220.

146 Nikolajewsky, 1934: 121–122; Spence, 1991: 48–49.

147 Geifman, 1993: 127–130.

148 For instance, Leontyeva shot a French tourist whom she mistook for former

Russian Minister of the Interior Peter Durnovo in August 1906 in Switzerland. She was tried by the Swiss and sentenced to four years' imprisonment. See Savinkov, 1972: 136.

149 Ascher, 1988: 211–242.

150 Savinkov, 1972: 155–170; Spence, 1991: 49.

151 Ascher, 1988: 275–303.

152 Fundaminsky, quoted in Savinkov, 1972: 178–179.

153 Savinkov, 1972: 179.

154 Ascher, 1988: 255.

155 Quoted in Ascher, 1988: 256.

156 Avrich, 2005b: 35–71; 91–119.

157 Ascher, 1988: 304–336.

158 Ascher, 1992: 17.

159 Savinkov, 1972: 196; Rubenstein, 1994: 187; Nikolajewsky, 1934: 135–136.

160 This account is derived from Boniece, 2003. See also Savinkov, 1972: 199.

161 Reprinted in Boniece, 2003: 588.

162 His wife had left him for a lover four years earlier. Boniece, 2003: 598.

163 Boniece, 2003: 606. It is interesting that women revolutionaries like Spiridonova and Zasulich were reduced to female stereotypes of innocence and purity, which completely ignored the role of politics in their action.

164 Quoted in Hildemeier, 2000: 119.

165 Savinkov, 1972: 203.

166 Nikolajewsky, 1934: 125–127; Rubenstein, 1994: 174–176; Savinkov, 1972: 221–230; Spence, 1991: 57–58.

167 Longuet and Silber, 1909: 151–163; Nikolajewsky, 1934: 137–148.

168 They were tried in the fall of 1906 and convicted. The bomb-maker was sentenced to ten years' hard labor and exile, and Moiseyenko was simply exiled from European Russia because the police had found no evidence against him. Moiseyenko married her and accompanied her to eastern Siberia. See Savinkov, 1972: 214.

169 It appears that Gerasimov believed his agent, despite all the evidence to the contrary. In the professional lexicon of intelligence work, this common mistake of an inexperienced case officer is called "falling in love with your agent." Gerasimov later on persisted in believing the lies that Azef told him. What is surprising is that Geifman (1993, 2000) seems to have believed Gerasimov's account despite all the evidence contradicting him. Savinkov's descriptions of his relationship with Azef and the PSR internal investigation are the most compelling accounts that are consistent with the facts.

170 Nikolajewsky, 1934: 149–159; Rubenstein, 1994: 195–202; Savinkov, 1972: 233–237.

171 Savinkov, 1972: 215–216; Nikolajewsky, 1934: 160–161.

172 The note is reprinted in Savinkov, 1972: 220–221.

173 Ascher, 1992: 78.

174 Nikolajewsky, 1934: 161.

175 Schleifman, 1988: 70–73.

176 Much later, in his memoirs, Gerasimov still insisted he did not know who planned the Dubasov attentat despite all the evidence that later surfaced. This is another example of Gerasimov "falling in love with" his agent.

177 Spence, 1991: 59–61.

178 Savinkov, 1972: 252–253.

179 Ascher, 1992: 42–80.

180 Ascher, 1992: 111–161.

181 Ascher, 1992: 162–215.

182 Ascher, 1992: 242.

183 Ascher, 1992: 240–244.

184 Ascher, 1992: 245–263. The figures come from page 248.

185 With their departure, Gerasimov lost his inside source within the Combat Unit, and with Savinkov's departure, we lose ours.

186 See Savinkov, 1972: 304–308.

187 Nikolajewsky, 1934: 208–209.

188 Savinkov, 1972: 306–307; Nikolajewsky, 1934: 210–211.

189 Ascher, 1992: 264–291.

190 Guerchouni, 1909: 271–325; Payne, 1957: 256–260. Gershuni's escape led to a crackdown on lax prison regimens. Sazonov was in the forefront of protest against cruel punishment of the prisoners through hunger strikes. Finally, on 28 November 1910, three months before his scheduled release, he could tolerate it no more and took his own life with an overdose of morphine. He wrote his family, "I believe that my suicide, deliberately committed, will arouse the attention of the public to the horrors of the Siberian prisons, and from the better members of society there will come a shout of protest. My comrades in prison will then know that voices are being raised against a government that makes torture and death common occurrences in prison life." Payne, 1957: 277. Apparently this intervention worked, and prisoners started to be treated with remarkable leniency until the Bolsheviks came to power.

191 Rubenstein, 1994: 223–224. Gotz had died of illness.

192 Nikolajewsky, 1934: 215–223; Ascher, 1992: 288–289; Rubenstein, 1994: 224–227.

193 Ascher, 1992: 326–355.

194 See Geifman, 1993: 123–222.

195 Ascher, 1992.

196 Nikolajewsky, 1934: 234–245.

197 Nikolajewsky, 1934: 268–302; Rubenstein, 1994: 249–287.

198 Nikolajewsky, 1934: 36–37.

199 Overstreet, 1951.

200 Savinkov, 1972: 10–12.

201 Savinkov, 1972: passim.

202 Le Carré, 1986.

203 Spence (1991: passim) shows that Azef's relationship with Savinkov was full of rivalry.

204 Chaliand and Blin, 2004: 189–213.

Chapter 7

1 See Chapter 5.

2 He became the inspiration for Maurice Leblanc's popular character Arsène Lupin.

3 Delpech, 2006: 10–46.

4 Quoted in Delpech, 2006: 52.

5 Delpech, 2006: 47–57.

6 Delpech, 2006: 57–75.

7 Delpech, 2006: 76–133.

8 Jacob, 2011: 17–22. His speech was reprinted in full in a pamphlet, "Why I have burglarized?"

9 Delpech, 2006: 160.

10 Jacob tried to escape 17 times from Guyana, studied law to help his fellow inmates, and organized a movement against the Guyana penitentiary. He was recalled to France in 1925 and pardoned in 1927. He then became a writer.

11 *Gazette des Tribunaux*, 14 March 1905: 4.

12 Quoted in Delpech, 2006: 206. The reference is to Jean Graves, nicknamed the "Pope of the Rue Mouffetard."

13 Delpech, 2006: 194–235. Half a century later, Jacob had grown disillusioned. "I don't believe that illegalism can free the individual in today's society. If he manages to escape from a few societal constraints by this means, the fight against society is not equal and this small gain will be offset by much heavier losses, resulting in the loss of freedom, the little freedom he had, and even the loss of his life." Maitron, 2007: 420.

14 Mercier, 1986.

15 No capital letter to emphasize equality.

16 Serge, 1937: 37–38.

17 Not in the common modern Freudian sense of the term but in the anarchist Max Stirner's (2005) sense.

18 Libertad, 1905: 2. See also Méric, 1926: 96–101.

19 Steiner, 2008: 25.

20 Serge, 1937: 37–38.

21 Maîtrejean, 2005: 73.

22 Maîtrejean, 1913: 2; Maitrejean, 2005: 117; Steiner, 2008: 15–18, 29–55.

23 *Le Matin*, 3 June 1908: 3.

24 Steiner, 2008: 56–62. It was later discovered that the first shots probably came from a police agent provocateur.

25 Michon, 1914: 190–194.

26 Serge, 2012: 15–16. Victor Serge was the nom de plume that Victor Kibaltchiche adopted after 1917. Before that, he used Le Rétif (the stubborn one) to write in *l'anarchie*.

27 Quoted in Michon, 1914: 195–196.

28 Quoted in Michon, 1914: 196–197; Serge, 2012: 16–18.

29 Serge, 2012: 19.

30 Le Rétif, 1908.

31 Serge, 2012: 23.

32 Le Rétif, 1909. The perpetrators were Paul Helfeld and Jacob Lepidus.

33 Serge, 2012: 19. Sokolov's real name was Abraham Hartenstein.

34 Quoted in R. Parry, 1987: 36.

35 Serge, 2012: 20.

36 Maîtrejean, 2005: 28.

37 Maîtrejean, 2005: 93.

38 Maîtrejean, 2005: 30.

39 Serge, 2012: 33.

40 Lavignette, 2008: 446, Serge, 2012: 25–26.

41 Lavignette, 2011: 8–50; Pagès, 2009.

42 Laut, 1910: 20.

43 Lavignette, 2008: 41–44; Lavignette, 2011: 51–57, 67–78.

44 Hervé, 1912: 229–231.

45 Hervé, 1912; Lavignette, 2011: 120–139. Hervé was finally pardoned and freed after 26 months of detention.

46 Le Rétif, 1910a: 2.

47 Lavignette, 2011: 163–176.

48 Lavignette, 2011: 211–217.

49 Serge, 2012: 35–36.

50 Serge, 2012: 26.

51 Serge, 2012: 36.

52 Serge, 2012: 41; Maîtrejean, 2005: 32–33.

53 Steiner, 2008: 235.

54 Lavignette, 2008: 133–134, 142–143.

55 Lavignette, 2008: 90–91, 103.

56 See Michon, 1914: 197.

57 Maîtrejean, 1913: 18 August: 2. The collection of her serial articles (Maîtrejean, 2005) skipped this installment.

58 Maîtrejean, 2005: 25–26, 39.

59 Maîtrejean, 2005: 40.

60 Garnier, 1912/1992: 182–183.

61 Maîtrejean, 1913: 18 August: 2.

62 Maîtrejean, 2005: 83–84.

63 Serge, 2012: 38–39.

64 Garnier, 1912/1992: 191.

65 Lavignette, 2008: 18–24, 352–356, 403–404; R. Parry, 1987: 64–72; Steiner, 2008: 100–102.

66 Serge, 2012: 39–40.

67 Callemin quoted in Maitron, 2007: 425.

68 Garnier, 1912/1992: 192.

69 Callemin's letter to his attorney on 4 April 1913, reproduced in Lavignette, 2008: 572.

70 Quoted in Maîtrejean, 2005: 46–47.

71 Maîtrejean, 2005: 47.

72 Bonnot's testament, reproduced in Lavignette, 2008: 361.

73 Lavignette, 2008; Steiner, 2008; R. Parry, 1987; Thomazo, 2009; Méric, 1926; Maitron, 2007.

74 Lavignette, 2008: 504–569.

75 Kibaltchiche and Maîtrejean got married in 1915 so she could visit him in prison.

Kibaltchiche was released in 1917. Banned from France, he went to Barcelona, where Maître-jean joined him. Eventually, he immigrated to Russia, where he became a famous revolutionary and writer under the name of Victor Serge. Metge and de Boë went to the penitentiary in Guyana. Metge served his sentence and stayed in Guyana until his death. De Boë escaped in 1923 and returned to Belgium, where he continued his political activism.

76 Le Rétif, 1912: 1.

77 André Girard, quoted in Maitron, 1992: 203.

78 Quoted in Steiner, 2008: 150.

79 Kibaltchiche's letter to Émile Armand, dated 22 January 1913, reprinted in Maitron, 1992: 204–207.

80 In Lavignette, 2008: 572.

81 Quoted in Lavignette, 2008: 575.

82 Serge, 2012: 40.

83 Serge, 2012: 47–48.

84 Serge, 2012: 51.

85 Serge, 2012: 51.

86 See Dedijer, 1966: 27–87, 202–204; Owings and Pribic, eds., 1984: viii–xvi.

87 Dedijer, 1966: 175, 226.

88 Dedijer, 1966: 178, 226.

89 Dedijer, 1966: 208–209.

90 Dedijer, 1966: 180–184.

91 Owings and Pribic, eds., 1984: xiii.

92 Gavrilo Princip, interview with Dr. Martin Pappenheim, in Armstrong, 1927: 704–705.

93 Owings and Pribic, eds., 1984: 57.

94 Dedijer, 1966: 237.

95 Dedijer, 1966: 238.

96 Dedijer, 1966: 241.

97 Dedijer, 1966: 241.

98 Dedijer, 1966: 243.

99 Quoted in Dedijer, 1966: 249.

100 Dedijer, 1966: 249; Owings and Pribic, eds., 1984: 51.

101 D. Smith, 2009: 21.

102 See Dedijer, 1966: 250–260; D. Smith, 2009: 20–27.

103 Luka Jukic, quoted in Dedijer, 1966: 264.

104 Dedijer, 1966: 262–266.

105 Dedijer, 1966: 266–267.

106 Dedijer, 1966: 268.

107 Dedijer, 1966: 270.

108 Dedijer, 1966: 271.

109 Jukic in Dedijer, 1966: 272.

110 Dedijer, 1966: 273–274.

111 Dedijer, 1966: 185–193.

112 Armstrong, 1927: 702.

113 Dedijer, 1966: 191.

114 Armstrong, 1927: 702.

115 Dedijer, 1966: 195; Armstrong, 1927: 707.

116 Dedijer, 1966: 277.

117 Dedijer, 1966: 237, 249.

118 Owings and Pribic, eds., 1984: xii, 308–319 (the reliability of this witness was challenged at the trial); Dedijer, 1966: 377–378.

119 Dedijer, 1966: 197; Owings and Pribic, eds., 1984: 55; Armstrong, 1927: 702.

120 Dedijer, 1966: 197. This was immediately after his arrest for assassinating Archduke Franz Ferdinand.

121 Owings and Pribic, eds., 1984: 55–56.

122 Dedijer, 1966: 272, 278–279.

123 Owings and Pribic, eds., 1984.

124 Nedeljko Cabrinovic, in Owings and Pribic, eds., 1984: 32.

125 Armstrong, 1927: 705; Dedijer, 1966: 185, 279; Owings and Pribic, eds., 1984: 113, 340, 388.

126 Owings and Pribic, eds., 1984: 32–33.

127 Dedijer, 1966: 201–202, 280–281; Owings and Pribic, eds., 1984: 17–21.

128 Owings and Pribic, eds., 1984: 3, 88–89, 534.

129 Armstrong, 1927: 705.

130 Namely, the reconstituted trial transcript in Owings and Pribic, eds., 1984, which had been subject to alterations (see Owings and Pribic, eds., 1984: xix–xxii); the notes of Princip's 1916 prison interview with Dr. Martin Pappenheim (Armstrong, 1927); and a careful reading of Dedijer, 1966, who occasionally falls victim to later speculations.

131 Dedijer, 1966: 288–290.

132 Owings and Pribic, eds., 1984: 56.

133 Owings and Pribic, eds., 1984: 89.

134 Armstrong, 1927: 705; Owings and Pribic, eds., 1984: 23–24, 57.

135 Owings and Pribic, eds., 1984: 25.

136 Owings and Pribic, eds., 1984: 25, 57.

137 Owings and Pribic, eds., 1984: 58.

138 Owings and Pribic, eds., 1984: 115–116.

139 Armtrong, 1927: 706.

140 Owings and Pribic, eds., 1984: 49; Didejer, 1966: 288–289.

141 Owings and Pribic, eds., 1984: 26–27.

142 Owings and Pribic, eds., 1984: 93–94.

143 Dedijer, 1966: 282–283.

144 Owings and Pribic, eds., 1984: 120. Ilic was a little inconsistent at the trial.

145 Dedijer, 1966: 264–265.

146 Owings and Pribic, eds., 1984: 118, 195.

147 Owings and Pribic, eds., 1984: 129.

148 Owings and Pribic, eds., 1984: 118, 130–131.

149 Owings and Pribic, eds., 1984: 140–142.

150 Quoted in Dedijer, 1966: 305.

151 Dedijer, 1966: 295–301; Owings and Pribic, eds., 1984.

152 Owings and Pribic, eds., 1984: 85.

153 Owings and Pribic, eds., 1984: 101.

154 Owings and Pribic, eds., 1984: 120–121.

155 Owings and Pribic, eds., 1984: 131–136.

156 Dedijer, 1966: 313–314.

157 Dedijer, 1966: 318.

158 Owings and Pribic, eds., 1984: 134.

159 Owings and Pribic, eds., 1984: 143.

160 Owings and Pribic, eds., 1984: 43–44.

161 Owings and Pribic, eds., 1984: 103. Dedijer, 1966: 318, found five versions of the reasons behind Grabez's failure to act.

162 Owings and Pribic, eds., 1984: 68.

163 Owings and Pribic, eds., 1984: 527–530.

164 D. Smith, 2009: 91; Dedijer, 1966: 393.

165 Quoted in Dedijer, 1966: 291.

166 Hoffman, 2006: 11–14, 2008. He claimed that this group was not anarchist, but Cabrinovic was foremost an anarchist and the rest of the group was strongly influenced by anarchism.

167 Sageman, 2004: 135.

168 Owings and Pribic, eds., 1984: 128.

169 Owings and Pribic, eds., 1984: 140–141.

170 Owings and Pribic, eds., 1984: vi.

171 Lukas, 1997.

172 Irwin, 2013: 1–75; McManigal, 1913.

173 Irwin, 2013: 72. See also Adams, 1966: 1–17.

174 Quoted in Irwin, 2013: 83.

175 Goldman, 1970: 479.

176 McManigal, 1913: 34.

177 T. Jones, 2012: 111–115, 122.

178 West, 1915: 127, 130–131.

179 Outraged, the miners started out an all-out insurrection, which ended with the introduction of neutral U.S. government troops. Eight months later, the miners called off the strike when their union ran out of money. Although the miners lost, the company eventually gave in to most of their demands, paving the way for further labor reforms.

180 Quoted in T. Jones, 2012: 167.

181 Avrich and Avrich, 2012: 223–230; T. Jones, 2012: 211–217.

182 Charles Plunkett, in Avrich, 2005a: 218. See also T. Jones, 2012: 226–228.

183 See Frost, 1968, and Gentry, 1967. After 23 years in prison, they were released and eventually pardoned for a crime they never committed.

184 Avrich and Avrich, 2012: 265–266.

185 This campaign of violence is described in detail in Avrich, 1991.

186 Watson, 2005.

187 Avrich, 1991: 63.

188 Avrich, 1991: 95.

189 Avrich, 1991: 59–60.

190 Avrich, 1991: 65.

191 Avrich, 1991: 66.

192 Avrich, 1991: 104.

193 Avrich, 1991: 102.

194 See Chapter 5.

195 Avrich, 1991: 105, speculated that Buda and Valdinoci came from Chicago and Youngstown, respectively, to plant the bomb.

196 Passante, 2008. The Wisconsin Supreme Court overturned the verdicts in April 1919, finding no evidence of a preconceived conspiracy to commit harm. The prisoners were then deported back to Italy.

197 Avrich, 1991: 156.

198 Avrich, 1991: 128–135.

199 Reprinted in Avrich, 1991: 137.

200 See Hagerdorn, 2007; Gage, 2009; and Murray, 1964.

201 Avrich, 1991: 140–147.

202 Avrich, 1991: 149–162. Avrich believes that Sacco and Vanzetti participated in this wave of bombings.

203 Avrich, 1991: 196.

204 Avrich, 1991: 135.

205 Avrich, 1991: 165–177; Hagerdorn, 2007; Murray, 1964.

206 Avrich, 1991: 197–199.

207 Avrich, 1991: 199–204.

208 Avrich, 1991: 193.

209 Quoted in Avrich, 1991: 204.

210 Avrich, 1991: 204–205. They were tried for these murders, convicted, and sentenced to death in July 1921. Despite a huge wave of protest against the unfairness of the proceedings, their appeal was rejected. They were electrocuted on 28 July 1927.

211 Avrich, 1991: 205.

212 Gage, 2009: 329–330, gives a list of the victims. See also Avrich, 1991: 206. Mario Buda sailed for Naples a few weeks later and died in Italy in 1963.

Chapter 8

1 See Reicher, 2003; Drury and Reicher, 2000; and Zomeren, Postmes, and Spears, 2008.

2 Apparently unprovoked attacks by foreign diaspora communities respond to an escalation of state violence abroad.

3 Unfortunately, western liberal democracies do not always live up to this standard. See the 1881 prosecution of Johann Most in Britain, the 1893 Scoundrel Laws in France, the late nineteenth-century prosecution of anarchists in the United States (all discussed in Chapter 5), and the 1917 Espionage Act in the United States banning criticism of the war under the charge of conspiracy of interfering with the draft (see Chapter 7).

4 See Chapter 5.

5 Like People's Will, the Combat Unit of the Socialist Revolutionary Party, the tragic bandits, or the Galleani group.

6 Like Ravachol or Vailland in Chapter 5.

7 For instance, the victory of the African National Congress in the Republic of South Africa.

8 Figner, 1991: 116.

9 See Della Porta, 2013, for an analysis of clandestine political violence, and Serge (2012: 47–48) for an illustration of this narrowing of cognitive horizons (see Chapter 7).

10 People's Will, the Terrorist Faction of People's Will, the French anarchists' campaign of violence, the PSR Combat Unit, the tragic bandits, and the Galleanists are examples of such obsession. This is also contrary to rational choice theory, which would predict that each of these setbacks would be a deterrent to further violence.

11 Kahneman, 2011.

12 See Bargh, Gollwitzer, and Oettingen, 2010: 288–306, for a review of this intriguing literature.

13 This was discovered about American troops in World War II: Stouffer et al., 1965: 105–191.

14 As demonstrated with some Russian and French anarchists (see Chapters 6 and 7).

15 For instance, People's Will's assassination of Alexander II, the Fenian Skirmishers' twin bombings of the Tower of London and Parliament, Caserio's assassination of President Carnot, and Buda's Wall Street bombing.

16 The gradual transformations of Land and Liberty into People's Will (see Chapter 4) is good example of this process.

17 Jones and Libicki, 2008: 18–20.

18 Cronin, 2009.

19 Furet (2007: 17, 221–794) also sees this period as a conflict between the Revolution and the Restoration.

20 See Whelehan, 2012, and McKenna, 2012.

21 Haslam, Reicher, and Platow, 2011: 109–120.

22 For instance, the indicators of radicalization published by the French government in January 2015 at http://www.stop-djihadisme.gouv.fr/decrypter.html are indicators of the global neo-jihadi protest community rather than its violent members.

23 Sageman, 2014, explains this alarmist tendency within state agencies.

24 Federal law on entrapment requires proof of a predisposition to violence for conviction.

25 See Aaronson, 2013, and Lustick, 2006, for an analysis of these tactics in the present global neo-jihadi wave of terrorism. An entrapment tactic was successfully used by the Okhrana in 1890 in Paris to turn the French population and government against Russian revolutionary émigrés in that city and led to the French-Russian entente but did not prevent later violence. See Longuet and Silber, 1909: 218–244; Fischer, 2010: 31–46; and Bataille, 1891: 217–258.

26 Mueller, 2006, and Lustick, 2006. The Great Fear of 1789 and the events leading to the Terror illustrate such panicky hysteria.

27 Sageman, 2016: 23–54.

28 See Sageman, 2016: 62–65.

29 For instance, the Italian attentats against Napoleon III (see Chapter 3).

30 The failure to understand the international dimension of the first World Trade Center bombing in 1993 unnecessarily delayed combating the global neojihadi threat against the United States.

31 See the Haymarket bombing trial, the Homestead attentat trial (Chapter 5), the Mooney-Billings and Sacco and Vanzetti frame-ups (Chapter 7), continuing to the 1960s trials against New Left militants and more recent trials against Muslims.

32 Like Grouvelle (Chapter 3), People's Will (Chapter 4), anarchists (Chapter 5), and the tragic bandits and Galleanists (Chapter 7).

33 Pinker, 2011.

Appendix

1 See Whelehan, 2012, and McKenna, 2012.

2 See Mandela, 2013.

3 See Harbi and Meynier, 2004 and Meynier, 2002.

4 See Delarue, 1994, and G. Fleury, 2002.

5 See Ayers, 2009; Gitlin, 1993; Hayden, 1988; H. Jacobs, ed., 1970; Rudd, 2009; Sale, 1973; Varon, 2004; Wilkerson, 2007.

6 See Fetscher and Rohrmoser, 1981; Jäger et al., 1981; Bäyer-Katte et al., 1982; Aust, 2008; and J. Smith and Moncourt, 2009.

7 See Della Porta, 1995.

8 See Ibrahim, 1980, 1982, 1988, and Kepel, 1993.

9 See Sageman, 2007: 9–32.

10 See Aho, 1995, and Levitas, 2002.

11 See Danzig et al., 2011.

12 See Aggoun and Rivoire, 2004; Labat, 1995; Lariège, 2005; Martinez, 1998; Mousaoui, 2006; Zerrouky, 2002.

13 I relied mostly on primary source material entered in the discovery for *Linde et al. v. Arab Bank*, 2015.

14 See Bergen, 2006; Coll, 2004; McDermott, 2005; National Commission on Terrorist Attacks Upon the United States, 2004; Sageman, 2004, 2008; Scheuer, 2002; and Wright, 2006.

15 See Ragin, 2000, 2008, as well as Smithson and Verkuilen, 2006.

16 Some perpetrators viewed themselves as soldiers defending their honor but not their comrades or the cause, like Fieschi and Lecomte, See Chapter 3.

17 See Ragin, 2000: 203–229.

18 See Chapter 3. This Henry, who carried out an attentat in 1846, should not be confused with Émile Henry of 1890s notoriety.

19 This is also the case for a minority of attacks commissioned from abroad in global neojihad terrorism.

Bibliography

Aaronson, Trevor, 2013, *The Terror Factory: Inside the FBI's Manufactured War on Terrorism*, Brooklyn, NY: Ig Publishing.

Abella, Alex, 2008, *Soldiers of Reason: The RAND Corporation and the Rise of the American Empire*, Orlando, FL: Harcourt.

Abou el Fadl, Khaled, 2005, *The Great Theft: Wrestling Islam from the Extremists*, New York: HarperCollins.

Académie Françoise, 1798, *Dictionnaire de l'Académie Françoise*, 5th ed., vol. 2: *L–Z*, Paris: J. J. Smits.

Adamic, Louis, 2008, *Dynamite: The Story of Class Violence in America*, Oakland, CA: AK Press.

Adams, Graham, 1966, *Age of Industrial Violence, 1910–15*, New York: Columbia University Press.

Adorno, T. W., Else Frenkel-Brunswik, Daniel Levinson, and Nevitt Sanford, 1950, *The Authoritarian Personality*, New York: Harper and Brothers.

Advielle, Victor, 1884, *Histoire de Gracchus Babeuf et du Babouvisme*, 2 vols., Paris: Chez Advielle.

Aggoun, Lounis, and Jean-Baptiste Rivoire, 2004, *Françalgérie, Crimes et Mensonges d'États: Histoire Secrète, de la Guerre d'Indépendance à la "Troisième Guerre" d'Algérie*, Paris: La Découverte.

Aho, James, 1995, *The Politics of Righteousness: Idaho Christian Patriotism*, Seattle: University of Washington Press.

Allport, Gordon, 1954, *The Nature of Prejudice*, Cambridge, MA: Addison-Wesley.

Alpert, Jane, 1981, *Growing Up Underground*, New York: William Morrow.

Altgeld, John, 1893/1986, *Reasons for Pardoning the Haymarket Anarchists*, Chicago: Charles H. Kerr.

Amann, Peter, 1975, *Revolution and Mass Democracy: The Paris Club Movement in 1848*, Princeton, NJ: Princeton University Press.

American Psychiatric Association, 2013, *Diagnostic and Statistical Manual of Mental Disorders*, 5th ed., Washington, DC: American Psychiatric Association.

Anderson, Benedict, 1991, *Imagined Communities: Reflections on the Origin and Spread of Nationalism,* rev. ed., London: Verso.

———, 2005, *Under Three Flags: Anarchism and the Anti-colonial Imagination,* London: Verso.

Andress, David, 2005, *The Terror: The Merciless War for Freedom in Revolutionary France,* New York: Farrar, Straus and Giroux.

Andrews, Richard, 1985, "Social Structures, Political Elites and Ideology in Revolutionary Paris, 1792–94: A Critical Evaluation of Albert Soboul's Les Sans-Culottes Parisiens en l'An II," *Journal of Social History* 19(1): 71–112.

Archives Parlementaires de 1787 à 1860, Recueil Complet des Débats Législatifs and Politiques des Chambres Françaises, 1st series (1789–1799), vol. VIII: *du 5 Mai 1789 au 15 Septembre 1789,* 1875, Paris: Librairie Administrative de Paul Dupont.

Archives Parlementaires de 1787 à 1860, Recueil Complet des Débats Législatifs and Politiques des Chambres Françaises, 1st series (1789–1799), vol. XV: *Assemblée Nationale Constituante, du 21 Avril 1790 au 30 Mai 1790,* 1883, Paris: Société d'Imprimerie et Librairie Administratives et des Chemins de Fer, Paul Dupont.

Archives Parlementaires de 1787 à 1860, Recueil Complet des Débats Législatifs and Politiques des Chambres Françaises, 1st series (1787–1799), vol. LX: *du 9 Mars 1793 au 30 Mars 1793,* 1901, Paris: Société d'Imprimerie et Librairie Administratives et des Chemins de Fer, Paul Dupont, Éditeur.

Archives Parlementaires de 1787 à 1860, Recueil Complet des Débats Législatifs and Politiques des Chambres Françaises, 1st series (1789–1799), vol. LXX: *du 30 Juillet 1793 au 9 Aout 1793,* 1906, Paris: Imprimerie et Librairie Administratives et des Chemins de Fer, Paul Dupont, Éditeur.

Archives Parlementaires de 1787 à 1860, Recueil Complet des Débats Législatifs and Politiques des Chambres Françaises, 1st series (1789–1799), vol. LXXIII: *du 25 Aout au 17 Septembre 1793,* 1908, Paris: Librairie Administrative Paul Dupont.

Archives Parlementaires de 1787 à 1860, Recueil Complet des Débats Législatifs and Politiques des Chambres Françaises, 1st series (1787–1799), vol. LXXIV: *du 12 Septembre 1793 au 22 Septembre 1793,* 1909, Paris: Librairie Administrative Paul Dupont.

Arena, Michael, and Bruce Arrigo, 2006, *The Terrorist Identity: Explaining the Terrorist Threat,* New York: New York University Press.

Armstrong, Hamilton, 1927, "Confessions of the Assassin Whose Deed Led to the World War," *Current History* 26(5): 699–707.

Asch, Solomon, 1956, "Studies of Independence and Conformity: A Minority of One Against a Unanimous Majority," *Psychological Monographs: General and Applied* 70(9): 1–70.

Ascher, Abraham, 1972, *Pavel Axelrod and the Development of Menshevism,* Cambridge, MA: Harvard University Press.

———, 1988, *The Revolution of 1905: Russia in Disarray,* Stanford, CA: Stanford University Press.

———, 1992, *The Revolution of 1905: Authority Restored*, Stanford, CA: Stanford University Press.

"The Assassin Makes a Full Confession: For Three Days Czolgosz Had Planned the Attack," 1901, *New York Times*, 8 September.

Atran, Scott, 2010, *Talking to the Enemy: Faith, Brotherhood, and the (Un)Making of Terrorists*, New York: HarperCollins.

Attentats et Complots contre Napoléon III: Histoire Complète des Attentats et des Complots jusqu'à ce Jour, 1870, Paris: A. Chevalier, Éditeur.

Aulard, Alphonse, 1902, *Paris pendant la Réaction Thermidorienne et sous le Directoire*, vol. V, Paris: Librairie Léopold Cerf.

———, 1903, *Paris sous le Consulat: Recueil de Documents pour l'Histoire de l'Esprit Public à Paris*, 4 vols., Paris: Librairie Léopold Cerf.

———, 1923, *La Théorie de la Violence et la Révolution Française, Discours prononcé au Congrès des Sociétés Savantes á la Sorbonne, le 6 Avril 1923*, Paris: Ligue des Droits de l'Homme.

Aust, Stephen, 2008, *The Baader Meinhof Complex*, London: Bodley Head.

Avorn, Jerry, et al., 1969, *Up Against the Ivy Wall: A History of the Columbia Crisis*, New York: Atheneum.

Avrich, Paul, 1976, *Russian Rebels, 1600–1800*, New York: W. W. Norton.

———, 1984, *The Haymarket Tragedy*, Princeton, NJ: Princeton University Press.

———, 1988, *Anarchist Portraits*, Princeton, NJ: Princeton University Press.

———, 1991, *Sacco and Vanzetti: The Anarchist Background*, Princeton, NJ: Princeton University Press.

———, 2005a, *Anarchist Voices: An Oral History of Anarchism in American*, Oakland, CA: AK Press.

———, 2005b, *The Russian Anarchists*, Oakland, CA: AK Press.

Avrich, Paul, and Karen Avrich, 2012, *Sasha and Emma: The Anarchist Odyssey of Alexander Berkman and Emma Goldman*, Cambridge, MA: Harvard University Press.

Ayers, Bill, 2009, *Fugitive Days: Memoirs of an Antiwar Activist*, Boston: Beacon Press.

Baczko, Bronislaw, 1989, *Comment Sortir de la Terreur: Thermidor et la Révolution*, Paris: Éditions Gallimard.

Baker, Keith Michael, 1987, "Politique et opinion publique sous l'Ancien Régime," *Annales: Économies, Sociétés, Civilisations* 42(1): 41–71.

Baker, Raymond, 2003, *Islam Without Fear: Egypt and the New Islamists*, Cambridge, MA: Harvard University Press.

Bakunin, Mikhail, 1869/1987, "Revolution, Terrorism, Banditry," in Laqueur and Alexander, eds., 1987: 65–68.

———, 1972, *Bakunin on Anarchy: Selected Works by the Activist-Founder of World Anarchism*, New York: Alfred A. Knopf.

Bandura, Albert, 1990, "Mechanisms of Moral Disengagement," in Reich, ed., 1990: 161–191.

Bantman, Constance, 2006, "Internationalism Without an International?

Cross-Channel Anarchist Networks, 1880–1914," *Revue Belge de philologie et d'histoire* 84(4): 961–981.

Bargh, John, Peter Gollwitzer, and Gabriele Oettingen, 2010, "Motivation," in Fiske, Gilbert, and Lindzey, eds., 2010: 268–316.

Barker, Eileen, 1984, *The Making of a Moonie: Choice or Brainwashing?* Oxford: Basil Blackwell.

Baron, Samuel, 1963, *Plekhanov: The Father of Russian Marxism*, Stanford, CA: Stanford University Press.

Bassiouni, Cherif, ed., 1975, *International Terrorism and Political Crimes*, Springfield, IL: Charles C. Thomas.

Bataille, Albert, 1883, *Causes criminelles et mondaines de 1882*, Paris: E. Dentu, Éditeur.

——, 1884, *Causes criminelles et mondaines de 1883*, Paris: E. Dentu, Éditeur.

——, 1886, *Causes criminelles et mondaines de 1885*, Paris: E. Dentu, Éditeur.

——, 1888, *Causes criminelles et mondaines de 1887–1888*, Paris: E. Dentu, Éditeur.

——, 1891, *Causes criminelles et mondaines de 1890*, Paris: E. Dentu, Éditeur.

——, 1892, *Causes criminelles et mondaines de 1891*, Paris: E. Dentu, Éditeur.

——, 1893, *Causes criminelles et mondaines de 1892*, Paris: E. Dentu, Éditeur.

——, 1894, *Causes criminelles et mondaines de 1893*, Paris: E. Dentu, Éditeur.

Baumeister, Roy, 1997, *Evil: Inside Human Violence and Cruelty*, New York: W. H. Freeman and Company.

Bäyer-Katte, Wanda von, Dieter Clässens, Hubert Feger, and Friedhelm Neidhardt, 1982, *Analysen zum Terrorismus*, vol. III: *Gruppenprozesse*, Opladen: Westdeutscher Verlag.

Bell, David, 2001, *The Cult of the Nation in France: Inventing Nationalism, 1680–1800*, Cambridge, MA: Harvard University Press.

Benjamin, Daniel, and Steven Simon, 2002, *The Age of Sacred Terror*, New York: Random House.

Bergen, Peter, 2006, *The Osama bin Laden I Know: An Oral History of al Qaeda's Leader*, New York: Free Press.

Berkman, Alexander, 1912, *Prison Memoirs of an Anarchist*, New York: Mother Earth Press.

Bernet, Anne, 2007, *Histoire générale de la Chouannerie*, Paris: Perrin.

Bernstein, I., 1909, *L'Affaire Azeff: Histoire et Documents*, Paris: No. 16 des Publications Périodiques de la Société des Amis du Peuple Russe, Librairie Stock.

Billington, James, 1980, *Fire in the Minds of Men: Origins of the Revolutionary Faith*, New York: Basic Books.

Bjørgo, Tore, and John Horgan, 2009, *Leaving Terrorism Behind: Individual and Collective Disengagement*, London: Routledge.

Blackwell, Alice Stone, ed., 1918, *The Little Grandmother of the Russian Revolution: Reminiscences and Letters of Catherine Breshkovsky*, Boston: Little, Brown.

Blanc, Louis, 1846, *Histoire de dix ans: 1830–1840,* 5th ed., 5 vols., Paris: Pagnerre, Éditeur.

Bloom, Mia, 2005, *Dying to Kill: The Allure of Suicide Terror,* New York: Columbia University Press.

Boniece, Sally, 2003, "The Spiridonova Case, 1906: Terror, Myth, and Martyrdom," *Kritika: Explorations in Russian and Eurasian History* 4(3): 571–606.

Bonney, Richard, 2004, *Jihad: From Qur'an to bin Laden,* Houndmills, Hampshire: Palgrave Macmillan.

Bookchin, Murray, 1998, *The Spanish Anarchists: The Heroic Years, 1868–1936,* Oakland, CA: AK Press.

Borowitz, Albert, 2005, *Terrorism for Self-Glorification: The Herostratos Syndrome,* Kent, OH: Kent State University Press.

Borum, Randy, 2004, *Psychology of Terrorism,* Tampa: University of South Florida.

Borum, Randy, Robert Fein, Bryan Vossekuil, and John Berglund, 1999, "Threat Assessment: Defining an Approach for Evaluating Risk of Targeted Violence," *Behavioral Sciences and the Law* 17: 323–337.

Bouhey, Vivien, 2008, *Les anarchistes contre la République: Contribution a l'histoire des réseaux sous la Troisième République (1880–1914),* Rennes: Presses Universitaires de Rennes.

Bourdin, Philippe, 2002, "La Terreur et la Mort," *Les Cahiers de Médiologie* 1: 79–89.

Braczko, Stanislaw, 1989, "Thermidorians," in Furet and Ozouf, eds., 2009: 400–413.

Bredin, Jean-Denis, 1988, *Sieyès: La clé de la Révolution française,* Paris: Éditions de Fallois.

Broido, Vera, 1977, *Apostles into Terrorists: Women and the Revolutionary Movement in the Russia of Alexander II,* New York: Viking Press.

Browning, Christopher, 1992, *Ordinary Men: Reserve Police Battalion 101 and the Final Solution in Poland,* New York: HarperCollins.

Bruce, Robert, 1989, *1877: Year of Violence,* Chicago: Ivan R. Dee.

Bruguière, Jean-Louis, 2009, *Ce que je n'ai pas pu dire: entretiens avec Jean-Marie Pontaut,* Paris: Éditions Robert Laffont.

Brunot, Ferdinand, 1937, *Histoire de la Langue Française, des Origines à 1900,* vol. IX: *La Révolution et l'Empire,* Paris: Librairie Armand Colin.

Buchez, Philippe, and Pierre Roux-Lavergne, eds., 1834, *Histoire Parlementaire de la Révolution Française, out Journal des Assemblées Nationales, Depuis 1789 jusqu'en 1815,* Paris: Paulin, Libraire.

Buford, Bill, 1993, *Among the Thugs,* New York: Vintage.

Buonarroti, Philippe, 1828, *Conspiration pour l'égalité dite de Babeuf, suivie du procès auquel elle donna lieu, et des pieces justificatives, etc., etc.,* 2 vols., Brussels: A la Librarie Romantique.

Burgat, François, 2005, *L'islamisme à l'heure d'Al-Qaida,* Paris: Éditions La Découverte.

Burgoyne, Arthur, 1979, *The Homestead Strike of 1892*, Pittsburgh: University of Pittsburgh Press.

Burke, Edmund, 1790/n.d., *Reflections on the Revolution in France*, New Rochelle, NY: Arlington House.

———, 1795/1999, *Selected Works of Edmund Burke*, vol. 3: *Letters on a Regicide Peace*, Indianapolis: Liberty Funds.

Burleigh, Michael, 2009, *Blood and Rage: A Cultural History of Terrorism*, New York: HarperCollins.

Burstin, Haim, 2005a, *L'Invention du Sans-culotte: Regard sur le Paris Révolutionnaire*, Paris: Odile Jacob.

———, 2005b, *Une Révolution à l'Oeuvre: Le Faubourg Saint-Marcel (1789–1794)*, Seyssel: Champ Vallon.

———, 2013, *Révolutionnaires: Pour une anthropologie politique de la Révolution française*, Paris: Vendémaire Éditions.

Bush, George, 2001, "Address to a Joint Session of Congress and the American People," United State Capitol, Washington, DC, 20 September, available at http://georgewbush-whitehouse.archives.gov/news/releases/2001/09/20010920-8.html.

Butterworth, Alex, 2010, *The World That Never Was: A True Story of Dreamers, Schemers, Anarchists and Secret Agents*, New York: Pantheon Books.

Cadoudal, Georges de, 1887, *Georges Cadoudal et la Chouannerie*, Paris: Librairie Plon.

Campardon, Émile, 1975, *Le Tribunal Révolutionnaire de Paris*, Geneva: Slatkine-Megariotis Reprints.

Camus, Albert, 1949, *Les Justes*, in Albert Camus, 1962, *Théâtre, Récits, Nouvelles*, Paris: Gallimard Bibliothèque de la Pléiade, 301–393.

———, 1951, *L'Homme Révolté*, in Albert Camus, 1965, *Essais*, Paris: Gallimard Bibliothèque de la Pléiade, 407–709.

Carr, Matthew, 2006, *The Infernal Machine: A History of Terrorism from the Assassination of Tsar Alexander II to Al-Qaeda*, New York: New Press.

Carrot, Georges, 2005, "La Police et la Révolution," in Michel Aubouin, Arnaud Teyssier, and Jean Tulard, eds., 2005, *Histoire et Dictionnaire de la Police du Moyen Age à nos Jours*, Paris: Bouqins, Éditions Robert Laffont,, 219–268.

Carton, Evan, 2006, *Patriotic Treason: John Brown and the Soul of America*, New York: Free Press.

Carus, Seth, 2000, "The Rajneeshees (1984)," in Jonathan Tucker, ed., 2000, *Toxic Terror: Assessing Terrorist Use of Chemical and Biological Weapons*, Cambridge, MA: MIT Press, 115–137.

Caserio, Sante, 1894, "Pleading," read at his trial in trial on 3 August; available at http://www.non-fides.fr/?Plaidoyer.

Casselle, Pierre, 2016, *L'Anti-Robespierre: Jérôme Pétion ou la Révolution pacifique*, Paris: Éditions Vendémiaire.

Cesari, Jocelyne, 2004, *L'Islam à l'épreuve de l'Occident*, Paris: Éditions La Découverte.

Chaliand, Gérard, and Arnaud Blin, 2004, *Histoire du Terrorisme: De l'Antiquité à Al Qaida*, Paris: Bayard.

Channing, Walter, 1902, "The Mental Status of Czolgosz, the Assassin of President McKinley," *American Journal of Insanity* 54(2): 1–46.

Chernyshevsky, Nikolai, 1863/1989, *What Is to Be Done?* Ithaca, NY: Cornell University Press.

Childs, Jessie, 2014, *God's Traitors: Terror and Faith in Elizabethan England*, Oxford: Oxford University Press.

Clarke, Ronald, and Graeme Newman, 2006, *Outsmarting the Terrorists*, Westport, CT: Praeger Security International.

Clay, Stephen, 2007, "Justice, vengeance et passé révolutionnaire: les crimes de la terreur blanche," *Annales Historiques de la Révolution Française*, no. 350: 109–133.

Cobb, Richard, 1970, *The Police and the People: French Popular Protest, 1789–1820*, Oxford: Oxford University Press.

———, 1987, *The People's Armies*, New Haven: Yale University Press.

Cohen, Stanley, 2002, *Folk Devils and Moral Panics: The Creation of the Mods and Rockers*, London: Routledge Classics.

Colombani, Jean-Marie, 2001, "Nous sommes tous Américains," *Le Monde*, 13 September.

Coll, Steve, 2004, *Ghost Wars: The Secret History of the CIA, Afghanistan, and bin Laden, from the Soviet Invasion to September 10, 2001*, New York: Penguin Books.

Collins, Randall, 2008, *Violence: A Micro-sociological Theory*, Princeton, NJ: Princeton University Press.

Confino, Michael, 1966, "Bakunin et Necaev: Les débuts de la rupture: introduction á deux lettres inédites de Michel Bakunin—2 et 9 Juin 1870," *Cahiers du Monde russe et soviétique* 7(4): 581–699.

———, 1989, "Idéologie et sémantique: Le vocabulaire politique des anarchistes Russes," *Cahiers du Monde russe et soviétique* 30(3–4): 255–284.

———, 1990, "Révolte Juvénile et Contre-Culture: Les Nihilistes Russes des 'Années 60,'" *Cahiers du Monde russe et soviétique* 31(4): 489–538.

Considérant, Victor, 1854, *Ma Justification*, Brussels: Imprimerie de K. Verbruggen.

Cooke, Michael, 2000, *Commanding Right and Forbidding Wrong in Islamic Thought*, Cambridge: Cambridge University Press.

Coolsaet, Rik, ed., 2011, *Jihadi Terrorism and the Radicalisation Challenge: European and American Experiences,* 2nd ed., Farnham, Surrey: Ashgate.

Corday, Charlotte, 1863, *Oeuvres Politiques de Chalotte de Corday, Décapitée à Paris le 17 Juillet 1793, réunies par un Bibliophile Normand (Ch. Renard)*, Caen: Le Gost, Libraire.

———, 1864, *Supplément aux Oeuvres de Charlotte de Corday, publiée par un Bibliophile Normand (Ch. Renard)*, Caen: Le Gost, Libraire.

Cour d'Assises de la Seine, 1838, *Affaire Huber: Attentat Contre la Vie du Roi*, Paris: A. Henry, Imprimeur de la Chambre des Députés.

———, 1855, "Affaire Pianori: Attentat contre la Vie de l'Empereur," *Journal des Débats Politiques et Littéraires*, 8 May: 2–3.

———, 1857, "Complot contre la Personne de l'Empereur," *Journal des Débats Politiques et Littéraires*, 7 August: 2–3; 8 August: 2; 4 September: 2.

———, 1858, *Procès de Orsini, de Rudio, Gomez, Pierri et Bernard, Attentat du 14 Janvier 1858, contre la Vie de S.M. Napoléon III, Empereur des Français— Audiences des 25 et 26 Février 1858*, Paris: G. Martin, Librairie.

———, 1864, "Complot contre la Vie de l'Empereur—Accusation contre Mazzini et autres," *Journal des Débats Politiques et Littéraires*, 26 February: 2–4; 27 February: 2–3.

———, 1867, "Attentat Commis sur la personne de l'Empereur Alexandre à l'issue de la revue passé au bois de Boulogne le 6 juin," *Journal des Débats Politiques et Littéraires*, 16 July: 1–2; 17 July: 1–2.

Cour d'Assises du Nord (Douai), 1855, "Affaire dite de Pérenchies—Machine Infernales—Tentative d'Assassinat contre la Personne de l'Empereur des Français—Complot contre la Sureté de l'État," *La Belgique Judiciaire* 13(66): 1041–1054.

Cour des Pairs, 1839, *Procès des Accusés des 12 et 13 Mai devant la Cour des Pairs contenant les faits préliminaires, les débats, les interrogatoires, les dépositions des témoins, les requisitoires, les plaidoiries, les répliques et l'arrêt de condamnation*, Paris: Pagnerre, Éditeur.

———, 1840, *Procès des Accusés des 12 et 13 Mai devant la Cour des Pairs, 2e Catégorie;—Blanqui et autres, contenant les faits préliminaires, les débats, les interrogatoires, les dépositions des témoins, les requisitoires, les plaidoiries, les répliques et l'arrêt de condamnation*, Paris: Pagnerre, Éditeur.

———, 1841, *Attentat du 13 Septembre 1841: Interrogatoires de Inculpés*, Paris: Imprimerie Royale.

Crenshaw, Martha, ed., 1995, *Terrorism in Context*, University Park: Pennsylvania State University Press.

———, 2011, *Explaining Terrorism: Causes, Processes and Consequences*, London: Routledge.

Croft, Lee, 2006, *Nikolai Ivanovich Kibalchich: Terrorist Rocket Pioneer*, Tempe, AZ: Institute for Issues in the History of Science.

Crone, Patricia, 2004, *God's Rule: Government and Islam, Six Centuries of Medieval Islamic Political Thought*, New York: Columbia University Press.

Cronin, Audrey, 2009, *How Terrorism Ends: Understanding the Decline and Demise of Terrorist Campaigns*, Princeton, NJ: Princeton University Press.

Czolgosz, Leon, 1901, *Signed Confession*, 6 September; available at http://www.shapell.org/manuscript.aspx?mckinley-assassin-confession.

Danzig, Richard, Marc Sageman, Terrance Leighton, Lloyd Hough, Hidemi Yuki, Rui Kotani, Zachary Hosford, 2011, *Aum Shinrikyo: Insights into How Terrorists Develop Biological and Chemical Weapons*, Washington, DC: Center for a New American Security.

Darrah, David, 1953, *Conspiracy in Paris: The Strange Career of Joseph Picot de*

Limoelan, Aristocrat, Soldier and Priest, and the Gunpowder Plot Against Napoleon on 3 Nivôse, Year IX (December 24, 1800), New York: Exposition Press.

Davis, Mike, 2007, *Buda's Wagon: A Brief History of the Car Bomb*, London: Verso.

Débats du Procès Instruit par la Haute-Cour de Justice, Séante à Vendôme, Contre Drouet, Babeuf, et autres; Recueillis par des Sténographes, 4 vols., 1797, Paris: Chez Baudouin Imprimeur du Corps Législatif.

Dedijer, Vladimir, 1966, *The Road to Sarajevo*, New York: Simon and Schuster.

Defrance, Eugène, 1909, *Charlotte Corday et la Mort de Marat*, Paris: Mercure de France.

Delarue, Jacques, 1994, *L'O.A.S. Contre de Gaulle, Nouvelle Édition*, Paris: Fayard.

Della Porta, Donatella, 1995, *Social Movements, Political Violence, and the State: A Comparative Analysis of Italy and Germany*, Cambridge: Cambridge University Press.

———, 2013, *Clandestine Political Violence*, New York: Cambridge University Press.

Della Porta, Donatella, and Mario Diani, 1999, *Social Movements: An Introduction*, Oxford: Blackwell.

Delpech, Jean-Marc, 2006, *Parcours et Reseaux d'un Anarchiste: Alexandre Marius Jacob, 1979–1954*, Nancy, France: Thèse de doctorat en histoire contemporaine à l'Université de Nancy II.

Desmarest, Pierre-Marie, 1833, *Témoignages Historiques ou Quinze Ans de Haute Police sous Napoléon*, Paris: Alphonse Levavasseur, Libraire.

Destrem, Jean, 1885, *Les Déportations du Consulat et de l'Empire*, Paris: Jean-maire, Librairie.

Drury, John, and Steve Reicher, 2000, "Collective Action and Psychological Change: The Emergence of New Social Identities," *British Journal of Social Psychology* 39: 579–604.

Dubois, Préfet de Police, 1801, *Rapports Officiels et Complets Fait au Gouvernement, par le Prefet de Police de Paris*, Paris: Imprimerie de Marchant.

Dumas, Alexandre (père), 1851, *Les Crimes Célèbres*, Paris: Librairie Théatrale—Bibliothèque de Ville et de Campagne.

Dupuy, 1997, *Les Chouans*, Paris: Hachettes Littératures—La Vie Quotidienne.

Engel, Barbara, and Clifford Rosenthal, eds., 1992, *Five Sisters: Women Against the Tsar: The Memoirs of Five Young Anarchist Women of the 1870s*, New York: Routledge.

Enyo, 2009, *Anatomie d'un Désastre: l'Occident, l'islam et la guerre au XXIe siècle*, Paris: Éditions Denoël.

Esposito, John, 1999, *The Islamic Threat: Myth or Reality?* New York: Oxford University Press.

———, 2002, *Unholy War: Terror in the Name of Islam*, New York: Oxford University Press.

Estignard, A., ed., 1892, *Le Parlement de Franche-Comté de son Installation a*

Besançon á sa Suppression, 1674–1790, vol. 2. Paris: A. Picard, Libraire-Éditeur.

Eude, Michel, 1983, "La Loi de Prairial," *Annales Historiques de la Revolution Française,* no. 254: 544–559.

Fanon, Frantz, 1961, *Les Damnés de la Terre,* Paris: François Maspero.

Faure, Sébastien, 1891, *L'Anarchie en Cour d'Assises,* Paris: La Révolte/Le Père Peinard.

Fehr, Ernst, and Simon Gächter, 2002, "Altruistic Punishment in Humans," *Nature* 415(6868): 137–140.

Fein, Robert, and Bryan Vossekuil, 1999, "Assassination in the United States: An Operational Study of Recent Assassins, Attackers, and Near-Lethal Approachers," *Journal of Forensic Sciences* 44(2): 321–333.

Fermé, Albert, 1869, *Les Conspirations sous le Second Empire: Complot de l'Hippodrome et de l'Opéra-Comique,* Paris: La Librairie de la Renaissance.

Ferro, Marc, ed., 2008, *Le Livre Noir du Colonialisme: XVIe–XXIe siècle: de l'extermination à la repentance,* Paris: Hachette Littératures, Collection Pluriels.

Festinger, Leon, Henry Riecken, and Stanley Schachter, 1964, *When Prophecy Fails: A Social and Psychological Study of a Modern Group That Predicted the Destruction of the World,* New York: Harper Torchbooks.

Fetscher, Iring, and Günter Rohrmoser, 1981, *Analysen zum Terrorismus,* vol. I: *Ideologien und Strategien,* Opladen: Westdeutscher Verlag.

Feuer, Lewis, 1969, *The Conflict of Generations: The Character and Significance of Student Movements,* New York: Basic Books.

Field, Daniel, 1976, *Rebels in the Name of the Tsar,* Boston: Houghton Mifflin.

Figner, Vera, 1991, *Memoirs of a Revolutionist,* DeKalb: Northern Illinois University Press.

———, 1992, *Vera Figner,* in Engel and Rosenthal, 1992: 1–58.

Fischer, Ben, 2010, *Okhrana: The Paris Operations of the Russian Imperial Police,* Washington, DC: Central Intelligence Agency, Center for the Study of Intelligence.

Fiske, Susan, Daniel Gilbert, and Gardner Lindzey, eds., 2010, *Handbook of Social Psychology,* 5th ed., Hoboken, NJ: John Wiley and Sons.

Fleury, Georges, 2002, *Histoire Secrète de l'OAS,* Paris: Bernard Grasset.

Fleury, Le Comte, 1897, *Les Grands Terroristes: Carrier à Nantes (1793–1794),* Paris: Librairie Plon.

Foner, Philip, ed., 1969, *The Autobiographies of the Haymarket Martyrs,* New York: Pathfinder.

Footman, David, 1968, *Red Prelude: A Life of A. I. Zhelyabov,* London: Barrie and Rockliff, Cresset Press.

Ford, Franklin, 1985, *Political Murder: From Tyrannicide to Terrorism,* Cambridge, MA: Harvard University Press.

Fouché, Joseph, 1824, *Mémoires de Joseph Fouché, Duc d'Otrante, Ministre de la Police Générale,* 2nd ed., Paris: Le Rouge, Libraire.

Fouquier, A., 1865–67, "La Machine Infernale de Senlis: Billon (1789)," *Causes Célèbres de tous les Peuples* 7(123): 1–16.

Franck-Carré, Paul, 1846, *Rapport fait à la Cour des Pairs, Attentat du 16 Avril 1846*, Paris: Imprimerie Royale.

Fraser, Antonia, 1997, *Faith and Treason: The Story of the Gunpowder Plot*, New York: Anchor Books.

Frost, Richard, 1968, *The Mooney Case*, Stanford, CA: Stanford University Press.

Furet, François, 2007, *La Révolution française*, Paris: Éditions Gallimard Quarto.

Furet, François, and Mona Ozouf, eds., 1989, *A Critical Dictionary of the French Revolution*, Cambridge, MA: Harvard University Press.

Furet, François, and Denis Richet, 2010, *La Révolution française*, Paris: Librairie Arthème Fayard/Pluriel.

Gage, Beverly, 2009, *The Day Wall Street Exploded: A Story of America in Its First Age of Terror*, New York: Oxford University Press.

Gambetta, Diego, ed., 2005, *Making Sense of Suicide Missions*, Oxford: Oxford University Press.

Gamson, William, 1992, *Talking Politics*, Cambridge: Cambridge University Press.

Garnier, Octave, 1912/1992, "Pourquoi j'ai cambriolé, pourquoi j'ai tué," in Maitron, 1992: 182–195.

Gaucher, Roland, 1965, *Les Terroristes*, Paris: Éditions Albin Michel.

Gazette des Tribunaux, Column run in contemporary periodicals, describing the day's proceedings in court. I chose to use *Le Figaro*, whose daily archives are found at http://gallica.bnf.fr/ark:/12148/cb34355551z/date.r=figaro.langEN.

Geertz, Clifford, 1973, *The Interpretations of Cultures*, New York: Basic Books.

Geifman, Anna, 1993, *Thou Shalt Kill: Revolutionary Terrorism in Russia, 1894–1917*, Princeton, NJ: Princeton University Press.

——, 2000, *Entangled in Terror: The Azef Affair and the Russian Revolution*, Wilmington, DE: Scholarly Resources.

Gentry, Curt, 1967, *Frame-up: The Incredible Case of Tom Mooney and Warren Billings*, New York: W. W. Norton.

George, Alexander, and Andrew Bennett, 2005, *Case Studies and Theory Development in the Social Sciences*, Cambridge, MA: MIT Press.

Gerges, Fawaz, 2005, *The Far Enemy: Why Jihad Went Global*, Cambridge: Cambridge University Press.

Gershoy, Leo, 1962, *Bertrand Barere: A Reluctant Terrorist*, Princeton, NJ: Princeton University Press.

Gillen, Jacques, 1997, *Les activité en Belgique d'un anthropologue anarchiste: Eugène Gaspar Marin (1883–1969)*, Brussels: Université Libre de Bruxelles, Faculté de Philosophie et lettres, mémoire pour licence en histoire contemporaine.

Gilovich, Thomas, Dale Griffin, and Daniel Kahneman, eds., 2002, *Heuristics and Biases: The Psychology of Intuitive Judgment*, Cambridge: Cambridge University Press.

Ginneken, Jaap van, 1992, *Crowds, Psychology, and Politics, 1871–1899*, Cambridge: Cambridge University Press.

Gisquet, Henri, 1840, *Mémoires de M. Gisquet, Ancien Préfet de Police, Écrits par Lui-même,* 4 vols., Paris: Marchant, Éditeur du Magasin Théatral.

Gitlin, Todd, 1993, *The Sixties: Years of Hope, Days of Rage*, New York: Bantam.

Gleason, Abbott, 1980, *Young Russia: The Genesis of Russian Radicalism in the 1860s*, New York: Viking Press.

Goldman, Emma, 1970, *Living My Life,* vol. 1, New York: Dover.

Gomez-Le Chevanton, Corinne, 2006, "Le Procès Carrier: enjeux politiques, pédagogie collective et construction mémorielle," *Annales Historiques de la Révolution Française*, no. 1, 73–92.

Goode, Erich, and Nachman Ben-Yehuda, 1994, *Moral Panics: The Social Construction of Deviance*, Oxford: Blackwell.

Goyens, Tom, 2007, *Beer and Revolution: The German Anarchist Movement in New York City, 1880–1914*, Urbana: University of Illinois Press.

Green, James, 2006, *Death in the Haymarket: A Story of Chicago, the First Labor Movement and the Bombing That Divided Gilded Age America*, New York: Anchor Books.

Greene, Joshua, 2013, *Moral Tribes: Emotion, Reason, and the Gap Between Us and Them*, New York: Penguin Press.

Gross, Feliks, 1969, "Political Violence and Terror in 19th and 20th Century Russia and Eastern Europe," in James Kirkham, Sheldon Levy, and William Crotty, 1969, *Assassinations and Political Violence*, vol. 8: *A Report to the National Commission on the Causes and Prevention of Violence*, Washington, DC: U.S. Government Printing Office: 421–476.

Gueniffey, Patrice, 2000, *La Politique de la Terreur*, Paris: Gallimard-Collection Tel.

Guérassimov, Alexandre, 1934, *Tsarisme et Terrorisme*, Paris: Imprimeur-Éditeur Plon.

Guerchouni, Grigouri, 1909, *Dans les cachots de Nicolas II*, Paris: Imprimerie Levé.

Guérin, Daniel, 2005, *No Gods, No Masters: An Anthology of Anarchism*, Oakland, CA: AK Press.

Gurr, Ted, 1970, *Why Men Rebel*, Princeton, NJ: Princeton University Press.

Habeck, Mary, 2006, *Knowing the Enemy: Jihadist Ideology and the War on Terror*, New Haven: Yale University Press.

Hafez, Mohammed, 2004, *Why Muslims Rebel: Repression and Resistance in the Islamic World*, Boulder, CO: Lynne Rienner Publishers, Inc.

Hagerdorn, Ann, 2007, *Savage Peace: Hope and Fear in American, 1919*, New York: Simon and Schuster.

Haidt, Jonathan, 2012, *The Righteous Mind: Why Good People Are Divided by Politics and Religion*, New York: Pantheon Books.

Harbi, Mohammed, and Gilbert Meynier, 2004, *Le FLN, documents et histoire, 1954–1962*, Paris: Fayard.

Hardman, J. B. S., 1934/1987, "Terrorism: A Summing Up in the 1930s," in Laqueur and Alexander, eds., 1987: 223–230.

Harmon-Jones, Eddie, and Judson Mills, eds., 1999, *Cognitive Dissonance: Progress on a Pivotal Theory in Social Psychology*, Washington, DC: American Psychological Association.

Haslam, Alexander, Penelope Oakes, Craig McGarty, John Turner, and Rina Onorato, 1995, "Contextual Changes in the Prototypicality of Extreme and Moderate Outgroup Members," *European Journal of Social Psychology* 25: 509–530.

Haslam, Alexander, and Stephen Reicher, 2007, "Identity Entrepreneurship and the Consequences of Identity Failure: The Dynamics of Leadership in the BBC Prison Study," *Social Psychology Quarterly* 70(2): 125–147.

———, 2012a, "Contesting the 'Nature' of Conformity: What Milgram and Zimbardo's Studies Really Show," *Public Library of Science Biology* 10(11): 1–4, available at http://www.plosbiology.org/article/info%3A-doi%2F10.1371%2Fjournal.pbio.1001426.

———, 2012b, "When Prisoners Take over the Prison: A Social Psychology of Resistance," *Personality and Social Psychology Review* 16(2): 154–179.

Haslam, Alexander, Stephen Reicher, and Megan Birney, 2014, "Nothing by Mere Authority: Evidence That in an Experimental Analogue of the Milgram Paradigm Participants Are Motivated Not by Orders but by Appeals to Science," *Journal of Social Issues* 70(3): 473–488.

Haslam, Alexander, Stephen Reicher, and Michael Platow, 2011, *The New Psychology of Leadership: Identity, Influence and Power*, Hove, East Sussex: Psychology Press.

Haslam, Alexander, Stephen Reicher, and Katherine Reynolds, 2012, "Identity, Influence, and Change: Rediscovering John Turner's Vision for Social Psychology," *British Journal of Social Psychology* 51: 201–218.

Haute Cour de Justice, 1870, "Affaire du Complot contre la Sûreté de l'État et la Vie de l'Empereur," *Journal des Débats Politiques et Littéraires*, 19 July: 3–4; 20 July: 3–4; 21 July: 3–4; 22 July: 3–4: 26 July: 3; 27 July: 3; 28 July: 3–4; 29 July: 3–4; 30 July: 3; 1 August: 3–4.

Hay, Douglas, 1983, *The Revolutionary Movement in the South of the Russian Empire, 1873–1883*, Ph.D. dissertation, University of Glasgow.

Hayden, Tom, 1988, *Reunion: A Memoir*, New York: Random House.

Heinzen, Karl, 1849/1987, "Murder," in Laqueur and Alexander, eds., 1987: 53–64.

Herman, Edward, and O'Sullivan, Gerry, 1989, *The Terrorism Industry: The Experts and Institutions That Shape Our View of Terror*, New York: Pantheon Books.

Hervé, Gustave, 1912, *Mes Crimes, ou, Onze ans de prison pour délits de presse*, Paris: Éditions de la "Guerre Sociale."

Higonnet, Patrice, 1989, "Sans-culottes," in Furet and Ozouf, eds., 1989: 393–399.

———, 1998, *Goodness Beyond Virtue: Jacobins During the French Revolution*, Cambridge, MA: Harvard University Press.

Hildermeier, Manfred, 2000, *The Russian Socialist Revolutionary Party Before the First World War*, New York: St. Martin's Press.

Hirschman, Albert, 1970, *Exit, Voice, and Loyalty: Responses to Decline in Firms, Organizations, and States*, Cambridge, MA: Harvard University Press.

Hodde, Lucien de la, 1850, *Histoire des sociétés secrètes et du parti républicain de 1830 à 1848: Louis-Philippe et la révolution de février, portraits, scenes de conspirations, faits inconnus*, Le Mans: Julien, Lanier, Éditeurs.

Hoffer, Eric, 1963, *The True Believer: Thoughts on the Nature of Mass Movements*, New York: Time Inc.

Hoffman, Bruce, 1998, *Inside Terrorism*, New York: Columbia University Press.

———, 2006, *Inside Terrorism,* rev. and expanded ed., New York: Columbia University Press.

———, 2008, "The Myth of Grass-Root Terrorism," *Foreign Affairs* 87(3): 133–138.

Hogg, Michael, and Scott Reid, 2006, "Social Identity, Self-Categorization, and the Communication of Group Norms," *Communication Theory* 16: 7–30.

Hogg, Michael, and Scott Tindale, eds., 2003, *Blackwell Handbook of Social Psychology: Group Processes*, Oxford: Blackwell.

Holyoake, George Jacob, 1900, *Sixty Years of an Agitator's Life,* vol. II, London: T. Fisher Unwin.

Homeland Security Policy Institute and Critical Incident Analysis Group, 2007, *NETworked Radicalization: A Counter-Strategy*, available at http://www.gwumc.edu/hspi/policy/NETworkedRadicalization.pdf.

Horgan, John, 2005, *The Psychology of Terrorism*, Abingdon, Oxon.: Routledge.

———, 2009, *Walking Away from Terrorism: Accounts of Disengagement from Radical and Extremist Movements*, London: Routledge.

Horgan, John, and Michael Boyle, 2008, "A Case Against 'Critical Terrorism Studies,'" *Critical Studies on Terrorism* 1(1): 51–64.

Hornsey, Matthew, 2008, "Social Identity Theory and Self-Categorization Theory: A Historical Review," *Social and Personality Psychology Compass* 2(1): 204–222.

Hue, Gustave, 1909, *Un Complot de Police sous le Consulat: La Conspiration de Ceracchi et Aréna (Vendémiaire an IX)*, Paris: Librairie Hachette.

Hugo, Victor, 1888, *Choses Vues*, Paris: G. Charpentier, Éditeurs.

Huntington, Samuel, 1996, *The Clash of Civilizations and the Remaking of World Order*, New York: Simon and Schuster.

Ibrahim, Saad Eddin, 1980, "Anatomy of Egypt's Militant Islamic Groups: Methodological Note and Preliminary Findings," *International Journal of Middle East Studies* 12: 423–453.

———, 1982, "Egypt's Islamic Militants," *MERIP Reports* 103 (February): 5–14.

———, 1988, "Egypt's Islamic Activism in the 1980s," *Third World Quarterly* 10(2): 632–657.

Ingraham, Barton, 1979, *Political Crime in Europe: A Comparative Study of France, Germany and England*, Berkeley: University of California Press.

Irwin, Lew, 2013, *Deadly Times: The 1910 Bombing of the* Los Angeles Times *and America's Forgotten Decade of Terror*, Guilford, CT: Lyons Press.

Ivanoskia, Praskovia, 1992, "Praskovia Ivanovskia," in Engel and Rosenthal, eds., 1992: 95–142.

Ivianski, Zeev, 2006, "The Terrorist Revolution: Roots of Modern Terrorism," in Rapoport, ed., 2006: 73–94.

Jackson, John, 2012, *Worker's Organisations and the Development of Worker-Identity in St. Petersburg, 1870–1895: A Study in the Formation of a Radical Worker-Intelligenty*, Ph.D. dissertation, University of Glasgow.

Jackson, Richard, Marie Breen Smyth, and Jeroen Gunning, eds., 2009, *Critical Terrorism Studies: A New Research Agenda*, London: Routledge.

Jacob, Alexandre, 2011, *Les travailleurs de la nuit*, Paris: L'Insomniaque.

Jacobs, Harold, ed., 1970, *Weatherman*, New York: Ramparts Press.

Jacobs, Ron, 1997, *The Way the Wind Blew: A History of the Weather Underground*, New York: Verso.

Jäger, Herbert, Gerhard Schmidtchen, Lieselotte Süllwold, and Lorenz Böllinger, 1981, *Analyzen zum Terrorismus,* vol. II: *Lebenslaufanalysen*, Opladen: Westdeutscher Verlag.

Jensen, Richard Bach, 2009, "The International Campaign Against Anarchist Terrorism, 1880–1930s," *Terrorism and Political Violence*, 21: 89–109.

Johns, A. Wesley, 1970, *The Man Who Shot McKinley: A New View of the Assassination of the President*, New York: A. S. Barnes.

Joll, James, 1980, *The Anarchists*, 2nd ed., Cambridge, MA: Harvard University Press.

Jones, Seth, and Libicki, Martin, 2008, *How Terrorist Groups End: Lessons for Countering al Qa'ida*, Santa Monica, CA: RAND Corporation.

Jones, Thai, 2012, *More Powerful Than Dynamite: Radicals, Plutocrats, Progressives, and New York's Year of Anarchy*, New York: Walker.

Juergensmeyer, Mark, 2000, *Terror in the Mind of God: The Global Rise of Religious Violence*, Berkeley: University of California Press.

Kahneman, Daniel, 2011, *Thinking, Fast and Slow*, New York: Farrar, Straus and Giroux.

Kahneman, Daniel, Paul Slovic, and Amos Tversky, eds., 1982, *Judgments Under Uncertainty: Heuristics and Biases*, Cambridge: Cambridge University Press.

Kahneman, Daniel, and Amos Tversky, eds., 2000, *Choices, Values, and Frames*, Cambridge: Cambridge University Press.

Kassow, Samuel, 1989, *Students, Professors, and the State in Tsarist Russia*, Berkeley: University of California Press.

Keniston, Kenneth, 1968, *Young Radicals: Notes on Committed Youth*, New York: Harcourt, Brace and World.

Kenny, Kevin, 1998, *Making Sense of the Molly Maguires*, Oxford: Oxford University Press.

Kepel, Gilles, 1993, *Muslim Extremism in Egypt: The Prophet and the Pharaoh*, Berkeley: University of California Press.

———, 2002, *Jihad: The Trail of Political Islam*, Cambridge, MA: Harvard University Press.

Khosrokhavar, Farhad, 2002, *Les Nouveaux martyrs d'Allah*, Paris: Flammarion.

Khoudiakoff, Ivan, 1889, *Mémoires d'un Révolutionnaire: Moeurs Russes*, Paris: Calmann Lévy.

King, Michael, and Donald Taylor, 2011, "The Radicalization of Homegrown Jihadists: A Review of Theoretical Models and Social Psychological Evidence," *Terrorism and Political Violence* 23(4): 602–622.

Kirchheimer, Otto, 1961, *Political Justice: The Use of Legal Procedure for Political Ends*, Princeton, NJ: Princeton University Press.

Kittrie, Nicholas, 2000, *Rebels with a Cause: The Minds and Morality of Political Offenders*, Boulder, CO: Westview Press.

Kittrie, Nicholas, and Eldon Wedlock, 1998a, *The Tree of Liberty: A Documentary History of Rebellion and Political Crime in America,* vol. 1: *Colonial Era to World War II*, rev. ed., Baltimore: Johns Hopkins University Press.

———, 1998b, *The Tree of Liberty: A Documentary History of Rebellion and Political Crime in America,* vol. 2: *Cold War to New World Order*, Baltimore: Johns Hopkins University Press.

Koestler, Arthur, 1941/1962, *Darkness at Noon*, New York: Time, Inc.

Krause, Paul, 1992, *The Battle for Homestead, 1890–1892: Politics, Culture, and Steel*, Pittsburgh: University of Pittsburgh Press.

Kropotkin, Peter, 1899/1971, *Memoirs of a Revolutionist*, New York: Dover.

Kruglanski, Arie, Xiaoyan Chen, Mark Dechesne, Shira Fishman, and Edward Orehek, 2009, "Fully Committed: Suicide Bombers' Motivation and the Quest for Personal Significance," *Political Psychology* 30(3): 331–357.

Kucherov, Samuel, 1952, "The Case of Vera Zasulich," *Russian Review* 11(2): 86–96.

Kuhn, Thomas, 1970, *The Structure of Scientific Revolutions,* 2nd ed., Chicago: University of Chicago Press.

Ladame, P., and E. Régis, 1907, *Le Régicide Lucheni: Étude d'Anthropologie Criminelle*, Paris: A. Maloine, Libraire-Éditeur.

Ladjouzi, Diane, 2000, "Les journées des 4 et 5 septembre 1793 à Paris. Un movement d'union entre le people, la Commune de Paris et la Convention pour un exécutif révolutionnaire," *Annales Historiques de la Révolution Française*, no. 321: 27–44.

Lakoff, George, 1987, *Women, Fire, and Dangerous Things: What Categories Reveal About the Mind*, Chicago: University of Chicago Press.

Lallié, Alfred, 1879, *Les Noyades de Nantes,* 2nd ed., Nantes: Libaros, Librairie-Éditeur.

Lamartine, Alphonse de, 1851, *Histoire des Girondes*, 2 vols., Brussels: Meline, Cans et Compagnie.

Lankford, Adam, 2013, *The Myth of Martyrdom: What Really Drives Suicide Bombers, Rampage Shooters, and Other Self-Destructive Killers*, New York: Palgrave Macmillan.

Laqueur, Walter, 1977, *Terrorism*, Boston: Little, Brown.

———, 1999, *The New Terrorism: Fanaticism and the Arms of Mass Destruction*, Oxford: Oxford University Press.

Laqueur, Walter, and Yonah Alexander, eds., 1987, *The Terrorism Reader: A Historical Anthology*, rev. ed., New York: Meridian.

Laurens, Henry, and Delmas-Marty, Mireille, eds., 2010, *Terrorismes: Histoire et Droit*, Paris: CNRS Éditions.

Laut, Ernest, 1910, "Comment débarrasser Paris des Apaches?" *Petit Journal Illustré*, 23 January, p. 20.

Lavignette, Frédéric, 2008, *La Bande à Bonnot: À Travers la Presse de l'Époque*, Lyon: Fage éditions.

———, 2011, *L'Affaire Liabeuf: Histoires d'une Vengeance*, Lyon: Fage éditions.

Law, Randall, 2009, *Terrorism: A History*, Cambridge: Polity Press.

Le Bon, Gustave, 1895/1963, *Psychologie des Foules*, Paris: Presses Universitaires de France.

———, 1912/1968, *The Psychology of Revolution*, Wells, VT: Fraser.

Le Carré, John, 1986, *A Perfect Spy*, New York: Knopf.

Lefebvre, Georges, 1962, *The French Revolution*, 2 vols., New York: Columbia University Press.

———, 1964, *The Thermidorians and the Directory: Two Phases of the French Revolution*, New York: Random House.

———, 1982, *The Great Fear of 1789: Rural Panic in Revolutionary France*, Princeton, NJ: Princeton University Press.

Lenin, Vladimir, 1902/1987, "Why the Social Democrats Must Declare War on the SR's," in Laqueur and Alexander, eds., 1987: 209–210.

Lenotre, G. (Louis Gosselin), 1912, *Les Noyades de Nantes*, Paris: Perrin.

Le Rétif [Victor Kibaltchiche], 1908, "Les Illégaux," *Le Communiste*, no. 14, 20 June.

———, 1909, "Anarchistes–Bandits," *Le Révolté*, no. 36, 6 February.

———, 1910a, "Le Bon Example," *l'anarchie*, no. 251, 27 January: 2.

———, 1910b, "Une tête va tomber," *l'anarchie*, no. 266, 12: 1.

———, 1912, "Les Bandits," *l'anarchie*, no. 352, 4 January: 1.

Lescure, M. de, 1864, "Les Chemises Rouges," *Le Figaro*, 5 June: 1–5; 9 June: 1–4; 12 June: 1–5; 16 June: 1–5; 19 June: 1–6.

Levitas, Daniel, 2002, *The Terrorist Next Door: The Militia Movement and the Radical Right*, New York: St. Martin's Press.

Lewis, Bernard, 1990, "The Roots of Muslim Rage," *Atlantic Monthly* 266: 47–60.

Lewis, Mark, 2014, *The Birth of the New Justice: The Internationalization of Crime and Punishment, 1919–1950*, Oxford: Oxford University Press.

Libertad, Albert, 1905, "Aux Résignés," *l'anarchie*, no. 1, 13 April: 2.

Lignereux, Aurélien, 2012, "Le moment terroriste de la chouannerie: des atteintes a l'ordre publique aux attentats contre le Premier Consul," *La Révolution Française*, vol. 1, available at http://lrf.revues.org/390.

Lih, Lars, 2006, *Lenin Rediscovered: "What Is to Be Done?" in Context*, Leiden: Brill.

Linde et al. v. Arab Bank, 2015, E.D.N.Y., 04 CV 02799 et al. (BMC).

Liubatovich, Olga, 1992, "Olga Liubatovich," in Engel and Rosenthal, eds., 1992: 143–201.

Loftus, Elizabeth, and Katcham, Katherine, 1994, *The Myth of Repressed Memory: False Memories and Allegations of Sexual Abuse*, New York: St. Martin's Griffin.

Longuet, Jean, and Silber, Georges, 1909, *Terroristes et policiers: Azev, Harting et cie–Etude historique et critique*, Paris: Librairie Félix Juven.

Lorédan, Jean, 1924, *La Machine Infernale de la Rue Nicaise (3 Nivôse an IX)*, Paris: Librairie Académique, Perrin, Libraires-Éditeurs.

Louessard, Laurent, 2000, *L'Épopée des Régicides: Passions et Drames, 1814–1848*, Paris: Soupir–L'Insomniaque.

Lukas, Anthony, 1997, *Big Trouble: A Murder in a Small Western Town Sets off a Struggle for the Soul of American*, New York: Simon and Schuster.

Lustick, Ian, 2006, *Trapped in the War on Terror*, Philadelphia: University of Pennsylvania Press.

Magen, Hippolyte, 1878, *Histoire du Second Empire (1848–1870)*, Paris: Librairie Illustrée.

Maher, Shiraz, 2006, "Campus Radicals," *Prospect*, 126 (24 September); available at http://www.prospectmagazine.co.uk/magazine/campusradicals/.

Maîtrejean, Rirette, 1913, "Souvenirs d'anarchie," serialized in 14 parts in *Le Matin*, 18–31 August 1913.

——, 2005, *Souvenirs d'anarchie: La vie quotidienne au temps de "la band à Bonnot" à la veille d'août 1914*, Quimperlé: Éditions La Digitale.

Maitron, Jean, 1992, *Ravachol et les anarchists*, Paris: Gallimard Collection folio-histoire.

——, 2007, *Le movement anarchiste en France: 1. Des origines à 1914*, Paris: Gallimard, Collection Tel.

Malandain, Gilles, 2008, "Un sentiment politique: la haine des Bourbons sous la Restauration," in Frédéric Chauvaud and Ludovic Gaussot, eds., *La Haine: Histoire et Actualité*, Rennes: Presses Universitaires de Rennes: 73–83.

——, 2012, "Les sens d'un mot: 'attentats,' de l'Ancien Régime à nos jours," *La Révolution Française*, vol. 1, available at http://lrf.revues.org/368.

Malato, Charles, 1894, "Some Anarchist Portraits," *Fortnightly Review*, no. 333, 1 September; available at http://libertarian-labyrinth.org/archive/Some_Anarchist_Portraits.

Malherbe, Michel, 2012, *La bande á Bonnot*, Paris: De Borée.

Mandela, Nelson, 2013, *Long Walk to Freedom: The Autobiography of Nelson Mandela*, New York: Little, Brown.

Markoff, John, 1996, *The Abolition of Feudalism: Peasants, Lords, and Legislators in the French Revolution*, University Park: Pennsylvania State University Press.

Marlowe, Frank, Colette Berbesque, et al., 2008, "More 'Altruistic' Punishment in Larger Societies," *Proceedings of the Royal Society B* 275: 587–590.

Marques, José, Dominic Abrams, Dario Páez, and Michael Hogg, 2003, "Social Categorization, Social Influence, and Rejection of Deviant Group Members," in Hogg and Tindale, eds., 2003: 400–424.

Marques, José, Vincent Yzerbyt, and Jacques-Philippe Leyens, 1988, "The 'Black Sheep Effect': Extremity of Judgments Towards In-Group Members as a Function of Group Identification," *European Journal of Social Psychology* 18: 1–16.

Martel de Porzou, Comte Aimé Denis de, 1885, *Les Historiens Fantaisistes: M. Thiers, Histoire du Consulat et de l'Empire, Deuxième Partie: La Pacification de l'Ouest, La Machine Infernale du 3 Novose An IX*, Paris: E. Dentu, Éditeur.

Martin, Jean-Clément, 2006, *Violence et* Révolution: Essai sur la Naissance d'un Mythe National, Paris: Éditions du Seuil.

———, 2002, "La Révolution Française: Généalogie de l'Ennemi," *Raisons Politiques* 1(5): 69–79.

———, 2012, *Nouvelle Histoire de la Révolution Française*, Paris: Perrin.

———, 2014, *La Guerre de Vendée, 1793–1800*, new ed., Paris: Points–Éditions du Seuil.

———, 2016, *Robespierre: La fabrication d'un monster*, Paris: Perrin.

Mathiez, Albert, 1965, *After Robespierre: The Thermidorian Reaction*, New York: Grosset and Dunlap: Universal Library.

Mayer, Arno, 2000, *The Furies: Violence and Terror in the French and Russian Revolutions*, Princeton, NJ: Princeton University Press.

Mazeau, Guillaume, 2009, *Le Bain de l'Histoire: Charlotte Corday et l'attentat contre Marat, 1793–2009*, Seyssel: Champ Vallon.

———, 2012, "Violence politique et transition démocratique: les attentats sous la Révolution française," *La Révolution Française*, vol. 1, available at http://lrf. revues.org/380.

McAdam, Doug, 1986, "Recruitment to High-Risk Activism: The Case of Freedom Summer," *American Journal of Sociology* 92(1): 64–90.

———, 1988, *Freedom Summer*, New York: Oxford University Press.

McAdam, Doug, Sidney Tarrow, and Charles Tilly, 2001, *Dynamics of Contention*, Cambridge: Cambridge University Press.

McCauley, Clark, 2008, Editor's welcome to the inaugural issue, *Dynamics of Asymmetric Conflict* 1(1): 1–5.

McCauley, Clark, and Sophia Moskalenko, 2011, *Friction: How Radicalization Happens to Them and Us*, New York: Oxford University Press.

McDermott, Terry, 2005, *Perfect Soldiers*, New York: HarperCollins.

McKenna, Joseph, 2012, *The Irish-American Dynamite Campaign: A History, 1881–1896*, Jefferson, NC: McFarland.

McManigal, Ortie, 1913, *The National Dynamite Plot: Being the authentic account of the attempts of Union Labor to destroy the Structural Iron Industry*, Los Angeles: Neale.

Meadowcroft, Jeff, 2011, *The History and Historiography of the Russian Worker-Revolutionaries of the 1870s*, Ph.D. dissertation, University of Glasgow.

Melucci, Alberto, 1996, *Challenging Codes: Collective Action in the Information Age*, Cambridge: Cambridge University Press.

Merari, Ariel, 2010, *Driven to Death: Psychological and Social Aspects of Suicide Terrorism*, New York: Oxford University Press.

Mercier, Lucien, 1986, *Les universités Populaires, 1899–1914: Éducation populaire et movement ouvrier au début du siècle*, Paris: les éditions ouvrières.

Méric, Victor, 1926, *Les bandits tragiques: les milieux anarchistes*, Paris: Simon Kra, Éditeur.

Merleau-Ponty, Maurice, 1947, *Humanisme et Terreur: Essai sur le Problème Communiste*, Paris: Éditions Gallimard.

Merriman, John, 2009, *The Dynamite Club: How a Bombing in Fin-de-Siècle Paris Ignited the Age of Modern Terror*, Boston: Houghton Mifflin Harcourt.

Merriman, John, 2014, *Massacre: The Life and Death of the Paris Commune*, New York: Basic Books.

Meynier, Gilbert, 2002, *Histoire Intérieure du FLN*, Paris: Fayard.

Michael, George, 2012, *Lone Wolf Terror and the Rise of Leaderless Resistance*, Nashville, TN: Vanderbilt University Press.

Michon, Emile, 1914, *Un peu de l'âme des bandits: étude de psychologie criminelle*, Paris: Dorbon-ainé.

Milgram, Stanley, 1974, *Obedience to Authority: An Experimental View*, New York: Harper & Row.

Miller, Martin, 1995, "The Intellectual Origins of Modern Terrorism in Europe," in Crenshaw, ed., 1995: 27–62.

———, 2013, *The Foundations of Modern Terrorism: State, Society and the Dynamics of Political Violence*, Cambridge: Cambridge University Press.

Moghaddam, Fathali, 2005, "The Staircase to Terrorism: A Psychological Exploration," *American Psychologist* 60(2): 161–169.

———, 2006, *From the Terrorists' Point of View: What They Experience and Why They Come to Destroy*, Westport, CT: Praeger Security International.

Mommsen, Wolfgang, and Gerhard Hirschfeld, eds., 1982, *Social Protest, Violence and Terror in Nineteenth- and Twentieth-Century Europe*, New York: St. Martin's Press.

Moore, Barrington, Jr., 1978, *Injustice: The Social Bases of Obedience and Revolt*, White Plains, NY: M. E. Sharpe.

Moore, David, 2001, "Bush Job Approval Highest in Gallup History: Widespread Public Support for War on Terrorism," Gallup News Service, 24 September; available at http://www.gallup.com/poll/4924/bush-job-approval-highest-gallup-history.aspx.

Morozov, Nikolai, 1880/1987, "The Terrorist Struggle," in Laqueur and Alexander, eds., 1987: 72–78.

Moscovici, Serge, 1981, *L'Âge des Foules: Un traité historique de psychologie des masses*, Paris: Librairie Arthème Fayard.

Most, Johann, 1885/1978, *Science of Revolutionary Warfare: A Handbook of Instruction regarding the Use and Manufacture of Nitroglycerine, Dynamite, Gun-Cotton, Fulminating Mercury, Bombs, Arsons, Poisons, etc.*, El Dorado, AZ: Desert Publications.

Mudd, Philip, 2013, *Takedown: Inside the Hunt for al Qaeda*, Philadelphia: University of Pennsylvania Press.

Mueller, John, 2006, *Overblown: How Politicians and the Terrorism Industry Inflate National Security Threats and Why We Believe Them*, New York: Free Press.

Münch, Philippe, 2010a, "Sophie Wahnich, la violence révolutionnaire et la Terreur: Note critique sur l'approche émotionnelle, Tracés. *Revue des Sciences Humaines* 19(2): 155–169.

———, 2010b, "La foule révolutionnaire, l'imaginaire du complot et la violence fondatrice: aux origines de la nation française (1789)," *Conserveries mémorielles*, no. 8, available at http://cm.revues.org/725#quotation.

Murray, Robert, 1964, *Red Scare: A Study in National Hysteria, 1919–1920*, New York: McGraw-Hill.

Naimark, Norman, 1983, *Terrorists and Social Democrats: The Russian Revolutionary Movement Under Alexander III*, Cambridge, MA: Harvard University Press.

National Commission on Terrorist Attacks upon the United States, 2004, *The 9/11 Commission Report,* New York: W. W. Norton.

Nechaev, Sergey, 1869/1987, "Catechism of the Revolutionist," in Laqueur and Alexander, eds., 1987: 68–72.

Nesser, Petter, 2012, "Individual Jihadist Operations in Europe: Patterns and Challenges," *CTC Sentinel* 5(1): 15–18.

Netanyahu, Benjamin, 1989, *International Terrorism: Challenge and Response*, New Brunswick, NJ: Transaction.

Newell, David, 1981, *The Russian Marxist Response to Terrorism, 1878–1917*, Ph.D. dissertation, Stanford University.

Nikolajewsky, Boris, 1934, *Aseff the Spy: Russian Terrorist and Police Stool*, Garden City, NY: Doubleday, Doran.

Nisbett, Richard, and Dov Cohen, 1996, *Culture of Honor: The Psychology of Violence in the South*, Boulder, CO: Westview.

Oakes, Penelope, Alexander Haslam, and John Turner, 1994, *Stereotyping and Social Reality*, Oxford: Blackwell.

Olson, Mancur, 1971, *The Logic of Collective Action: Public Goods and the Theory of Groups*, New York: Schocken Books.

Orsini, Felice, 1857, *Memoirs and Adventures,* Edinburgh: Thomas Constable.

Overstreet, Bonaro, 1951, *Understanding Fear in Ourselves and Others*, New York: Harper and Brothers.

Owings, W. A. Dolph, and Elizabeth Pribic, eds., 1984, *The Sarajevo Trial: The Monumental Story of the Assassination That Began World War I*, 2 vols., Chapel Hill, NC: Documentary Publications.

Packe, Michael St. John, 1957, *The Bombs of Orsini*, London: Secker and Warburg.

Pagès, Yves, 2009, *L'homme hérissé: Liabeuf, tueur de flics*, Paris: Baleine Noire.

Palmer, R. R., 1941/1989, *Twelve Who Ruled: The Year of the Terror in the French Revolution*, Princeton, NY: Princeton University Press.

Pantucci, Raffaello, 2011, *A Typology of Lone Wolves: Preliminary Analysis of Lone*

Islamist Terrorists, The International Centre for the Study of Radicalisation and Political Violence (ICSR), King's College London.

Parry, Albert, 1976, *Terrorism: From Robespierre to the Weather Underground*, Mineola, NY: Dover.

Parry, Richard, 1987, *The Bonnot Gang: The Story of the French Illegalists*, London: Rebel Press.

Passante, Anna, 2008, "Anarchy in Bay View," BayViewCompass.com, available at http://bayviewcompass.com/archives/245.

Payne, Robert, 1950, *Zero: The History of Terrorism*, New York: John Day.

——, 1957, *The Terrorists: The Story of the Forerunners of Stalin*, New York: Funk and Wagnalls.

Pernicone, Nunzio, 2009, *Italian Anarchism, 1864–1892*, Oakland, CA: AK Press.

Perrie, Maureen, 1982, "Political and Economic Terror in the Tactics of the Russian Socialist-Revolutionary Party Before 1914," in Mommsen and Hirschfeld, eds., 1982: 63–79.

Perry, Simon, and Badi Hasisi, 2015, "Rational Choice Rewards and the Jihadist Suicide Bomber," *Terrorism and Political Violence* 27(1): 53–80.

Pinker, Steven, 2011, *The Better Angels of Our Nature: Why Violence Has Declined*, New York: Penguin Books.

Pipes, Richard, 2003, *The Degaev Affair: Terror and Treason in Tsarist Russia*, New Haven: Yale University Press.

Pomper, Philip, 1970, *The Russian Revolutionary Intelligentsia*, Arlington Heights, IL: AHM Publishing.

——, 1995, "Russian Revolutionary Terrorism," in Crenshaw, ed., 1995: 63–101.

——, 2010, *Lenin's Brother: The Origins of the October Revolution*, New York: W. W. Norton.

Porter, Cathy, 1976, *Fathers and Daughters: Russian Women in Revolution*, London: Virago.

Post, Jerrold, 2007, *The Mind of the Terrorist: The Psychology of Terrorism from the IRA to al-Qaeda*, New York: Palgrave Macmillan.

Procès de Alibaut devant la Cour des Pairs, 1836, Paris: Pagnerre, Éditeur.

Procès de Fieschi et de ses complices devant la Cour des Pairs, 1836, Bordeaux: Imprimerie et Lithographie de Henry Faye.

Procès de la Conspiration des Patriotes de 1816, 1816, Paris: Paris, Imprimeur-Libraire.

Procès des Anarchistes devant la Police Correctionnelle et la Cour d'Appel de Lyon, 1883, Lyon: Imprimerie Nouvelle.

Procès Fieschi devant la Cour des Pairs, Débats, 1836, vols. 2 and 3, Paris: Pagnerre, Éditeur.

Procès Instruit par le Tribunal Criminel du Département de la Seine, Contre Demerville, Céracchi, Aréna et autres . . . , Recueilli par des Sténographes, Pluviôse an IX, 1801, Paris: Imprimerie de la République.

Procès Instruit par le Tribunal Criminel du Département de la Seine, Contre les nommés Saint-Réjant, Carbon et autres . . . , *Recueilli par des Sténographes*, Floréal an IX, 1801, Paris: Imprimerie de la République.

Pronin, Emily, Carolyn Puccio, and Lee Ross, 2002, "Understanding Misunderstanding: Social Psychological Perspectives," in Gilovich, Griffin, and Kahneman, eds., 2002: 636–665.

"Propaganda by Deed: The Greenwich Observatory Bomb of 1894," 2005, Royal Museum Greenwich; available at http://www.rmg.co.uk/explore/astronomy-and-time/astronomy-facts/history/propaganda-by-deed-the-greenwich-observatory-bomb-of-1894.

Quinet, Edgar, 1865/n.d., *La Révolution, en trois tomes, quatorzième édition*, Paris: Librairie Hachette et Cie.

Ragin, Charles, 2000, *Fuzzy-Set Social Science*, Chicago: University of Chicago Press.

———, 2008, *Redesigning Social Inquiry: Fuzzy Sets and Beyond*, Chicago: University of Chicago Press.

Rapoport, David, 1984, "Fear and Trembling: Terrorism in Three Religious Traditions," *American Political Science Review* 78(3): 658–677.

———, 2001, "The International World as Some Terrorists Have Seen It: A Look at a Century of Memoirs," in Rapoport, ed., 2001: 32–58.

———, 2002, "Four Waves of Modern Terrorism," *Anthropoetics* 8: 46–73.

———, ed., 2006, *Terrorism: Critical Concepts in Political Science*, Abingdon, Oxon.: Routledge.

———, 2008, "Before the Bombs, There Were the Mobs: American Experiences with Terror," *Terrorism and Political Violence* 20(2): 167–194.

Rapport, Mike, 2010, *1848: Year of Revolution*, New York: Basic Books.

Regina v. Simon Bernard, 1858, Proceedings at the Special Commission held at the Justice Hall, Old Bailey, in John Wallis, ed., 1898, *Reports of State Trials, New Series*, vol. VIII: *1850 to 1858*, London: Her Majesty's Stationery Office: 887–1064.

Regina v. Johann Most, 1881, Old Bailey Proceedings Online, 15 May (35) (t18810523-541); available at http://www.oldbaileyonline.org/browse.jsp?id=def1-541-18810523anddiv=t18810523-541.

Regina v. Patrick O'Donnell, 1883, Old Bailey Proceedings Online, 30 November (48) (t18831119-75); available at http://www.oldbaileyonline.org/browse.jsp?id=t18831119-75-offence-1anddiv=t18831119-75#highlight.

Regnault, Élias, 1884, *Histoire de Huit Ans, 1840–1848, Faisant Suite à L'Histoire de Dix Ans, 1830–1840 par M. Louis Blanc et Complétant le Règne de Louis-Philippe, Sixième Édition*, 3 vols., Paris: Félix Alcan, Éditeur.

Reich, Walter, ed., 1990, *Origins of Terrorism: Psychologies, Ideologies, Theologies, States of Mind*, Washington, DC: Woodrow Wilson Center Press.

Reicher, Stephen, 2003, "The Psychology of Crowd Dynamics," in Hogg and Tindale, eds., 2003: 182–208.

Reicher, Stephen, and Alexander Haslam, 2006, "Rethinking the Psychology of Tyranny: The BBC Prison Study," *British Journal of Social Psychology*, 45: 1–40.

Reicher, Stephen, Alexander Haslam, and Joanne Smith, 2012, "Working Toward the Experimenter: Reconceptualizing Obedience Within the Milgram Paradigm as Identification-Based Followership," *Perspectives on Psychological Science* 7(3): 315–324.

Reicher, Stephen, Nick Hopkins, Mark Levine, and Rakshi Rath, 2005, "Entrepreneurs of Hate and Entrepreneurs of Solidarity: Social Identity as a Basis for Mass Communication," *International Review of the Red Cross* 87(860): 621–637.

Reitman, Janet, 2013, "Jahar's World," *Rolling Stone*, 17 July; available at http://www.rollingstone.com/culture/news/jahars-world-20130717.

Report of the Committee Appointed to Investigate the Railroad Riots in July, 1877, 1878, Harrisburg, PA: Lane S. Hart, State Printer.

Reppetto, Thomas, 2012, *Battleground New York City: Countering Spies, Saboteurs, and Terrorists Since 1861*, Washington, DC: Potomac Books.

Reynolds, David, 2006, *John Brown Abolitionist: The Man Who Killed Slavery, Sparked the Civil War, and Seeded Civil Rights*, New York: Alfred A. Knopf.

Roberts, J. M., 1972, *The Mythology of the Secret Societies*, London: Watkins Publishing.

Robespierre, Maximilien, 1954, *Oeuvres Complètes de Maximilien Robespierre, Tome VIII, Discours: Octobre 1791–Septembre 1792*, Paris: Presses Universitaires de France.

———, 1967, *Oeuvres Complètes de Maximilien Robespierre, Tome X, Discours: 27 Juillet 1793–27 Juillet 1794*, Paris: Presses Universitaires de France.

Robinson, J. H., ed., 1906, *Readings in European History*, vol. 2, Boston: Ginn.

Robiquet, Paul, 1910, *Buonarroti et la Secte des Égaux*, Paris: Librairie Hachette et Cie.

Rolland-Boulestreau, Anne, 2015, *Les Colonnes Infernales: Violences et guerre civile en Vendée militaire (1794–1795)*, Paris: Libraire Arthème Fayard.

Roosevelt, Theodore, 1901, First Annual Message, 3 December; available at The American Presidency Project at http://www.presidency.ucsb.edu/ws/?pid=29542.

Rose, R. B., 1978, *Gracchus Babeuf: The First Revolutionary Communist*, Stanford, CA: Stanford University Press.

———, 1983, *The Making of the Sans-Culottes: Democratic Ideas and Institutions in Paris, 1789–92*, Manchester: Manchester University Press.

Rosemont, Franklin, and David Roediger, 2012, *Haymarket Scrapbook*, anniversary ed., Oakland, CA: AK Press.

Rosenfeld, Jean, ed., 2011, *Terrorism, Identity and Legitimacy*, Abington, Oxon.: Routledge.

Ross, Lee, Mark Lepper, and Andrew Ward, 2010, "History of Social Psychology: Insights, Challenges, and Contributions to Theory and Application," in Fiske, Gilbert, and Lindzey, 2010: 3–50.

Ross, Lee, and Richard Nisbett, 1991, *The Person and the Situation: Perspective of Social Psychology*, New York: McGraw-Hill.

Rousseau, Jean-Jacques, 1962, *Du Contrat Social*, Paris: Garnier Frères.

Roy, Olivier, 2004, *Globalized Islam: The Search for a New Ummah*, New York: Columbia University Press.

Rubenstein, Richard, 1994, *Comrade Valentine: The True Story of Azef the Spy—The Most Dangerous Man in Russia at the Time of the Last Czars*, New York: Harcourt Brace.

Rudd, Mark, 2009, *Underground: My Life with SDS and the Weathermen*, New York: William Morrow.

Rudé, George, 1959, *The Crowd in the French Revolution*, Oxford: Oxford University Press.

———, 1964, *The Crowd in History: A Study of Popular Disturbances in France and England, 1730–1848*, New York: John Wiley and Sons.

Sageman, Marc, 2004, *Understanding Terror Networks*, Philadelphia: University of Pennsylvania Press.

———, 2007, *Modern Bioterrorism*, Report Prepared for the Department of Homeland Security, Directorate of Science and Technology, unpublished.

———, 2008, *Leaderless Jihad: Terror Networks in the Twenty-First Century*, Philadelphia: University of Pennsylvania Press.

———, 2014, "The Stagnation in Terrorism Research," *Terrorism and Political Violence* 26(4): 565–580.

———, 2016, *Misunderstanding Terrorism*, Philadelphia: University of Pennsylvania Press.

Sale, Kirkpatrick, 1973, *SDS*, New York: Random House.

Salmon, André, 1959/2008, *La Terreur Noire*, Montreuil: Édition l'Échappée.

Salomé, Karine, 2010a, "L'Attentat de la Rue Nicaise en 1800: L'irruption d'une violence inédite?" *Revue d'Histoire du XIX Siècle* 40(1): 59–75.

———, 2010b, *L'Ouragan Homidice: L'Attentat Politique en France au XIXe Siècle*, Seyssel: Champ Vallon.

Savinkov, Boris, 1972, *Memoirs of a Terrorist*, Millwood, New York: Kraus Reprint.

Schaack, Michael, 1889, *Anarchy and Anarchists: A History of the Red Terror and the Social Revolution in American and Europe; Communism, Socialism, and Nihilism in Doctrine and in Deed; The Chicago Haymarket Conspiracy and the Detection and Trial of the Conspirators*, Chicago: F. J. Schulte.

Schacter, Daniel, ed., 1995, *Memory Distortion: How Minds, Brains, and Societies Reconstruct the Past*, Cambridge, MA: Harvard University Press.

———, 1996, *Searching for Memory: The Brain, the Mind, and the Past*, New York: Basic Books.

———, 2001, *The Seven Sins of Memory: How the Mind Forgets and Remembers*, Boston: Houghton Mifflin.

Schama, Simon, 1989, *Citizens: A Chronicle of the French Revolution*, New York: Alfred A. Knopf.

Scheler, Auguste, 1855, *Annuaire Statistique and Historique Belge, Deuxième Année*, Bruxelles: Kiessling, Schnée et Companie, Éditeurs.

[Scheuer, Michael], 2002, *Through Our Enemy's Eyes: Osama bin Laden, Radical Islam, and the Future of America*, Washington, DC: Brassey's.

Schiller, Friedrich von, 1972, *Wilhelm Tell*, Chicago: University of Chicago Press.

Schleifman, Nurit, 1988, *Undercover Agents in the Russian Revolutionary Movement: The SR Party, 1902–14*, London: Macmillan.

Schmid, Alex, 1983, *Political Terrorism: A Research Guide to Concepts, Theories, Data Bases and Literature*, Amsterdam: North-Holland.

Schmidle, Robert, 2009, "Positioning Theory and Terrorist Networks," *Journal for the Theory of Social Behaviour* 40: 65–78.

Schuurman, Bart, and Quirine Eijkman, 2013, "Moving Terrorism Research Forward: The Crucial Role of Primary Sources," *ICCT Background Note* (June), The Hague: International Center for Counter-Terrorism.

Schwartz, Seth, Curtis Dunkel, and Alan Waterman, 2009, "Terrorism: An Identity Theory Perspective," *Studies in Conflict and Terrorism* 32: 537–559.

Semelin, Jacques, 2007, *Purify and Destroy: The Political Uses of Massacre and Genocide*, New York: Columbia University Press.

Sen, Amartya, 2006, *Identity and Violence: The Illusion of Destiny*, London: Penguin Books.

Serge, Victor, 1937, "Méditation sur l'anarchie," *Esprit, Revue Internationale*, no. 55, 1 April: 29–43.

———, 2012, *Memoirs of a Revolutionary*, New York: New York Review Books.

Serman, William, 1986, *La Commune de Paris (1871)*, Paris: Librairie Arthème Fayard.

Seth, Ronald, 1966, *The Russian Terrorists: The Story of the Narodniki*, London: Barrie and Rockliff.

Sieyès, Emmanuel, 1789/1988, *Qu'est-ce que le Tiers-État?* Paris: Flammarion–Champs Classiques.

Silber, Mitchell, 2012, *The Al Qaeda Factor: Plots Against the West*, Philadelphia: University of Pennsylvania Press.

Silber, Mitchell, and Arvin Bhatt, 2007, *Radicalization in the West: The Homegrown Threat*, New York: New York Police Department Intelligence Division, at http://www.nypdshield.org/public/SiteFiles/documents/NYPD_Report-Radicalization_in_the_West.pdf.

Siljak, Ana, 2008, *Angel of Vengeance: The "Girl Assassin," the Governor of St. Petersburg, and Russia's Revolutionary World*, New York: St. Martin's Press.

Silke, Andrew, 1998, "Cheshire-Cat Logic: The Recurring Theme of Terrorist Abnormality in Psychological Research," *Psychology, Crime and Law* 4: 51–69.

———, ed., 2003, *Terrorists, Victims and Society: Psychological Perspectives on Terrorism and Its Consequences*, Chichester, England: John Wiley and Sons.

Simon, Jeffrey, 2013, *Lone Wolf Terrorism: Understanding the Growing Threat*, Amherst, NY: Prometheus Books.

Slavin, Morris, 1986, *The Making of an Insurrection: Parisian Sections and the Gironde*, Cambridge, MA: Harvard University Press.

Smith, David, 2009, *One Morning in Sarajevo: 28 June 1914*, London: Phoenix.

Smith, J., and André Moncourt, 2009, *The Red Army Faction: A Documentary History*, vol. 1: *Projectiles for the People*, Oakland, CA: PM Press.

Smith, Joanne, and Alexander Haslam, eds., 2012, *Social Psychology: Revisiting the Classic Studies*, Los Angeles: Sage.

Smithson, Michael, and Jay Verkuilen, 2006, *Fuzzy Set Theory: Applications in the Social Sciences*, Thousand Oaks, CA: Sage.

Snow, David, Sarah Soule, and Hanspeter Kriesi, 2007, eds., *The Blackwell Companion to Social Movements*, Oxford: Blackwell.

Soboul, Albert, 1975, *The French Revolution 1787–1799: From the Storming of the Bastille to Napoleon*, New York: Vintage Books.

———, 1980, *The Sans-Culottes*, Princeton, NJ: Princeton University Press.

Société d'Avocats et de Publicistes, 1827a, *Causes politiques célèbres du XIXe siècle: Procès de Saint-Rejeant, Carbon, Mlle de Cicé et autres (Machine Infernale)*, Paris: H. Langlois Fils et Cie, Éditeurs.

Société d'Avocats et de Publicistes, 1827b, *Causes politiques célèbres du XIXe siècle: Procès de Louvel*, Paris: H. Langlois Fils et Cie, Éditeurs.

Sommier, Isabelle, 2008, *La violence politique et son deuil: L'après 68 en France et en Italie*, Rennes: Presses Universitaires de Rennes.

Spears, Russell, and Sabine Otten, 2012, "Discrimination: Revisiting Tajfel's Minimal Group Studies," in Smith and Haslam, eds., 2012: 160–177.

Spence, Richard, 1991, *Boris Savinkov: Renegade on the Left*, Boulder, CO: East European Monographs, distributed by Columbia University Press.

Spiridovitch, Alexander, 1930, *Histoire du terrorisme russe, 1886–1917*, Paris: Payot.

Spitzer, Alan, 1971, *Old Hatreds and Young Hopes: The French Carbonari Against the Bourbon Restoration*, Cambridge, MA: Harvard University Press.

Stampnitzky, Lisa, 2013, *Disciplining Terror: How Experts Invented "Terrorism,"* Cambridge: Cambridge University Press.

Stark, Rodney, and William Bainbridge, 1985, *The Future of Religion: Secularization, Revival and Cult Formation*, Berkeley: University of California Press.

Steiner, Anne, 2008, *Les en-dehors: anarchistes individualistes et illégalistes* à la *Belle Époque*, Montreuil: Éditions L'Échappée.

———, 2012, *Le Goût de l'Émeute: Manifestations et violences de rue dans Paris et sa banlieue à la "belle époque."* Montreuil: Éditions l'Échappée.

Stekelenburg, Jacquelien van, 2014, "Going All the Way: Politicizing, Polarizing, and Radicalizing Identity Offline and Online," *Sociology Compass*: 1–15, 10.1111/soc4.12157.

Stekelenburg, Jacquelien van, and Bert Klandermans, 2009, "Social Movement Theory: Past, Present and Prospects," in Stephen Ellis and Ineke van Kessel, eds., 2009, *Movers and Shakers: Social Movements in Africa*, Leiden: Brill, 19–43.

Stepniak, Sergei [Sergei Kravchinsky], 1883, *Underground Russia: Revolutionary Profiles and Sketches from Life*, New York: Charles Scribner's Sons.

Sterling, Claire, 1982, *The Terror Network: The Secret War of International Terrorism*, New York: Berkley Books.

Stern, Susan, 2007, *With the Weathermen: The Personal Journal of a Revolutionary Woman*, Piscataway, NJ: Rutgers University Press.

Stirner, Max, 2005, *The Ego and His Own: The Case of the Individual Against Authority*, Mineola, NY: Dover.

Stone, Geoffrey, 2004, *Perilous Times: Free Speech in Wartime, from the Sedition Act of 1798 to the War on Terrorism*, New York: W. W. Norton.

Stouffer, Samuel, Arthur Lumsdaine, Marion Lumsdaine, Robin Williams, Brewster Smith, Irving Janis, Shirley Star, Leonard Cottrell, 1965, *The American Soldier: Combat and Its Aftermath*, vol. II, New York: John Wiley and Sons.

Tackett, Timothy, 2000, "Conspiracy Obsession in a Time of Revolution: French Elites and the Origins of the Terror, 1789–1792," *American Historical Review* 105(3): 691–713.

———, 2003, *When the King Took Flight*, Cambridge, MA: Harvard University Press.

———, 2004, "La Grande Peur et le complot aristocratique sous la Révolution française," *Annales historiques de la Révolution française* 335: 1–17.

———, 2006, *Becoming a Revolutionary: The Deputies of the French National Assembly and the Emergence of a Revolutionary Culture (1789–1790)*, University Park: Pennsylvania State University Press.

———, 2011, "Rumor and Revolution: The Case of the September Massacres," *French History and Civilization* 4: 54–64.

Taine, Hippolyte, 1904, *Les Origines de la France Contemporaine, V: La Révolution–La Conquête Jacobine*, vol. 1, Paris: Librairie Hachette et Cie.

———, 2002, *The French Revolution*, 3 vols., Indianapolis: Liberty Fund.

Tajfel, Henri, 1970, "Experiments in Intergroup Discrimination," *Scientific American* 223: 96–102.

———, 1982, "Social Psychology of Intergroup Relations," *Annual Review of Psychology*, 33: 1–39.

Tajfel, Henri, and John Turner, 1979, "An Integrative Theory of Intergroup Conflict," in W. G. Austin and S. Worchel, eds., *The Social Psychology of Intergroup Relations*, Monterey, CA: Brooks/Cole: 33–48.

Tardy, Jean-Noël, 2012, "Tuer le tyran ou la tyrannie? Attentat et conspiration politique: distinctions et affinités en France de 1830 à 1870," *La Révolution Française*, vol. 1; available at http://lrf.revues.org/438.

———, 2015, *L'Âge des Ombres: Complots, conspirations et sociétés secrètes au XIXe siècle*, Paris: Les Belles Lettres.

Taylor, Maxwell, 1988, *The Terrorist*, London: Brassey's Defense Publishers.

Taylor, Maxwell, and P. M. Currie, eds., 2012, *Terrorism and Affordance*, London: Continuum.

Tessendorf, K. C., 1986, *Kill the Tsar! Youth and Terrorism in Old Russia*, New York: Atheneum.

Tetlock, Phillip, 2009, *Expert Political Judgment: How Good Is It? How Can We Know?* Princeton, NJ: Princeton University Press.

Thomas, Tom, 1970, "The Second Battle of Chicago 1969," in Jacobs, ed., 1970: 196–225.

Thomazo, Renaud, 2009, *Morts aux bourgeois!* Paris: Larousse.

Thompson, E. P., 1966, *The Making of the English Working Class*, New York: Vintage Books.

Tilly, Charles, 2005, *Identities, Boundaries and Social Ties*, Boulder, CO: Paradigm.

Tocqueville, Alexis de, 1986, *De la Démocratie en Amérique; Souvenirs; L'Ancien Régime et la Révolution*, Paris: Bouquins, Éditions Robert Laffont.

Trautmann, Frederic, 1980, *The Voice of Terror: A Biography of Johann Most*, Westport, CT: Greenwood Press.

Trifonov, Yuri, 1978, *The Impatient Ones*, Moscow: Progress Publishers.

Turner, John, 1991, *Social Influence*, Pacific Grove, CA: Brooks/Cole.

——, 1996, "Henri Tajfel: An Introduction," in W. Peter Robinson, ed., 1996, *Social Groups and Identities: Developing the Legacy of Henri Tajfel*, Oxford: Butterworth-Heinemann, 1–23.

Turner, John, Michael Hogg, Penelope Oakes, Stephen Reicher, and Margaret Wetherell, 1987, *Rediscovering the Social Group: A Self-Categorization Theory*, Oxford: Blackwell.

Turner, John, Penelope Oakes, Alexander Haslam, and Craig McGarty, 1994, "Self and Collective: Cognition and Social Context," *Personality and Social Psychology Bulletin* 20(5): 454–463.

Tversky, Amos, and Daniel Kahneman, 1982, "Availability: A Heuristic for Judging Frequency and Probability," in Kahneman, Slovic, and Tversky, 1982: 163–178.

Ulam, Adam, 1977, *In the Name of the People: Prophets and Conspirators in Prerevolutionary Russia*, New York: Viking Press.

Varennes, Henri, 1895, *De Ravachol á Caserio (notes d'audience)*, Paris: Garnier Frères.

Varon, Jeremy, 2004, *Bringing the War Home: The Weather Underground, the Red Army Faction, and Revolutionary Violence in the Sixties and Seventies*, Berkeley: University of California Press.

Venturi, Franco, 2001, *Roots of Revolution: A History of the Populist and Socialist Movements in 19th Century Russia,* rev. ed., London: Phoenix Press.

Verhoeven, Claudia, 2009, *The Odd Man Karakozov: Imperial Russia, Modernity, and the Birth of Terrorism*, Ithaca, NY: Cornell University Press.

Wahnich, Sophie, 2008, *La Longue Patience du Peuple: 1792. Naissance de la République*, Paris: Éditions Payot and Rivages.

——, 2012, *In Defense of the Terror: Liberty or Death in the French Revolution*, London: Verso.

Wallon, H., 1880–82, *Histoire du Tribunal Révolutionnaire de Paris*, 6 vols., Paris: Librairie Hachette et Cie.

Walzer, Michael, 2000, *Just and Unjust Wars: A Moral Argument with Historical Illustrations,* 3rd ed., New York: Basic Books.

———, 2004, *Arguing About War*, New Haven: Yale University Press.

Waresquiel, Emmanuel de, 2014, *Fouché: Les silences de la pieuvre*, Paris: Éditions Tallandier/Librairie Arthème Fayard.

Warren, Robert Penn, 1993, *John Brown: The Making of a Martyr*, Nashville, TN: J. S. Sanders

Watson, Bruce, 2005, *Bread and Roses: Mills, Migrants, and the Struggle for the American Dream*, New York: Viking.

Weber, Max, 1978, *Economy and Society*, 2 vols., Berkeley: University of California Press.

Weimann, Gabriel, 2006, *Terror on the Internet: The New Arena, the New Challenges*, Washington, DC: United States Institute of Peace Press.

West, George, 1915, *United States Commission on Industrial Relations: Report on the Colorado Strike*, Washington, DC: United States Government Printing Office.

Whelehan, Niall, 2012, *The Dynamiters: Irish Nationalism and Political Violence in the Wider World, 1867–1900*, Cambridge: Cambridge University Press.

Wicker, Allan, 1969, "Attitudes Versus Actions: The Relationship of Verbal and Overt Behavioral Responses to Attitude Objects," *Journal of Social Issues* 25(4): 41–78.

Wickham, Carrie Rosefsky, 2002, *Mobilizing Islam: Religion, Activism and Political Change in Egypt*, New York: Columbia University Press.

Wiktorowicz, Quintan, ed., 2004, *Islamic Activism: A Social Movement Theory Approach*, Bloomington: Indiana University Press.

———, 2005, *Radical Islam Rising: Muslim Extremism in the West*, Oxford: Rowman and Littlefield.

Wilkerson, Cathy, 2001, Review of *Fugitive Days* by Bill Ayers, *Z Magazine*, December.

———, 2007, *Flying Close to the Sun: My Life and Times as a Weatherman*, New York: Seven Stories Press.

Wright, Lawrence, 2006, *The Looming Tower: Al-Qaeda and the Road to 9/11*, New York: Alfred A. Knopf.

Young, Stephen, 1980, *The Role of the Radical Fraternity in the Turn to Political Terror Within Russian Revolutionary Populism: A Statistical Analysis and Group Biography of Activists with the Populist Movement of the 1870's*, Ph.D. dissertation, University of Chicago.

Zamoyski, Adam, 2015, *Phantom Terror: Political Paranoia and the Creation of the Modern State, 1789–1848*, New York: Basic Books.

Zasulich, Vera, 1992, "Vera Zasulich," in Engel and Rosenthal, 1992: 59–94.

Zimbardo, Philip, 2007, *The Lucifer Effect: Understanding How Good People Turn Evil*, New York: Random House.

Zinn, Howard, 1999, *A People's History of the United States: 1492–Present*, New York: HarperCollins.

Zlataric, Bogdan, 1975, "History of International Terrorism and Its Legal Control," in Bassiouni, ed., 1975: 474–484.

Zomeren, Martijn van, Tom Postmes, and Russell Spears, 2008, "Toward an Integrative Social Identity Model of Collective Action: A Quantitative Research Synthesis of Three Socio-Psychological Perspectives," *Psychological Bulletin* 134: 504–535.

Index

abolitionists, political violence of, 415n20
Admiral, Henry, 88, 103
African Americans, police killings of, 365
African National Congress (ANC), 434n7;
    military wing of, 382
aggression: out-group, 37–38; against prototypes,
    108; retribution against, 38; against symbols,
    37. *See also* attentats politiques; state
    aggression
Alexander I (tsar of Russia), 111; Mikhailov's
    attentat against, 212
Alexander II (tsar of Russia): assassination of,
    214–19, 434n15; Berezowski's attentat against,
    160–62, 404n136; counterterrorism measures
    of, 210–11; edict against political prisoners,
    196; Emancipation Statute of, 153, 154, 157, 163,
    267, 404n5; Karakozov's attentat on, 156–60;
    liberal reforms of, 152–54; memorial mass for,
    294; and Mezentsev assassination, 195;
    People's Will's attentat against, 206–10, 379;
    police of, 160; Polish nationalist attentat on,
    160–62; reactionary ministers of, 160;
    Soloviev's attentat on, 198–200; on Zasulich
    trial, 191
Alexander III (tsar of Russia), 218; attentat on,
    222; ministers of, 219–20
Alexandrov, Peter, 190–91
Alexeev, Peter, 181–82
Alfonso XII (king of Spain), attentat against,
    192
Alibaud, Louis, 390n101; attentat against
    Louis-Philippe, 119–22; government press on,
    121; military career of, 119; as republican hero,
    121–22; self-sacrifice of, 122; suicide attempt,
    120; trial and execution of, 121; during Trois
    Glorieuses, 119; underground press on, 122;
    weapons of, 120

Allsop, Thomas, 139; explosive device of, 138;
    trial of, 141
al Qaeda, 361; Bush on, 1–3
Altgeld, Governor John, 233, 416n37
American Christian Patriots, 382; ideological
    thesis for, 383
American Revolution, political arena of, 48
l'anarchie (newsletter), 318, 319, 322, 329; at
    Romainville, 325–27; shutdown of, 331
anarchists: Belgian, 320–22, 325; free love
    among, 235; hostility toward police, 333;
    ideology of, 262; imagined political
    community of, 251; martyrs, 234, 235, 242,
    258, 260; on Marx, 151; peaceful, 228–29; in
    political process, 370; pretended, 251;
    scientific faction of, 326; self-categorization
    by, 228; self-sacrifice by, 262; social identity
    of, 262, 333; socialism of, 320; Spanish,
    251–52; in trade unions, 370; turn to violence,
    228. *See also* political actors, violent;
    terrorists
anarchists, French, 239–42; banditry by, 251, 259,
    325, 434n14; Bonnot and, 328; links among,
    242; martyrs, 240; police brutality against,
    243; precursors of, 122; publications of,
    418n100; self-categorization of, 319; social
    identity of, 239; sympathizers with, 418n100;
    in trade union movement, 260
anarchists, Italian, 224–26; ideological thesis for,
    383; nonviolence of, 379; propaganda of the
    deed, 382; spontaneous violence of, 382. *See
    also* Galleani group
anarchists, U.S.: in Lexington Avenue bombing,
    352; picketing of Rockefeller, 355; prosecution
    of, 433n3; social identity of, 371; stereotypes
    of, 233; trials of, 365. *See also* political
    violence, U.S.

A c k n o w l e d g m e n t s

Writing a book is often the culmination of a long process. This one has been a decade in the making. It came out of my interest in trying to understand political violence when I was privileged to gain access to primary sources and actual perpetrators of such violence. I must thank David Cohen for first giving me this opportunity as the New York Police Department's first and still only scholar in residence. My stay with the department was enriched by long conversations with Mitch Silber, who has become a good friend. After the Fort Hood tragedy, Richard Zahner, the deputy chief of staff of the U.S. Army (intelligence), provided me with another such opportunity by asking me to come on board and become his advisor. In the army, I benefitted from long talks with David Clark. Bob Ashley, the International Security Assistance Force deputy chief of staff for intelligence, invited me to come to Afghanistan to help fight insider attacks on ISAF troops. This allowed me to interview a dozen perpetrators. After my return to the United States, I was asked to be an expert witness in about a dozen terrorist trials and was able to interview more people directly connected with political violence. I would like to thank the countless number of lawyers who made this possible. In addition, I have interviewed many people who had been involved in political violence but had moved on with their lives. These interviews revealed the complexity of their lives which was completely overshadowed by their heinous acts and totally absent from secondary sources, on which most terrorism research is based. It is this first-hand experience that left me dissatisfied with all the available simplistic models of the turn to political violence and convinced me to write a more nuanced account of this process that might better fit the everyday reality of their lives.

This book is an attempt to make sense of all this confusing data. From it, I slowly generated my model of the turn to political violence. From my search for a perspective framing this model, it seems that the work of Alex Haslam and Stephen Reicher on social identity was most relevant. However, since I could not write about my experience and my interviews because of various secrecy and nondisclosure agreements, I turned to history to illustrate my model. This was a lonely process of reading primary source documents and many transcripts of terrorist trials in the West of the past two centuries. I would like to thank the few people who read drafts of this book and provided me with excellent suggestions on how to improve it. They include David Rapoport, Alex Littlefield, Elizabeth Benson, and Lara Heimert. I also thank Rafe Sagalyn for being my agent, negotiating my contract for this book.

I would also like to thank the team at the University of Pennsylvania Press, especially Peter Agree, Noreen O'Connor-Abel, Joyce Ippolito, and their professional staff that edited and marketed this book. Finally, this book could not have been possible without the full support of my wife, Jody, and son, Joseph, as they encouraged me in this lonely enterprise. This study was self-funded without any institutional support on my own time and effort. For long periods of time when I was exploring new possibilities, I was absent from their lives. I am sorry for this lost time despite the fact that they never complained about it. On the contrary, their love provided me with the peace of mind and strength allowing me to forge ahead on this project. Jody also read and edited multiple drafts of these chapters.

I thank all these people who helped shape this book into what it is.

Lightning Source UK Ltd.
Milton Keynes UK
UKOW08n0705100517

300881UK00010B/160/P